Exam 4-6 Sat

DICK WINKIER

Ch 6, 7, 8, 9

FINITE MATHEMATICS
FOR BUSINESS, ECONOMICS
AND SOCIAL SCIENCE

Duxbury Press
North Scituate
Massachusetts

FINITE MATHEMATICS

JAMES RADLOW *University of New Hampshire*

*for Business,
Economics and
Social Science*

Finite Mathematics for Business, Economics, and Social Science
was edited and prepared for composition by Penelope Rohrbach.
Interior design was provided by Dorothy Booth. The cover was
designed by Joseph Landry.

Duxbury Press
A Division of Wadsworth, Inc.

Library of Congress Cataloging in Publication Data

Radlow, James, 1925–
  Finite mathematics for business, economics, and
social science.

  Includes index.
  1. Mathematics—1961– I. Title.
QA39.2.R32   510   78-13783
ISBN 0-87872-182-7

Printed in the United States of America
1 2 3 4 5 6 7 8 9 — 83 82 81 80 79

contents

CHAPTER
ONE

CHAPTER
TWO

preface

This book is designed for a finite mathematics course that emphasizes applications.

From the table of contents, the book does not look very different from other finite mathematics books. I treat linear equations and inequalities, matrix algebra, linear programming, probability, functions, and functional models.

What do I do that is different? One major difference is in *tone*. I have tried to be informal and unintimidating—to make contact with students instead of holding them at a distance. To see how I go about this, please look at the pages addressed "To the Student." Any expectations raised by these pages are, I hope, sustained by the text.

Specifically, I try to explain mathematical concepts clearly, to avoid abstraction, to nail down ideas by means of verbal and mathematical examples and worked-out problems. There are many real-world applications. They occur throughout the text, in many of the exercises, and above all in the sections that are specifically devoted to applications. I hasten to add that no application in the book assumes any previous knowledge of business, economics, or social science.

In *organization*, I have tried to respond to the fact that there are a number of equally valid ways of ordering the material. As the flow chart on p. x shows, the response has been to present each of the three main topics in the book (linear algebra, probability, functions) in a largely self-contained group of chapters. After the first two chapters (labeled "Preliminaries" in the flow chart), it is possible to move either to chapters 3, 4 and 5 to study linear algebra and linear programming or to chapters 10, 11 and 12 to study functions and functional models. Probability chapters 6, 7 and 8 can be studied without reference to the rest of the book, but matrix multiplication (Chapter 4) is a prerequisite for Chapter 9.

As the preceding description shows, Chapters 1 through 9 provide a course in finite mathematics. A different organization (for example: Chapters 1, 2, 10, 11, 12, 3, 4 in that order) would give emphasis to functions and functional models. The flow chart on this page, shows other organizational possibilities.

Sections that are starred in the table of contents can be omitted without loss of continuity. But if section 2.5 on the line of best fit is omitted, then the curve-fitting material in sections 10.6 and 11.4 must also be omitted.

A class that is heavily weighted with business and economics students would have a natural interest in the starred sections 4.4 (input-output analysis) and 5.5 (the simplex method). With this in mind, I have made a special effort to present input-output analysis and the simplex method in a clear and interesting way.

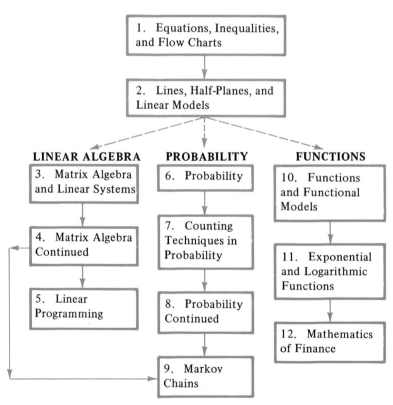

PRELIMINARIES

1. Equations, Inequalities, and Flow Charts

2. Lines, Half-Planes, and Linear Models

LINEAR ALGEBRA

3. Matrix Algebra and Linear Systems

4. Matrix Algebra Continued

5. Linear Programming

PROBABILITY

6. Probability

7. Counting Techniques in Probability

8. Probability Continued

9. Markov Chains

FUNCTIONS

10. Functions and Functional Models

11. Exponential and Logarithmic Functions

12. Mathematics of Finance

ACKNOWLEDGMENTS

I have been very much helped by the comments and suggestions of the reviewers: Margaret R. Brittan, University of Denver; Richard Butterworth, Massasoit Community College; Edward L. Keller, California State University, Hayward; Herbert C. Kranzer, Adelphi University; and Melvin A. Mitchell, Clarion State College.

Barbara Chambers, George Mason University; Howard Connors, University of South Dakota; and Michael Spinelli, Virginia Commonwealth University have been similarly helpful.

I am especially grateful to Marie Gaudard, Richard E. Johnson, Tim Kelly, and Donovan Van Osdol of the University of New Hampshire for their valuable suggestions.

Among others who have helped, and whose help is appreciated, I note: Dean Richard S. Davis of the University of New Hampshire, who made it possible for me to do extensive class-testing of the manuscript; my students and teaching assistants, for their friendly interest and helpful comments; my expert mathematical typists Nan Collins, Jean Gahan and Janet Lord; Edward L. Francis, managing editor of Duxbury Press and my personal editor, for all the help he gave me and organized for me through his staff.

To the student

The bullfight is not a sport in the Anglo-Saxon sense of the word, that is, it is not an equal contest or an attempt at an equal contest between a bull and a man.

—ERNEST HEMINGWAY

The contest between you and the mathematics you can learn from this book is not a sport in the Anglo-Saxon sense either.

WHAT YOU HAVE ON YOUR SIDE:

1. **Motivation.** The title of this book says that it is mathematics for students of business, economics, and social science. This is true. The mathematics in the book will help you in your courses and in your career. (This does not mean that you are about to study a dull cookbook. But you will not be reading an equally dull rhapsody on the beauties of mathematics either.)

2. **An easy beginning.** This book does not assume that you remember everything you have ever learned. Topics from high school algeba that you need to know are discussed in various sections of the first two chapters. (If you do remember it all, you can skip or skim these sections.)

3. **You do not have to be good at math** to succeed in this course. I know this from experience. Many students who have taken a course based on this book have done very well with it. These were not math or science or engineering majors. They were students who had (most of them) done poorly in math in high school. They expected a difficult uninteresting course again. They were pleasantly surprised.

4. **Examples.** There is nothing abstract here. Every concept is illustrated by concepts you can understand.

5.   **Worked-out problems.** Before you are asked to do an exercise, you are prepared for it. Word problems, which you may find hard (many high school and college students do), get special attention. The rules of Section 1.6 (together with the data table approach explained in the same section), give you a step-by-step method for translating word problems into mathematical form. Later chapters continue the careful step-by-step approach.

6.   **Flow charts** (explained in Chapter 1) are used a number of times to explain new procedures of practical importance. They enable you to see at a glance what is going on. They also help you to make a procedure self-correcting.

chapter one

EQUATIONS, INEQUALITIES, AND FLOW CHARTS

THE first five sections of this chapter review some high school math. You may need this review, or it may be better to skip these sections.

Since real-world problems are usually expressed in words, it is good to know how to translate words into equations. Section 1.6 gives a systematic way to do this.

Sections 1.7 and 1.8 show you how to read and write flow charts. Nowadays, most business and economics people expect you to have these skills.

1.1 EQUATIONS AND VARIABLES

A statement involving a sign of equality ($=$) is called an *equation*. As examples,

$$2 + 2 = 4$$

is a *true equation,* while

$$2 + 2 = 22$$

is a *false equation.*

    The equation

$$x + 2 = 13$$

is neither true nor false. If x has the value 11, we have the true equation

$$11 + 2 = 13$$

If x has the value 7, we have the false equation

$$7 + 2 = 13$$

    An equation like $x + 2 = 13$, which is neither true nor false, is called a *conditional equation.* The symbol x in the equation, which may be given various values, is called a *variable.* The value $x = 11$, which makes $x + 2 = 13$ a true equation, is called a *solution* of the equation.

DEFINITION   **Solution of an Equation in One Variable**

A solution of a conditional equation in one variable x is a value of x that makes the equation true.

    Equations in one variable may have one solution, no solutions, or infinitely many solutions.

EXAMPLE 1 $3x = 5$

has one solution: $x = \frac{5}{3}$ makes the equation true.

EXAMPLE 2 $x + 3 = x + 5$

has no solutions: the choice of *any* number for x makes the equation false.

EXAMPLE 3 $3x = 5x$

has one solution: $x = 0$.

EXAMPLE 4 $2x + 3x = 5x$

has infinitely many solutions: the choice of *any* number for x makes the equation true.

EXERCISES *for Section 1.1*

Give your own examples of:

1. an equation   2. a true equation

3. a false equation   4. a conditional equation

5. a variable   6. a solution

Verify the following statements:

7. $\dfrac{1}{x} = 5$ has one solution.

8. $\dfrac{1}{x} = 0$ has no solutions.

9. $\dfrac{1}{x} = \dfrac{3}{3x}$ has infinitely many solutions (but $x = 0$ is not a solution).

10. $3(x + 4) = 3x + 12$ has infinitely many solutions.

11. $3x + 4 = x + 12$ has one solution.

12. $3(x + 4) = 3(x + 5)$ has no solution.

13. $3(x + 4) = 4(x + 3)$ has one solution: $x = 0$.

State the number of solutions (one, none, or infinitely many) for each of the following equations. If there is one solution, find it.

14. $7x = 18$ 15. $22x = 23x$

16. $x - 3 = 14$ 17. $x - 3 = 14 - x$

18. $x - 3 = 14 + x$ 19. $x - 3 = x - 3$

20. $13x = 0$ 21. $\dfrac{x}{13} = 0$

22. $\dfrac{13}{x} = 0$ 23. $\dfrac{1}{x - 1} = \dfrac{1}{x - 2}$

24. $\dfrac{1}{x - 1} = \dfrac{2}{x - 2}$ 25. $\dfrac{1}{x - 1} = \dfrac{1}{x - 1}$

1.2 SOLVING LINEAR EQUATIONS IN ONE VARIABLE

Sometimes different equations have the same solution. For example, the three equations

$$2x - 14 = 0$$

$$\tfrac{1}{2}x - 3\tfrac{1}{2} = 0$$

$$x - 7 = 0$$

all have the solution $x = 7$. The three equations are called *equivalent equations*.

DEFINITION   Equivalent Equations

If two or more equations have the same solution, they are called *equivalent equations*.

To solve an equation, transform it into simpler and simpler equivalent equations. First, let's look at an example, and then we will explain the basic principle.

EXAMPLE 1:   SOLVING AN EQUATION

Start with:
$$3x - 7 = 5$$

Add 7 to both sides:
$$3x - 7 + 7 = 5 + 7$$

$$3x = 12$$

Divide both sides by 3:
$$\frac{3x}{3} = \frac{12}{3}$$

Answer:
$$x = 4$$

The basic principle used in Example 1 is this: Performing the same *legal operations* of arithmetic on both sides of an equation leads to an equivalent equation.

What are *legal operations?*

For an answer, let's look at which operations of arithmetic are legal and which are illegal and then look at some examples of both.

LEGAL OPERATIONS

1. Addition or subtraction of the same number to both sides of an equation is legal.

2. Multiplying or dividing both sides of an equation by the same nonzero number is legal.

Example 1 used legal operations to transform an equation into simpler equivalent equations. Here is another example:

EXAMPLE 2: OPERATING LEGALLY

Start with:
$$3x + 4 = -\sqrt{3}x + 11$$

Subtract 4 from both sides:
$$3x + 4 - 4 = -\sqrt{3}x + 11 - 4$$

$$3x = -\sqrt{3}x + 7$$

Add $\sqrt{3}x$ to both sides:
$$3x + \sqrt{3}x = -\sqrt{3}x + 7 + \sqrt{3}x$$

$$= -\sqrt{3}x + \sqrt{3}x + 7$$

$$3x + \sqrt{3}x = 7$$

Rewrite the left side:
$$(3 + \sqrt{3})x = 7$$

Divide both sides by $3 + \sqrt{3}$:
$$\frac{3 + \sqrt{3}}{3 + \sqrt{3}}x = \frac{7}{3 + \sqrt{3}}$$

Answer:
$$x = \frac{7}{3 + \sqrt{3}}$$

Since legal operations transform an equation into equivalent equations, illegal operations must transform an equation into non-equivalent equations.

EXAMPLES: ILLEGAL OPERATIONS

1. Multiplying both sides of an equation by 0 is illegal. As an illustration: The equation $3x = 5$ has the one solution $x = \frac{5}{3}$. But if we multiply both sides of $3x = 5$ by 0, we have $0 \cdot 3x = 0 \cdot 5$, or $0 \cdot x = 0$, which has infinitely many solutions.

2. Dividing both sides of an equation by 0 is illegal. Notice that it is possible to do this without realizing that you are. To illustrate: The equation $3x = 5x$ has the one solution $x = 0$. But if we divide both sides of $3x = 5x$ by x, we have the false equation $3 = 5$. (The step of dividing by x was a concealed division by 0.)

Notice that multiplying by zero is generally legal (but illegal as an operation on equations). Dividing by zero is always and everywhere illegal.

Multiplying and dividing by zero are not the only illegal operations on equations. Any operation that transforms an equation into a non-equivalent equation is illegal. For example, common mistakes, such as performing a legal operation on some but not *all* terms of an equation, are illegal operations. To illustrate: If we have

$$8 = 2x + 1$$

it is legal to divide both sides by 2. Doing so leads to the equivalent equation

$$4 = x + \tfrac{1}{2}$$

It is a common mistake to forget to divide the last term on the right side of $8 = 2x + 1$ by 2. This would give

$$4 = x + 1$$

which is not equivalent to $8 = 2x + 1$.

All the equations used as examples in this section are of the form

$$ax + b = 0 \qquad (a \neq 0)$$

or can be put in that form. For example, $\frac{1}{2}x - 3\frac{1}{2} = 0$ is of the form $ax + b = 0$, with $a = \frac{1}{2}$ and $b = -3\frac{1}{2}$. And $8 = 2x + 1$ is equivalent to $2x - 7 = 0$, which is of the form $ax + b = 0$, with $a = 2$ and $b = -7$.

> **DEFINITION** Linear Equation in One Variable
>
> An equation of the form
>
> $$ax + b = 0 \qquad (a \neq 0)$$
>
> or any equation equivalent to this equation is called a
> *linear equation in one variable.*

Let's apply legal operations to the linear equation $ax + b = 0$ $(a \neq 0)$. If we add $-b$ to both sides, we have $ax = -b$. If we divide both sides by a $(a \neq 0)$, we have $x = -b/a$. To check that $x = (-b/a)$ is a solution of $ax + b = 0$ $(a \neq 0)$, we write

$$ax + b = a\left(\frac{-b}{a}\right) + b = -b + b = 0$$

> The linear equation
>
> $$ax + b = 0 \qquad (a \neq 0)$$
>
> has one solution:
>
> $$x = \frac{-b}{a}$$

Notice that an equation like $3x + 4 = 5x + 6$ is a linear equation, since it can be put into the form $2x + 2 = 0$.

PROBLEM 1 Solve the equation $4x + 7 = 11x - 15$.

SOLUTION

Add 15 to both sides:

$$4x + 7 + 15 = 11x - 15 + 15$$

$$4x + 22 = 11x$$

Subtract $4x$ from both sides:

$$4x + 22 - 4x = 11x - 4x$$

$$7x = 22$$

Divide both sides by 7:

$$\frac{7x}{7} = \frac{22}{7}$$

Answer:

$$x = \frac{22}{7}$$

PROBLEM 2   Solve the equation $\dfrac{y-1}{3} = 4 - 21y$.

SOLUTION

Multiply both sides by 3: $y - 1 = 12 - 63y$

Add 1 to both sides: $y = 13 - 63y$

Add $63y$ to both sides: $64y = 13$

Divide both sides by 64: $y = \dfrac{13}{64}$

PROBLEM 3   Solve the equation $36 - 8x = 45 - 8x$.

SOLUTION

Add $8x$ to both sides:

$$36 = 45$$

A legal operation has led to a false equation. We conclude that the equation $36 - 8x = 45 - 8x$ *has no solution.*

Before going on, let's look back at Problem 2. The first step in the solution was to multiply both sides of the equation by 3. This simplified the equation. There is a similar first step in the next problem.

PROBLEM 4   Solve the equation $\dfrac{x-1}{2} = \dfrac{x-2}{3}$.

SOLUTION   Multiplying by 2 will simplify the left side of the equation, and multiplying by 3 will simplify the right side. Multiplying by $2 \cdot 3 = 6$ will simplify both sides at once. (The number 6 is called the *least common denominator* of the fractional expressions in the equation.) After multiplying by 6, we can simplify a little further:

$$6\left(\frac{x-1}{2}\right) = 6\left(\frac{x-2}{3}\right)$$

$$3(x-1) = 2(x-2)$$

$$3x - 3 = 2x - 4$$

Add 3 to both sides:

$$3x = 2x - 1$$

Subtract $2x$ from both sides:

$$x = -1$$

The strategy used in Problem 4 also works for an equation like

$$\frac{1}{3x+7} = \frac{2}{8x-6}$$

In this case the least common denominator is $(3x+7)(8x-6)$. If we multiply both sides of the equation by $(3x+7)(8x-6)$, we have

$$8x - 6 = 2(3x + 7)$$

and can go on from there to find the solution, which is $x = 10$. (*Suggestion:* Check that solution. In fact, it is a good idea to check every numerical statement in this book. It is an easy way to make sure you are in touch.)

PROBLEM 5   Find the solution of

$$\frac{1}{t-2} + \frac{8}{t+5} = 0$$

SOLUTION   Multiply both sides of the equation by the least common denominator $(t-2)(t+5)$. This gives

$$t + 5 + 8(t - 2) = 0$$

which can be rewritten as

$$t + 5 + 8t - 16 = 0$$

or as

$$9t - 11 = 0$$

Add 11 to both sides:

$$9t = 11$$

Divide both sides by 9:

$$t = \tfrac{11}{9}$$

Check: Substitute $t = \tfrac{11}{9}$ in the original equation. This gives:

$$\frac{1}{(11/9) - 2} + \frac{8}{(11/9) + 5} = \frac{1}{-7/9} + \frac{8}{56/9} = -\frac{9}{7} + \frac{72}{56} = 0$$

PROBLEM 6   Find the solution of

$$\frac{1}{2x - 2} = \frac{1}{3x - 3}$$

SOLUTION   Multiply both sides of the equation by the least common denominator $(2x - 2)(3x - 3)$. This leads to:

$$3x - 3 = 2x - 2$$

Add 3 to both sides:

$$3x = 2x + 1$$

Subtract $2x$ from both sides:

$$x = 1$$

Check: We cannot set $x = 1$ in the original equation, since that would amount to dividing by 0 on both sides of the equation. Therefore $x = 1$ is *not* the solution.

Q. Where did we go wrong?
A. We multiplied by $(2x - 2)(3x - 3)$. If $x = 1$, this means we multiplied by $(2 - 2)(3 - 3) = (0)(0) = 0$. That was an illegal operation. The equation in Problem 6 does not have a solution.

In the last worked-out problem of this section, we solve a linear equation that does not at first sight look like a linear equation.

PROBLEM 7   Find the solution of

$$(x + 1)^2 + (x + 2)^2 = 2(x + 3)^2$$

SOLUTION   We have

$$(x + 1)^2 = (x + 1)(x + 1) = x^2 + 2x + 1$$
$$(x + 2)^2 = (x + 2)(x + 2) = x^2 + 4x + 4$$
$$2(x + 3)^2 = 2(x + 3)(x + 3) = 2(x^2 + 6x + 9)$$

Rewrite the given equation:

$$(x^2 + 2x + 1) + (x^2 + 4x + 4) = 2x^2 + 12x + 18$$

or:

$$2x^2 + 6x + 5 = 2x^2 + 12 + 18$$

Subtract $2x^2$ from both sides:

$$6x + 5 = 12x + 18$$

Subtract $6x + 18$ from both sides:

$$-13 = 6x$$

Divide both sides by 6:

$$x = \frac{-13}{6}$$

EXERCISES   *for Section 1.2*

Solve each of the following equations by applying legal operations.

1. $5x + 2 = 26$

2. $8x + 5 = 47$

3. $4x + 5 = 2x + 13$

4. $\frac{1}{3}x - 5 = x$ *check*

5. $8 = 2y + 11$

6. $2 - 8x = 5x - 31$

7. $3x + 4 = 7x - 6$

8. $5t - 4 = 12 - 4t$

9. $7x + \frac{1}{3} = 3x - \frac{3}{2}$

10. $-4(3x + 2) = 5(5x - 4)$

11. $2x - 8 = 4x + 2$

12. $\frac{1}{3}y - \frac{6}{7} = 13 - \frac{4}{3}y$

13. $3(\frac{1}{4}x + 2) + 4(\frac{3}{4}x + 9) = -4$

14. $3(y - 6) = 4 - (5 + 2y)$

15. $\frac{x - 12}{2} = \frac{77 - x}{11}$

16. $6x + 3 = \frac{4}{3}x - 12$

17. $\frac{4}{9} + \frac{1}{3t} = \frac{3}{t}$

18. $\frac{y - 5}{4} = \frac{68 - y}{9}$

19. $\dfrac{3x - 2}{3x + 2} = \dfrac{1}{5}$

20. $\dfrac{2x - 3}{3x - 2} = \dfrac{2}{3}$

21. $\dfrac{2x + 4}{6} - 3 = \dfrac{4x + 3}{5} - 4$

22. $\dfrac{3x - 2}{3x + 2} = \dfrac{2x + 3}{2x + 5}$

23. $\dfrac{1}{5 - t} + \dfrac{4}{7 + t} = 0$

24. $\dfrac{7t - 2}{6} - 4t = \dfrac{13t - 17}{16}$

25. $\dfrac{1}{2x} = \dfrac{5}{4x + 2}$

26. $2x^3 + 6x + 4 = 2x^2(x - 3) + 3(2x^2 + 5x + 2)$

27. $\dfrac{3}{x^2 - x - 7} = \dfrac{6}{2x^2 + x + 8}$

1.3 THE NUMBER LINE AND THE PROPERTY OF ORDER

Let's choose a line, a unit of length, and a fixed point on the line called the *origin*. Then attach the number 0 to the origin, positive numbers to distances measured to the right of the origin, and negative numbers to distances measured to the left of the origin. The result (see the figure) is known as a *number line*. The arrow at the right of the line indicates the positive direction. It is understood that the number line extends infinitely in both directions.

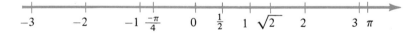

The number associated with each point on the number line is called the *coordinate* of that point. The coordinates of 11 numbers are marked in the figure. These numbers—and all other numbers that are coordinates of points on the number line—are called *real numbers*. Every real number is the coordinate of one and only one point on the number line. Every point on the number line corresponds to one and only one real number. We sometimes say that there is a *one-to-one correspondence* between the real numbers and the points on the number line.

If we locate the points on the number line that correspond to a real number and its negative (for example, 3 and −3), we see that both these points are at the same distance from the origin. This leads to the idea of the *absolute value* of a real number.

DEFINITION   Absolute Value

The absolute value of a real number is the distance of the corresponding point on the number line from the origin.

Since distance is always positive or zero—that is, we can go some distance or no distance but not a *negative* amount of distance—the absolute value of a real number is always positive or zero.

EXAMPLES: ABSOLUTE VALUE

1.   The absolute value of 3 is 3. Notation: $|3| = 3$.

2.   The absolute value of -3 is 3. Notation: $|-3| = 3$.

3.   The only real number a with the property that $|a| = 0$ is the number 0.

Numbers become larger as we move to the right along the number line. In mathematical language we say that the real numbers have the property of *order*. This means that we have the relations "greater than" and "less than" among real numbers. The symbols for these relations are $>$ ("is greater than") and $<$ ("is less than"). If a and b are distinct real numbers, we write

$a > b$ if a is to the right of b on the number line

$a < b$ if a is to the left of b on the number line

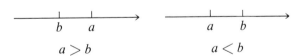

As special cases,

$a > 0$ means "a is positive"

$a < 0$ means "a is negative"

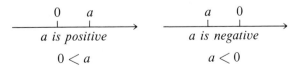

EXAMPLES: GREATER THAN AND LESS THAN

1. $4 > 3$ (4 is to the right of 3)

2. $3 < 4$ (3 is to the left of 4)

3. $3.1416 > 3.14159$ (3.1416 is to the right of 3.14159)

4. $-50 < -30$ (-50 is to the left of -30)

Notice that examples 1 and 2 are the same inequality stated in different ways. If example 4 is not intuitively clear, think of it in terms of temperatures: 50 degrees below zero is colder than 30 degrees below zero.

In defining "greater than" and "less than" by means of the number line, we are giving geometric definitions. We can also give algebraic definitions:

$$a > b \quad \text{if and only if} \quad (a - b) > 0$$

$$a < b \quad \text{if and only if} \quad (a - b) < 0$$

Using these definitions, we can redo the examples just given:

1. $4 > 3$ ($4 - 3 = 1 > 0$)

2. $3 < 4$ ($3 - 4 = -1 < 0$)

3. $3.1416 > 3.14159$ ($3.1416 - 3.14159 = 0.00001 > 0$)

4. $-50 < -30$ ($-50 - (-30) = -50 + 30 = -20 < 0$)

EXERCISES *for Section 1.3*

Find a simpler expression, not involving absolute values, for each of the following:

1. $|-8|$ **2.** $|5|$ **3.** $-|-7|$

4. $|-9 + 6|$ **5.** $|3 - 10|$ **6.** $|-6 - (-7)|$

7. $|-6| - |-7|$ **8.** $|\sqrt{2} - 2|$ **9.** $|2 - \sqrt{2}|$

10. $|-3| + |-4|$ **11.** $|(-3)(-4)|$ **12.** $|-3| + |5|$

13. $|-3 + 5|$ **14.** $|-6| \cdot |-7|$ **15.** $|-5| \div 5$

16. $|11 + (-8)|$ **17.** $|11| + |-8|$

18. $|x + 1|$ if $x > -1$

19. $|x + 1|$ if $x < -1$

In the following pairs of numbers, determine which number is to the right of the other on the number line.

20. 6, 13

21. $-6, -13$

22. $\frac{4}{7}, -\frac{5}{7}$

23. $-\frac{5}{8}, \frac{4}{8}$

The algebraic definition of the symbols $>$ and $<$ says that $a > b$ if and only if $(a - b)$ is positive; $a < b$ if and only if $(a - b)$ is negative. Use this definition to supply the correct symbol, $>$ or $<$, between the two numbers in each of the following pairs.

24. $\frac{2}{5}, \frac{5}{7}$

25. $-\frac{2}{5}, -\frac{5}{7}$

26. $0.333, \frac{1}{3}$

27. $-0.333, -\frac{1}{3}$

28. $\pi, 3.14$

29. $-\pi, -3.14$

30. $|3 + 7|, 3 + 6$

31. $|-7 + 3|, 6 - 3$

32. $|x + 7|, x + 6$
    (*Hint:* Consider the cases $x > -7$ and $x < -7$ separately.)

1.4 INEQUALITIES

Mathematical statements containing the symbols $>$ or $<$ are called *inequalities*. Numerical inequalities are either *true*, like

$$\pi > 3 \qquad -\pi < -3$$

or *false*, like

$$-7 > -6 \qquad -6 < -6$$

An inequality like

$$x + 2 > 7$$

which is true when $x = 12$ and false when $x = 1$, is called a *conditional inequality* in the variable x. We solve a conditional inequality in one variable by finding all the values of that variable that make the inequality true.

EXAMPLES: SOLUTIONS OF INEQUALITIES IN ONE VARIABLE

1. $x + 2 > 7$ is solved by all $x > 5$

2. $x + 2 < -7$ is solved by all $x < -9$

3. $x + 3 > x + 5$ has no solution

4. $3x > 5x$ is solved by all $x < 0$

The solutions just given were found by inspection. To solve inequalities systematically, we must apply the addition and multiplication rules. Notice that each of these rules tells you whether or not the operation changes the *sense* of the inequality: that is, whether or not it changes the direction of the inequality sign. The rules say that addition and subtraction do not change the direction of the inequality sign. Neither does multiplication or division by a positive number. But multiplication or division by a negative number does change the direction of the inequality sign.

ADDITION RULE FOR INEQUALITIES

If $a > b$ and c is any number, then $a + c > b + c$.

EXAMPLE: Since $-3 > -5$, we have $-3 + 10 > -5 + 10 \, (7 > 5)$. Also, $-3 - 12 > -5 - 12 \, (-15 > -17)$. The second illustration shows that subtracting the same number from both sides of an inequality does not change the sense of the inequality.

POSITIVE MULTIPLICATION RULE FOR INEQUALITIES

If $a > b$ and c is any *positive* number, then $ac > bc$.

EXAMPLE: Since $-3 > -5$, we have $(-3)(4) > (-5)(4)$. Also, $(-3)(\frac{1}{4}) > (-5)(\frac{1}{4})$. Notice that dividing both sides of an inequality by the same positive number does not change the sense of the inequality.

NEGATIVE MULTIPLICATION RULE FOR INEQUALITIES

If $a > b$ and d is any *negative* number, then $ad < bd$.

EXAMPLE: Since $-3 > -5$, we have $(-3)(-1) < (-5)(-1)$ [$3 < 5$] and also $(-3)(-\frac{1}{4}) < (-5)(-\frac{1}{4})$ [$\frac{3}{4} < \frac{5}{4}$]. In other words: Multiplying or dividing both sides of an inequality by the same negative number changes the sense of the inequality.

Now we will see how to apply the addition rule and the two multiplication rules to solve inequalities in one variable.

PROBLEM 1   Solve the inequality $3x + 7 > 16$.

SOLUTION   Subtract 7 from each side:

$$3x > 9$$

Multiply both sides by the positive number $\frac{1}{3}$:

$$x > 3$$

PROBLEM 2   Solve the inequality $2 - x < 5$.

SOLUTION   Subtract 2 from each side:

$$-x < 3$$

Multiply both sides by the negative number -1:

$$x > -3$$

PROBLEM 3   Solve the inequality $-2x + 10 > 6$.

SOLUTION   Multiply both sides by -1:

$$2x - 10 < -6$$

Add 10 to both sides:

$$2x < 4$$

Divide each side by 2:

$$x < 2$$

Notice that each of the three problems we have solved has an infinite number of solutions. This is typical of inequalities.

Solve each of the following inequalities.

1. $4x - 6 < 8$ **2.** $3x - 2 > 5$

3. $5x - 2 > 4$ **4.** $2x + 11 > 6$

5. $x - 4 < 6$ **6.** $4 - x < 7$

7. $13 < 4 - 7x$

For what number or numbers (if any) will the following statements be true?

8. $x > 7$ and $-x < -7$ **9.** $x > 0$ and $-x < 0$

10. $2x - 11 > 14$ and $11 - 2x < -14$

11. $2x - 11 > 14$ and $33 - 6x < -42$

12. $3x - 4 > 7$ and $3x - 104 > -93$

13. $2x - 18 < 24$ and $9 - x < -12$

Use the addition and multiplication rules for inequalities to solve:

14. $5x - 4 > 7x + 2$ **15.** $9 + 3x < 27 - 2x$

16. $x + 2 > 2x - 3$ **17.** $(3x - 2)^2 < 9x^2 + 5$

18. $7x - 2 < \dfrac{4x - 2}{5}$ **19.** $12 - 6x < 12 - 5x$

1.5   GRAPHS OF INEQUALITIES IN ONE VARIABLE

In Section 1.2 we studied the linear equation in one variable

(1.1) $$ax + b = 0 \qquad (a \neq 0)$$

We now say: If an inequality can be written in the form

(1.2) $$ax + b > 0 \qquad (a \neq 0)$$

it is a *linear inequality in one variable.*

Sometimes we have the problem of finding all values of x that solve either (1.1) or (1.2). If we introduce the symbol $\geq$ ("is greater than or equal to"), we can write the problem to be solved in the form

(1.3) $$ax + b \geq 0 \qquad (a \neq 0)$$

We can also use the symbol $\leq$ ("is less than or equal to") to consider inequalities of the type

(1.4) $$ax + b \leq 0 \qquad (a \neq 0)$$

Inequalities like (1.3) or (1.4) can be solved by the methods we used in Section 1.4.

PROBLEM 1 Solve the inequality $x - 3 \leq 16$.

SOLUTION Add 3 to both sides:

$$x \leq 19$$

PROBLEM 2 Solve the inequality $2x - 5 \geq 4x + 11$.

SOLUTION Add 5 to both sides:

$$2x \geq 4x + 16$$

Subtract $4x$ from each side:

$$-2x \geq 16$$

Divide each side by the negative number -2:

$$x \leq -8$$

If we mark all points on the number line whose coordinates satisfy a given equation or inequality, our result is called the *graph* of that equation or inequality. The typical linear equation in one variable has one solution. Its graph consists of one point. But linear inequalities in one variable usually have infinitely many solutions. Their graphs contain infinitely many points.

EXAMPLES: GRAPHS OF INEQUALITIES

1. In Problem 1 of Section 1.4 we found that $3x + 7 > 16$ is solved by

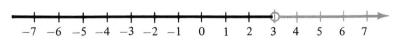

$x > 3$. The graph is an *open ray,* a semi-infinite line starting at $x = 3$ and extending infinitely far to the right. The word *open* means that the starting point 3 does not belong to the graph. In the figure, this is indicated by the hollow dot at 3.

2. In Problem 2 of this section, we found that the inequality $2x - 5 \geq 4x + 11$ is solved by $x \leq -8$. The graph is a *ray,* starting at

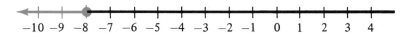

$x = -8$ and extending infinitely far to the left. The starting point -8 belongs to the graph. This is indicated by the solid dot at -8 in the figure.

3. The set of all numbers greater than -1 and less than 3 can be denoted by $-1 < x < 3$. The graph of this set of numbers is an *open interval,* as

shown in the figure. The open dots show that -1 and 3 do not belong to the graph.

4. We can define all numbers greater than or equal to -2 and less than or equal to 1 by $-2 \leq x \leq 1$. The graph of this set of numbers is a *closed*

interval. The solid dots at -2 and 1 in the figure show that these points belong to the graph.

5. The graph of the set of numbers defined by $-2 < x \leq 3$ is an *interval.* In this case the interval is neither open nor closed. Rather, it is open at the

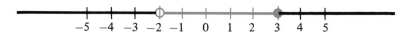

left (-2 does not belong to the graph) and closed at the right (3 does belong to the graph), as shown in the figure.

As you can see from the examples, the graph of an inequality gives a pictorial representation of its meaning. The ideas in the examples are applied in the next three problems.

PROBLEM 3   Graph the inequality

$$-6 < 3x + 2 \leq 5$$

SOLUTION   We begin by solving the inequality. Notice that we can apply our rules for inequalities to all three members of the inequality at the same time. Add -2 to all three members:

$$-8 < 3x \leq 3$$

Divide all three by 3:

$$-8/3 < x \leq 1$$

The graph is an interval (open on the left and closed on the right), as shown in the figure.

PROBLEM 4   Graph the inequality

$$\frac{4x}{x + 2} > 3$$

SOLUTION   To solve the inequality, we will multiply both sides by $x + 2$. But $x + 2$ can be positive or negative. We must consider the two cases separately. (Why? Because the inequality has different senses in the two cases.)

CASE 1 $(x + 2) > 0$, or $x > -2$. Multiply both sides of the inequality by the positive number $(x + 2)$:

$$4x > 3x + 6$$

Subtract $3x$ from both sides:

$$x > 6$$

The result $x > 6$ is compatible with the assumption $x > -2$.

CASE 2 $(x + 2) < 0$, or $x < -2$. Multiply both sides of the inequality by the negative number $(x + 2)$:

$$4x < 3x + 6$$

Subtract $3x$ from both sides:

$$x < 6$$

The result is compatible with the assumption $x < -2$ only if we exclude the interval $-2 \leq x < 6$. We therefore have the solution

$$x < -2$$

in Case 2.

The graph of Case 1 is an open ray, and the graph of Case 2 is a non-overlapping open ray. The graph of the inequality is shown in the figure. It consists of the points on the number line *exterior* to the closed interval $-2 \leq x \leq 6$.

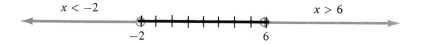

PROBLEM 5   Graph the inequality

$$\frac{3x}{x+1} < 2$$

SOLUTION   As in the last problem, we must distinguish two cases.

CASE 1 $(x + 1) > 0$, or $x > -1$. Multiply both sides of the inequality by the positive number $(x + 1)$:

$$3x < 2x + 2$$

Subtract $2x$ from both sides:

$$x < 2$$

Since $x > -1$ by assumption, the inequality is satisfied for

$$-1 < x < 2$$

CASE 2 $(x + 1) < 0$, or $x < -1$. Multiply both sides of the inequality by the negative number $(x + 1)$:

$$3x > 2x + 2$$

This gives:

$$x > 2$$

which is contrary to the assumption $x < -1$. The inequality has no solution in Case 2.

The graph of the inequality is an open interval, as shown in the figure. All the points of the graph are contributed by the solution in

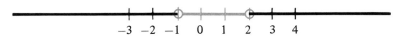

Case 1. Since there is no solution in Case 2, the graph for that case is *empty:* It contains no points.

EXERCISES *for Section 1.5*

Solve:

1. $2x + 2 \geq -1$ **2.** $3x - 4 \leq 6$

3. $3x + 2 \geq 14 - 5x$ **4.** $2x - 1 \leq 9 + \frac{1}{2}x$

5. $\frac{2}{3}x + 4 \geq x - 3$ **6.** $5x + 8 \geq 2x - 9$

7. $4x + 2 \geq 3x - 2$

Graph each of the following inequalities:

8. $\frac{1}{3}x + \frac{1}{2} \geq 4 - \frac{1}{6}x$ **9.** $7(2x - 1) \geq 3(11 - 2x)$

10. $-5 < x < 4$ **11.** $-3 \leq 2x \leq 3$

12. $-6 < x + 2 < 4$ **13.** $4 \leq 3x - 2 < 12$

14. $\dfrac{3x - 8}{6} > 0$ **15.** $5 < \frac{1}{3}(2x + 1) < 9$

16. $\dfrac{1}{3} > \dfrac{5}{4 - x}$ **17.** $\dfrac{1}{x} > \dfrac{3}{4}$

18. $\dfrac{x}{x - 4} > 0$ **19.** $\dfrac{3}{1 - 2x} < 1$

20. $\dfrac{1}{x + 2} < \dfrac{3}{x}$ **21.** $\dfrac{6x}{x - 5} \geq 7$

22. $\dfrac{3x - 12}{5x - 12} < 1$ **23.** $\dfrac{4x - 7}{3x + 4} < 5$

1.6 PROBLEMS LEADING TO EQUATIONS AND INEQUALITIES

All the mathematical techniques explained in this book can be applied to useful problems in business or economics. But if there are *n* such techniques, then there is an *n*-plus-first technique that may be most useful of all: the technique of translating real-world problems into mathematical problems. Our first examples of this technique are problems stated in words. Each problem contains a single unknown quantity expressed in terms of known quantities. Each problem is translated into a linear equation or inequality in one variable. Once the translation is complete, the solution is easy.

RULES FOR TRANSLATING AND SOLVING WORD PROBLEMS

1. Read the problem.

2. Decide which quantities are known and which are unknown. List the known and unknown quantities.

3. Denote one of the unknown quantities by a variable.

4. Express the other unknown quantities in the problem in terms of that variable.

5. The data of the problem will now lead to an equation or inequality in one variable. (If not, read the problem again and carry out step 2 in a different way.)

6. Solve the equation or inequality.

7. Solve the problem.

8. Check your solution. If it checks, you are through. If not, read the problem again. Carry out step 2 again. Go to step 3.

We are about to work through a number of examples of the application of these rules. Then there will be exercises in which you will be asked to apply the rules. In the worked-out problems, everything goes as on roller skates. In student-worked exercises, things may not be so smooth. What to do? Notice that the rules allow for trouble at step 5 and at step 8. The rules tell you:

WHAT TO DO IF THE RULES DO NOT WORK

1. Repeat step 1.

2. Repeat step 2.

3. Go to step 3.

In other words: Reread the problem. Carefully. Re-decide which quantities are known and which are unknown. (You may have missed one of the known or unknown quantities the first time you carried out step 2.) Then proceed.

It is sometimes convenient to carry out steps 1 through 4 of the rules by setting up a data table. For examples of how this is done, see worked-out Problems 1 and 3. The data table approach can help you get started on a word problem. It can also help you redo a problem that does not check out.

Finally, remember that it takes practice to get the knack of roller skating.

PROBLEM 1   A corporation bought a fleet of 56 cars last week. The cars were of two types: compact cars, at a price of $4200 each, and intermediate cars, at a price of $4800 each. The total cost of the 56 cars was $245,400. How many cars of each type did the corporation buy?

SOLUTION

STEP 1   Read the problem.

STEP 2   The unknown quantities are: the number of compact cars bought, the number of intermediate cars bought, the total cost of the compact cars, and the total cost of the intermediates. The known quantities are: the total number of cars bought, the cost of each compact car, the cost of each intermediate car, and the total cost.

STEP 3   Denote the number of compact cars bought by C.

STEP 4   Then the number of intermediate cars bought is $56 - C$. The total cost of the compact cars is $4200C$. The total cost of the intermediates is $4800(56 - C)$.

STEP 5   The cost of all the cars is $245,400. This gives:

Author Assumes: $C_{II} = 56 - C_{I}$

[handwritten annotations:]

$C_I(4200) + (56 - C_I)(4800) = 245,400$

$4200\, C_I + (56)(4800) - 4800\, C_I = 245,400$

$-600\, C_I + 268,800 = 245,400$

$ \quad -245,400 \quad +600$

$+600 \quad C_I = -245$

$600\, C_I = 23,400$

$C_I = \dfrac{23,400}{600} = 39$

$$4200C + 4800(56 - C) = 245,400$$

STEP 6 Solve the equation:

$$4200C + 268,800 - 4800C = 245,400$$

or:

$$-600C = 23,400$$

or:

$$C = 39$$

STEP 7 If $C = 39$, then $56 - C = 17$. In words: The corporation bought 39 compact cars and 17 intermediates.

STEP 8 $4200(39) + 4800(17) = 245,400$. The solution checks.

THE DATA TABLE FOR PROBLEM 1 Step 1 of the rules amounts to setting up the following table and step 2 amounts to filling it in as much as possible with known data. The four blank

	Number Bought	Cost per Car	Total Cost
Compact cars		4200	
Intermediate cars		4800	
Both types	56		245,400

spaces in the first two rows correspond to the four unknown quantities. Step 3 fills in one of the blank spaces (number of compact cars $= C$) and step 4 fills in the other blank spaces.

	Number Bought	Cost per Car	Total Cost
Compact cars	C	4200	$4200C$
Intermediate cars	$56 - C$	4800	$4800(56 - C)$
Both types	56		245,400

The data table is complete. (The remaining blank space, if we were to fill it in, would give the average cost per car: $245,400 \div 56 = \$4382.14$. Since we do not care about this fact, we do not fill in the space.) For a check, notice that the last column of the table gives

$$4200C + 4800(56 - C) = 245,400$$

as in step 5.

PROBLEM 2   Five oil companies form a partnership to build a pipeline. Each company will pay one fifth of the building cost. Three other oil companies wish to join the partnership. If they are admitted as equal partners, each of the original 5 will pay $75 million less than under the original plan. How much will the pipeline cost?

SOLUTION

STEP 1   Read the problem.

STEP 2   The unknown quantities are: the cost of the pipeline, the cost to each of 5 companies under the first plan, and the cost to each of 8 companies under the second plan. The known quantities are: the equal-shares arrangement (under either plan) and the amount saved by each of the original 5 companies if the second plan goes into effect.

STEP 3   Denote the cost, in megabucks (1 megabuck = $1 million), of the pipeline by C.

STEP 4   Then the cost to each of 5 companies under the first plan is $C/5$. The cost to each of 8 companies under the second plan is $C/8$.

STEP 5   Each of the original 5 companies pays 75 megabucks less under the second plan. This means that:

$$\left(\frac{C}{8}\right) = \left(\frac{C}{5}\right) - 75$$

STEP 6   Solve the equation:

$$5C = 8C - 3000$$

or: $$C = 1000.$$

STEP 7   The cost of the pipeline is 1000 megabucks, or $1 billion.

STEP 8   Under the first plan, each of 5 companies pays $(1000/5) = 200$ megabucks. Under the second plan, each of 8 companies pays $(1000/8) = 125$ megabucks. Each of the original 5 would save 75 megabucks. The solution checks.

The next two problems translate into inequalities.

PROBLEM 3   A silver mine produces two grades of ore. Grade I is 0.18% silver and Grade II is 0.1% silver. If 1600 tons of ore are mined in a day, how few of these can be Grade I ore if at least 2.4 tons of silver are to be produced?

SOLUTION

STEP 1 Read the problem. The words "how few" and "at least" in the last sentence tell us that the problem will lead to an inequality.

STEP 2 There are three unknown quantities: the number of tons of Grade I and Grade II ore that are mined, and the number of tons of silver produced. The known quantities are: the fraction (0.0018) of silver in Grade I ore; the fraction (0.001) of silver in Grade II ore; the total number of tons (1600) of ore mined in a day; and the least amount (2.4 tons) of silver desired.

STEP 3 Denote the number of tons of Grade I ore by T.

STEP 4 Then the number of tons of Grade II ore will be $1600 - T$. The total number of tons of silver will be $0.0018T + 0.001(1600 - T)$.

STEP 5 The total amount of silver must be at least 2.4 tons:

$$0.0018T + 0.001(1600 - T) \geq 2.4$$

STEP 6 Solve the inequality:

$$0.0008T + 1.6 \geq 2.4$$

or: $$0.0008T \geq 0.8$$

or: $$T \geq 1000$$

STEP 7 No fewer than 1000 tons of Grade I ore must be mined to produce at least 2.4 tons of silver.

STEP 8 1000 tons of Grade I ore give 1.8 tons of silver. 600 tons of Grade II ore give 0.6 tons of silver. The total is 2.4 tons of silver. If the 1600 tons include fewer than 1000 tons of Grade I ore, then fewer than 2.4 tons of silver are produced. For example: Let 900 tons of Grade I and 700 tons of Grade II ore be mined in a day. Then the tonnage of silver is

$$0.0018(900) + 0.001(700) = 2.32$$

or less than 2.4.

THE DATA TABLE FOR PROBLEM 3 Step 1 of the rules corresponds to setting up the following table and step 2 corresponds to filling it in as much as possible with known data.

	Amount of Ore (Tons)	Fraction of Silver	Amount of Silver (Tons)
Grade I		0.0018	
Grade II		0.001	
Total	1600		at least 2.4

The four blank spaces in the first two rows represent unknown quantities. Step 3 fills in one of these (number of tons of Grade I ore $= T$) and step 4 fills in the other three:

	Amount of Ore (Tons)	Fraction of Silver	Amount of Silver (Tons)
Grade I	T	0.0018	$(0.0018)T$
Grade II	$1600 - T$	0.001	$(0.001)(1600 - T)$
Total	1600		at least 2.4

To check the table, notice that the last column gives

$$(0.0018)T + (0.001)(1600 - T) \geq 2.4$$

as in step 5.

PROBLEM 4   You have $88,000 to invest. You will invest twice as much at 12% as at 8%, and you will invest all the rest of the money at 10%. How little can you invest at 12% if you want an income of at least $9200?

SOLUTION

STEP 1   Read the problem. Notice that the last sentence contains the words "how little" and "at least." These words tell us that the problem will lead to an inequality.

STEP 2   There are three unknown quantities: the amounts to be invested at 8%, at 12%, and at 10%. The known quantities are: the total amount to be invested; the comparative amounts to be invested at 12% and 8%; the fact that everything you do not invest at 12% or 8% will be invested at 10%; and the least amount of income desired.

STEP 3   Denote the amount to be invested at 8% by x.

STEP 4   Then the amount you invest at 12% is $2x$. The amount you invest at 10% is $88,000 - 3x$. (This is all that is left after you invest x dollars at 8% and $2x$ dollars at 12%.)

STEP 5   The total income from the 3 investments must be at least 9200. That is, it must be greater than or equal to $9200. This gives:

$$0.08x + 0.12(2x) + 0.10(88,000 - 3x) \geq 9200$$

STEP 6   Solve the inequality:

$$0.02x + 8800 \geq 9200$$

or: $$0.02x \geq 400$$

or: $$x \geq 20,000$$

STEP 7 If $x \geq 20,000$, then $2x \geq 40,000$. The least amount you can invest at 12% is $40,000.

STEP 8 With $40,000 invested at 12% and $20,000 invested at 8%, you must have $28,000 invested at 10%. The total return is:

$$0.12(40,000) + 0.08(20,000) + 0.10(28,000) = 9200$$

If you invest more than $40,000 at 12%, your return will be greater than $9200. For example: If you invest $50,000 at 12%, $25,000 at 8%, and the remaining $13,000 at 10%, your total return will be $9300.

EXERCISES *for Section 1.6*

1. An IRS office audited the returns of 2800 middle- and high-income taxpayers last year. The average middle-income taxpayer was found to have underpaid by $670, and the average high-income taxpayer was found to have underpaid by $19,300. If the total underpayment was $18,643,000, how many taxpayers of each type were audited?

2. A food processor has 5000 gallons of maple syrup. How many gallons of cane sugar syrup can he add to the maple syrup, to produce a mixture containing 2% maple syrup? *245,000 gal*

3. RST Corporation has a 17-member board of directors. The board voted in favor of a motion to increase dividends on RST stock by 10 cents a share. But if two of the directors favoring the increase had changed their votes, the motion would have failed by one vote. How many directors voted to increase dividends?

4. Barb and Chris can each do a data processing job in 8 hours. Angela can do the same job in 6 hours. If all three work together, how long will it take them to do the data processing?

5. A retired investor has one fourth of his money in 8% bonds, one third of his money in 9% bonds, and the rest in stocks yielding 4%. If his income from these three investments is $47,000 a year, how much money does he have?

6. Since becoming popular seven years ago, a rock group has given a total of 13 concerts in Oakland and Boston. Their performance fees per concert are $79,000 in Oakland and $87,000 in Boston. If the 13 concerts have earned them $1,043,000, how many have been held in each of the two cities? *11 in Oak, 2 in Boston*

7. Ransom, Tate and Company, publishers, brought out two new books last spring: a novel and a book of poems. The profit per copy was $6.70 for the novel and $5.30 for the book of poems. Total sales of the two books were 185,000 copies. If the total profit was $1,235,300, how many copies of each book were sold?

8. The New York Nicks played 84 basketball games this season. Some of the games were televised and some were not. The average profit on each untelevised game was $46,342, and the average profit on each televised game was $67,961. If the toal profit for the season was $4,389,965, how many of the Nicks' games were televised?

9. EXCO produces copiers with a copying speed of 900 copies per minute. WYCO produces a competing model with a speed of 3600 copies per minute. RST Corporation plans to buy 40 copiers: some from EXCO and the rest from WYCO. RST requires a total copying capacity of at least 80,000 copies per minute. What is the largest number of copiers it can buy from EXCO?

10. A television actor must pay 10% of his income to an agent, 12% of it to his first wife, 13% to his second wife, and 25% to the IRS. He and his third wife need $90,000 a year for basic living expenses. If he wants to save more than $130,000 each year, how large must his annual income be?

11. The Calder Motor Company (CMC) is bringing out a new car called the Caldermobile. CMC has factories in both Detroit and Stuttgart. The Caldermobile will be manufactured in both locations. The selling price will be $5000. The profit margin will be 13% on Detroit-built cars and 18% on Stuttgart-built cars. If CMC sells 60,000 Caldermobiles next year, and if the profit on these must be at least $48 million, how many of the cars can be built in Detroit?

12. An insurance company has issued group accident insurance to a group of 900 barkeepers. The rates are such that the company loses an average of $120 per year per barkeeper. The company also issues group accident insurance to a group of 2100 college professors. At current rates it earns an average profit of $35 per professor per year. The company wishes to earn an average profit of at least $15 per year per person from the two groups. It cannot raise the barkeepers' rates. How much per year must the professors' rates be raised?

13. An investor has a system for assigning a risk factor to stocks she buys. At present she has invested equal amounts in stocks with risk factors of 58, 67, and 45. She will shortly invest the same amount in a fourth stock. What risk factor can this fourth stock have if her average risk factor is to be less than 60 but not below 55?

14. Sunny Acres Peanut Butter is produced in Birmingham and Montgomery. The Birmingham product is 18% peanuts and the Montgomery product is 23% peanuts. By mixing the two, Sunny Acres produces a peanut butter that always contains between 20% and 22% peanuts. The current production schedule (after a successful advertising campaign) calls for 15 million tons of Sunny Acres Peanut Butter to be produced next year. How much of this amount can be produced in Birmingham?

1.7

THE RULES OF THE GAME AT A GLANCE: VERBAL FLOW CHARTS

By now you should have discovered that success in doing word problems is certain when you have rules telling you what to do, what order to do it in, and even what to do if you make a mistake.

Again and again in this book, rules are given for solving problems in the mathematics of business and economics. To make the step-by-step instructions in these rules easier to follow, they will often be presented in a pictorial form called a *flow chart*. The first example, Figure 1.1, is the flow chart form of the rules given in Section 1.6; looking at the figure, you will see symbols of four types.

A *dashed box* indicates the beginning or end of the procedure.

A *box* contains a command.

A *circle* contains a question to be answered.

Arrows point to the next step in the procedure.

The flow chart contains almost exactly the same words as the rules in Section 1.6. We have simply enclosed each step of these rules in a suitably shaped box and joined the boxes by a trail of arrows. But you will note three differences.

HOW THE FLOW CHART DIFFERS FROM THE RULES

1. Step 5 of the rules is converted into a question and enclosed in a circle. Two clearly marked alternatives, YES ↓ and ⟶, flow out of the circle.
NO

2. The same is true for step 8.

3. The self-correcting cycle, the "what to do if the rules do not work" part of the rules, is very clearly displayed in the flow chart.

In other words: The flow chart focuses our attention on key steps of the procedure for translating and solving word problems. It displays alternatives in a format that cannot be easily misunderstood.

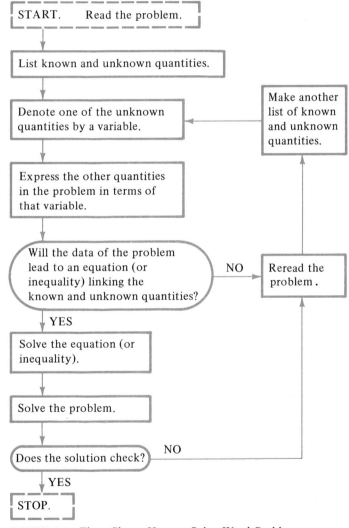

FIGURE 1.1 Flow Chart: How to Solve Word Problems

Now let's look at some examples of the use of the flow chart to solve word problems.

PROBLEM 1   An airport limousine travels north from Logan Airport in Boston at the rate of 50 miles per hour. A private car following the same route travels at the rate of 55 miles per hour. The limousine leaves Logan Airport at 5:30 P.M. and the private car leaves at 5:45 P.M. At what time will the car overtake the limousine?

SOLUTION   We read the problem and then follow the other instructions given by the flow chart.

> List known and unknown quantities.

The *known quantities* are: the speed of the limousine, the speed of the car, the departure time of the limousine, and the departure time of the car. The *unknown quantities* are: the number of minutes the car travels before it overtakes the limousine, and the number of minutes the limousine travels before it is overtaken.

> Denote one of the unknown quantities by a variable.

Let the car travel for M minutes before it overtakes the limousine. (The variable is M).

> Express the other quantities in the problem in terms of that variable.

The limousine (with a 15-minute start) travels for $M + 15$ minutes before it is overtaken. Since the car travels $55/60$ miles in a minute, it travels $55M/60$ miles in M minutes. Since the limousine travels $50/60$, or $5/6$, miles in a minute, it travels $(5/6)(M + 15)$ miles in $M + 15$ minutes.

> Will the data of the problem
> lead to an equation linking
> the known and unknown quantities?

YES. By the definition of M as the overtake time, we have:

$$\frac{55M}{60} = \frac{5}{6}(M + 15)$$

> Solve the equation.

$$55M = 50(M + 15)$$

$$\text{or:} \quad 5M = 750$$

$$\text{or:} \quad M = 150$$

> Solve the problem.

The overtake time is 150 minutes, or 2 hours and 30 minutes. The car started at 5:45 P.M. It overtakes the limousine at 8:15 P.M.

> Does the solution check?

In 150 minutes, the car has traveled $150(55/60) = 137.5$ miles. In 165 minutes, the limousine has traveled $165(5/6) = 137.5$ miles.

The solution checks. **STOP.**

PROBLEM 2 A developing nation is trying to encourage small farmers. At the start of its land program, it has 100 million acres in small farms. It adds 12 million acres per year in small farms by clearing the jungle. Large estates comprise 200 million acres at the start of the land program. The large estates increase by 10 million acres per year through jungle-clearing. After how many years will the small farm acreage amount to more than 80% of the large estate acreage?

SOLUTION   Read the problem. Then proceed as follows.

List known and unknown quantities.

The *known* quantities are: the number of acres in small farms and in large estates at the beginning of the program, and their yearly increase. The *unknown* quantities are: the number of acres in small farms and large estates at the end of the program, and the number of years it takes for the program to reach its goal.

Denote one of the unknown
quantities by a variable.

Let $G=$ the number of years before the program reaches its goal.

Express the other quantities
in the problem in terms of
that variable.

The number of acres in small farms at the end of the program is (in millions of acres) $100 + 12G$. The number of acres in large estates at the end of the program is (in millions of acres) $200 + 10G$.

Will the data of the problem
lead to an inequality linking
the known and unknown quantities?

YES. By the definition of the goal of the program,

$$100 + 12G > 0.80(200 + 10G)$$

Solve the inequality.

$$100 + 12G > 160 + 8G$$
$$\text{or:} \qquad 4G > 60$$
$$\text{or:} \qquad G > 15$$

Solve the problem.

The goal of the program is met after 15 years.

Does the solution check?

In 15 years, the small farm acreage is $100 + 12(15) = 280$ million acres. The large estate acreage at that time is $200 + 10(15) = 350$ million acres. The small farm acreage is exactly 80% of the large estate acreage at that time. As the program continues *after* 15 years, the small farm acreage will come to be more than 80% of the large estate acreage. Suppose, for example, that the program continues for 16 years. At that time $100 + 12(16) = 292$ million acres; $200 + 10(16) = 360$ million acres; and 292 is more than 80% of 360.

The solution checks. STOP.

Flow charts are often used to describe nonmathematical situations. As examples, Figures 1.2 and 1.3 are flow charts telling how to prepare a watermelon and how to study for a math exam.

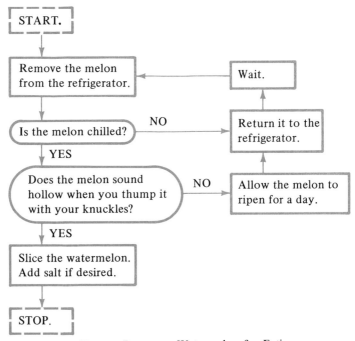

FIGURE 1.2   How to Prepare a Watermelon for Eating

COMMENT: Figure 1.2 focuses attention on the (circled) questions: Is the melon chilled? Does the knuckle-thumping test show that the melon is ripe?

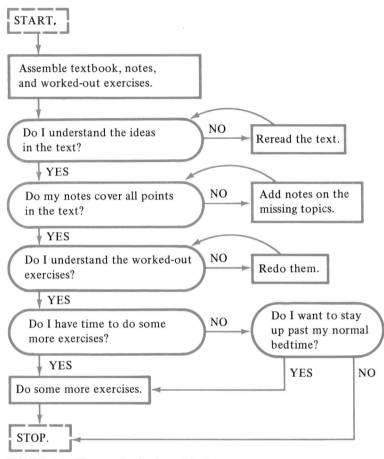

FIGURE 1.3 How to Study for a Math Exam

Figure 1.3 is intended to be useful. It does not, for example, tell you to memorize anything. By the time you have checked over the text, your notes, and the homework exercises you have worked out, you will understand and remember everything you need to know. Doing more exercises (if you have the time) is all you can possibly do to prepare yourself further for a math exam.

$D\sigma$
$1-6$

Use a step-by-step procedure to solve each of the following word problems. Use the flow chart on page 33 as your guide.

1. A leopard has killed and eaten a young baboon. Knowing that the adult baboons will be on his trail, he then sets off on his escape route. The leopard's rate of speed is 20 miles per hour for 3 hours, and 15 miles per hour for the next 3 hours. Exhausted he then slows down to 5 miles per hour but keeps going. The baboons discover the evidence of the leopard's kill and set out on the trail $1\frac{1}{2}$ hours after he does. Their rate of speed is a steady 10 miles per hour, and they can keep it up for 20 hours. Will the baboons ever catch the leopard? If so, how long will it take?

$W + 15 = \# wks$
until caught up

2. Professor X teaches a 30-week course in organizational behavior. He assigns reading at the rate of 220 pages per week for the first 15 weeks, and 195 pages per week for the next 15 weeks. His students read at a steady pace of 35 pages per day, 6 days per week. Will they be caught up with their reading during the 30 weeks? If so, when?

220×15
$+ 195 \times_\circ^i W$
$= (35)(6)(W+15)$

3. Portland Pride, a super-horse who dominated racing as a 3-year-old, has been bought by a business syndicate for $20,500,000. They have put him out to stud. His quarters cost $275,000 to build, and the expenses of maintaining him in health and comfort are $50,000 per year. Portland Pride's stud fee is $68,000. He services 50 mares a year. After how many years does the syndicate start to earn a profit on its investment? *NOTE:* We assume that the loss of interest on the money invested in Portland Pride is exactly made up for by tax write-offs.

4. Peary Paper Company manufactures paper towels, facial tissue, and toilet paper. Its investment in timberlands, logging camps, pulp mills, and paper goods factories is $238,750,000. Advertising expense is $3 million a year, and this expense increases at the rate of $400,000 a year. Net income from paper goods sales is $26 million a year. Peary makes weekly price adjustments that increase its net income by $7 million a year. How long will it be before Peary is earning more than 20% (before taxes) on its investment?

5. As in the last problem, Peary has an investment of $238,750,000; yearly advertising expense of $3 million, which increases by $400,000 a year; yearly income of $26 million, which increases by $7 million a year. Then the U.S. government enters the picture. Federal environmental regulations force Peary to spend $8 million on antipollution devices. The cost of maintaining these devices increases by $750,000 a year. Now how long will it be before Peary's earnings on investment exceed a pre-tax 20%?

6. Public Benefactor Company (PBC), an electric utility company, has decided to go nuclear. Its customers now consume 950 megawatt hours (MWh) of electricity per year. This quantity will go up by 100 MWh per year. PBC's current nuclear generating capacity is 30 MWh per year. As new nuclear plants come onstream, PBC's nuclear generating capacity will increase by 150 MWh per year. When will PBC be able to provide 75 to 80 percent of its customers' needs through nuclear capacity?

In each of the following, write a flow chart showing a procedure for:

7. Hanging a picture on the wall
8. Watching a live football game
9. Watching a televised football game
10. Putting a refill in a ball-point pen
11. Scrambling eggs
12. Watering a cactus plant
13. Starting a car
14. Changing a flat tire
15. Studying for an exam (not a math exam, unless you disagree with the flow chart in Figure 1.3, p. 38).
16. You name it.

17. The flow chart for watermelon-preparing (Figure 1.2) includes a knuckle-thumping test for ripeness. Another test is to press your thumb against the end of the watermelon opposite the stem. If the watermelon springs back when your thumb is released, it is ripe. Modify the flow chart so that it tells the watermelon preparer to carry out both tests for ripeness before slicing the watermelon.

18. The flow chart for studying for a math exam (Figure 1.3) assumes that all the material on the exam has been covered in class. Now suppose you are told that you will have to know a section of the text that was not covered in class. Modify the flow chart so that it includes instructions to learn and review the additional material.

1.8 ARITHMETICAL FLOW CHARTS

The word problem flow chart in the last section (Figure 1.1) contained such verbal instructions as: "List the known and unknown quantities." To use the flow chart, it is necessary to know what is meant by a known and an unknown quantity. The flow charts for watermelon-preparing and studying assumed an understanding of instructions like "Slice watermelon" and of questions like "Do I understand the worked-out exercises?"

Some much simpler examples follow. The flow charts contain only arithmetical instructions. They can be used by anyone who knows how to add, subtract, multiply, and divide. *If you can write such a flow chart, you can communicate your ideas to people who do not know as much mathematics as you do.* This widely recognized fact explains why it is useful to learn the technique of writing flow charts. In many businesses and government offices today, you are expected to have this skill, just as you are expected to know how to write a letter. (A secretary will type your letter. A programmer will turn your flow chart into a computer program.)

The problems and exercises in this section are restricted to high school algebra. In later chapters you will see how to apply flow-charting to problems of decision-making and allocation of resources, as well as to other problems of interest in business and economics.

PROBLEM 1 If a, b, c, and d are given numbers, find $\dfrac{a}{b} + \dfrac{c}{d}$.

SOLUTION We know from high school algebra that

$$\frac{a}{b} + \frac{c}{d} = \frac{ad + bc}{bd}$$

The flow chart gives step-by-step arithmetical instructions for obtaining this result.

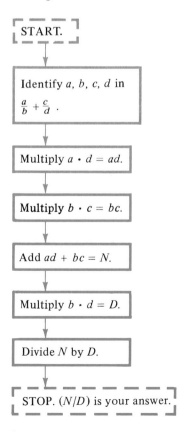

START.

Identify a, b, c, d in $\frac{a}{b} + \frac{c}{d}$.

Multiply $a \cdot d = ad$.

Multiply $b \cdot c = bc$.

Add $ad + bc = N$.

Multiply $b \cdot d = D$.

Divide N by D.

STOP. (N/D) is your answer.

EXAMPLE 1: Suppose the addition to be performed is:

$$\tfrac{6}{7} + \tfrac{10}{11}$$

Then $a = 6$, $b = 7$, $c = 10$, and $d = 11$. We have $ad = 66$, $bc = 70$, and $ad + bc = 136 = N$. Next, $bd = 77 = D$. The answer is $N/D = (\tfrac{136}{77})$.

PROBLEM 2 If a, b, c, and d are given numbers, find $\dfrac{a}{b} \div \dfrac{c}{d}$.

SOLUTION The answer, again, is elementary:

$$\frac{a}{b} \div \frac{c}{d} = \frac{ad}{bc}$$

Arithmetical instructions for obtaining the answer are in the flow chart.

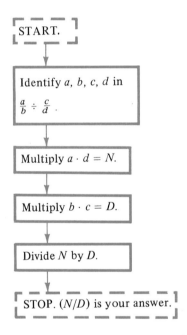

EXAMPLE 2: Carry out the division:

$$\tfrac{7}{8} \div \tfrac{3}{4}$$

Here $a = 7$, $b = 8$, $c = 3$, and $d = 4$. We write $ad = 28 = N$, $bc = 24 = D$. The answer is $(N/D) = (\tfrac{28}{24})$. (The result is not in lowest terms, but putting it in lowest terms was not part of the problem.)

PROBLEM 3   If a is a given number, find the absolute value $|a|$.

SOLUTION   From high school algebra we know that the absolute value $|a|$ is given by:

$$|a| = a \quad \text{if } a \geq 0$$
$$= -a \quad \text{if } a < 0$$

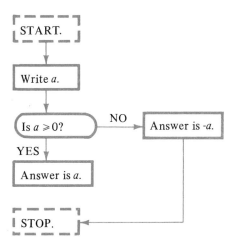

EXAMPLE 3: Let $a = 7$. Since $7 > 0$, $|7| = 7$. Next let $a = -4$. Since $-4 < 0$, $|-4| = -(-4) = 4$.

PROBLEM 4   If a is a given integer and $a \geq 0$, determine whether a is odd or even.

SOLUTION   If a is divisible by 2, then it is even. Otherwise a is odd. We might therefore write a flow chart as follows:

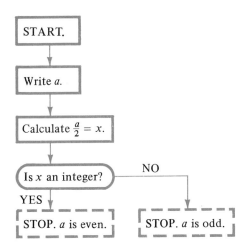

43

The flow chart is not of the purely arithmetical type, since the question enclosed in the circle requires a knowledge of what is meant by an integer. We want instructions that can be understood by a person—or a computer—whose only capacity is the ability to do arithmetic. Here is another flow chart for answering the question, "Is the nonnegative integer a even?"

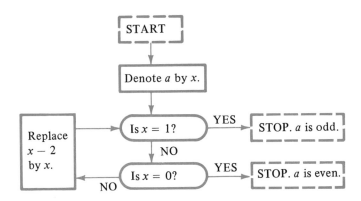

In this case the questions in the circles can be answered by a person (or computer) who can identify the numbers 1 and 0. The flow chart is the type we want.

EXAMPLE 4: Let $a = 3$. Following the flow chart, we set $3 = x$. Then $x \neq 1$. Next $x \neq 0$. The number $x - 2 = 3 - 2 = 1$. We replace $x - 2 = 1$ by x. Then $x = 1$ and a is odd.

Now consider a large number. For example, let $a = 5358979323846264$. We recognize at once that a is even. To get the same result from our flow chart, we have to use the flow chart a great many times: 5358979323846264 times, to be precise. This suggests an improved flow chart. We simply write

Denote the last digit of a by x.

in place of

Denote a by x.

The rest of the flow chart is unchanged.

If *a*, *b*, *c*, and *d* are given numbers, write flow charts for

1. $\dfrac{a}{b} - \dfrac{c}{d}$

2. $\dfrac{a}{b} \cdot \dfrac{c}{d}$

---

3. If *a* is a given number, write a flow chart for finding $|a - 7|$.

4. If *a* is a given number (positive, negative, or 0), write a flow chart for finding a^3.

5. If *a* is a given number, write a flow chart for finding the answer to the question: Is a^2 even?

---

6. If *a*, *b*, and *c* are given numbers, the following six instructions tell you how to calculate $ax^2 + bx + c$ for any given value of *x*.

    1. Identify *a*, *b*, and *c*.
    2. Make a choice of *x*.
    3. Multiply *x* by *a*.
    4. Add *b*.
    5. Multiply by *x*.
    6. Add *c*.

  (i) Carry out the instructions for $a = 2$, $b = 3$, $c = 4$, and $x = 6$.
 (ii) Write a flow chart corresponding to the six instructions.
(iii) If *a*, *b*, *c*, and *d* are given numbers, write a flow chart for calculating $ax^3 + bx^2 + cx + d$ for any given value of *x*.

7. Choose any positive number *x*, and carry out the instructions in the following flow chart. (For example: Suppose you start with $x = 10$. Then the instruction

> Replace $x + 2$ by y.

means: Set $y = 12$.) Find the number *y*.

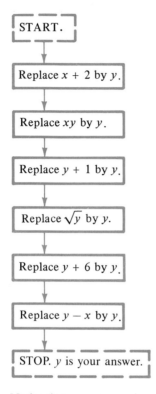

START.

Replace $x + 2$ by y.

Replace xy by y.

Replace $y + 1$ by y.

Replace $\sqrt{y}$ by y.

Replace $y + 6$ by y.

Replace $y - x$ by y.

STOP. y is your answer.

Notice that your answer is $y = 7$ for any choice of x. Can you explain that?

8. Following the general approach of the flow chart in Exercise 7, write a flow chart for calculating $6x^3 + 17x^2 - 3x + 8$ for any given value of x. Compare the result with the flow chart in Exercise 6(iii).

---

9. Carry out the instructions in the flow chart (page 47) with the choice $a = 2$. (*HINT:* Notice that the process is repetitive. On the first go-around, you should find $y = \frac{3}{2}$. Since $|(\frac{3}{2})^2 - 2| = 0.25 > 0.01$, you must repeat the process. A repetition should give $y = \frac{17}{12}$. In this case $|y^2 - 2| < 0.01$ and $y = \frac{17}{12}$ is the answer.)

10. Carry out the instructions in the flow chart of Exercise 9 for $a = 64$, $a = 62$.

The flow chart in Exercise 9 gives a process for finding an approximation to $\sqrt{a}$, the square root of the positive number a. The process is repetitive, as many approximation methods are. Another way of finding the approximation is as follows:

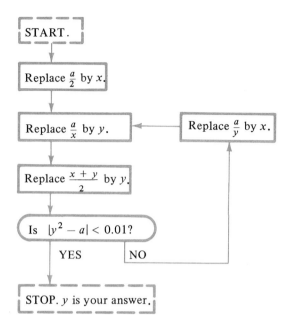

RULE

If x is an approximation to $\sqrt{a}$, then the formula

$$y = \frac{x}{2} + \frac{a}{2x}$$

gives a better approximation.

EXAMPLE: We have $\sqrt{16} = 4$. This suggests $x = 4$ as an approximation to $\sqrt{17}$. By the rule,

$$y = \tfrac{4}{2} + \tfrac{17}{8} = 4\tfrac{1}{8}$$

gives a better approximation to $\sqrt{17}$. A still better approximation is given by using $x = 4\tfrac{1}{8}$ as a first approximation, and the process can be continued as desired.

11. Using the rule, find a good approximation to $\sqrt{62}$. Compare this result with the result you obtained in Exercise 10.

12. Show how the rule can be translated into the flow chart of Exercise 9, *provided* that the criterion of a good approximation y is that $|y^2 - a| < 0.01$. (If the criterion is, for example, $|y^2 - a| < 0.001$, the flow chart is slightly different.)

chapter two

LINES, HALF-PLANES, AND LINEAR MODELS

LINEAR equations and inequalities in two variables can be studied algebraically and also geometrically. We will do both in this chapter. Many of the topics may be familiar from high school, and you may want to do some skipping or skimming, but you will very definitely be leaving the world of high school math when you study this chapter. You will find out how to apply linear equations to problems of sales prediction, cost analysis, and price and wage equilibrium.

COORDINATES IN THE PLANE

By choosing an origin and a unit of length on a line, we can assign a coordinate to each point on the line. We describe the process by saying that we *coordinatize* the line.

To coordinatize the plane, we begin with two perpendicular lines and a unit of length. The point of intersection of the lines is called the *origin of coordinates,* marked O in Figure 2.1. The horizontal line is called the *x-axis,* and the vertical line is called the *y-axis.* Each axis is coordinatized, as shown in Figure 2.1. The arrows indicate the positive x- and y-directions. The point O serves as an origin for both axes.

If P is any point in the plane, we draw lines through P perpendicular to the x-axis and the y-axis (Figure 2.2). The first line intersects the x-axis at a point $x = a$, called the *x-coordinate* of P. The second line similarly determines a point $y = b$, the *y-coordinate* of P. More briefly, we say that the point P determines the *ordered pair* (a, b). Notice that the x-coordinate is placed first in an ordered pair.

If we begin with an ordered pair (a, b), we can reverse the construction by drawing a line through $x = a$ parallel to the y-axis, and a line through $y = b$ parallel to the x-axis. The lines meet at one and only one point P. (See Figure 2.2 again.)

To sum up: Each point in the plane determines one and only one ordered pair; each ordered pair of real numbers determines one and only one point in the plane. We have coordinatized the plane.

EXAMPLES: POINTS AND ORDERED PAIRS

1. The origin O corresponds to the ordered pair $(0, 0)$.

2. The point on the x-axis that is 17 units to the left of the origin determines the ordered pair $(-17, 0)$.

3. The point on the y-axis that is $\sqrt{2}$ units above the origin determines the ordered pair $(0, \sqrt{2})$.

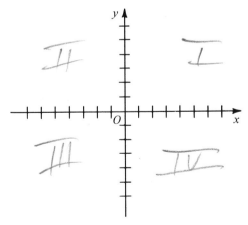

FIGURE 2.1

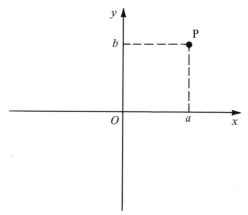

FIGURE 2.2

4. The points corresponding to the ordered pairs A $(2, \frac{5}{2})$, B $(-3, 1)$, C $(-2, -1)$, and D $(4, -\frac{1}{2})$ are marked in Figure 2.3.

5. The axes divide the plane into four *quadrants*, labeled I, II, III, and IV, as shown in Figure 2.4. The signs of the *x*- and *y*-coordinates of a point determine which quadrant it belongs to.

Q. Why do we coordinatize the plane?
A. We want to have a geometric way of talking about ordered pairs, since ordered pairs are solutions of equations and inequalities in two variables. For example, the equation

$$x + y = 1$$

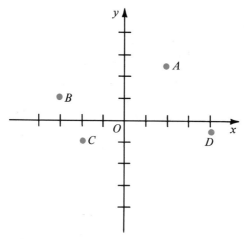

FIGURE 2.3

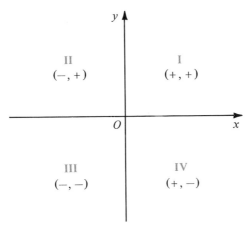

FIGURE 2.4

has the ordered pair solution $(1, 0)$, since $x = 1$ and $y = 0$ give

$$x + y = 1 + 0 = 1$$

The ordered pairs $(0, 1)$, $(2, -1)$, $(\frac{1}{2}, \frac{1}{2})$, and infinitely many others are also solutions of $x + y = 1$. Of course, infinitely many ordered pairs are non-solutions of the equation. For example, $(2, 0)$ is a non-solution because $2 + 0 = 2 \neq 1$.

As a second example, the inequality

$$x + y > 1$$

is solved by the ordered pair $(1, 1)$, since $x = 1$ and $y = 1$ give

$$x + y = 1 + 1 = 2 > 1$$

There are infinitely many ordered pair solutions of $x + y > 1$, such as $(2, 0)$, $(0, 2)$, $(\frac{1}{2}, 1)$, and $(-10, 12)$. There are also infinitely many non-solutions. For example, any ordered pair solution of $x + y = 1$ is a non-solution of $x + y > 1$.

Now, to put all this together: The points in the plane corresponding to the ordered pair solutions of an equation (or inequality) in two variables make up the *graph* of the equation (or inequality). We have just talked about the ordered pair solutions of $x + y = 1$ and $x + y > 1$. In Figure 2.5, the line passing through the three marked points A $(0, 1)$, B $(1, 0)$, C $(2, -1)$ is the graph of $x + y > 1$. The shaded area to the right of the line is the graph of $x + y > 1$. The points D $(0, 2)$, E $(1, 1)$, F $(2, 0)$ in the shaded area are solutions of the inequality.

What makes the graph of $x + y = 1$ a straight line? How do you know it doesn't curve in and out between the points marked A, B and C, as in Figure 2.6? You do not know, but once you have studied Section 2.2, you

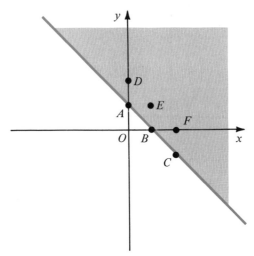

FIGURE 2.5

will know that any linear equation in two variables

$$ax + by + c = 0$$

(where a and b are not both zero) has a straight line as its graph. You will also know that the graph of the corresponding linear inequality in two variables

$$ax + by + c > 0$$

(again, where a and b are not both zero) consists of all points in the plane to one side of the line $ax + by + c = 0$. The set of all points to one side of a line is called a *half-plane*. Here are two examples:

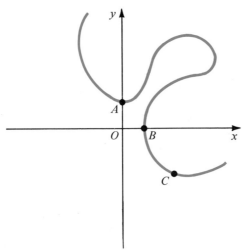

FIGURE 2.6

EXAMPLE 1: The points to the right of the *y*-axis form a half-plane (Figure 2.7a). Any point in this half-plane has a positive *x*-coordinate.

EXAMPLE 2: The points below the *x*-axis form a half-plane (Figure 2.7b). Any point in this half-plane has a negative *y*-coordinate.

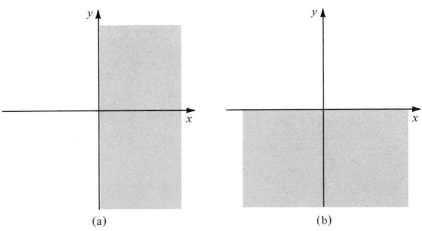

(a)   (b)

FIGURE 2.7

The next four problems are examples of graphing linear equations and inequalities.

PROBLEM 1   Graph the equation

$$2x + 3y = 4$$

SOLUTION   The first step is to find ordered pair solutions of the equation. This is easy. For any choice of *y*, we can find a corresponding value of *x* by solving a linear equation in one variable. As examples (notice that each arrow → means "corresponds to"):

$y = 0 \rightarrow 2x = 4 \rightarrow x = 2$ $(2, 0)$ is a solution

$y = 2 \rightarrow 2x + 6 = 4 \rightarrow x = -1$ $(-1, 2)$ is a solution

$y = -2 \rightarrow 2x - 6 = 4 \rightarrow x = 5$ $(5, -2)$ is a solution

Of course, we could have started by choosing *x* and determining the corresponding value of *y*. As examples (again, each arrow → means "corresponds to"):

$x = 0 \rightarrow 3y = 4 \rightarrow y = \frac{4}{3}$ $(0, \frac{4}{3})$ is a solution

$x = 1 \rightarrow 2 + 3y = 4 \rightarrow y = \frac{2}{3}$ $(1, \frac{2}{3})$ is a solution

$x = -4 \rightarrow -8 + 3y = 4 \rightarrow y = 4$ $(-4, 4)$ is a solution

The points corresponding to the six ordered pairs we have determined are marked in Figure 2.8. All these points lie on the straight line shown in the figure. The straight line is the graph of the equation.

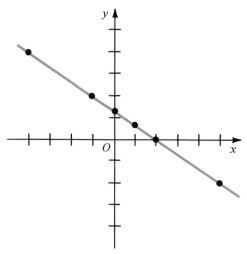

FIGURE 2.8 Graph of $2x + 3y = 4$

PROBLEM 2   Graph the set of points in the plane satisfying

$$y \geq 0$$

SOLUTION   The points with positive y-coordinates form a half-plane. The half-plane contains all points above the x-axis. Since the x-axis is determined by $y = 0$, our graph consists of the x-axis and of all points above it. Such a graph is called a *closed half-plane*. The word "closed" refers to the fact that the line bounding the half-plane, namely the x-axis, is included in the graph (Figure 2.9).

PROBLEM 3   Graph the set of points in the plane satisfying

$$-2 \leq x \leq 2$$

SOLUTION   A line through $(2, 0)$ perpendicular to the x-axis contains all points in the plane with x-coordinate 2. A parallel line through $(-2, 0)$ contains all points with x-coordinate -2. All points whose x-coordinates satisfy $-2 < x < 2$ lie between these two lines. The graph of $-2 \leq x \leq 2$ is called an *infinite vertical strip*. See Figure 2.10. The strip is *closed*, since it includes the bounding lines $x = -2$ and $x = 2$.

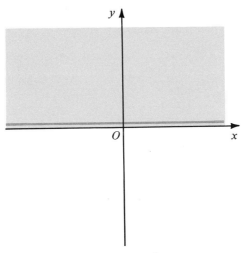

FIGURE 2.9 Graph of $y \geq 0$

PROBLEM 4 Graph the inequality

$$x - 3y > 4$$

SOLUTION We begin by graphing the equation

$$x - 3y = 4$$

By applying the same method we used in Problem 1, we can find ordered pair solutions of the equation. Some of these solutions are listed in the table on p. 56.

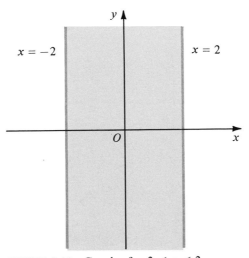

FIGURE 2.10 Graph of $-2 \leq x \leq 2$

x	1	0	4	-2	-5	7
y	-1	$-\frac{4}{3}$	0	-2	-3	1

The graph of $x - 3y = 4$ is a line. The six ordered pairs in the table correspond to six points on the line. The graph of the inequality consists of all points to one side of the line. Which side? To find out, we simply test a point. If $y = 0$, the inequality is satisfied only for $x > 4$. For example, the point $(5, 0)$ is a solution of the inequality. The graph of $x - 3y > 4$ is the half-plane shaded in Figure 2.11. The half-plane is *open* since it does not include the bounding line $x - 3y = 4$.

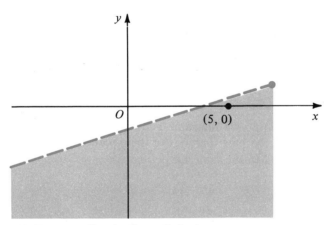

FIGURE 2.11   Graph of $x - 3y > 4$

EXERCISES   *for Section 2.1*

Coordinatize the plane by drawing a set of axes. Then locate and mark the given ordered pairs:

1. $(4, 0)$, $(0, -2)$, $(7, 5)$, $(6, -3)$ **2.** $(4, -7)$, $(2, 4)$, $(0, 0)$, $(-4, -4)$

3. $(1, -1)$, $(-3, 0)$, $(0, 5)$, $(6, 6)$ **4.** $(-4, 9)$, $(0, 5)$, $(8, 0)$, $(-5, 8)$

5. $(-9, -4)$, $(-4, -9)$, $(0, -4)$, $(5, 9)$, $(9, 4)$

Graph each of the following equations:

6.	$x + 1 = 0$	**7.**	$y - 2 = 0$
8.	$2x - 14 = 0$	**9.**	$3y + 15 = 0$
10.	$\dfrac{1}{x} = 2$		

Graph each of the following inequalities:

11.	$y > 2$	**12.**	$x \leq -1$
13.	$2x + 6 > 0$	**14.**	$7y - 21 \leq 0$
15.	$\dfrac{1}{y} < 3$		

Give the ordered pair description of the points:

16. in the first quadrant (*not* including the axes)

17. in the third quadrant (including the axes)

18. above the line $y = 2$

19. on or below the line $y = -3$

20. to the left of the line $x = \frac{1}{2}$

21. on or to the right of the line $x = -7$

Graph each of the following equations:

22.	$x + y = 2$	**23.**	$5x - 2y = 8$
24.	$2x - 5y = 7$	**25.**	$3y - 8x = 16$
26.	$2x - 8y = 19$	**27.**	$2x + 10y = 5$

Graph each of the following inequalities:

28.	$x + y > 2$	**29.**	$5x - 2y < 8$
30.	$2x - 5y \leq 7$	**31.**	$3y - 8x > 16$
32.	$2x - 8y \leq 19$	**33.**	$2x + 10y > 5$

Define each of the following by means of an inequality:

34. the half-plane below the line $x + 4y - 7 = 0$

35. the half-plane above the line $3x - 5y + 6 = 0$

36. the closed half-plane bounded by $3x - 6y + 4 = 0$ and containing the point $(2, -1)$

37. the closed half-plane bounded by $3x - 6y + 4 = 0$ and containing the point $(-3, 4)$

38. the closed half-plane bounded by $4x + 2y = 7$ and containing the point $(1, 1)$

Graph the set of points in the plane satisfying:

39. $-1 \leq x \leq 1$ **40.** $-2 \leq x \leq 3$

41. $1 < x < 4$ **42.** $1 < x \leq 4$

43. $-2 \leq y \leq 2$ **44.** $-1 \leq x \leq 1$ and $y > 0$

45. $x > 0$ and $-2 \leq y \leq 2$ **46.** $x > 1$ and $y > 2$

47. $x < -1$ and $y < 1$

2.2

LINES AND HALF-PLANES

In this section we will see the following:

1. A linear equation in two variables is the equation of a line. (This explains why the word "linear" is used to describe such equations.)

2. The graph of a linear inequality in two variables is a half-plane.

We begin with some examples.

2.2A Graphing Linear Equations

PROBLEM 1   Graph the equation

$$y = x$$

SOLUTION   The ordered pairs $(0, 0)$ and $(1, 1)$ are solutions of $y = x$. Draw the line through $(0, 0)$ and $(1, 1)$. (The line passes through the first and third quadrants, as shown in Figure 2.12. To be precise, it bisects the right angle between the positive x- and y-axes.) *Perpen-*

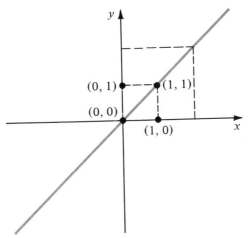

FIGURE 2.12 Graph of $y = x$

diculars dropped from $(1, 1)$ to the x- and y-axes have the same length. This is also true of perpendiculars dropped from any other point on the line.

If this does not seem obvious, look at Figure 2.13, which is a redrawn version of Figure 2.12. Triangles OAB and OPQ are similar; so are OAC and OPR. All these triangles are isosceles right triangles.

In other words, any point on the line has *equal* x- and y-coordinates. Moreover, all points in the plane with equal x- and y-coordinates are on the line. Since any ordered pair that solves $y = x$ is made up of two equal numbers, we see that the line through $(0, 0)$ and $(1, 1)$ is the graph of $y = x$.

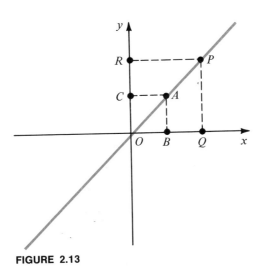

FIGURE 2.13

PROBLEM 2   Graph the equation

$$y = ax \qquad (a \neq 0)$$

SOLUTION   The ordered pairs $(0, 0)$ and $(1, a)$ are solutions of $y = ax$. Draw the line through $(0, 0)$ and $(1, a)$. (For the moment let's take $a > 0$.) If we drop perpendiculars from $(1, a)$ to the x- and y-axes, we find that the lengths of these perpendiculars are in the ratio $a : 1$ (Figure 2.14). By looking at Figure 2.15, which is a redrawn version of Figure 2.14, we see that this is also true of perpendiculars dropped from any other point on the line. For example, triangles OAB and OPQ are similar. This means that the ratios of lengths of corresponding sides are equal. Specifically, since A is the point $(1, a)$

$$\frac{\overline{AB}}{\overline{OB}} = \frac{\overline{PQ}}{\overline{OQ}} = \frac{a}{1}$$

If the coordinates of P are (x, y), then $\overline{PQ} = y$ and $\overline{OQ} = x$, so that

$$\frac{y}{x} = \frac{a}{1}$$

or
$$y = ax$$

But P can be *any* point on the line. In other words: Any point on the line corresponds to an ordered pair solution of $y = ax$.

By using the similar triangles of Figure 2.15, we also see that any point in the plane such that $y = ax$ is on the line. The line through $(0, 0)$ and $(1, a)$ is the graph of $y = ax$.

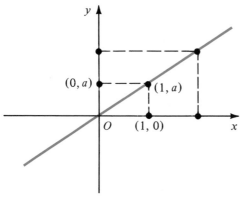

FIGURE 2.14   Graph of $y = ax$ $(a \neq 0)$

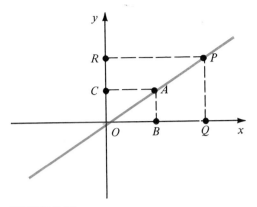

FIGURE 2.15

We have taken $a > 0$. If $a < 0$, the inclination of the line is different (see Figure 2.16). Again, the line through $(0, 0)$ and $(1, a)$ is the graph of $y = ax$.

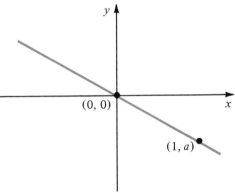

FIGURE 2.16 Graph of $y = ax$ $(a < 0)$ *where's b*

PROBLEM 3   Graph the equation

$$y = ax + b \quad (a \neq 0, b \neq 0).$$

SOLUTION   The ordered pairs $(0, b)$ and $(1, a + b)$ are solutions of $y = ax + b$. Draw the line through $(0, b)$ and $(1, a + b)$. Let's take $a > 0$ and $b > 0$, as in Figure 2.17. The point O' is $(0, b)$, and the point A' is $(1, a + b)$. The dashed line through the points O $(0, 0)$ and A $(1, a)$ is the graph of $y = ax$. Notice that O' is b units above O and A' is b units above A. *Every point on the line through $O'A'$ is b units above a corresponding point on the line through OA.* The two lines are

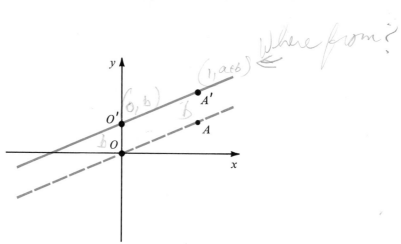

Where from?

FIGURE 2.17 Graph of $y = ax + b$ $(a \neq 0, b \neq 0)$

parallel. By proceeding exactly as we did in solving Problem 2, we can see that the line through $(0, b)$ and $(1, a + b)$ is the graph of $y = ax + b$.

Q. What if $a < 0$, or $b < 0$, or both?
A. The picture will not look like Figure 2.17. But it is still true that the line through $(0, b)$ and $(1, a + b)$ is the graph of $y = ax + b$.

EXERCISES *for Section 2.2A*

Graph each of the following equations:

1. $y = -x$

2. $x = 2y$

3. $2x = 3y + 4$

4. $x = cy + d$ $(c \neq 0, d \neq 0)$.

5. Graph the equations

$$y = -3x$$
$$y = -3x - 1$$
$$y = -3x + 2$$

and compare the results. What do the three graphs have in common? What do the three equations have in common?

6. Graph the equations

$$y = -3x + 2$$
$$y = 3x + 2$$

$$y = 2$$
$$y = \tfrac{2}{3}x + 2$$

and compare the results. What do the four graphs have in common? What do the four equations have in common?

2.2B The Equation of a Line

Suppose A and B are not both zero. Then:

The graph of the linear equation in two variables
$$Ax + By + C = 0$$
is a line.

There are two special cases.

The case $A = 0$. The equation reduces to
$$By + C = 0$$
or:
$$y = -\frac{C}{B}$$

The graph is a *horizontal line* passing through the point $\left(0, -\dfrac{C}{B}\right)$.

The case $B = 0$. The equation reduces to
$$Ax + C = 0$$
or:
$$x = -\frac{C}{A}$$

The graph is a *vertical line* passing through the point $\left(-\dfrac{C}{A}, 0\right)$.

If $A \neq 0$ and $B \neq 0$, the equation reduces to

$$y = -\frac{A}{B}x - \frac{C}{B}$$

Equations of this type were discussed in Problem 3 on page 61. The graph of the equation is a line passing through the points $\left(0, -\dfrac{C}{B}\right)$ and $\left(1, -\dfrac{(A + C)}{B}\right)$.

To sum up: If the linear equation in two variables reduces to a *one*-variable equation, its graph is a *horizontal line* (y = const.) or a *vertical line* (x = const.). Otherwise, the graph is a line that is neither horizontal or vertical.

The inclination of a non-vertical line is measured by its *slope*.

DEFINITION 1 Slope of a Line

A line $y = ax + b$ is said to have slope a.

EXAMPLES: SLOPE

1. A horizontal line has slope zero.

2. In Figure 2.18, the lines L_1, L_2, and L_3 have *positive* slope.

3. If a line with equation $y = ax + b$ has positive slope, then the parallel line $y = ax$ passes through the first and third quadrants.

4. In Figure 2.19, the lines L_a, L_b, and L_c have *negative* slope.

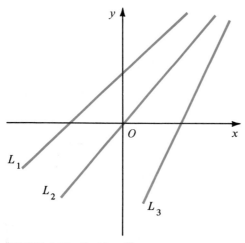

FIGURE 2.18 Positive Slope

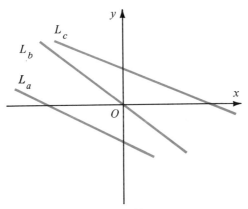

FIGURE 2.19 Negative Slope

5. If a line with equation $y = ax + b$ has negative slope, then the parallel line $y = ax$ passes through the second and fourth quadrants.

6. The following are equations of lines with slope 3: $y = 3x$, $y = 3x + 7$, and $y = 3x - 2$.

7. Some lines with slope -2 are: $y = -2x$, $y = -2x - 18$, and $y = -2x + \sqrt{7}$.

8. An equation of the form $x = c$ cannot be put in the form $y = ax + b$. The line $x = c$ is vertical, and the slope of a vertical line is not defined.

The next two problems illustrate the correspondence between linear equations and lines.

PROBLEM 1   Graph the equation

$$x + 2y = 6$$

SOLUTION   Since the equation is linear, its graph is a line. The ordered pair solutions $(0, 3)$ and $(6, 0)$ give us two points that determine the line (see Figure 2.20). Notice that the equation may be rewritten $y = -\frac{1}{2}x + 3$. This form of the equation shows that the slope of the line is $-\frac{1}{2}$.

PROBLEM 2   Find the equation of the line passing through the points $(-3, 1)$ and $(0, 7)$.

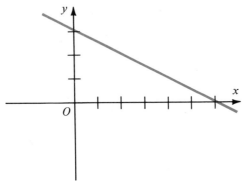

FIGURE 2.20 Graph of $x + 2y = 6$

SOLUTION   Draw the line through the two given points (Figure 2.21). The line has positive slope. Its equation is of the form $y = ax + b$.

    We determine a and b from a knowledge of the two points $(-3, 1)$ and $(0, 7)$. Since $(0, 7)$ is on the line, we have $b = 7$. Since $(-3, 1)$ is on the line, we have (setting $y = 1$ and $x = -3$ in $y = ax + b$)

$$1 = -3a + b = -3a + 7$$

or $a = 2$. The equation of the line is

$$y = 2x + 7$$

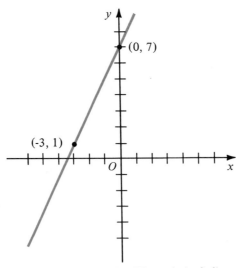

FIGURE 2.21 The Line Through $(-3, 1)$ and $(0, 7)$

The slope is the positive number 2.

Check: The ordered pairs $(-3, 1)$ and $(0, 7)$ satisfy the equation $y = 2x + 7$.

We have defined the slope of a line by means of its equation. If the equation is $y = ax + b$, then by definition the slope is a. Sometimes we want to determine the slope of a line without finding its equation. To understand how this can be done, consider the line $y = ax + b$. Two of the points on the line are $(0, b)$ and $(1, a + b)$. As shown in Figure 2.22, if we draw lines parallel to the axes through $(1, a + b)$, they meet at $(1, b)$. The triangle with vertices $(0, b), (1, a + b), (1, b)$ has base 1 and altitude a. The ratio $a : 1 = a$ is precisely the slope. The same ratio prevails for *any* two points on the line. We have the following definition.

DEFINITION 2   Slope of a Line

If $P_1\ (x_1, y_1)$ and $P_2\ (x_2, y_2)$ are any two points, then the slope of the line passing through P_1 and P_2 is

$$a = \text{slope} = \frac{y_2 - y_1}{x_2 - x_1}$$

To illustrate this second definition of slope, consider the line with slope a passing through the point $Q(0, b)$, as shown in Figure 2.23. If $P(x, y)$ is an arbitrary point on the line, then our definition gives

$$a = \text{slope} = \frac{y - b}{x - 0} = \frac{y - b}{x}$$

or: $y - b = ax$, or: $y = ax + b$

which is the equation of the line.

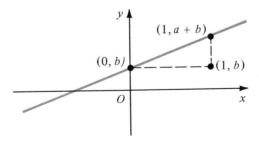

FIGURE 2.22

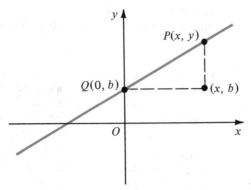

FIGURE 2.23

EXAMPLES: SLOPE OF A LINE

1. The slope of the line through $(0, 3)$ and $(6, 0)$ is

$$\frac{0 - 3}{6 - 0} = -\frac{3}{6} = -\frac{1}{2}$$

(see Problem 1, p. 65).

2. The slope of the line through $(-3, 1)$ and $(0, 7)$ is

$$\frac{7 - 1}{0 - (-3)} = \frac{6}{3} = 2$$

(see Problem 2, p. 65).

3. The slope of the line through $(17, 4)$ and $(-\sqrt{2}, 4)$ is

$$\frac{4 - 4}{17 - (-\sqrt{2})} = \frac{0}{17 + \sqrt{2}} = 0$$

The line is the horizontal line $y = 4$.

Definition 2 of the slope of a line really saves work in some problems. Try, for example, to solve Problem 4 by using the definition of slope on p. 64.

PROBLEM 3   Find the slope of the line that passes through the points $(1, 42)$ and $(-3, 30)$.

SOLUTION   By definition,

$$\text{slope} = \frac{y_2 - y_1}{x_2 - x_1}$$

$$= \frac{30 - 42}{-3 - 1} = \frac{-12}{-4} = 3$$

Why not the larger first?

$+42 - 30$ $\frac{12}{4} = 3$

$1 - (-3)$

doesn't matter

PROBLEM 4   The line L_1 passes through the points $(-2, 8)$ and $(17, -30)$. The line L_2 passes through the points $(16, -35)$ and $(-4, 5)$. Are L_1 and L_2 parallel?

SOLUTION   To answer the question, we find the slopes of L_1 and L_2. If they are equal, the lines are parallel. By definition:

$$\text{slope of } L_1 = \frac{-30 - 8}{17 - (-2)} = \frac{-38}{19} = -2$$

$$\text{slope of } L_2 = \frac{5 - (-35)}{-4 - 16} = \frac{40}{-20} = -2$$

The lines are parallel.

EXERCISES *for Section 2.2B*

Give three examples of:

1. horizontal lines
2. vertical lines
3. lines with positive slope
4. lines with negative slope
5. lines passing through only the first and third quadrants
6. lines passing through only the second and fourth quadrants
7. lines passing through only the first and fourth quadrants
8. lines passing through only the first and second quadrants

9. lines with slope 0.75

10. lines with slope $-\frac{1}{2}$

Graph each of the following linear equations.

11. $3x + 4y = 9$

12. $\frac{1}{2}x + \frac{1}{3}y = 1$

13. $x = \frac{1}{2}y - 2$

Find an equation for the line through the two given points, then graph the line.

14. $(-3, -6), (-2, -2)$ **15.** $(-1, -2), (0, 0)$

16. $(4, 7), (-7, -4)$ **17.** $(2, -2), (2, 5)$

Find the slope of line through the two given points.

18. $(-4, 3), (5, -2)$ **19.** $(0, -2), (-2, 0)$

20. $(4, 3), (-3, 4)$ **21.** $(6, 7), (-7, -6)$

22. $(1, -3), (7, -3)$ **23.** $(4, 0), (1, 1)$

---

24. Show that the slope of the line through any two of the three points

$$(2, 0), (3, 3), (0, -6)$$

is the same. From this fact, we see that the three points are *collinear* (that is, they lie on the same line).

25. Use the idea in Exercise 24 to find out if the three points

$$(0, -2), (2, -1), (4, 2)$$

are collinear.

26. Now find out if the three points

$$(0, -4), (4, 0), (2, 2)$$

are collinear.

---

27. Is the line L_1 through $(2, -5)$ and $(19, 12)$ parallel to the line L_2 through $(-4, -5)$ and $(-3, -6)$?

28. Is the line determined by $(3, 7)$ and $(12, 18)$ parallel to the line determined by $(-4, -5)$ and $(5, 6)$?

---

29. Find an equation for the line with slope 0 through the point $(17, -1)$.

30. Find an equation for the line with slope 2 through the point $(1, 3)$.

31. Find an equation for the line with slope $-\frac{1}{2}$ through the point $(0, 1)$.

32. Find an equation of the line through the point $(2, 3)$ and parallel to the line $y = 7x - 6$.

33. Find an equation of the line through the point $(-4, -1)$ and parallel to the line $3x + 5y + 7 = 0$.

2.2C Linear Inequalities and Half-Planes

A *half-plane* consists of all points to one side of a line. The bounding line may or may not be included in the half-plane. If it is, the half-plane is *closed*. If not, the half-plane is *open*.

EXAMPLES: OPEN AND CLOSED HALF-PLANES

1. The half-planes $x > 1$, $y < -2$ (shaded in Figure 2.24) are open half-planes. The bounding lines $x = 1$ and $y = -2$ of the half-planes are dashed to show that they are not included in the half-planes.

2. The half-planes $x \leq -\frac{3}{2}$, $y \geq \frac{1}{2}$ (shaded in Figure 2.25) are closed half-planes. The bounding lines $x = -\frac{3}{2}, y = \frac{1}{2}$ are shown as solid lines since they are included in the half-planes.

Suppose a half-plane is bounded by a line $y = ax + b\,(a \neq 0)$. If (x, y) is a point *above* the line (Figure 2.26), then it belongs to the graph of $y > ax + b$. Similarly, a point *below* the line belongs to the graph of $y < ax + b$.

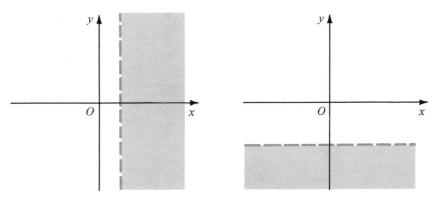

FIGURE 2.24 Open Half-Planes

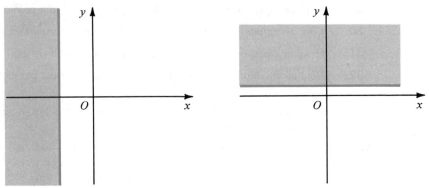

FIGURE 2.25 Closed Half-Planes

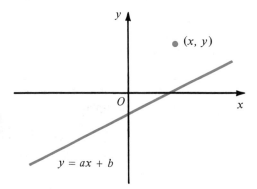

$y = ax + b$

FIGURE 2.26

> The graph of $y > ax + b$ is the half-plane lying above the line $y = ax + b$.
>
> The graph of $y < ax + b$ is the half-plane lying below the line $y = ax + b$.

The closed half-planes $y \geq ax + b, y \leq ax + b$ are defined in the same way. For example, the graph of $y \geq ax + b$ consists of all points on or above the line $y = ax + b$.

PROBLEM 1   Graph the inequality

$$2x + 3y \geq 6$$

SOLUTION   The inequality can be rewritten as:

$$3y \geq -2x + 6$$

or as:

$$y \geq -\tfrac{2}{3}x + 2$$

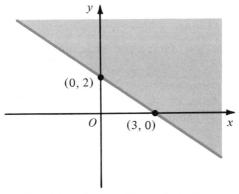

FIGURE 2.27   Graph of $2x + 3y \geq 6$

The graph is the closed half-plane above the line $y = -\tfrac{2}{3}x + 2$. Since the points $(0, 2)$ and $(3, 0)$ are on the line, the graph is as shown in Figure 2.27. The bounding line is solid since the half-plane is closed.

PROBLEM 2   Graph the inequality

$$x + y > 1$$

SOLUTION   The inequality can be rewritten as:

$$y > -x + 1$$

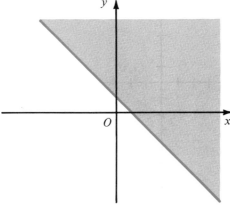

FIGURE 2.28   Graph of $x + y > 1$

The graph is the open half-plane above the line $y = -x + 1$. The line is easy to graph: two of its points are $(1, 0)$ and $(0, 1)$. Figure 2.28 duplicates Figure 2.5. But Figure 2.5 was obtained by arm-waving. Now we have an easy systematic method for graphing linear inequalities.

ARM-
WAVING?

PROBLEM 3   Graph the inequality

$$2x - 3y \geq 6$$

SOLUTION   The inequality can be rewritten:

$$-3y \geq -2x + 6$$

or:

$$3y \leq 2x - 6$$

or:

$$y \leq \tfrac{2}{3}x - 2$$

The graph is the closed half-plane below the line $y = \tfrac{2}{3}x - 2$. Two points on the line are: $(0, -2)$ and $(3, 0)$. The graph is shown in Figure 2.29.

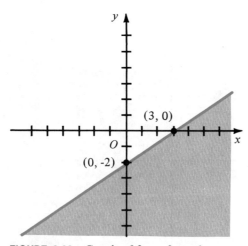

FIGURE 2.29   Graph of $2x - 3y \geq 6$

Graph each of the following inequalities:

1. $y \leq 3x + 2$ **2.** $y - x \geq 4$

3. $x + 2y < 2$ **4.** $x - 3y > 4$

5. $y > -4x + 5$ **6.** $x < 3y + 4$

7. $8x + 4y \geq 5$ **8.** $4x + 5 > 3y$

9. $3y - 9x + 4 > 0$

Write an inequality corresponding to each of the following:

10. the open half-plane below the line $6x + 4y - 5 = 0$

11. the open half-plane above the line $2y - 8x + 5 = 0$

12. the closed half-plane below the line $3x - 2y + 4 = 0$

13. the closed half-plane above the line $2x - 5y + 7 = 0$

14. the closed half-plane bounded by $y + 3x + 7 = 0$ and containing the point $(-2, 3)$

15. a closed half-plane bounded by $7x + 8y - 10 = 0$ and containing the point $(-2, 3)$

16. the closed half-plane bounded by $2x + 3y + 4 = 0$ and *not* containing the point $(-7, -6)$

2.3 APPLYING LINEAR EQUATIONS TO REAL-WORLD PROBLEMS

The best way to show how linear equations are applied is to give examples.

EXAMPLE 1: LINEAR SALES PREDICTION

Calder Motor Company invested $190 million in the manufacture of the Smog Moratorium, an antipollution device. The device earned the approval of the Environmental Conservation Agency since it markedly reduced hydrocarbon and other emissions from Calder engines. Unfortunately, the operation of the Smog Moratorium produced various substances that were said to be increasing the U.S. annual death rate by 10 per million. The alleged news received publicity because it was mentioned on a national TV program. A fuss was made, and Calder weekly sales started dropping. Calder economists prepared a table and graph. The variables were:

x = number of weeks since alleged news was first publicized

y = weekly sales of Calder cars, in thousands.

x	0	1	2	3	4	5
y	26	24	22	20	18	16

T. R. Matthews, senior economist at Calder, explained the graph to the Calder board. Since the line in Figure 2.30 contained the two points (0, 26) and (5, 16), it was easy for him to show that weekly sales (in thousands) over the five-week period could be described by the linear equation

$$y = -2x + 26$$

"A slope of -2 is disastrous!" he said. Pointing to the dotted line on the graph, he predicted that in five more weeks at this rate Calder sales would be down to 6000 cars a week.

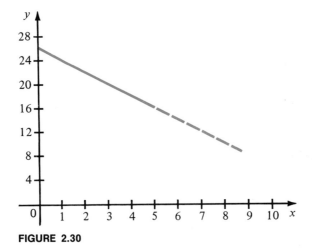

FIGURE 2.30

Various solutions were proposed by board members:

1. a public relations campaign challenging the alleged scientific data and the alleged death figures;

2. a public relations campaign emphasizing the number of jobs likely to be lost if the Smog Moratorium could no longer be manufactured.

3. an advertising campaign on the theme "The Smog Moratorium is working! America's cities are coming out from under their blanket of smog!" The campaign would completely ignore the alleged death figures.

The board decided to implement plans 2 and 3. The countercampaign began to take effect in three weeks. Six weeks after that, Calder economists had a new table and a new graph to show the board. The variables were:

x = number of weeks since countercampaign impacted public

y = weekly sales of Calder cars, in thousands

x	0	1	2	3	4	5
y	12	16	20	24	28	32

The equation of the sales line was:

$$y = 4x + 12$$

The slope was +4, and the dotted line showing hypothetical sales looked very good (Figure 2.31).

EXAMPLE 2: LINEAR COST ANALYSIS

Quality Books, Inc. publishes paperback books. It has acquired paperback rights to the highly successful novel *The Family*. Quality has paid $1 million for these rights. The firm expects to recover its money (and earn a slight profit) by selling over a million copies of *The Family*. The editor-in-chief calculates that the cost C in dollars of publishing N copies will be:

$$C = \tfrac{1}{2}N + 1{,}000{,}000$$

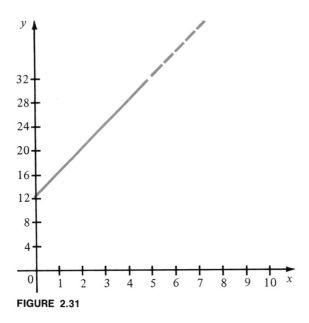

FIGURE 2.31

The equation says that the cost of publishing *no* copies is $1 million, the sum paid for the rights. This amount is called the *fixed cost* of publication. The *variable cost* per book is the average amount it costs to print, bind, advertise, and distribute each copy. As the equation indicates, the variable cost is half a dollar per copy. The equation

$$C = \tfrac{1}{2}N + 1{,}000{,}000$$

is the equation of a line with slope $\tfrac{1}{2}$. To graph the line conveniently, we choose the units such that 1 unit corresponds to 1 million for either N (copies sold) or C (cost in dollars of publication). The line is then drawn through the two points $(0, 1)$ ($N = 0$, $C = 1$ million) and $(2, 2)$ ($N = C = 2$ million). See Figure 2.32.

Suppose that Quality Books sells 1 million copies of *The Family*. The total cost will be

$$C = \tfrac{1}{2}(1{,}000{,}000) + 1{,}000{,}000$$
$$= \$1{,}500{,}000$$

Sellers of the book pay the publisher $1.50 per copy. (Buyers of the book pay the bookseller $2.45 per copy.) One million copies will therefore bring in $1.5 million, which exactly matches the total cost. The point where costs exactly match receipts is called the *break-even point*.

If Quality sells 1,200,000 copies of the book, the total receipts will be

$$(1{,}200{,}000)(1\tfrac{1}{2}) = \$1{,}800{,}000$$

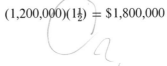

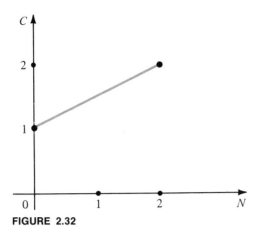

FIGURE 2.32

The total cost will be

$$C = \tfrac{1}{2}(1{,}200{,}000) + 1{,}000{,}000$$
$$= \$1{,}600{,}000$$

There will be a profit of $200,000.

If *The Family* sells 2 million copies in paperback (as the publishers hope), the receipts will be $3 million, and the total cost will be

$$C = \tfrac{1}{2}(2{,}000{,}000) + 1{,}000{,}000$$

or $2 million. The profit will be $1 million.

We see that a paperback publisher's profits go up very rapidly once the break-even point is passed. The same principle applies to many other businesses, but the facts are rarely as simple as those just described. For example, the variable cost of producing an item may go up as sales increase beyond a company's expectations. The company might have to subcontract some of its production of the big-selling item, or pay overtime to its own production workers.

The concept of *depreciation* is well known to every car owner. Depreciation is largest in the first year one owns a new car, next largest in the second year, and fairly steady after the third year. The first example of linear depreciation reflects these realities.

EXAMPLE 3: LINEAR DEPRECIATION OF A CAR

Miles Malone bought a high-quality, prestigious sedan for $18,000. Three years later it was worth $5500. From that point on, the car loses 2% of its $5500 value each month. The value y of the car in dollars after x months will be

$$y = 5500 - 5500(0.02)x$$

or:

$$y = -110x + 5500$$

The graph of this equation is a line with slope -110. (The car loses value at the rate of $110 a month.) If Malone keeps his car for 20 more months, its value will be

$$-110(20) + 5500 = \$3300$$

The following table gives value y of the car against month x of ownership (after month 36):

x (month)	0	5	10	15	20
y (value)	5500	4950	4400	3850	3300

Figure 2.33 shows this set of data in a graph. The choice of units is different on the two axes. Whatever the choice of units, the graph of depreciation at a steady rate is a *line*. This is why such depreciation is called *linear*. The slope -110 of the line is, of course, unaffected by the choice of units.

For record-keeping or income tax purposes, the assets of a business are sometimes assumed to depreciate linearly even when they do not.

**EXAMPLE 4: LINEAR DEPRECIATION IN THE
            RAG TRADE**

Frieda Franklin is in the rag trade. That is, she is a dress designer and

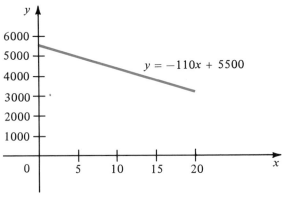

FIGURE 2.33

manufacturer. She calculates that any dresses she has not sold by the end of the buying season have zero value. In making a quarterly report to her stockholders, she lists the value of dresses on hand (10 weeks before the end of the season) as $210,000, and estimates that 10% of this value will be lost each week the dresses are unsold. After x weeks, the estimated value y of the dresses is:

$$y = 210,000 - (210,000)(0.10)x$$

or:

$$y = -21,000x + 210,000$$

dollars. If the dresses remain unsold for 6 weeks, their value will decline to

$$-21,000(6) + 210,000 = \$84,000$$

In drawing the graph (Figure 2.34), we choose different units on the two axes. The very steep downward slope ($-21,000$) of the line says that you need strong nerves in the rag trade.

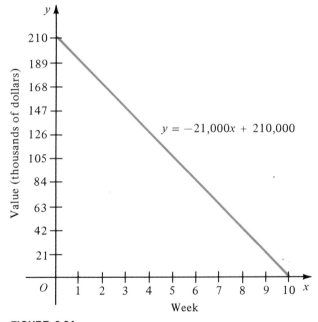

FIGURE 2.34

EXERCISES *for Section 2.3*

The following exercises are divided into five groups. The first two groups (Exercises 1–13) contain exercises in linear sales prediction. The third group (Exercises 14–19) contains exercises in linear cost analysis. The last two groups (Exercises 20–26) contain exercises in linear depreciation.

Universal Mills, one of the leading millers in Minneapolis, sells three well-known breakfast cereals: the healthful Raisin Soy, the "natural" cereal Good Morning, and the big-selling Sugar Yummies. All three cereals are competitive in their markets, and all three are intelligently and adequately advertised. Sales are expected to continue in their present patterns for the next 8 to 9 months at least. The company's market research department has tabulated sales of the three cereals for the past 6 months. In each of the three following tables:

x = number of months since the beginning of the 6 months
y = number of thousand boxes of the cereal sold in the preceding month

1. Choose convenient units for x and y and graph the data in Table 1. If the points you have graphed lie on a line, find the equation and slope of the line.

TABLE 1 RAISIN SOY Sales

x	0	1	2	3	4	5
y	90	91.75	93.5	95.25	97	98.75

TABLE 2 GOOD MORNING Sales

x	0	1	2	3	4	5
y	130	142	154	166	178	190

TABLE 3 SUGAR YUMMIES Sales

x	0	1	2	3	4	5
y	480	491	502	513	524	535

2. Repeat for Table 2.

3. Repeat for Table 3.

4. (This question depends on Exercises 2 and 3). Looking at Tables 2 and 3, you may think that sales of Good Morning are rising faster than sales of Sugar Yummies. Is this true? Does it follow from your answers to Exercises 2 and 3? If present trends continue far into the future, will Good Morning ever outsell Sugar Yummies? If so, when?

Universal Mills needs large stocks of grains and other ingredients to produce its three cereals. These stocks will be bought and set aside when prices are at their lowest. It would be poor business to buy too little or too much. The estimates of future cereal sales called for in the next three exercises will help management decide how much of each ingredient will be needed.

5. To make a buying decision about soybeans, management would like an estimate of Raisin Soy sales 8 months after sales reached 97,000 boxes a month. Does your answer to Exercise 1 allow you to make such an estimate? If so, how many boxes will be sold at that time?

6. Oats, raisins, and honey are among the ingredients in Good Morning. Sales estimates are needed for 3 months, 5 months, and 8 months past the data point (5, 190). Use your answer to Exercise 2 to make the required estimates.

7. A writer in a major women's magazine has just announced that eating a pound of Sugar Yummies a day will make any woman thin. Top Universal Mills executives find this claim somewhat hard to believe, but they are not about to argue with it. Market research estimates that the equation for monthly sales over the next 6 months will be

$$y = 97x + 535$$

A company vice-president who took a quick look at this equation said, "We will have to increase our buying of ingredients for the next six months by 50%!" Was he correct?

Good Old Fashioned Entertainment (GOFE) is a corporation that bought and renovated a large number of old movie houses. It then showed good double features in these movie houses for a price of one dollar. GOFE's planning specialist had the data shown in Tables 1, 2, and 3 (p. 84) after 6 months of operation.

8. Choose suitable units for x and y, and graph the ordered pairs $(1, 9)$, $(2, 20)$, etc., in Table 1. If the 6 points lie on a line, find the equation and slope of the line.

TABLE 1

x	1	2	3	4	5	6
y	9	20	31	42	53	64

x = number of months GOFE has been in business
y = number of paid admissions per month, in tens of thousands

TABLE 2

x	1	2	3	4	5	6
y	8	11	14	17	20	23

x = number of months GOFE has been in business
y = number of boxes of popcorn sold per month, in thousands

TABLE 3

x	1	2	3	4	5	6
y	93	208	323	438	553	668

x = number of months GOFE has been in business
y = cash receipts (admissions, sales of popcorn and other refreshments) per month, in thousands of dollars

9. Repeat for Table 2.

10. Repeat for Table 3.

11. GOFE's management set a goal of 1,200,000 paid admissions a month by the end of the first year of operation. Can you use your answer to Exercise 8 to predict if this goal will be met? If so, when?

12. GOFE's planning specialist thinks that popcorn sales are doing slightly better than he expected. His original prediction was for sales of 40,000 boxes of popcorn a month at the end of GOFE's first year. Now he predicts sales of

41,000 boxes a month at the end of the first year. Does your answer to Exercise 9 support his prediction? Can you predict popcorn sales at the end of GOFE's first 15 months in business?

13. GOFE needs monthly cash receipts of $1,500,000 to stay in business. It does not seem likely that receipts will reach this point at the end of GOFE's first year. Use your answer to Exercise 10 to predict when monthly receipts will reach or exceed $1,500,000. Now adopt the point of view of a hard-headed investor in GOFE. Explain why you do or do not think GOFE will be in business at the end of its second year.

Quality Books did not have very good luck with its would-be best-seller *The Family*. The book got a lot of attention on talk shows. The critics all described *The Family* as wholesome, heartwarming, and absorbing. The owners of Quality Books were delighted, so they ordered an increased printing of *The Family*. They thought their only problem would be investing the profits. The following table shows what happened in the 6 months following paperback publication of *The Family*. The variables are:

x	1	2	3	4	5	6
y	9672	8231	7619	5802	2811	343

x = number of months since paperback *The Family* appeared

y = number of copies (not *thousands* of copies, but *copies*) sold in preceding month

The editors at Quality Books decided to do the cost analysis contained in the following questions.

14. The fixed cost of publishing *The Family* was the million dollars paid for paperback rights. The variable cost per copy *would* have been half a dollar, with large sales. With the tiny sales shown in the table, the variable cost per copy was $10. Use this data to write a linear equation giving the cost C in dollars of publishing N copies of *The Family*. Graph the equation. Compare the slope of the line with the slope of the line in Figure 2.32.

15. What is the total cost of publishing *The Family* after 1 month? 3 months? 6 months?

16. Quality Books received $1.50 for each copy of *The Family* that was sold. How much had the firm lost on the book after 1 month? 3 months? 6 months?

In the old days, authors were paid a royalty for each copy of a paperback book sold instead of receiving a fixed sum independent of the number of copies sold. If this system had been adopted for *The Family* and if the author received a 25-cent royalty for each copy, losses on the book would have been much smaller. Explain this by answering the following questions.

17. Write a linear equation for the cost C in dollars of publishing N copies of the book, under the royalty system. Graph the equation. Compare the slope of the line with the slope of the line in your answer to Exercise 14.

18. Give the total cost of publishing *The Family* after 1, 3, and 6 months under the royalty system.

19. Compare the losses under the royalty system with the losses you calculated in answering Exercise 16.

Kris Keitel bought a used Honda for $550. After riding the bike for 22 months, she sold it for $220.

20. Assume the bike depreciated linearly. Draw a graph showing the depreciation.

21. Find the equation of the line you graphed in Exercise 20.

22. From your answer to Exercise 21: How much value did the bike lose each month? How much was it worth (theoretically) after 9 months? 11 months? 13 months?

Jack Adams, an instructor in a college's physical education department, constructed his own weight room at home. Jack bought secondhand weights, mats, and benches; built racks and bars himself; and bought a new Universal machine. The total cost of the weight room was $2300. He deducted that amount from his next year's income tax. The IRS called him in. "Mr. Adams," the auditor said, "the cost of your weight room is a deductible professional expense, but you cannot deduct it all at once." The following questions explore the choices open to Jack Adams.

23. He could assume the weight room had a useful life of 20 years. This would mean linear depreciation from a value of $2300 to a value of zero over that period. Draw a graph illustrating this choice of depreciation method. (Your variables should be x = year, from 0 to 20; y = value, from 2300 to 0.) Write an equation corresponding to the graph. How much will Jack be able to claim as a deduction each year if he follows the 20-year method?

24. He might assume the weight room would lose $1800 of its value in 10 years. If the depreciation is linear, draw a graph picturing the assumed loss of value. (For variables, take x = year, from 0 to 10; y = value, from 2300 to 500). Write a linear equation connecting the variables x and y. Compare the tax deductions given by the 10-year and 20-year methods.

The weight room takes up 10% of the floor space of Jack Adams' house. He could therefore list 10% of the $3500 annual cost of running his house as a tax deduction. Suppose he does this.

25. If Jack also uses the 20-year method of Exercise 23, write an equation and draw a graph showing how the total amount he deducts will grow from year to year. [Variables: x = year; y = total amount deducted by year x. The first data point is $(0, 0)$.]

26. Repeat Exercise 25 for the 10-year method of Exercise 24.

2.4 SYSTEMS OF TWO LINEAR EQUATIONS

If a line is the graph of a linear equation, then two lines must be the graph of two linear equations. Figure 2.35 shows the graph of the linear equations

(2.1)
$$\begin{cases} 2x - 3y = 7 \\ 4x + 3y = 5 \end{cases}$$

The lines intersect at one point. The meaning is clear: Each point on a line is an ordered pair solution of the corresponding linear equation. The point at which the two lines intersect is therefore an ordered pair solution of the *two* corresponding equations.

According to Figure 2.35, the two equations (2.1) have one and only one solution in common: the ordered pair $(2, -1)$.

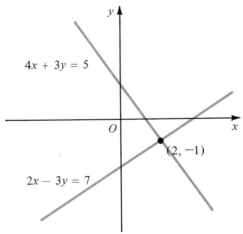

FIGURE 2.35 Graph of
$$\begin{cases} 2x - 3y = 7 \\ 4x + 3y = 5 \end{cases}$$

We see that the problem of simultaneously solving two linear equations in two variables can be solved graphically. The problem can also be solved algebraically as follows. Add the two equations:

$$\begin{array}{rcl} 2x - 3y &=& 7 \\ 4x + 3y &=& 5 \\ \hline 6x &=& 12 \end{array}$$

or:

$$x = 2$$

If $x = 2$, then $2x - 3y = 7$ only for $y = -1$. If $x = 2$, then $4x + 3y = 5$ only for $y = -1$. The ordered pair $(2, -1)$ is therefore the simultaneous solution of the two equations or, as we shall say, the *solution of the system*.

The system (2.1) was easy to solve, since one of the variables dropped out when we added the two equations. For a slightly more complicated example, consider the system

$$(2.2) \qquad \begin{cases} x - 3y = 9 \\ 2x + y = 4 \end{cases}$$

Neither of the variables drops out if we add the two equations. Instead, we can multiply the second equation of the system by 3, and then add. This will make y drop out:

$$\begin{array}{rcl} x - 3y &=& 9 \\ 6x + 3y &=& 12 \\ \hline 7x &=& 21 \end{array}$$

or:

$$x = 3$$

If we set $x = 3$ in either of the equations, we find that

$$y = -2$$

The solution of the system is $(3, -2)$.

The algebraic method we have just used to solve systems (2.1) and (2.2) is called the *addition method*.

The idea of the addition method is to transform the two equations of a system in such a way that addition causes one of the variables to drop out. In the case of system (2.1), no transformation was necessary: we merely added. For system (2.2), we had to transform by multiplying the second equation of the system by 3. For a system like

$$\begin{cases} 3x + 4y = 5 \\ 2x + 3y = 1 \end{cases}$$

we might multiply the first equation by 3 and the second by -4 before adding. (This would eliminate y. If we prefer to eliminate x, we multiply the first equation by 2 and the second by -3 before adding.)

Sometimes the addition method shows that a system does not have a solution. For example, take

(2.3)
$$\begin{cases} 3x - y = 4 \\ 6x - 2y = 3 \end{cases}$$

Multiply the first equation of the system by -2, and add:

$$\begin{array}{r} -6x + 2y = -8 \\ 6x - 2y = 3 \\ \hline 0 = -5 \end{array}$$

The result is a false equation. The system has no solution. Why not? If we rewrite the system as

$$\begin{cases} y = 3x - 4 \\ y = 3x - \frac{3}{2} \end{cases}$$

we see (Figure 2.36) that the lines corresponding to the equation have the same slope. The lines are parallel, and therefore never intersect. A system like (2.3), which has no solution, is called *inconsistent*. (By contrast, systems like (2.1) and (2.2), which have solutions, are called *consistent*.)

There is one more case to watch out for. Consider the system

(2.4)
$$\begin{cases} 3x - 4y + 12 = 0 \\ 9x - 12y + 36 = 0 \end{cases}$$

Multiply the first equation of the system by -3 and add:

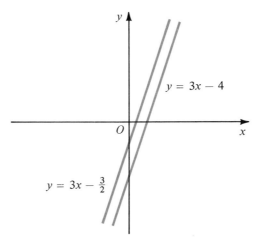

FIGURE 2.36 Graph of
$$\begin{cases} y = 3x - 4 \\ y = 3x - \frac{3}{2} \end{cases}$$

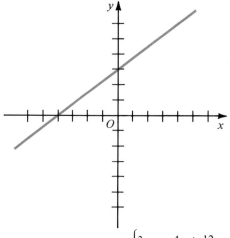

FIGURE 2.37 Graph of $\begin{cases} 3x - 4y + 12 = 0 \\ 9x - 12y + 36 = 0 \end{cases}$

$$\begin{array}{r} -9x + 12y - 36 = 0 \\ 9x - 12y + 36 = 0 \\ \hline 0 = 0 \end{array}$$

The result is a true equation. The system (2.4) has infinitely many solutions because the two equations of the system are constant multiples of one another. They have the same line as a graph (Figure 2.37), and each point on the line corresponds to a solution of the system. Such a system is called *dependent*.

Q. What do we do about systems where we do not need the addition method?

A. If we have a system like

$$2y = -6$$

$$7x + 5y = 34$$

adding the equations would certainly be counterproductive. Instead, we solve the one-variable equation $2y = -6$. Then we substitute the solution $y = -3$ into the second equation. The solution of the system is $(x, y) = (7, -3)$. Things are always just that simple when one of the equations in a system is a one-variable equation. That possibility is the first one considered in Figure 2.38.

In each of the following four problems, we will use the addition method to classify the given system as consistent, inconsistent, or dependent.

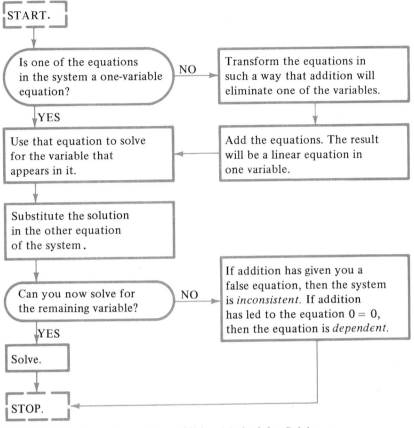

FIGURE 2.38 Flow Chart: The Addition Method for Solving a System of Two Linear Equations in Two Variables

If the system is consistent, we will find the solution. If it is inconsistent or dependent, we explain why.

PROBLEM 1
$$\begin{cases} 3x + 4y = 5 \\ 2x + 3y = 1 \end{cases}$$

SOLUTION Multiply the first equation of the system by 3 and the second by -4. Add:

$$\begin{array}{rcl} 9x + 12y & = & 15 \\ -8x - 12y & = & -4 \\ \hline x & = & 11 \end{array}$$

The system is *consistent*. By substituting $x = 11$ in either equation of the system, we find $y = -7$. The solution of the system is $(11, -7)$.

PROBLEM 2
$$\begin{cases} 5x + 5y = 10 \\ -3x - 3y = -6 \end{cases}$$

SOLUTION   Multiply the first equation of the system by 3 and the second equation by 5. Add:

$$\begin{array}{r} 15x + 15y = 30 \\ -15x - 15y = -30 \\ \hline 0 = 0 \end{array}$$

The system is *dependent*. The equations of the system are constant multiples of one another: as graphs, they have the same line.

PROBLEM 3
$$\begin{cases} 4x + 2y = 3 \\ 2x + y = 5 \end{cases}$$

SOLUTION   Multiply the second equation of the system by -2. Add:

$$\begin{array}{r} 4x + 2y = 3 \\ -4x - 2y = -10 \\ \hline 0 = -7 \end{array}$$

The system is *inconsistent*. If we rewrite the system in the form

$$y = -2x + \tfrac{3}{2}$$
$$y = -2x + 5$$

we see that the graphs of the two linear equations are distinct lines with the same slope (parallel lines), which of course have no point in common.

PROBLEM 4
$$\begin{cases} 2x + 3y = 1 \\ 4x + 2y = -1 \end{cases}$$

SOLUTION   Multiply the first equation of the system by -2. Add:

$$\begin{array}{r} -4x - 6y = -2 \\ 4x + 2y = -1 \\ \hline -4y = -3 \end{array}$$

or:

$$y = \tfrac{3}{4}$$

The system is *consistent*. If we substitute $y = \tfrac{3}{4}$ in either equation, we find $x = -\tfrac{5}{8}$. The solution of the system is $(-\tfrac{5}{8}, \tfrac{3}{4})$.

Graph each of the following systems. From the graph, classify the system as consistent, inconsistent, or dependent. If the equations are consistent, find their solution from the graph.

1.
$$\begin{cases} 2x - y = 5 \\ y = 2x + 7 \end{cases}$$

2.
$$\begin{cases} y - 3x = 5 \\ 3x + y + 3 = 0 \end{cases}$$

3.
$$\begin{cases} x - 3y = 1 \\ 5x + 6y = 2 \end{cases}$$

4.
$$\begin{cases} 8x - 2y = 3 \\ y = 4x - 7 \end{cases}$$

5.
$$\begin{cases} y = 5 + 3x \\ 6x + 2y = 0 \end{cases}$$

Use the addition method to classify each of the following systems of equations as consistent, inconsistent, or dependent. Find the solution of each consistent pair of equations.

6.
$$\begin{cases} 5x + 2y = 18 \\ 4x - 2y = 5 \end{cases}$$

7.
$$\begin{cases} 4x - y - 4 = 0 \\ 2x + 3y - 2 = 0 \end{cases}$$

8.
$$\begin{cases} p + 4q = 9 \\ 3p = 2q + 10 \end{cases}$$

9.
$$\begin{cases} 3x - 2y = 17 \\ 2x - 2y = -23 \end{cases}$$

10.
$$\begin{cases} y = 2 - x \\ 3x + y = 5 \end{cases}$$

11.
$$\begin{cases} 4u - 3v = -9 \\ 5u + 2v = 56 \end{cases}$$

12.
$$\begin{cases} 3x + 2y = 4 \\ y = 4 - 3x \end{cases}$$

13.
$$\begin{cases} 6x + 2y = 4 \\ y = 4 - 3x \end{cases}$$

14.
$$\begin{cases} 4x - 2y = 7 \\ 5x - 2y = 9 \end{cases}$$

15.
$$\begin{cases} 9x - 4y = 6 \\ 6x - 3y = 5 \end{cases}$$

16.
$$\begin{cases} 3a - 4b + 2 = 0 \\ b = 4 + a \end{cases}$$

17.
$$\begin{cases} 4a - 2b + 2 = 0 \\ b = 1 + 2a \end{cases}$$

18.
$$\begin{cases} 6x + 4y = 4 \\ x + 8y = 3 \end{cases}$$

19.
$$\begin{cases} 3p + 7q = 1 \\ 6p + 14q = 1 \end{cases}$$

20.
$$\begin{cases} x + 3y = -3 \\ -3x + y = 5 \end{cases}$$

21.
$$\begin{cases} 4x + 5y - 5 = 0 \\ 7x - 3y - 4 = 0 \end{cases}$$

22.
$$\begin{cases} 17x + 2y - 9 = 0 \\ 3x - 3y - 7 = 0 \end{cases}$$

23.
$$\begin{cases} m - 3n = 4 \\ m + 3n = -7 \end{cases}$$

24. $\begin{cases} 2x + y = 7 \\ -2x + 2y = -7 \end{cases}$

25. $\begin{cases} x + 2y = 7 \\ x - 2y = -7 \end{cases}$

26. $\begin{cases} x + 2y = 7 \\ x + 2y = -7 \end{cases}$

27. $\begin{cases} 4x + 3y = 16 \\ 12x - 4y = 48 \end{cases}$

28. $\begin{cases} 11x + 9y = 39 \\ 4x = 6y - 5 \end{cases}$

29. $\begin{cases} 9m - 6n = 3 \\ 3m - 2n = 1 \end{cases}$

30. $\begin{cases} \dfrac{x}{4} + \dfrac{y}{3} = 1 \\ \dfrac{x}{5} - \dfrac{y}{4} = -1 \end{cases}$

31. $\begin{cases} \dfrac{x}{4} + \dfrac{y}{3} = 1 \\ \dfrac{x}{4} + \dfrac{y}{3} = -1 \end{cases}$

2.5 THE LINE OF BEST FIT AND THE METHOD OF AVERAGES

Applying linear equations in Section 2.3 was very easy. The data always led to a linear equation. We then chose convenient units and graphed the equation.

Things are not usually that simple in the real world. In Figure 2.30, for example, T. R. Matthews graphed y (weekly sales) against x (weeks since alleged news first came out). Car sales fell at a steady rate of two (thousand) units per week. This is so uniform that one can suspect a slight misrepresentation of the data. Actually, Matthews did smooth things out a bit. The correct figures were:

x	0	1	2	3	4	5
y	25.8	24.1	21.4	19.3	17.8	15.3

The points are marked on the axes of Figure 2.39. Looking at the points, we see that they do not all lie on the same line, but they do come reasonably close to it. Matthews decided to give an easy-to-follow picture of the data by

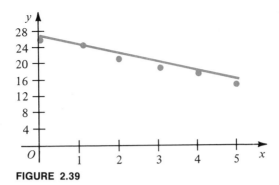

FIGURE 2.39

simply drawing the line that seemed to come closest to all the points. Such a line is called a *line of best fit*. The line of best fit he drew is shown in Figure 2.39. It is in fact the line shown in Figure 2.30. Once he had drawn the line, Matthews thought it would be best to avoid confusing the board of directors with higher mathematics. He therefore adjusted the data to fit his line.

The decision was unwise. The directors had the correct sales figures, and they asked Matthews why he was using inaccurate numbers. He had to pull out Figure 2.39 and explain about his line of best fit.

He was then asked how he knew his line of best fit was better than some other line he might have drawn. Matthews tried to give a clear, convincing answer. He explained the *method of averages* for finding the line of best fit.

Boiled down to essentials, what he said was:

1. He assumed the data could be described by a line

$$y = ax + b$$

2. As a first step in determining a and b, he substituted the sales data into the equation. Since he had data for weeks 0 through 5, this gave him 6 equations ($x = 0, 1, 2, 3, 4, 5$, and corresponding values for y):

$$\begin{cases} 25.8 = b \\ 24.1 = a + b \\ 21.4 = 2a + b \end{cases}$$

$$\begin{cases} 19.3 = 3a + b \\ 17.8 = 4a + b \\ 15.3 = 5a + b \end{cases}$$

3. He divided the six equations into two groups of three (note the

brackets above) and added the three equations in each group to obtain the system

$$\begin{cases} 71.3 = 3a + 3b \\ 52.4 = 12a + 3b \end{cases}$$

4. To solve for a and b, Matthews subtracted the second equation of the system from the first. This gave:

$$18.9 = -9a$$

or:

$$a = -2.1$$

He then found that:

$$b = 25.9$$

5. His method of averages result for the line of best fit was:

$$y = -2.1x + 25.9$$

Finally Matthews rounded off his figures to the nearest tenth, which gave the equation $y = -2x + 26$.

If you did not find the Matthews explanation all that clear, the following worked-out problems showing how to use the method of averages may help.

PROBLEM 1   Find a line of best fit for the points (2, 20), (5, 17), (10, 13), (14, 10), (16, 9), (20, 6), (23, 3).

SOLUTION   Assume an equation

$$y = ax + b$$

for the line of best fit. Substitute the coordinates of the seven points into the equation:

$$\begin{cases} 20 = 2a + b \\ 17 = 5a + b \\ 13 = 10a + b \\ 10 = 14a + b \end{cases}$$

$$\begin{cases} 9 = 16a + b \\ 6 = 20a + b \\ 3 = 23a + b \end{cases}$$

Group the equations as indicated by the brackets. Add the four equations in the first group, and then the three equations in the second group. The resulting two equations are:

$$\begin{cases} 60 = 31a + 4b \\ 18 = 59a + 3b \end{cases}$$

To solve the system, multiply the first equation by 3 and the second by −4. Add:

$$\begin{aligned} 180 = & \quad 93a + 12b \\ -72 = & -236a - 12b \\ \hline 108 = & -143a \end{aligned}$$

or:

$$a = -0.755$$

The corresponding value for b is:

$$b = 20.85$$

Our line of best fit is:

$$y = -0.755x + 20.85$$

The line and the given points are graphed in Figure 2.40.

PROBLEM 2   Find a line of best fit for the data in the table:

x	0	5	10	15	20	25	30	35	40
y	0.5	4.2	7.3	10.7	13.2	17.5	19.6	22.4	26.2

SOLUTION   Use the method of averages. Assume that the line of best fit has the equation

$$y = ax + b$$

Substitute the data into the assumed equation. This gives nine equations:

$$\begin{cases} 0.5 = \quad\quad b \\ 4.2 = \quad 5a + b \\ 7.3 = 10a + b \\ 10.7 = 15a + b \\ 13.2 = 20a + b \end{cases}$$

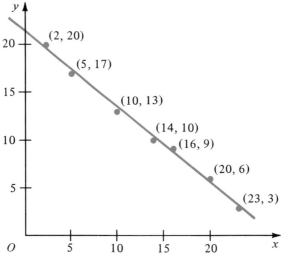

(2, 20)
(5, 17)
(10, 13)
(14, 10)
(16, 9)
(20, 6)
(23, 3)

FIGURE 2.40   Graph of the Line of Best Fit for Problem 1

$$\begin{cases} 17.5 = 25a + b \\ 19.6 = 30a + b \\ 22.4 = 35a + b \\ 26.2 = 40a + b \end{cases}$$

Divide the equations into two groups: take the first five equations as the first group, and the next four as the second. Add the two groups separately to obtain the system

$$\begin{cases} 35.9 = 50a + 5b \\ 85.7 = 130a + 4b \end{cases}$$

Multiply the first equation of the system by 4 and the second by -5. Add:

$$-284.9 = -450a$$

or:

$$a = 0.633$$

Then solve for b. The result is:

$$b = 0.85$$

The method of averages result for the line of best fit is:

$$y = 0.633x + 0.85$$

The line is graphed in Figure 2.41. The points close to the line are the

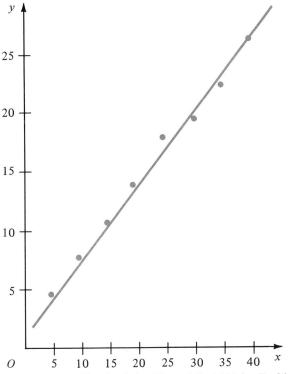

FIGURE 2.41 Graph of the Line of Best Fit for Problem 2

graphs of the ordered pairs given in the table: (0, 0.5), (5, 4.2), and so on. The line appears to go through only one of these points: (40, 26.2). As for the others, the line is the line of best fit.

EXERCISES *for Section 2.5*

In each of the following exercises, find a line of best fit for the given points by applying: (a) a graphical method, and (b) the method of averages.

1. (3, 29), (5, 26), (7, 22), (10, 15), (11, 12), (13, 8), (15, 3)

2. (11.5, 6.5), (8, 7.5), (7, 8.5), (4.5, 9), (4, 9.5), (2, 10), (1.5, 10.5)

3. (10, 25), (25, 30), (30, 40), (40, 45), (50, 60), (75, 75), (80, 85)

4. (9, 26), (9, 24), (10, 20), (11, 19), (12, 14), (14, 8), (16, 1)

5. (23.3, 6.7), (30, 20.7), (36.7, 36.7), (43.3, 43.3), (46.7, 56.7)

6. (7.5, 30), (10, 25), (20, 22.5), (25, 17.5), (32.5, 15), (37.5, 7.5), (47.5, 5)

By applying the method of averages, find a line of best fit for the data in each of the following tables.

7.

x	18	30	36	42	54	60	72	78	90
y	80	75	60	55	50	40	30	15	5

8.

x	5	8	10	12	15	16	18
y	0.64	0.78	0.88	0.95	1.07	1.10	1.16

9.

x	20	38	62	74	92
y	117.35	117.71	118.18	118.43	111.77

10.

x	12	24	40	48	60
y	97.32	97.65	98.07	98.30	98.61

11.

x	4.4	6.4	7.8	9.0	10.0	11.0	11.8	12.6
y	2.62	2.92	3.15	3.35	3.52	3.67	3.81	3.95

12.

x	1	2	3	4	5	6	7	8
y	34.2	31.7	29.3	26.7	24.0	21.5	18.0	16.6

13.

x	38	50	60	72	80	90	100
y	80.8	82.6	84.15	85.9	87.15	88.5	90.2

14.

x	7.2	10.4	11.8	13.4	19.2	24.4
y	53.1	58.1	60.6	62.9	72.0	80.1

15. The graph in Figure 2.31 was based on smoothed-out data. The actual data were as follows:

x	0	1	2	3	4	5
y	11.8	16.3	21.1	22.6	27.7	31.3

Apply the method of averages to find a line of best fit for the actual data. Graph the line and compare it with the line in Figure 2.31.

16. On p. 82, Table 2 gives sales of Good Morning over a period of six months. The table was based on smoothed-out data. The correct figures were:

x	0	1	2	3	4	5
y	117	135	149	167	179	186

By applying the method of averages, find a line of best fit for these figures. Making use of this line, answer Exercise 2 on p. 83 and Exercise 6 on p. 83. Compare your answers with the answers based on the smoothed-out data.

17. On p. 82, Table 3 gives sales of Sugar Yummies over a period of six months. The table is not quite accurate. A corrected table is:

x	0	1	2	3	4	5
y	464	489	497	506	526	531

Find a line of best fit for these figures by means of the method of averages. Using this line, answer Exercise 3 on p. 83. Using this line together with your answer to Exercise 16, answer Exercise 4 on p. 83. Compare the result with the answer you gave on the basis of the smoothed-out data.

2.6 LINEAR MODELS OF EQUILIBRIUM

In a free marketplace, prices are determined by supply and demand. There are three possibilities:

1. If demand is high, producers try to benefit by raising the price and increasing the supply of the product.

2. If demand is stable, producers neither raise nor lower the price or the supply.

3. If demand is low, producers may lower the price to increase the demand or may lower the supply to increase the price, or may do both.

EXAMPLES: HIGH, STABLE, AND LOW DEMAND

1. High demand: A hit movie tends to be shown at premium admission prices, and at a larger-than-average number of movie houses.

2. High demand: Just after World War II, there was an immense unsatisfied demand for consumer goods. A clever entrepreneur brought out (and sold) a large number of ballpoint pens—then a new item—at a price of $10 each.

3. Stable demand: Thirty years after the post–World War II era, ballpoint pens had saturated the writing tool market in the United States. Demand could not possibly go up, but it did not go down either. The price remained stable.

4. Low demand: A worldwide recession in the mid-seventies sharply reduced the demand for copper. Prices fell. Copper producers decreased their production in the hope of getting better prices.

5. Low demand: The 1975 model year was a time of low demand for American automobiles. (One reason was that many potential buyers found the prices too high.) At various times in the year, manufacturers lowered prices by offering small price rebates. Demand went up slightly.

6. Low demand: Skyrocketing beef prices led to a greatly lowered demand for beef in 1974. Prices paid to cattle-raisers fell sharply. The cattle-raisers (who were operating at a loss) lowered the supply by reducing their herds. Prices went up again.

As the illustrations show, prices and supplies tend to go up when demand is high and to go down when demand is low. When supply and demand are in balance, and there is a price that keeps them in balance, we say that the market is in *equilibrium*. The price at which this occurs is an *equilibrium price*. The corresponding supply and demand are called the *equilibrium supply* and the *equilibrium demand*. If the data on supply and demand can be described by linear equations, we say that we have *linear models* of supply and demand. If we graph the lines describing supply and demand, we expect to have a situation like the one illustrated in Figure 2.42. The variables there are:

$$x = \text{price}$$

$$y = \text{number of items}$$

The supply and demand lines meet at a point P. The x-coordinate of P is the equilibrium price. The y-coordinate of P is the equilibrium number of items: the equilibrium supply/demand. Figure 2.42 pictures a *linear model of equilibrium in the marketplace*. The following example shows how the manufacturer's production and pricing policies led to equilibrium in the market for a certain computer.

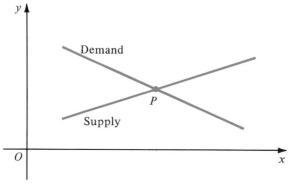

FIGURE 2.42

EXAMPLE 1: EQUILIBRIUM IN THE MARKETPLACE

Adam Smith, chief economist for HAL (a computer manufacturer), found that the demand for HAL computers went down as prices for the computer went up. Smith studied the data, which was fairly close to being linear, and calculated a line of best fit. His line had the equation

$$D = -\tfrac{5}{4}x + 54$$

where D = number of HAL computers in demand

x = price (in millions of dollars) of a HAL computer

The demand equation gives a good approximation to the facts. When HAL sold for $8 million, the equation correctly shows that the company had orders for 44 computers. The company could not manufacture 44 computers, and management raised the price to $12 million. Demand then dropped to 39.

The buoyant market for HAL computers greatly stimulated production. Economist Smith's evaluation of the data led him to the equation

$$S = 3x - 14$$

where S = number of HAL computers in supply

and x, as before, is the price. The equation shows that the company was prepared to supply 10 computers at a price of $8 million. By raising the price to $12 million, management was able to finance the building of a second factory. The company was then able to manufacture 22 computers. The supply was still below the demand, but management was not sure it ought to risk building a third factory. The facts were as follows:

1. With a third factory, HAL would be able to produce over 30 computers a year.

2. The price per HAL computer would have to go up by about $3 million, and the number of orders might go down sharply.

Adam Smith was asked for his advice. He noted that his linear equations

$$S = 3x - 14 \quad \text{and} \quad D = -\tfrac{5}{4}x + 54$$

described the supply and demand situation for $x = 8$ and $x = 12$. (The equations were also approximately correct for several prices the company had tried between $8 million and $12 million). He went on: "It would be foolish to assume that the trends shown by these linear equations will continue indefinitely. It would be just as foolish not to assume that they will continue through another round or two of price increases."

Smith had graphed his two linear equations, as shown in Figure 2.43 (the x-coordinate gives price, and the y-coordinate gives the number of computers in supply or in demand). The solid lines describe the past. The broken lines describe a possible future. If the trends shown in the graph were to continue, the two lines would meet at $x = 16$. The corresponding y-value would be 34.

In other words: At a price of $16 million, the expected demand would be for 34 computers, and this would also be the expected supply. (That is, the company could finance a third factory if it could sell HAL computers at 16 million dollars each).

Adam Smith also explained that the price determined by the supply and demand lines is called the *equilibrium price*. The corresponding number of computers in demand is the *equilibrium demand*. The corresponding supply (the same number) is the *equilibrium supply*.

Finally, he showed that he did not have to draw a graph to find the

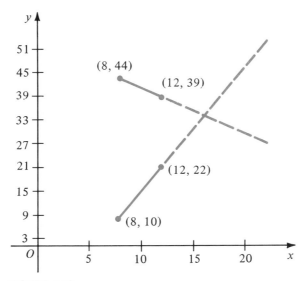

FIGURE 2.43

equilibrium price, the equilibrium demand, or the equilibrium supply. All he had to do was set

$$S = D$$

or

$$3x - 14 = -\tfrac{5}{4}x + 54$$

The solution of this linear equation in one variable is the equilibrium price:

$$x = 16$$

The corresponding equilibrium supply and demand are:

$$S = 3(16) - 14 = 34$$

$$D = -\tfrac{5}{4}(16) + 54 = 34$$

HAL management found out what they wanted to know. A third factory was built, the computer price was raised to $16 million, and the company made a large profit selling 34 computers a year.

The supply of labor for a given job is determined by the going wage scale. Everyone knows, for example, of the hordes of workers attracted to Alaska by high wages paid in the pipeline construction industry. As a contrary example, certain New England shipyards cannot hire all the skilled workers they need because they offer low wages. If we want to study equilibrium in the labor market, it does not matter what sort of labor we are talking about. We therefore choose the following example.

EXAMPLE 2: AN EQUILIBRIUM FISTFUL OF DOLLARS

Certain western movies show us the bounty-hunter in action. A bounty-hunter is prepared to kill a criminal outlaw for a reward, or bounty. If the bounty is too low to attract anyone into this specialized line of work, criminals will be unpunished. If the bounty is too high, the best men will retire after a few successful hunts. The profession will be left to beginners.

Experience has shown that the number N of men attracted to bounty-hunting in a certain territory is given by the equation

$$N = 7x$$

where x is the bounty (in thousands of dollars) offered for a murderer. For example: If the bounty $x = 5$ ($5000), there will be 35 bounty-hunters. This is too many: most of them will be too inexperienced to survive for very long.

The number S of skillful bounty-hunters attracted by a bounty of x thousand dollars is known to be

$$S = -7.5x + 29$$

If the bounty $x = 5$, there will be no skilled bounty-hunters available.

Ideally, all bounty-hunters should be skilled men. When does this happen? When

$$N = S$$

or

$$7x = -7.5x + 29$$

The solution is:

$$x = 2$$

The equilibrium fistful of dollars is $2000. If this is the bounty for murderers, there will be 14 men on the hunt and every one of them will be good at the job.

The following two problems give further examples of how equilibrium is reached in the marketplace and in the labor market.

PROBLEM 1 When the price of a famous soft drink was raised to $1.00 a bottle, sales collapsed to 300,000 bottles a day. A quick market analysis was ordered. Data was collected, and it led to the linear equation

$$D = -50,000x + 5,300,000$$

where D = number of bottles in demand each day

x = price per bottle, in cents

It was obviously necessary to lower the price. The equation showing the supply, S, that the company was prepared to manufacture at a price of x cents a bottle was:

$$S = 60,000x - 2,400,000$$

Find the equilibrium price and the equilibrium supply/demand of the soft drink.

SOLUTION   Set $S = D$. This gives:

$$60,000x - 2,400,000 = -50,000x + 5,300,000$$

or:

$$100,000x = 7,700,000$$

or:

$$x = 70¢$$

as the equilibrium price. The equilibrium supply/demand corresponding to this price was 1,800,000 bottles per day.

PROBLEM 2   A large conglomerate decided to invest in the construction of an undersea city in the Gulf of Mexico. The underwater construction would require a workforce of at least 3000 experienced underwater workers (known as "sand hogs"). Sand hogs are in short supply, and the work seemed dangerous even for them. Data provided by contractors showed that the supply of sand hogs who would work on the city could be described by

$$S = 30x - 1001$$

where S = number of sand hogs who would work on the city at x dollars an hour

x = hourly wage offered

Calculations by the company's planning staff gave the equation

$$D = -60x + 11{,}203$$

for the number D of sand hogs it would be profitable to hire at x dollars an hour. Find the equilibrium hourly wage and the corresponding number for S and D.

SOLUTION   Set $S = D$. This gives:

$$30x - 1001 = 60x + 11{,}203$$

or:

$$90x = 12{,}204$$

or:

$$x = \$135.60 \text{ an hour}$$

At this wage,

$$S = D = 3067$$

qualified sand hogs will work on the project.

EXERCISES *for Section 2.6*

The following exercises are divided into four groups. The first two groups (Exercises 1–13) contain exercises on equilibrium in the marketplace. The last two groups (Exercises 14–29) give exercises on equilibrium in the labor market.

The novel *The Family*, which did very well in hardcover and very poorly in paperback, has been made into a movie. Great work by the director-scriptwriter and by some of the best actors in America has produced a movie that everyone wants to see. Market research has led to the equation

$$\text{if } D = 0 \qquad D = 7(0) + 74 = 74$$
$$D(3.50) = -7(3.50) + 74$$
$$= 49.5 \text{ million}$$
$$D = -7x + 74$$

where D = number of people (in millions) who want to see the movie this year

x = the admission price, in dollars

1. How many million people will want to see *The Family* if admission is free?

2. How many will want to see *The Family* if admission is $10?

3. Graph the equation $D = -7x + 74$.

The owners of the movie *The Family* have a real problem. Demand for the movie is fantastic, but the supply of seats at movie houses is limited. The supply of seats is given by the equation

$$S = \tfrac{39}{5}x$$

where S = number of seats (in millions) that will be available at movie houses this year

x = admission price (in dollars)

4. How many million seats will be available if the admission price is $1? if it is $5? if it is $10?

5. Graph the equation $S = \tfrac{39}{5}x$ on the same axes you used for graphing $D = -7x + 74$.

6. From the graph in Exercise 5: What is the equilibrium price for showing the movie this year?

7. Use algebra to find the equilibrium price and the equilibrium supply/demand for the movie this year.

Aztec, a Mexican manufacturer, is producing a subcompact car called the Aztec Princess. This is a roomy and sturdy automobile with strong acceleration and high gas mileage. It is also exceptionally attractive. Market research in the U.S. shows that demand for the car will be

$$D = -4000x + 26,000,000$$

where D = number of people who will buy the car

x = U.S. price of the car, in dollars

8. How many Aztec Princesses can be sold in the U.S. at a price of $1000? at a price of $5000?

9. Choose suitable units, and graph the equation $D = -4000x + 26,000,000$.

The Mexican automobile industry is still in its infancy. The supply of Princesses for export to the U.S. is given by the equation

$$S = 200x + 100,000$$

where S = number of Aztec Princesses the company is prepared to export to the U.S.

x = price of the car, in dollars

Note: If $x = 0$, $S = 100,000$. This is not a mistake. It means that Aztec would be willing to send 100,000 free Princesses to the U.S, merely to show what a terrific car it is. Fortunately, this is not necessary.

10. How many cars would Aztec send to the United States at a price of $3000? at a price of $10,000?

11. Graph the equation $S = 200x + 100,000$ on the same axes you used (in answering Exercise 9) to graph $D = 4000x + 26,000,000$.

12. From your answer to Exercise 11: What is the equilibrium price of the Aztec Princess? What is the equilibrium supply/demand?

13. Use algebra to find the equilibrium price and the equilibrium supply/demand for the Aztec Princess.

Sunpower is a successful new corporation in the field of solar energy. It needs at least 500 scientists (physicists and chemists) to work at its Nevada plant. Sunpower's business is so good that it will pay very well for the right scientists. The equation expressing this fact is:

$$D = -\tfrac{5}{2}x + 2470$$

where D = number of scientists Sunpower is willing to hire

x = average number of dollars per week Sunpower will pay these scientists.

14. How many scientists would Sunpower be willing to hire at an average salary of $400 a week?

15. How many would the company hire at an average of $600 a week?

16. Choose suitable units, and graph the equation $D = -\tfrac{5}{2}x + 2470$.

Sunpower's recruiters found that many capable scientists were interested in solar energy. But very few wanted to work and live in Nevada. The number available was given by the equation

$$S = \tfrac{13}{4}x - 1831$$

where S = number of scientists willing to work for Sunpower in Nevada

x = weekly salary offered by Sunpower

17. Will any scientists work for as little as $400 a week? for $500? for $600?

18. How many would be willing to work for $1000 a week?

19. Graph the equation $S = \tfrac{13}{4}x - 1831$ on the same axes you used in graphing $D = -\tfrac{5}{2}x + 2470$.

20. Use the graph in Exercise 19 to find the equilibrium salary for scientists at Sunpower's Nevada plant.

21. Answer Exercise 20 by using algebra. Find the equilibrium scientists' supply/demand at the equilibrium salary.

West Side Hospital wants to add a large number of nurses to its staff. The equation describing what the hospital will pay is~ *The # nurses desired*

$$D = -\tfrac{3}{7}x + 251$$

where D = the number of nurses in demand for the West Side Hospital
x = monthly salary offered by the hospital

22. Is West Side Hospital willing to pay the new nurses $700 a month?

23. How many nurses would the hospital be willing to hire at $350 a month?

24. Graph the equation $D = -\tfrac{3}{7}x + 251$.

West Side Hospital is a municipal institution, and it does not have much money to spend on nurses. This explains the low salaries that are offered. The business manager of the hospital finds that the supply of nurses is given by:

$$S = \tfrac{2}{3}x - 370$$

25. Would any nurses be willing to work for $450 a month?

26. How many nurses would be willing to work for $600 a month?

27. Graph the equation $S = \tfrac{2}{3}x - 370$ on the same axes you used in graphing $D = -\tfrac{3}{7}x + 251$.

28. From the graph you drew in answering Exercise 27: What is the equilibrium monthly salary for new staff nurses at the West Side Hospital?

29. By using algebra, find the equilibrium monthly salary and the corresponding equilibrium supply of (and demand for) nurses.

chapter three

MATRIX ALGEBRA AND LINEAR SYSTEMS

REAL-WORLD data often comes to us in the form of the rectangular blocks of numbers called data tables. Matrix algebra helps us to deal with such tables. Basically, it is a way of bringing order into blocks of raw numbers so that we are not simply overwhelmed by masses of data.

The easiest ideas of matrix algebra lead to the convenient method of solving systems of linear equations, explained in Sections 3.1 and 3.2 and applied in Section 3.3.

3.1 MATRICES, LINEAR SYSTEMS, AND LEGAL ROW OPERATIONS

The Bureau of Labor Statistics regularly publishes figures on what it costs a family of four to live moderately well. It costs different amounts in different parts of the country. Some of the September 1976 dollar figures for three cities are shown in Table 3.1.

TABLE 3.1 Cost, in Dollars, for a Family of Four to Live
Moderately Well in Three U.S. Cities,
September 1976.

City	Total Budget	Food	Shelter	Transportation	
Boston	27,000	4363	5943	1607	1435
Chicago	22,592	3967	4198	1575	1335
Houston	20,090	3967	3794	1393	1376

These figures (and thousands of others like them) are stored in computer memories for rapid retrieval, updating, cross-comparing, trend-spotting, and all the rest of what is done with cost-of-living figures. The name of the city and the name of the budget item are stored *once*. From that point on, the computer stores only a rectangular array of figures. The information in Table 3.1 would be stored as:

$$\begin{pmatrix} 27{,}000 & 4363 & 5943 & 1607 \\ 22{,}592 & 3967 & 4198 & 1575 \\ 20{,}090 & 3967 & 3794 & 1393 \end{pmatrix}$$

This rectangular array, or *matrix,* duplicates the numbers in Table 3.1 and also the precise row-and-column order of these numbers.

DEFINITION Matrix

A rectangular array of numbers is called a *matrix* (plural, *matrices*).

The rectangular array we have used for an example has 3 rows and 4 columns, so it is called a 3 × 4 (read "three by four") matrix. Each of the 12 numbers in the matrix has an ordered pair *address* of the form (row number, column number). As an example, the number 1575 has the address (2, 4). We also say that 1575 is the (2, 4) *entry*. Two other examples: 3794 is the (3, 3) entry; 22,592 has the address (2, 1).

To repeat: Each address (and each entry number) is an ordered pair. In our example, the (1, 2) entry 4363 and the (2, 1) entry 22,592 are differently placed in the matrix and are different numbers. Notice that we also distinguish between the (2, 2) and (3, 2) entries: same number, different addresses.

PROBLEM 1   For each of the following matrices, give the *size* (number of rows × number of columns) and identify the second row and the second column.

$$A = \begin{pmatrix} 1 & 2 \\ 4 & -3 \end{pmatrix}$$

$$B = \begin{pmatrix} 3 & 7 \\ -5 & 9 \\ 7 & 12 \end{pmatrix}$$

$$C = \begin{pmatrix} -4 & 2 & 5 \\ 3 & 8 & -5 \end{pmatrix}$$

SOLUTION   The matrix **A** has 2 rows and 2 columns; **B** has 3 rows and 2 columns; **C** has 2 rows and 3 columns. Therefore: **A** is 2 × 2, **B** is 3 × 2, and **C** is 2 × 3. We have the following second-row list:

$$(4 \quad -3) \qquad \text{for } A$$
$$(-5 \quad 9) \qquad \text{for } B$$
$$(3 \quad 8 \quad -5) \qquad \text{for } C$$

The second-column list is:

$$\begin{pmatrix} 2 \\ -3 \end{pmatrix} \text{ for } A \qquad \begin{pmatrix} 7 \\ 9 \\ 12 \end{pmatrix} \text{ for } B \qquad \begin{pmatrix} 2 \\ 8 \end{pmatrix} \text{ for } C$$

PROBLEM 2   In the matrix **B** of Problem 1, what are the addresses of −5, 12, and 7?

SOLUTION   The number −5 is in the second row and first column. Its address is (2, 1). Similarly: 12 is in the third row and second column, with address (3, 2). And 7, which occurs twice in the matrix, naturally has two addresses: (3, 1) and (1, 2).

PROBLEM 3   In the matrix **C** of Problem 1, identify the (2, 2), (1, 3), and (3, 1) entries.

SOLUTION   The (2, 2) entry is 8 and the (1, 3) entry is 5. The (3, 1) entry cannot be identified since the matrix **C** has only two rows.

The first, the easiest, and probably the most useful application of matrices is in solving systems of linear equations. Before demonstrating the matrix method, we want to point out that the term *linear equation* is not restricted to equations in two variables like $2x + 3y = 4$. An equation in three, four, five, or any number of variables is also called a linear equation, provided that the variables occur only in the first degree.

EXAMPLES: LINEAR AND NONLINEAR EQUATIONS

1. The equations

$$7x_1 + 8x_2 + 9x_3 = 10$$
$$3x_1 - 7x_5 + 14x_{12} = 15x_{27} - 8$$

are linear equations since the variables occur only in the first degree.

2. Each of the equations

$$3x_1 + 5x_2 + 7\sqrt{x_3} = 8$$
$$4x_1 + 6x_2 + 8x_1x_3 = 9$$
$$5x_1 + 7x_1^2 + 9x_8 = 10$$

contains a term that is not of first degree. Therefore each equation is nonlinear.

A two by two linear system (two variables, two equations) like

$$\begin{cases} x + 2y = 3 \\ 4x + 5y = 6 \end{cases}$$

can be represented by the matrix

$$\begin{pmatrix} 1 & 2 & 3 \\ 4 & 5 & 6 \end{pmatrix}$$

The first and second columns of the matrix give the coefficients of the first and second variables of the system and its third column lists the constants. The matrix is called the *augmented matrix* of the system because the column of constants *augments,* or supplements, the array of coefficients of the linear system. Similarly, the three by three system

$$\begin{cases} 3x_1 + 2x_2 + 3x_3 = 1 \\ -5x_1 \qquad - 2x_3 = 2 \\ 7x_1 + 7x_2 + 6x_3 = 4 \end{cases}$$

has the augmented matrix

$$\begin{pmatrix} 3 & 2 & 3 & 1 \\ -5 & 0 & -2 & 2 \\ 7 & 7 & 6 & 4 \end{pmatrix}$$

Notice that we must list coefficients of the first, second, and third variables in corresponding columns of the matrix. This leaves the last column for constants.

PROBLEM 4 Write a linear system that has the augmented matrix

$$\mathbf{A} = \begin{pmatrix} 1 & 2 & -1 & -3 & 1 & 4 \\ 3 & 4 & 2 & 0 & 3 & 11 \\ 0 & -1 & 0 & 3 & -1 & 5 \end{pmatrix}$$

SOLUTION **A** is a 3 × 6 matrix. It corresponds to a three by five system: three equations, five variables. The last column in **A** specifies the column of constants on the right side of the system. If we label the variables x_1, x_2, x_3, x_4, x_5, then the linear system corresponding to **A** is:

$$x_1 + 2x_2 - x_3 - 3x_4 + x_5 = 4$$
$$3x_1 + 4x_2 + 2x_3 + 3x_5 = 11$$
$$-x_2 + 3x_4 - x_5 = 5$$

We had a simple method for solving linear equations in one variable in Section 1.2. Given an equation, we used *legal operations* to derive successively simpler equivalent equations until we arrived at an equation with an obvious solution.

In Section 2.4, we used the *addition method* to solve systems of two linear equations in two variables. The idea behind that method was to transform the equations of the system in such a way that adding them would eliminate one of the variables. Basically, we transformed a given system into successively simpler equivalent systems having the same solution. To make this process clear, we will redo Problem 1 of Section 2.4. Steps ♦ through 5 (p. 117) give successive equivalent systems at the left and corresponding augmented matrices at the right.

	System	*Augmented Matrix*

1. Start with:

$$3x + 4y = 5$$
$$2x + 3y = 1$$

$$\begin{pmatrix} 3 & 4 & 5 \\ 2 & 3 & 1 \end{pmatrix}$$

2. Multiply the first equation by 3 and the second by -4:

$$9x + 12y = 15$$
$$-8x - 12y = -4$$

$$\begin{pmatrix} 9 & 12 & 15 \\ -8 & -12 & -4 \end{pmatrix}$$

3. Add the second equation to the first:

$$x + 0 = 11$$
$$-8x - 12y = -4$$

$$\begin{pmatrix} 1 & 0 & 11 \\ -8 & -12 & -4 \end{pmatrix}$$

4. Add 8 times the first equation to the second equation:

$$x \qquad = 11$$
$$0 - 12y = 84$$

$$\begin{pmatrix} 1 & 0 & 11 \\ 0 & -12 & 84 \end{pmatrix}$$

5. Divide the second equation by -12:

$$x \qquad = 11$$
$$y = -7$$

$$\begin{pmatrix} 1 & 0 & 11 \\ 0 & 1 & -7 \end{pmatrix}$$

The final system gives the solution $(x, y) = (11, -7)$, exactly as on p. 91. And the final augmented matrix gives the same information in matrix form. The point of it all is that *we obtained the successive equivalent systems by carrying out legal operations on the equations of the system.*

The corresponding augmented matrices *could* have been obtained by carrying out corresponding operations on the rows of the matrices. For example, the matrix in step 2 could have been obtained by carrying out two operations on the matrix in step 1: multiplying each entry in the first row by 3, and then multiplying each entry in the second row by -4. Similarly, the matrix in step 4 results from one operation on the matrix in step 3: adding 8 times each entry of the first row to the corresponding entry of the second row.

The operations on augmented matrices that we have been talking about are called *row operations* since they are always carried out on the rows of these matrices. They are also called *legal,* since they correspond to legal operations on linear equations. Combining the two names, we call these matrix operations *legal row operations.*

The point to remember is that legal row operations transform the augmented matrix of a linear system into augmented matrices of equivalent linear systems with the same solution.

There are three legal row operations:

LEGAL ROW OPERATIONS

1. Interchanging any two rows of a matrix is legal.

2. Multiplying any row of a matrix by a nonzero number is legal.

3. Adding a multiple of one row of a matrix to another row is legal.

It is understood that legal operation 2 includes *dividing* a row by a nonzero number, and legal operation 3 includes *subtracting* a multiple of one row from another.

The following examples are designed to illustrate the mechanics of carrying out legal row operations. The examples also introduce some notations that we will use when we apply the operations to solve linear systems.

EXAMPLES: OPERATING LEGALLY ON THE ROWS OF A MATRIX

Start with the matrix

$$\begin{pmatrix} 3 & 4 & 3 & 7 \\ 4 & 6 & -3 & -11 \\ 2 & -8 & 4 & 0 \end{pmatrix}$$

Interchange rows 1 and 3:

$$\begin{pmatrix} 3 & 4 & 3 & 7 \\ 4 & 6 & -3 & -11 \\ 2 & -8 & 4 & 0 \end{pmatrix} \times \begin{pmatrix} 2 & -8 & 4 & 0 \\ 4 & 6 & -3 & -11 \\ 3 & 4 & 3 & 7 \end{pmatrix}$$

Notice the use of the crossed arrows as a symbol for row interchange.

Divide row 1 of the matrix on the right by 2. (This means: Divide *all entries* of row 1 by 2. Notice that R_1 is a brief notation for row 1.)

$$\begin{pmatrix} 2 & -8 & 4 & 0 \\ 4 & 6 & -3 & -11 \\ 3 & 4 & 3 & 7 \end{pmatrix} \xrightarrow{\frac{1}{2}R_1} \begin{pmatrix} 1 & -4 & 2 & 0 \\ 4 & 6 & -3 & -11 \\ 3 & 4 & 3 & 7 \end{pmatrix}$$

Subtract 4 times row 1 from row 2. (This means: From each entry of row 2, subtract 4 times the corresponding entry of row 1.) Also *subtract* 3 times row 1 from row 3:

$$\begin{pmatrix} 1 & -4 & 2 & 0 \\ 4 & 6 & -3 & -11 \\ 3 & 4 & 3 & 7 \end{pmatrix} \begin{matrix} \\ R_2 - 4R_1 \\ R_3 - 3R_1 \end{matrix} \begin{pmatrix} 1 & -4 & 2 & 0 \\ 0 & 22 & -11 & -11 \\ 0 & 16 & -3 & 7 \end{pmatrix}$$

Now we give some examples of solving linear systems. In each case we form the augmented matrix of the system, and then we apply legal row operations until we arrive at a matrix corresponding to an obvious solution. For example, the matrix

$$\begin{pmatrix} 1 & 0 & 5 \\ 0 & 2 & 8 \end{pmatrix}$$

corresponds to $x = 5$, $2y = 8$, or $(x, y) = (5, 4)$. Notice that the particular legal operations we apply in solving the following problems are not the *only* ones that will work. To make sure that they do work, we check each solution.

PROBLEM 5   Solve the linear system

$$3x - 2y = 19$$
$$x + y = 23$$

SOLUTION   We apply legal row operations to the augmented matrix of the system:

$$\begin{pmatrix} 3 & -2 & 19 \\ 1 & 1 & 23 \end{pmatrix} \begin{pmatrix} 1 & 1 & 23 \\ 3 & -2 & 19 \end{pmatrix} \begin{matrix} \\ R_2 - 3R_1 \end{matrix} \begin{pmatrix} 1 & 1 & 23 \\ 0 & -5 & -50 \end{pmatrix}$$

$$-\tfrac{1}{5}R_2 \quad \begin{pmatrix} 1 & 1 & 23 \\ 0 & 1 & 10 \end{pmatrix} \quad R_1 - R_2 \quad \begin{pmatrix} 1 & 0 & 13 \\ 0 & 1 & 10 \end{pmatrix}$$

The last matrix corresponds to: $(x, y) = (13, 10)$.
Check: Substitute $(13, 10)$ in the original system:

$$3(13) - 2(10) = 19 \; \checkmark$$

$$13 + 10 = 23 \; \checkmark$$

PROBLEM 6 Find the intersection point of the lines with equations $3x + 4y - 4 = 0$ and $5x + 2y - 8 = 0$.

SOLUTION The equations of the two lines form a two by two linear system. We apply legal operations to the augmented matrix of the system until we have reduced the matrix to a form giving us an obvious solution:

$$\begin{pmatrix} 3 & 4 & 4 \\ 5 & 2 & 8 \end{pmatrix} \quad R_2 - R_1 \quad \begin{pmatrix} 3 & 4 & 4 \\ 2 & -2 & 4 \end{pmatrix}$$

$$\tfrac{1}{2}R_2 \quad \begin{pmatrix} 3 & 4 & 4 \\ 1 & -1 & 2 \end{pmatrix} \quad \begin{pmatrix} 1 & -1 & 2 \\ 3 & 4 & 4 \end{pmatrix}$$

$$R_2 - 3R_1 \quad \begin{pmatrix} 1 & -1 & 2 \\ 0 & 7 & -2 \end{pmatrix} \quad R_1 + \tfrac{1}{7}R_2 \quad \begin{pmatrix} 1 & 0 & \tfrac{12}{7} \\ 0 & 7 & -2 \end{pmatrix}$$

The last matrix corresponds to $x = \tfrac{12}{7}$, $7y = -2$. Therefore the point of intersection is $(x, y) = (\tfrac{12}{7}, -\tfrac{2}{7})$.
Check:

$$3(\tfrac{12}{7}) + 4(-\tfrac{2}{7}) - 4 = 0 \; \checkmark$$

$$5(\tfrac{12}{7}) + 2(-\tfrac{2}{7}) - 8 = 0 \; \checkmark$$

Sometimes a linear system does not have a solution. To show how the matrix method operates in such cases, let's simply repeat two examples from Section 2.4.

PROBLEM 7   Solve the linear system

$$\begin{cases} 3x - y = 4 \\ 6x - 2y = 3 \end{cases}$$

SOLUTION   We work with the augmented matrix:

$$\begin{pmatrix} 3 & -1 & 4 \\ 6 & -2 & 3 \end{pmatrix} \quad \boxed{R_2 - 2R_1} \quad \begin{pmatrix} 3 & -1 & 4 \\ 0 & 0 & -5 \end{pmatrix}$$

The second row of the matrix on the right corresponds to the false equation $0 \cdot x + 0 \cdot y = -5$. The system is *inconsistent*.

PROBLEM 8   Solve the linear system

$$\begin{cases} 3x - 4y = 12 \\ 9x - 12y = 36 \end{cases}$$

SOLUTION   We perform a legal row operation on the augmented matrix of the system:

$$\begin{pmatrix} 3 & -4 & 12 \\ 9 & -12 & 36 \end{pmatrix} \quad \boxed{R_2 - 3R_1} \quad \begin{pmatrix} 3 & -4 & 12 \\ 0 & 0 & 0 \end{pmatrix}$$

The second row corresponds to the equation $0 \cdot x + 0 \cdot y = 0$. This equation is true, but it gives no information: any ordered pair (x, y) is a solution. The system is *dependent*.

EXERCISES *for Section 3.1*

1.   Table 3.1 gave the total budget together with food, housing, and transportation expenses for a family of four to live moderately well in Boston, Chicago, or Houston in September 1976. Such a family also required the following dollar amounts for clothing: in Boston, $1435; in Chicago, $1335; in Houston, $1376. Use this information to prepare an expanded version of Table 3.1. Then write the matrix corresponding to the expanded table.

2.   Bureau of Labor Statistics figures, comparable to those listed in Table 3.1,

give the following cost-of-living data for San Francisco, Detroit, Portland Maine, and Orlando, Florida, in that order. *Total budgets:* $24,073; $22,947; $21,733; $19,737. *Food:* $3991; $4011; $4295; $3477. *Housing:* $4476; $4477; $4017; $4358. *Transportation:* $1448; $1355; $1305; $1400. *Clothing:* $1405; $1303; $1435; $1226. Write this data in matrix form in two different ways: (a) rows corresponding to cities, columns to budget items; (b) rows corresponding to budget items, columns to cities.

---

3. Give the *size* of the following matrices, and also identify row 2 and column 3 in each matrix.

$$A = \begin{pmatrix} 3 & 4 & 15 & 10 & 0 \\ 5 & 12 & 0 & 4 & 10 \end{pmatrix}$$

$$B = \begin{pmatrix} -3 & 2 & -3 & 8 \\ 2 & 1 & -6 & 1 \\ 3 & -2 & 7 & 3 \\ -4 & 0 & 5 & 4 \end{pmatrix}$$

$$C = \begin{pmatrix} 534 & 657 & 1016 \\ 346 & 198 & 3141 \\ 2531 & 4551 & 216 \end{pmatrix}$$

4. In the matrix **A** of Exercise 3, what are the addresses of 3, 15, 4, and 12?

5. In the matrix **B** of Exercise 3, what are the addresses of -6, 5, 3, and 1?

6. In the matrix **C** of Exercise 3, identify the $(3, 1)$, $(2, 3)$, and $(3, 2)$ entries.

---

7. Write the matrix whose three rows are (2 4), (1 -1), and (3 5) in that order.

8. Write the matrix whose three rows are (5 11 4), (-1 3 1), and (0 2 2) in that order.

9. Write the matrix whose columns are

$$\begin{pmatrix} 5 \\ 2 \\ 6 \end{pmatrix} \text{ and } \begin{pmatrix} 7 \\ 4 \\ 5 \end{pmatrix}$$

in that order.

10. Write the matrix whose columns are

$$\begin{pmatrix} 6 \\ 0 \\ 7 \\ 3 \\ 11 \end{pmatrix} \begin{pmatrix} 3 \\ 7 \\ 8 \\ 7 \\ 6 \end{pmatrix} \begin{pmatrix} 19 \\ 21 \\ 53 \\ 55 \\ 44 \end{pmatrix}$$

in that order. Write another matrix having the same columns.

Write linear systems corresponding to each of the following augmented matrices:

11. $\begin{pmatrix} 9 & 1 & 1 \\ 4 & 6 & 8 \end{pmatrix}$ **12.** $\begin{pmatrix} 3 & 2 & 3 \\ 9 & 0 & 2 \end{pmatrix}$

13. $\begin{pmatrix} 6 & 7 & 2 & 1 \\ 0 & 6 & 9 & 5 \end{pmatrix}$ **14.** $\begin{pmatrix} 1 & 0 & 0 & 5 & 1 \\ 2 & 7 & 7 & 8 & 9 \\ 8 & 6 & 4 & 3 & 5 \end{pmatrix}$

Write the augmented matrix of each of the following linear systems:

15.
$$\begin{cases} 3x + 4y = 5 \\ x + y = 8 \\ x - 5y = -6 \end{cases}$$

16.
$$\begin{cases} 8x_2 + 8x_3 + 6x_4 = 2 \\ 2x_1 + x_2 + 9x_3 + 9x_4 = 8 \\ 6x_1 + 6x_2 + 2x_3 + 6x_4 = 7 \\ 3x_3 + 8x_4 = 1 \end{cases}$$

17.
$$\begin{cases} 2x_1 + 3x_2 - 2x_3 = 4 \\ x_1 + 4x_2 - 3x_3 = 6 \end{cases}$$

18. $3x - 2y = 7$

The next three exercises refer to the matrix

$$\mathbf{L} = \begin{pmatrix} 1 & 9 \\ 2 & 6 \end{pmatrix}$$

19. Write the matrix obtained by interchanging the rows of **L.**

20. Write the matrix obtained by: (a) multiplying row 1 of **L** by 4; (b) dividing row 2 of **L** by -2.

21. Write the matrix obtained by multiplying row 2 of **L** by $\frac{1}{2}$ and adding the result to row 1 of **L.**

The next three exercises refer to the matrix

$$\mathbf{M} = \begin{pmatrix} 1 & 0 & 2 \\ 5 & 7 & 3 \\ 8 & 3 & 4 \\ 9 & 6 & -2 \end{pmatrix}$$

22. Write the matrix obtained by interchanging rows 2 and 3 of **M.**

23. Write the matrix obtained by: (a) multiplying row 4 of **M** by 1.5; (b) dividing row 1 of **M** by 1.7.

24. Write the matrix obtained by multiplying row 3 of **M** by -3 and adding the result to row 1.

The next four exercises refer to the matrix

$$\mathbf{N} = \begin{pmatrix} 2 & 4 & 1 & 5 & 7 \\ 9 & 6 & 8 & 2 & 1 \\ 5 & 0 & 8 & 1 & 8 \end{pmatrix}$$

25. Write the matrix obtained by interchanging rows 1 and 3 of **N.**

26. Write the matrix obtained from **N** by: (a) multiplying row 2 by 3; (b) multiplying row 1 by -4; (c) dividing row 3 by 8.

27. Write the matrix obtained from **N** by adding twice row 1 to row 3.

28. Write the matrix obtained from **N** by first adding row 1 to row 2 and then multiplying row 2 of the result by 3. In the result, multiply row 3 by 2 and add it to row 1.

---

29. Find the solution of the system

$$\begin{cases} 4x + 3y = 2 \\ 5x + 4y = 1 \end{cases}$$

by carrying out the following steps:

a. Write the augmented matrix of the system. Call it **A**.
b. Subtract row 1 of **A** from row 2. Call the result **B**.
c. Subtract 4 times row 2 of **B** from row 1. Call the result **C**.
d. Add row 1 of **C** to row 2. Call the result **D**.
e. Interchange the rows of **D**. Call the result **E**.
f. Write a linear system corresponding to the augmented matrix **E**.

30. Find the solution of the system

$$\begin{cases} 2x + 3y = 5 \\ x - 2y = 6 \end{cases}$$

by carrying out the following steps:
a. Write the augmented matrix of the system. Call it **A**.
b. Subtract twice row 2 of **A** from row 1. Call the result **B**.
c. Divide row 1 of **B** by 7. Call the result **C**.
d. Add twice row 1 of **C** to row 2. Call the result **D**.
e. Interchange the rows of **D**. Call the result **E**.
f. Write a linear system corresponding to the augmented matrix **E**.

The linear systems in the next three exercises are to be solved by the method used in Exercises 29 and 30. In each case, write the augmented matrix of the system and then use legal row operations to simplify that matrix to the point where the solution can be read off, as in the matrix

$$\begin{pmatrix} 1 & 0 & 2 \\ 0 & 1 & 3 \end{pmatrix}$$

which corresponds to $x = 2$, $y = 3$.

31. Solve:

$$\begin{cases} 2x + 3y = 5 \\ 3x + 4y = 6 \end{cases}$$

32. Solve:

$$\begin{cases} 9x + 7y = 5 \\ 3x + 8y = -4 \end{cases}$$

33. Solve:

$$\begin{cases} \frac{1}{4}x + \frac{1}{5}y = 1 \\ \frac{1}{6}x + \frac{1}{7}y = \frac{1}{3} \end{cases}$$

Use legal row operations to solve the linear system whose augmented matrix is:

34. $\begin{pmatrix} 3 & 4 & 7 \\ 4 & -1 & 3 \end{pmatrix}$

35. $\begin{pmatrix} \frac{1}{3} & \frac{1}{2} & 0 \\ \frac{1}{6} & \frac{1}{8} & \frac{1}{2} \end{pmatrix}$

36. $\begin{pmatrix} 4 & -3 & 5 \\ 6 & 2 & 1 \end{pmatrix}$

The systems in the next four exercises do not have solutions. In each case, show this by writing the augmented matrix of the system and then using legal row operations to simplify that matrix. *Hint:* The augmented matrix of a system without a solution is easily recognized. See Problems 7 and 8 at the end of Section 3.1.

37. $\begin{cases} 2x + 3y = 5 \\ 4x + 6y = 7 \end{cases}$

38. $\begin{cases} \frac{1}{4}x + \frac{1}{5}y = 1 \\ \frac{1}{8}x + \frac{1}{10}y = 2 \end{cases}$

39. $\begin{cases} 19x + 27y = 46 \\ 38x + 54y = 92 \end{cases}$

40. $\begin{cases} \frac{1}{6}x + \frac{1}{7}y = \frac{1}{3} \\ 21x + 18y = 42 \end{cases}$

Use matrix methods to find the intersection point, *if there is one,* of each of the following pairs of lines:

41. $\begin{cases} 2x + 5y = 3 \\ 2x - 5y = 8 \end{cases}$

42. $\begin{cases} 6x + 2y + 1 = 0 \\ 5x - y - 8 = 0 \end{cases}$

43. $\begin{cases} x + 5y = 0 \\ y = 3x + 7 \end{cases}$

44. $\begin{cases} 3x + 2y = 14 \\ 6x + 4y = 28 \end{cases}$

45. $\begin{cases} y = 3x + 2 \\ y = 3x + 6 \end{cases}$

46. $\begin{cases} y = 4x + 7 \\ x = 5y + 8 \end{cases}$

3.2 LINEAR SYSTEMS: THE ECHELON METHOD

The last three worked-out problems in Section 3.1 were examples of the three possible cases for two by two linear systems. We saw that two by two systems can have one solution, infinitely many solutions, or no solutions.

Similar possibilities exist for higher order systems. *Higher order* means: more than two equations, more than two variables, or both. An example is an eight by six system: eight equations, six variables.

To study a higher order system, we start by forming the system's augmented matrix. (Example: For an eight by six system, the augmented matrix is 8×7.) By applying legal row operations, we then reduce the augmented matrix to a form that immediately tells us whether the corresponding system has one solution, no solutions, or infinitely many solutions.

Caution. If your interest is in real-world applications, you may be inclined to dismiss the infinitely-many-solutions case as impractical mathematical talk. However, if *your* real-world system of linear equations has infinitely many solutions, then there are a great many ways for you to meet your objectives. You are in an ideal position for bargaining and maneuvering. That is what real-world systems are all about.

Now for the mathematics. The job is to reduce an augmented matrix to a useful form. Here are some examples of matrices in useful form. (System variables will be labeled x_1, x_2, and so on.)

EXAMPLE 1: Augmented matrix of a four by four system.

$$\mathbf{A} = \begin{pmatrix} 1 & 0 & 0 & 0 & 2 \\ 0 & 1 & 0 & 0 & 3 \\ 0 & 0 & 1 & 0 & 4 \\ 0 & 0 & 0 & 1 & 5 \end{pmatrix} \qquad (4 \times 5 \text{ matrix})$$

tells us that $x_1 = 2$, $x_2 = 3$, $x_3 = 4$, $x_4 = 5$. The system has one solution.

EXAMPLE 2: Augmented matrix of a three by two system.

$$\mathbf{B} = \begin{pmatrix} 1 & 0 & -6 \\ 0 & 1 & 15 \\ 0 & 0 & 35 \end{pmatrix} \qquad (3 \times 3 \text{ matrix})$$

corresponds to an inconsistent system, since the third row says that $0 \cdot x_2 = 35$, which is never true. The system has no solution.

EXAMPLE 3: Augmented matrix of a two by three system.

$$\mathbf{C} = \begin{pmatrix} 1 & 0 & 0 & 1 \\ 0 & 0 & 1 & 2 \end{pmatrix} \qquad (2 \times 4 \text{ matrix})$$

tells us that $x_1 = 1$, x_2 is *arbitrary* (that is, it can be given any value at all), $x_3 = 2$. There are infinitely many solutions: not surprising when there are more variables than equations.

EXAMPLE 4: Augmented matrix of a four by four system.

$$\mathbf{D} = \begin{pmatrix} -14 & 1 & 1 & 1 & -16 \\ 0 & 3 & 1 & 1 & 18 \\ 0 & 0 & 2 & 1 & 13 \\ 0 & 0 & 0 & 1 & 5 \end{pmatrix} \qquad (4 \times 5 \text{ matrix})$$

corresponds to a system with one solution: $x_1 = 2$, $x_2 = 3$, $x_3 = 4$, $x_4 = 5$. *Check:* The fourth row of the matrix says that $x_4 = 5$; the third row gives us $2x_3 + x_4 = 13$, or $x_3 = 4$; etc. As a further check, you can apply legal row operations to reduce the matrix **D** to the matrix **A** of Example 1.

The matrices **A, B, C,** and **D** of our four examples are said to be in *echelon form.*

DEFINITION   Echelon Form

A matrix is in echelon form if each of its rows starts with more zeros then the preceding row.

The word *echelon* is an old-fashioned military and naval term. For example the warships of a fleet are said to be in echelon if they are arranged in a slanting line relative to their direction of travel (Figure 3.1).

Any matrix can be put in echelon form. All we need to do is apply legal row operations. Problems 5, 6, 7, and 8 of the last section show how it is done. Here are two more examples.

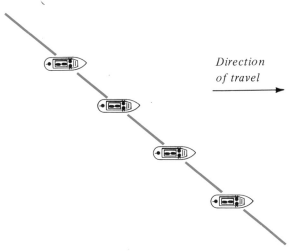

FIGURE 3.1 Fleet of Four Warships in Echelon

PROBLEM 1 Put the matrix

$$
\begin{pmatrix}
1 & 2 & 3 \\
4 & 5 & 6 \\
7 & 8 & 9
\end{pmatrix}
$$

in echelon form.

SOLUTION Apply legal row operations:

$$
\begin{pmatrix}
1 & 2 & 3 \\
4 & 5 & 6 \\
7 & 8 & 9
\end{pmatrix}
\begin{array}{c} R_2 - 4R_1 \\ R_3 - 7R_1 \end{array} \!\!\!>
\begin{pmatrix}
1 & 2 & 3 \\
0 & -3 & -6 \\
0 & -6 & -12
\end{pmatrix}
\begin{array}{c} R_3 - 2R_2 \end{array} \!\!\!>
\begin{pmatrix}
1 & 2 & 3 \\
0 & -3 & -6 \\
0 & 0 & 0
\end{pmatrix}
$$

PROBLEM 2 Put the matrix

$$
\begin{pmatrix}
2 & 3 & 4 & 5 \\
1 & 1 & 1 & 2 \\
3 & 5 & 7 & 9
\end{pmatrix}
$$

in echelon form.

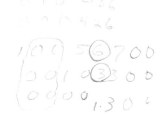

Legal row operations give us:

$$\begin{pmatrix} 2 & 3 & 4 & 5 \\ 1 & 1 & 1 & 2 \\ 3 & 5 & 7 & 9 \end{pmatrix} \begin{array}{c} R_1 - 2R_2 \\ \\ R_3 - 3R_2 \end{array} \Rightarrow \begin{pmatrix} 0 & 1 & 2 & 1 \\ 1 & 1 & 1 & 2 \\ 0 & 2 & 4 & 3 \end{pmatrix}$$

$$\begin{array}{c} \\ R_3 - 2R_1 \end{array} \Rightarrow \begin{pmatrix} 0 & 1 & 2 & 1 \\ 1 & 1 & 1 & 2 \\ 0 & 0 & 0 & 1 \end{pmatrix} \Rrightarrow \begin{pmatrix} 1 & 1 & 1 & 2 \\ 0 & 1 & 2 & 1 \\ 0 & 0 & 0 & 1 \end{pmatrix}$$

In *Animal Farm*, George Orwell said, "All animals are equal but some animals are more equal than others." It is also the case that some echelon form matrices are more equal—or more useful—than others. For example, let's compare the matrix **A** of Example 1 on p. 127 with the matrix **D** of Example 4 on p. 128. Both matrices correspond to the same linear system. But matrix **A** gives us the solution of the system immediately. Matrix **D** gives us only one variable immediately, and we have to solve for the rest. The difference is small when we have only 4 variables, but not so small if there are 40 variables. Real-world linear systems (remember that the real world embraces Texaco, MacDonald's, and the IRS, among others) frequently run to hundreds or even thousands of variables. We really have to care about putting matrices in the most useful possible form. The form we want is called the *reduced echelon form*.

DEFINITION   Reduced Echelon Form

A matrix is in reduced echelon form:
1. if it is in echelon form

2. when there are nonzero entries in a row, then the first nonzero entry is a 1.

3. when a column contains the beginning 1 of any row, then all the other entries in that column are zero.

Notice that the matrix **A** of Example 1 satisfies the definition. Here are some more examples (and nonexamples).

EXAMPLE 5: These matrices are in reduced echelon form:

$$\begin{pmatrix} 1 & 0 & 4 & 4 \\ 0 & 1 & -3 & 2 \\ 0 & 0 & 0 & 0 \end{pmatrix} \qquad \begin{pmatrix} 1 & 0 & 0 & 0 & 0 \\ 0 & 1 & 0 & 8 & 0 \\ 0 & 0 & 1 & 9 & 0 \\ 0 & 0 & 0 & 0 & 1 \end{pmatrix} \qquad \begin{pmatrix} 1 & 2 & 0 & 3 \\ 0 & 0 & 1 & 8 \end{pmatrix}$$

EXAMPLE 6: These matrices are not in reduced echelon form: why?

$$\begin{pmatrix} 1 & 3 & 0 & 0 & 4 \\ 0 & 0 & 1 & 2 & 3 \\ 0 & 0 & 0 & 1 & 5 \end{pmatrix} \qquad \begin{pmatrix} 1 & 9 & 10 \\ 0 & 1 & 11 \\ 0 & 0 & 1 \end{pmatrix} \qquad \begin{pmatrix} 0 & 1 & 0 \\ 1 & 0 & 0 \\ 0 & 0 & 1 \end{pmatrix}$$

Problems 1 and 2 showed how a matrix can be put in echelon form by means of legal row operations. To find the reduced echelon form of those matrices, we apply further legal row operations.

PROBLEM 3   Find the reduced echelon form of the matrices in Problems 1 and 2.

SOLUTION   Working with the echelon form obtained in Problem 1, we have:

$$\begin{pmatrix} 1 & 2 & 3 \\ 0 & -3 & -6 \\ 0 & 0 & 0 \end{pmatrix} \xrightarrow{-\frac{1}{3}R_2} \begin{pmatrix} 1 & 2 & 3 \\ 0 & 1 & 2 \\ 0 & 0 & 0 \end{pmatrix} \xrightarrow{R_1 - 2R_2} \begin{pmatrix} 1 & 0 & -1 \\ 0 & 1 & 2 \\ 0 & 0 & 0 \end{pmatrix}$$

In the case of the echelon form matrix of Problem 2, we merely need to *clear* the second and third columns (that is, to clear the second column of the nonzero term in its first row and the fourth column of its nonzero terms in the first and second rows):

$$\begin{pmatrix} 1 & 1 & 1 & 2 \\ 0 & 1 & 2 & 1 \\ 0 & 0 & 0 & 1 \end{pmatrix} \xrightarrow[R_2 - R_3]{R_1 - R_2} \begin{pmatrix} 1 & 0 & -1 & 1 \\ 0 & 1 & 2 & 0 \\ 0 & 0 & 0 & 1 \end{pmatrix}$$

$$\xrightarrow{R_1 - R_3} \begin{pmatrix} 1 & 0 & -1 & 0 \\ 0 & 1 & 2 & 0 \\ 0 & 0 & 0 & 1 \end{pmatrix}$$

This section closes with three examples of solving linear systems. In each case we put the augmented matrix of the system in reduced echelon form and then read off the solution.

PROBLEM 4   Solve the linear system

$$\begin{cases} 2x_1 + 3x_2 + 5x_3 = 23 \\ x_1 - x_2 - x_3 = -4 \\ x_1 - 2x_2 + 3x_3 = 6 \end{cases}$$

SOLUTION   The reduced echelon form of the augmented matrix of the system is obtained as follows:

$$\begin{pmatrix} 2 & 3 & 5 & 23 \\ 1 & -1 & -1 & -4 \\ 1 & -2 & 3 & 6 \end{pmatrix} \begin{array}{c} R_1 - 2R_2 \\ \\ R_3 - R_2 \end{array} \begin{pmatrix} 0 & 5 & 7 & 31 \\ 1 & -1 & -1 & -4 \\ 0 & -1 & 4 & 10 \end{pmatrix} \begin{pmatrix} 1 & -1 & -1 & -4 \\ 0 & 5 & 7 & 31 \\ 0 & -1 & 4 & 10 \end{pmatrix}$$

why?

$$\begin{array}{c} R_1 - R_3 \\ R_2 + 5R_3 \\ -R_3 \end{array} \begin{pmatrix} 1 & 0 & -5 & 14 \\ 0 & 0 & 27 & 81 \\ 0 & 1 & -4 & -10 \end{pmatrix} \begin{pmatrix} 1 & 0 & -5 & -14 \\ 0 & 1 & -4 & -10 \\ 0 & 0 & 27 & 81 \end{pmatrix}$$

$$\begin{array}{c} \\ \tfrac{1}{27}R_3 \end{array} \begin{pmatrix} 1 & 0 & -5 & -14 \\ 0 & 1 & -4 & -10 \\ 0 & 0 & 1 & 3 \end{pmatrix} \begin{array}{c} R_1 + 5R_3 \\ R_2 + 4R_3 \end{array} \begin{pmatrix} 1 & 0 & 0 & 1 \\ 0 & 1 & 0 & 2 \\ 0 & 0 & 1 & 3 \end{pmatrix}$$

We see that $x_1 = 1$, $x_2 = 2$, $x_3 = 3$.
Check:

$$2(1) + 3(2) + 5(3) = 23$$
$$1 - 2 - 3 = -4$$
$$1 - 2(2) + 3(3) = 6$$

PROBLEM 5   Solve the linear system

$$\begin{cases} x_1 + 2x_2 + 7x_3 = 4 \\ 4x_1 + 9x_2 + 31x_3 = 21 \\ 2x_1 + 4x_2 + 14x_3 = 9 \end{cases}$$

SOLUTION We put the augmented matrix of the system in reduced echelon form:

$$\begin{pmatrix} 1 & 2 & 7 & 4 \\ 4 & 9 & 31 & 21 \\ 2 & 4 & 14 & 9 \end{pmatrix} \xrightarrow[\;R_3 - 2R_1\;]{R_2 - 4R_1} \begin{pmatrix} 1 & 2 & 7 & 4 \\ 0 & 1 & 3 & 5 \\ 0 & 0 & 0 & 1 \end{pmatrix} \xrightarrow{R_1 - 2R_2} \begin{pmatrix} 1 & 0 & 1 & -6 \\ 0 & 1 & 3 & 5 \\ 0 & 0 & 0 & 1 \end{pmatrix}$$

$$\xrightarrow[\;R_2 - 5R_3\;]{R_1 + 6R_3} \begin{pmatrix} 1 & 0 & 1 & 0 \\ 0 & 1 & 3 & 0 \\ 0 & 0 & 0 & 1 \end{pmatrix}$$

The last row of the matrix corresponds to the false equation $0 \cdot x_1 + 0 \cdot x_2 + 0 \cdot x_3 = 1$. Therefore the system has no solution.

PROBLEM 6 Solve the linear system

$$\begin{cases} x_1 + 2x_2 + x_3 = 2 \\ 4x_1 - 7x_2 - 5x_3 = 2 \\ 2x_1 - x_2 - x_3 = 2 \end{cases}$$

SOLUTION Starting with the augmented matrix, we have:

$$\begin{pmatrix} 1 & 2 & 1 & 2 \\ 4 & -7 & -5 & 2 \\ 2 & -1 & -1 & 2 \end{pmatrix} \xrightarrow[\;R_3 - 2R_1\;]{R_2 - 4R_1} \begin{pmatrix} 1 & 2 & 1 & 2 \\ 0 & -15 & -9 & -6 \\ 0 & -5 & -3 & -2 \end{pmatrix} \xrightarrow{R_2 - 3R_3} \begin{pmatrix} 1 & 2 & 1 & 2 \\ 0 & 0 & 0 & 0 \\ 0 & -5 & -3 & -2 \end{pmatrix}$$

$$\xrightarrow{-\frac{1}{5}R_3} \begin{pmatrix} 1 & 2 & 1 & 2 \\ 0 & 0 & 0 & 0 \\ 0 & 1 & \frac{3}{5} & \frac{2}{5} \end{pmatrix} \xrightarrow{\;\times\;} \begin{pmatrix} 1 & 2 & 1 & 2 \\ 0 & 1 & \frac{3}{5} & \frac{2}{5} \\ 0 & 0 & 0 & 0 \end{pmatrix} \xrightarrow{R_1 - 2R_2} \begin{pmatrix} 1 & 0 & \frac{1}{5} & \frac{3}{5} \\ 0 & 1 & \frac{3}{5} & \frac{2}{5} \\ 0 & 0 & 0 & 0 \end{pmatrix}$$

The last matrix is the augmented matrix of the system

$$\begin{cases} x_1 - \frac{1}{5}x_3 = \frac{3}{5} \\ x_2 + \frac{3}{5}x_3 = \frac{2}{5} \\ 0 = 0 \end{cases}$$

The equation $0 = 0$ is always true, but it does not give us any information. We are left with two equations in three variables. If we assign *any* value to x_3, we can solve for x_1 and x_2. For example:

$$\text{if } x_3 = 0, \text{ then } x_1 = \tfrac{3}{5} \text{ and } x_2 = \tfrac{2}{5}$$

$$\text{if } x_3 = 1, \text{ then } x_1 = \tfrac{4}{5} \text{ and } x_2 = -\tfrac{1}{5}$$

and so on. The system has infinitely many solutions.

EXERCISES *for Section 3.2*

For each of the following matrices: (a) Is the matrix in echelon form (and if not, why not?) (b) Is the matrix in reduced echelon form (and if not, why not)?

1. $\begin{pmatrix} 1 & 0 & 4 \\ 0 & 1 & 3 \\ 0 & 0 & 2 \end{pmatrix}$

2. $\begin{pmatrix} 1 & 0 & 1 & 7 \\ 0 & 1 & 0 & 6 \\ 0 & 0 & 1 & 3 \end{pmatrix}$

3. $\begin{pmatrix} -2 & 1 & 0 \\ 0 & 4 & 5 \end{pmatrix}$

4. $\begin{pmatrix} 1 & 1 & 1 & 1 \\ 0 & 1 & 1 & 2 \\ 0 & 0 & 1 & 3 \\ 0 & 0 & 0 & 4 \end{pmatrix}$

5. $\begin{pmatrix} 1 & 2 \\ 0 & 3 \\ 0 & 4 \\ 0 & 5 \end{pmatrix}$

6. $\begin{pmatrix} 1 & 0 & 0 & 0 & 3 \\ 0 & 1 & 0 & 0 & 5 \\ 0 & 0 & 0 & 1 & 7 \end{pmatrix}$

7. $\begin{pmatrix} 0 & 0 & 0 & 1 & 0 & 4 \\ 0 & 1 & 0 & 0 & 3 & 6 \\ 1 & 0 & 4 & 0 & 0 & 5 \end{pmatrix}$

8. $\begin{pmatrix} 1 & 0 & 0 & 0 & 1 \\ 0 & 0 & 1 & 0 & 2 \\ 0 & 0 & 0 & 1 & 1 \\ 0 & 0 & 0 & 0 & 0 \end{pmatrix}$

Find: (a) an echelon form and (b) the reduced echelon form of each of the following matrices:

9. $\begin{pmatrix} 1 & 2 \\ 3 & 4 \end{pmatrix}$

10. $\begin{pmatrix} 5 & 6 \\ 7 & 8 \end{pmatrix}$

11. $\begin{pmatrix} 1 & 2 & 3 \\ 4 & 5 & 6 \end{pmatrix}$

12. $\begin{pmatrix} 7 & 8 \\ 9 & 8 \\ 7 & 6 \end{pmatrix}$

13. $\begin{pmatrix} 1 & 2 & 3 & -1 \\ 4 & 5 & 6 & -2 \end{pmatrix}$

14. $\begin{pmatrix} 3 & -4 & 12 & -5 \\ 4 & 1 & 1 & -8 \\ 4 & -1 & -8 & 10 \end{pmatrix}$

15. $\begin{pmatrix} 1 & 2 & 1 & 7 \\ 2 & 3 & 3 & 16 \\ 2 & 3 & 4 & 19 \end{pmatrix}$

16. $\begin{pmatrix} 1 & 2 & 2 & -5 \\ 4 & 5 & -7 & 3 \end{pmatrix}$

17. $\begin{pmatrix} 2 & 1 & 3 & 9 \\ 3 & -6 & -4 & 7 \\ 5 & 2 & 7 & 22 \end{pmatrix}$

18. $\begin{pmatrix} 15 & -8 & 20 & 0 \\ 2 & 9 & -6 & 18 \\ 4 & 7 & -4 & 27 \end{pmatrix}$

19. $\begin{pmatrix} 2 & 1 & -3 & -7 \\ 1 & -2 & 1 & 4 \\ 3 & 4 & 1 & 2 \end{pmatrix}$

20. $\begin{pmatrix} 5 & 9 & 5 & 27 \\ 3 & 3 & 2 & 8 \\ 4 & 5 & 3 & 14 \end{pmatrix}$

21. $\begin{pmatrix} 2 & -3 & 5 & 8 \\ 4 & 6 & 2 & 1 \\ 6 & -9 & 15 & 5 \end{pmatrix}$

22. $\begin{pmatrix} -2 & 4 & 1 & 25 \\ 1 & 2 & -1 & -3 \\ 3 & -3 & 2 & -11 \end{pmatrix}$

23. $\begin{pmatrix} 4 & 4 & 3 & 3 & 3 \\ 3 & 4 & 5 & 2 & 8 \\ 6 & 7 & 7 & 4 & 7 \end{pmatrix}$

24. $\begin{pmatrix} 2 & 3 & -1 & 5 \\ 3 & -2 & 2 & 5 \\ 3 & 11 & -5 & 10 \end{pmatrix}$

25. $\begin{pmatrix} 3 & -1 & -3 & 10 \\ 7 & -2 & -4 & 14 \\ 6 & 2 & -6 & 15 \end{pmatrix}$

26. $\begin{pmatrix} 2 & 3 & -1 & 19 \\ 3 & -2 & 3 & 7 \end{pmatrix}$

27. $\begin{pmatrix} 1 & 0 & -4 & 2 \\ 2 & 2 & 3 & 5 \\ -2 & 4 & 1 & 6 \end{pmatrix}$

28. $\begin{pmatrix} 1 & 3 \\ 4 & 0 \\ 7 & 8 \\ -5 & 6 \end{pmatrix}$

29.
$$\begin{pmatrix} 3 & 2 & 4 & -6 & 8 & 15 \\ 9 & -3 & -8 & 7 & -9 & 29 \\ 4 & 7 & -10 & 11 & -2 & 57 \end{pmatrix}$$

Solve each of the following linear systems by putting the augmented matrix of the system in reduced echelon form:

30. $\begin{cases} 3x + y = 5 \\ 2x - 4y = -6 \end{cases}$

31. $\begin{cases} x + 10y = 12 \\ 3x - y = 5 \end{cases}$

32. $\begin{cases} 7x - 7y = 37 \\ 5x - 8y = -13 \end{cases}$

33. $\begin{cases} 3x - 5y = -2 \\ -9x + 15y = 6 \end{cases}$

34. $\begin{cases} 3x - 5y = -2 \\ -9x + 15y = -6 \end{cases}$

35. $\begin{cases} 3x - 4y = 1 \\ 4x - 3y = 13 \end{cases}$

36. $\begin{cases} -2x + 23y = 15 \\ 7x - 9y = 19 \end{cases}$

37. $\begin{cases} 2x_1 + 3x_2 + 7x_3 = 15 \\ 5x_1 + 4x_2 - 4x_3 = -2 \\ -2x_1 + x_2 + 2x_3 = -1 \end{cases}$

38. $\begin{cases} 7x_1 - 8x_2 + 9x_3 = 18 \\ 6x_1 + 5x_2 - 4x_3 = 4 \\ -3x_1 + 2x_2 + x_3 = 4 \end{cases}$

39. $\begin{cases} x_1 + 3x_2 + x_3 = -1 \\ 3x_1 - 6x_2 - 4x_3 = -31 \\ 2x_1 + 6x_2 + 2x_3 = -2 \end{cases}$

40. $\begin{cases} x_1 + 2x_2 + x_3 = 0 \\ 2x_1 + 3x_2 + 4x_3 = 0 \\ 2x_1 - 3x_3 + 5x_3 = 0 \end{cases}$

41. $\begin{cases} 8x_1 + 7x_2 + x_3 = 10 \\ 4x_1 + 5x_3 = 16 \\ -2x_1 + 4x_2 + x_3 = 14 \end{cases}$

42. $\begin{cases} x_1 + x_2 - x_3 = 3 \\ 3x_1 + 5x_2 + 4x_3 = 7 \\ 5x_1 + 7x_2 + 2x_3 = 12 \end{cases}$

43. $\begin{cases} 3x_1 + 4x_2 + 3x_3 = 7 \\ 4x_1 + 6x_2 - 3x_3 = -11 \\ 2x_1 - 8x_2 + 4x_3 = 0 \end{cases}$

44. $\begin{cases} 2x_1 + x_2 + x_3 = 11 \\ 2x_1 + 2x_2 + x_3 = 5 \\ 3x_1 + 3x_2 + 2x_3 = 11 \end{cases}$

45. $\begin{cases} x_1 + 2x_2 + 3x_3 = 4 \\ 4x_1 + 3x_2 + 2x_3 = 1 \\ 6x_1 + 7x_2 + 8x_3 = 9 \end{cases}$

3.3 APPLICATIONS OF LINEAR SYSTEMS

The known and unknown quantities in a real-world problem may be connected through linear equations.

If they are, and if we can find those equations, we can solve them by the echelon method. The real-world interpretation of the variables then gives the solution of the problem.

The following three examples show how it is done.

EXAMPLE 1: ECA TRIES SECTOR ANALYSIS

The Environmental Conservation Agency (ECA) has decided to study a new concept in pollution control.

This new concept is called *sector analysis*.

The idea behind sector analysis is that many allegedly harmful substances are *really* harmful only when they are concentrated in one sector: air, water, soil, or food.

As an example: Arsenic from crop dusting can be very harmful to earthworms if it remains in the soil, but the same arsenic will be relatively harmless if it is spread around into the atmosphere, the water supply, and the food supply.

Dr. Melody Moore, the inventor of sector analysis, will be publishing a report and recommendations on the concept. Let's see how she uses linear systems.

The report is designed to show how sector analysis works for four substances: radioactive waste, asbestos, mercury, and vinyl chloride. According to ECA's count, the environment now contains:

1. 383 ECA units* of radioactive waste from nuclear reactors;

2. 258 ECA units of asbestos from various industries (steel, building, automobile brakes, breweries, etc.);

3. 145 ECA units of mercury from industrial and agricultural products;

4. 124 ECA units of vinyl chloride from the manufacture and processing of plastics.

*ECA units give the ECA estimate of the potential harmfulness of a potentially harmful substance.

Table 3.2 shows how many ECA units of each substance can be harmlessly absorbed by each of the four environmental sectors *each month*.

TABLE 3.2 Four Potentially Harmful Substances and Four Environmental Sectors (Absorption Capacities in ECA Units Per Month)

Substance	Units Absorbed by Air	Units Absorbed by Water	Units Absorbed by Soil	Units Absorbed by Food
Radioactive Waste	2	6	4	3
Asbestos	0.5	2	5	2.5
Mercury	1	0.5	3.5	0.5
Vinyl Chloride	0.8	0.8	2.4	0.8

In how many months can the four sectors absorb the 383 units of radioactive waste, 258 units of asbestos, 145 units of mercury, and 124 units of vinyl chloride now floating around in the environment?

Since the *how many months* question tells exactly what is unknown, Dr. Moore lets:

x_1 = the number of months needed for the *air* sector to do its share of the harmless absorption job

and she lets x_2, x_3, and x_4 be the number of months required by the water, soil, and food sectors to do their share. The first row of Table 3.2 then gives her the equation

$$2x_1 + 6x_2 + 4x_3 + 3x_4 = 383$$

where 383 is the known number of units of radioactive waste in the environment. Rows 2, 3, and 4 of the table lead to:

$$0.5x_1 + 2x_2 + 5x_3 + 2.5x_4 = 258$$
$$x_1 + 0.5x_2 + 3.5x_3 + 0.5x_4 = 145$$
$$0.8x_1 + 0.8x_2 + 2.4x_3 + 0.8x_4 = 124$$

The total number of equations is four. Since there are four variables, it is a four by four linear system, and the corresponding augmented matrix is:

$$\begin{pmatrix} 2 & 6 & 4 & 3 & 383 \\ 0.5 & 2 & 5 & 2.5 & 258 \\ 1 & 0.5 & 3.5 & 0.5 & 145 \\ 0.8 & 0.8 & 2.4 & 0.8 & 124 \end{pmatrix}$$

The reduced echelon form of the matrix is then found in the usual way. (It takes seven sets of legal row operations to find it.) The result—with numbers in the last column rounded off to integers—is:

$$\begin{pmatrix} 1 & 0 & 0 & 0 & 23 \\ 0 & 1 & 0 & 0 & 27 \\ 0 & 0 & 1 & 0 & 28 \\ 0 & 0 & 0 & 1 & 21 \end{pmatrix}$$

This means that $x_1 = 23$, $x_2 = 27$, $x_3 = 28$, and $x_4 = 21$. Dr. Moore's conclusions are as follows:

1. The sector analysis concept works, at least for the four substances the report studies: the 383 ECA units of radioactive waste, etc.

2. The proof is that all four substances (in the quantities now present) can be harmlessly absorbed if we allow them to spread out into the *air* sector for 23 months, the *water* supply sector for 27 months, the *soil* sector for 28 months, and the national *food* supply sector for 21 months.

Dr. Moore seems to be saying—and proving—that pollution would just naturally disappear. If she were right, ECA would have much less pollution monitoring to do, and it would find it much easier to live within its budget. Some people at the agency liked Dr. Moore's report very much.

The next example describes some contrary thinking that went on at ECA.

EXAMPLE 2: ECA HAS DOUBTS ABOUT SECTOR ANALYSIS

Some of Dr. Moore's fellow scientists at ECA did some tough thinking about the sector analysis concept. They made the following points:

1. The Moore report showed that current levels of four potentially harmful substances would eventually be absorbed by the environment.

2. That left just one difficulty. While current levels were being absorbed, ongoing production would lead to new and higher levels of the four substances.

3. Conclusion: Sector analysis is a good policy, but it is not enough. ECA must issue new and more detailed guidelines for protecting the environment.

The new ECA policy would be to stay on top of the pollution problem month by month. There would be three ways of taking care of every potentially harmful substance: *countermeasures* (regulations to change manufacturing methods or waste disposal methods), industry-installed *emission controls* (like the "scrubbers" in some factory smokestacks), and after-emission *waste treatment* (like the burying of radioactive waste in abandoned salt mines).

All three methods were already being applied under old guidelines, but the scientists did not think they were going far enough. Table 3.3 shows ECA units per month produced by asbestos and vinyl chloride. The table also shows how many ECA units of each substance are removed under the old guidelines.

TABLE 3.3 Monthly Production and Control of Asbestos and Vinyl Chloride (in ECA Units per Month)

Substance	ECA Units	Counter-measures	Emission Controls	Waste Treatment
Asbestos	30	4	3	7
Vinyl Chloride	20	2	4	3

If we add up the control figures, we see that $4 + 3 + 7 = 14$ ECA units per month of asbestos are controlled, as against 30 produced.

Similarly, 9 ECA units per month of vinyl chloride are controlled, and 20 units are produced.

According to Dr. Moore, sector analysis, or harmless absorption, would take up the slack. But ECA does not believe in the sector analysis concept any more. The new position is to increase countermeasures, emission controls, and waste treatment to the point where controls exactly match production.

But how large should the increases be? ECA's expert on linear systems had a suggestion. He would multiply countermeasures by a number t_1, emission controls by a number t_2, and waste treatment by a number t_3. Then he would use Table 3.3 to write two equations:

$$4t_1 + 3t_2 + 7t_3 = 30$$
$$2t_1 + 4t_2 + 3t_3 = 20$$

He would solve for t_1, t_2, and t_3. Then ECA would know how much to increase controls to take care of the exact number of ECA units produced by asbestos and vinyl chloride.

It looked good. ECA's research director gave the go-ahead and the linear systems expert set to work. He wrote the augmented matrix of the system:

$$\begin{pmatrix} 4 & 3 & 7 & 30 \\ 2 & 4 & 3 & 20 \end{pmatrix}$$

Then he used a few legal row operations to put the matrix in reduced echelon form:

$$\begin{pmatrix} 1 & 0 & 1.9 & 6 \\ 0 & 1 & -0.2 & 2 \end{pmatrix}$$

The equations corresponding to the reduced echelon form are:

$$\begin{cases} t_1 \qquad + 1.9t_3 = 6 \\ \qquad t_2 - 0.2t_3 = 2 \end{cases}$$

or:

$$\begin{cases} t_1 = 6 - 1.9t_3 \\ t_2 = 2 + 0.2t_3 \end{cases}$$

Mathematically, this amounts to saying that the system has infinitely many solutions. Any and all of these solutions can be obtained by assigning a value to t_3 and then determining t_1 and t_2. A few of the results are listed in the following table:

t_1	4.1	3.15	2.675	2.2	1.725	1.25	0.775	0.3	0.0625
t_2	2.2	2.3	2.35	2.4	2.45	2.5	2.55	2.6	2.625
t_3	1	1.5	1.75	2	2.25	2.5	2.75	3	3.125

Notice that the choices are reasonable. For example, it makes no sense for t_1, t_2, or t_3 to be negative. Therefore such a choice as $t_3 = 4$ would be unreasonable because then t_1 would be negative.

ECA was truly pleased with these results, for they gave the agency many alternative ways of controlling pollution. Depending on the political and engineering realities, ECA could shift from one set of guidelines to another and still get its job done. Here are three examples:

POLICY CHOICE 1: ECA works with $t_1 = 4.1$, $t_2 = 2.2$, and $t_3 = 1$. Using these multipliers in Table 3.3 gives the results shown in Table 3.4. The

TABLE 3.4

Substance	ECA Units	Counter-measures	Emission Controls	Waste Treatment
Asbestos	30	16.4	6.6	7
Vinyl Chloride	20	8.2	8.8	3

guidelines described by Table 3.4 put the main burden for controlling asbestos on countermeasures. For vinyl chloride, countermeasures take second place to emission controls.

POLICY CHOICE 2: ECA works with $t_1 = 2.2$, $t_2 = 2.4$, and $t_3 = 2$. Table 3.3 then gives the results shown in Table 3.5. The guidelines are now designed to emphasize waste treatment to control asbestos, and to emphasize emission controls for vinyl chloride.

TABLE 3.5

Substance	ECA Units	Counter-measures	Emission Controls	Waste Treatment
Asbestos	30	8.8	7.2	14
Vinyl Chloride	20	4.4	9.6	6

POLICY CHOICE 3: ECA works with $t_1 = 0.3$, $t_2 = 2.6$, and $t_3 = 3$. These multipliers change Table 3.3 into Table 3.6. The guidelines in this table very strongly emphasize waste treatment to control asbestos, and waste treatment is relied on almost to the same extent as emission controls for vinyl chloride.

TABLE 3.6

Substance	ECA Units	Counter-measures	Emission Controls	Waste Treatment
Asbestos	30	1.2	7.8	21
Vinyl Chloride	20	0.6	10.4	9

EXAMPLE 3: THE COMPUTER MARKET

The idea of *equilibrium in the marketplace* was explained in Section 2.6. Example 1 of that section showed how the manufacturers adjusted the price of HAL computers to bring supply and demand into equilibrium—and to send company profits into high orbit.

No good moneymaker lasts forever. Competitors get into the market. Or, as it is said in the business world, every good market becomes fragmented.

In the case of HAL computers, the company itself fragmented within 10 years of its first big success.

It happened this way. Each of three hard-driving project managers set to work developing a second-generation HAL computer. The computers they produced could do anything the original HAL could do, but each of them also had special capabilities. The computers and their specialities were H-1000 (engineering and science), H-2000 (business and economics), and H-3000 (sociology and opinion research).

Each of the three managers thought his computer could succeed alone, and each of them got financing to split off from HAL and to set up a separate company. The three new companies were named after the computers they manufactured: H-1000, H-2000, and H-3000.

H-1000 did not have to do much competing: it gave computer-using scientists and engineers the second-generation performance they wanted at a first-generation price of $16 million. Orders (83) were far ahead of productive capacity (29). Management raised the price and increased production several times. At $20 million, orders were down 19% to 67, and annual production was up 28% to 37.

More increases in price and production were in the cards. Management wanted these increases to go far enough but not too far. Abel Smith, H-1000's economist, was given the job of finding a theoretical equilibrium price. Smith set up a system of three equations in three variables. The variables were S (number of H-1000 computers in supply), D (number of H-1000 computers in demand), and x (price of an H-1000 computer in millions of dollars). The equations (based on the data given in the last paragraph, and derived in the same way as Adam Smith's equations for HAL on pp. 104–106) were:

$$D = -4x + 147$$

$$S = 2x - 3$$

$$S = D$$

The augmented matrix of the system (with columns 1, 2, and 3 corresponding to the variables x, D, and S) was:

$$\begin{pmatrix} 4 & 1 & 0 & 147 \\ 2 & 0 & -1 & 3 \\ 0 & 1 & -1 & 0 \end{pmatrix}$$

Legal row operations led to the reduced echelon form:

$$\begin{pmatrix} 1 & 0 & 0 & 25 \\ 0 & 1 & 0 & 47 \\ 0 & 0 & 1 & 47 \end{pmatrix}$$

Abel Smith therefore predicted that an equilibrium price of $25 million would go along with an equilibrium demand (and supply) of 47 computers. So management contracted for a new factory with an annual production rate of 10 computers, and it raised the price per computer to $25 million.

It was different for the H-2000 and H-3000. They were supposed to have designed-in specialities, but computer users in business, economics, sociology, and opinion research just did not see it that way. H-2000 and H-3000 found themselves competing head-to-head in one and the same market. Supply, demand, and prices for the two computers were interrelated. If either company raised prices, it would lose business to the other.

What happened? Confusion. Prices were raised and lowered chaotically for some 16 months. When things settled down, economists for H-2000 and H-3000 tried (separately) to describe the supply–demand-price picture for the benefit of their companies. The H-2000 description (which turned out to be a little more accurate) consisted of six equations in six variables. The variables S_1, D_1, and x_1 were supply, demand, and price for H-2000 computers; S_2, D_2, and x_2 were supply, demand, and price for H-3000 computers. The equations relating these variables were:

$$\begin{cases} D_1 = -2x_1 + 3x_2 + 104 \\ S_1 = 2x_1 + 12x_2 - 226 \\ S_1 = D_1 \end{cases}$$

$$\begin{cases} D_2 = 4x_1 - 5x_2 + 116 \\ S_2 = 7x_1 + 2x_2 - 138 \\ S_2 = D_2 \end{cases}$$

Charles Smith, head of H-2000's quantitative analysis staff, explained these equations to management. First he gave some examples to show that the equations checked with the facts. Then he pointed out that they checked with common sense. For example, the two demand equations show that raising H-2000's price would lower demand for it and raise demand for H-3000. The supply equations show that raising H-2000's price would increase the supply of both computers. And so on. All very sensible.

From experience with HAL, management understood about equilibrium price, equilibrium supply, and equilibrium demand in a *one*-product market. Charles Smith introduced a new idea: In a *two*-product market as described by his system of six equations, a solution of the system is called an *equilibrium solution*. In other words, if the system has a solution, then that solution describes a market in equilibrium.

Charles Smith showed that his system does have a solution. How did he show it? Since he had six equations in six variables—x_1, x_2, S_1, S_2, D_1, D_2—the obvious way was to write a 6 × 7 augmented matrix and use legal row operations to put the matrix in reduced echelon form. This is obvious, but it's not intelligent. Charles Smith's way was to replace his six by six system with a two by two system before attempting to find a solution. He did this by eliminating S_1 and D_1 from the first set of three equations, and by eliminating S_2 and D_2 from the second set. The result (as you can check by looking back at the equations above) was:

$$\begin{cases} -2x_1 + 3x_2 + 104 = 2x_1 + 12x_2 - 226 \\ 4x_1 - 5x_2 + 116 = 7x_1 + 2x_2 - 138 \end{cases}$$

or:

$$\begin{cases} 4x_1 + 9x_2 = 330 \\ 3x_1 + 7x_2 = 254 \end{cases}$$

The solution is $x_1 = 24$, $x_2 = 26$. Returning to the original system on p. 144, we see that this gives $D_1 = S_1 = 134$ and $D_2 = S_2 = 82$.

Is there any practical meaning in the claim that this is an equilibrium solution? Well, yes. Charles Smith knew from recent experience that H-3000 would follow H-2000's lead in pricing. Moreover, H-3000 could be counted on to set a higher price, with the expectation of selling fewer computers but making more money per computer. This is just the way it turned out. Charles Smith's equilibrium solution was very close to the actual market equilibrium that held for the next several years.

Note: If there are more than two products competing, the linear equilibrium system contains more than 6 equations: 9 if there are 3 products, 12 if there are 4, and so on.

The equations of equilibrium may have more than one solution. They may have infinitely many solutions. That is good. It means that there are infinitely many ways to reach market equilibrium. (It may also mean that the equations are not the best.)

Finally, the system may not have a solution. Then market equilibrium is impossible. A real-world example of a market that is not in equilibrium is the world market for oil: since world demand for oil goes up even when the price goes up, OPEC will continue raising prices as long as it has oil to sell.

Forest Industries is a company that controls 66 million acres of forest and farmland in the U.S., Canada, and Brazil. The company is in many businesses: pulp and paper, lumber, plywood, poles for telephone and power lines, agriculture, and real estate. Exercises 1–4 are concerned with some of these businesses.

1. New Hampshire Logging (a division of Forest Industries) will cut 4092 acres of medium-quality forest and 10,410 acres of low-quality forest this year. The timber will be used to supply small sawmills and small pulp mills in northern New England. Each small sawmill needs all the timber provided by 100 acres of medium-quality forest and 50 acres of low-quality forest. Each small pulp mill needs all the timber produced by 12 acres of medium-quality forest and 210 acres of low-quality forest. How many small sawmills and how many small pulp mills can New Hampshire Logging supply this year?

2. Forest Industries has extensive agricultural holdings in Louisiana. The company's Rice Industries and Sugar Industries divisions in that state are among the largest U.S. producers of rice and sugar cane.

To produce a market-ready ton of rice demands 5 pounds of fertilizer and 13 hours of labor. Rice Industries' per-ton cost for fertilizer and labor is $46.30.

To produce a market-ready ton of sugar demands 4 pounds of fertilizer and 15 hours of labor. Sugar Industries' per-ton cost of fertilizer and labor is $51.30.

If Rice Industries and Sugar Industries pay the same amounts for fertilizer and labor, then what do they pay for a pound of fertilizer? What is their hourly cost for labor?

3. Like all efficiently run companies, Forest Industries expands production to supply booming markets and cuts back on products for declining markets. Recent figures for four Forest Industries products in the three sections of the U.S. show the following after-tax profit per year for each dollar invested.

	Region		
Product	*Sunbelt*	*Mid-America*	*East*
White Paper	0.11	0.12	0.16
Bleached Boards	0.23	0.17	0.11
Milk Cartons	0.05	0.03	0.01
Pulp	0.11	0.14	0.13

After studying these figures, Forest Industries management decides that milk carton production will not be expanded because profit margins are so low. To test other options, management asks the following questions:

a. *What product or products do we want to emphasize in future investments?* To answer this question, staff analysts let

x_1 = the number of megabucks (1 megabuck = \$1 million) invested in expanding white paper production (the same number x_1 is used in all three sections of the U.S.)

x_2 = the number of megabucks invested in bleached board mill expansion (the same number x_2 in all three sections)

x_3 = the number of megabucks in pulp mill expansion (the same number x_3 in all three sections)

Then, assuming that profit margins will be the ones given in the table, they ask: What must x_1, x_2, and x_3 be to give total profits of 13.55 megabucks in the Sunbelt, 13.58 megabucks in mid-America, and 13.21 megabucks in the East?
What conclusion do you draw from the answer?

b. *What section of the country offers the best climate for future expansion?* The analysis staff tries to answer this question by letting

y_1 = the number of megabucks invested in plant expansions for each of the three products (same number for white paper, for bleached boards, for pulp) in the Sunbelt

y_2 = the number of megabucks invested in the expansion of each of the three products in mid-America

y_3 = the number of megabucks invested in expansion for each of the three products in the East

Then (with the table's profit margins assumed) they ask: What values of y_1, y_2, and y_3 will give profits of 13.58 megabucks in white paper production, 14.21 megabucks in bleached board production, and 12.64 megabucks in pulp production?
What investment conclusion can be drawn from the answer?

4. The various divisions of Forest Industries harvest and sell timber for four purposes: *poles* (for telephone lines and utility company power lines), *lumber* (for sawmills), *plywood* (low-quality lumber) and *pulp* (for carton- and papermaking). Company forests in North and South America are of four types: 20-, 30-, 40-, and 50-year growth. (The ages give the number of years since the forest was last cut. Older forests contain more of the larger trees that are suitable for high-profit uses such as poles and lumber.) The number of units of timber suitable for each of the four purposes in 10,000 acres of 20-, 30-, 40-, or 50-year forest is shown in the following table. The units are T-units, company-devised units used for measuring board-feet of usable timber (or equivalent tons of pulp).

| | Age of Forest, in Years | | | |
Use	20	30	40	50
Poles	1	3	7	8
Lumber	2	4	6	6
Plywood	9	4	3	2
Pulp	12	3	2	1

In this next year, Forest Industries will want to have enough timber to supply 483 T-units for poles, 508 T-units for lumber, 561 T-units for plywood, and 549 T-units for pulp. How many 10,000-acre tracts of 20-, 30-, 40-, and 50-year forest must be harvested to meet these needs?

Maxim's is the largest French restaurant in Southern California. It is so large that it employs four master chefs. The next five exercises are concerned with the restaurant and its chefs.

5. In addition to the four master chefs, Maxim's employs a small army of assistant chefs and kitchen workers. Assistant chefs earn $78 per day, and kitchen workers earn $24 per day. The daily payroll for assistant chefs and kitchen workers is $14,520. After a wage increase of 12% for assistant chefs and 7% for kitchen workers, the daily payroll climbs to $15,770.40. How many assistant chefs and how many kitchen workers are employed at Maxim's?

6. A fund-raising dinner for a political candidate was held at Maxim's. The guests were all married couples. Tickets were priced in a way that was supposed to amuse the guests:

> $100 per couple if neither husband nor wife had been married before
>
> $500 per couple if neither husband nor wife had been married more than once before
>
> $1000 per couple for all other couples

The dinner was held in the main dining room, which seats 375 couples. Since the management is sympathetic to the candidate, it charged his campaign committee only $30,000 for food and service. After the dinner was over, the committee found that it had sold 364 tickets, that it had sold twice as many $500 tickets as $100 tickets, and that it had a profit (after deducting the $30,000 in costs) of $318,800. How many tickets of each kind were sold?

7. Maxim's has been very successful with the Big Maxim, a $15 imitation of a well-known fast-food hamburger. A Big Maxim consists of steak tartare on French bread. The menu explains that steak tartare à la Maxim's is a mixture of steak with other ingredients. In fact, it is a mixture of steak @ $2.70 per pound, poultry @ $1.50 per pound, and mutton @ $1.95 per pound. To keep customers satisfied, the mixture must have a fat content of 18%. The fat content per ingredient is 24% for steak, 12% for poultry, and 18% for mutton. The master chefs want their steak tartare mixture to have the 18% fat content and to cost exactly $2.00 per pound. What proportions of steak, poultry, and mutton should they use?

8. Maxim's has recently started serving a Sunday brunch. Actually, they serve four of them, all in different price ranges. Each brunch requires the services of specialists in the preparation of salads, seafood, and dessert fruits. The man-hours required to serve each brunch are shown in the following table:

| | Specialist | | |
| | | | |
Brunch	Salads	Seafood	Fruits
I	0.1	0.5	0.3
II	0.2	1.1	0.7
III	0.3	1.0	0.4
IV	0.4	1.3	0.5

The master chef in charge of the kitchen on Sunday mornings has a skeleton staff to work with: 40 man-hours of salad specialist time, 160 man-hours of seafood specialist time, and 60 man-hours of fruit specialist time. Suppose that customers will buy all the brunches that these specialists concoct. Can the chef in charge make use of all the available kitchen staff time?

9. Maxim's offers its dinner patrons 50-year-old brandy and rare liqueurs. These items cannot be replaced. To avoid running out of them too quickly, the management has devised a rationing system. Each master chef is allotted a certain number of ounces of brandy and liqueur for each dinner he supervises. The figures are as follows:

	Master Chef 1	Master Chef 2	Master Chef 3	Master Chef 4
Brandy	2	3	5	6
Liqueur	10	10	16	30

The totals to be served to all diners each evening are 1375 ounces of brandy and 6250 ounces of liqueur. Three questions arose:

a. Master Chef 3 glanced at these numbers and said, "Gentlemen, you must take me for a fool! Under these conditions I can preside over no more than 69 dinners each evening." Was he a fool? Or was he being taken for one?

b. Master Chef 4, noticing that he required more brandy and more liqueur per patron than Master Chef 3, concluded that he would be able to supervise fewer than 69 dinners each evening. Far fewer. Was he right?

c. The management predicted that there would be evenings on which Master Chef 1 supervised more than 500 dinners. Could this happen? Can you give a numerical example?

Cage Realty is the leading real estate agency in a small college town. They claim to offer places to live for everyone from 18-year-old students to 80-year-old retirees. In fact, their listings include rooms, apartments, trailers, condominiums, duplexes, and single-family houses.

10. Cage Realty has noticed that rooms and apartments are in competition for the student dollar. If rooms are too expensive, students rent (and share) apartments. But if prevailing room rents are too low, then rooms are withdrawn from the market. (It is a lot of strain for homeowners to rent out a room or two, so they will not do it if the return is too small.) And if there are no rooms to be had, then apartment rents go up. These realities are described in the following equations, in which S_1, D_1, and x_1 are supply, demand, and price for rooms; and S_2, D_2, and x_2 are the same quantities for apartments. (Price = cost per person per month in dollars.)

$$\begin{cases} D_1 = -3x_1 + 6x_2 + 309 \\ S_1 = x_1 + 11x_2 - 746 \\ S_1 = D_1 \end{cases} \qquad \begin{cases} D_2 = 8x_1 - 2x_2 + 556 \\ S_2 = 11x_1 + 4x_2 - 539 \\ S_2 = D_2 \end{cases}$$

What are the equilibrium prices, supply, and demand for rooms and apartments?

11. Exercise 10 is concerned with rooms and apartments that are within walking distance of the college campus. Students who are willing to live 8 to 10 miles from campus have a larger choice of apartments. They have also found that taking over the payments on a trailer is sometimes cheaper than renting an apartment. Let price be dollar cost per person per month. Let x_1, D_1, and S_1 be price, demand, and supply for trailers. Let x_2, D_2, and S_2 be price, demand, and supply for apartments. Cage Realty has discovered that the following equations describe the trailer–apartment competition for the student market.

$$\begin{cases} D_1 = -5x_1 + 7x_2 + 786 \\ S_1 = 2x_1 + 19x_2 - 1412 \\ S_1 = D_1 \end{cases} \qquad \begin{cases} D_2 = 8x_1 + 13.5x_2 + 829 \\ S_2 = 13x_1 + 22.5x_2 - 795 \\ S_2 = D_2 \end{cases}$$

Find the equilibrium price, supply, and demand for trailers and for apartments.

12. Single-family houses have become very expensive in the college town served by Cage Realty. If teachers and other college employees are in the housing market, they are usually looking for a condominium or a duplex. Let x_1, S_1, and D_1 be the selling price (in thousands of dollars), the supply, and the demand for a condominium. Let x_2, S_2, and D_2 be the same quantities for a duplex. Cage Realty's market equilibrium equations are:

$$\begin{cases} D_1 = -8x_1 + 5x_2 + 287 \\ S_1 = 7x_1 + 9x_2 - 376 \\ S_1 = D_1 \end{cases} \qquad \begin{cases} D_2 = 4x_1 + 5x_2 + 205 \\ S_2 = 26x_1 + 11x_2 - 773 \\ S_2 = D_2 \end{cases}$$

What is the equilibrium selling price of a condominium? Of a duplex? What are the equilibrium supply and demand for these items?

13. Cage Realty also has many clients who can afford single-family houses. Their choice is between existing houses and new houses. Let x_1 be the price in thousands of dollars of an existing house, and let S_1 and D_1 be the supply and demand for existing houses. Let x_2, S_2, and D_2 have the same meanings for new houses. The agents at Cage Realty have found that the single-family housing market can be described by the following equations:

$$\begin{cases} D_1 = -11x_1 + 13x_2 + 1747 \\ S_1 = 3x_1 + 21x_2 - 579 \\ S_1 = D_1 \end{cases} \qquad \begin{cases} D_2 = 4x_1 + 5x_2 + 1452 \\ S_2 = 24x_1 + 16x_2 - 1816 \\ S_2 = D_2 \end{cases}$$

What are the equilibrium prices, supply, and demand for existing and new single-family houses?

chapter four

MATRIX ALGEBRA
CONTINUED

SECTIONS 4.1, 4.2, and 4.3 show how to add, subtract, multiply, and divide in matrix algebra. This part of the subject is called *matrix arithmetic.*

Section 4.4 applies matrix arithmetic to *input–output analysis,* the most realistic and interesting application we have come to so far. (Input–output analysis is a technique of mathematical economics, but you do not need any background in economics to understand what is said about it here.)

4.1 MATRIX ARITHMETIC: ADDITION AND MULTIPLICATION BY A NUMBER

Matrices are very convenient for classifying data. To make use of all the information in a matrix—or in several matrices—we sometimes need to do matrix arithmetic. Let's begin by defining equality of matrices:

EXAMPLES: EQUAL AND UNEQUAL MATRICES

1. The equation

$$\begin{pmatrix} 1 & 2 & 3 \\ 4 & 5 & 6 \end{pmatrix} = \begin{pmatrix} 1 & 2 & 3 \\ 4 & 5 & x \end{pmatrix}$$

is correct if and only if $x = 6$.

2. No matter what values x and y have,

$$\begin{pmatrix} 1 & 2 & 3 \\ 4 & 5 & 6 \end{pmatrix} \neq \begin{pmatrix} 1 & 2 & 3 & x \\ 4 & 5 & 6 & y \end{pmatrix}$$

since the matrices are of different sizes.

3. Although the matrices are of the same size,

$$\begin{pmatrix} 7 & 8 & 9 \\ 6 & 5 & 4 \end{pmatrix} \neq \begin{pmatrix} 7 & 9 & 8 \\ 6 & 5 & 4 \end{pmatrix}$$

since the $(1, 2)$ and $(1, 3)$ entries are unequal.

Now we can define matrix addition and subtraction.

HOW TO ADD AND SUBTRACT MATRICES

If **A** and **B** are matrices of the same size, then the sum **A** + **B** is obtained by adding corresponding entries of **A** and **B**. Similarly, the difference **A** − **B** is obtained by subtracting corresponding entries of **A** and **B**.

EXAMPLES: ADDITION AND SUBTRACTION OF MATRICES; ZERO MATRIX

1. If

$$A = \begin{pmatrix} 1 & 2 & 3 \\ 4 & 5 & 6 \end{pmatrix} \quad \text{and} \quad B = \begin{pmatrix} 7 & 8 & 9 \\ 10 & 11 & 12 \end{pmatrix}$$

then

$$A + B = \begin{pmatrix} 1+7 & 2+8 & 3+9 \\ 4+10 & 5+11 & 6+12 \end{pmatrix} = \begin{pmatrix} 8 & 10 & 12 \\ 14 & 16 & 18 \end{pmatrix}$$

and

$$A - B = \begin{pmatrix} 1-7 & 2-8 & 3-9 \\ 4-10 & 5-11 & 6-12 \end{pmatrix} = \begin{pmatrix} -6 & -6 & -6 \\ -6 & -6 & -6 \end{pmatrix}$$

2. If

$$A = \begin{pmatrix} 1 & 2 & 3 \\ 4 & 5 & 6 \end{pmatrix} \quad \text{and} \quad B = \begin{pmatrix} 3 & 2 & 1 & 4 \\ 9 & 8 & 7 & 7 \end{pmatrix}$$

then we cannot define either the sum $A + B$ or the difference $A - B$ since A and B are of different sizes.

3. If A and B are equal, then $A - B$ is the *zero matrix*. For example,

$$\begin{pmatrix} 1 & 2 & 3 \\ 4 & 5 & 6 \end{pmatrix} - \begin{pmatrix} 1 & 2 & 3 \\ 4 & 5 & 6 \end{pmatrix} = \begin{pmatrix} 0 & 0 & 0 \\ 0 & 0 & 0 \end{pmatrix}$$

If A is any matrix and 0 is the zero matrix *of the same size,* then $A + 0 = A$. For example,

$$\begin{pmatrix} 7 & 10 \\ 8 & 11 \\ 9 & 12 \end{pmatrix} + \begin{pmatrix} 0 & 0 \\ 0 & 0 \\ 0 & 0 \end{pmatrix} = \begin{pmatrix} 7 & 10 \\ 8 & 11 \\ 9 & 12 \end{pmatrix}$$

In real-world applications, we may use matrix addition to extract information from hundreds of matrices (of the same size) at once. To keep the arithmetic simple, the following illustrative problem contains only 2 matrices. But the principle is the same for 200 matrices.

PROBLEM 1   Aztec, the Mexican car company, now manufactures five models in the U.S.: Princess, Indio, Ramita, Lobo, and Tigre. Their first year's production at the Baton Rouge, Kenosha, and San Diego factories is given in Table 4.1, and their second year's production is given in Table 4.2. What was the total production of each of the five models at Baton Rouge, at Kenosha, and at San Diego in the first two years of production?

TABLE 4.1   Aztec USA: Year 1 Production

	Baton Rouge	Kenosha	San Diego
Princess	50,680	50,432	46,395
Indio	41,587	22,980	37,793
Ramita	27,946	25,015	31,703
Lobo	19,419	15,007	13,629
Tigre	11,850	7,948	4,174

TABLE 4.2   Aztec USA: Year 2 Production

	Baton Rouge	Kenosha	San Diego
Princess	65,351	61,190	119,003
Indio	54,586	75,260	113,069
Ramita	41,645	41,556	35,085
Lobo	20,500	19,630	21,251
Tigre	13,589	14,410	17,434

SOLUTION   The entries in Table 4.1 give us a year 1 production matrix:

$$\mathbf{P} = \begin{pmatrix} 50,680 & 50,432 & 46,395 \\ 41,587 & 22,980 & 37,793 \\ 27,946 & 25,015 & 31,703 \\ 19,419 & 15,007 & 13,629 \\ 11,850 & 7,948 & 4,174 \end{pmatrix}$$

The entries in Table 4.2 give us a year 2 production matrix:

$$
\mathbf{Q} = \begin{pmatrix}
65{,}351 & 61{,}190 & 119{,}003 \\
54{,}586 & 75{,}260 & 113{,}069 \\
41{,}645 & 41{,}556 & 35{,}085 \\
20{,}500 & 19{,}630 & 21{,}251 \\
13{,}589 & 14{,}410 & 17{,}434
\end{pmatrix}
$$

Since the matrices $\mathbf{P}$ and $\mathbf{Q}$ are the same size, we can add them. If we write $\mathbf{P} + \mathbf{Q} = \mathbf{R}$, we have

$$
\mathbf{R} = \begin{pmatrix}
116{,}031 & 111{,}622 & 165{,}398 \\
96{,}173 & 98{,}240 & 150{,}862 \\
69{,}591 & 66{,}571 & 66{,}788 \\
39{,}919 & 34{,}637 & 34{,}880 \\
25{,}439 & 22{,}358 & 21{,}608
\end{pmatrix}
$$

If we label the five rows of $\mathbf{R}$ with the model names Princess, Indio, Ramita, Lobo, and Tigre, and the three columns with the factory locations Baton Rouge, Kenosha, and San Diego, we have all 15 of the production numbers we want. For example, the total production of Ramitas at Kenosha in years 1 and 2 is 66,571. (To save space, we will not give the data table form of the matrix $\mathbf{R}$).

Matrix arithmetic includes two kinds of matrix multiplication. The first (and by far the simpler) is multiplication of a matrix by a number:

HOW TO MULTIPLY A MATRIX BY A NUMBER

To multiply a matrix $\mathbf{B}$ by a number c, multiply each entry of $\mathbf{B}$ by the number c.

EXAMPLE: MULTIPLYING A MATRIX BY A NUMBER

$$3 \begin{pmatrix} 15 & 6 & -8 \\ -4 & 0 & 11 \end{pmatrix} = \begin{pmatrix} 45 & 18 & -24 \\ -12 & 0 & 33 \end{pmatrix}$$

PROBLEM 2   As is shown by Tables 4.1 and 4.2, Aztec produced many more cars in year 2 than in year 1. The explanation was simple: there was great demand for Aztec cars in year 1. The company therefore expanded all three of its U.S. factories and (naturally) increased its work force. As a result, Aztec's investment in producing cars was 20% higher in year 2 than in year 1. Management expected production of all five models at all three plants to go up by 25%. Was this really what happened in year 2?

SOLUTION   To answer the question, we multiply the production matrix **P** by 1.25. Then we compare the result with **Q**. An easy way to compare is to calculate the matrix

$$\mathbf{M} = \mathbf{Q} - 1.25\mathbf{P}$$

If every entry in the matrix **M** is positive, then production of all five models at all three plants increased by at least 25% in year 2.

By carrying out the multiplication, we find (with numbers rounded off to the nearest integer) that:

$$1.25\mathbf{P} = \begin{pmatrix} 63{,}350 & 63{,}040 & 57{,}994 \\ 51{,}984 & 28{,}725 & 47{,}241 \\ 34{,}933 & 31{,}269 & 39{,}629 \\ 24{,}274 & 18{,}759 & 17{,}036 \\ 14{,}813 & 9{,}935 & 5{,}218 \end{pmatrix}$$

To find $\mathbf{M} = \mathbf{Q} - 1.25\mathbf{P}$, we merely subtract 1.25**P** from the production matrix **Q** of Problem 1. The result is:

$$\mathbf{M} = \begin{pmatrix} 2{,}001 & -1{,}850 & 61{,}009 \\ 2{,}602 & 46{,}535 & 65{,}828 \\ 6{,}712 & 10{,}287 & -4{,}544 \\ -3{,}774 & 871 & 4{,}215 \\ -1{,}224 & 4{,}475 & 12{,}216 \end{pmatrix}$$

If we label the rows and columns of **M** in the manner of Tables 4.1 and 4.2, we see that 11 of Aztec's 15 production goals were met. The Baton Rouge plant was least efficient: its production of Lobo and Tigre models failed to meet the year 2 goals. Kenosha was slightly below target for the Princess model, but it far exceeded its goal for the Indio model. San Diego was below target for the Ramita model but exceptionally productive otherwise.

EXERCISES *for Section 4.1*

In each of the following exercises, determine the value of x, *if there is one,* that makes **A** = **B**.

1. $\mathbf{A} = \begin{pmatrix} 10 & 8 & 4 \\ 4 & 8 & x \end{pmatrix}$ $\mathbf{B} = \begin{pmatrix} 10 & 8 & 4 \\ 4 & 8 & 10 \end{pmatrix}$

2. $\mathbf{A} = \begin{pmatrix} 2 & 2 & 2 \\ 2 & 2 & x \end{pmatrix}$ $\mathbf{B} = \begin{pmatrix} x & 2 & 2 \\ 2 & 2 & 2 \end{pmatrix}$

3. $\mathbf{A} = \begin{pmatrix} 0 & x & 2 \\ 3 & 1 & 0 \\ 1 & 2 & 3 \end{pmatrix}$ $\mathbf{B} = \begin{pmatrix} x & 2 & 0 \\ 3 & 1 & 0 \\ 1 & 2 & 3 \end{pmatrix}$

4. $\mathbf{A} = \begin{pmatrix} 1 & 4 \\ 2 & 5 \\ 3 & x \end{pmatrix}$ $\mathbf{B} = \begin{pmatrix} 1 & 2 & 3 \\ 4 & 5 & x \end{pmatrix}$

In each of the following exercises, determine the values of x and y, *if there are any,* that make **A** = **B**:

5. $\mathbf{A} = \begin{pmatrix} x & 2 & 4 \\ 1 & x & 2 \\ 2 & 4 & y \end{pmatrix}$ $\mathbf{B} = \begin{pmatrix} 1 & 2 & 4 \\ 1 & 1 & 2 \\ 2 & 4 & 7 \end{pmatrix}$

6. $\mathbf{A} = \begin{pmatrix} x & 1 & 1 \\ 2 & x^2 & 2 \\ 3 & 3 & y \end{pmatrix}$ $\mathbf{B} = \begin{pmatrix} 3 & 1 & 1 \\ 2 & 9 & 2 \\ 3 & 3 & 4 \end{pmatrix}$

7. $\mathbf{A} = \begin{pmatrix} y & 3 & 4 \\ 2 & 2 & 1 \end{pmatrix}$ $\mathbf{B} = \begin{pmatrix} 7 & 3 & 4 \\ x & x & 1 \end{pmatrix}$

8. $\mathbf{A} = \begin{pmatrix} -35 & -8 & -33 \\ 9 & 5 & 7 \end{pmatrix}$ $\mathbf{B} = \begin{pmatrix} xy & -8 & -33 \\ 9 & x & y \end{pmatrix}$

The matrices **A, B, C,** and **D** referred to in Exercises 9 to 16 are:

$$\mathbf{A} = \begin{pmatrix} 2 & 3 \\ 9 & 4 \end{pmatrix} \quad \mathbf{B} = \begin{pmatrix} -1 & -2 \\ -4 & -5 \end{pmatrix}$$

$$\mathbf{C} = \begin{pmatrix} 1 & 2 \\ 4 & 5 \end{pmatrix} \quad \mathbf{D} = \begin{pmatrix} 1 & 2 & 3 \\ 9 & 4 & 5 \end{pmatrix}$$

9. Calculate **A** + **B**.

10. Calculate **B** + **C** and **B** − **C**.

11. Calculate 3**A**.

12. Calculate −2**B**.

13. Calculate 3**C** − 4**B**.

14. Calculate 2**D** + **B** − 3**C**.

15. What matrix should be added to **B** to obtain **A**?

16. What matrix should be added to **A** to obtain **B**?

The matrices **P, Q, R,** and **S** referred to in the next 10 exercises are:

$$\mathbf{P} = \begin{pmatrix} 15 & -3 & 6 \\ 2 & 4 & 3 \end{pmatrix} \quad \mathbf{Q} = \begin{pmatrix} 4 & -2 \\ -3 & -1 \end{pmatrix}$$

$$\mathbf{R} = \begin{pmatrix} 45 & -9 \\ 6 & 12 \end{pmatrix} \quad \mathbf{S} = \begin{pmatrix} 1.5 & -.3 & .6 \\ .2 & .4 & .3 \end{pmatrix}$$

17. Calculate 0.7**P**.

18. Calculate 7**S**.

19. Calculate $\frac{1}{4}$**Q**.

20. Calculate $\frac{1}{3}$**R**.

21. Factor 10 out of the matrix **P**.

22. Factor 3 out of the matrix **R**.

23. If x is a number, can you solve the equation $x\mathbf{P} = \mathbf{S}$?

24. Can you solve $x\mathbf{S} = \mathbf{P}$?

25. Can you solve $x\mathbf{Q} = \mathbf{R}$?

26. Can you solve $x\mathbf{R} = \mathbf{P}$?

Over the years, Forest Industries has bought out a great many small companies. Along with the physical assets and experienced personnel of these smaller companies, Forest Industries has inherited certain business problems. For example, small loggers are often liberal in extending credit and lackadaisical in collecting overdue accounts. Table 1 shows the number of Forest Industries' overdue accounts in various categories in the year 1974. Table 2 gives the same data for the year 1975. The accounts are classified according to the dollar amount owed and the number of days overdue.

TABLE 1

Amount (Dollars)	30 Days	60 Days	90 Days
0 to 20,000	997	858	602
20,001 to 50,000	574	477	412
50,001 to 100,000	469	356	341

TABLE 2

Amount (Dollars)	30 Days	60 Days	90 Days
0 to 20,000	1144	417	323
20,001 to 50,000	658	360	332
50,001 to 100,000	614	436	138

27. Prepare a table showing the total number of overdue accounts in each of the 9 categories over the 24-month period 1974–1975.

28. Prepare a table showing the increase or decrease in the number of accounts in each category from 1974 to 1975.

29. Forest Industries management would like to see a 20% decrease in the number of overdue accounts in each of the nine categories from 1975 to 1976. Prepare a table showing management's goals for 1976.

30. One of Forest Industries' vice-presidents points out that 30-day accounts are not lethal. He suggests that the goal for 1976 should be to increase 30-day accounts by 20% and decrease the rest by 15%. Prepare a table showing his overdue accounts goals for 1976.

The next three exercises are based on data concerning the common stocks of six well-known companies. For each company Table 3 shows the October 1976 price of one share of its common stock; the annual earnings per share (that is, the total annual amount earned by the company divided by the total number of common stock shares outstanding); and the dividend paid on one share in one year. All amounts are in dollars.

TABLE 3

Company	Recent Price	Earnings per Share	Dividends per Year
E.I. duPont	118.75	9.99	4.99
Union Carbide	58.25	6.31	2.50
Eastman Kodak	85.5	4.00	2.05
Quaker Oats	21.25	2.31	0.91
J. C. Penney	48.25	3.58	1.30
Holiday Inns	10.75	1.27	0.40

31. Table 3 was compiled at a time when corporate earnings were said to be on an upswing. Suppose that the earnings per share of each of the six companies increase by exactly 20% in one year. Suppose also that the dividend payout and share price of each increases by exactly 20% in the same period. Write the 18-entry matrix containing the new data. Write a second matrix whose entries give the one-year gain in price, earnings, and dividends for each of the six common stocks.

32. Suppose that earnings per share for each of the six companies increase by exactly 20% in one year. Suppose that dividends do not increase in that period, but that each of the six stock prices increases by 20%. Write a matrix incorporating these facts. Write a second matrix showing the change in the price/earnings/dividends picture for the six stocks over the one-year period.

33. Let **A** be the 18-entry matrix with the same rows and columns as Table 3. Then calculate 1.2**A** and also 0.2**A**. Are these the matrices you obtained in Exercise 31? In Exercise 32? If the two matrices you obtained in Exercise 32 are **B** and **C**, calculate 1.2**A** − **B** and 0.2**A** − **C**.

Pet food sales have increased enormously since the mid-1960s. Four top-selling brands are the soybean-based TLC (for cats) and Call of the Wild (for dogs); and the all-meat Simba and White Fang. Table 4 gives the sales of the four brands in three cities on *one day* in 1975. The figures are in *tons*, the unit used by supermarket people to measure pet food sales.

TABLE 4

Pet Food	Boston	Indianapolis	Phoenix
TLC	42	24	25
Simba	45	33	31
Call of the Wild	29	49	30
White Fang	21	53	34

34. The average retail price of the pet food described in the table was 32¢ a pound. Assume that every pound described in the table sold for exactly 32¢. Then prepare a table giving the dollar volume of sales of each of the four pet foods in each of the three cities on November 18, 1975.

35. Pet food sales nationwide increased 14% from 1974 to 1975. Assume that the 14% figure held for each of the four foods and each of the three cities listed in Table 4. Then prepare a table giving the same information as the table, backdated to November 18, 1974.

36. Dwight David Hill, the advertising executive who named the four brands of pet food and planned the advertising campaigns that put them over, predicts that their sales will have increased 15% from November 18, 1975, to November 18, 1976. He predicts a further increase of 17% from November 18, 1976, to November 18, 1977. Assume that each of the four pet foods (in each of the three cities) is to show the same percentage increase in those two one-year periods. Then prepare a table showing Hill's projection of November 18, 1977, sales.

4.2 MULTIPLYING A MATRIX BY A MATRIX

A matrix with only one row is called a *row vector* and a matrix with only one column is called a *column vector*. The number of entries in a vector gives its *dimension*. As examples:

$$(1 \quad 7 \quad -8 \quad 5)$$

is a four-dimensional row vector, and

$$\begin{pmatrix} 6 \\ -3 \\ 19 \\ 12 \end{pmatrix}$$

is a four-dimensional column vector. For another kind of example, consider the matrix

$$\begin{pmatrix} 29 & 71 & -56 \\ 38 & -4 & 666 \end{pmatrix}$$

The row vector

$$\mathbf{R}_1 = (29 \quad 71 \quad -56)$$

is made up of the entries in the first row of the matrix, and the row vector

$$\mathbf{R}_2 = (38 \quad -4 \quad 666)$$

is made up of the entries in the second row of the matrix. Similarly, the three column vectors

$$\mathbf{C}_1 = \begin{pmatrix} 29 \\ 38 \end{pmatrix} \qquad \mathbf{C}_2 = \begin{pmatrix} 71 \\ -4 \end{pmatrix} \qquad \mathbf{C}_3 = \begin{pmatrix} -56 \\ 666 \end{pmatrix}$$

are made up of the entries in the first, second, and third columns of the matrix.

We will find it useful to define the product of a row vector and a column vector:

HOW TO MULTIPLY A ROW VECTOR BY A COLUMN VECTOR

If **A** is a row vector and **B** is a column vector of the same dimension, then the product **AB** is a *number* obtained by multiplying corresponding entries of **A** and **B** and then adding all these products.

A few examples will show how (and how not to) multiply row vectors by column vectors.

EXAMPLES: MULTIPLYING A ROW VECTOR BY A COLUMN VECTOR

1. If

$$\mathbf{A} = (1 \quad 2 \quad 3 \quad 4) \quad \text{and} \quad \mathbf{B} = \begin{pmatrix} 5 \\ 6 \\ 7 \\ 8 \end{pmatrix}$$

then

$$\mathbf{AB} = 1 \cdot 5 + 2 \cdot 6 + 3 \cdot 7 + 4 \cdot 8$$
$$= 70$$

2. If

$$\mathbf{A} = (-3 \quad \tfrac{7}{2} \quad 15 \quad -8) \quad \text{and} \quad \mathbf{B} = \begin{pmatrix} -12 \\ -24 \\ 13 \\ 0 \end{pmatrix}$$

then

$$\mathbf{AB} = (-3)(-12) + (\tfrac{7}{2})(-24) + (15)(13) + (-8)(0)$$
$$= 147$$

3. If

$$\mathbf{A} = (1 \quad 2 \quad 3 \quad 4) \quad \text{and} \quad \mathbf{B} = \begin{pmatrix} 5 \\ 6 \\ 7 \end{pmatrix}$$

then **AB** is not defined since the dimensions of the two vectors are different.

4. If

$$\mathbf{A} = (7 \quad 8 \quad 9) \quad \text{and} \quad \mathbf{B} = (3 \quad 4 \quad 6)$$

then the dimensions of **A** and **B** are the same, but the product **AB** is not defined since both vectors are row vectors. Similarly, if

$$C = \begin{pmatrix} 7 \\ 8 \\ 9 \end{pmatrix} \quad \text{and} \quad D = \begin{pmatrix} 3 \\ 4 \\ 6 \end{pmatrix}$$

then the product **CD** is not defined.

5. Consider the equation

$$\mathbf{AX} = b$$

where **A** is a *known* row vector, **X** is an *unknown* column vector of the same dimension, and b is a given number. Can we solve the equation? In general, we can solve it in infinitely many ways. For example, let

$$\mathbf{A} = (7 \quad -5 \quad 4), \quad \mathbf{X} = \begin{pmatrix} x_1 \\ x_2 \\ x_3 \end{pmatrix}, \quad \text{and} \quad b = 8.$$

Then **AX** $= b$ means:

$$7x_1 - 5x_2 + 4x_3 = 8$$

which is one equation in three variables. There are infinitely many solutions.

If you can multiply a row vector by a column vector, you can also multiply a matrix by a matrix. Before seeing how, we should emphasize that the product

row vector × column vector

is defined *only* for vectors of the same dimension. Similarly, the product

matrix × matrix

is defined *only* when the number of columns in the matrix on the left equals the number of rows in the matrix on the right. The multiplication rule for matrices shows why we need to make this restriction:

HOW TO MULTIPLY A MATRIX BY A MATRIX

The matrix product

$$\mathbf{MN} = \mathbf{P}$$

is defined if the row vectors $\mathbf{R}_1, \mathbf{R}_2, \ldots$ formed by the rows of **M** have the same dimension as the column vectors $\mathbf{C}_1, \mathbf{C}_2, \ldots$ formed by the columns of **N**. The (i, j) entry of **P** is the product $\mathbf{R}_i \mathbf{C}_j$.

In words: The entry in the *ith row* and *jth column* of **P** is the product of the *ith row vector* of **M** and the *jth column vector* of **N**.

EXAMPLES: MATRIX MULTIPLICATION

1. As an easy special case, let's first multiply a row vector by a matrix:

$$(1 \quad 2 \quad 3)\begin{pmatrix} 3 & 4 \\ 2 & 6 \\ 1 & -5 \end{pmatrix}$$

$$= (1 \cdot 3 + 2 \cdot 2 + 3 \cdot 1 \quad 1 \cdot 4 + 2 \cdot 6 + (3)(-5))$$
$$= (10 \quad 1)$$

The product is a 1×2 matrix. The way this comes about is shown in the *size equation:*

$$(1 \times 3) \cdot (3 \times 2) = (1 \times 2)$$

2. For another easy case, we multiply a matrix by a column vector:

$$\begin{pmatrix} 3 & 6 \\ 2 & 4 \\ 7 & -1 \end{pmatrix}\begin{pmatrix} 9 \\ -5 \end{pmatrix} = \begin{pmatrix} 3 \cdot 9 + 6(-5) \\ 2 \cdot 9 + 4(-5) \\ 7 \cdot 9 + (-1)(-5) \end{pmatrix} = \begin{pmatrix} -3 \\ -2 \\ 68 \end{pmatrix}$$

The size equation here is:

$$(3 \times 2) \cdot (2 \times 1) = (3 \times 1)$$

3. Next we multiply a matrix by a matrix:

$$\begin{pmatrix} 3 & 3 & 7 \\ 5 & 6 & 2 \end{pmatrix}\begin{pmatrix} 12 & 2 \\ 4 & 1 \\ -8 & 2 \end{pmatrix}$$

$$= \begin{pmatrix} 3 \cdot 12 + 3 \cdot 4 + 7(-8) & 3 \cdot 2 + 3 \cdot 1 + 7 \cdot 2 \\ 5 \cdot 12 + 6 \cdot 4 + 2(-8) & 5 \cdot 2 + 6 \cdot 1 + 2 \cdot 2 \end{pmatrix}$$

$$= \begin{pmatrix} -8 & 23 \\ 68 & 20 \end{pmatrix}$$

As a check on the size of the result, we note the size equation:

$$(2 \times 3) \cdot (3 \times 2) = (2 \times 2)$$

Note: In 1, 2, and 3 we have size equations of the form

$$(i \times j) \cdot (j \times k) = (i \times k)$$

In words: If an $(i \times j)$ matrix is multiplied on the right by a $(j \times k)$ matrix, the result is an $(i \times k)$ matrix.

4. If **M** is of size $(i \times j)$, **N** is of size $(h \times k)$, and $h \neq j$, then the matrix product **MN** is not defined. For example, the product

$$\begin{pmatrix} 1 & 2 & 3 \\ 4 & 5 & 6 \\ 7 & 8 & 9 \end{pmatrix} \begin{pmatrix} 10 & 11 & 12 \\ 13 & 14 & 15 \end{pmatrix}$$

is not defined, since the number of columns in the matrix on the left is not equal to the number of rows in the matrix on the right. Another way of saying this is: the rows of the left matrix form vectors of dimension 3, and the columns of the right matrix form vectors of dimension 2. Multiplication is impossible.

5. We can write systems of linear equations in a convenient matrix form. For example, the system

$$3x_1 - x_2 - 2x_3 = 7$$
$$4x_1 + 2x_2 - 3x_3 = 5$$
$$7x_1 - 5x_2 - 6x_3 = 13$$

can be written in the form

$$\mathbf{AX = B}$$

where

$$\mathbf{A} = \begin{pmatrix} 3 & -1 & -2 \\ 4 & 2 & -3 \\ 7 & -5 & -6 \end{pmatrix} \quad \mathbf{X} = \begin{pmatrix} x_1 \\ x_2 \\ x_3 \end{pmatrix} \quad \text{and} \quad \mathbf{B} = \begin{pmatrix} 7 \\ 5 \\ 13 \end{pmatrix}$$

The matrix **A** is called the *coefficient matrix* of the system. It lists the coefficients of x_1, x_2, and x_3 in the equations of the system.

This section closes with four problems. Problems 1 and 2 are further examples of matrix multiplication; Problem 3 applies matrix multiplication to a linear system; and Problem 4 is a real-world application.

PROBLEM 1   If

$$\mathbf{M} = \begin{pmatrix} 1 & 2 \\ 2 & -1 \end{pmatrix} \quad \text{and} \quad \mathbf{N} = \begin{pmatrix} 2 & 1 \\ 0 & 4 \end{pmatrix}$$

find **MN** *and* **NM** if possible.

SOLUTION   Since **M** is a 2 × 2 matrix and **N** is a 2 × 2 matrix, the products **MN** *and* **NM** are both defined and both will be 2 × 2 matrices. We have:

$$\mathbf{MN} = \begin{pmatrix} 1 & 2 \\ 2 & -1 \end{pmatrix}\begin{pmatrix} 2 & 1 \\ 0 & 4 \end{pmatrix} = \begin{pmatrix} 2 & 9 \\ 4 & -2 \end{pmatrix}$$

$$\mathbf{NM} = \begin{pmatrix} 2 & 1 \\ 0 & 4 \end{pmatrix}\begin{pmatrix} 1 & 2 \\ 2 & -1 \end{pmatrix} = \begin{pmatrix} 4 & 3 \\ 8 & -4 \end{pmatrix}$$

Notice that **MN** $\neq$ **NM**.

NOTE: If a matrix product **MN** is defined, it is not always possible to define the product **NM** because the sizes may be wrong. But if it *is* possible, we almost always find that **MN** $\neq$ **NM** as in Problem 1. For another such example, let **M** be any (3 × 4) matrix and let **N** be any (4 × 3) matrix. Then **MN** $\neq$ **NM** since the first product is (3 × 3) and the second product is (4 × 4).

PROBLEM 2   Can the matrices

$$\mathbf{A} = \begin{pmatrix} 8 & 4 & 2 & 2 & 6 \\ 6 & 3 & 3 & 6 & 2 \\ 0 & 3 & 8 & 4 & 1 \end{pmatrix} \quad \text{and} \quad \mathbf{B} = \begin{pmatrix} 3 & 8 & 7 & 3 \\ 2 & 5 & 9 & 6 \\ 6 & 6 & 5 & 4 \\ 2 & 2 & 1 & 3 \\ 4 & 2 & 6 & 1 \end{pmatrix}$$

be multiplied? If so: What is the size of **AB?** What is the (2, 3) entry?

SOLUTION The size equation for multiplying **A** by **B** is $(3 \times 5) \cdot (5 \times 4) = (3 \times 4)$. Therefore the product **AB** is defined, and its size is (3×4). The $(2, 3)$ entry of **AB** is the product of $\mathbf{R}_2$ (from **A**) by $\mathbf{C}_3$ (from **B**). We find that:

$$(6 \quad 3 \quad 3 \quad 6 \quad 2) \begin{pmatrix} 7 \\ 9 \\ 5 \\ 1 \\ 6 \end{pmatrix} = 42 + 27 + 15 + 6 + 12 = 102$$

NOTE: The product **BA** is not defined, since **B** has 4 columns and **A** has 3 rows.

PROBLEM 3 Write the linear system

$$2x_1 + 3x_2 = 5$$
$$-5x_1 - 2x_2 = 4$$

in matrix form. Then use matrix multiplication to find the result of changing the variables from x_1, x_2 to y_1, y_2 by means of:

$$x_1 = 3y_1 - 7y_2$$
$$x_2 = -9y_1 + 5y_2$$

SOLUTION The matrix form of the given system is

$$\mathbf{AX} = \mathbf{B}$$

where the coefficient matrix is

$$\mathbf{A} = \begin{pmatrix} 2 & 3 \\ -5 & -2 \end{pmatrix}$$

and

$$\mathbf{X} = \begin{pmatrix} x_1 \\ x_2 \end{pmatrix} \qquad \mathbf{B} = \begin{pmatrix} 5 \\ 4 \end{pmatrix}$$

The change from x_1, x_2 to y_1, y_2 has the matrix form

$$\mathbf{X} = \mathbf{CY}$$

where

$$\mathbf{C} = \begin{pmatrix} 3 & -7 \\ -9 & 5 \end{pmatrix}$$

and

$$X = \begin{pmatrix} x_1 \\ x_2 \end{pmatrix} \qquad Y = \begin{pmatrix} y_1 \\ y_2 \end{pmatrix}$$

If we substitute **CY** for **X** in **AX = B**, we have

$$\textbf{ACY} = \textbf{B}$$

Multiplication gives us:

$$\textbf{AC} = \begin{pmatrix} 2 & 3 \\ -5 & -2 \end{pmatrix}\begin{pmatrix} 3 & -7 \\ -9 & 5 \end{pmatrix}$$

$$= \begin{pmatrix} -21 & 1 \\ 3 & 25 \end{pmatrix}$$

Therefore the linear system in the variables y_1, y_2 is:

$$\begin{cases} -21y_1 + y_2 = 5 \\ 3y_1 + 25y_2 = 4 \end{cases}$$

Check: Substitute in the original system:

$$2x_1 + 3x_2 = 2(3y_1 - 7y_2)$$
$$+ 3(-9y_1 + 5y_2)$$
$$= -21y_1 + y_2$$

and so on.

PROBLEM 4   The numbers in Tables 4.1 and 4.2 (see Section 4.1, Problem 1) show that Aztec manufactures a great many cars at its factories in Baton Rouge, Kenosha, and San Diego. Aztec also sells a great many cars. Three of its leading dealers are in Denver, Wichita, and Lincoln. Table 4.3 shows the profit to the dealer on each of the five Aztec models. (Profit margins differ because of different costs of doing business in the three cities and different accounting methods at

TABLE 4.3   Profit To Dealer

Models →	Princess	Indio	Ramita	Lobo	Tigre
Denver	290	310	360	400	540
Wichita	280	300	370	390	550
Lincoln	270	260	350	410	560

Dealer ↓

the three dealerships. All figures are for the second year Aztec manu-factured cars in the U.S.)

Aztec sent each of the three dealers exactly the same number of cars during the model year. Table 4.4 shows the number shipped to each dealer from each factory.

TABLE 4.4

Factory	Baton Rouge	Kenosha	San Diego
Princess	1267	1261	1159
Indio	1036	575	944
Ramita	699	625	793
Lobo	485	375	341
Tigre	296	198	104

In a report it had to make to the Mexican government, Aztec was required to calculate the total profit earned by each of the three dealers on cars shipped to it from each of the three factories. (*NOTE:* All cars shipped to the dealers were sold.) How can this calculation be carried out, and what were the results?

SOLUTION   Table 4.3 leads to the 3 × 5 unit profit matrix

$$\mathbf{A} = \begin{pmatrix} 290 & 310 & 360 & 400 & 540 \\ 280 & 300 & 370 & 390 & 550 \\ 270 & 260 & 350 & 410 & 560 \end{pmatrix}$$

and Table 4.4 leads to the 5 × 3 shipping matrix

$$\mathbf{B} = \begin{pmatrix} 1267 & 1261 & 1159 \\ 1036 & 575 & 944 \\ 699 & 625 & 793 \\ 485 & 375 & 341 \\ 296 & 198 & 104 \end{pmatrix}$$

The product **AB** = **C** is a 3 × 3 total profit matrix:

$$\mathbf{C} = \begin{pmatrix} 1{,}298{,}264 & 1{,}029{,}616 & 1{,}111{,}548 \\ 1{,}276{,}140 & 1{,}011{,}980 & 1{,}091{,}320 \\ 1{,}220{,}710 & 973{,}350 & 1{,}033{,}970 \end{pmatrix}$$

If you want to check the arithmetic, a hand-held calculator is recommended.

The entries in **C**, as recorded in Table 4.5, give the total dollar profits earned by each of the three dealers on cars shipped from each of the three factories.

TABLE 4.5

	Baton Rouge	Kenosha	San Diego
Denver	$1,298,264	$1,029,616	$1,111,548
Wichita	$1,276,140	$1,011,980	$1,091,320
Lincoln	$1,220,710	$ 973,350	$1,033,970

for Section 4.2

1. Write the matrix whose rows are the row vectors
$$\mathbf{R}_1 = (2 \quad 6 \quad 6 \quad 7) \quad \text{and} \quad \mathbf{R}_2 = (1 \quad 0 \quad 7 \quad 1)$$

2. Write the matrix whose rows are the row vectors
$$\mathbf{R}_1 = (9 \quad 0 \quad 4 \quad 2) \quad \text{and} \quad \mathbf{R}_2 = (8 \quad 9 \quad 8 \quad 7)$$

3. Write the matrix whose columns are the column vectors
$$\mathbf{C}_1 = \begin{pmatrix} 7 \\ 4 \\ 2 \end{pmatrix} \quad \mathbf{C}_2 = \begin{pmatrix} 8 \\ 1 \\ 2 \end{pmatrix} \quad \mathbf{C}_3 = \begin{pmatrix} 8 \\ 7 \\ 6 \end{pmatrix}$$

4. Write the matrix whose columns are the column vectors
$$\mathbf{C}_1 = \begin{pmatrix} 0 \\ 8 \end{pmatrix} \quad \mathbf{C}_2 = \begin{pmatrix} 6 \\ 2 \end{pmatrix} \quad \mathbf{C}_3 = \begin{pmatrix} 5 \\ 9 \end{pmatrix} \quad \mathbf{C}_4 = \begin{pmatrix} 4 \\ 4 \end{pmatrix}$$

If
$$\mathbf{A} = (2 \quad 1 \quad 7 \quad 3), \qquad \mathbf{B} = (9 \quad 4 \quad 2 \quad 2)$$

$$\mathbf{C} = \begin{pmatrix} 8 \\ 9 \\ -5 \\ 4 \end{pmatrix} \quad \text{and} \quad \mathbf{D} = \begin{pmatrix} 2 \\ -7 \\ -5 \\ 3 \end{pmatrix}$$

what are the following products?

5. AC   **6. AD**   **7. DA** $= \begin{pmatrix} 4, & 4 \end{pmatrix}$

8. BC   **9. BD**   **10. AB**

Wrong Answer in Back of Book

If

$$\mathbf{M} = (2 \quad 8 \quad 6 \quad 8) \qquad \mathbf{N} = (4 \quad 3 \quad 7)$$

$$\mathbf{P} = \begin{pmatrix} 4 \\ 6 \\ 6 \\ 8 \end{pmatrix} \qquad \mathbf{Q} = \begin{pmatrix} 1 \\ 2 \\ 5 \\ 0 \end{pmatrix} \qquad \mathbf{R} = \begin{pmatrix} 9 \\ 6 \\ 5 \end{pmatrix}$$

then what are the following products?

11. MP   **12. MQ**   **13. MR**

14. MN   **15. NP**   **16. NQ**

17. NR

Each of the following linear equations can be written in the form $\mathbf{AX} = b$, where $\mathbf{A}$ is a row vector, $\mathbf{X}$ is a column vector, and b is a number. Find $\mathbf{A}$, $\mathbf{X}$, and b if:

18. $19x_1 + 20x_2 = 21$

19. $4x_1 + 5x_2 + 7x_3 = 7$

20. $3x_2 + 4x_3 = 5$

21. $4x_1 + 5x_2 + 8x_3 = 0$

22. $x_1 + x_3 + 2x_5 + 3x_7 = 6$

23. $2x_1 + 3x_2 + 6x_3 + 9 = 5x_1 + 4x_2 + 4x_3 + 1$ *EASY*

24. $x_5 + 5 = 7x_1 + 5x_2 + x_4 + 2$

If

$$\mathbf{E} = (1 \quad -1), \qquad \mathbf{F} = (2 \quad 3), \qquad \mathbf{G} = \begin{pmatrix} 2 \\ -6 \end{pmatrix} \qquad \mathbf{H} = \begin{pmatrix} 4 & -7 \\ 0 & 5 \end{pmatrix}$$

then what are the following products?

25. EH   **26. FH**   **27. HG**

28. GH   **29. GF**   **30. GE**

If

$$\mathbf{J} = (8 \quad 2 \quad 0) \qquad \mathbf{K} = (7 \quad 6 \quad -7)$$

$$\mathbf{R} = \begin{pmatrix} 0 \\ -6 \\ 3 \end{pmatrix} \quad \mathbf{S} = \begin{pmatrix} -8 & 0 \\ 4 & 2 \\ 3 & 6 \end{pmatrix} \quad \mathbf{T} = \begin{pmatrix} -9 & 4 & 0 \\ 6 & 1 & -8 \\ 3 & 2 & 0 \end{pmatrix}$$

then what are the following products?

31. JS **32. JT** **33. KS**

34. KT **35. KR** **36. RK**

37. SR **38. TR**

In each of the following cases: Is the product **AB** defined? Is the product **BA** defined?

39. **A** is a 7 × 3 matrix, **B** is a 3 × 7 matrix

40. **A** is a 7 × 3 matrix, **B** is a 3 × 6 matrix

41. **A** is a 7 × 3 matrix, **B** is a 6 × 7 matrix

42. **A** is a 9 × 5 matrix, **B** is a 5 × 7 matrix

43. **A** is a 6 × 4 matrix, **B** is a 6 × 5 matrix

44. **A** is a 4 × 3 matrix, **B** is a 4 × 4 matrix

What can you say about the sizes of the matrices **C** and **D** if:

45. **CD** is a 3 × 3 matrix and **DC** is a 4 × 4 matrix? 3×4 $D = 4 \times 3$

46. **CD** and **DC** are both 3 × 3 matrices?

47. **CD** is a 4 × 4 matrix and **DC** is a number?

48. **CD** is a 3 × 5 matrix?

49. **CD** is a 3 × 5 matrix and **DC** is not defined?

50. **(CD) C** is a 3 × 5 matrix? $C = 3 \times 5$
$D = 5 \times 3$

Any linear system can be written in the form **AX** = **B,** where **A** is the coefficient matrix of the system and **X** and **B** are column vectors. For each of the following systems, write **A, X,** and **B:**

51. $x + y = 4$

  $4x + 3y = 5$

52.
$$y = 8$$
$$3x + 2y = 6$$

53.
$$8x_2 + 8x_3 + 6x_4 = 2$$
$$2x_1 + x_2 + 9x_3 + 9x_4 = 8$$
$$x_1 \qquad\qquad + 7x_4 = 3$$
$$3x_1 + 4x_2 + 8x_3 - 8x_4 = 0$$

54.
$$2.7x_1 + 6.2x_2 = 3$$
$$6.8x_2 + 8.6x_3 = 1$$
$$9.2x_3 + 4.7x_4 = 9$$
$$5.3x_1 + 3x_4 = 7$$

If

$$\mathbf{A} = \begin{pmatrix} 3 & 0 \\ 1 & 5 \end{pmatrix} \qquad \mathbf{B} = \begin{pmatrix} 1 & 2 \\ 2 & -6 \end{pmatrix} \qquad \mathbf{C} = \begin{pmatrix} 4 & 9 \\ 9 & 4 \end{pmatrix}$$

what are the following products?

55. AB **56. BA** **57. AC**

58. CA **59. BC** **60. CB**

If

$$\mathbf{D} = \begin{pmatrix} 2 & 6 \\ -7 & 8 \end{pmatrix} \qquad \mathbf{E} = \begin{pmatrix} 1 & 4 \\ 4 & 1 \end{pmatrix} \qquad \mathbf{F} = \begin{pmatrix} -9 & -3 \\ -3 & -9 \end{pmatrix}$$

what are the following products?

61. DE **62. ED** **63. DF**

64. FD **65. EF** **66. FE**

If

$$\mathbf{G} = \begin{pmatrix} 2 & 2 \\ 8 & -6 \end{pmatrix} \qquad \mathbf{H} = \begin{pmatrix} 2 & -4 & 4 \\ -9 & 7 & 9 \end{pmatrix}$$

$$\mathbf{J} = \begin{pmatrix} 7 & 0 & 0 \\ 1 & -1 & 0 \\ 2 & 3 & 3 \end{pmatrix} \qquad \mathbf{K} = \begin{pmatrix} 5 & 0 & 1 \\ 4 & 0 & 1 \\ 2 & -8 & 2 \end{pmatrix}$$

what are the following products?

67. GH   **68. HJ**   **69. HK**

70. JH   **71. JK**   **72. KJ**

Some of the exercises for Section 4.1 were concerned with Forest Industries. Those exercises (numbers 27–31) referred to overdue accounts on Forest Industries' books in 1974 and 1975. The facts were summarized in Tables 1 and 2. Some of these overdue accounts would eventually be paid and some would not. Forest Industries had three methods of collecting the money: *waiting* (and trusting); *refusing* to extend further credit until an outstanding account is paid; and *discipline* (a long-range attack on the problem: a manager who extends credit unwisely, loses his or her job). Success ratios for the three methods are shown in Table 5 (based on results up to 1974) and Table 6 (based on results up to 1975). Notice that the success ratios depend on both the method used and the amount overdue.

TABLE 5

	Dollar Amount Owed		
Method	0 to 20,000	20,001 to 50,000	50,001 to 100,000
Waiting	0.7	0.6	0.5
Refusing	0.8	0.7	0.6
Discipline	0.6	0.7	0.8

TABLE 6

	Dollar Amount Owed		
Method	0 to 20,000	20,001 to 50,000	50,001 to 100,000
Waiting	0.7	0.65	0.45
Refusing	0.83	0.74	0.62
Discipline	0.66	0.78	0.9

73. Make use of Table 1, Table 5, and matrix multiplication to prepare a table showing the number of 30-, 60-, and 90-day overdue accounts Forest Industries might have collected in 1974 by following each of the three collection methods.

74. Make use of Table 2, Table 6, and matrix multiplication to prepare a table showing the number of 30-, 60-, and 90-day overdue accounts Forest Industries might have succeeded with in 1975 by following each of the three collection methods.

Three of the exercises for Section 4.1 (numbers 31, 32, and 33) were based on Table 3, which gave the October 1976 prices, earnings, and dividends for six common stocks. Dr. Miles Malone bought 100 shares of each of these common stocks and paid the prices shown in Table 3. (To keep things simple, we will ignore commissions and other minor expenses.) By adding the six prices in column 1 of Table 3 and multiplying by 100, we see that Malone invested $34,275. From column 2 of Table 3, we see that the earnings of Malone's six stocks totaled $2746. Finally, column 3 of Table 3 shows that Malone's annual dividend income from the 600 shares was $1215. Since $1215 \div 34,275 = 0.035$, we see that Malone's return on his investment was a mere 3.5%. This return is not very worthwhile, but Malone's broker had told him that dividends would be up 20% in a year. This increase would give a rate of return of 4.2%, which is still not exciting. Malone's broker had also told him that stock prices would be up 20% in a year. If this happens, his $34,275 investment will be worth $41,130. This sounds good—if it happens. Malone wanted some other opinions. Four optimistic (or "bullish") investment advisers gave him estimates of one-year price, earnings, and dividend increases for his six stocks (Table 7). Malone also consulted four pessimistic (or "bearish") investment advisers. Their estimates of price, earnings, and dividend increases (or decreases) for his six stocks are shown in Table 8.

TABLE 7

Adviser			Stock			
	duPont	Carbide	Kodak	Quaker	Penney	Holiday
I	0.18	0.19	0.16	0.26	0.27	0.16
II	0.35	0.34	0.15	0.19	0.18	0.41
III	0.29	0.28	0.14	0.21	0.22	0.19
IV	0.33	0.34	0.12	0.17	0.18	0.42

TABLE 8

Adviser			Stock			
	duPont	Carbide	Kodak	Quaker	Penney	Holiday
A	0.01	0.02	0.05	0.14	0.15	−0.06
B	0.04	0.03	0.11	0.07	0.13	−0.05
C	−0.02	−0.01	−0.12	0.06	0.08	−0.13
D	−0.12	−0.13	−0.23	0.04	0.05	−0.17

75. Prepare a table showing the October 1977 total price, total earnings, and total annual dividends of Malone's 600 shares of stock if bullish advisers I, II, III, or IV are correct in their optimistic predictions.

76. Prepare a table showing the October 1977 total price, total earnings, and total annual dividends of Malone's 600 shares of stock if bearish advisers A, B, C, or D are correct in their pessimistic predictions.

4.3

THE INVERSE OF A MATRIX

A matrix with the same number of rows and columns is called a *square matrix*. The number of rows (and columns) is called the *order* of the square matrix. For example,

$$\begin{pmatrix} 9 & 5 & 1 & 7 \\ 1 & 4 & 2 & 6 \\ 1 & 6 & 0 & 1 \\ 6 & 7 & 0 & 3 \end{pmatrix}$$

is a square matrix of order 4.

If **A** and **B** are square matrices of the same order, then the matrix products **AB** and **BA** are both defined. Usually **AB** $\neq$ **BA**. (For an example, see Problem 1 of Section 4.2). But notice the case

$$\begin{pmatrix} 1 & 2 \\ 3 & 4 \end{pmatrix} \begin{pmatrix} 1 & 0 \\ 0 & 1 \end{pmatrix} = \begin{pmatrix} 1 & 0 \\ 0 & 1 \end{pmatrix} \begin{pmatrix} 1 & 2 \\ 3 & 4 \end{pmatrix} = \begin{pmatrix} 1 & 2 \\ 3 & 4 \end{pmatrix}$$

The square matrix

$$\mathbf{I} = \begin{pmatrix} 1 & 0 \\ 0 & 1 \end{pmatrix}$$

is called the *identity matrix* of order 2. It has the property

$$\mathbf{AI} = \mathbf{IA} = \mathbf{A}$$

for any square matrix **A** of order 2. There are also identity matrices of order

3, order 4, order 5, and so on. Every identity matrix is a square matrix with 1's along its main diagonal [entries (1, 1), (2, 2), and so on] and 0's everywhere else. And every such matrix has the identity property $\mathbf{AI} = \mathbf{IA} = \mathbf{A}$, if $\mathbf{A}$ is a square matrix of the same order as $\mathbf{I}$. As another example (which you should check), we have:

$$\begin{pmatrix} 7 & 6 & -1 \\ -5 & 4 & 7 \\ 9 & -2 & 3 \end{pmatrix} \begin{pmatrix} 1 & 0 & 0 \\ 0 & 1 & 0 \\ 0 & 0 & 1 \end{pmatrix} = \begin{pmatrix} 1 & 0 & 0 \\ 0 & 1 & 0 \\ 0 & 0 & 1 \end{pmatrix} \begin{pmatrix} 7 & 6 & -1 \\ -5 & 4 & 7 \\ 9 & -2 & 3 \end{pmatrix} = \begin{pmatrix} 7 & 6 & -1 \\ -5 & 4 & 7 \\ 9 & -2 & 3 \end{pmatrix}$$

Sometimes the product of two square matrices is an identity matrix. As an example: If

$$\mathbf{A} = \begin{pmatrix} 1 & 2 \\ 3 & 5 \end{pmatrix} \quad \text{and} \quad \mathbf{B} = \begin{pmatrix} -5 & 2 \\ 3 & -1 \end{pmatrix}$$

then

$$\mathbf{AB} = \begin{pmatrix} 1 & 0 \\ 0 & 1 \end{pmatrix} \quad \text{and} \quad \mathbf{BA} = \begin{pmatrix} 1 & 0 \\ 0 & 1 \end{pmatrix}$$

or

$$\mathbf{AB} = \mathbf{BA} = \mathbf{I}$$

In such a case we say that $\mathbf{B}$ is the *inverse* of $\mathbf{A}$, and we write

$$\mathbf{B} = \mathbf{A}^{-1}$$

NOTE: We can also say that $\mathbf{A}$ is the inverse of $\mathbf{B}$. In fact, if $\mathbf{B} = \mathbf{A}^{-1}$, then $\mathbf{A} = \mathbf{B}^{-1}$. Both equations mean the same thing: $\mathbf{AB} = \mathbf{BA} = \mathbf{I}$.

What are inverses good for? One application is to linear systems. Suppose that

$$\mathbf{AX} = \mathbf{K}$$

is a linear system with a square coefficient matrix $\mathbf{A}$. (This way of writing a linear system was explained on p. 167–168.) If $\mathbf{A}$ has an inverse $\mathbf{A}^{-1}$, we will now see that

$$\mathbf{X} = \mathbf{A}^{-1}\mathbf{K}$$

EXAMPLE 1: USING A⁻¹ TO SOLVE AX = K

First we need to know that an identity matrix is an identity for anything it can multiply. For example,

$$\begin{pmatrix} 1 & 0 & 0 \\ 0 & 1 & 0 \\ 0 & 0 & 1 \end{pmatrix} \begin{pmatrix} x_1 \\ x_2 \\ x_3 \end{pmatrix} = \begin{pmatrix} x_1 \\ x_2 \\ x_3 \end{pmatrix}$$

Now for the solution of $\mathbf{AX} = \mathbf{K}$: We multiply both sides of $\mathbf{AX} = \mathbf{K}$ by $\mathbf{A}^{-1}$:

$$\mathbf{A}^{-1}\mathbf{AX} = \mathbf{A}^{-1}\mathbf{K}$$

Since $\mathbf{A}^{-1}\mathbf{A} = \mathbf{I}$ and $\mathbf{IX} = \mathbf{X}$, we have

$$\mathbf{X} = \mathbf{A}^{-1}\mathbf{K}$$

For an illustration, write

$$x_1 + 2x_2 = 8$$
$$3x_1 + 5x_2 = 9$$

in the form $\mathbf{AX} = \mathbf{K}$. In other words, write

$$\mathbf{A} = \begin{pmatrix} 1 & 2 \\ 3 & 5 \end{pmatrix} \qquad \mathbf{X} = \begin{pmatrix} x_1 \\ x_2 \end{pmatrix} \qquad \mathbf{K} = \begin{pmatrix} 8 \\ 9 \end{pmatrix}$$

We have just seen that

$$\mathbf{A}^{-1} = \begin{pmatrix} -5 & 2 \\ 3 & -1 \end{pmatrix}$$

Therefore

$$\mathbf{X} = \mathbf{A}^{-1}\mathbf{K} = \begin{pmatrix} -22 \\ 15 \end{pmatrix}$$

or: $\qquad\qquad\qquad x_1 = -22, \qquad x_2 = 15$

Check: $\qquad\qquad\qquad (-22) + 2(15) = 8$

$$3(-22) + 5(15) = 9$$

There is one difficulty in using an inverse matrix to solve a linear system. We have to calculate the inverse. And what is the best way to calculate an inverse? You guessed it: by solving a linear system.

CAUTION: Do not assume the worst. Inverse matrices can be worthwhile for solving linear systems. A real-world application at the end of this section will prove it. Inverses also have other practical uses, some of which will be explained in Section 4.4.

EXAMPLE 2: CALCULATING THE INVERSE OF A MATRIX

Suppose that the matrix

$$\mathbf{A} = \begin{pmatrix} 2 & 3 \\ 1 & 2 \end{pmatrix}$$

has an inverse **B**. We write

$$\mathbf{B} = \begin{pmatrix} x_1 & y_1 \\ x_2 & y_2 \end{pmatrix}$$

and attempt to determine x_1, x_2, y_1, and y_2 from the equation $\mathbf{AB} = \mathbf{I}$, or

$$\begin{pmatrix} 2 & 3 \\ 1 & 2 \end{pmatrix} \begin{pmatrix} x_1 & y_1 \\ x_2 & y_2 \end{pmatrix} = \begin{pmatrix} 1 & 0 \\ 0 & 1 \end{pmatrix}$$

Test Question

Matrix multiplication gives us the two linear systems

$$\begin{cases} 2x_1 + 3x_2 = 1 \\ x_1 + 2x_2 = 0 \end{cases} \qquad \begin{cases} 2y_1 + 3y_2 = 0 \\ y_1 + 2y_2 = 1 \end{cases}$$

The two systems have the same coefficient matrix and different augmented matrices. We solve both systems at once by using the echelon method. That is, we write the *doubly* augmented matrix

$$\mathbf{D} = \left(\begin{array}{cc|cc} 2 & 3 & 1 & 0 \\ 1 & 2 & 0 & 1 \end{array} \right)$$

with a vertical line separating the shared coefficient matrix from the separate columns of constants. Then we apply legal row operations to **D:**

$$\left(\begin{array}{cc|cc} 2 & 3 & 1 & 0 \\ 1 & 2 & 0 & 1 \end{array} \right) \quad \boxed{R_1 - 2R_2}$$

$$\left(\begin{array}{cc|cc} 0 & -1 & 1 & -2 \\ 1 & 2 & 0 & 1 \end{array} \right) \quad \boxed{\begin{array}{c} -R_1 \\ R_2 + 2R_1 \end{array}}$$

$$\begin{pmatrix} 0 & 1 & | & -1 & 2 \\ 1 & 0 & | & 2 & -3 \end{pmatrix} \times \begin{pmatrix} 1 & 0 & | & 2 & -3 \\ 0 & 1 & | & -1 & 2 \end{pmatrix}$$

We conclude that:

$$x_1 = 2 \qquad x_2 = -1$$
$$y_1 = -3 \qquad y_2 = 2$$

$\mathbf{B} = \mathbf{A}^{-1}$ is therefore determined:

$$\mathbf{A}^{-1} = \begin{pmatrix} 2 & -3 \\ -1 & 2 \end{pmatrix}$$

To check, we multiply:

$$\begin{pmatrix} 2 & 3 \\ 1 & 2 \end{pmatrix} \begin{pmatrix} 2 & -3 \\ -1 & 2 \end{pmatrix} = \begin{pmatrix} 1 & 0 \\ 0 & 1 \end{pmatrix}$$

Let's summarize the work in Example 2. We started with a 2×2 matrix $\mathbf{A}$. Then we augmented $\mathbf{A}$ with a 2×2 identity matrix $\mathbf{I}$. The result was a 2×4 matrix $\mathbf{D}$. For convenience we will call $\mathbf{D}$ an *identity-augmented matrix*, and we will write $\mathbf{D} = (\mathbf{A}|\mathbf{I})$. The vertical line separates $\mathbf{A}$ from $\mathbf{I}$. By using legal row operations we transformed the identity-augmented matrix $\mathbf{D}$ to reduced echelon form. In the process, $\mathbf{A}$ was transformed into $\mathbf{I}$, and $\mathbf{I}$ was transformed into $\mathbf{A}^{-1}$.

In symbols: Legal row operations reduced $(\mathbf{A}|\mathbf{I})$ to $(\mathbf{I}|\mathbf{A}^{-1})$.

The same method can be applied to any 2×2 matrix. Here is an example:

PROBLEM 1   Calculate the inverse of

$$\begin{pmatrix} 3 & -4 \\ -5 & 7 \end{pmatrix}$$

SOLUTION   Augment the given matrix with the 2×2 identity matrix and apply legal row operations to the identity-augmented matrix:

$$\begin{pmatrix} 3 & -4 & | & 1 & 0 \\ -5 & 7 & | & 0 & 1 \end{pmatrix} \begin{array}{c} 5R_1 \\ 3R_2 \end{array} \Longrightarrow \begin{pmatrix} 15 & -20 & | & 5 & 0 \\ -15 & 21 & | & 0 & 3 \end{pmatrix} \begin{array}{c} \\ R_2 + R_1 \end{array} \Longrightarrow$$

$$\begin{pmatrix} 15 & -20 & | & 5 & 0 \\ 0 & 1 & | & 5 & 3 \end{pmatrix} \quad \boxed{R_1 + 20R_2} \quad \begin{pmatrix} 15 & 0 & | & 105 & 60 \\ 0 & 1 & | & 5 & 3 \end{pmatrix}$$

$$\boxed{\tfrac{1}{15}R_1} \quad \begin{pmatrix} 1 & 0 & | & 7 & 4 \\ 0 & 1 & | & 5 & 3 \end{pmatrix}$$

The required inverse is

$$\begin{pmatrix} 7 & 4 \\ 5 & 3 \end{pmatrix}$$

Check:

$$\begin{pmatrix} 7 & 4 \\ 5 & 3 \end{pmatrix}\begin{pmatrix} 3 & -4 \\ -5 & 7 \end{pmatrix} = \begin{pmatrix} 1 & 0 \\ 0 & 1 \end{pmatrix}$$

Does every 2×2 matrix have an inverse? Suppose that

$$\begin{pmatrix} 1 & -3 \\ 2 & -6 \end{pmatrix}$$

has an inverse

$$\begin{pmatrix} x_1 & y_1 \\ x_2 & y_2 \end{pmatrix}$$

Then

$$\begin{pmatrix} 1 & -3 \\ 2 & -6 \end{pmatrix}\begin{pmatrix} x_1 & y_1 \\ x_2 & y_2 \end{pmatrix} = \begin{pmatrix} 1 & 0 \\ 0 & 1 \end{pmatrix}$$

But if we multiply the matrices on the left, we have

$$\begin{pmatrix} x_1 & -3x_2 & y_1 & -3y_2 \\ 2x_1 & -6x_2 & 2y_1 & -6y_2 \end{pmatrix} = \begin{pmatrix} 1 & 0 \\ 0 & 1 \end{pmatrix}$$

or

$$\begin{cases} x_1 - 3x_2 = 1 \\ 2x_1 - 6x_2 = 0 \end{cases} \qquad \begin{cases} y_1 - 3y_2 = 0 \\ 2y_1 - 6y_2 = 1 \end{cases}$$

We have, in fact, two inconsistent systems. Since inconsistent linear systems have no solution, the given matrix has no inverse. Would we have discovered this by applying the method of Problem 1? Let's try it and see.

PROBLEM 2   Calculate, if possible, the inverse of

$$\begin{pmatrix} 1 & -3 \\ 2 & -6 \end{pmatrix}$$

SOLUTION   We form the identity-augmented matrix consisting of the given matrix and (to its right) the 2 × 2 identity matrix. Then we reduce the identity-augmented matrix:

$$\left(\begin{array}{cc|cc} 1 & -3 & 1 & 0 \\ 2 & -6 & 0 & 1 \end{array}\right) \quad \boxed{R_2 - 2R_1} \quad \left(\begin{array}{cc|cc} 1 & -3 & 1 & 0 \\ 0 & 0 & -2 & 1 \end{array}\right)$$

We cannot continue. The given matrix cannot be transformed into **I**. Its inverse does not exist.

Conclusion: If our matrix-inverting method fails to work, then the given matrix has no inverse.

We do not have to confine matrix-inverting to 2 × 2 matrices. Our method can be applied to a square matrix of any order. If it works, it produces the inverse. If it fails to work, then there is no inverse. To make sure you have it straight, study the flow chart in Figure 4.1.

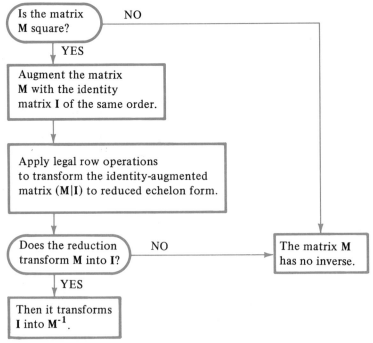

FIGURE 4.1   Flow Chart: How to Invert a Matrix **M**

PROBLEM 3   Calculate, if possible, the inverse of

$$\mathbf{M} = \begin{pmatrix} 4 & 0 & 5 \\ 0 & 1 & -6 \\ 3 & 0 & 4 \end{pmatrix}$$

SOLUTION   **M** is square. We apply legal row operations to put the identity-augmented matrix **(M|I)** into reduced echelon form:

$$\left(\begin{array}{ccc|ccc} 4 & 0 & 5 & 1 & 0 & 0 \\ 0 & 1 & -6 & 0 & 1 & 0 \\ 3 & 0 & 4 & 0 & 0 & 1 \end{array}\right) \quad \boxed{R_1 - R_3} \quad \left(\begin{array}{ccc|ccc} 1 & 0 & 1 & 1 & 0 & -1 \\ 0 & 1 & -6 & 0 & 1 & 0 \\ 3 & 0 & 4 & 0 & 0 & 1 \end{array}\right)$$

$$\boxed{R_3 - 3R_1} \quad \left(\begin{array}{ccc|ccc} 1 & 0 & 1 & 1 & 0 & -1 \\ 0 & 1 & -6 & 0 & 1 & 0 \\ 0 & 0 & 1 & -3 & 0 & 4 \end{array}\right) \quad \boxed{\begin{array}{c} R_1 - R_2 \\ R_2 + 6R_3 \end{array}} \quad \left(\begin{array}{ccc|ccc} 1 & 0 & 0 & 4 & 0 & -5 \\ 0 & 1 & 0 & -18 & 1 & 24 \\ 0 & 0 & 1 & -3 & 0 & 4 \end{array}\right)$$

The reduction has transformed **M** into **I** and **I** into **M^{-1}**:

$$\mathbf{M}^{-1} = \begin{pmatrix} 4 & 0 & -5 \\ -18 & 1 & 24 \\ -3 & 0 & 4 \end{pmatrix}$$

PROBLEM 4   Calculate, if possible, the inverse of

$$\mathbf{N} = \begin{pmatrix} 4 & 5 & 6 \\ 1 & 2 & 3 \\ 7 & 8 & 9 \end{pmatrix}$$

SOLUTION   **N** is square. We apply legal row operations to the identity-augmented matrix **(N|I)**:

$$\left(\begin{array}{ccc|ccc} 4 & 5 & 6 & 1 & 0 & 0 \\ 1 & 2 & 3 & 0 & 1 & 0 \\ 7 & 8 & 9 & 0 & 0 & 1 \end{array}\right) \quad \boxed{\begin{array}{c} R_1 - 4R_2 \\ \\ R_3 - 7R_2 \end{array}} \quad \left(\begin{array}{ccc|ccc} 0 & -3 & -6 & 1 & -4 & 0 \\ 1 & 2 & 3 & 0 & 1 & 0 \\ 0 & -6 & -12 & 0 & -7 & 0 \end{array}\right) \quad \boxed{R_3 - 2R_1}$$

$$\left(\begin{array}{ccc|ccc} 0 & -3 & -6 & 1 & -4 & 0 \\ 1 & 2 & 3 & 0 & 1 & 0 \\ 0 & 0 & 0 & -2 & 1 & 0 \end{array}\right)$$

The row of zeros shows that **N** cannot be transformed into **I**. Therefore the matrix **N** has no inverse.

Finally, let's discuss the application of inverses in solving linear systems. It does not seem to make much sense to solve a linear system by calculating the inverse of the coefficient matrix. After all, we have to use the echelon method to find the inverse, and we might just as well apply the method directly to the linear system.

But some problems lead to a number of linear systems, all of which have the same coefficient matrix but different columns of constants. For example, we might have three systems:

$$\mathbf{AX} = \mathbf{K}_1 \qquad \mathbf{AX} = \mathbf{K}_2 \qquad \mathbf{AX} = \mathbf{K}_3$$

If we can calculate $\mathbf{A}^{-1}$, we have the three solutions:

$$\mathbf{X} = \mathbf{A}^{-1}\mathbf{K}_1 \qquad \mathbf{X} = \mathbf{A}^{-1}\mathbf{K}_2 \qquad \mathbf{X} = \mathbf{A}^{-1}\mathbf{K}_3$$

It is the efficient way. Here is a practical example:

PROBLEM 5   In Section 3.3 we saw that the market equilibrium problem for the H-2000 and the H-3000 could be reduced to the solution of the linear system

(4.1)
$$\begin{cases} 4x_1 + 9x_2 = 330 \\ 3x_1 + 7x_2 = 254 \end{cases}$$

The number 330 came from the supply and demand equations for the H-2000, and the number 254 came from the supply and demand equations for the H-3000.

As competition between the two computer companies continued, there were changes in the supply–demand picture and in the corresponding equations. There was a new market equilibrium, which could be described by the linear system

(4.2)
$$\begin{cases} 4x_1 + 9x_2 = 341 \\ 3x_1 + 7x_2 = 262 \end{cases}$$

The trend expressed by the change from (4.1) to (4.2) accelerated. The next time there was a market equilibrium, its description led to the linear system

(4.3)
$$\begin{cases} 4x_1 + 9x_2 = 423 \\ 3x_1 + 7x_2 = 325 \end{cases}$$

What can be said about the prices x_1 (for H-2000) and x_2 (for H-3000) over the period covered by the three systems of equilibrium equations?

SOLUTION Write the three systems in matrix form. We have:

4.1 $$\mathbf{AX} = \mathbf{K}_1$$

4.2 $$\mathbf{AX} = \mathbf{K}_2$$

4.3 $$\mathbf{AX} = \mathbf{K}_3$$

where

$$\mathbf{A} = \begin{pmatrix} 4 & 9 \\ 3 & 7 \end{pmatrix} \qquad \mathbf{X} = \begin{pmatrix} x_1 \\ x_2 \end{pmatrix}$$

and

$$\mathbf{K}_1 = \begin{pmatrix} 330 \\ 254 \end{pmatrix} \qquad \mathbf{K}_2 = \begin{pmatrix} 341 \\ 262 \end{pmatrix} \qquad \mathbf{K}_3 = \begin{pmatrix} 423 \\ 325 \end{pmatrix}$$

To find the inverse of **A**, we apply legal row operations to the identity-augmented matrix **(A|I)**:

$$\left(\begin{array}{cc|cc} 4 & 9 & 1 & 0 \\ 3 & 7 & 0 & 1 \end{array}\right) \xrightarrow{\ R_1 - R_2\ } \left(\begin{array}{cc|cc} 1 & 2 & 1 & -1 \\ 3 & 7 & 0 & 1 \end{array}\right)$$

$$\xrightarrow{\ R_2 - 3R_1\ } \left(\begin{array}{cc|cc} 1 & 2 & 1 & -1 \\ 0 & 1 & -3 & 4 \end{array}\right) \xrightarrow{\ R_1 - 2R_2\ } \left(\begin{array}{cc|cc} 1 & 0 & 7 & -9 \\ 0 & 1 & -3 & 4 \end{array}\right)$$

We see that:

$$\mathbf{A}^{-1} = \begin{pmatrix} 7 & -9 \\ -3 & 4 \end{pmatrix}$$

The solution of system (4.1) is:

$$\mathbf{X} = \mathbf{A}^{-1}\mathbf{K}_1 = \begin{pmatrix} 7 & -9 \\ -3 & 4 \end{pmatrix}\begin{pmatrix} 330 \\ 254 \end{pmatrix} = \begin{pmatrix} 24 \\ 26 \end{pmatrix}$$

or $x_1 = 24$, $x_2 = 26$. This checks with the result found in Chapter 3. System (4.2) has the solution

$$\mathbf{X} = \mathbf{A}^{-1}\mathbf{K}_2 = \begin{pmatrix} 7 & -9 \\ -3 & 4 \end{pmatrix}\begin{pmatrix} 341 \\ 262 \end{pmatrix} = \begin{pmatrix} 29 \\ 25 \end{pmatrix}$$

or $x_1 = 29$, $x_2 = 25$. And system (4.3) gives

$$\mathbf{X} = \mathbf{A}^{-1}\mathbf{K}_3 = \begin{pmatrix} 7 & -9 \\ -3 & 4 \end{pmatrix}\begin{pmatrix} 423 \\ 325 \end{pmatrix} = \begin{pmatrix} 36 \\ 31 \end{pmatrix}$$

or $x_1 = 36$, $x_2 = 31$.

Mathematically, we see that an inverse matrix can be useful in solving a number of linear systems that share the same coefficient matrix.

The business interpretation of the mathematics is interesting. Notice two points:

1. The matrix **A** was the same for all three systems. This shows that the supply–demand picture did not change much. H-2000 always sold more computers than H-3000.

2. H-2000's price went from $24 million up to $29 million up to $36 million. H-3000's price went from $26 million down to $25 million up to $31 million.

During the period covered by system (4.1), H-2000 sold more computers than H-3000 (the exact numbers are given in Chapter 3), but it had to be satisfied with a lower price. In the market conditions described by systems (4.2) and (4.3), H-2000 was establishing a strong competitive advantage: more sales *and* a higher price. Customers obviously thought that H-2000 had a much better computer than H-3000.

EXERCISES *for Section 4.3*

If

$$\mathbf{A} = (1 \quad 2) \qquad \mathbf{B} = \begin{pmatrix} 3 \\ 4 \end{pmatrix} \qquad \mathbf{C} = \begin{pmatrix} 5 & 6 \\ 7 & 8 \end{pmatrix}$$

and **I** is the second order identity matrix, what are the following matrix products?

1. AI	2. IA	3. BI
4. IB	5. CI	6. IC

If

$$D = \begin{pmatrix} 1 & 2 \\ 3 & 4 \\ 5 & 6 \end{pmatrix} \quad E = \begin{pmatrix} 4 & 6 & 8 \\ 3 & 7 & 5 \end{pmatrix} \quad F = \begin{pmatrix} 1 & 1 & 9 \\ 3 & 4 & 6 \\ 8 & 7 & 5 \end{pmatrix}$$

and **I** is the third order identity matrix, what are the following matrix products?

7. DI   **8. ID**   **9. EI**

10. IE   **11. FI**   **12. IF**

---

13. Check to see if either

$$\begin{pmatrix} 2 & 1 \\ -5 & -3 \end{pmatrix} \quad \text{or} \quad \begin{pmatrix} 2 & -1 \\ -5 & 3 \end{pmatrix}$$

is the inverse of

$$\begin{pmatrix} 3 & 1 \\ 5 & 2 \end{pmatrix}$$

14. Check to see if

$$\begin{pmatrix} -2 & 3 \\ 5 & 7 \end{pmatrix} \quad \text{or} \quad \begin{pmatrix} -2 & 5 \\ 3 & 7 \end{pmatrix} \quad \text{or} \quad \begin{pmatrix} -2 & 5 \\ 3 & -7 \end{pmatrix}$$

is the inverse of

$$\begin{pmatrix} 7 & 5 \\ 3 & 2 \end{pmatrix}$$

Calculate, if possible, the inverse of:

15. $\begin{pmatrix} 8 & 11 \\ 5 & 7 \end{pmatrix}$ $\begin{pmatrix} 7 & -11 \\ -5 & 8 \end{pmatrix}$ **16.** $\begin{pmatrix} 5 & 24 \\ 6 & 29 \end{pmatrix}$

17. $\begin{pmatrix} -6 & 9 \\ 2 & 3 \end{pmatrix}$ $\begin{pmatrix} -\frac{1}{12} & \frac{1}{4} \\ \frac{1}{18} & \frac{1}{6} \end{pmatrix}$ **18.** $\begin{pmatrix} 1 & 2 \\ 3 & 4 \end{pmatrix}$

19. $\begin{pmatrix} 5 & -4 \\ 3 & -2 \end{pmatrix}$ done   **20.** $\begin{pmatrix} 1 & 3 \\ 3 & 8 \end{pmatrix}$

21. Make use of the inverse you found in Exercise 15 to solve the linear systems

$$\begin{cases} 8x + 11y = -3 \\ 5x + 7y = -2 \end{cases} \quad \text{and} \quad \begin{cases} 8x + 11y = 9 \\ 5x + 7y = 6 \end{cases}$$

22. Make use of the inverse you found in Exercise 19 to solve the linear systems

$$\begin{cases} 5x - 4y = 6 \\ 3x - 2y = 8 \end{cases} \quad \text{and} \quad \begin{cases} 5x - 4y = 7 \\ 3x - 2y = 9 \end{cases}$$

23. Check to see if either

$$\begin{pmatrix} 1 & -\frac{2}{3} & \frac{5}{3} \\ -1 & \frac{4}{3} & -\frac{10}{3} \\ 1 & 1 & 2 \end{pmatrix} \quad \text{or} \quad \begin{pmatrix} 1 & -\frac{2}{3} & \frac{5}{3} \\ -1 & \frac{4}{3} & -\frac{10}{3} \\ 1 & 1 & -2 \end{pmatrix}$$

is the inverse of

$$\begin{pmatrix} 2 & 1 & 0 \\ 4 & -1 & 5 \\ 1 & -1 & 2 \end{pmatrix}$$

24. Find the value of x that makes

$$\tfrac{1}{10}\begin{pmatrix} 4 & 3 & x \\ -2 & 1 & x \\ 2 & -1 & x \end{pmatrix}$$

the inverse of

$$\begin{pmatrix} 1 & -2 & 1 \\ 2 & 1 & -3 \\ 0 & 1 & 1 \end{pmatrix}$$

25. Find the value of x that makes

$$\begin{pmatrix} 0 & 0 & \frac{1}{4} \\ 0 & -\frac{1}{2} & x \\ \frac{1}{3} & -\frac{1}{6} & -x \end{pmatrix}$$

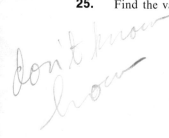

the inverse of

$$\begin{pmatrix} 2 & -1 & 3 \\ 1 & -2 & 0 \\ 4 & 0 & 0 \end{pmatrix}$$

Calculate, if possible, the inverse of:

26. $\begin{pmatrix} 1 & 2 & 3 \\ 0 & 1 & 4 \\ 0 & 0 & 1 \end{pmatrix}$ **27.** $\begin{pmatrix} 1 & -3 & 2 \\ 0 & 1 & 5 \\ 0 & 0 & 1 \end{pmatrix}$

28. $\begin{pmatrix} 0 & 0 & 1 \\ 0 & 1 & 3 \\ 1 & 7 & -9 \end{pmatrix}$ **29.** $\begin{pmatrix} 0 & 1 & 4 \\ 0 & 0 & 1 \\ 1 & 8 & 8 \end{pmatrix}$

30. $\begin{pmatrix} 3 & -4 & 1 \\ 2 & 0 & 6 \\ 1 & -5 & -7 \end{pmatrix}$ **31.** $\begin{pmatrix} 2 & 1 & 1 \\ 0 & 2 & 4 \\ -1 & -1 & -1 \end{pmatrix}$

32. $\begin{pmatrix} 1 & 1 & 1 \\ 2 & 1 & 1 \\ -3 & 4 & 5 \end{pmatrix}$

33. Make use of the inverse you found in Exercise 31 to solve the linear systems

$$\begin{cases} 2x_1 + x_2 + x_3 = -7 \\ \quad\quad 2x_2 + 4x_3 = 26 \\ -x_1 - x_2 - x_3 = -2 \end{cases} \quad \text{and} \quad \begin{cases} 2x_1 + x_2 + x_3 = 18 \\ \quad\quad 2x_2 + 4x_3 = -48 \\ -x_1 - x_2 - x_3 = -3 \end{cases}$$

34. Make use of the inverse you found in Exercise 32 to solve the linear systems

$$\begin{cases} x_1 + x_2 + x_3 = -7 \\ 2x_1 + x_2 + x_3 = 3 \\ -3x_1 + 4x_2 + 5x_3 = 12 \end{cases} \quad \text{and} \quad \begin{cases} x_1 + x_2 + x_3 = 8 \\ 2x_1 + x_2 + x_3 = 13 \\ -3x_1 + 4x_2 + 5x_3 = 6 \end{cases}$$

In the next two exercises, linear systems are used to describe three stages of market equilibrium. Find an inverse matrix that can be used to solve all three systems. Then carry out the solution process.

35.
$$\begin{cases} 4x_1 + 5x_2 = 1055 \\ 3x_1 + 6x_2 = 1095 \end{cases} \qquad \begin{cases} 4x_1 + 5x_2 = 1122 \\ 3x_1 + 6x_2 = 1224 \end{cases} \qquad \begin{cases} 4x_1 + 5x_2 = 1189 \\ 3x_1 + 6x_2 = 1254 \end{cases}$$

36.
$$\begin{cases} 7x_1 + 12x_2 = 2198 \\ 5x_1 + 9x_2 = 1624 \end{cases} \qquad \begin{cases} 7x_1 + 12x_2 = 2230 \\ 5x_1 + 9x_2 = 1648 \end{cases} \qquad \begin{cases} 7x_1 + 12x_2 = 2257 \\ 5x_1 + 9x_2 = 1680 \end{cases}$$

Find and use an inverse matrix to solve both linear systems:

37.
$$\begin{cases} 6x_1 - x_2 - 5x_3 = -1 \\ -7x_1 + x_2 + 5x_3 = 2 \\ -10x_1 + 2x_2 + 11x_3 = 3 \end{cases} \quad \text{and} \quad \begin{cases} 6x_1 - x_2 - 5x_3 = 4 \\ -7x_1 + x_2 + 5x_3 = -5 \\ -10x_1 + 2x_2 + 11x_3 = -6 \end{cases}$$

38.
$$\begin{cases} x_1 + x_2 - 3x_3 = 5 \\ 2x_1 + 5x_2 + x_3 = 4 \\ x_1 + 3x_2 + 2x_3 = 1 \end{cases} \quad \text{and} \quad \begin{cases} x_1 + x_2 - 3x_3 = 8 \\ 2x_1 + 5x_2 + x_3 = 6 \\ x_1 + 3x_2 + 2x_3 = 2 \end{cases}$$

4.4

INPUT–OUTPUT ANALYSIS

Let's imagine a horrendous national emergency:

1. It is definitely known that a monster earthquake along the San Andreas fault exactly 37 months from now will destroy California.

2. It is also definitely known that this disaster can be prevented by some far-out engineering that can move the earthquake 300 miles west into the Pacific.

3. The projected cost of the engineering is incredible. It is not certain that the U.S. economy can provide all the steel, lumber, aluminum, petroleum, lead, concrete, machinery, electronics, geologists, physicists, civil engineers, and construction workers needed to do the job.

4. The only alternative to the engineering is to relocate the 22 million Californians whose lives are threatened by the quake. Since the relocation would be permanent (when we say California would be destroyed, we mean it would slide into the Pacific and be no more), the U.S. economy would be faced with the super-

colossal task of increasing its output of goods and services by about 10%. And this would have to be done without the fertile California land or the rich California economy.

We are assuming that everyone understands the emergency and the choices, that Congress has authorized the administration to do all that must be done, and that the President is ready to set the wheels in motion.

But: which way?

It would really be unwise to spend two years and half a trillion dollars on the engineering only to find out that the job cannot be finished in time because of shortages of construction materials.

It would be just as unwise to write off California and relocate all those people, only to find out when it is too late that Operation Rescue California (ORC) would have been feasible after all.

In short: California and the U.S. need to know in advance whether or not the U.S. economy can generate the material and human resources needed to make ORC work. And they need to know quickly. And accurately.

Can it be done?

Well, we think so. We think that the President's economic advisers would get the ORC data, combine it with all the known data about current U.S. production of absolutely everything that's produced, and use *input-output analysis* to find out whether the python (U.S. economy) could expect to swallow the pig (ORC) or vice versa.

What Is Input–output Analysis?

Input–output analysis uses matrices to study the interdependence of producing and consuming sectors in an industrial economy. The basic insight is that every sector is both a producer and a consumer.*

EXAMPLE 1: STEEL AND COAL

The steel industry consumes coal (among other items) to produce steel. The coal industry consumes steel in the form of machinery (among other items) to produce coal.

Example 1 left out the primary factor in all production (and consumption): labor. The next example includes labor. It also uses the terms

---

*Input–output analysis is the creation of the economist Wassily W. Leontief, who used an 83-sector model of the U.S. economy. The main idea was to show the interconnections of the various sectors. Leontief was the Nobel prizewinner in economics in 1973. There is a profile of him in the October 29, 1973 issue of *Newsweek*.

output (for production) and *input* (for consumption). Every one of the five basic items in Example 2 is both output and input.

EXAMPLE 2: STEEL, COAL, LABOR, FOOD, MACHINERY

To have an output of steel, you need an input of coal. For an output of coal, you need an input of machinery. For an output of machinery, you need an input of steel. For outputs of steel, coal and machinery, you need inputs of labor. To have an output of labor, you need an input of food. For an output of food, you need an input of machinery. For that you need steel. For that you need coal. For all of these you need labor. For that you need food. For that you need machinery. And so on: back to the beginning and round and round again.

Before going on to a numerical example, we want to note that input–output analysis can be applied to a productive unit of any reasonable size: a nation, a region, a state, or as in the case of Example 3, a county within a state.

EXAMPLE 3: A TWO-INDUSTRY INPUT–OUTPUT TABLE

Yoknapatawpha County has two industries: agriculture and manufacturing. Table 4.6 gives the input–output picture for these two industries over a period of one year. The units are megabucks (million of dollars). We see that agriculture has a total output of 154 megabucks, and industry a total output of 98 megabucks, during the year. Row 1 of the table shows what happened to the 154 megabucks of agricultural output: 12 megabucks of output were kept back (for seed and livestock); 16 megabucks of output went to manufacturing (cotton and other fibers); and 126 megabucks of output went to final demand (consumption by households, investment, taxes—in other words, demand from outside the two-industry system). From the second row of the table we see that the 98-megabuck total of manufactured goods was divided into a 22-megabuck input to agriculture (agricultural machinery); a 30-megabuck input to manufacturing (machines to make machines); and a 46-megabuck input to final demand (consumer goods, investment, taxes).

TABLE 4.6

Industries	Inputs to Agriculture	Inputs to Manufacturing	Final Demand	Total Outputs
Agriculture	12	16	126	154
Manufacturing	22	30	46	98

Table 4.6 is a descriptive device: it tells us what the two-industry economy of Yoknapatawpha County looks like right now. But final demand may change: households may want to consume more; industries may need to invest more in land, buildings, or machinery; governments may increase tax rates. If we want to know how the economy must change to meet changes in final demand, then we must convert our input–output table into an input–output analysis.

EXAMPLE 4:   A TWO-INDUSTRY INPUT–OUTPUT ANALYSIS

We work with Table 4.6. Out first step (the reason for it will be clear in a moment) is to divide each item in column 1 by the row 1 total, and then to divide each item in column 2 by the row 2 total. The other items in Table 4.6 are left unchanged. The result is Table 4.7. The numbers in columns 1 and 2 of the table are *input–output coefficients*. We see that each dollar of agricultural output requires 8 cents of agricultural input and 14 cents of manufacturing input. Column 2 gives similar information for manufacturing.

TABLE 4.7

Industries	Inputs to Agriculture	Inputs to Manufacturing	Final Demand	Total Outputs
Agriculture	0.08	0.16	126	154
Manufacturing	0.14	0.31	46	98

Columns 1 and 2 together describe the input–output structure of Yoknapatawpha County's two-industry economy. We write

$$\mathbf{A} = \begin{pmatrix} 0.08 & 0.16 \\ 0.14 & 0.31 \end{pmatrix}$$

and call **A** the *structural matrix* of the economy. The entries in column 3 of the table give us the *demand vector* **D** and the entries in column 4 make up the *total output vector* **X.** We have

$$\mathbf{D} = \begin{pmatrix} 126 \\ 46 \end{pmatrix} \quad \text{and} \quad \mathbf{X} = \begin{pmatrix} 154 \\ 98 \end{pmatrix}$$

Total output is divided into two parts:

AX = the part of total output used as input by the two industries

D = the part of total output used to meet final demands

Therefore

$$X = AX + D$$

or

$$(I − A)X = D$$

where **I** is the second order identity matrix. If the matrix (**I** − **A**) has an inverse, then we can multiply both sides of the matrix equation (**I** − **A**)**X** = **D** by (**I** − **A**)$^{-1}$ to find:

$$(I − A)^{-1}(I − A)X = (I − A)^{-1}D$$

$$X = (I − A)^{-1}D$$

output vector = structural matrix INVERSE · demand vector

which is the key equation of input–output analysis. Why? Because it says: Give me the structural matrix (**A**) of your economy, give me the demand vector (**D**), and I will tell you the total output vector (**X**) you need to satisfy that demand.

As a check on the equation, let's see if it will give us the correct output for Yoknapatawpha County's two-industry economy. From the structural matrix **A** we calculate

$$I − A = \begin{pmatrix} 1 & 0 \\ 0 & 1 \end{pmatrix} − \begin{pmatrix} 0.08 & 0.16 \\ 0.14 & 0.31 \end{pmatrix} = \begin{pmatrix} 0.92 & -0.16 \\ -0.14 & 0.69 \end{pmatrix}$$

and we then find the inverse matrix

$$(I − A)^{-1} = \begin{pmatrix} 1.13 & 0.26 \\ 0.23 & 1.5 \end{pmatrix}$$

To check that we have the correct inverse we have to show that (**I** − **A**)(**I** − **A**)$^{-1}$ = (**I** − **A**)$^{-1}$(**I** − **A**) = **I**. It is understood that we round off the decimals. For example, it turns out that

$$(I − A)(I − A)^{-1} = \begin{pmatrix} 1.0028 & -0.0008 \\ 0.0005 & 0.9986 \end{pmatrix}$$

which rounds off to **I**. Next, we have

$$(I − A)^{-1}D = \begin{pmatrix} 142.38 + 11.96 \\ 28.98 + 69.00 \end{pmatrix} = \begin{pmatrix} 154.34 \\ 97.98 \end{pmatrix}$$

which rounds off to

$$\mathbf{X} = \begin{pmatrix} 154 \\ 98 \end{pmatrix}$$

The total output vector is correct.

Now suppose that final demand in Yoknapatawpha County changes. Suppose it is not **D,** but instead

$$\mathbf{D}_1 = \begin{pmatrix} 252 \\ 230 \end{pmatrix}$$

The total output $\mathbf{X}_1$ needed to meet this demand is

$$(\mathbf{I} - \mathbf{A})^{-1}\mathbf{D}_1 = \begin{pmatrix} 344.56 \\ 402.96 \end{pmatrix}$$

which rounds off to

$$\mathbf{X}_1 = \begin{pmatrix} 345 \\ 403 \end{pmatrix}$$

A little arithmetic will make the meaning of the answer clearer. Comparing **D** with $\mathbf{D}_1$, we see that final demand for agricultural output doubled (from 126 to 252 megabucks) and that final demand for manufacturing output quintupled (from 46 to 230 megabucks). If we did not know about input–output analysis, we might say that the way to meet this increased demand would be to double total agricultural output and quintuple total manufacturing output. Such an approach is incorrect, since it ignores the fact that each industry needs inputs from the other. Comparing **X** with $\mathbf{X}_1$, we see that total agricultural output has to increase by a factor of 2.24 $(345 \div 154)$ and that total manufacturing output has to increase by a factor of 4.11 $(403 \div 98)$.

NOTE: The incorrect solution (doubling agricultural output, quintupling manufacturing output) will provide more manufactured goods than are in demand, and fewer agricultural products. Check this statement mathematically to be sure you understand the importance of input–output analysis.

Now that you know what input–output analysis is, consider these two illustrative problems. The first is a continuation of Examples 3 and 4. The second reconsiders the Operation Rescue California (ORC) emergency described at the beginning of this section. We will apply input–output analysis to a simplified version of ORC.

PROBLEM 1   Tables 4.6 and 4.7 give input–output data for the 1977 economy of Yoknapatawpha County. For a more detailed picture, we now include *households,* which contribute labor to the economy and consume food and manufactures. The result is Table 4.8. Notice that comparable final demand items are smaller than they were in Tables 4.6 and 4.7. The reason is that consumption by households is now given in a separate column.

TABLE 4.8

Sectors	Inputs to Agriculture	Inputs to Manufacturing	Inputs to Households	Final Demand	Total Outputs
Agriculture	12	16	87	39	154
Manufacturing	22	30	25	21	98
Households	26	11	19	7	63

Suppose that final demand in the three-sector economy changes from

$$D = \begin{pmatrix} 39 \\ 21 \\ 7 \end{pmatrix} \quad \text{to} \quad D_1 = \begin{pmatrix} 78 \\ 84 \\ 42 \end{pmatrix}$$

What total output is required to meet the new demand?

SOLUTION   The total output vector X_1 corresponding to the demand vector D_1 is

$$X_1 = (I - A)^{-1}D_1$$

where A is the structural matrix of the three-sector economy and I is the third order identity matrix. We are assuming that $(I - A)$ has an inverse.

To find A, we divide column 1 of Table 4.8 by the row 1 total, column 2 by the row 2 total, and column 3 by the row 3 total. The result (with decimals rounded off to three figures) is:

$$A = \begin{pmatrix} 0.078 & 0.163 & 1.380 \\ 0.143 & 0.306 & 0.397 \\ 0.169 & 0.112 & 0.302 \end{pmatrix}$$

This gives

$$\mathbf{I} - \mathbf{A} = \begin{pmatrix} 0.922 & -0.163 & -1.380 \\ -0.143 & 0.694 & -0.397 \\ -0.169 & -0.112 & 0.698 \end{pmatrix}$$

Using the matrix-inverting method explained in Section 4.3 (and a hand-held calculator, for the arithmetic), we find that

$$(\mathbf{I} - \mathbf{A})^{-1} = \begin{pmatrix} 2.263 & 1.381 & 5.259 \\ 0.8585 & 2.111 & 2.898 \\ 0.6857 & 0.6728 & 3.172 \end{pmatrix}$$

The total output required to meet the demand

$$\mathbf{D}_1 = \begin{pmatrix} 78 \\ 84 \\ 42 \end{pmatrix}$$

is therefore

$$\mathbf{X}_1 = (\mathbf{I} - \mathbf{A})^{-1}\mathbf{D}_1 = \begin{pmatrix} 513.39 \\ 366.00 \\ 243.22 \end{pmatrix}$$

Since the units are megabucks, this means that the required total outputs are: agriculture, \$513,390,000; manufacturing, \$366,000,000; households, \$243,220,000. (The output of households consists of labor: agricultural labor, manufacturing labor, and direct inputs to households. Direct inputs to households are services performed by beauticians, dentists, preachers, etc.)

NOTE: To check the arithmetic leading to the total output vector $\mathbf{X}_1$, we multiply $\mathbf{X}_1$ by $(\mathbf{I} - \mathbf{A})$. The result should be $\mathbf{D}_1$. We find:

$$(\mathbf{I} - \mathbf{A})\mathbf{X}_1 = \begin{pmatrix} 78.04 \\ 84.03 \\ 42.01 \end{pmatrix}$$

which rounds off to

$$\begin{pmatrix} 78 \\ 84 \\ 42 \end{pmatrix} = \mathbf{D}_1$$

PROBLEM 2   Project ORC is scheduled to take three years to complete. Preliminary studies have shown that the first year will be crucial: if first-year goals are met, ORC floats; if not, it sinks. To get a quick answer about that first year, we can divide the U.S. economy into three sectors: raw materials, manufacturing, and labor. The input–output figures for the three-sector economy (in billions of dollars per year) are given in Table 4.9. The raw materials sector includes extractive industries such as agriculture, logging, and mining; the manufacturing sector includes nonextractive industries and all businesses; and the labor sector includes everyone in the U.S. (even the smallest child is linked to the economy as a consumer). The first

TABLE 4.9

Sector	Inputs to Raw Materials	Inputs to Manufacturing	Inputs to Labor	Final Demand	Total Output
Raw Materials	340	216	48	246	850
Manufacturing	425	144	24	127	720
Labor	85	72	48	35	240

year of ORC will create immense new demands. In place of the demand vector

$$\mathbf{D} = \begin{pmatrix} 246 \\ 127 \\ 35 \end{pmatrix}$$

shown in the final demand column of Table 4.9, the economy will have to meet a demand of

$$\mathbf{D}_1 = \begin{pmatrix} 664 \\ 368 \\ 109 \end{pmatrix}$$

The total demand (obtained by adding the three entries in $\mathbf{D}_1$) is well over \$1 trillion. Notice that the difference between the $\mathbf{D}_1$ total and the $\mathbf{D}$ total is \$733 billion. This is the first-year cost of ORC. Can the U.S. economy manage it? To help find out, do an input–output analysis and calculate the total output vector $\mathbf{X}_1$ corresponding to the demand vector $\mathbf{D}_1$.

SOLUTION We want to use the basic equation

$$\mathbf{X}_1 = (\mathbf{I} - \mathbf{A})^{-1}\mathbf{D}_1$$

The demand vector $\mathbf{D}_1$ is given, and the structural matrix $\mathbf{A}$ of the three-sector U.S. economy will be calculated from Table 4.9. $\mathbf{I}$ is the third order identity matrix, and $(\mathbf{I} - \mathbf{A})^{-1}$ will be calculated by the matrix-inverting method of Section 4.3. [Since we have a real-world problem, we expect $(\mathbf{I} - \mathbf{A})^{-1}$ to exist. If by any chance it does not, that will show up when we try to calculate the inverse.]

To calculate the structural matrix $\mathbf{A}$, we divide column 1 of Table 4.9 by the row 1 total, column 2 by the row 2 total, and column 3 by the row 3 total. The result is:

$$\mathbf{A} = \begin{pmatrix} 0.4 & 0.3 & 0.2 \\ 0.5 & 0.2 & 0.1 \\ 0.1 & 0.1 & 0.2 \end{pmatrix}$$

which leads to:

$$\mathbf{I} - \mathbf{A} = \begin{pmatrix} 0.6 & -0.3 & -0.2 \\ -0.5 & 0.8 & -0.1 \\ -0.1 & -0.1 & 0.8 \end{pmatrix}$$

To find the inverse by the method of Section 4.3, we find it convenient to rewrite this as:

$$\mathbf{I} - \mathbf{A} = \begin{pmatrix} \dfrac{3}{5} & -\dfrac{3}{10} & -\dfrac{1}{5} \\ -\dfrac{1}{2} & \dfrac{4}{5} & -\dfrac{1}{10} \\ -\dfrac{1}{10} & -\dfrac{1}{10} & \dfrac{4}{5} \end{pmatrix}$$

The advantage of using fractions instead of decimals is that we avoid round-off errors. For example, the first step of the inverting process is to multiply row 1 of the identity-augmented matrix $(I - A|I)$ by $\frac{5}{3}$. If we were to use decimals, we would multiply by a rounded-off number: 1.667, say.

Our calculations (with a hand-held calculator used only in the last step) give:

$$(I - A)^{-1} = \begin{pmatrix} 2.75 & 1.14 & 0.830 \\ 1.79 & 2.01 & 0.699 \\ 0.568 & 0.393 & 1.44 \end{pmatrix}$$

Check: It is left to you to show that $(I - A)^{-1}(I - A) = (I - A)(I - A)^{-1} = I$, with all entries correct to three figures. Another way to check the result is to calculate $(I - A)^{-1}D$, where D is the demand vector formed from column 4 of Table 4.9. The result

$$(I - A)^{-1} \begin{pmatrix} 246 \\ 127 \\ 35 \end{pmatrix} = \begin{pmatrix} 850.33 \\ 720.08 \\ 240.04 \end{pmatrix}$$

checks out with the total output vector X formed from column 5 of Table 4.9.

To solve our problem, we multiply $(I - A)^{-1}$ by D_1 to find X_1. We have:

$$(I - A)^{-1} \begin{pmatrix} 664 \\ 368 \\ 109 \end{pmatrix} = \begin{pmatrix} 2335.99 \\ 2004.43 \\ 678.74 \end{pmatrix} = X_1$$

This is the total output vector corresponding to the demand vector D_1.

If we add the three entries in X_1, we have the total post-ORC output of the three-sector U.S. economy. The sum of the numbers is 5019.16. Since the units are billions of dollars per year, the required yearly output is over $5 trillion.

By contrast, the pre-ORC total output (obtained by adding the three entries in column 5 of Table 4.9) is 1810, or less than $2 trillion per year.

Input–output analysis has shown that the yearly output of the U.S. economy would have to grow by over $3 trillion (in other words, almost triple) to make the first year of ORC feasible. This looks impossible. It also looks impossible to stand by and see California swept into the Pacific. A nonmathematical guess is that ORC would somehow or other get financed and completed and that it would be a very good thing for all sectors of the U.S. economy, especially the parts of those sectors located in California.

EXERCISES *for Section 4.4*

Each of the following input–output tables refers to a two-industry economy. The units are megabucks. In each case, use the table to find the *structural matrix* of the economy, the *demand vector*, and the *total output vector*.

1.

Industry	Input to Wheat	Input to Wool	Final Demand	Total Output
Wheat	12	22	86 ×2	120
Wool	36	44	30 ×3	110

2.

Industry	Input to Fisheries	Input to Mining	Final Demand	Total Output
Fisheries	3582	915	1473	5970
Mining	597	1220	1233	3050

3.

Industry	Input to Aerospace	Input to Banks	Final Demand	Total Output
Aerospace	3864	1368	4428	9660
Banks	1932	228	120	2280

4.

Industry	Input to Rice	Input to Lumber	Final Demand	Total Output
Rice	548	1122	1070	2740
Lumber	1096	187	587	1870

5.

Industry	Input to Cars	Input to Corn	Final Demand	Total Output
Cars	7525	804	2421	10750
Corn	430	268	642	1340

In the following exercises, it is assumed that the structural matrix of an economy remains the same while demand changes.

6. In the economy described by Exercise 1, demand for wheat doubles and demand for wool triples. What is the new total output vector?

7. In the economy described by Exercise 2, the demand for fish products goes down to 1320 megabucks and the demand for minerals produced by mining goes up to 1560 megabucks. What total output vector satisfies these new demands?

8. In the economy described by Exercise 3, the aerospace industry falls on hard times: demand for its products goes down to 1150 megabucks. The final demand for banking services goes down as well: to 80 megabucks. Nevertheless, the structural matrix of the economy is unchanged. What total outputs correspond to the new circumstances?

9. In the economy described by Exercise 4, demand for rice goes to 1220 megabucks and demand for lumber goes to 690 megabucks. What is the new total output vector?

10. In the economy described by Exercise 5, demand for cars zooms to 4870 megabucks, and demand for corn is unchanged. What are the new total outputs of cars and corn?

In each of the following exercises, the given matrix is the structural matrix of a three-industry economy. The given vector is a demand vector for that economy. Use this data to construct a complete input–output table for the three industries. Notice that the table will consist of three rows and five columns.

HINT: The economies described are the same as those given in Exercises 1–5. (Exercise 11 corresponds to Exercise 1, Exercise 12 to Exercise 2, etc.) In each case a labor sector has been added. The table you construct should partially coincide with the corresponding two-industry table. To be precise: the (1, 1), (1, 2), (2, 1), and (2, 2) entries should be the same. The (1, 5) and (2, 5) entries of the new table should be the same as the (1, 4) and (2, 4) entries of the corresponding two-industry table. Why does all this happen? No deep reason. It's just that we cooked up the demand vectors that make it happen.

11. $\mathbf{A}_1 = \begin{pmatrix} 0.1 & 0.2 & 0.2 \\ 0.3 & 0.4 & 0.3 \\ 0.1 & 0.2 & 0.2 \end{pmatrix}$ $\qquad \mathbf{D}_1 = \begin{pmatrix} 70 \\ 6 \\ 30 \end{pmatrix}$

12. $\mathbf{A}_2 = \begin{pmatrix} 0.6 & 0.3 & 0.5 \\ 0.1 & 0.4 & 0.3 \\ 0.2 & 0.2 & 0.1 \end{pmatrix}$ $\qquad \mathbf{D}_2 = \begin{pmatrix} 358 \\ 564 \\ 203 \end{pmatrix}$

13. $\mathbf{A}_3 = \begin{pmatrix} 0.4 & 0.6 & 0.5 \\ 0.2 & 0.1 & 0.01 \\ 0.1 & 0.1 & 0.1 \end{pmatrix}$ $\mathbf{D}_3 = \begin{pmatrix} 3478 \\ 101 \\ 516 \end{pmatrix}$

14. $\mathbf{A}_4 = \begin{pmatrix} 0.2 & 0.6 & 0.5 \\ 0.4 & 0.1 & 0.3 \\ 0.1 & 0.2 & 0.1 \end{pmatrix}$ $\mathbf{D}_4 = \begin{pmatrix} 455 \\ 218 \\ 459 \end{pmatrix}$

15. $\mathbf{A}_5 = \begin{pmatrix} 0.7 & 0.6 & 0.5 \\ 0.04 & 0.2 & 0.1 \\ 0.02 & 0.05 & 0.04 \end{pmatrix}$ $\mathbf{D}_5 = \begin{pmatrix} 1121 \\ 382 \\ 2214 \end{pmatrix}$

chapter five

LINEAR PROGRAMMING

LINEAR programming is a simple mathematical technique for solving planning and decision-making problems. It has applications in industry, in agriculture, in military planning, in government at all levels. This chapter will introduce you to the key ideas of linear programming.

Systems of linear inequalities, the foundation of the subject, are covered in Section 5.1. The approach is geometric, as in Section 2.2C, and it is therefore restricted to two variables.

Section 5.2 tells you how to formulate a linear programming problem mathematically. The next two sections explain a geometrical solution method—a graph-drawing method, really.

We explain the algebraic approach to linear programming in Section 5.5. This approach, called the *simplex method,* is essential for solving realistic problems involving many, many variables. To keep the arithmetic at the pencil-and-paper level, we have explained simplex in terms of two-variable problems (with one three-variable example, at the end of the section).

5.1 SYSTEMS OF LINEAR INEQUALITIES IN TWO VARIABLES

An ordered pair solution of a system of inequalities in two variables satisfies all the inequalities in the system. A non-solution fails to satisfy one or more of the inequalities.

EXAMPLE 1: If (x, y) is an ordered pair solution of the system

$$x > -2$$
$$y < 1$$

then $x > -2$ *and* $y < 1$. If (x, y) is a non-solution of the system, then $x \le -2$ or $y \ge 1$, or both.

EXAMPLE 2: Among the solutions of the system

$$x + y > 1$$
$$2x - 3y \ge 6$$

are $(3, 0)$, $(4, -1)$, and $(6, 2)$. Some of the non-solutions are $(2, -1)$, which does not satisfy the first inequality; $(4, 1)$, which does not satisfy the second; and $(0, 0)$, which does not satisfy either inequality.

There is an easy graphical method for solving any system of linear inequalities in x and y:

1. Graph all the inequalities of the system on one set of axes.

2. The region of intersection of all these graphs is the graph of the system. (If there is no region of intersection, then the system has no solutions).

Now, if you have forgotten how to graph an inequality, reread pp. 71–74. And if you are puzzled because this method for *solving* a system just seems to be a method for *graphing* the system, do not worry. The points in the plane corresponding to the ordered pair solutions of a system of inequalities make up the *graph of the system*. Once you have graphed a system, you have solved it. Let's look further at the first two examples:

EXAMPLE 1 REVISITED: The graph of $x > -2$ is the open half-plane to the right of the line $x = -2$, and the graph of $y < 1$ is the open half-plane below the line $y = 1$. The doubly shaded region of intersection of the two graphs (shown in Figure 5.1) is the graph of the system.

EXAMPLE 2 REVISITED: The inequality $x + y > 1$ was graphed in Figure 2.28, and the inequality $2x - 3y \ge 6$ was graphed in Figure 2.29. Figure 5.2 shows both graphs on one set of axes. The doubly shaded region of intersection is the graph of the system.

> **PROBLEM 1** The lines $3x + 4y = 12$ and $7x + 2y = 14$ divide the plane into four regions. Explain which of these regions is the graph of the system

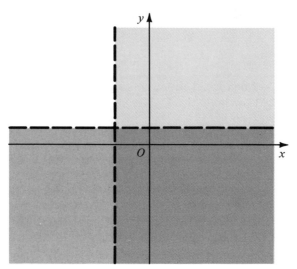

FIGURE 5.1 Graph of the System

$$\begin{cases} x > -2 \\ y < 1 \end{cases}$$

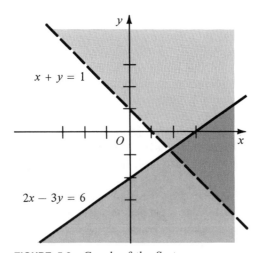

FIGURE 5.2 Graph of the System

$$\begin{cases} x + y > 1 \\ 2x - 3y \geq 6 \end{cases}$$

$$\begin{cases} 3x + 4y \le 12 \\ 7x + 2y \ge 14 \end{cases}$$

and draw the graph.

SOLUTION   The two lines are graphed in Figure 5.3. Since the lines intersect, they divide the plane into four regions. By using the methods of pp. 71–74, we find that $3x + 4y \le 12$ defines the closed half-plane below the line $3x + 4y = 12$, and that $7x + 2y \ge 14$ defines the closed half-plane above the line $7x + 2y = 14$. The shaded region in Figure 5.3 is the intersection of the two half-planes.

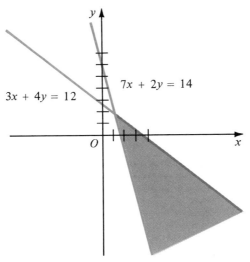

FIGURE 5.3   Graph of the System

$$\begin{cases} 3x + 4y \le 12 \\ 7x + 2y \ge 14 \end{cases}$$

PROBLEM 2   Graph and discuss the system

$$\begin{cases} 3x + 5y \ge 15 \\ 12x + 20y \le 27 \end{cases}$$

SOLUTION   We begin by graphing the lines $3x + 5y = 15$ and $12x + 20y = 27$. The lines and the shaded half-plane graphs of the two inequalities are shown in Figure 5.4.

Since the bounding lines $3x + 5y = 15$ and $12x + 20y = 27$ are parallel, the two half-planes do not intersect. This means that the system of inequalities has no solutions.

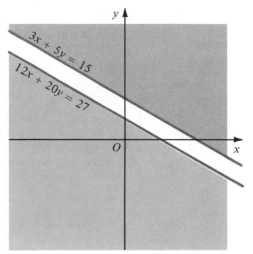

FIGURE 5.4 Graph of the System

$$\begin{cases} 3x + 5y \geq 15 \\ 12x + 20y \leq 27 \end{cases}$$

PROBLEM 3 Graph the system

$$\begin{cases} 3x + 5y < 15 \\ 12x + 20y > 27 \end{cases}$$

SOLUTION The graph of the first inequality is the half-plane below the line $3x + 5y = 15$, and the graph of the second inequality is the half-plane above the line $12x + 20y = 27$. The region of intersection of the two graphs is the infinite strip between the parallel lines bounding the half-planes. See Figure 5.5.

The next two worked-out problems show systems of more than two inequalities in the two variables x and y. In each case the graph of the system is enclosed on all sides, or *bounded*. (A graph is *unbounded* if it is not enclosed on all sides. Figures 5.1 through 5.5 are examples of unbounded graphs.)

PROBLEM 4 Graph the system

$$\begin{cases} 4x + 7y - 28 \leq 0 \\ 2x - 3y + 6 \geq 0 \\ \qquad\qquad y \geq -2 \end{cases}$$

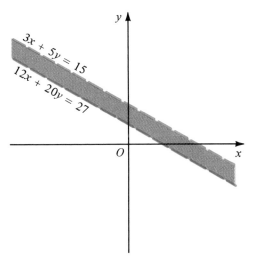

FIGURE 5.5 Graph of the System

$$\begin{cases} 3x + 5y < 15 \\ 12x + 20y > 27 \end{cases}$$

SOLUTION   The three inequalities define three half-planes. The bounding lines are shown, with the triangular region of intersection shaded, in Figure 5.6.

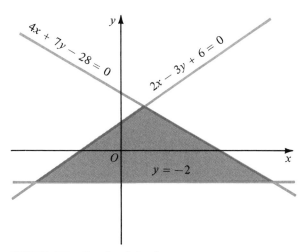

FIGURE 5.6 Graph of the System

$$\begin{cases} 4x + 7y - 28 \leq 0 \\ 2x - 3y + 6 \geq 0 \\ \qquad y \qquad \geq -2 \end{cases}$$

PROBLEM 5   Graph the system

$$\begin{cases} 3x + 5y \leq 15 \\ 12x + 20y \geq 27 \\ x < 6 \\ y < 5 \end{cases}$$

SOLUTION   The graph of the first two inequalities is a parallel strip, as in Problem 3. (In the present case the bounding lines are included.) The half-plane graphs of the third and fourth inequalities cut off the strip on the right and left. Figure 5.7 shows that the graph of the system is a bounded four-sided region.

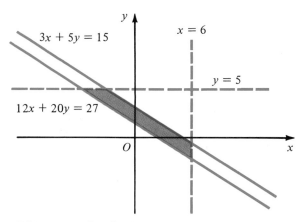

FIGURE 5.7   Graph of the System

$$\begin{cases} 3x + 5y \leq 15 \\ 12x + 20y \geq 27 \\ x < 6 \\ y < 5 \end{cases}$$

EXERCISES   *for Section 5.1*

In each of the following exercises, you are given three ordered pairs and a system of inequalities. Examine each of the three ordered pairs to see if it is a solution or a non-solution of its system.

15.
$$\begin{cases} x + y \geq 4 \\ x \geq 0 \\ y \geq 0 \end{cases}$$

16.
$$\begin{cases} x + y < 4 \\ x \geq 0 \\ y \geq 0 \end{cases}$$

17.
$$\begin{cases} y + 3x \leq 11 \\ y > 27 - 3x \end{cases}$$

18.
$$\begin{cases} 7x + 9y < 4 \\ 11.9x + 15.3y > 6.8 \end{cases}$$

19.
$$\begin{cases} x + y \leq 3 \\ x - y \geq 0 \\ y \leq 3 \end{cases}$$

20.
$$\begin{cases} x < 3 \\ x \geq -3 \\ x < y \end{cases}$$

21.
$$\begin{cases} 5x + 2y \geq 8 \\ x - y \leq 3 \\ 3x - 6y \geq 4 \end{cases}$$

22.
$$\begin{cases} x \geq 4 \\ x \leq 14 \\ y \geq 0 \\ y \leq 21 \\ x + y \leq 29 \end{cases}$$

23.
$$\begin{cases} x + y \leq 4 \\ x - y \leq 3 \\ -x + y \leq 2 \\ -x - y \leq 1 \end{cases}$$

Find a system of inequalities whose graph is:

24. the infinite strip bounded by $2x + 3y = 4$ and $10x + 15y = 18$, including the bounding lines

25. the exterior of the infinite strip bounded by $3x - 5y = 8$ and $6x - 10y = 12$, *not* including the lines bounding the strip

26. the triangle bounded by $x = 0$, $y = 0$, and $x + y = 4$, including the bounding lines

27. the triangle bounded by $x - y = 0$, $x + y = 7$, and $2x - 5y = 11$, including the bounding lines

28. the triangle enclosed by (and including) the lines $x + y = 0$, $2x + 3y - 4 = 0$, and $-2x + 4y + 7 = 0$

29. the bounded region enclosed by (and including) the lines $x = -1$, $y = 3$, $7x - 8y = 3$, and $14x - 16y = 24$

30. the bounded region enclosed by (and including) the lines $x + y = 40$, $x = 0$, $y = 0$, and $2x + 3y = 90$

31. the bounded region enclosed by (and including) $2x + y = 10$, $3x + 4y = 20$, $x = 0$, and $y = 0$

1. $(-3, 3)$; $(0, -4)$; $(-4, 0)$
$$\begin{cases} x < -2 \\ y > -3 \end{cases}$$

2. $(4, 3)$; $(3, 3)$; $(5, -3)$
$$\begin{cases} x > 3 \\ y < 4 \end{cases}$$

3. $(7, -4)$; $(-12, 8)$; $(-12, -8)$
$$\begin{cases} x + y \leq 3 \\ x - 3y \geq 5 \end{cases}$$

4. $(2, 0)$; $(2, -7)$; $(-8, 5)$
$$\begin{cases} 2y - 3x \leq 5 \\ 3x + 2y \leq 5 \end{cases}$$

5. $(-6, 2)$; $(-3, 3)$; $(3, -3)$
$$\begin{cases} x + 3y \leq 6 \\ 3x - 2y \leq 4 \\ y \geq 0 \end{cases}$$

6. $(1, 3)$; $(1, 4)$; $(\frac{4}{3}, 3)$
$$\begin{cases} y \leq 3x \\ 3x + 2y \leq 10 \\ y \geq 3 \end{cases}$$

---

7. Since the lines $3x + 2y = -2$ and $5x + 7y = 4$ intersect, they divide the plane into four regions. *Without* drawing the graph, explain which of these regions is described by the system

$$\begin{cases} 3x + 2y \geq -2 \\ 5x + 7y \leq 4 \end{cases}$$

Then check your answer by drawing the graph.

8. Repeat Exercise 7 for the system

$$\begin{cases} 2x - 9y \geq 4 \\ 3x - 12y \leq 9 \end{cases}$$

9. Repeat Exercise 7 for the system

$$\begin{cases} 4x + 3y - 10 \leq 0 \\ 6x - y - 4 \geq 0 \end{cases}$$

10. Repeat Exercise 7 for the system

$$\begin{cases} 2x - 3y + 2 \geq 0 \\ 4x - 5y - 4 \leq 0 \end{cases}$$

Find the region, if there is one, whose points satisfy all the inequalities i system:

11, $$\begin{cases} x - 3y \leq 6 \\ x - y \leq 0 \end{cases}$$

12. $$\begin{cases} 3x + 2y \geq 6 \\ 2x - 5y \leq 10 \end{cases}$$

13. $$\begin{cases} 3x + y > 4 \\ y < 4 - 3x \end{cases}$$

14. $$\begin{cases} x + y < 3 \\ 3x - 2y \geq 7 \end{cases}$$

5.2   LINEAR PROGRAMMING: SETTING UP THE PROBLEM

Real-world limitations, or *constraints,* on time, money, and resources can sometimes be expressed as linear inequalities. Usually several such constraints operate at once. Then the real-world problem leads to a system of inequalities. Section 5.1 showed that a system of inequalities may have infinitely many solutions. But the real world may not care about finding all mathematically *feasible* solutions of a problem. It will care about the best, or *optimal,* solution.

If we have to find the optimal solution of a system of linear inequalities, we say that we have a *linear programming* problem. (The term "linear" refers to the linearity of the inequalities. The term "programming" is used as a synonym for "planning.") Before looking at examples of linear programming, let's see what is meant by real-world constraints, feasible solutions, and optimal solutions.

EXAMPLES: CONSTRAINTS, FEASIBLE SOLUTIONS, AND OPTIMAL SOLUTIONS

1.   The city government of Metropolitan Area #37 must provide its citizens with elementary and secondary education; police, fire, and health protection; and so on. It must also avoid overburdening businesses and homeowners with property taxes. Faced with all these *constraints,* City Hall probably feels that any solution that keeps it from being voted out of office is a *feasible solution.* City Hall's *optimal solution* is to provide essential municipal services at lowest cost. (*NOTE:* It is understood that all possible municipal bonds have been floated, and that all possible federal funds have been obtained.)

2.   CPV Chemical, like other major manufacturers, depends heavily on its research department. Two kinds of research are carried on: short-term, or developmental, research on current products, and long-term research aimed at creating basically new products. (Short-term research safeguards year-to-year profits, and long-term research will keep CPV competitive 10 years from now.) There are two *constraints* on CPV's research effort: the *time* of the research staff is limited, and the amount of *money* that can be invested in research is also limited. What is the best way to allocate research time and money? One *feasible solution* is to concentrate on short-term research exclusively. (This will maximize profits for the next few years, and it may be argued that nobody knows what will happen after that.) Another feasible solution is to devote all efforts to long-term research. (The argument here is that CPV will have a rocky time of it for the short term, but that it will emerge as the industry's leader when the long-term research begins to pay off.) The *optimal solution* (according to CPV's management) is a combination of short-term and long-term research designed to give the company a steady 15% annual growth rate.

Now let's look at some examples of translating real-world problems of the linear programming type into mathematical form. In each case the real-world constraints will lead to a system of linear inequalities in two variables. And real-world requirements will lead to the linear programming problem of finding the optimal solution of the system. Sections 5.3 and 5.4 will show how such solutions are found. In this section the focus is on setting up the problem.

EXAMPLE 1: WYOTEX INCREASES ENERGY PRODUCTION

Wyotex is an energy corporation that started life as Texoil, a Texas oil company. Nowadays the company combines its oil holdings with substantial interests in Wyoming coal.

Ted Jones is Wyotex's CEO (chief executive officer). Each year he authorizes the drilling of oil wells and the expansion of coal mines. The average costs in moneyblocks (1 moneyblock = $100 million) are:

2 moneyblocks to drill a well

3 moneyblocks to expand a mine

The return on these operations can be measured in KC units of energy (1 KC unit = the electric power used by Kansas City, Kansas, in one year). Average annual returns are:

1 KC unit for each oil well drilled

2 KC units for each coal mine expanded

Ted Jones wants to increase Wyotex's annual energy production by at least 4 KC units this year. How can he do that at least cost?

TRANSLATING EXAMPLE 1 INTO MATHEMATICAL FORM: We begin by listing the known quantities. These are: the average cost and

TABLE 5.1

	Per Well Drilled	Per Mine Expanded	Total Required
KC Units	1	2	at least 4
Cost (Moneyblocks)	2	3	

energy return for each well drilled and each mine expanded; and the minimum number of KC units of energy that must be added to Wyotex's production this year. Table 5.1 summarizes what is known.

The unknown quantities are the number of wells drilled and the number of mines expanded. These numbers are to be determined in such a way that the energy production requirement will be met at lowest cost.

Let x be the number of wells drilled and let y be the number of mines expanded. Since each well costs 2 moneyblocks and each mine costs 3 moneyblocks, the total cost, C, is

$$C = 2x + 3y$$

moneyblocks. Since the energy return is 1 KC unit per well and 2 KC units per mine, the total return is

$$x + 2y$$

KC units of energy. To meet Ted Jones's requirement, the return must be at least 4 units:

$$x + 2y \geq 4$$

Neither x nor y can be negative. This gives

$$x \geq 0 \quad \text{and} \quad y \geq 0$$

Therefore any ordered pair (x, y) satisfying

$$x \geq 0$$
$$y \geq 0$$
$$x + 2y \geq 4$$

is a *feasible solution* to Ted Jones's problem. The feasible solution that makes the cost

$$C = 2x + 3y$$

as small as possible is the *optimal solution,* and this is what Ted Jones really wants.

EXAMPLE 2: SUNPOWER'S SCINTILLATING STRATEGY

Sunpower, the Nevada-based solar energy firm, manufactures two types of solar collectors for home heating: the Suntrap (which uses mirrors) and the Sunstream (which uses water in glass tubes).

To manufacture one Suntrap requires

$4\frac{1}{3}$ minutes of work by skilled craftsmen

$8\frac{2}{3}$ minutes of work by automated machines

To manufacture one Sunstream collector requires

$8\frac{2}{3}$ minutes of work by skilled craftsmen

$4\frac{1}{3}$ minutes of work by automated machines

The working day in the factory—for both craftsmen and machines—is 8 hours and 40 minutes.

Because the profit on each Suntrap is $50 and the profit on each Sunstream is $70, management is thinking seriously of phasing out Suntrap production and concentrating on Sunstreams. (The Sunstream collector is more expensive, but fossil fuel costs are rising so fast that Sunpower can sell any and all of the solar collectors it manufactures.) Before deciding to go full-bore on Sunstream manufacture, management has the facts studied by linear programming to find the optimal daily production mix for company profits.

TRANSLATING EXAMPLE 2 INTO MATHEMATICAL FORM: The known quantities are: the manpower time and machine time needed to manufacture each Suntrap and each Sunstream; the working time per day for both workers and machines; and the profit for each Suntrap and each Sunstream. Table 5.2 summarizes these facts.

We do not know how many solar collectors of each type are to be

TABLE 5.2

	Per Suntrap	*Per Sunstream*	*Total Available*
Skilled Labor Time (Minutes)	$\frac{13}{3}$	$\frac{26}{3}$	at most 520
Machine Time (Minutes)	$\frac{26}{3}$	$\frac{13}{3}$	at most 520
Profit (Dollars)	50	70	

manufactured per day to maximize Sunpower's profit. The optimal solution will be found in Section 5.3. When we have it, we will be able to answer management's original question: Does it make sense to concentrate production on Sunstream collectors? In this section, we will merely set up the mathematical problem.

Let x be the number of Suntraps to be manufactured each day, and let y be the number of Sunstreams to be manufactured each day. Since the profit is $50 per Suntrap and $70 per Sunstream, the total daily profit, P, is

$$P = 50x + 70y$$

dollars. Each Suntrap requires $4\frac{1}{3}$, or $\frac{13}{3}$, minutes of skilled labor, and each Sunstream requires $8\frac{2}{3}$, or $\frac{26}{3}$, minutes. The total amount of skilled labor for x Suntraps and y Sunstreams is therefore

$$\tfrac{13}{3}x + \tfrac{26}{3}y$$

minutes per day. Since 8 hours and 40 minutes—or 520 minutes—are available each day, we have

$$\tfrac{13}{3}x + \tfrac{26}{3}y \le 520$$

The machine time available each day is also 520 minutes. From the data in Table 5.2, we have

$$\tfrac{26}{3}x + \tfrac{13}{3}y \le 520$$

Neither x nor y can be negative:

$$x \ge 0 \quad \text{and} \quad y \ge 0$$

To sum up: Any ordered pair (x, y) satisfying

$$x \ge 0$$
$$y \ge 0$$
$$\tfrac{13}{3}x + \tfrac{26}{3}y \le 520$$
$$\tfrac{26}{3}x + \tfrac{13}{3}y \le 520$$

is a *feasible solution* of Sunpower's production problem. The feasible solution that leads to the largest possible value of the profit

$$P = 50x + 70y$$

is the *optimal solution* Sunpower's management is looking for.

EXAMPLE 3: FEEDING THE ANIMALS

Dr. Borza is in charge of nutrition at the animal experiment laboratories on the Planet of the Apes. The human animals under her care are given two kinds of food: meat table scraps and mixed table scraps. One hundred grams (g) of meat table scraps contain

10 g of protein

16 g of fat

4 g of carbohydrates

The mixed table scraps consist of bread, cereal, vegetables, and other nonmeat leftovers. One hundred grams of these scraps contain

5 g of protein

2 g of fat

50 g of carbohydrates

As a scientist, Dr. Borza wants each of her animals to have a healthful daily diet of

at least 60 g of protein

at least 30 g of fat

at least 120 g of carbohydrates

As an administrator, Dr. Borza wants to save some money. The cost of the scraps is

$3 for 100 g of meat scraps

$2 for 100 g of mixed scraps

Dr. Borza wants to know how many grams of each type of table scraps will give an animal a healthful diet at the lowest possible cost.

TRANSLATING EXAMPLE 3 INTO MATHEMATICAL FORM: As in Examples 1 and 2, we begin by listing the known quantities and summarizing this information in a data table.

The known quantities in Example 3 are the nutritional content (number of grams of protein, fat, and carbohydrates) of each 100 g of meat scraps and mixed scraps; the cost of each 100 g of meat scraps and each 100 g of mixed scraps; and the minimum nutritional requirements of each animal. Table 5.3 displays this data in summary form.

We do not know how many grams of table scraps of each kind are needed to give the animals a healthful diet. Of course, there are many

TABLE 5.3

	Per 100 g of Meat Scraps	Per 100 g of Mixed Scraps	Total Required
Protein (Grams)	10	5	at least 60
Fat (Grams)	16	2	at least 30
Carbohydrates (Grams)	4	50	at least 120
Cost (Dollars)	3	2	

feasible answers. For example: 1000 g of each kind of table scraps will meet the nutritional needs. But the cost would be an unreasonable $50 per day per animal. The optimal answer will deliver adequate nutrition at the lowest possible cost.

As in the other examples of this section, we have exactly two unknown quantities. Let x be the number of hundreds of grams of meat scraps and y the number of hundreds of grams of mixed scraps to be fed each animal each day. The cost of this diet will be

$$C = 3x + 2y$$

dollars. The number of grams of protein, fat, and carbohydrates in x hundred grams of meat table scraps and y hundred grams of mixed table scraps is given in Table 5.3. Since each animal's minimum daily requirement of protein is 60 grams, we have the inequality

$$10x + 5y \geq 60$$

The data for fat and carbohydrates give us

$$16x + 2y \geq 30$$

$$4x + 50y \geq 120$$

Since animals are not fed a negative number of grams of any kind of table scraps, we have

$$x \geq 0 \quad \text{and} \quad y \geq 0$$

We conclude that any ordered pair (x, y) satisfying

$$x \geq 0$$
$$y \geq 0$$
$$10x + 5y \geq 60$$
$$16x + 2y \geq 30$$
$$4x + 50y \geq 120$$

is a *feasible solution* of the nutritional problem. A feasible solution that leads to the minimum value of

$$C = 3x + 2y$$

is an *optimal solution* of Dr. Borza's administrative problem.

EXAMPLE 4: ENVIRONMENTAL STRUCTURES PLANS SUPERIOR ESTATES

Environmental Structures is developing a small tract along the shores of Lake Superior. Future homeowners in Superior Estates will choose between two popular models: the Florida Sunshine House (with many large windows) and the Energy-Efficient House (with no windows at all on the north side). These models were designed by the company's own architects, and Environmental Structures is proud of the response they have been getting from the public. For the past four years the company has been able to sell as many of them as its construction crews can build.

After a foundation has been poured, two crews work on each house: the wood crew does carpentry, glass and roofing and the metal crew does the plumbing and wiring. Building a Florida Sunshine House takes

  34 hours of metal crew work

  85 hours of wood crew work

Building an Energy-Efficient House consumes

  68 hours of metal crew work

  34 hours of wood crew work

Each crew is on the job for 1360 hours a season. (The building season is 25 weeks. The average work week per worker is 54 hours and 24 minutes.)

There are many feasible ways to use the 1360 hours of construction labor. (For example, Environmental Structures can feasibly build 10 houses of each type in a season.) Is there an optimal way that will earn Environmental Structures the largest possible profit? That depends on prices and profit margins. In fact, the optimum construction mix can and does vary from year to year.

To explain: In pricing its two models, Environmental Structures tries to stay very close to the price charged by competitive builders. Buyers lose confidence in a builder who undersells or is undersold.) This means that the prices of the Florida Sunshine and Energy-Efficient houses change considerably from one year to the next. Profit margins change along with prices.

TABLE 5.4

	Year 1	Year 2	Year 3	Year 4
Florida Sunshine House	6	9	11	12
Energy-Efficient House	7	3	22	27

Table 5.4 gives the profit per house (in thousands of dollars) over four successive years.

Common sense suggests that the way to earn the largest possible profit in year 2 was to build nothing but Florida Sunshine Houses and that the optimal way to do things in year 4 was to build nothing but Energy-Efficient Houses. Management made exactly that decision in those two years. Was management right? When we do the linear programming, in Section 5.4, we will answer that question.

There is no obvious common-sense solution for year 1 or year 3. Linear programming is needed. We formulate the problem in this section and give the details of the linear programming solution (with the slightly surprising results for one year) in Section 5.4.

TRANSLATING EXAMPLE 4 INTO MATHEMATICAL FORM: Since we have different profit data in each of four years, we have four separate problems to solve.

More precisely, the feasible solutions will be the same each year, but the optimal solution may be different.

To find the feasible solutions, we must look at the construction labor data. Table 5.5 summarizes what we know.

Let x be the number of Florida Sunshine Houses built in one season, and let y be the number of Energy-Efficient Houses built in one season. Since nobody builds a negative number of houses, our first constraints are

$$x \geq 0 \quad \text{and} \quad y \geq 0$$

We see from Table 5.5 that x Florida Sunshine Houses take $34x$ hours of

TABLE 5.5

	Per Florida Sunshine House	Per Energy-Efficient House	Total Available (per Season)
Metal Crew Labor (Hours)	34	68	at most 1360
Wood Crew Labor (Hours)	85	34	at most 1360

metal crew work, and that y Energy-Efficient Houses take $68y$ hours of metal crew work. Since the metal crew is on the job for no more than 1360 hours per season, we have

$$34x + 68y \leq 1360$$

In the same way, the known facts about wood crew labor tell us that

$$85x + 34y \leq 1360$$

The optimal construction mix in any given year will satisfy all the restrictions we have stated so far, and will also maximize Environmental Structures' profit in that year.

If we look at Table 5.4, we see that the profit in year 1 (P_1) is

$$P_1 = 6x + 7y$$

thousand dollars. The profits in years 2, 3, and 4 will be written P_2, P_3, and P_4. Table 5.4 says that those profits (in thousands of dollars) are

$$P_2 = 9x + 3y$$
$$P_3 = 11x + 22y$$
$$P_4 = 12x + 27y$$

To sum up: We can find all feasible solutions of Environmental Structures' problem by solving the system of inequalities

$$x \geq 0$$
$$y \geq 0$$
$$34x + 68y \leq 1360$$
$$85x + 34y \leq 1360$$

The feasible solution that leads to the largest possible value of

$$P_1 = 6x + 7y$$

is the optimal solution in year 1. Feasible solutions that maximize P_2, P_3, and P_4 are optimal solutions in those respective years.

As a numerical illustration, Table 5.6 lists the year-by-year profits for

TABLE 5.6

Florida Sunshine Houses Built per Season	Energy-Efficient Houses Built per Season	P_1	P_2	P_3	P_4
12	8	128	132	308	360
4	18	150	90	440	534

two feasible construction mixes. It is left to you to check out the arithmetical facts: that (12, 8) and (4, 18) are feasible solutions; and that the yearly profits are as shown.

EXERCISES *for Section 5.2*

In each of the following cases:

a. List the known and unknown quantities.
b. Introduce variables x and y to represent the unknown quantities.
c. Express the main quantity of interest (profit or cost, usually) in terms of x and y.
d. Express the given conditions as a system of linear inequalities in x and y.
e. Formulate the linear programming problem: to find the *feasible* solution (x, y) of the system of inequalities that leads to the *optimal* value of the main quantity of interest (profit, cost, or what have you).

Do not try to solve the problem you have formulated.

1. Ted Jones guides the destinies of Wyotex Energy Corporation with great ability, but he is less skillful with his personal investments. He has decided to have his money handled for him by professional money managers. Some of his money will go into East Texas Real Estate Investment Trust (ETREIT), and some will go into Los Angeles Mutual Fund (LAMFUND). These outfits sell shares to substantial investors only:

> each ETREIT share costs $80,000
> each LAMFUND share costs $100,000

The estimated annual returns on these shares are enticing:

> each ETREIT share is supposed to bring in $8000 per year
> each LAMFUND share is supposed to bring in $9000 per year

Assume that Ted Jones believes these estimates. If he wants a return of at least $72,000 per year, how many shares of ETREIT and how many shares of LAMFUND will give him this return for the least amount invested?

2. Dr. Peter Frank is a famous baby doctor. He has invented many ingenious procedures that help really sick babies. Most of his practice, however, is pure routine: regular physicals and inoculations against childhood diseases.

> Each *regular physical* takes up 20 minutes of Dr. Frank's time and 30 minutes of his nurse's time.
> Each *inoculation* takes up 5 minutes of Dr. Frank's time and 15 minutes of his nurse's time.

Dr. Frank is not willing to spend any more than 3 hours and 20 minutes a day on this routine part of his practice. The nurse who assists him with physicals and inoculations works for no more than 7 hours and 30 minutes a day. If Dr. Frank's profit is $16 for each regular physical and $7 for each inoculation, how many of each should he schedule each day to earn the most money?

3. A hotel restaurant specializes in fund-raising dinners. At one such fund-raiser, the restaurant is supposed to serve each guest a dinner containing at least 12 g of fat and at least 42 g of sugar. The fat and sugar are to be provided by:

> a *chicken* dish containing 3 g of fat and 6 g of sugar per 100 g
>
> a *dessert* containing 3 g of fat and 15 g of sugar per 100 g

The cost of 100 g of the chicken dish is $.80 and the cost of 100 g of the dessert is $1.20.

The restaurant manager wants to meet the requirement of at least 12 g of fat and at least 42 g of sugar per guest at *lowest cost*. How many hundred grams of the chicken dish and how many hundred grams of the dessert should the manager serve to each guest?

4. BAT (Bluegrass Air Traffic), a Kentucky-based airline serving mid-America and the Sunbelt, makes money because its aircraft are well maintained and its safety record is superb. BAT rules for maintaining airplanes are:

> No airplane can make more than 14 day flights and 12 night flights per week.
>
> In any 24-hour period, an airplane can make no more than 3 day flights and 2 night flights *or* 2 day flights and 4 night flights.

Every BAT airplane obeys these rules.

BAT also has a money-making rule: Get as much flight time as possible out of the well-maintained aircraft. With that rule in mind, how many hours would BAT like each of its day flights to last, and how many hours would it like each of its night flights to last?

5. Leningrad flu, a new flu strain first noticed (and named) by doctors in Helsinki, is now a serious public health threat in the U.S. Immunizing vaccines have been developed; the problem is to deliver them efficiently. In Megalopolis, for example, a force of 2700 doctors and 10,800 nurses is ready to do the job. It is known that

> An *A group* (1 doctor, 5 nurses) can give 950 flu shots a day.
>
> A *B group* (1 doctor, 3 nurses) can give 650 flu shots a day.

If the objective is to deliver as many flu shots as possible in a day, how many A groups and how many B groups should be assembled in Megalopolis?

6. Election Associates is a political image-building firm. There are two associates: Carl Swanson and Patricia Grant. They are specialists who perform only two image-building tasks:

Effective presentation jobs (helping politicians to present their ideas in a way that will get them media coverage) require 1 week of Carl's time and 3 weeks of Pat's time.

Whole new image jobs (helping politicians to present themselves in totally new ways with—they hope—appeal to totally new groups of voters) require 1 week of Carl's time and 5 weeks of Pat's time.

Carl, who is close to retirement, can do image-building work for 7 weeks a year at most.

Pat, who is just beginning her career as a political image-builder, can work at it for as many as 30 weeks a year.

Election Associates charges $110,000 for an effective presentation job and $250,000 for a whole new image job. (Since they have helped many politicians win elections, they have a long waiting list for both jobs.) If they want their total yearly fees to be as high as possible, how many effective presentation jobs and how many whole new image jobs should they schedule?

7. As we explained in Exercise 6, Pat Grant was just starting her career as a political image-builder while her partner Carl was just finishing his. She would have preferred a more active associate, and was not too unhappy when Carl retired.

Pat's new partnership was with Gilbert Greene and Barbara Black-lock. The partners continued to specialize in effective presentation jobs and whole new image jobs. But they introduced something new: all three of them worked together on each image-building job, and it was really efficient.

Each *effective presentation job* now required 0.4 weeks of Gil Greene's time; 1.2 weeks of Barb Blacklock's time; and 1 week of Pat Grant's time.

Each *whole new image job* required 1.2 weeks of Gil Greene's time; 0.6 weeks of Barb Blacklock's time; and 1 week of Pat Grant's time.

The partnership agreement was that no one of the three associates would work at image-building for more than 24 weeks a year.

It is understood that the demand for Election Associates's services was overwhelming. Little wonder: they were holding the line on prices. It was still $110,000 for an effective presentation job and $250,000 for a whole new image job.

How many effective presentation jobs and how many whole new image jobs did they schedule each year, to keep their total yearly fees as high as possible?

8. A. E. Trapper, the behaviorist psychologist is no longer satisfied to observe how his laboratory rats perform on tests. Instead, he gives them pills of two types: *S-pills* (serenity pills) and *E-pills* (euphoria pills). Then he measures front-brain, mid-brain, and rear-brain pleasure. The following table shows the results Dr. Trapper has found. (The units for pleasure are T-units, or Trapper units.)

Pill	T-Units of Pleasure		
	Front-brain	*Mid-brain*	*Rear-brain*
S	2	5	1
E	1	8	6

Trapper wants to know the least *number* of pills (S-pills, E-pills, or both) he can give a rat if he wants the rat to experience at least 12 T-units of front-brain pleasure, at least 24 T-units of mid-brain pleasure, and at least 28 T-units of rear-brain pleasure?

HINT: The quantity to be minimized is $N = x + y$.

9. A. E. Trapper continues to be interested in the S-pills and E-pills described in Exercise 8. Now he feeds them to cats. After experimenting, Trapper has put together some "improved" pills that give his cats the same number of T-units of pleasure that the original pills gave to his rats:

Pill	T-Units of Pleasure		
	Front-brain	*Mid-brain*	*Rear-brain*
"Improved" S	2	5	1
"Improved" E	1	8	6

Trapper wants his cats to experience

> at most 12 units of front-brain pleasure
> at least 24 units of mid-brain pleasure
> at most 28 units of rear-brain pleasure

What is the least number of pills that will produce these effects?

10. East End Engineering (EEE) has factories in Suffolk County, New York, and in Connecticut. It is often necessary to transport large numbers of EEE workers between these two factory locations. In the past that has been done by bus. With the recent introduction of hovercraft service across Long Island Sound, it has become much more efficient to transport workers by hovercraft.

One day EEE had to transport 1500 workers from Suffolk County to Connecticut and back again. It would take a large number of hovercraft to do this. The available types were:

> large hovercraft, which carry 150 passengers and are operated by a crew of 9
>
> jumbo hovercraft, which carry 300 passengers and are operated by a crew of 12

There were 72 crew members available that day.

It would cost $2800 to charter a large hovercraft for the round trip, and $5400 to charter a jumbo hovercraft. How many hovercraft of each type should EEE charter to transport its 1500 workers at lowest cost?

11. Prince Johannes von Thurn is the current head of a thousand-year-old family. His family owns 80,000 acres of forest and farm in the southern part of West Germany. The farmland is kept in top condition through the liberal use of two excellent fertilizers: mixture *Bavaria* and mixture *Regensburg*. The nitrogen, potassium, and phosphate contents of these mixtures are as follows:

Each 50-kilogram (kg) bag of mixture Bavaria contains 1 kg of nitrogen, 1 kg of potassium, and 2 kg of phosphate.

Each 50-kg bag of mixture Regensburg contains 3 kg of nitrogen, 1 kg of potassium, and 1 kg of phosphate.

The cost per 50-kg bag is 30 marks for mixture Bavaria and 50 marks for mixture Regensburg.

Suppose that one of the prince's farm managers wants to obtain at least

900 kg of nitrogen

500 kg of potassium

600 kg of phosphate

to fertilize a small tract of land. How many 50-kg bags of mixture Bavaria and how many 50-kg bags of mixture Regensburg will provide him with these chemicals at lowest cost?

NOTE: A kilogram is 100 g, or 2.2046 lb. A mark was worth $.41 at one point in 1976.

12. One of the specialties of The Organic Market is its home-baked bread. Two types are most popular: Soya-Wheat Bread and Wheat-Soya Bread. A baker's dozen (13 loaves) of Soya-Wheat Bread requires, among other ingredients,

2 lb of soya flour

9 lb of wheat flour

1.5 lb of milk powder

A baker's dozen of Wheat-Soya Bread requires, among other ingredients,

0.5 lb of soya flour

7.5 lb of wheat flour

4.5 lb of milk powder

One day the lady who baked this bread had in her larder

5 lb of soya flour

33 lb of wheat flour

13.5 lb of milk powder

plus ample supplies of all other bread-making ingredients. Her profit for bread-baking is

$5 for each baker's dozen of Soya-Wheat loaves

$7 for each baker's dozen of Wheat-Soya loaves

If she wants to make as much money as possible, how many loaves of each type should she bake with the soya flour, wheat flour, and milk powder she has on hand?

5.3 GEOMETRICAL SOLUTIONS OF LINEAR PROGRAMMING PROBLEMS

Section 5.2 contained four examples of linear programming problems in two variables x and y. Notice that each problem contained a *third* variable: the linear cost

$$C = 2x + 3y$$

in Example 1; the linear profit

$$P = 50x + 70y$$

in Example 2; and so on. Since the third variable expresses the goal, or objective, of the problem it is called the *objective variable*. The objective variable is always a linear expression of the form

$$ax + by$$

where a and b are positive constants. If $x \geq 0$ and $y \geq 0$, this means that the objective variable is nonnegative.

A linear programming problem always has two ingredients: a system of inequalities and an objective variable. Among all feasible solutions of the system, we want the one optimal solution corresponding to the smallest (or largest) value of the objective variable. A smallest-value problem is called a *minimum* problem and a largest-value problem is called a *maximum* problem.

Example 1 of Section 5.2 led to the following minimum problem.

PROBLEM 1   **WYOTEX INCREASES ENERGY PRODUCTION (CONTINUED)**

Find the ordered pair solution (x, y) of the system of inequalities

$$x \geq 0$$

$$y \geq 0$$

$$x + 2y \geq 4$$

that makes the objective variable

$$C = 2x + 3y$$

as small as possible.

GEOMETRICAL SOLUTION   We begin by graphing the system of inequalities. The methods of Section 5.1 show that the graph is the shaded first-quadrant region shown in Figure 5.8. Since each point of the graph is a feasible solution of this problem, the graph of the system of inequalities is called the *feasible region* of the linear programming problem.

Next question: How do we find the feasible point (x, y) that minimizes the objective variable $C = 2x + 3y$?

We will try to give a geometrical answer. The objective variable C denotes cost, and the smallest possible cost is $C = 0$. We do not really expect to get away with zero cost, but just to keep ourselves honest, we will consider that possibility along with some more realistic values: $C = 3$, $C = 6$, $C = 12$, etc. To do this geometrically, we

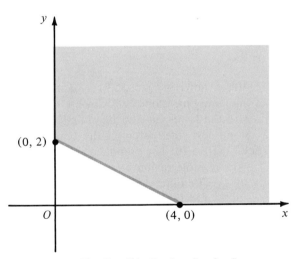

FIGURE 5.8   The Feasible Region for the System

$$\begin{cases} x \geq 0 \\ y \geq 0 \\ x + 2y \geq 4 \end{cases}$$

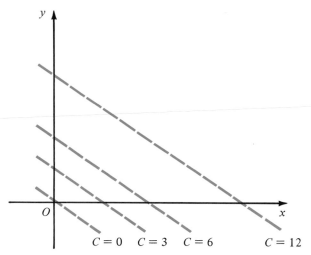

FIGURE 5.9 Lines of Constant Cost for Problem 1

simply graph the lines

$$2x + 3y = 0$$

$$2x + 3y = 3$$

$$2x + 3y = 6$$

$$2x + 3y = 12$$

etc.

The result (as shown in Figure 5.9) is a *family* of parallel lines. (Every line of the family has slope $-\frac{2}{3}$). Since C represents cost, we refer to the lines of the family as *cost lines,* or *lines of constant cost.*

    Some cost lines intersect the feasible region and some do not. (See Figure 5.10) The optimal solution (x, y) of this problem is a point *in* the feasible region and *on* the intersecting cost line that is closest to $C = 0$. Figure 5.10 shows that the optimal solution is $(x, y) = (0, 2)$ and that the corresponding cost is 6.

    The real-world meaning of this problem is that Wyotex can meet its energy goal at lowest cost by expanding 2 coal mines and not drilling any oil wells at all. This would cost 6 moneyblocks, or $600 million.

    Example 2 of Section 5.2 led to the following maximum problem.

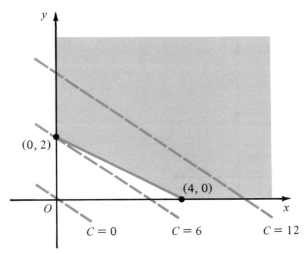

$C = 0$ $C = 6$ $C = 12$

FIGURE 5.10 The Geometry of Problem 1

PROBLEM 2 SUNPOWER'S SCINTILLATING STRATEGY (CONTINUED)

Find the ordered pair solution (x, y) of the system of inequalities

$$x \geq 0$$

$$y \geq 0$$

$$\tfrac{13}{3}x + \tfrac{26}{3}y \leq 520$$

$$\tfrac{26}{3}x + \tfrac{13}{3}y \leq 520$$

that makes the objective variable

$$P = 50x + 70y$$

as large as possible.

GEOMETRICAL SOLUTION   Graphing the system of inequalities will give us the feasible region for Problem 2.

As in Problem 1, the nonnegativity conditions $x \geq 0$ and $y \geq 0$ limit the feasible region to the closed first quadrant. The other two inequalities in the system give the upper boundary and the right-hand boundary of the feasible region. Figure 5.11 shows the first-quadrant segments of those two boundary lines. The feasible region is shaded.

Now we want to find the feasible point (x, y) that makes $P = 50x + 70y$ a maximum. The geometrical method is to graph the

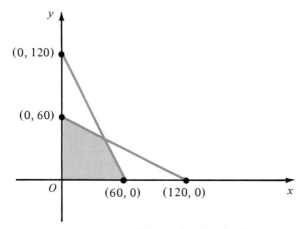

FIGURE 5.11 The Feasible Region for the System

$$\begin{cases} x \geq 0 \\ y \geq 0 \\ \tfrac{13}{3}x + \tfrac{26}{3}y \leq 520 \\ \tfrac{26}{3}x + \tfrac{13}{3}y \leq 520 \end{cases}$$

lines of constant profit $P = 50x + 70y$ for various values of P. These profit lines form a parallel family since they all have slope $-\tfrac{5}{7}$. Some lines of the family intersect the feasible region and some do not. Looking at Figure 5.12, we see that the highest profit line intersecting the feasible region goes through exactly one feasible point. That maximum-profit point (marked M in the figure) is the optimal solution of this problem.

Geometrically, the optimal point M is the point of intersection of the upper and right-hand boundary lines of the feasible region. The equations of these two lines are

$$\tfrac{13}{3}x + \tfrac{26}{3}y = 520$$
$$\tfrac{26}{3}x + \tfrac{13}{3}y = 520$$

and the solution of the system of two equations is $x = 40$, $y = 40$.

Since the optimal solution is $(40, 40)$, the largest possible profit is

$$P = 50(40) + 70(40) = 4800$$

In real-world terms: Sunpower's best strategy is to manufacture 40 Suntraps and 40 Sunstreams per day. This leads to a daily profit of $4800. In Section 5.2 we noted that Sunpower's management was

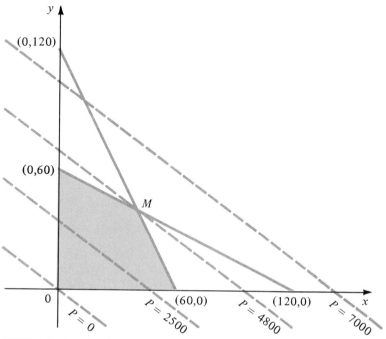

FIGURE 5.12 The Geometry of Problem 2

thinking of dropping Suntraps in favor of all-out production of the more profitable Sunstreams. Figure 5.12 shows that the most profitable form of this strategy is represented by the feasible point $(0, 60)$. Since that point lies on the profit line $P = 4200$, the all-Sunstream strategy falls $600 per day short of being optimal.

EXERCISES *for Section 5.3*

1. Find the solution (x, y) of

$$x \geq 0$$
$$y \geq 0$$
$$5x + 2y \geq 10$$

that minimizes the objective variable $C = 13x + 5y$.

2. Find the solution (x, y) of

$$x \geq 0$$
$$y \geq 0$$
$$5x + 4y \geq 24$$
$$x + 4y \geq 16$$

that minimizes the objective variable $C = 3x + 4y$.

3. Find the solution (x, y) of

$$x \geq 0$$
$$y \geq 0$$
$$2x + 3y \leq 15$$
$$3x + y \leq 12$$

that maximizes the objective variable $P = 3x + 5y$.

4. Find the solution (x, y) of

$$x \geq 0$$
$$y \geq 0$$
$$x + y \leq 10$$
$$x + 2y \geq 12$$

that minimizes the objective variable $C = 7x + 8y$.

5. Find the solution (x, y) of

$$x \geq 0$$
$$y \geq 0$$
$$4x + 3y \leq 24$$
$$x + 2y \leq 11$$

that makes $P = 3.5x + 3y$ a maximum.

6. Maximize $P = 7x + 5y$, subject to:

$$x \geq 0$$
$$y \geq 0$$
$$x + 2y \leq 10$$
$$3x + 2y \leq 18$$

7. Maximize $P = 13x + 21y$, subject to:

$$x \geq 0$$
$$y \geq 0$$
$$2x + 3y \leq 40$$
$$2x + y \leq 20$$

8. Minimize $C = 14x + 13y$, subject to:

$$x \geq 0$$
$$y \geq 0$$
$$x + y \geq 7$$
$$3x + y \geq 11$$

9. Maximize $P = 17x + 11y$, subject to:

$$x \geq 0$$
$$y \geq 0$$
$$3x + 2y \leq 18$$
$$4x + 8y \leq 40$$

10. Minimize $C = 9x + 5y$, subject to:

$$x \geq 0$$
$$y \geq 0$$
$$x + 3y \geq 18$$
$$5x + 3y \geq 30$$

Find the geometrical solution of the linear programming problem you formulated in solving the following exercises in Section 52:

11. Exercise 1

12. Exercise 2

13. Exercise 3

14. Exercise 4

15. Exercise 5

16. Exercise 6

THE CORNER POINT PRINCIPLE

Our solutions of Problems 1 and 2 (in Section 5.3) have a common geometrical feature. Figures 5.13a and 5.13b (they're simply Figures 5.8 and 5.11, redrawn) show this plainly. The points $(0, 2)$ and M $(40, 40)$ are the

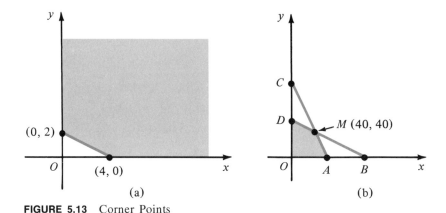

FIGURE 5.13 Corner Points

optimal solutions of Problems 1 and 2. In each case the optimal solution is at a *corner point* of the feasible region.

DEFINITION   Feasible Corner Point

A corner point of the feasible region, or *feasible corner point,* is a point *in* the feasible region (and therefore feasible) and *at* the intersection of two boundary lines (and therefore a corner point).

**EXAMPLES: FEASIBLE AND NONFEASIBLE
                        CORNER POINTS**

1.   The corner points $(0, 2)$ and $(4, 0)$ in Figure 5.13a are feasible.

2.   The corner points O, A, M, and D in Figure 5.13b are feasible. The point B in that figure is a corner point (the intersection of the boundary lines $y = 0$ and $\frac{13}{3}x + \frac{26}{3}y = 520$) but not a feasible corner point since it is not in the feasible region. Similarly, the point C is a corner point but not a feasible corner point.

3.   Suppose that the unbounded shaded region in Figure 5.14 is the feasible region for a problem. Then the points marked A and C are feasible corner points. The point marked B is at the intersection of the boundary lines L_1 and L_2 and therefore a corner point, but it is not a feasible corner point.

4.   Suppose that the bounded shaded region in Figure 5.15 is a feasible

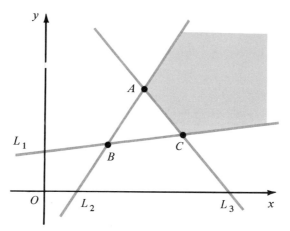

FIGURE 5.14

region. Then the points O, A, B, F, and G are feasible corner points. The points C, D, and E are corner points but not feasible.

Our interest in corner points is justified by the *corner point principle:*

> **THE CORNER POINT PRINCIPLE**
>
> If a linear programming problem has an optimal solution, then that solution is at a corner point of the feasible region.

Notice that a linear programming problem may fail to have an optimal

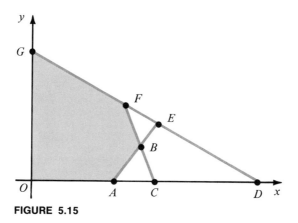

FIGURE 5.15

solution. For example, we cannot solve a maximum problem in an un-bounded region. This fact is illustrated by the following alternate version of Problem 1.

PROBLEM 1   Find the ordered pair solution (x, y) of the system of inequalities

$$x \geq 0$$
$$y \geq 0$$
$$x + 2y \geq 4$$

that makes the objective variable

$$z = 2x + 3y$$

as *large* as possible.

SOLUTION   Figure 5.8 shows the feasible region. The lines on which $z = 2x + 3y$ is constant are the same as the cost lines shown in Figures 5.9 and 5.10. But there is no line of *largest* z passing through the feasible region. As examples: $z = 1$ million, $z = 1$ billion, $z = 1$ trillion, etc., all intersect the region. The problem has no optimal solution.

There is a second no-solution case. If the feasible region has no points in it, then there are no feasible solutions and certainly there is no optimal solution. For example, the feasible region in a problem may be as in Figure 5.16: the first-quadrant region above the line L_1 and below the line L_2. Such

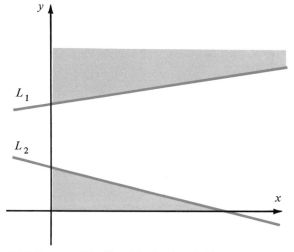

FIGURE 5.16   The Feasible Region Is Empty

a region is called *empty*. Can a real-world problem lead to an empty feasible region? Yes it can, if the real-world constraints are so severe that they cannot all be met at once. For example, an investor who demands a 20% annual return on capital and also a high degree of safety may find that there is no way to meet both objectives.

Taking account of the corner point principle and the two no-solution possibilities, we can now give a step-by-step method for solving linear programming problems in two variables.

RULES FOR SOLVING LINEAR PROGRAMMING PROBLEMS GEOMETRICALLY

1. Make sure that the problem has the two basic ingredients: a system of linear inequalities in x and y (including the two inequalities $x \geq 0$, $y \geq 0$), and a linear objective variable of the form $z = ax + by$, where a and b are positive constants.

2. Graph the system of inequalities. The graph is the feasible region of the problem. If the feasible region is empty, there is no solution. If the feasible region is nonempty, continue to step 3 if the region is unbounded, or to step 4 if the region is bounded.

3. If the feasible region is unbounded, there are two cases to consider. The maximum problem (of finding the largest possible value of the objective variable) has no solution. The minimum problem (finding the smallest possible value of the objective variable) does have a solution. To find it, proceed to step 5.

4. If the feasible region is bounded, the maximum and minimum problems both have solutions. Go on to step 5.

5. Determine the feasible corner points. This step is partly geometric and partly algebraic. The graph of the feasible region shows which corner points are feasible. Then find the coordinates of the feasible corner points by inspection or by solving a system of two linear equations. (The second method was used in Section 5.3 in the solution of Problem 2.)

6. Calculate the value of the objective variable at each of the feasible corner points determined in step 5. One of these points will give the optimal value of the objective variable.

Example 3 of Section 5.2 led to a minimum problem. For the solution, we turn to our step-by-step method.

PROBLEM 2   FEEDING THE ANIMALS (CONTINUED)

Find the ordered pair solution (x, y) of the system of inequalities

$$x \geq 0$$
$$y \geq 0$$
$$10x + 5y \geq 60$$
$$16x + 2y \geq 30$$
$$4x + 50y \geq 120$$

that makes the objective variable

$$C = 3x + 2y$$

as small as possible.

SOLUTION

STEP 1   The problem has the two basic ingredients.

STEP 2   The system of inequalities is graphed in Figure 5.17. The feasible region (shaded) is nonempty.

STEP 3   The feasible region is unbounded. Since the problem is a *minimum* problem, there will be an optimal solution.

STEP 4   Not applicable.

STEP 5   Figure 5.17 shows that there are four feasible corner points. The intersection of L_1 $(16x + 2y = 30)$ and $x = 0$ gives $(0, 15)$. The intersection of L_3 $(4x + 50y = 120)$ and $y = 0$ gives $(30, 0)$. Solving the system

$$\begin{cases} 16x + 2y = 30 \\ 10x + 5y = 60 \end{cases}$$

gives us the feasible corner point $(0.5, 11)$, and the system

$$\begin{cases} 10x + 5y = 60 \\ 4x + 50y = 120 \end{cases}$$

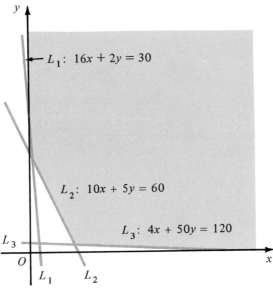

L_1: $16x + 2y = 30$

L_2: $10x + 5y = 60$

L_3: $4x + 50y = 120$

L_3

O

L_1 L_2

x

y

FIGURE 5.17   The Feasible Region for the System

$$\begin{cases} x \geq 0 \\ y \geq 0 \\ 10x + 5y \geq 60 \\ 16x + 2y \geq 30 \\ 4x + 50y \geq 120 \end{cases}$$

gives us (5, 2).

Notice that the intersection point of the boundary lines $16x + 2y = 30$ and $4x + 50y = 120$ is not a feasible corner point.

STEP 6   The objective variable $C = 3x + 2y$ has the following values at the four feasible corner points:

(x, y)	$(0, 15)$	$(30, 0)$	$(0.5, 11)$	$(5, 2)$
$C = 3x + 2y$	30	90	23.5	19

The optimal (lowest) value of the objective variable is 19. The optimal solution corresponding to this value is (5, 2).

The real-world interpretation is that Dr. Borza can feed her animals healthfully at lowest cost on a daily diet of 500 g of meat table scraps and 200 g of mixed table scraps. Antiscientific politicians complain that $19 a day is still a lot of money to spend on feeding animals. But Dr. Borza is a great political fence-mender, and she's kept her laboratories well funded up to now.

Example 4 of Section 5.2 led to a problem involving one system of inequalities and *four* different objective variables to maximize. Finding all four optimal solutions by drawing families of profit lines would require a great deal of graph drawing. (If it were all done on one graph, it would also be very messy.) The step-by-step method based on the corner principle is much more convenient.

PROBLEM 3   ENVIRONMENTAL STRUCTURES PLANS SUPERIOR ESTATES (CONTINUED)

Find the ordered pair solutions (x, y) of the system of inequalities

$$x \geq 0$$
$$y \geq 0$$
$$34x + 68y \leq 1360$$
$$85x + 34y \leq 1360$$

that maximize each of the following objective variables:

$$P_1 = 6x + 7y$$
$$P_2 = 9x + 3y$$
$$P_3 = 11x + 22y$$
$$P_4 = 12x + 27y$$

SOLUTION

STEP 1   We have four linear programming problems, and each one has the two basic ingredients. The system of inequalities is the same for all four problems, but the objective variables are different.

STEP 2   The graph of the system of inequalities is drawn in Figure 5.18. The feasible region is shaded. Since there is something to shade, the region is, of course, nonempty.

STEP 3   Not applicable.

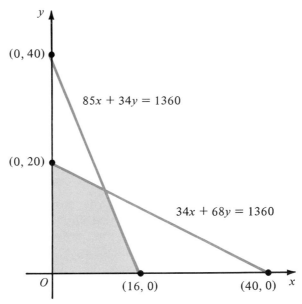

FIGURE 5.18   The Feasible Region for the System

$$\begin{cases} x \geq 0 \\ y \geq 0 \\ 34x + 68y \leq 1360 \\ 85x + 34y \leq 1360 \end{cases}$$

STEP 4   The feasible region is bounded. The four maximum problems have solutions.

STEP 5   There are four feasible corner points. Three of them can be read off the graph: $(16, 0)$, $(0, 0)$, and $(0, 20)$. By solving the system

$$34x + 68y = 1360$$
$$85x + 34y = 1360$$

we find that the fourth corner point has the coordinates $(10, 15)$.

STEP 6   All the objective variables vanish at $(0, 0)$. At the other three corner points, we have the following values:

Corner Point	P_1	P_2	P_3	P_4
$(0, 20)$	140	60	440	540
$(10, 15)$	165	135	440	525
$(16, 0)$	96	144	176	192

The optimal values of the objective variables and the corresponding optimal solutions are:

Objective Variable	Optimal Value	Optimal Solution
P_1	165	(10, 15)
P_2	144	(16, 0)
P_3	440	(0, 20) *and* (10, 15)
P_4	540	(0, 20)

Everything seems to be in order except for one small (or maybe not so small) point: P_3 has the same allegedly optimal value of 440 at two feasible corner points.

Is 440 the optimal value of P_3?

Is the optimal solution (0, 20), (10, 15), or something else?

To explain what is happening, we have to return to the lines of constant profit approach. Since $P_3 = 11x + 22y$, the profit line corresponding to a profit of 440 is

$$11x + 22y = 440$$

which is equivalent to

$$x + 2y = 40$$

The upper boundary of the feasible region is the line $34x + 68y = 1360$, and this is also equivalent to $x + 2y = 40$. In other words: The line of constant profit 440 coincides with the upper boundary of the feasible region. The objective variable P_3 has the same optimal value at (0, 20), at (10, 15), and at every point of the line segment joining those two points. Notice that this result does not contradict the corner point principle.

We can now answer the questions asked in Section 5.2.

Environmental Structures management was right about year 2: the (16, 0) all–Florida Sunshine strategy gave Superior Estates an optimal profit of $144,000. Management was also right about year 4: the (0, 20) choice led to an optimal $540,000 per year.

The most profitable choice for year 1 was to build 10 Florida Sunshine Houses and 15 Energy-Efficient Houses. This gave a profit of $165,000.

In year 3, Superior Estates had six ways of earning an optimal $440,000. These optimal programs were (0, 20), (2, 19), (4, 18), (6, 17), (8, 16), and (10, 15). The first and last are the corner point optimal solutions. The other four optimal solutions are points on the line segment joining $(0, 20)$ and $(10, 15)$. [*NOTE:* There are infinitely many points (x, y) on the line segment, but x and y must both be integers for a practical solution.]

From the management point of view, it was nice to have all this freedom of choice for year 3. A problem with just one optimal solution may be very neat mathematically. But experienced managers prefer to have more than one optimal choice since they know that business conditions may change at any moment, and they want to stay flexible.

EXERCISES *for Section 5.4*

1. Minimize $C = 3x + 5y$, subject to:
$$x \geq 0$$
$$y \geq 0$$
$$x \leq 9$$
$$y \leq 8$$
$$2x + 3y \geq 6$$

2. Maximize $P = 57x + 38y$, subject to:
$$x \geq 0$$
$$y \geq 0$$
$$4x + y \leq 4$$
$$x + 5y \leq 5$$

3. Maximize $P = 14x + 42y$, subject to:
$$x \geq 0$$
$$y \geq 0$$
$$x + y \leq 2$$
$$x \geq y$$
$$x + 3y \leq 3$$

4. Maximize $P = 9x + 5y$, subject to:
$$x \geq 0$$
$$y \geq 0$$
$$5x - 6y \geq -30$$
$$5x + 3y \leq 60$$

5. Maximize $P = 50x + 20y$, subject to:

$$x \geq 0$$
$$y \geq 0$$
$$3x + y \leq 8$$
$$2x + y \leq 7$$

6. Maximize $P = 10x + 4y$, subject to:

$$x \geq 0$$
$$y \geq 0$$
$$3x + y \leq 12$$
$$2x + y \leq 9$$

7. Maximize $P = 11x + 17y$, subject to:

$$x \geq 0$$
$$y \geq 0$$
$$x + 3y \leq 21$$
$$2x + 3y \leq 24$$
$$2x + y \leq 16$$

8. Find the minimum and maximum of $V = 5x + 8y$, subject to:

$$x \geq 0$$
$$y \geq 0$$
$$3x + y \leq 12$$
$$2x + 3y \leq 15$$
$$x + y \geq 2$$

9. Find the minimum and maximum of $V = 80x + 120y$, subject to:

$$x \geq 0$$
$$y \geq 0$$
$$2x + 3y \geq 6$$
$$x + 3y \leq 21$$
$$2x + 3y \leq 24$$
$$2x + y \leq 16$$

---

10. Dr. Borza's problem in feeding her animals was stated in Example 3 of Section 5.2 and solved in Problem 3 of this section. Things have changed. Dr. Borza is no longer able to get neatly sorted packages of meat scraps and mixed scraps for her animals. Instead she has to buy unsorted table scraps from two neighborhoods of a nearby city: SoHo and the East Village.

One hundred grams of SoHo table scraps contain 12 grams of protein, 1 gram of fat and 8 grams of carbohydrates.

One hundred grams of East Village table scraps contain 4 grams of protein, 10 grams of fat, and 22 grams of carbohydrates.

Dr. Borza's ideas on nutrition have changed a little, too. She now wants the daily diet of each of her animals to include at least 56 grams of protein, at least 24 grams of fat, and at most 134 grams of carbohydrates.

The cost of 100 grams of SoHo scraps is $2.10 and the cost of 100 grams of East Village scraps is $.60.

If Dr. Borza's animals are to have the diet she wants for them at minimum cost, how many hundred grams of SoHo and East Village scraps are required?

Apply the rules for solving linear programming problems geometrically to find the optimum solution of the problem you formulated in the following exercises of Section 5.2:

11. Exercise 7   **12.** Exercise 8   **13.** Exercise 9

14. Exercise 10   **15.** Exercise 11   **16.** Exercise 12

5.5 THE SIMPLEX METHOD

We now want to give an algebraic approach to linear programming. Because real-world problems often involve a hundred or so variables and many hundreds of constraints, a graph-drawing approach is impossible. The corner principle still applies, but it is necessary to define "corner" in an algebraic way. Having done that, we can locate all the corners, separate out the feasible corners, calculate the objective variable at each feasible corner, and find the optimal solution if there is one.

This makes it sound easy. It is, but not if you do the corner-searching the brute force way. There are troubles at each stage when you just forge ahead:

1. Locating a corner requires solving a system of equations, and there may be many to solve. For example, if there are 7 variables and 15 constraints, which is a *small* real-world problem, there are 6435 corners to locate.

2. Suppose you have found some thousands of corners. Which are the feasible ones? Only a fraction of them, usually. Without a graph to help, they are hard to find.

3. Once you have located all the feasible corners, you have to calculate the objective variable at each one and compare them all. If, at the end, you discover that the *second* of a few thousand feasible corners gave the optimal solution, you feel like a parrot killed with a broom.

What is really needed (after we have an algebraic definition of "corner") is a method that is clever in two ways at once: clever at locating the feasible corners, and clever at searching through them until the optimal one is found. If the method is really clever, it will tell you to *stop* as soon as you find the optimal solution. (If you find it early in the game, you benefit.)

There is such a method, and it is called *simplex*. As the name suggests, the method is simple. It is also fiendishly clever.

To show how simplex works, we will redo the Sunpower problem that was solved by the profit-line method in Section 5.3. The problem is to find the solution (x, y) of the system

$$\tfrac{13}{3}x + \tfrac{26}{3}y \le 520$$

$$\tfrac{26}{3}x + \tfrac{13}{3}y \le 520$$

$$x \ge 0 \quad \text{and} \quad y \ge 0$$

that maximizes the objective variable

$$P = 50x + 70y$$

Preparing for Simplex

Simplex works with equations, not with inequalities. As a preparatory step, we therefore replace all the inequalities in the problem (except for $x \ge 0$ and $y \ge 0$) by equations. This is easy to do: we replace the first inequality in the system by

$$\tfrac{13}{3}x + \tfrac{26}{3}y + u = 520$$

for some $u \ge 0$ and the second inequality by

$$\tfrac{26}{3}x + \tfrac{13}{3}y + v = 520$$

for some $v \ge 0$. The variables u and v are called *slack variables* because they take up the slack (that is, make up the difference) between the left and right sides of the two inequalities.

Our linear programming problem now looks like this:

Maximize

$$P = 50x + 70y$$

subject to the nonnegativity conditions

$$x \geq 0$$
$$y \geq 0$$
$$u \geq 0$$
$$v \geq 0$$

and the constraint equations

$$\tfrac{13}{3}x + \tfrac{26}{3}y + u = 520$$
$$\tfrac{26}{3}x + \tfrac{13}{3}y + v = 520$$

Before we can proceed with the solution, we need an algebraic way to locate corners. This is as follows: *to locate a corner, set any two of the four variables x, y, u, v equal to zero.* You can check this rule by looking at the results in Figure 5.19 (which is simply a redrawn version of Figure 5.11 with the labeling changed). One corner is the origin: $x = y = 0$. The constraint equations show that $u = 0$ is the line

$$\tfrac{13}{3}x + \tfrac{26}{3}y = 520$$

and that $v = 0$ is the line

$$\tfrac{26}{3}x + \tfrac{13}{3}y = 520$$

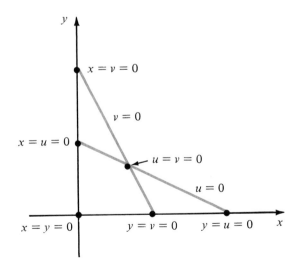

FIGURE 5.19

These two lines are shown in Figure 5.19. Their intersection is the corner $u = v = 0$. We say that u and v are the *corner variables* for that corner. Similarly, x and y are the corner variables for the origin. The other corners in the figure are also marked with their corner variables. Notice that two of the corners ($x = v = 0$ and $y = u = 0$) are not in the feasible region. We will see what happens to these corners when we apply the simplex method.

Start-up of Simplex

There is one corner at which all four variables are known and do not have to be calculated. This corner is the origin. There we have

$$x = y = 0 \qquad u = v = 520$$

The objective variable $P = 50x + 70y$ is really a fifth variable in the problem, and it is known at that corner, too:

$$P(0, 0) = 50 \cdot 0 + 70 \cdot 0 = 0$$

We get simplex started by noting that any increase in either x or y will increase the objective variable (or profit) P. Since y has a larger coefficient than x (70 instead of 50), the variable to increase is y.

Let's increase y as much as the constraints allow us to. If the constraints allow us to increase y indefinitely—which they do not, in this problem—then the feasible region is unbounded. If the feasible region is bounded, then increasing y as much as we can should take us from $(0, 0)$ to a new feasible corner.

To check this out, we set $x = 0$ in the two constraint equations. This gives:

$$\tfrac{26}{3}y + u = 520$$

$$\tfrac{13}{3}y + v = 520$$

The first of these equations says that we can increase y to 60. (At that point, $u = 0$. If $y > 60$, then $u < 0$, which is not allowed.) The second equation says that we can increase y to 120. (At that point, $v = 0$.)

Conclusion: We can increase y from 0 to 60. When we do so, we reach the corner

$$x = u = 0$$

At this corner ($x = 0$, $y = 60$) the objective variable

$$P(0, 60) = 50(0) + 70(60) = 4200$$

which is a big improvement over the value at $(0, 0)$. But it is not the optimal solution. How does simplex carry on from here? The answer is what makes the simplex method clever.

Why Simplex Is Clever

The objective variable $P = 50x + 70y$ was expressed in terms of the corner variables x and y at $(0, 0)$. Therefore we saw at once that P could be increased by increasing y.

To keep simplex working, we again put ourselves in a situation where there is no possible doubt about what to do next. We are now at the corner $(x, y) = (0, 60)$, where the corner variables are x and u. (In other words: $x = u = 0$ corresponds to $x = 0$ and $y = 60$). *We express P in terms of the corner variables x and u.* This is done by means of the constraint equation

$$\tfrac{13}{3}x + \tfrac{26}{3}y + u = 520$$

which gives us

$$y = 60 - \tfrac{1}{2}x - \tfrac{3}{26}u$$

Since $P = 50x + 70y$, we find that:

$$P = 15x - \tfrac{105}{13}u + 4200$$

(*Check:* $x = u = 0$ gives $P = 4200$.)

We see at once that the way to increase P is to increase x. Notice that we do not want to increase u since doing so would decrease P.

How much can we increase x? We look at the constraint equations. The first equation has been rewritten as

$$y = 60 - \tfrac{1}{2}x - \tfrac{3}{26}u$$

and we make use of this in rewriting the second constraint equation as

$$v = 260 - \tfrac{13}{2}x - \tfrac{1}{2}u$$

Set $u = 0$. Then the rewritten constraint equations become

$$y = 60 - \tfrac{1}{2}x$$

$$v = 260 - \tfrac{13}{2}x$$

The first of these equations says that we can increase x up to 120. (At that point, $y = 0$. If $x > 120$, then $y < 0$, which is not allowed.) The second equation says that we can increase x to 40. (At that point, $v = 0$).

Conclusion: We can increase x from 0 to 40 and no further. At $x = 40$, $u = 0$. Since we have had $u = 0$ throughout this search for an improved corner, we have reached the corner

$$u = v = 0$$

Has this helped? To find out, we express P in terms of the corner variables u and v. This is done by rewriting the two constraint equations as

$$x = 40 - \tfrac{1}{13}u - \tfrac{2}{13}v$$

$$y = 40 - \tfrac{2}{13}u - \tfrac{1}{13}v$$

Since $P = 50x + 70y$, we have

$$P = 4800 - \tfrac{190}{13}u - \tfrac{170}{13}v$$

At $u = v = 0$, the objective variable $P = 4800$. To move to a new corner, we would have to increase either u or v. But any such increase would decrease P. Therefore $u = v = 0$ is the optimal corner, and $P = 4800$ is the optimal solution.

The result checks with the solution we found in Section 5.3. More significantly, we see that

>   simplex told us how to keep going

>   simplex told us when to stop

Simplex is just as clever as was claimed. Notice, by the way, that the nonfeasible corners in Figure 5.19 ($x = v = 0$ and $y = u = 0$) never entered the simplex calculations. The reason is that simplex never led us out of the feasible region. Simplex never wastes our time.

Speaking of time-wasting, we have been doing simplex the long way to make sure it was understandable. Now that the method is clear, we will redo the same problem efficiently, using matrices.

Saying Simplex with Matrices

To put the Sunpower problem (or any linear programming problem) in matrix form, we must: (1) replace inequalities by equations through introducing slack variables, and (2) include the definition of the objective variable in the system of equations. In the Sunpower case, the problem is to find nonnegative values of x, y, u, and v *satisfying*

$$\tfrac{13}{3}x + \tfrac{26}{3}y + u \qquad\qquad = 520$$

$$\tfrac{26}{3}x + \tfrac{13}{3}y \qquad + v \qquad = 520$$

$$-50x - 70y \qquad\qquad + P = 0$$

and *maximizing* $P = 50x + 70y$.

The augmented matrix of the system of equations is called the *initial matrix*. We will find it helpful to label the rows and columns of the initial matrix:

$$
\begin{array}{c}
 \\
u \\
v \\
P
\end{array}
\begin{array}{cccccc}
x & y & u & v & P & \\
\left(\begin{array}{ccccc}
\tfrac{13}{3} & \tfrac{26}{3} & 1 & 0 & 0 & 520 \\
\tfrac{26}{3} & \tfrac{13}{3} & 0 & 1 & 0 & 520 \\
-50 & -70 & 0 & 0 & 1 & 0
\end{array}\right)
\end{array}
$$

Columns 3, 4, and 5 of the matrix form an identity matrix. The variables u, v, and P corresponding to these columns are called *basic variables.* (They also appear as row labels.) The variables x and y corresponding to columns 1 and 2 are called *nonbasic,* or *corner, variables.*

Simplex will now consist of two steps, which we repeat as many times as necessary.

STEP 1 *Find a corner variable to increase.* If there is a negative number in the last row of the initial matrix, then there is a corner variable to increase. Given a choice of negative numbers, as in the example we are now doing, we choose the number of largest absolute value. Since $|-70| > |-50|$, this gives us the second column, or y column. In the next step, y will change from a corner variable to a basic variable. We call y the *incoming variable.*

STEP 2 *Find a new corner variable to take the place of the incoming variable.* Divide the row 1 and row 2 entries of the y column into the corresponding entries of column 6. The entry that yields the smallest positive quotient (the row 1 entry, in our example) is called the *pivot* and is circled. We apply legal row operations to transform the pivot into a 1 and then to clear the pivot column:

$$
\begin{array}{c}
 \\
u \\
v \\
P
\end{array}
\begin{array}{cccccc}
x & y & u & v & P & \\
\frac{13}{3} & \boxed{\frac{26}{3}} & 1 & 0 & 0 & 520 \\
\frac{26}{3} & \frac{13}{3} & 0 & 1 & 0 & 520 \\
-50 & -70 & 0 & 0 & 1 & 0
\end{array}
\quad \frac{3}{26}R_1
$$

$$
\begin{pmatrix}
\frac{1}{2} & 1 & \frac{3}{26} & 0 & 0 & 60 \\
\frac{26}{3} & \frac{13}{3} & 0 & 1 & 0 & 520 \\
-50 & -70 & 0 & 0 & 1 & 0
\end{pmatrix}
\quad
\begin{array}{l}
R_2 - \frac{13}{3}R_1 \\[4pt]
R_3 + 70R_1
\end{array}
$$

$$
\begin{array}{c}
 \\
y \\
v \\
P
\end{array}
\begin{array}{cccccc}
x & y & u & v & P & \\
\frac{1}{2} & 1 & \frac{3}{26} & 0 & 0 & 60 \\
\frac{13}{2} & 0 & -\frac{1}{2} & 1 & 0 & 260 \\
-15 & 0 & \frac{105}{3} & 0 & 1 & 4200
\end{array}
$$

Columns 2, 4, and 5 now form an identity matrix. Therefore the new basic variables are y, v, and P. (Notice that the rows are relabeled to indicate this fact.) The new corner variables are x and u. We call u the *outgoing variable* because it is no longer a basic variable.

The last row of our transformed matrix contains a negative entry in column 1. We therefore repeat step 1 and step 2. The location of the pivot entry (circled) shows us that x is the incoming variable and that v is the outgoing variable. The arrows marked IN and OUT are a shorthand reminder of this:

$$
\begin{array}{c}
\text{IN} \\
\downarrow
\end{array}
$$

$$
\begin{array}{c}
\\
y \\
\text{OUT} \to v \\
P
\end{array}
\begin{pmatrix}
x & y & u & v & P & \\
\frac{1}{2} & 1 & \frac{3}{26} & 0 & 0 & 60 \\
\boxed{\frac{13}{2}} & 0 & -\frac{1}{2} & 1 & 0 & 260 \\
-15 & 0 & \frac{105}{13} & 0 & 1 & 4200
\end{pmatrix}
\begin{array}{l}
\\
\frac{2}{13}R_2 \\
\\
\end{array}
$$

$$
\begin{pmatrix}
\frac{1}{2} & 1 & \frac{3}{26} & 0 & 0 & 60 \\
1 & 0 & -\frac{1}{13} & \frac{2}{13} & 0 & 40 \\
-15 & 0 & \frac{105}{13} & 0 & 1 & 4200
\end{pmatrix}
\begin{array}{l}
R_1 - \frac{1}{2}R_2 \\
\\
R_3 + 15R_2
\end{array}
$$

$$
\begin{array}{c}
\\
y \\
x \\
P
\end{array}
\begin{pmatrix}
x & y & u & v & P & \\
0 & 1 & \frac{2}{13} & -\frac{1}{13} & 0 & 40 \\
1 & 0 & -\frac{1}{13} & \frac{2}{13} & 0 & 40 \\
0 & 0 & \frac{90}{13} & \frac{30}{13} & 1 & 4800
\end{pmatrix}
$$

All the entries in the last row of the matrix are now nonnegative. Step 1 says there is no corner variable to increase. In other words: Simplex has arrived at the optimal solution. The last column of the matrix lists the optimal values of the basic variables y, x, and P in that order: $y = 40$, $x = 40$, and $P = 4800$.

It should be clear that the ideas behind doing ("saying") simplex with matrices are exactly the ones we used in saying simplex without matrices. (If you have any doubts, check it all through. Notice that not every step of the matrix method corresponds to a step of the non-matrix method.) The matrix method is the one to use because you do not have to rethink it every time. You just follow the steps. The matrix method is the one that is programmed into computers for solving linear programming problems with large numbers of variables and constraints.

256   **LINEAR PROGRAMMING**   **CH. 5**

The simplex method as presented here will work only under certain conditions, which we will call first-round conditions:

FIRST-ROUND CONDITIONS

1. The problem must be a maximum problem.

2. The variables and the coefficients of the system must all be nonnegative.

3. The constraints must all be stated with the sign $\leq$.

4. The origin $x = y = 0$ (or, in three variables, $x_1 = x_2 = x_3 = 0$) must be a feasible corner.

Variations of the simplex method can be used to solve linear programming problems that do not meet these conditions. Now that you know the basic method, you should not have any trouble learning the variations. There is not enough here (and this course does not have enough time) to say any more about simplex or about the applications of linear programming. If you want to pursue the subject, J. E. Strum, *Introduction to Linear Programming* (San Francisco: Holden-Day, 1972) is outstanding. It is written with the beginning student in mind.

Before going on to worked-out problems, we want to note that the simplex method can be summarized in two sets of rules:

SIMPLEX PRELIMINARIES

P,1. Make sure that the first-round conditions are satisfied. (If any of them are not satisfied, our method does not apply. The corner-point method of Section 5.4 may work.)

P,2. Introduce slack variables. Set up the initial matrix. Label it; the corner variables are x, y (x_1, x_2, x_3 in three variables); the basic variables are the slack variables and the objective variable.

SIMPLEX IN ACTION

1. Find a corner variable (the incoming variable) to increase.

2. Find a new corner variable (the outgoing variable)

to take the place of the incoming variable. (Circle the pivot entry. The pivot column locates the incoming variable and the pivot row locates the outgoing variable.) Transform the matrix by clearing the pivot column. Relabel the rows. (The incoming variable becomes a basic variable; it takes the place of the outgoing variable.)

3. If the transformed matrix is optimal (no negative entries in the last row, which means that there are no corner variables to increase), then its last column gives the optimal values of the basic variables. Otherwise, return to step 1.

The rules do not say anything about arithmetical errors. They occur frequently. When you think you have an optimal solution, be sure to check. The way to check is to substitute your optimal values for the basic variables in the initial system (the constraint equations, plus the equation defining the objective variable). The corner variables are easy to substitute: they have the value zero. If everything checks, you are all right. If not, go back through the arithmetic until you find your error.

The details of steps 1 and 2 of the rules are given on p. 255. Some of the omitted details are included in Figure 5.20, which is a flow chart version of the rules.

PROBLEM 1   Maximize $P = 7x + 9y$ subject to

$$x \geq 0$$

$$y \geq 0$$

$$3x + 4y \leq 12$$

SOLUTION   We follow our two sets of rules (preliminaries first, then simplex in action):

P,1.   The first-round conditions are satisfied.

P,2.   Introduce a slack variable u. The system

$$\begin{cases} 3x + 4y + u & = 12 \\ -7x - 9y & + P = 0 \end{cases}$$

leads to the initial matrix

$$\begin{array}{c} \\ u \\ P \end{array} \begin{array}{cccc} x & y & u & P \\ \left(\begin{array}{cccc} 3 & 4 & 1 & 0 \\ -7 & -9 & 0 & 1 \end{array} \right. & \left. \begin{array}{c} 12 \\ 0 \end{array} \right) \end{array}$$

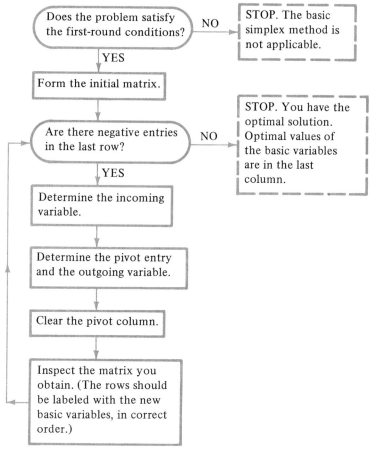

FIGURE 5.20 Flow Chart: Applying the Simplex Method to
Solve a Linear Programming Problem. The first
two boxes on the left—and the first box on the
right—cover the simplex preliminaries (rules P,1
and P,2). The remaining six boxes in the chart correspond to the three steps of "simplex in action."

STEP 1 Since $|-9| > |-7|$, the incoming variable is y.

STEP 2 The only possible choices for the pivot and the outgoing
variable are 4 and u. We have:

$$
\begin{array}{c}
\quad\quad\quad\quad\quad\text{IN} \\
\quad\quad\quad\quad\quad\downarrow \\
\begin{array}{cccc}
x & y & u & P
\end{array} \\
\begin{array}{cc}
\text{OUT} \rightarrow u \\
P
\end{array}
\left(
\begin{array}{cccc}
3 & \boxed{4} & 1 & 0 & 12 \\
-7 & -9 & 0 & 1 & 0
\end{array}
\right)
\end{array}
$$

$$0.25R_1 \quad \begin{pmatrix} 0.75 & 1 & 0.25 & 0 & 3 \\ -7 & -9 & 0 & 1 & 0 \end{pmatrix}$$

$$\begin{array}{c} \\ \\ R_2 + 9R_1 \end{array} \quad \begin{array}{c} \\ y \\ P \end{array} \begin{array}{ccccc} x & y & u & P & \\ \left(0.75 \right. & 1 & 0.25 & 0 & 3 \\ \left. -0.25 \right. & 0 & 2.25 & 1 & 27 \end{array}$$

STEP 3   The transformed matrix is not optimal. Return to step 1.

STEP 1 REPEATED   The only choice for the incoming variable is x.

STEP 2 REPEATED   The pivot is 0.75. The outgoing variable is y. We clear the pivot column:

$$\text{OUT} \rightarrow \begin{array}{c} y \\ P \end{array} \begin{array}{ccccc} x & y & u & P & \\ \left(\boxed{0.75} \right. & 1 & 0.25 & 0 & 3 \\ \left. -0.25 \right. & 0 & 2.25 & 1 & 27 \end{array}$$

$$\tfrac{4}{3}R_1 \quad \begin{pmatrix} 1 & \tfrac{4}{3} & \tfrac{1}{3} & 0 & 4 \\ -0.25 & 0 & 2.25 & 1 & 27 \end{pmatrix}$$

$$R_2 + 0.25R_1 \quad \begin{array}{c} x \\ P \end{array} \begin{array}{ccccc} x & y & u & P & \\ \left(1 \right. & \tfrac{4}{3} & \tfrac{1}{3} & 0 & 4 \\ \left. 0 \right. & \tfrac{1}{3} & \tfrac{7}{3} & 1 & 28 \end{array}$$

STEP 3 REPEATED   The transformed matrix is optimal. The optimal values of the basic variables are $x = 4$, $P = 28$.

Check: Substitute $x = 4$, $P = 28$, $y = u = 0$ into the initial system (step P,2):

$$3x + 4y + u = 12 + 0 + 0 = 12 \ \checkmark$$

$$-7x - 9y + P = -28 - 0 + 28 = 0 \ \checkmark$$

PROBLEM 2   Maximize $P = 14x + 15y$ subject to:

$$x \geq 0$$
$$y \geq 0$$
$$2x + 5y \leq 19$$
$$7x + 3y \leq 23$$

SOLUTION   Again we follow our rules.

P,1. The first-round conditions are satisfied.

P,2. We introduce the slack variables u and v and have the initial system:

$$2x + 5y + u \qquad\qquad = 19$$
$$7x + 3y \qquad + v \qquad = 23$$
$$-14x - 15y \qquad\qquad + P = 0$$

The initial matrix is:

$$
\begin{array}{c}
\\
u \\
v \\
P
\end{array}
\begin{array}{c}
\begin{array}{ccccc}
x & y & u & v & P
\end{array} \\
\left(
\begin{array}{ccccc|c}
2 & 5 & 1 & 0 & 0 & 19 \\
7 & 3 & 0 & 1 & 0 & 23 \\
-14 & -15 & 0 & 0 & 1 & 0
\end{array}
\right)
\end{array}
$$

STEP 1   The incoming variable is y.

STEP 2   The pivot is 5, which means that the outgoing variable is u. We transform the matrix by clearing the pivot column:

$$
\begin{array}{c}
\\
\text{OUT} \rightarrow u \\
v \\
P
\end{array}
\begin{array}{c}
\begin{array}{ccccc}
x & \overset{\text{IN}}{\underset{\downarrow}{y}} & u & v & P
\end{array} \\
\left(
\begin{array}{ccccc|c}
2 & \boxed{5} & 1 & 0 & 0 & 19 \\
7 & 3 & 0 & 1 & 0 & 23 \\
-14 & -15 & 0 & 0 & 1 & 0
\end{array}
\right)
\end{array}
\quad \boxed{0.2\mathrm{R}_1}
$$

$$
\left(
\begin{array}{ccccc|c}
0.4 & 1 & 0.2 & 0 & 0 & 3.8 \\
7 & 3 & 0 & 1 & 0 & 23 \\
-14 & -15 & 0 & 0 & 1 & 0
\end{array}
\right)
\quad
\begin{array}{l}
\mathrm{R}_2 - 3\mathrm{R}_1 \\
\mathrm{R}_3 + 15\mathrm{R}_1
\end{array}
$$

$$\begin{array}{c} & x & y & u & v & P \\ y & \begin{pmatrix} 0.4 & 1 & 0.2 & 0 & 0 & 3.8 \\ 5.8 & 0 & -0.6 & 1 & 0 & 11.6 \\ -8 & 0 & 3 & 0 & 1 & 57 \end{pmatrix} \\ \begin{array}{c} v \\ P \end{array} & \end{array}$$

STEP 3 The transformed matrix is not optimal. Return to step 1.

STEP 1 REPEATED The incoming variable is x.

STEP 2 REPEATED The pivot is 5.8 and the outgoing variable is v. We clear the pivot column:

IN
↓

$$\begin{array}{cc} & x \quad y \quad\quad u \quad\quad v \quad P \\ y & \begin{pmatrix} 0.4 & 1 & 0.2 & 0 & 0 & 3.8 \\ (5.8) & 0 & -0.6 & 1 & 0 & 11.6 \\ -8 & 0 & 3 & 0 & 1 & 57 \end{pmatrix} \end{array}$$

OUT → v ... $\frac{5}{29}R_2$

$$\begin{pmatrix} 0.4 & 1 & 0.2 & 0 & 0 & 3.8 \\ 1 & 0 & -\frac{3}{29} & \frac{5}{29} & 0 & 2 \\ -8 & 0 & 3 & 0 & 1 & 57 \end{pmatrix} \quad \begin{array}{l} R_1 - 0.4R_2 \\ \\ R_3 + 8R_2 \end{array}$$

$$\begin{array}{c} & x & y & u & v & P \\ y & \begin{pmatrix} 0 & 1 & \frac{7}{29} & -\frac{2}{29} & 0 & 3 \\ 0 & 0 & -\frac{3}{29} & \frac{5}{29} & 0 & 2 \\ 1 & 0 & \frac{63}{29} & \frac{40}{29} & 1 & 73 \end{pmatrix} \\ \begin{array}{c} x \\ P \end{array} & \end{array}$$

STEP 3 REPEATED The transformed matrix is optimal. The optimal values of the basic variables are: $y = 3$, $x = 2$, $P = 73$.

Check: Substitute $y = 3$, $x = 2$, $P = 73$, $u = v = 0$ in the initial system:

$$2x + 5y + u = 4 + 15 + 0 = 19 \; ✔$$
$$7x + 3y + v = 14 + 9 + 0 = 23 \; ✔$$
$$-14x - 15y + P = -28 - 45 + 73 = 0 \; ✔$$

Problem 3 is our first example of a linear programming problem in three variables.

PROBLEM 3   Maximize $P = 5x_1 + 6x_2 + 8x_3$ subject to:

$$x_1 \geq 0$$
$$x_2 \geq 0$$
$$x_3 \geq 0$$
$$x_1 + x_2 + x_3 \leq 4$$
$$2x_1 + x_2 + x_3 \leq 5$$
$$x_1 + x_2 + 2x_3 \leq 6$$

SOLUTION   Our rules apply very nicely to the three-variable case:
P,1.   The first-round conditions are satisfied.
P,2.   We introduce the slack variables $u, v,$ and w. The initial system is

$$
\begin{aligned}
x_1 + x_2 + x_3 + u &= 4 \\
2x_1 + x_2 + x_3 + v &= 5 \\
x_1 + x_2 + 2x_3 + w &= 6 \\
-5x_1 - 6x_2 - 8x_3 + P &= 0
\end{aligned}
$$

and the initial matrix is

	x_1	x_2	x_3	u	v	w	P	
u	1	1	1	1	0	0	0	4
v	2	1	1	0	1	0	0	5
w	1	1	2	0	0	1	0	6
P	-5	-6	-8	0	0	0	1	0

STEP 1   The incoming variable is x_3.

STEP 2   The pivot is 2 and the outgoing variable is w. We clear the pivot column:

	x_1	x_2	x_3	u	v	w	P		
u	1	1	1	1	0	0	0	4	
v	2	1	1	0	1	0	0	5	
OUT → w	1	1	②	0	0	1	0	6	$0.5R_3$
P	-5	-6	-8	0	0	0	1	0	

IN ↓ (x_3)

$$\begin{pmatrix} 1 & 1 & 1 & 1 & 0 & 0 & 0 & 4 \\ 2 & 1 & 1 & 0 & 1 & 0 & 0 & 5 \\ 0.5 & 0.5 & 1 & 0 & 0 & 0.5 & 0 & 3 \\ -5 & -6 & -8 & 0 & 0 & 0 & 1 & 0 \end{pmatrix} \begin{array}{l} R_1 - R_3 \\ R_2 - R_3 \\ \\ R_4 + 8R_3 \end{array}$$

$$\begin{array}{c c c c c c c c} & x_1 & x_2 & x_3 & u & v & w & P \\ u & 0.5 & 0.5 & 0 & 1 & 0 & -0.5 & 0 & 1 \\ v & 1.5 & 0.5 & 0 & 0 & 1 & -0.5 & 0 & 2 \\ x_3 & 0.5 & 0.5 & 1 & 0 & 0 & 0.5 & 0 & 3 \\ P & -1 & -2 & 0 & 0 & 0 & 4 & 1 & 24 \end{array}$$

STEP 3 Since the transformed matrix is not optimal, we return to step 1.

STEP 1 REPEATED The incoming variable is x_2.

STEP 2 REPEATED The pivot is 0.5 and the outgoing variable is u. We transform the matrix by clearing the pivot column:

$$\begin{array}{c c c c c c c c} & & \text{IN} & & & & & \\ & & \downarrow & & & & & \\ & x_1 & x_2 & x_3 & u & v & w & P \\ \text{OUT} \to u & 0.5 & (0.5) & 0 & 1 & 0 & -0.5 & 0 & 1 \\ v & 1.5 & 0.5 & 0 & 0 & 1 & -0.5 & 0 & 2 \\ x_3 & 0.5 & 0.5 & 1 & 0 & 0 & 0.5 & 0 & 3 \\ P & -1 & -2 & 0 & 0 & 0 & 4 & 1 & 24 \end{array} \quad 2R_1$$

$$\begin{pmatrix} 1 & 1 & 0 & 2 & 0 & -1 & 0 & 2 \\ 1.5 & 0.5 & 0 & 0 & 1 & -0.5 & 0 & 2 \\ 0.5 & 0.5 & 1 & 0 & 0 & 0.5 & 0 & 3 \\ -1 & -2 & 0 & 0 & 0 & 4 & 1 & 24 \end{pmatrix} \begin{array}{l} \\ R_2 - 0.5R_1 \\ R_3 - 0.5R_1 \\ R_4 + 2R_1 \end{array}$$

$$\begin{array}{c c c c c c c c} & x_1 & x_2 & x_3 & u & v & w & P \\ x_2 & 1 & 1 & 0 & 2 & 0 & -1 & 0 & 2 \\ v & 1 & 0 & 0 & -1 & 1 & 1 & 0 & 1 \\ x_3 & 0 & 0 & 1 & -1 & 0 & 1 & 0 & 2 \\ P & 1 & 0 & 0 & 4 & 0 & 2 & 1 & 28 \end{array}$$

STEP 3 REPEATED   The transformed matrix is optimal. The optimal values of the basic variables are: $x_2 = 2$, $v = 1$, $x_3 = 2$, $P = 28$.

Check: Substitute $x_2 = 2$, $v = 1$, $x_3 = 2$, $P = 28$, $x_1 = u = w = 0$ in the initial system:

$$x_1 + x_2 + x_3 + u = 0 + 2 + 2 + 0 = 4 \ ✔$$
$$2x_1 + x_2 + x_3 + v = 0 + 2 + 2 + 1 = 5 \ ✔$$
$$x_1 + x_2 + 2x_3 + w = 0 + 2 + 4 + 0 = 6 \ ✔$$
$$-5x_1 - 6x_2 - 8x_3 + P = -0 - 12 - 16 + 28 = 0 \ ✔$$

EXERCISES *for Section 5.5*

In each of the following cases: Does the problem meet the four first-round conditions stated on p. 257? If not, why not?

1. Maximize $P = 24x + 36y$, subject to:

$$x \geq 0$$
$$y \geq 0$$
$$2x + 2y \leq 9$$
$$3x + 2y \leq 10$$

2. Maximize $P = 24x + 36y$, subject to:

$$x \geq 0$$
$$y \geq 0$$
$$3x + 2y \leq 6$$
$$2x + 4y \leq 21$$
$$3x + 2y \geq 24$$
$$3x + 2y \leq 16$$

3. Maximize $P = 24x + 36y$, subject to:

$$x \geq 3$$
$$y \geq 0$$
$$7x + 8y \leq 16$$
$$3x + 11y \leq 13$$

4. Maximize $P = 24x + 36y$, subject to:

$$x \geq 0$$
$$y \geq 0$$
$$17x + 58y \leq 202$$
$$221x - 234y \leq 5886$$

5. Minimize $P = 24x + 36y$, subject to:

$$x \geq 0$$
$$y \geq 0$$
$$8x + 7y \leq 24$$
$$13x + 17y \leq 169$$

When we say simplex with matrices, we must: (1) replace inequalities by equations through introducing slack variables; (2) include the definition of the objective variable in the system of equations; and (3) write the initial matrix—that is, the augmented matrix of the system of equations resulting from operations (1) and (2).

Do these three things for each of the following problems. *Do not try to solve any of these problems.* Notice that your answer should be a 3 × 6 matrix in each case. Columns 3, 4, and 5 of the matrix should form an identity matrix.

6. Maximize $P = 5x + 4y$, subject to:

$$x \geq 0$$
$$y \geq 0$$
$$6x + y \leq 66$$
$$x + 6y \leq 48$$

7. Maximize $P = 13x + 6y$, subject to:

$$x \geq 0$$
$$y \geq 0$$
$$3x + 8y \leq 32$$
$$2x + 7y \leq 31$$

8. Maximize $P = 94x + 804y$, subject to:

$$x \geq 0$$
$$y \geq 0$$
$$9x + 7y \leq 22$$
$$7x + 2y \leq 17$$

9. Maximize $P = 45x + 110y$, subject to:

$$x \geq 0$$
$$y \geq 0$$
$$2x + 5y \leq 95$$
$$6x + 7y \leq 56$$

The simplex method can be applied to each of the following problems. In each case: (1) form the initial matrix; (2) identify the basic variables; and (3) identify the nonbasic or corner variables.

10. Maximize $P = 11x + 13y$, subject to:

$$x \geq 0$$
$$y \geq 0$$
$$8x + 7y \leq 19$$

11. Maximize $P = 76x + 85y$, subject to:

$$x \geq 0$$
$$y \geq 0$$
$$9x + 29y \leq 58$$

12. Maximize $P = 17x + 28y$, subject to:

$$x \geq 0$$
$$y \geq 0$$
$$5x + 4y \leq 25$$
$$2x + 3y \leq 13$$

13. Maximize $P = 0.4x + 0.6y$, subject to:

$$x \geq 0$$
$$y \geq 0$$
$$4x + 2y \leq 8$$
$$x + y \leq 6$$

14. Maximize $P = 12x + 24y$, subject to:

$$x \geq 0$$
$$y \geq 0$$
$$x + 2y \leq 3$$
$$3x + 4y \leq 5$$
$$6x + 7y \leq 8$$

15. Maximize $P = 2x_1 + 3x_2 + 4x_3$, subject to:

$$x_1 \geq 0$$
$$x_2 \geq 0$$
$$x_3 \geq 0$$
$$2x_1 + 3x_2 + 4x_3 \leq 27$$
$$3x_1 + 2x_2 + 2x_3 \leq 39$$

16. Maximize $P = 0.4x_1 + 0.2x_2 + 0.3x_3$, subject to:

$$x_1 \geq 0$$
$$x_2 \geq 0$$
$$x_3 \geq 0$$
$$2x_1 + 3x_2 + 2x_3 \leq 19$$
$$3x_1 + 4x_2 + 2x_3 \leq 21$$

Write the linear programming problem corresponding to each of the following initial matrices. In assigning variables, use x, y, and P for a two-variable problem and x_1, x_2, x_3, and P for a three-variable problem.

17.
$$\begin{pmatrix} 8 & 2 & 1 & 0 & 7 \\ -9 & -29 & 0 & 1 & 0 \end{pmatrix}$$

18.
$$\begin{pmatrix} 8 & 8 & 1 & 0 & 18 \\ -6 & -30 & 0 & 1 & 0 \end{pmatrix}$$

19.
$$\begin{pmatrix} 4 & 2 & 1 & 0 & 0 & 45 \\ 7 & 3 & 0 & 1 & 0 & 73 \\ -8 & -61 & 0 & 0 & 1 & 0 \end{pmatrix}$$

20.
$$\begin{pmatrix} 3 & 2 & 1 & 0 & 0 & 47 \\ 11 & 14 & 0 & 1 & 0 & 53 \\ -42 & -99 & 0 & 0 & 1 & 0 \end{pmatrix}$$

21.
$$\begin{pmatrix} 12 & 3 & 1 & 0 & 0 & 0 & 32 \\ 7 & 98 & 0 & 1 & 0 & 0 & 88 \\ 55 & 86 & 0 & 0 & 1 & 0 & 211 \\ -157 & -822 & 0 & 0 & 0 & 1 & 0 \end{pmatrix}$$

22.

$$\begin{pmatrix} 63 & 77 & 1 & 0 & 0 & 0 & 326 \\ 80 & 59 & 0 & 1 & 0 & 0 & 710 \\ 46 & 74 & 0 & 0 & 1 & 0 & 692 \\ -536 & -1091 & 0 & 0 & 0 & 1 & 0 \end{pmatrix}$$

23.

$$\begin{pmatrix} 2 & 7 & 6 & 1 & 0 & 0 & 0 & 33 \\ 6 & 0 & 7 & 0 & 1 & 0 & 0 & 35 \\ 6 & 5 & 7 & 0 & 0 & 1 & 0 & 48 \\ -8 & -9 & -10 & 0 & 0 & 0 & 1 & 0 \end{pmatrix}$$

24.

$$\begin{pmatrix} 1 & 3 & 1 & 1 & 0 & 0 & 0 & 64 \\ 3 & 5 & 8 & 0 & 1 & 0 & 0 & 79 \\ 5 & 4 & 1 & 0 & 0 & 1 & 0 & 53 \\ -8 & -4 & -8 & 0 & 0 & 0 & 1 & 0 \end{pmatrix}$$

In each of the following cases, identify: the incoming variable; the pivot; the outgoing variable.

25.

$$\begin{array}{c} \\ u \\ P \end{array}\begin{array}{cccc} x & y & u & P \\ \end{array}$$

$$\begin{array}{c} u \\ P \end{array}\begin{pmatrix} 1 & 4 & 1 & 0 & 13 \\ -8 & -4 & 0 & 1 & 0 \end{pmatrix}$$

26.

$$\begin{array}{ccccc} x & y & u & P \\ \end{array}$$

$$\begin{array}{c} u \\ P \end{array}\begin{pmatrix} 8 & 7 & 1 & 0 & 56 \\ -9 & -4 & 0 & 1 & 0 \end{pmatrix}$$

27.

$$\begin{array}{cccccc} x & y & u & v & P \\ \end{array}$$

$$\begin{array}{c} u \\ v \\ P \end{array}\begin{pmatrix} 1 & 8 & 1 & 0 & 0 & 24 \\ 3 & 6 & 0 & 1 & 0 & 39 \\ -9 & -8 & 0 & 0 & 1 & 0 \end{pmatrix}$$

28.

$$\begin{array}{cccccc} x & y & u & v & P \\ \end{array}$$

$$\begin{array}{c} u \\ v \\ P \end{array}\begin{pmatrix} 3 & 6 & 1 & 0 & 0 & 12 \\ 6 & 7 & 0 & 1 & 0 & 73 \\ -4 & -5 & 0 & 0 & 1 & 0 \end{pmatrix}$$

29.

	x	y	u	v	w	P	
u	29	35	1	0	0	0	350
v	12	17	0	1	0	0	340
w	28	40	0	0	1	0	280
P	-9	-92	0	0	0	1	0

30.

	x_1	x_2	x_3	u	v	P	
u	3	3	6	1	0	0	29
v	4	0	3	0	1	0	38
P	-9	-4	-12	0	0	1	0

31.

	x_1	x_2	x_3	u	v	w	P	
u	6	5	5	1	0	0	0	66
v	3	5	4	0	1	0	0	36
w	4	9	5	0	0	1	0	48
P	-8	-5	-7	0	0	0	1	0

Carry through steps 1 and 2 of simplex for each of the following initial matrices. (Do not repeat the steps. That is: Do not try to obtain the optimal matrix of the problem.) Then explain which variables are the *old* corner variables and basic variables, and which are the *new* corner variables and basic variables.

32.
$$\begin{pmatrix} 8 & 4 & 1 & 0 & 24 \\ -2 & -6 & 0 & 1 & 0 \end{pmatrix}$$

33.
$$\begin{pmatrix} 6 & 6 & 1 & 0 & 36 \\ -9 & -2 & 0 & 1 & 0 \end{pmatrix}$$

34.
$$\begin{pmatrix} 9 & 7 & 1 & 0 & 0 & 49 \\ 2 & 6 & 0 & 1 & 0 & 48 \\ -38 & -41 & 0 & 0 & 1 & 0 \end{pmatrix}$$

35.
$$\begin{pmatrix} 2 & 8 & 1 & 0 & 0 & 18 \\ 2 & 4 & 0 & 1 & 0 & 16 \\ -16 & -13 & 0 & 0 & 1 & 0 \end{pmatrix}$$

36.

$$\begin{pmatrix} 4 & 9 & 8 & 1 & 0 & 0 & 0 & 20 \\ 3 & 6 & 9 & 0 & 1 & 0 & 0 & 12 \\ 1 & 7 & 2 & 0 & 0 & 1 & 0 & 6 \\ -9 & -2 & -3 & 0 & 0 & 0 & 1 & 0 \end{pmatrix}$$

Use the simplex method to:

37. Maximize $P = 29x + 19y$, subject to:

$$x \geq 0$$
$$y \geq 0$$
$$6x + 18y \leq 54$$

38. Maximize $P = 4x + 5y$, subject to:

$$x \geq 0$$
$$y \geq 0$$
$$11x + 22y \leq 66$$

39. Maximize $P = 5x + 9y$, subject to:

$$x \geq 0$$
$$y \geq 0$$
$$3x + 4y \leq 24$$
$$x + 2y \leq 10$$

40. Maximize $P = 21x + 31y$, subject to:

$$x \geq 0$$
$$y \geq 0$$
$$2x + 3y \leq 15$$
$$3x + y \leq 12$$

41. Maximize $P = 34x_1 + 59x_2 + 51x_3$, subject to:

$$x_1 \geq 0$$
$$x_2 \geq 0$$
$$x_3 \geq 0$$
$$x_1 + x_2 + x_3 \leq 4$$
$$2x_1 + x_2 + x_3 \leq 5$$
$$x_1 + x_2 + 2x_3 \leq 6$$

42. Maximize $P = 2x_1 + 5x_2 + 3x_3$, subject to:

$$x_1 \geq 0$$
$$x_2 \geq 0$$
$$x_3 \geq 0$$
$$x_1 + 6x_2 + 3x_3 \leq 16$$
$$x_1 + 2x_2 + 4x_3 \leq 24$$
$$x_1 + 3x_2 + x_3 \leq 12$$

43. Maximize $P = 6x_1 + 5x_2 + 2x_3$, subject to:

$$x_1 \geq 0$$
$$x_2 \geq 0$$
$$x_3 \geq 0$$
$$x_1 + 3x_2 + 2x_3 \leq 6$$
$$x_1 + 2x_2 + 4x_3 \leq 8$$
$$3x_1 + 2x_2 + 4x_3 \leq 12$$

---

44. Fakes Unlimited is a group of three artists who paint and sell fake modern paintings: simulated Rothkos, simulated Pollocks, and simulated Mondrians. The three artists, whom we will call A, B and C, cooperate on each painting. The table shows the number of hours that each artist spends on each painting:

	A	B	C
Rothko	1	2	1
Pollock	6	3	3
Mondrian	1	1	1

Artist A is willing to put in as many as 70 hours per week; artist B, as many as 40 hours; and artist C, up to 30 hours. The profits of their labors are $600 for a Rothko, $900 for a Pollock, and $200 for a Mondrian. If Fakes Unlimited wants to maximize its profits over a 30-week period, how many simulations of each type does simplex say it should produce and what will the maximum profit be?

45. Wyotex Energy Corporation is interested in building its corporate image. Following an ad agency's advice, Wyotex plans to do its image-building with a media mix: commercial TV, public TV, and print media. The agency has some figures:

1 megabuck spent on TV commercials (very dignified, very soft sell) builds the company's image with 5 million people

1 megabuck spent on public TV (paying for cultural programs, with just a line of credit for Wyotex) builds the company's image with 7 million people

1 megabuck spent on print media (ads explaining how everyone will benefit from higher oil and gas prices) builds the company's image with 13 million people.

Wyotex plans to spend up to 50 megabucks ($50 million) on image-building. Of this money, no more than 30 megabucks will be spent on both kinds of TV. No more than 20 megabucks will be spent on public TV and print media together. No more than 15 megabucks will be spent on print media. Under these management-imposed constraints: How much does simplex say Wyotex should spend on each of the three media, to build the company's image with the largest number of people?

HINT: There are three variables but four constraints. Be sure to introduce four slack variables.

chapter six

PROBABILITY

REAL-WORLD data often gives us an uncertain picture of a real-world problem. The data may be inaccurate, incomplete, or only partly relevant. A knowledge of probability helps us to make reasonable decisions on the basis of uncertain data.

This chapter introduces the basic concepts of probability. There are many examples. Some are real-world examples, and others use ideas that can be applied in real-world situations.

6.1 PROBABILITY MODELS

Probability means *likelihood* in both ordinary language and in mathematics. To make the probability concept more precise—and more useful—we need to define a few key words. These are words from ordinary language, but they are used in a special way in probability.

The first key word is *experiment*. In ordinary language, experiments (in laboratories or elsewhere) are procedures used to test theories. In probability, an experiment is merely an activity whose outcome is observable but not predictable.

EXAMPLES: EXPERIMENTS

1. Tossing a coin once is an experiment.

2. Tossing a coin 10,000 times is an experiment.

3. Selecting a group of 500 people and finding out how many of them smoke is an experiment.

4. Recording the price of wheat in Chicago for 90 days in succession is an experiment. (The results are subject to so many economic, political, and climatic forces that they cannot be predicted.)

Since the experiments we are talking about are probability experiments, we are obviously going to want to talk about the probability, or likelihood, of something happening in each case. To do this, we have to say exactly what item or items of data we want to record. Each individual item of data that may result from an experiment is called an *outcome* of the experiment. (*Outcome* is our second key word.) The collection of all possible outcomes is called the *sample space* of the experiment. (The sample space is so named because it includes a sample of each allowable outcome.)

Before looking at some examples of outcomes and sample spaces, note that the possible outcomes of an experiment are not dictated by the experiment. They are our choice, our way of describing an experiment so that its results are useful.

EXAMPLES: OUTCOMES AND SAMPLE SPACES

1. The outcome of tossing a coin may be H (head) or T (tail). The sample space would then be {H, T}. We denote the sample space of an experiment by the letter S. In the present case, we have

$$S = \{H, T\}$$

2. If two coins are tossed at the same time, the outcomes may be recorded as M (they match: two heads or two tails) or D (they do not match). The sample space would then be

$$S = \{M, D\}$$

Alternately, we might want to record the number of heads: 0, 1, or 2. The sample space for this description of the experiment is

$$S = \{0, 1, 2\}$$

3. If a coin is tossed 10,000 times, we may be interested in the total number of heads. There are 10,001 possible outcomes in the experiment: 0 heads, 1 head, 2 heads, . . . , 10,000 heads. Our sample space is

$$S = \{0, 1, 2, \ldots, 10{,}000\}$$

The very same sample space can be used for recording the total number of tails in the 10,000 tosses. But suppose that we want to record each outcome of the 10,000-toss experiment in the form

$$(n(H), n(T))$$

where $n(H)$ is the total number of heads in the 10,000 tosses and $n(T)$ is the total number of tails. In that case we would have $0 \le n(H) \le 10{,}000$, $0 \le n(T) \le 10{,}000$, and $n(H) + n(T) = 10{,}000$. The sample space would consist of 10,001 ordered pairs:

$$S = \{(0, 10{,}000), (1, 9999), \ldots, (10{,}000, 0)\}$$

4. Wheat farmers, grain dealers, and commodities speculators are interested in the price of wheat in Chicago 90 days from now. That price may be considered to be the outcome of an experiment. (The price will be observable, but it is certainly not predictable.) If it is assumed that the price per bushel will not go lower than 10 cents or higher than $10 (or 1000 cents), then the sample space containing all possible outcomes of the experiment is

$$S = \{10, 11, 12, \ldots, 1000\}$$

5. Rolls-Royces are carefully examined for defects before they are sent out of the factory. The examination process may be thought of as a probability experiment. Possible outcomes are 0, 1, 2, 3, . . . defects. (The three dots indicate that there can be any positive number of defects.) The sample space consists of all nonnegative integers:

$$S = \{0, 1, 2, 3, \ldots\}$$

6. Let's assume that the Rolls-Royce factory classifies its cars as follows, according to the number of inspection defects: G (good—no more than 5 defects); F (fair—6 to 15 defects); M (marginal—16 to 25 defects); J (junked—more than 25 defects). The sample space for this set of outcomes is:

$$S = \{G, F, M, J\}$$

Now we will use the concepts of experiment, outcome, and sample space as a framework for discussing probabilities.

Suppose that an experiment is performed (or imagined). Then every outcome in the sample space S of that experiment has a certain likelihood, or probability, of occurring. If A is one of those outcomes, we will use the symbol $P(A)$ (read "P of A") for the *probability* of A—that is, for the probability that A occurs.

$P(A)$ *will be a number measuring the likelihood that A is the outcome of the experiment.*

In some cases $P(A)$ can be estimated from past results in performing the experiment. This amounts to predicting the future from a knowledge of the past. In probability it is called the *empirical* method.

Suppose, for example, that you have a coin that may or may not be well balanced. Your experiment is to toss the coin. The sample space for each toss is $S = \{H, T\}$. If you toss the coin 80 times and if the outcome is H (heads) 32 of those times, then the fraction

$$\frac{n(H)}{N} = \frac{\text{number of heads}}{\text{number of tosses}} = \frac{32}{80} = .4$$

gives an empirical estimate of the probability that H will be the outcome when you next toss that particular coin. Since $n(H)$ is the *frequency* of heads in N tosses, the fraction $n(H)/N$ is the *relative frequency* of heads in N tosses.

A probability that is defined as a relative frequency is called an *empirical probability*.

DEFINITION   Empirical Probability

The *empirical probability* of an outcome is defined as the *relative frequency* of occurrence of that outcome.

If an outcome A occurs $n(A)$ times in N repetitions of an experiment, this means that the empirical probability $P(A)$ is given by:

$$P(A) = \frac{n(A)}{N}$$

In the example of the coin that is tossed 80 times (with $n(H) = 32$ and $n(T) = 48$), the empirical probability of heads is given by

$$P(H) = \frac{n(H)}{N} = \frac{32}{80} = .4$$

as we have seen, and the empirical probability of tails is given by

$$P(\text{T}) = \frac{n(\text{T})}{N} = \frac{48}{80} = .6$$

Empirical probabilities are the ones to use whenever relative frequency data is available.

EXAMPLE 1: EMPIRICAL PROBABILITIES IN REAL ESTATE SALES

A good real estate broker knows how to sell a house to a solid prospect. If outcomes for solid prospects are recorded as A (sale made) and B (no sale), then the sample space is $S = \{A, B\}$. Sales data for a very successful broker over a period of several months might be:

N (number of solid prospects) 75

$n(A)$ (number of sales made) 48

For that broker, the empirical probability of making a sale to a solid prospect would be

$$P(A) = \frac{n(A)}{N} = \frac{48}{75} = .64$$

Since $n(A) = 48$, then $n(B) = 75 - 48$, or 27. Therefore

$$P(B) = \frac{n(B)}{N} = \frac{27}{75} = .36$$

for that broker.

The empirical approach is based on the idea that an experiment can be repeated under the same conditions. This is certainly the way things work in a coin-tossing experiment: the same coin can be tossed in the same way again and again. By contrast, a real estate broker's clients are not all alike; neither are the properties that the broker sells. Example 1 assumes that it makes sense to ignore the differences when classifying 75 clients as "solid prospects." Experience has shown that such assumptions are reasonable and useful.

Our knowledge of the empirical probability $P(A)$ does not tell us whether or not the broker in Example 1 will sell a house to the next solid prospect. But the fact that $P(A) = .64$ suggests that the broker will sell houses to approximately 64 of the next 100 solid prospects. It is in this sense that an empirical probability is a measure of likelihood.

The relative frequency approach to probability is especially easy to apply when all the outcomes in a sample space are known or assumed to occur with the same frequency. For example, suppose that you toss a perfectly balanced coin. Then the two outcomes H, T in the sample space

$$S = \{H, T\}$$

will occur with the same frequency. If you toss the coin 100 times ($N = 100$), you will then have $n(H) = n(T) = 50$, and

$$P(H) = \frac{n(H)}{N} = \frac{50}{100} = \frac{1}{2}$$

$$P(T) = \frac{n(T)}{N} = \frac{50}{100} = \frac{1}{2}$$

In this case, and in others like it, we say that all the outcomes in the sample space are *equally likely*. Or we may refer to the sample space as an *equally likely sample space*.

The example of tossing a perfectly balanced coin shows how we calculate the probability of an outcome in an equally likely sample space.

DEFINITION   Probability in an Equally Likely Sample Space

If each of the outcomes in a sample space is equally likely, then each outcome has the same probability of occurrence.

If an equally likely sample space contains k outcomes $A_1, A_2, \ldots, A_k$, the definition says that

$$P(A_1) = P(A_2) = \cdots = P(A_k)$$

To evaluate these probabilities, we use the relative frequency approach with imagined data. Imagine that the experiment whose possible outcomes are $A_1, A_2, \ldots, A_k$ is repeated $100k$ times. Then, by the definition of "equally likely," each of the k outcomes occurs 100 times. This is true, for example, of A_1, which gives

$$P(A_1) = \frac{n(A_1)}{N} = \frac{100}{100k} = \frac{1}{k}$$

Since $P(A_1) = P(A_2) = \cdots = P(A_k)$, we have the following rule:

If $S = \{A_1, A_2, \ldots, A_k\}$ is an equally likely sample space, then

$$P(A_1) = P(A_2) = \cdots = P(A_k) = \frac{1}{k}$$

A briefer way to state the probabilities is:

$$P(A_i) = \frac{1}{k} \qquad \text{for } i = 1, 2, \ldots, k$$

Here is an application:

EXAMPLE 2: SELECTING A WINNER IN AN EQUALLY LIKELY SAMPLE SPACE

For a sales promotion, a manufacturer will give a snowmobile to someone in the town of Moulton Bay. There are 376 people in Moulton Bay. Their names are typed on slips of paper, which are then put into a drum. After the drum has been revolved, the slip containing the name of the winner will be selected by a blindfolded manufacturer's representative. Three questions:

Q,1. If you live in Moulton Bay, what is your probability of winning the snowmobile?

Q,2. Eleven people in Moulton Bay have the last name Johnson. What is the probability that the snowmobile winner will be named Johnson?

Q,3. What is the probability that the winner will *not* be named Johnson?

Now for the answers:

A,1. All outcomes of the drawing are equally likely. Since there are 376 possible outcomes, your probability of winning is $\frac{1}{376}$.

A,2. Imagine that the drawing is repeated 376,000 times. Since each of the outcomes is equally likely, the name Johnson will occur

11,000 times. The probability that the winner will be named Johnson is $\frac{11,000}{376,000} = \frac{11}{376}$.

A,3.   There are 365 non-Johnsons in Moulton Bay. As in A,2, let's imagine 376,000 drawings. Among these, names other than Johnson will occur 365,000 times. The probability that the winner is *not* named Johnson is $\frac{365,000}{376,000} = \frac{365}{376}$.

So far we have defined probabilities as relative frequencies. For empirical probabilities, the relative frequencies are based on data. For probabilities in equally likely sample spaces, the relative frequencies are based on *imagined* data.

It is not always convenient, or even possible, to work with the relative frequency approach. A probability that is assigned without reference to actual or imagined frequency data is called a *subjective probability*. There is no formula for calculating or even describing a subjective probability, but the following example will show how such a probability may be arrived at and what it means.

**EXAMPLE 3:   SUBJECTIVE PROBABILITY IN
                     OIL EXPLORATION**

Major oil companies spend tens of millions of dollars drilling offshore wells in certain areas of the world's oceans. Why in those particular areas? Because management has been told some such thing as: "There is a probability of .85 that we will find large pools of oil in offshore tract #1047."

Now that probability of .85 is not based on relative frequency data, for the simple reason that no one has ever drilled in offshore tract #1047 before. It is certainly not based on the assumption that the outcomes of finding or not finding oil are equally likely. Then what is it based on?

The basis for assigning the probability of .85 would (we think) be a careful comparison between the geological structure of tract #1047 and the geological structures of other offshore tracts with known exploration records. Calling such a probability a *subjective probability* indicates that it represents an opinion. But it is an expert's opinion, based on knowledge and experience. The subjective approach to assigning a probability is as logical as any other. And sometimes, as in the oil exploration business, the subjective way is the only possible way to assign a probability to an outcome.

Finally; subjective probabilities are assigned without reference to relative frequency data, but they can be (and usually are) interpreted as relative frequencies. An oil-strike probability of .85 is interpreted by management as: "If we sink 100 wells in circumstances like the present ones, then 85 of those wells will give us good oil strikes."

From what has been said so far, it may seem that probability goes off in three different directions. But the fact that all probabilities can be interpreted as relative frequencies pulls the subject together.

Look at the following list of the fundamental properties that all probabilities have. Alongside each property is the relative frequency interpretation that intuitively justifies including that property in the list.

Property		*Relative Frequency Interpretation*
1.	If A is an outcome in a sample space S, then $$P(A) \geq 0$$	1. In N repetitions of the experiment, A occurs $n(A)$ times. The integer $n(A)$ may be zero, or it may be positive. It cannot be negative. Therefore $P(A) = n(A)/N \geq 0$.
2.	$P(A) \leq 1$	2. If the experiment is repeated N times and A occurs every one of those times, then $n(A) = N$ and $P(A) = N/N = 1$. In all other cases, $n(A) < N$ and $P(A) < 1$.
3.	If a sample space S contains k outcomes: $$S = \{A_1, A_2, \ldots, A_k\}$$ then $$P(A_1) + P(A_2) + \cdots + P(A_k) = 1$$	3. In N repetitions of the experiment, the only possible outcomes are $A_1, A_2, \ldots, A_k$. Therefore $$n(A_1) + n(A_2) + \cdots + n(A_k) = N$$ Dividing both sides of the equation by N gives: $$\frac{n(A_1)}{N} + \frac{n(A_2)}{N} + \cdots + \frac{n(A_k)}{N} = \frac{N}{N} = 1$$ or $$P(A_1) + P(A_2) + \cdots + P(A_k) = 1$$

NOTE: It is convenient to combine property 1 and property 2 by writing

$$0 \leq P(A) \leq 1$$

The meaning of $P(A) = 1$ is that A must happen or is certain. The meaning of $P(A) = 0$ is that A cannot happen or is impossible. Such an outcome may even be omitted from the sample space. For example: In tossing a coin, we might consider three outcomes: H (heads), T (tails), and E (edge). This gives the sample space $S = \{H, T, E\}$. If we regard the outcome E (which would be the coin landing on its edge and staying there) as impossible, we write $P(E) = 0$. Or we may omit E from the sample space. From now on we will say: If an outcome is not listed in the sample space of an experiment, then that outcome has probability 0, relative to that experiment.

At this point let's look carefully at what the subject of probability is about and what it is not about.

It should now be clear that the subject of probability refers only to possible outcomes of experiments. Such experiments may be real or conceptual (that is, they may be carried out or imagined). In either case, they must be describable in terms of outcomes, and therefore in terms of a sample space containing all possible outcomes. Statements like "this smiling child is probably happy" or "the truth will probably never be known" cannot be referred to the experiment–outcome–sample space framework. They are meaningful statements, but they are not part of our subject.

To use probabilities to describe a real-world activity, we must set up a *probability model* for that activity. This is done by following four rules:

RULES FOR SETTING UP A PROBABILITY MODEL

1. Make certain that the activity being described is an *experiment:* observable, but not predictable.

2. Specify the *sample space* of the experiment. That is: List every possible *outcome*.

3. Assign a *probability* to each outcome. These probabilities may be *empirical, equally likely,* or *subjective.*

4. Check out the *fundamental properties* of the probabilities assigned in step 3. Each probability must be ≥ 0 and ≤ 1, and the sum of all the probabilities must be equal to 1.

In symbols, we define a probability model as follows:

DEFINITION   Probability Model

A *probability model* for an experiment is defined by a sample space such as

$$S = \{A_1, A_2, \ldots, A_k\}$$

together with probability assignments $P(A_1)$, $P(A_2), \ldots, P(A_k)$ satisfying:

PROPERTY 1 $0 \leq P(A_i) \leq 1$ for $i = 1, 2, \ldots, k$

PROPERTY 2 $P(A_1) + P(A_2) + \cdots + P(A_k) = 1$

Now let's see how all this works out in practice.

PROBABILITY MODELS: EXAMPLES AND NONEXAMPLES

1. Our sample space for coin-tossing is $S = \{H, T\}$. If we assign the probabilities $P(H) = P(T) = \frac{1}{2}$, then properties 1 and 2 are satisfied and we have a probability model.

2. If $S = \{H, T\}$ and if we assign the probabilities $P(H) = \frac{2}{3}$, $P(T) = \frac{1}{3}$, then properties 1 and 2 are satisfied. We have a second probability model for coin-tossing.

NOTE: Examples 1 and 2 show that we may have two probability models for the same experiment. The model we choose is the one that best describes real-world experience. In tossing a *particular* coin, we may find that our first model fits the facts, or our second, or perhaps a third, with $P(H) = .45$ and $P(T) = .55$.

3. Let's return to the example of Rolls-Royce inspection (p. 276). We use the same space $S = \{G, F, M, J\}$. Suppose that an employee assigns probabilities (based on inspection records, which means that these are empirical probabilities) as follows: $P(G) = .5$, $P(F) = .4$, $P(M) = .3$, $P(J) = .01$. These probabilities satisfy property 1, but they do not satisfy property 2, since

$$P(G) + P(F) + P(M) + P(J) = 1.21$$

Suppose that the records are then restudied and that the new results are $P(G) = .455$, $P(F) = .355$, $P(M) = .189$, $P(J) = .001$. These probabilities again satisfy property 1 and they also satisfy property 2. Since they are the probabilities of outcomes in a sample space, they give us a probability model for Rolls-Royce inspections.

4. The year is moving toward its end. Connie Carpenter, a bank trust officer, has a big chunk of trust department money to invest in common stocks. She feels uncertain about the market but she has been feeling that way for six months and it is time for her to make a move. As a conservative banker, Connie plans to invest in big solid companies—the Dow Jones Industrials, pretty much. Therefore she really cares about where the DJIA (Dow Jones Industrial Average) is going in the next 12 months.

In 1977 the DJIA started out at about 1000 and fell to about 800. Judging the future by the past, Connie's sample space for next year has 3 DJIA outcomes in it: R (rise to 1000), F (fall below 800), J (jiggle around between 800 and 1000). Connie writes:

$$S = \{R, F, J\}$$

For a probability model to guide her investment decisions, she may follow a certain famous expert who assigns the probabilities

$$P(R) = .7 \qquad P(F) = .1 \qquad P(J) = .2$$

These probabilities have properties 1 and 2. Connie has a probability model.

Experts have been known to be wrong, however, so it is prudent to seek other opinions. A second expert assigns:

$$P(R) = .1 \qquad P(F) = .6 \qquad P(J) = .3$$

Properties 1 and 2 are satisfied again. The sample space, together with these probabilities for the outcomes, gives Connie a second perfectly valid probability model.

Connie Carpenter had a clear choice. Since both models were based on subjective probability assignments, she tried to introduce some objectivity by examining the track records of the alleged experts. Each of them had been predicting for over 20 years. Connie had enough material to apply the relative frequency approach in assigning probabilities of correctness to the two experts' readings of the future. She did this and based her investment strategy on the results. Connie knew perfectly well that this careful approach did not guarantee investment success. But she was paid to be cautious, not to be all-knowing. She had been cautious.

1. Two bank tellers each toss a coin to decide who is going to work at the drive-up window that day. What is a good sample space for the experiment?

2. One of the skiers waiting for a chair lift at Waterville Valley is asked how many years she has been skiing. Give a sample space for the experiment.

3. Inspector Callahan of the SFPD (San Francisco Police Department) conducts a probability experiment: For each of 20 nights, he records the number of violent crimes reported to the SFPD between the hours of 9 P.M. and 1 A.M. Give a sample space that describes the inspector's experiment.

4. The worldwide corporation ROOF (Riches of the Ocean Floor) is in the undersea mining business. After discussing the pros and cons of eight promising ocean mining projects, management makes its choice by drawing straws. What sample space describes the straw-drawing experiment?

5. An unsymmetrical coin is tossed 12 times and the number of heads is recorded. Give a sample space for this experiment.

6. Each one of 143 ticket-buyers on TWA's Flight 307 is asked: "Do you wish to sit in the no-smoking section of the aircraft?" The number of yes answers is recorded (and used in making up a seating plan). Construct a sample space for the experiment.

7. Digital Equipment Corporation (DEC) is the leader in minicomputers, and its stock is held by many technologically oriented investors. One of these investors observes and records the price of DEC over a period of 25 stock market days. During that time, DEC moves from 45 to 58. (It goes up, down, and up again. The company is excellent, but the stock is volatile.) Construct a sample space for the investor's experiment.

8. Suppose that the technologically oriented investor in Exercise 7 records not only the daily price of DEC for 25 days, but also the change in price from the preceding day. What sample space would you now use to describe his experiment?

9. The investor described in Exercises 7 and 8 is basically interested only in his profit or loss. He owns 1000 shares of DEC, which he bought at $50. If DEC's price is $55, his profit is $5000. If DEC's price is $48, his loss is $2000. (Commissions and other transaction costs are neglected.) Construct a sample space for the investor's 25-day profit/loss experiment.

10. A bag of marbles contains 10 red marbles and 10 green marbles. (The marbles are alike except for color.) If the marbles are well shaken and one of them is drawn, find the probability that the marble drawn is: (a) red; (b) blue; (c) green; (d) not yellow.

11. What is the probability that the next person you meet was born on a Tuesday?

12. What sample space would you choose for the tossing of a two-headed coin? For each toss, what probability would you assign to the outcome H (heads)? What probability would you assign to the outcome T (tails)?

13. Three-card Monte is a game played with three cards: the Ace of Hearts, the Ace of Diamonds, and the Ace of Spades. The cards are shown to the player by the dealer, and then placed face down on a table. The dealer shifts the three cards about the table with a few deft movements. He then invites a player to say which card is the Ace of Spades. A foolish person assumes that he can follow the movement of the cards, and bets accordingly. He usually loses. A sensible person knows that the dealer's hand is quicker than the player's eye and therefore bets at random. What is the probability that a sensible player will choose the *black* Ace rather than one of the *red* Aces?

14. Election Associates, the political image-building firm, specializes in two types of image-building: the *effective presentation job* (which helps politicians deal with the media) and the *whole new image job* (which helps politicians who want to appeal to totally new voter groups). A survey of Election Associates' work by a team of political scientists has revealed that 100 of the firm's *effective presentation* clients and 100 of their *whole new image* clients benefited (or failed to benefit) as follows:

	Much Better Image	Better Image	No Change in Image	Worse Image	Total Failure
Effective Presentation Jobs	25	32	18	14	11
Whole New Image Jobs	22	30	19	17	12

By taking the relative frequency approach, calculate the probability that the political image of an Election Associates client will:

a. benefit by an effective presentation job
b. not lose by an effective presentation job
c. not be benefited by a whole new image job
d. be improved by a whole new image job

15. The encroachments of agribusiness on the family farm are well known. But the fact is that family farms tend to be more efficient than large corporate-owned farms. (One reason: Family farms are worked by *owners,* not by employees.) A survey of 500 family farms in Iowa showed that 300 of the 500 produced a bushel of wheat at a lower cost than an average agribusiness competitor; 90 produced a bushel of wheat at the same cost as an average agribusiness competitor; and 110 produced a bushel of wheat at a higher cost than an average agribusiness competitor. Assuming that the 500 farms in the survey are representative of family farms in Iowa, use the relative frequency approach to calculate the probabilities that:

a. a family farm is a more efficient wheat-producer than an agribusiness competitor
b. a family farm is at least as efficient a wheat-producer as an agribusiness competitor
c. a family farm is a less efficient wheat-producer than an agribusiness competitor

16. Games played with dice (Monopoly, for instance) normally use *two* dice. But let's assume that a single die is rolled. Then the sample space is:

$$S = \{1, 2, 3, 4, 5, 6\}$$

The die is rolled 500 times with the following results:

Outcome	Frequency
1	85
2	90
3	80
4	85
5	81
6	79

We have the following questions:

a. Calculate the relative frequency of each outcome.
b. Adopting the relative frequency or empirical approach, assign a probability to each of the six outcomes.
c. Do you now have a probability model for the experiment of rolling the die?

17. A single die is rolled. You do not have a data table like the one given in Exercise 16. If you believe that the die is symmetrical, and that it is rolled fairly, what probabilities would you assign to the following outcomes?

a. 2   b. 4   c. 6
d. 3   e. 5   f. 7
g. an even number   h. an odd number

Finally: Do the probabilities you assign in answering these questions give you a probability model?

18. Dr. Miles Malone tells his patient: "You have a 95% probability of surviving this operation." (This means that the survival probability is .95).

Is Dr. Malone's assertion an example of the *subjective* approach to assigning probabilities? Suppose that the patient dies. Does this change your answer?

19. Which of the three methods of assigning probabilities—the equal likelihood approach, the relative frequency or empirical approach, or the subjective approach—would be appropriate in assigning probabilities for each of the following?

   a. a 38-inch two-year old growing to an adult height of 76 inches
   b. a swine flu vaccine recipient being paralyzed by Guion-Barré syndrome
   c. one of the two major party candidates being elected president
   d. the DJIA being *up* for the day, on the first business day of 1989
   e. the outcome of tossing a symmetrical coin being H (heads) on the 936th toss of 1500 tosses

20. Health records are kept for 1000 heavy smokers (one pack or more a day) over a period of 20 years, from ages 30 to 50. The results of the experiment are as follows:

Outcome	Number
Healthy at age 50	212
Dead before age 50	123
Lung cancer	284
Heart disease	381

There are some obvious conclusions. To spell them out, adopt the relative frequency approach to probability and answer the following questions.

   a. What is the probability that a person who smokes heavily from ages 30 to 50 will be healthy at age 50?
   b. What is the probability that such a person will still be alive at age 50?
   c. What is the probability that such a person will be suffering from lung cancer or heart disease (both linked to smoking) at age 50?
   d. Do you now have a probability model for the 20-year smoking experiment?

21. Tobacco industry spokesmen studied the data in Exercise 20 and made the following criticisms:

   (i) The 123 persons who died before age 50 did not necessarily die because they were smokers. (Some, for example, died in car accidents.)
   (ii) At least some of the 284 lung cancer victims in the group had been exposed to other causes of lung cancer, such as asbestos, vinyl chloride, and aerosol propellants.
   (iii) The 381 heart disease sufferers had been exposed to harmful chemicals in community water supplies, to fatty foods, to car exhaust emission, to alcohol, and to stress.

The tobacco industry people restudied the results of the 20-year experiment involving 1000 heavy smokers and decided that there were really five outcomes to consider:

A_1: healthy at age 50
A_2: death before age 50 *not linked to smoking*
A_3: lung cancer *not linked to smoking*
A_4: heart disease *not linked to smoking*
A_5: death or disease possibly linked to smoking

They assigned the following probabilities to these outcomes:

$$P(A_1) = .25 \qquad P(A_2) = .10$$

$$P(A_3) = .16 \qquad P(A_4) = .27 \qquad P(A_5) = .21$$

To absorb the implications of the tobacco industry probability assignments, answer three questions:

a. Construct the data table corresponding to the tobacco industry's probability assignments.
b. Do you find any significant differences or discrepancies between the tobacco industry data table and the table given in Exercise 20?
c. The tobacco industry's criticisms may or may not be valid. Is their probability model valid?

6.2 THE PROBABILITY OF AN EVENT

A collection of outcomes in a sample space is called an *event*.

EXAMPLE 1: EVENTS AT ROLLS-ROYCE

In Section 6.1 we defined a four-outcome sample space for inspecting Rolls-Royces:

$$S = \{G, F, M, J\}$$

We have events in S consisting of 0 outcomes, 1 outcome, 2 outcomes, 3 outcomes, and 4 outcomes.

There is only one event in S containing 0 outcomes. We denote it by Ø (a zero with a slash through it). The event Ø is called the *empty* event because we are talking about something impossible. Even at Rolls-Royce, for example, it is impossible for an inspector to find a negative number of defects in a car.

Including Ø, the total number of events in the sample space is 16. They include such events as $\{G, F, M\}$. The meaning of $\{G, F, M\}$ is that one of the three outcomes occurs: G *or* F *or* M. We will look at that further in a moment. The complete list of events in S is

{G}	{G, F}	{F, J}	{G, M, J}
{F}	{G, M}	{M, J}	{F, M, J}
{M}	{G, J}	{G, F, M}	{G, F, M, J}
{J}	{F, M}	{G, F, J}	{∅}

Notice that the sample space S is one of the 16 possible events. It is the only four-outcome event in S.

Now to explain. Remember how we defined the four symbols G, F, M, J: G means 0 to 5 defects; F means 6 to 15 defects; M means 16 to 25 defects; and J means more than 25 defects. Two events at Rolls-Royce inspections are:

$$E_1 = \{\text{the inspector finds fewer than 16 defects}\}$$
$$= \{G, F\}$$

$$E_2 = \{\text{the inspector finds more than 5 defects}\}$$
$$= \{F, M, J\}$$

From the verbal descriptions of the events, we see that E_1 means *either* G *or* F. And E_2 means one of the three outcomes F, M, and J. A reasonable question is: If we know the probabilities of the outcomes G, F, M, and J, can we find the probabilities of the events E_1 and E_2?

Sometimes we are more interested in the probability of an event, or collection of outcomes, than we are in the probabilities of the individual outcomes.

EXAMPLE 2: VENUS SPACEFLIGHT

Let's suppose that the first manned spacecraft is to be sent to Venus. It has been engineered to go to Venus, land, shelter the astronauts in the Venusian atmosphere, and return to Earth. One possible sample space for outcomes of the mission might contain the outcomes A_1 (disaster on launch from Earth), A_2 (disaster on flight to Venus), A_3 (disastrous soft landing on Venus), A_4 (disaster during exploration of the planet), A_5 (unsuccessful sheltering from the elements inside the spacecraft), A_6 (unsuccessful launch from Venus), A_7 (unsuccessful return flight), A_8 (unsuccessful landing on Earth), A_9 (success in all eight stages of the mission).

The engineering group responsible for sheltering problems has worked to make $P(A_5)$ as small as possible. The group responsible for launchings has tried to minimize the probability of the event $\{A_1, A_6\}$. (Can the probability of this event be calculated if $P(A_1)$ and $P(A_6)$ are known? We will discuss that in a moment.) The astronauts making the trip are interested in $P(A_1)$ before launch, in $P(A_2)$ as the flight begins, in $P(A_3)$ before landing, and so on to $P(A_8)$. In other words, they are interested in the probability of lack of success for every stage of the mission, one at a time. They are also interested in the total probability of disaster ahead. For example: If they complete the first four stages successfully, their immediate worry is about $P(A_5)$, but they will also be thinking about the probability of the four-outcome event $\{A_5, A_6, A_7, A_8\}$. Putting things positively, they are interested above all in $P(A_9)$.

A key question in Examples 1 and 2—and in many other probability examples—is: If we have assigned probabilities to the *outcomes* in a sample space, can we then calculate the probabilities of the *events* in that sample space? The answer is given by the following definition.

DEFINITION   Probability of an Event

The probability of an event is the sum of the probabilities of the outcomes making up that event.

As an illustration: If A and B are outcomes in a sample space, and E is the event $\{A, B\}$ then

$$P(E) = P(A) + P(B)$$

As further illustrations, let's continue with Examples 1 and 2.

EXAMPLE 1 CONTINUED: PROBABILITIES OF EVENTS AT ROLLS-ROYCE

The probabilities of the outcomes G, F, M, and J were given in Section 6.1: $P(G) = .455, P(F) = .355, P(M) = .189,$ and $P(J) = .001.$ Since we have defined $E_1 = \{G, F\}$ and $E_2 = \{F, M, J\}$, we have

$$P(E_1) = P(G) + P(F) = .455 + .355 = .810$$

$$P(E_2) = P(F) + P(M) + P(J) = .355 + .189 + .001 = .545$$

If we think of probabilities as relative frequencies, then the probability assignments $P(G) = .455, P(F) = .355$ say that long-term inspection results will show approximately 455 cars out of 1000 in the range G and 355 of the same 1000 in the range F. In other words, $455 + 355 = 810$ out of 1000 will be in the G *or* F range. This is precisely the meaning of the result $P(E_1) = .810.$

**EXAMPLE 2 CONTINUED: PROBABILITIES OF
VENUS SPACEFLIGHT EVENTS**

Probabilities have been assigned to the various outcomes of the Venus mission. (The method used in assigning the probabilities was the subjective approach. That is, they were assigned on the basis of expert knowledge of the results of past spaceflights—manned and unmanned—and of the reliability of aerospace contractors who manufactured the various spacecraft components.) The probabilities are listed in the table:

Outcome	A_1	A_2	A_3	A_4	A_5	A_6	A_7	A_8	A_9
Probability	.035	.015	.025	.025	.035	.015	.015	.015	.820

Notice that the table provides a probability model for the flight: we have listed all the outcomes in the sample space, we have a probability for each outcome, and these probabilities have properties 1 and 2.

Let's define a few events and calculate their probabilities. We write:

$$E_1 = \{A_1, A_6\}$$
$$E_2 = \{A_1, A_2, A_3\}$$
$$E_3 = \{A_5, A_6, A_7, A_8\}$$
$$E_4 = \{A_1, A_2, A_3, A_4, A_5, A_6, A_7, A_8\}$$

By the definition of the probability of an event, we then have

$$P(E_1) = P(A_1) + P(A_6) = .035 + .015 = .05$$
$$P(E_2) = P(A_1) + P(A_2) + P(A_3) = .035 + .015 + .025 = .075$$

and in the same way:

$$P(E_3) = .035 + .015 + .015 + .015 = .08$$
$$P(E_4) = .035 + .015 + 2(.025) + .035 + 3(.015) = .18$$

Sample spaces, outcomes, and events can be pictured by means of diagrams. This geometric approach makes the concepts more tangible.

The sample space for any probability example can be illustrated by a large rectangle (Figure 6.1). Outcomes are represented by points in the rectangle. The point corresponding to an outcome is called a *sample point*. Figure 6.2 represents Example 1.

Since an event is a collection of outcomes, the geometric equivalent of an event is a circle (or other closed curve) enclosing the sample points corresponding to those outcomes. Figure 6.3 shows the events $E_1 = \{G, F\}$, $E_2 = \{F, M, J\}$ in the Rolls-Royce sample space. The figure illustrates a fact

S

FIGURE 6.1 Sample Space *S*

that we have not emphasized: the events E_1 and E_2 have the outcome F in common. In geometric language, we say that F is the *intersection* of E_1 and E_2.

The circles representing E_1 and E_2 in Figure 6.3 are called *Venn diagrams*.

The Venn diagram illustration of Example 2 is shown in Figure 6.4. We have sample points representing the nine outcomes in the sample space, and circles for the events E_1, E_2, E_3, and E_4 defined on p. 293.

Figure 6.4 illustrates the concept of intersection—and the related concept of non-intersection—in several ways:

A_1 is the intersection of E_1 and E_2.

A_6 is the intersection of E_1 and E_3.

E_2 and E_3 do not intersect.

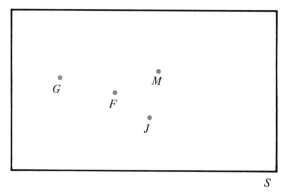

S

FIGURE 6.2 Sample Space *S*; Sample Points G, M, F, J

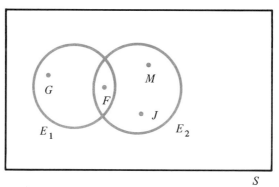

FIGURE 6.3 Sample Space $S = \{G, M, F, J\}$; Events
$E_1 = \{G, F\}$, $E_2 = \{F, M, J\}$

The intersection of E_1 and E_4 consists of 2 sample points: A_1 and A_6. (Another way of saying this is: The intersection of E_1 and E_4 is E_1.)

The intersection of E_2 and E_4 is E_2.

The intersection of E_3 and E_4 is E_3.

The intersection of E_1, E_2, and E_3 is $\emptyset$, the empty event. (E_1 and E_2 have a nonempty intersection. So do E_1 and E_3. But there is no outcome that is included in all three of the events E_1, E_2, and E_3, and therefore no sample point that belongs to all three of the circles representing these events.)

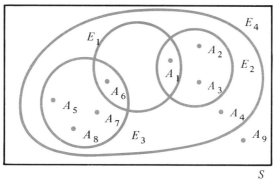

FIGURE 6.4 Sample Space $S = \{A_1, A_2, \ldots, A_9\}$; Events
$E_1 = \{A_1, A_6\}$, $E_2 = \{A_1, A_2, A_3\}$, $E_3 = \{A_5, A_6, A_7, A_8\}$, and
$E_4 = \{A_1, A_2, \ldots, A_8\}$

PROBLEM 1   Jim McCarthy has invested in three fast-food franchises. He believes that each of the three will be either a big-profit or a small-profit operation. (Since he has been extremely successful with fast-food restaurants in the past, he does not even consider the possibility of a losing operation). List all the outcomes in his experiment, and draw a Venn diagram showing these outcomes as sample points.

SOLUTION   Let B denote the big-profit result, and let C denote the small-profit result for any one of the three operations. Every outcome in the sample space for the three-franchise experiment is an *ordered triple* $(-, -, -)$. Each of the three places in the ordered triple is occupied by one of the two letters B, C. The sample space therefore contains the eight outcomes

$$A_1 = (B, B, B) \qquad A_5 = (C, B, B)$$
$$A_2 = (B, B, C) \qquad A_6 = (C, B, C)$$
$$A_3 = (B, C, B) \qquad A_7 = (C, C, B)$$
$$A_4 = (B, C, C) \qquad A_8 = (C, C, C)$$

and we write

$$S = \{A_1, A_2, A_3, A_4, A_5, A_6, A_7, A_8\}$$

A Venn diagram illustrating this description of the McCarthy experiment is shown in Figure 6.5.

PROBLEM 2   Four events that may occur in the experiment described in Problem 1 are:

$E_1 = \{$at least 2 of the 3 franchises are big-profit operations$\}$

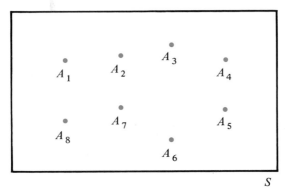

FIGURE 6.5   Sample Space and Sample Points for Problem 1

$E_2 = \{$at least 2 of the 3 franchises are small-profit operations$\}$

$E_3 = \{$1 of the 3 franchises is a big-profit operation$\}$

$E_4 = \{$1 of the 3 franchises is a small-profit operation$\}$

Describe E_1, E_2, E_3, and E_4 in terms of the eight outcomes $A_1, A_2, \ldots, A_8$ listed in the solution of Problem 1. Draw the Venn diagrams corresponding to these descriptions. Specify the intersections (and non-intersections) of the events with one another.

SOLUTION   By using the definitions of the four events E_1, E_2, E_3, and E_4 and of the eight outcomes $A_1, A_2, \ldots, A_8$ in S, we find that:

$$E_1 = \{A_1, A_2, A_3, A_5\}$$
$$E_2 = \{A_4, A_6, A_7, A_8\}$$
$$E_3 = \{A_4, A_6, A_7\}$$
$$E_4 = \{A_2, A_3, A_5\}$$

The descriptions are illustrated by the Venn diagrams in Figure 6.6. We see that the intersection of E_1 and E_4 is $\{A_2, A_3, A_5\}$ and that the intersection of E_2 and E_3 is $\{A_4, A_6, A_7\}$. These are the only nonempty intersections. Notice, for example, that the intersection of E_1 and E_2 is $\emptyset$, the empty event.

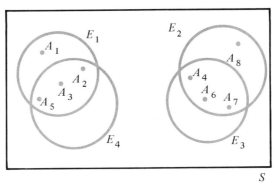

FIGURE 6.6   Sample Space, Sample Points, and Events for Problem 2

We will make further use of Venn diagrams in Sections 6.3 and 6.4.
Putting aside the geometric approach for the moment, we can sum up Sections 6.1 and 6.2 by giving the following five rules for calculating the probability of an event. Rules 1, 2, and 3 tell how to construct a probability model; rules 4 and 5 tell how to apply the model.

NOTE: We always have $0 \leq P(E) \leq 1$ ($P(E) \geq 0$, since the probabilities of the outcomes in *E* are all ≥ 0. $P(E) \leq 1$, since we cannot have $P(E) > 1$.) As special cases: The empty event is impossible, and the occurrence of *some* event in *S* is certain, which gives us $P(0) = 0 \qquad P(S) = 1$

We will apply these rules in solving one last problem.

PROBLEM 3   The following table records deaths, decade by decade, among a group of 100,000 Americans from ages 20 to 100.

Age in Years (By Decades)	Number Living at Beginning of Decade	Number Dying During the Decade
20–30	100,000	7,767
30–40	92,233	7,918
40–50	84,315	8,962
50–60	75,353	12,832
60–70	62,521	20,983
70–80	41,538	25,950
80–90	15,588	14,676
90–100	912	912

Suppose that a life insurance company uses the table in calculating premiums for a 20-year-old person. Find the probability that the company will assign to each of the three events:

$$E_1 = \{\text{the person dies by age 40}\}$$

$$E_2 = \{\text{the person dies by age 50}\}$$

$$E_3 = \{\text{the person dies by age 70}\}$$

SOLUTION First we construct a probability model by applying rules 1, 2, and 3:

1. There are eight outcomes in the sample space: A_1 (person dies in decade 20–30); A_2 (person dies in decade 30–40); A_3 (person dies in decade 40–50); and so on to A_8 (person dies in decade 90–100).

2. We use the empirical approach in assigning probabilities to the eight outcomes. This means that the *relative frequency* of death in a given decade is taken as the *probability* of death in that decade. (Since the original group numbers 100,000, the relative frequency of death in any decade is equal to the number dying in that decade divided by 100,000.) We therefore have:

Outcome	Probability
A_1	.07767
A_2	.07918
A_3	.08962
A_4	.12832
A_5	.20983
A_6	.25950
A_7	.14676
A_8	.00912

3. Each of the eight probabilities we have calculated has property 1. Since the sum of all eight probabilities is 1, property 2 holds as well. Thus we have a valid probability model.

Rules 4 and 5 make use of the model:

4. From the definitions of the events E_1, E_2, and E_3 and the outcomes $A_1, A_2, \ldots, A_8$, we have

$$E_1 = \{A_1, A_2\}$$
$$E_2 = \{A_1, A_2, A_3\}$$
$$E_3 = \{A_1, A_2, A_3, A_4, A_5\}$$

5. Therefore the company will assign the following probabilities to the events E_1, E_2, E_3:

$$P(E_1) = P(A_1) + P(A_2) = .07767 + .07918 = .15685$$
$$P(E_2) = P(A_1) + P(A_2) + P(A_3)$$
$$= .07767 + .07918 + .08962$$
$$= .24647$$

$$P(E_3) = P(A_1) + P(A_2) + P(A_3) + P(A_4) + P(A_5)$$
$$= .07767 + .07918 + .08962 + .12832 + .20983$$
$$= .58462$$

EXERCISES *for Section 6.2*

1. An experiment has a three-outcome sample space

$$S = \{A, B, C\}$$

There are eight events in S. List them.

2. The sample space for rolling a single die is

$$S = \{1, 2, 3, 4, 5, 6\}$$

What is the total number of events in S? List the events in S made up of one or more of the outcomes 2, 4, 5.

3. *Beat the Odds* is a book on how to apply probability to games of chance. Careful examination of the book shows that there are anywhere from 1 to 7 printing errors on each page. The probabilities of these outcomes are:

Number of Errors	1	2	3	4	5	6	7
Probability		.29	.21	.17	.13	.09	.08	.03

If a page of the book is selected by chance, find the probability that:

a. there are no more than 2 errors on the page
b. there are at least 3 errors on the page
c. there are 5 or more errors on the page

4. Iowa is basketball country, and no one was surprised when 250 girls turned out for the first meeting of the women's basketball squad at the University of Iowa. The 250 girls were classified by height, with the following results:

Height Range	Number in Range
64 inches or under	17
Over 64 to 66 inches	30
Over 66 to 68 inches	40
Over 68 to 70 inches	48
Over 70 to 72 inches	60
Over 72 inches	55

If one of these girls is selected (by drawing her name out of a hat, or by some other experiment of chance whose outcome cannot be predicted), what is the probability that her height is:

a. under 5 feet, 6 inches?
b. over 5 feet, 8 inches?
c. between 5 feet, 6 inches and 6 feet?

5. Since it is hard to believe that anything so complex and varied as human intelligence can be measured by a single number, the validity of IQ tests for humans is now being seriously questioned. But some experimental psychologists find IQ scores useful in the classification of laboratory rats. For example, C. C. Brigham does experiments with 100 rats and has the following estimates for their IQs:

IQ Scores	Number of Rats
90–99	10
100–109	14
110–119	21
120–129	33
130–139	22

If Brigham makes a chance selection of one of these rats, what is the probability that the rat he selects has:

a. an IQ under 110?
b. an IQ over 120?
c. an IQ higher than 110 but lower than 130?

Draw diagrams to illustrate the sample space, the sample points, and the events described by questions a, b, and c of:

6. Exercise 3

7. Exercise 4

8. Exercise 5

9. In 1949 Dr. Arie Haagen-Smit, a Cal Tech biochemist, discovered that Pasadena's auto-caused smog contained ozone and other harmful oxidants. Since 1960, Congress has attempted to deal with auto-caused air pollution by setting standards that must be met by all cars sold in the U.S. The standards (embodied in the Clean Air Act) set permissible limits for emission of hydrocarbons, carbon monoxide, and nitrogen oxides. Suppose that a car is selected at random (that is, in a purely chance way) from a carmaker's production line and inspected for compliance with the Clean Air Act standards. Then the inspector will grade the car P (pass) or F (fail) in each of three emission categories: hydrocarbons, carbon monoxide, and nitrogen oxide. Since the car to be tested has been selected by chance, the inspector is conducting a probability experiment.

a. List all the outcomes of the experiment.
b. Draw a diagram that represents these outcomes as sample points.

10. Among the possible events in the car inspection experiment described in Exercise 9, we have:

$E_1 = \{$the car passes in exactly 2 of the 3 categories$\}$
$E_2 = \{$the car passes in at least 2 of the 3 categories$\}$
$E_3 = \{$the car passes in no more than 2 of the 3 categories$\}$

Describe E_1, E_2, and E_3 in terms of the outcomes you listed in answering part a of Exercise 9. Draw Venn diagrams showing these events and their intersections, if any, with one another.

11. In answering part a of Exercise 9, you constructed a sample space for the car inspection experiment. Now:

a. Convert your sample space into a probability model by assigning a probability to each of the outcomes on your list. (*NOTE:* The probabilities may be assigned in any way you like, provided that the result is a valid probability model.)
b. Use your probability model to calculate the probabilities of the events E_1, E_2, and E_3 described in Exercise 10.

12. The original owner of a car may dispose of it within a few months or may keep it for years. A survey of 1000 cars gave the following results:

Time in Hands of Original Owner	Number of Cars
1 year or less	92
over 1 year to 2 years	163
over 2 years to 3 years	225
over 3 years to 4 years	188
over 4 years to 5 years	175
over 5 years to 6 years	84
over 6 years	73

Suppose that these results are typical for car owners in the U.S. Then use the rules on p. 298 to construct a probability model (based on the empirical approach) that will allow you to calculate the probability of each of the following events for the typical owner of a new car:

$E_1 = \{$the owner keeps the car for less than 2 years$\}$
$E_2 = \{$the owner keeps the car for more than 5 years$\}$
$E_3 = \{$the owner keeps the car for more than 2 years but less than 5 years$\}$

13. Black lung disease is the plague of underground mining in Appalachia. Since 1969, victims of the disease have been considered totally and permanently disabled and have received Social Security payments on that basis. Social Security Administration records give the following health data for 10,000 miners:

Years Employed as Miner	Number in Good Health at Beginning of Year	Number of Cases of Black Lung Disease During the Year
0–1	10,000	547
1–2	9,453	567
2–3	8,886	583
3–4	8,303	597
4–5	7,706	607
5–6	7,099	612
6–7	6,487	611

7–8	5,876	604
8–9	5,272	594
9–10	4,678	578
10–11	4,100	559
11–12	3,541	536
12–13	3,005	511
13–14	2,494	479
14–15	2,015	443
15–16	1,572	402
16–17	1,170	359
17–18	811	315
18–19	496	272
19–20	224	224

Assume that this health data is typical for underground miners in Appalachia. By applying the rules on p. 298 (using the empirical approach, in rule 2), calculate the probability of each of the following events in the working life of a typical underground miner:

E_1 = {contracts black lung disease within 3 years}
E_2 = {contracts black lung disease within 5 years}
E_3 = {contracts black lung disease within 7 years}
E_4 = {contracts black lung disease within 15 years}

6.3   RELATING AND COMBINING EVENTS

Sometimes events are most conveniently specified by relating them to other events. As a first example: If E is an event in S, then the event *not-E* (that is, E does not occur) is also an event in S.

DEFINITION   Complement of an Event

The event made up of all outcomes in S that are not in E is called the *complement* of E. The complement of E will be denoted by E^c.

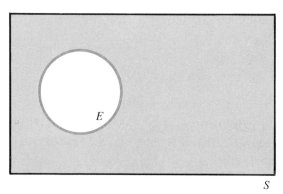

FIGURE 6.7 E^c Is Shaded

Figure 6.7 is a Venn diagram illustrating the idea of the complement of an event. Here are some examples:

EXAMPLE 1: Let a sample space contain five outcomes:

$$S = \{A_1, A_2, A_3, A_4, A_5\}$$

If we define the event $E = \{A_1, A_3, A_4\}$, then $E^c = \{A_2, A_5\}$. Notice that the complement of E^c is E. In symbols: $(E^c)^c = E$.

EXAMPLE 2: In Section 6.2 we defined the Rolls-Royce events

$$E_1 = \{G, F\} \qquad E_2 = \{F, M, J\}$$

The complements of these events are:

$$E_1{}^c = \{M, J\} \qquad E_2{}^c = \{G\}$$

The Rolls-Royce sample space also includes the events ∅ and S. The complements are:

$$\emptyset^c = S \qquad S^c = \emptyset$$

These equations hold for any and every sample space, since every sample space includes the empty event ∅ and the full sample space S.

The definition of E^c shows that all the outcomes in a sample space S are contained in either E or E^c. Our definition of the probability of an event (as given in Section 6.2) shows that

$$P(E) + P(E^c) = P(S) = 1$$

By simple arithmetic we have:

$$P(E^C) = 1 - P(E)$$

EXAMPLE 2 CONTINUED: The probabilities of the Rolls-Royce events E_1 and E_2 were calculated in Section 6.2. We saw (p. 292) that

$$P(E_1) = .810 \qquad P(E_2) = .545$$

Since $P(M) = .189$, $P(J) = .001$, $P(G) = .455$, we find that

$$P(E_1{}^C) = P(M) + P(J) = .190$$

$$P(E_2{}^C) = .455$$

or: $P(E_1{}^C) = 1 - P(E_1)$; $P(E_2{}^C) = 1 - P(E_2)$.

If E and F are events in S, then the event that *both E and F occur* is also an event in S.

DEFINITION   Intersection of Two Events

The event made up of all outcomes in S that are in both E and F is called the *intersection* of E and F. The intersection of E and F will be denoted by $E \cap F$.

Notice that this verbal definition is in agreement with the geometric concept of intersection that was introduced in Section 6.2. There, the concept was illustrated by means of Figures 6.3 and 6.4. In this section, we will omit sample points when we draw Venn diagrams. (The diagrams can refer to *any* sample space if we do not specify the sample points.) Figures 6.8 and 6.9 illustrate the intersection (and non-intersection) concepts.

The non-intersection case illustrated in Figure 6.9 is described symbolically by $E \cap F = \emptyset$ (the intersection of the two events is the empty event) or verbally by the statement "E and F are *mutually exclusive* events."

EXAMPLE 3: If E is any event in any sample space, and E^C is its complement, then

$$E \cap E^C = \emptyset$$

Why? Because E and E^C have no outcomes in common. (And their Venn diagrams have no sample points in common.)

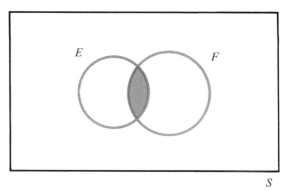

FIGURE 6.8 $E \cap F$ Is Shaded

EXAMPLE 4: In addition to the four Venus spaceflight events defined on p. 293, we will write:

$$E_5 = \{A_2, A_3, A_4\}$$
$$E_6 = \{A_5, A_8, A_9\}$$

Then we have the following as examples:

$$E_1 \cap E_5 = E_1 \cap E_6 = \emptyset$$
$$E_2 \cap E_5 = \{A_2, A_3\}$$
$$E_2 \cap E_6 = E_3 \cap E_5 = \emptyset$$
$$E_3 \cap E_6 = \{A_5, A_8\}$$

E_1 and E_5 are mutually exclusive events. So are E_1 and E_6; E_2 and E_6; and E_3 and E_5.

Suppose that we know $P(E)$ and $P(F)$. Do we then have a simple way

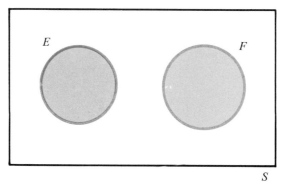

FIGURE 6.9 E and F Are Shaded ($E \cap F = \emptyset$)

of calculating the probability of $E \cap F$? No, we do not. All that we can say is that the intersection *may* contain 0 outcomes (geometrically: 0 sample points), or *may* contain as many outcomes as one of the two events E, F. This state of affairs is summed up by inequalities:

$$0 \leq P(E \cap F) \leq P(E)$$
$$0 \leq P(E \cap F) \leq P(F)$$

EXAMPLE 4 CONTINUED: In Section 6.2 we found that:

$$P(E_1) = .05 \qquad P(E_2) = .075 \qquad P(E_3) = .08$$

From the known probabilities of A_2, A_3, A_4, A_5, A_8, and A_9 (see the table on p. 293), we have

$$P(E_5) = .015 + .025 + .025 = .065$$
$$P(E_6) = .035 + .015 + .820 = .87$$

We also have:

$$P(\{A_2, A_3\}) = .015 + .025 = .04$$
$$P(\{A_5, A_8\}) = .035 + .015 = .05$$

Therefore $P(E_2 \cap E_5) = .04$, so that

$$P(E_2 \cap E_5) < P(E_2) \qquad P(E_2 \cap E_5) < P(E_5)$$

Similarly, $P(E_3 \cap E_6) = .05$, which gives us

$$P(E_3 \cap E_6) < P(E_3) \qquad P(E_3 \cap E_6) < P(E_6)$$

And of course:

$$P(E_1 \cap E_5) = P(E_1 \cap E_6) = 0$$
$$P(E_2 \cap E_6) = P(E_3 \cap E_5) = 0$$

If E and F are events in S, then the event *either E or F or both occur* is another event in S.

DEFINITION   Union of Two Events

The event made up of all outcomes in S that are either in E or in F or in both E and F is called the *union* of E and F. The union of E and F will be denoted $E \cup F$.

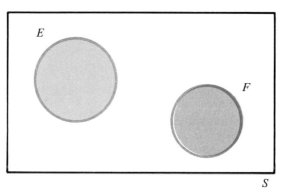

FIGURE 6.10 $E \cup F$ Is Shaded ($E \cap F = \emptyset$)

Two Venn diagrams, Figures 6.10 and 6.11, illustrate the concept of the union of two events.

EXAMPLE 5: If E is any event in any sample space, and E^C is its complement, then

$$E \cup E^C = S$$

As a special case:

$$\emptyset \cup S = S$$

EXAMPLE 6: In Example 4, we referred to five space flight events: E_1, E_2, E_3 (as defined on p. 293) and the newly defined events E_5 and E_6. Applying the concept of union, we have:

$$E_1 \cup E_5 = \{A_1, A_2, A_3, A_4, A_6\}$$
$$E_1 \cup E_6 = \{A_1, A_5, A_6, A_8, A_9\}$$
$$E_2 \cup E_5 = \{A_1, A_2, A_3, A_4\}$$
$$E_3 \cup E_6 = \{A_5, A_6, A_7, A_8, A_9\}$$

In calculating the probability of the union of two events, we have to look at two cases. If E and F are mutually exclusive, as illustrated in Figure 6.10, the number of outcomes in $E \cup F$ is the number of outcomes in E plus the number in F. Therefore:

$$\boxed{\text{If } E \cap F = \emptyset, \text{ then } P(E \cup F) = P(E) + P(F).}$$

If E and F are not mutually exclusive, then the two events have at least one outcome in common. In other words: $P(E) + P(F)$ will be greater than $P(E \cup F)$, since any outcome in $E \cap F$ is counted twice. (The Venn diagram in Figure 6.11 shows this clearly.) The remedy? Subtract the probabilities of the doubly counted outcomes:

$$\boxed{P(E \cup F) = P(E) + P(F) - P(E \cap F)}$$

Notice that this second result applies perfectly well to the case $E \cap F = \emptyset$, since $P(\emptyset) = 0$.

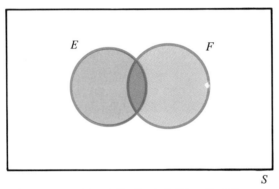

FIGURE 6.11 $E \cup F$ Is Shaded $(E \cap F \neq \emptyset)$

EXAMPLE 6 CONTINUED: We now calculate the probabilities of the five unions listed in Example 6, and also check the results:

$$P(E_1 \cup E_5) = P(E_1) + P(E_5) - P(E_1 \cap E_5)$$
$$= .05 + .065 - 0 = .115$$

Check: $P(\{A_1, A_2, A_3, A_4, A_6\})$
$$= .035 + .015 + .025 + .025 + .015 = .115$$

$$P(E_1 \cup E_6) = P(E_1) + P(E_6) - P(E_1 \cap E_6)$$
$$= .05 + .87 - 0 = .92$$

Check: $P(\{A_1, A_5, A_6, A_8, A_9\})$
$$= .035 + .035 + .015 + .015 + .820 = .920$$

$$P(E_2 \cup E_5) = P(E_2) + P(E_5) - P(E_2 \cap E_5)$$
$$= .075 + .065 - .04 = .10$$

Check:
$$P(\{A_1, A_2, A_3, A_4\})$$
$$= .035 + .015 + .025 + .025 = .100$$

$$P(E_3 \cup E_6) = P(E_3) + P(E_6) - P(E_3 \cap E_6)$$
$$= .08 + .87 - .05 = .90$$

Check:
$$P(\{A_5, A_6, A_7, A_8, A_9\})$$
$$= .035 + .015 + .015 + .015 + .820 = .900$$

To sum up:

In Section 6.2 we defined an event as a collection of outcomes in a sample space. The sum of the probabilities of those outcomes gave the probability of the event.

Here we define events by relating them to other events, and we calculate probabilities by means of the equation

$$P(E^C) = 1 - P(E)$$

or the equation

$$P(E \cup F) = P(E) + P(F) - P(E \cap F)$$

We have applied these equations to several examples, and we will close this section by looking at three more examples.

PROBLEM 1 By using the table given in Problem 3 of Section 6.2, we were able to calculate the probabilities of events we called E_1, E_2, and E_3; namely, that a 20-year old person would die by age 40, by age 50, or by age 70. Now use the methods of this section (and the data table on pp. 289–299) to calculate the probabilities of the following events for a 20-year old person:

$$F_1 = \{\text{the person lives to age 40 or older}\}$$
$$F_2 = \{\text{the person lives to age 50 or older}\}$$
$$F_3 = \{\text{the person lives to age 70 or older}\}$$

SOLUTION The events F_1, F_2, and F_3 are the complements of E_1, E_2, and E_3:

$$F_1 = E_1{}^C \qquad F_2 = E_2{}^C \qquad F_3 = E_3{}^C$$

This means that

$$P(F_1) = P(E_1{}^C) = 1 - P(E_1)$$
$$P(F_2) = P(E_2{}^C) = 1 - P(E_2)$$
$$P(F_3) = P(E_3{}^C) = 1 - P(E_3)$$

We know the probabilities of E_1, E_2, and E_3 (see p. 300) and we therefore have

$$P(F_1) = 1 - .15685 = .84315$$

$$P(F_2) = 1 - .24647 = .75353$$

$$P(F_3) = 1 - .58462 = .41538$$

PROBLEM 2 An experienced franchise operator assigned the following probabilities to the eight possible outcomes of the Jim McCarthy experiment defined in Problem 1 of Section 6.2:

Outcome	A_1	A_2	A_3	A_4	A_5	A_6	A_7	A_8
Probability	.05	.06	.07	.15	.09	.16	.19	.23

Use these probabilities together with the methods of Section 6.2 to calculate the probabilities of:

$$E_1 = \{A_1, A_2, A_3, A_5\}$$

$$E_3 = \{A_4, A_6, A_7\}$$

Then use the methods of this section to calculate the probabilities of:

$$E_2 = \{A_4, A_6, A_7, A_8\}$$

$$E_4 = \{A_2, A_3, A_5\}$$

$$E_1 \cap E_4$$

$$E_2 \cap E_3$$

$$E_2 \cup E_3$$

SOLUTION By the methods of Section 6.2, we have

$$P(E_1) = P(A_1) + P(A_2) + P(A_3) + P(A_5)$$
$$= .05 + .06 + .07 + .09 = .27$$

and

$$P(E_3) = P(A_4) + P(A_6) + P(A_7)$$
$$= .15 + .16 + .19 = .50$$

Next we see that $E_2 = E_1{}^C$, and this gives us

$$P(E_2) = 1 - P(E_1) = 1 - .27 = .73$$

Since $E_4 \cup A_1 = E_1$, and $E_4 \cap A_1 = \emptyset$, we have

$$P(E_4 \cup A_1) = P(E_4) + P(A_1) = P(E_1)$$

or

$$P(E_4) = P(E_1) - P(A_1)$$
$$= .27 - .05 = .22$$

As we saw in solving Problem 2 of Section 6.2 (see Figure 6.6):

$$E_1 \cap E_4 = \{A_2, A_3, A_5\} = E_4$$
$$E_2 \cap E_3 = \{A_4, A_6, A_7\} = E_3$$

Therefore

$$P(E_1 \cap E_4) = P(E_4) = .22$$
$$P(E_2 \cap E_3) = P(E_3) = .50$$

and

$$P(E_1 \cup E_4) = P(E_1) + P(E_4) - P(E_1 \cap E_4)$$
$$= P(E_1) = .27$$

$$P(E_2 \cup E_3) = P(E_2) + P(E_3) - P(E_2 \cap E_3)$$
$$= P(E_2) = .73$$

PROBLEM 3   John Waller, account executive for a national brokerage house, is about to make the sale of his life. He has 1,250,000 shares of Forest Industries stock to sell, and two possible clients. The clients are Tubefund (a TV employee pension fund) and Sunbankinc (a major Sunbelt bank with a big trust department). The probability that Tubefund will decide to buy the stock is .51, the probability that Sunbankinc will decide to buy is .58, and the probability that *both* will decide to buy is .32. Since there is a $125,000 commission involved, account executive Waller is interested in the answers to two probability questions: What is the probability that *at least one* of the two clients will decide to buy the stock? What is the probability that *neither* will decide to buy the stock?

SOLUTION   Suppose that Waller defines the events

$$E = \{\text{Tubefund decides to buy}\}$$
$$F = \{\text{Sunbankinc decides to buy}\}$$

Then he can use the definitions of complement, union, and intersection to write

$$E^C = \{\text{Tubefund decides } not \text{ to buy}\}$$
$$F^C = \{\text{Sunbankinc decides } not \text{ to buy}\}$$
$$E \cup F = \{\text{at least 1 of the 2 clients decides to buy}\}$$

$E \cap F = \{\text{both clients decide to buy}\}$

$E^C \cap F^C = \{\text{both clients decide } not \text{ to buy}\}$

Since John Waller knows $P(E)$, $P(F)$, and $P(E \cap F)$, he has:

$$P(E \cup F) = P(E) + P(F) - P(E \cap F)$$
$$= .51 + .58 - .32 = .77$$

That is, the probability that at least one of the two clients will decide to buy the stock is .77.

To answer his second question, Waller notices that what he wants is $P(E^C \cap F^C)$. He draws a Venn diagram (Figure 6.12), which shows him that $E^C \cap F^C$ is the complement of $E \cup F$. Therefore

$$P(E^C \cap F^C) = 1 - P(E \cup F)$$
$$= 1 - .77 = .23$$

That is, the probability that neither of the two clients will buy the stock is .23. (*NOTE:* The event "neither will buy" is simply another way of saying "both decide *not* to buy.")

Check: $P(E^C \cup F^C) = P(E^C) + P(F^C) - P(E^C \cap F^C)$
$$= .49 + .42 - .23 = .68$$

A little thought (aided by reference to a Venn diagram, if necessary) shows that $(E^C \cup F^C)$ is the complement of $(E \cap F)$. Therefore we should have

$$P(E^C \cup F^C) = 1 - P(E \cap F)$$
$$= 1 - .32 = .68$$

and this is exactly what we do have. Everything checks.

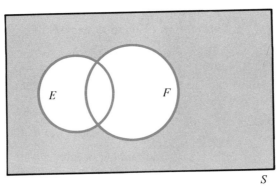

FIGURE 6.12 $E^C \cap F^C$ Is Shaded

EXERCISES *for Section 6.3*

A sample space is defined by

$$S = \{A_1, A_2, A_3, A_4, A_5, A_6, A_7, A_8, A_9, A_{10}\}$$

and the events E, F, G in S are defined by

$$E = \{A_1, A_3, A_5, A_7, A_9\}$$
$$F = \{A_1, A_2, A_3, A_4, A_5, A_6\}$$
$$G = \{A_5, A_6, A_7, A_8, A_9, A_{10}\}$$

Use the definitions of the *complement of an event*, the *intersection of two events* and the *union of two events* to specify each of the following:

1. E^C	**2.** F^C	**3.** G^C
4. $E \cap F$	**5.** $E \cap G$	**6.** $F \cap G$
7. $F \cap E$	**8.** $G \cap E$	**9.** $G \cap F$
10. $E \cup F$	**11.** $E \cup G$	**12.** $F \cup G$
13. $E \cap F^C$	**14.** $E^C \cap F$	**15.** $E^C \cap F^C$
16. $E \cap G^C$	**17.** $E^C \cap G$	**18.** $E^C \cap G^C$
19. $F \cap G^C$	**20.** $F^C \cap G$	**21.** $F^C \cap G^C$
22. $E^C \cup F$	**23.** $E \cup F^C$	**24.** $E^C \cup F^C$
25. $E^C \cup G$	**26.** $E \cup G^C$	**27.** $E^C \cup G^C$
28. $F^C \cup G$	**29.** $F \cup G^C$	**30.** $F^C \cup G^C$
31. $E^C \cup E$	**32.** $F^C \cap F$	**33.** $G \cup \emptyset$
34. $E \cap \emptyset$	**35.** $E^C \cap \emptyset$	**36.** $E^C \cup \emptyset$
37. $F \cap S$	**38.** $F \cup S$	**39.** $F^C \cup S$

Use the symbols for complement, union, and intersection to describe the events that are shaded in the following Venn diagrams:

40.

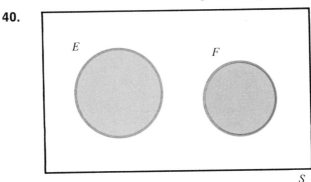

41.

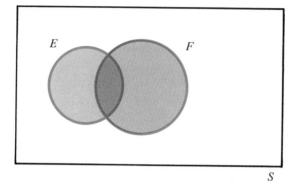

S

42.

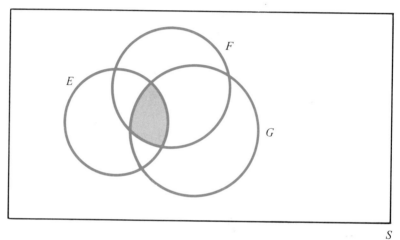

S

43.

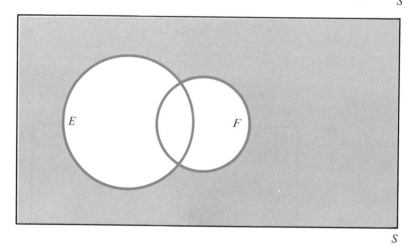

S

Let *U*, *V*, and *W* be events in a sample space *S*. Draw Venn diagrams in which you shade in the events symbolized by:

44. U^C

45. $U^C \cup V$

46. $U \cap V \cap W$ (if the intersection is not empty)

47. $V^C \cup W^C$

48. $V^C \cap W^C$

A sample space S contains seven outcomes:

$$S = \{A_1, A_2, A_3, A_4, A_5, A_6, A_7\}$$

The probabilities that these outcomes will occur are shown in the following table:

Outcome	A_1	A_2	A_3	A_4	A_5	A_6	A_7
Probability	.23	.16	.13	.12	.14	.13	.09

49. Applying the methods of Section 6.2, calculate the probabilities of the events

$$E = \{A_1, A_2, A_3, A_5, A_7\}$$
$$F = \{A_2, A_4, A_5, A_6\}$$
$$G = \{A_3, A_5, A_6, A_7\}$$

Make use of your answer to Exercise 49 together with the methods of Section 6.3 to calculate the probability that:

50. At least one of the events E, F occurs.

51. At least one of the events E, G occurs.

52. At least one of the events F, G occurs.

53. Both E and F occur.

54. Both E and G occur.

55. Both F and G occur.

56. Neither E nor F occurs.

57. Neither E nor G occurs.

58. Neither F nor G occurs.

---

59. In Exercise 13 of Section 6.2, you calculated the probabilities of certain events in the working life of a typical underground miner in Appalachia. Use those results to calculate the probabilities of the following events in the working life of such a miner:

$F_1 = \{$free of black lung disease after 3 years in the mines$\}$
$F_2 = \{$free of black lung disease after 5 years in the mines$\}$
$F_3 = \{$free of black lung disease after 7 years in the mines$\}$
$F_4 = \{$free of black lung disease after 15 years in the mines$\}$

An investment adviser who is known for her thoroughness and conservatism believes that certain stocks will double their dividend payouts in the next decade. She believes that this is true of:

IBM, with probability .68

John Deere, with probability .61

Mobil, with probability .57

For the benefit of clients who might want to buy two of the three stocks, she assigns

probability .35 to IBM *and* Deere doubling their dividends in the next decade

probability .32 to IBM *and* Mobil doubling their dividends in the next decade

probability .26 to Deere *and* Mobil doubling their dividends in the next decade

If the investment adviser believes her own probability assignments, and if she knows how to calculate the probabilities of complements and unions of events, what probabilities would she assign to the following events?

60. IBM or Deere or both will double their dividends in the next decade.

61. IBM or Mobil or both will double their dividends in the next decade.

62. Mobil or Deere or both will double their dividends in the next decade.

63. Neither IBM nor Deere will double its dividend in the next decade.

64. Neither IBM nor Mobil will double its dividend in the next decade.

65. Neither Mobil nor Deere will double its dividend in the next decade.

Driving conditions in the Upper Midwest in the winter of 1976–77 were extremely bad. Nick Lobatchevski put his car in the barn and took to driving into Minneapolis in a troika. Since a troika is an open vehicle, it may not be the commuter's best choice. One morning when it was −70°F, Nick found he was getting drowsy as he drove along. He had to admit to himself that there was a probability of .45 that he would freeze to death before he reached shelter. Out of the corner of his eye, he glimpsed a pack of wolves closing in on his horses. Nick thought that the wolves had a very good chance—probability .67, he thought—of tearing the horses (and himself) to death before they reached shelter. "Lobatchevski," he murmured, "you will be a lucky man if you freeze to death before you are eaten."

(One possibility he had in mind was that he would be eaten *while* freezing to death: he assigned a probability of .28 to this unpleasing prospect.) To occupy his mind, he asked two obvious questions:

66. What is the probability that I will either freeze to death or be eaten by the wolves or both?

67. What is the probability that I will neither freeze to death nor be eaten by the wolves?

EQUALLY LIKELY OUTCOMES

If a simple game of chance is played with symmetrical equipment, we believe that all the outcomes are equally likely. The example of coin-tossing ($S = \{H, T\}$, $P(H) = P(T) = \frac{1}{2}$) was given in Section 6.1. Here are some further examples.

EXAMPLES: SIMPLE GAMES OF CHANCE

1. A symmetrical die is given a fair roll. The sample space is $S = \{1, 2, 3, 4, 5, 6\}$. Each of the 6 outcomes is assigned a probability of $\frac{1}{6}$.

2. A card is chosen from a well-shuffled standard deck of 52 cards. The sample space contains 52 outcomes. Each of them is assigned a probability of $\frac{1}{52}$.

3. Two well-balanced coins (one is a quarter, the other a half dollar) are tossed. Possible sample spaces (see p. 275) are:

$$S = \{M, D\}$$

(the coins match or do not match) and

$$S = \{0, 1, 2\}$$

(0, 1, or 2 heads). A third possibility is

$$S = \{HH, HT, TH, TT\}$$

where HH means (heads for the quarter, heads for the half dollar), HT means (heads for the quarter, tails for the half dollar), etc.

All three of these sample spaces correctly describe the experiment of tossing the two coins. But they are not all *equally likely* sample spaces. To see this, suppose that we assign equal probability to each outcome in each sample space. This gives

$$P(M) = P(D) = \tfrac{1}{2}$$
$$P(0) = P(1) = P(2) = \tfrac{1}{3}$$
$$P(HH) = P(HT) = P(TH) = P(TT) = \tfrac{1}{4}$$

Since the coins are perfectly balanced, it is reasonable to assume that the third set of probability assignments is correct ("Correct" here means "in agreement with long-term relative frequency data"). The first sample space is also an equally likely sample space. (It is less precise than the third. The description "M" does not tell us if the outcome was HH or TT.) But the probability assignments for the second sample space are not in agreement with the other two. For example, the outcome 0 in that sample space is the same as the outcome TT in the third sample space. If $P(TT) = \tfrac{1}{4}$ is "correct" in the relative frequency sense, then $P(0) = \tfrac{1}{3}$ must be "incorrect."

The example of tossing two coins shows the need for caution in assigning equal probability to each of the outcomes in a sample space. If you make such an assignment, you must be sure that you have counted up all the outcomes *one by one*. As an aid in the one by one counting of outcomes, we introduce the idea of the *tree diagram*. For the tossing of two coins, we start from the *root* of the tree and draw two *branches* to represent the outcomes of tossing one of the coins (the quarter, say), as in Figure 6.13.

Each of the two points H and T then serves as a root for branches representing the outcomes of tossing the half dollar (Figure 6.14).

If we put Figures 6.13 and 6.14 together, we have a tree diagram for the tossing of two coins (Figure 6.15). Each of the four topmost branches in the figure represents an outcome of the experiment. The tree diagram is a visual equivalent of the sample space $S = \{HH, HT, TH, TT\}$, which gave us all four of the equally likely outcomes of tossing two coins.

Tree diagrams are especially useful when there are many outcomes in

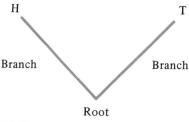

FIGURE 6.13

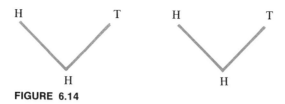

FIGURE 6.14

a sample space. Problem 2, on p. 325, will provide an example of this fact.

Now let's turn from simple games of chance to another illustration of equally likely outcomes: *random sampling*.

DEFINITION Random Sampling

Suppose that a selection is made from among a number of items. If the selection is made in such a way that every item is equally likely to be chosen, then the selection is said to be *random* and the procedure is called *random sampling*.

Everyone has heard of one or more of the applications of random sampling: they include opinion polling, market research, and industrial quality control. Professionals in these fields use sophisticated techniques that cannot be explained here. But the following examples will certainly show the connection between random sampling and equally likely outcomes.

EXAMPLES: RANDOM SAMPLING

1. What percentage of the 3,987,636 men, women, and children in Los

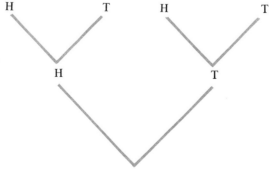

FIGURE 6.15

Angeles drink a pint or more of milk per day? To find this out without questioning everyone, we may poll a random sample of 1000 people. "Random" means that every one of the 3,987,636 *Angelenos* is equally likely to be one of the sample of 1000. (The idea behind it all is that a random sample is a representative sample.)

2. Manufacturers want the percentage of defective items coming off their assembly lines to be vanishingly small. It is not usually possible to inspect every item. Therefore the quality control procedure is to inspect only a small random sample of the items in each production run. "Random" means that every item is equally likely to be chosen for the sample. The percentage of defective items in the sample is expected to be the same as in the total production run.

The probability model that goes along with assigning equal probability to each outcome in a sample space is called the *equiprobable model*.

DEFINITION   Equiprobable Model

If a sample space S contains N equally likely outcomes, then the assignment of probability $1/N$ to each outcome defines the *equiprobable model*.

Notice that the equiprobable model has the properties required of a probability model: $1/N$ lies between 0 and 1; and the sum of the probabilities of all N outcomes in S is $N(1/N) = 1$.

To visualize the equiprobable model, we draw a Venn diagram containing sample points to represent the outcomes. Figure 6.16 is such a

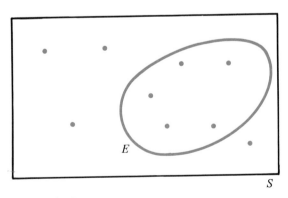

FIGURE 6.16

diagram. The sample space S contains nine sample points (representing nine outcomes). The five-outcome event E is represented by a closed curve containing five sample points. Since each of the nine points in S represents an outcome with probability $\frac{1}{9}$, it is clear that the five-outcome event E has probability $\frac{5}{9}$. This suggests the following definition:

DEFINITION   Probability of an Event (Equiprobable Model)

If the outcomes in a sample space S are equally likely, and if E is an event in S, then

$$P(E) = \frac{\text{number of outcomes in } E}{\text{number of outcomes in } S}$$

We usually write $n(E)$ (read "n of E") for the number of outcomes in E, $n(S)$ for the number of outcomes in S, and

$$P(E) = \frac{n(E)}{n(S)}$$

for the equiprobable model.

Now let's look at some problems that involve calculating the probability of an event in the equiprobable model. The concepts of complement, intersection, and union of events will be used in some of the calculations.

PROBLEM 1   A pair of symmetrical dice is given a fair roll. What is the probability that:

a.   each of the dice shows the same number on its top face?

b.   the sum of the numbers on the top faces is greater than 4?

c.   there is at least one 4 showing on the two top faces?

SOLUTION   The outcome of rolling two dice can be described by an ordered pair: (3, 5), for example, means that die 1 shows 3 and die 2 shows 5. Our sample space S—containing all possible outcomes for a roll of two dice—is given by:

$$S = \begin{cases} (1,1) & (1,2) & (1,3) & (1,4) & (1,5) & (1,6) \\ (2,1) & (2,2) & (2,3) & (2,4) & (2,5) & (2,6) \\ (3,1) & (3,2) & (3,3) & (3,4) & (3,5) & (3,6) \\ (4,1) & (4,2) & (4,3) & (4,4) & (4,5) & (4,6) \\ (5,1) & (5,2) & (5,3) & (5,4) & (5,5) & (5,6) \\ (6,1) & (6,2) & (6,3) & (6,4) & (6,5) & (6,6) \end{cases}$$

We have $n(S) = 36$. Any one of the 36 equally likely outcomes has probability $\frac{1}{36}$.

The event described in question a contains six outcomes:

$$A = \{(1,1), (2,2), (3,3), (4,4), (5,5), (6,6)\}$$

This means that

$$P(A) = \frac{n(A)}{n(S)} = \frac{6}{36} = \frac{1}{6}$$

Let's use the letter B for the event described in question b. B^C, the complement of B, contains six outcomes:

$$B^C = \{(1,1), (1,2), (1,3), (2,1), (2,2), (3,1)\}$$

Therefore

$$P(B^C) = \frac{n(B^C)}{n(S)} = \frac{1}{6}$$

and

$$P(B) = 1 - P(B^C) = \frac{5}{6}$$

As a check, we count the outcomes in B. The count gives us $n(B) = 30$, and

$$P(B) = \frac{n(B)}{n(S)} = \frac{5}{6}$$

To answer question c, we write

$$C = \{\text{at least one 4 on the two dice}\}$$

A count of outcomes gives us $n(C) = 11$ and

$$P(C) = \frac{n(C)}{n(S)} = \frac{11}{36}$$

For an alternate solution, we define the events

$$C_1 = \{4 \text{ on the first die}\}$$
$$C_2 = \{4 \text{ on the second die}\}$$

and their intersection, the one-outcome event

$$C_1 \cap C_2 = \{(4, 4)\}$$

We have $C = C_1 \cup C_2$ and therefore (see p. 310).

$$P(C) = P(C_1) + P(C_2) - P(C_1 \cap C_2)$$

Since $n(C_1) = n(C_2) = 6$ and $n(C_1 \cap C_2) = 1$, we have

$$P(C_1) = P(C_2) = \frac{1}{6} \qquad P(C_1 \cap C_2) = \frac{1}{36}$$

and

$$P(C) = \frac{11}{36}$$

as before.

PROBLEM 2   A retired investor owns shares of common stock in Chase Manhattan Bank, Morgan Guaranty Trust, Burroughs, Digital Equipment Corporation, and IBM (two banks and three computer companies). All five stocks are up sharply, and the investor decides to sell his shares in two of the five. Since he mistrusts his judgment, he will choose the two to be sold at random. (He will choose one of the five at random, and then he will choose one of the remaining four at random.) What is the probability that the two he sells will be:

a.   the two bank stocks?

b.   two of the three computer stocks?

c.   one bank and one computer stock?

SOLUTION   The experiment has two stages: (1) one of the five stocks is randomly selected; (2) one of the four remaining stocks is randomly selected.

We will call the bank stocks B_1, B_2 and the computer stocks C_1, C_2, and C_3. To count all possible outcomes of the investor's two choices, we draw a tree diagram (Figure 6.17).

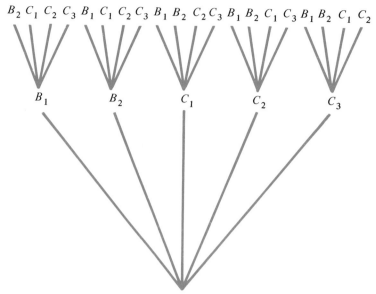

$$B_2\ C_1\ C_2\ C_3\ B_1\ C_1\ C_2\ C_3\ B_1\ B_2\ C_2\ C_3\ B_1\ B_2\ C_1\ C_3\ B_1\ B_2\ C_1\ C_2$$

$$B_1 \qquad B_2 \qquad C_1 \qquad C_2 \qquad C_3$$

FIGURE 6.17

The tree has 20 topmost branches, and 20 is the total number of equally likely outcomes in the sample space S of the experiment. We write

$$n(S) = 20$$

To answer question a, we notice from the tree diagram that the bank–bank event (which we will call event E) can happen in two ways only: $n(E) = 2$. Therefore

$$P(E) = \frac{n(E)}{n(S)} = \frac{2}{20} = \frac{1}{10}$$

Question b is answered in the same way. We will call the computer–computer event F, and we see from the tree diagram that $n(F) = 6$. This gives us

$$P(F) = \frac{n(F)}{n(S)} = \frac{6}{20} = \frac{3}{10}$$

To answer question c, we define the events

$G = \{$a bank stock is selected, then a computer stock is selected$\}$

$H = \{$a computer stock is selected, then a bank stock is selected$\}$

The event we are interested in is $J = G \cup H$. Since G and H are mutually exclusive events ($G \cap H = \emptyset$), we have

$$P(J) = P(G) + P(H) = \frac{n(G) + n(H)}{n(S)}$$

Since $n(G) = n(H) = 6$, the result is

$$P(J) = \frac{6}{10}$$

As a check, we notice that $P(E) + P(F) + P(J) = 1$. This is as it should be. The events E, F, and J are mutually exclusive, and their union contains all the outcomes in S.

PROBLEM 3   Sun Honey is a grower of extra-high-quality oranges that it sells by mail. A clerk is about to choose 2 oranges to complete a shipment. If the 2 oranges are chosen randomly from a box of 100 oranges—90 perfect, 10 blemished—what is the probability that:

a. both of the randomly selected oranges will be perfect?

b. both of the randomly selected oranges will be blemished?

SOLUTION   The experiment is: choose one of the 100 oranges at random, then choose one of the remaining 99 oranges at random.
  If we imagine a tree diagram representing this experiment, it would contain 100 branches starting at the root and 99 branches starting from each of these 100 branches. The number of topmost branches of the imagined tree would therefore be 9900. This is the total number of outcomes in the sample space S. We write:

$$n(S) = 9900$$

  For the clerk to choose 2 perfect oranges, he must *first* choose one of the 90 perfect oranges and *second* choose one of the 89 remaining perfect oranges. To count the number of perfect–perfect outcomes, we again imagine a tree diagram. There are 90 "perfect" branches starting at the root and 89 "perfect" branches starting from each of the 90. The number of topmost "perfect–perfect" branches is therefore $90 \cdot 89 = 8010$. If we call the perfect–perfect event A, then $n(A) = 8010$ and

$$P(A) = \frac{n(A)}{n(S)} = \frac{8010}{9900} = \frac{89}{110} = .809$$

Finally, the tree diagram illustrating the blemished–blemished outcome would have 10 "blemished" branches starting at the root and 9 "blemished" branches starting from each of the 10. The number of topmost "blemished–blemished" branches is $10 \cdot 9 = 90$. If we call the blemished–blemished event B, this gives us $n(B) = 90$ and

$$P(B) = \frac{n(B)}{n(S)} = \frac{90}{9900} = \frac{1}{110} = .009$$

Check: Notice first that

$$P(A \cup B) = P(A) + P(B) = \frac{9}{11}$$

All the outcomes in the sample space that are not contained in A or B are contained in

$$C_1 = \{\text{blemished–perfect}\} \quad \text{or} \quad C_2 = \{\text{perfect–blemished}\}$$

By imagining the tree diagram again, we see that

$$n(C_1) = 10 \cdot 90 = 900 \qquad n(C_2) = 90 \cdot 10 = 900$$

If we write $C = C_1 \cup C_2$, then $n(C) = 1800$ and

$$P(C) = \frac{1800}{9900} = \frac{2}{11}$$

Result: $P(A) + P(B) + P(C) = 1$, which checks.

EXERCISES *for Section 6.4*

1. A well-balanced coin is given two successive fair tosses. The sample space is

$$S = \{\text{HH, HT, TH, TT}\}$$

What is the probability of getting at least one head? What is the probability of getting exactly two heads?

2. A well-balanced coin is given three successive fair tosses. This means that the sample space for the experiment contains eight outcomes. If each of these outcomes is equally likely, then what is the probability of getting at least two heads? What is the probability of getting exactly two heads?

3. Luther Wilcox has had a spectacularly successful career as a TV programming boss. We can now reveal his methods. Every show Wilcox allows on the air must have exactly six sponsors. (He thinks six is his lucky number.) After the show has been aired, one of the six sponsors is chosen at random. Then Wilcox personally calls the top executive in the sponsor's advertising department and asks what he thinks of the show. If the executive does not like the show, Wilcox drops it.

    a. If two of the sponsors dislike the show, what is the probability that Wilcox will call one of the two?

    b. If three of the sponsors dislike the show, what is the probability that Wilcox will call one of the three?

    c. If four of the sponsors dislike the show (and two like it), what is the probability that Wilcox will call one of the two who like it?

4.   A pair of symmetrical dice (one red, one green) is given a fair roll. What is the probability that:

    a. 3 shows on the top face of the red die, 4 on the top face of the green die?

    b. 3 shows on the top face of one of the dice, 4 on the top face of the other?

    c. the sum of the numbers on the top faces is 6?

For the next two exercises, note that a positive integer greater than one is called a *prime* if it has no factors except one and itself. Examples of primes are 2, 3, and 29.

5.   A number is chosen at random from among the first 12 positive integers. What is the probability that the number chosen is a prime?

6.   A number is chosen at random from among the first 30 positive integers. What is the probability that the number chosen is a prime?

Two different numbers are selected at random from among the 4 prime numbers 3, 7, 11, 17.

7.   Draw a tree diagram showing all the possible outcomes of the experiment.

8.   What is the probability that the sum of the two randomly selected numbers will be less than 21?

A film director plans to remake the James Bond movie *You Only Live Twice*. The director's idea is to have both the hero and the villain played by actors dressed in ape suits, but what species of apes has not been decided. He will make his choice from among four actors—two dressed in chimpanzee suits, one dressed in a gorilla suit, and one dressed in an orangutan suit.

9.   Draw a tree diagram to show the number of outcomes if the director casts one of the four ape-suited actors as the hero and one of them as the villain. [*NOTE:* One casting choice is the ordered pair (chimp 1 for the hero, chimp 2 for the villain). The tree diagram will show you all the other choices.]

10. Assume that the director's casting choices are made at random. This means that each of the outcomes in the tree diagram of Exercise 9 is equally likely. Calculate the probability of each of the following choices:

    a. chimp 1 for the hero, chimp 2 for the villain
    b. chimp for the hero, gorilla for the villain
    c. orang for the hero, gorilla for the villain

---

11. Four parking lot customers have arrived to pick up their cars. Customer 1 owns a Cordoba, customer 2 a Granada, customer 3 a Z-car, and customer 4 a Volaré. An inexperienced parking lot attendant has mixed up the ignition keys and hands them out at random.

    a. Draw a tree diagram showing all the ways in which the keys can be handed out.
    b. Find the probability that customers 1 and 4 get the correct car keys.

The Surgical Review Board (SRB) at a hospital keeps an especially close watch on any surgeon who performs a large number of operations. For each 21 operations by such a surgeon, SRB investigates. SRB's method is to choose 2 of the 21 cases at random, and then to investigate these closely. If the surgeon's skill or judgment have been below average in either of these cases, the surgeon is asked to transfer to another hospital.

12. If the surgeon's skill or judgment were below average in only *1* of the 21 cases, what is the probability that SRB's random choice of 2 cases will include that 1?

13. If the surgeon's skill or judgment were below average in *5* of the 21 cases, what is the probability that SRB will ask the surgeon to transfer to another hospital?

chapter seven

COUNTING TECHNIQUES IN PROBABILITY

I F all the outcomes in a sample space S are equally likely, then we calculate the probability of an event E in S by *counting:* counting the number of outcomes in E, counting the number of outcomes in S.

In Section 6.4 we did our counting by listing the outcomes (as in worked-out Problem 1), drawing a tree diagram (as in Problem 2), or imagining a tree diagram (as in Problem 3).

When we study more realistic problems—in which, for example, the sample space may contain millions of outcomes—we need to do our counting more systematically. The first three sections of this chapter explain three useful counting techniques. In showing how these techniques are applied, this chapter gives special emphasis to random sampling and quality control applications.

Section 7.4 applies the counting technique of Section 7.3 to algebra. The result is the *binomial formula,* which we will need in Chapter 8.

THE MULTIPLICATION PRINCIPLE

An example will show how our first counting technique works.

PROBLEM 1   If the movies are to be believed, plainclothes police teams in San Francisco always contain one veteran officer and one rookie. The lieutenant in charge of SF Precinct 37 had 15 veterans and 18 rookies reporting for duty on January 2, 1978. How many different plainclothes teams could the lieutenant send out on the streets that day?

SOLUTION   The question being asked is: How many (veteran, rookie) *ordered pairs* can be found if there are 15 veterans $v_1, v_2, \ldots,$ v_{15} and 18 rookies $r_1, r_2, \ldots, r_{18}$ to choose from?
     For the answer, we arrange the possible ordered pairs in a rectangular array:

$$(v_1, r_1) \quad (v_1, r_2) \quad \cdot \ \cdot \ \cdot \quad (v_1, r_{18})$$

$$(v_2, r_1) \quad (v_2, r_2) \quad \cdot \ \cdot \ \cdot \quad (v_2, r_{18})$$

$$(v_{15}, r_1) \quad (v_{15}, r_2) \quad \cdot \ \cdot \ \cdot \quad (v_{15}, r_{18})$$

Row 8 of the array (if we wrote it out) would show that v_8 (veteran #8) can be teamed with any one of the 18 rookies. Column 9 would show that r_9 (rookie #9) can be teamed with any one of the 15 veterans. And so on. Each possible (veteran, rookie) team appears once and only once. To find how many of them there are, multiply: $15 \cdot 18 = 270$ possible teams.

Problem 1 illustrates the multiplication principle.

MULTIPLICATION PRINCIPLE

If there are m possible outcomes $(a_1, a_2, \ldots, a_m)$ of a first choice and n possible outcomes $(b_1, b_2, \ldots, b_n)$ of a second choice, then the number of (first choice, second choice) ordered pairs is mn.

The choices can also be called *decisions*. Or we can talk about stage 1 and stage 2 of a *two-stage experiment*.

PROBLEM 2   A stock trader has done very well with auto stocks in 1977. He does not think there is much bounce left in the autos, and his strategy for 1978 has two stages. Early in the year he will buy 1 of 3 consumer-oriented stocks, and at mid-year he will switch his money into 1 of 5 high-technology stocks. If he stays with the 8 stocks, how many possible choices does this strategy give him?

SOLUTION   There are 3 consumer-oriented and 5 high-technology stocks to choose from. The number of (consumer-oriented, high-technology) pairs is $3 \cdot 5 = 15$.

NOTE: This problem can also be solved by drawing or imagining a tree diagram. But the multiplication principle is quicker.

PROBLEM 3   A snake-fancier reaches into a cage containing 15 live mice and randomly chooses a mouse to feed to his hogback rattlesnake. Twenty-four hours later he randomly chooses one of the mice from the cage to feed his coppermouth moccasin. (We assume that no mice have been born in the cage—or died in it—during the 24-hour period.) How many possible outcomes are there for this two-stage probability experiment?

SOLUTION   We want to know how many (first-day mouse, second-day mouse) ordered pairs are possible. Since there are 15 mice to choose from on the first day and 14 mice to choose from on the second day, the multiplication principle says that there are $15 \cdot 14 = 210$ two-stage choices.

The multiplication principle can be applied to experiments with more than two stages. For example, there is a three-stage multiplication principle:

THREE-STAGE MULTIPLICATION PRINCIPLE

If there are m choices in the first stage, n choices in the second stage, and p choices in the third stage of a three-stage experiment, then the number of possible (first-choice, second-choice, third-choice) triplets is mnp.

Problem 4 will illustrate the three-stage principle and Problem 5, the 10-stage principle. The principle works in just the same way for 10 stages as it does for 2, 3, and so on.

PROBLEM 4   Drawbridge Mutual Fund ("combining safety with growth") has had some financial problems lately. Its management expects to increase the fund's cash position by selling one of Drawbridge's 14 drug stock holdings, one of its 13 chemical stock holdings, and one of its 18 petroleum stock holdings. How many possible choices are there for the drug-chemical-petroleum troika?

SOLUTION   There are 14 possible drug choices, 13 chemical choices, and 18 petroleum choices. The three-stage multiplication principle says that the number of possible (drug, chemical, petroleum) triplets is $14 \cdot 13 \cdot 18 = 3276$.

PROBLEM 5   There are 18,500,000 listed 10-digit telephone numbers in the U.S. (Example: 603-862-2320.) If a child at play lifts a telephone receiver and randomly dials a 10-digit number, what is the probability that this number will be one of the listed numbers?

SOLUTION   The child is conducting a 10-stage probability experiment. Since there are 10 choices at each stage, the number of possible outcomes is

$$10^{10} = \underbrace{10 \cdot 10 \cdot 10 \cdot \ldots \cdot 10}_{10 \text{ times}}$$

In other words: If S is the sample space for the experiment, then

$$n(S) = 10^{10}$$

The number of outcomes in the event

$$E = \{\text{child dials a listed number}\}$$

is given:

$$n(E) = 18{,}500{,}000$$

If we assume that all outcomes are equally likely,

$$P(E) = \frac{n(E)}{n(S)} = \frac{18{,}500{,}000}{10^{10}} = .00185$$

EXERCISES *for Section 7.1*

1. How many 2-digit numbers can you make up using the numbers 3, 5, 7, and 9 if: (a) repetitions are allowed; (b) repetitions are not allowed?

2. How many 3-digit numbers can you make up using the numbers 3, 5, 7, and 9 if: (a) repetitions are allowed; (b) repetitions are not allowed?

3. To order a dinner for two at Mee Hong, you choose one dish from column A and one from column B. If there are 9 dishes in column A and 7 in column B, how many dinners for two can be ordered?

4. To order a dinner for three at Mee Hong, you choose 2 dishes from among the 9 listed in column A, and 1 of the 7 listed in column B. How many dinners for three can be ordered if: (a) 2 different dishes are ordered from column A? (b) 2 orders of the same dish are chosen from column A?

5. How many different 2-letter words can be formed in which the first letter is a vowel and the second letter is a consonant? (*NOTE:* The words do not have to be dictionary-defined words. For example, *Eq* is one of the possibilities.)

6. How many different 3-letter words can be formed in which the first letter is a vowel, the second letter is a consonant, and the third letter is chosen from among B, D, G, J, M, R, V, Z?

7. Suppose that n distinguishable coins are tossed at the same time. Find the number of possible outcomes if $n = 2$; if $n = 3$; if $n = 4$.

8. Suppose that n dice are rolled at the same time. (The dice are distinguishable. For example, each die may be of a different color.) Find the number of possible outcomes if $n = 2$; $n = 3$; $n = 4$.

9. If a client asks an account executive at the New York Stock Exchange firm of Fenton Carlsbad Kelley for buying advice, the executive must recommend 1 basic-industry stock, 1 high-technology stock, and 1 mineral-resource stock. The executive is allowed to tailor his choices to the client's needs: he has a list of 9 basic-industry stocks, 6 high-technology stocks, and 8 mineral-resource stocks from which to make his recommendations. With these restrictions, how many possible 3-stock portfolios can a Fenton Carlsbad Kelley account executive recommend to a client?

$(_9C_1)(_6C_1)(_8C_1)$

$= 9 \cdot 6 \cdot 8 = 432$

The Fenton Carlsbad Kelley stock lists mentioned in Exercise 9 contain some winners and some losers. (A winner makes money for the client, a loser loses it.) To be precise: 5 of the basic-industry stocks are winners and 4 are losers; 1 of the high-technology stocks is a winner and 5 are losers; 4 of the mineral-resource stocks are winners and 4 are losers. Suppose that an account executive follows the rules explained in Exercise 9 and recommends a 3-stock portfolio to a client.

10. How many such portfolios contain 3 winners? How many contain 3 losers?

2

11. How many such portfolios contain 2 winners? How many contain 2 or more winners?

12. How many recommendable portfolios contain 2 losers? How many contain 2 or more losers?

WIN: $(5)(1)(4) = 20$

LOSE $(4)(5)(4) = 80$

In the next three exercises, assume that the account executive does *not* exercise his personal judgment. Each of the 9 possible choices from the basic-industry list, each of the 6 possible choices from the high technology list, and each of the 8 possible choices from the mineral resource list is therefore equally likely.

13. Use your answers to Exercises 9 and 10 to calculate the probability that an account executive recommends: (a) 3 winners; (b) 3 losers.

14. From Exercises 9 and 11, calculate the probabilities of: (a) 2 winners; (b) 2 or more winners.

15. From Exercises 9 and 12, calculate the probabilities of: (a) 2 losers; (b) 2 or more losers.

7.2 ORDERED SAMPLES AND PERMUTATIONS

Our second counting technique is closely related to sample-taking. Two examples will explain some key terms.

EXAMPLE 1: A professional soup-taster will sample one teaspoon of a new soup and grade the flavor, and then repeat with a second teaspoon and a third teaspoon. If these samples are taken from an 8-ounce cup of soup (8 ounces = 48 teaspoons), we say that the taster has taken a *sample of size 3* from a *population of size 48*. Since the taster has identified the first, second, and third teaspoon, his sample is *ordered*. Since he does not return the tasted soup to the cup, the sample is *without replacement*.

EXAMPLE 2:   Cleopatra has had 7 husbands. This is a *sample of size 7* from the *male population*. Since the names of husbands 1, 2, 3, 4, 5, 6, and 7 are known, the sample is *ordered*. Since husbands 5 and 6 were the same man, the sample is *with replacement*.

Let's say it again. If we have *n* objects—things or people or choices or outcomes in a sample space—and if we select *r* of these objects, then we have taken a *sample of size r* from a *population of size n*. We assume that the choices are made one by one and that we know which object was chosen first, second, and so on to the *r*th choice. In other words, we assume that the sample is *ordered*. After each choice, we do or do not return the chosen object to the population before making our next choice. If we do, it is *sampling with replacement*. If we do not, it is *sampling without replacement*.

EXAMPLES: SAMPLING WITH AND WITHOUT REPLACEMENT

1.   We select 13 cards from a standard deck. (This is a sample of size 13 from a population of 52 cards.) The sample will be *ordered:* we will note which card is chosen first, which is chosen second, and so on to the thirteenth card. If each of the 13 cards is returned to the deck after it is chosen, we have *sampling with replacement*. If each of the 13 cards is put aside—that is, not returned to the deck after it is chosen—then we have *sampling without replacement*.

2.   There are 130 moose in a certain area of Canada. Wildlife specialists sample this population every year. The sample size is 20. That is: 20 moose are captured, examined, identified with an ear tag, and released. This is sampling with replacement. The hope is that each year's sample will include some previously sampled moose.

3.   Every Rolls-Royce is inspected before it leaves the factory, but this sort of thing is not possible for high-volume car production. Instead, a small sample of each day's production is chosen for inspection. After a car has been inspected, it is sent on its way. (Gross defects are repaired. Small ones are left for the dealer to take care of.) This is sampling without replacement.

We want to be able to calculate the number of possible ways of choosing a sample of size *r* from a collection of *n* objects. As the following worked-out problem shows, the number we get depends on whether the sampling is with or without replacement.

PROBLEM 1   A president, vice-president, and treasurer are to be elected from among the 9 directors of the Wyotex Energy Corporation. How many ways are there to choose the 3 officers (a) if a director can be elected to more than one office—even to all three? (b) if no director can be elected to more than one office?

SOLUTION   In question a, there are 9 possible choices for each of the 3 offices. By the multiplication principle, the number of ways to choose the 3 officers is:

$$9 \cdot 9 \cdot 9 = 729$$

In question b, any one of the 9 directors can be elected president. Once that choice has been made, any one of 8 directors can be elected vice-president. Finally, any one of 7 directors can be elected treasurer. The multiplication principle shows that the number of ways to elect the 3 officers in question b is

$$9 \cdot 8 \cdot 7 = 504$$

Problem 1 shows us that the number of ways of choosing a sample of size 3 from a collection of 9 objects is

$$9^3 = 9 \cdot 9 \cdot 9$$

if the sampling is with replacement, and

$$9(9 - 1)(9 - 2)$$

if the sampling is without replacement.

The same rules work for choosing a sample of size r from a collection of n objects:

The number of ways of choosing a sample of size r from a collection of n objects is

$$n^r = \underbrace{n \cdot n \cdot \ldots \cdot n}_{r \text{ times}}$$

if the sampling is with replacement, and

$$n(n - 1)(n - 2) \cdots (n - r + 1)$$

if the sampling is without replacement.

NOTE: In the case of sampling with replacement, r can be larger than n. But if we have sampling without replacement, r must be smaller than or equal to n: $r \leq n$.

A sample without replacement is sometimes called a *rearrangement,* or *permutation.*

Suppose, for example, that a sales manager wants to assign 6 star sales representatives to 6 key territories. Each way of making these assignments is a sample without replacement of size 6 from a population of size 6. Each way of making the assignments is also a permutation of the 6 sales representatives. We know that there are

$$6 \cdot 5 \cdot 4 \cdot 3 \cdot 2 \cdot 1 = 720$$

ways of taking the sample. Therefore we also know that there are 720 permutations of the 6 sales representatives—or of any 6 objects.

If the sample size is smaller than the population size, we can still see that a sample and a permutation are the same thing. It is understood that this refers to samples without replacement. It is also understood (we assumed it once for all on p. 337) that all the samples we are talking about are *ordered.*

For an example, suppose that NASA has 19 equally qualified astronauts ready to go on a mission that requires 5 astronauts. These mission astronauts will be *ordered:* as Captain, Command Module Pilot, Lunar Module Pilot, Flight Engineer, and Communications Officer. The number of samples without replacement of size 5 from a population of size 19 gives NASA

$$19 \cdot 18 \cdot 17 \cdot 16 \cdot 15 = 1{,}395{,}360$$

ways of choosing the mission astronauts. The self-same number is also called the *number of permutations of 19 objects taken 5 at a time.*

We use the symbol $_nP_r$ (read "NPR") for the *number of permutations of n objects taken r at a time.* Therefore our example says that

$$_{19}P_5 = 19 \cdot 18 \cdot 17 \cdot 16 \cdot 15$$

Our example also illustrates the fact that the number of permutations of n objects taken r at a time is identical with the number of samples without replacement of size r from a population of size n:

$$_nP_r = n(n-1)(n-2) \cdots (n-r+1)$$

Our sales manager example says that

$$_6P_6 = 6 \cdot 5 \cdot 4 \cdot 3 \cdot 2 \cdot 1$$

This illustrates the fact that

$$_nP_n = n(n-1)(n-2) \cdots 1$$

The symbol $_nP_n$ (read "NPN") is called "the number of permutations of n objects" (If you want to be extra-fussy, you can say "n objects taken n at a time," but that is not really necessary.)

The best way to remember—and understand—the formula

$$_nP_r = n(n-1)(n-2) \cdots (n-r+1)$$

is to notice that the right side of the equation is the product of r consecutive integers, the highest of which is n. As examples:

$$_5P_3 = 5 \cdot 4 \cdot 3$$

is the product of 3 consecutive integers, the highest of which is 5;

$$_{17}P_6 = 17 \cdot 16 \cdot 15 \cdot 14 \cdot 13 \cdot 12$$

is the product of 6 consecutive integers, the highest of which is 17; and

$$_8P_8 = 8 \cdot 7 \cdot 6 \cdot 5 \cdot 4 \cdot 3 \cdot 2 \cdot 1$$

is the product of 8 consecutive integers, the highest of which is 8.

PROBLEM 2   Vampireman, a well-known daytime disc jockey, has 11 records he wants to play but he has only enough time left on his program to play 7 records. In how many ways can he choose and arrange these records?

SOLUTION   Vampireman wants to take a sample of size 7 from a collection of 11 objects. We assume that no selection will be played twice. This says that the sampling is without replacement. Vampireman can do his choosing and arranging in

$$_{11}P_7 = 11 \cdot 10 \cdot 9 \cdot 8 \cdot 7 \cdot 6 \cdot 5 = 1,663,200$$

ways.

The formula for $_nP_r$ becomes simpler if we define *factorials*.

EXAMPLES: FACTORIALS

$$1! = 1$$
$$2! = 2 \cdot 1 = 2$$
$$3! = 3 \cdot 2 \cdot 1 = 6$$
$$5! = 5 \cdot 4 \cdot 3 \cdot 2 \cdot 1 = 120$$

Notice that

$$6! = 6 \cdot 5 \cdot 4 \cdot 3 \cdot 2 \cdot 1 = 6(5!)$$

This illustrates the fact that

$$(n + 1)! = (n + 1)(n!)$$

---

for any positive integer n. If we set $n = 0$ in the boxed formula, we get

$$1! = (1)(0!)$$

Since $1! = 1$, we must take

$$0! = 1$$

to keep things consistent.

To apply factorials to permutations, we start with

$$_nP_n = n(n - 1) \cdots 1 = n!$$

Since $_nP_n$ is the number of permutations of n objects taken n at a time, we see from the multiplication principle that

$$_nP_n = {_nP_r} \cdot {_{n-r}P_{n-r}}$$

In words: We can rearrange n objects taken r at a time in $_nP_r$ ways. We can rearrange the remaining $(n - r)$ objects in $_{n-r}P_{n-r}$ ways. The multiplication principle therefore says that $_nP_n = {_nP_r} \cdot {_{n-r}P_{n-r}}$. As examples:

$$_4P_4 = {_4P_2} \cdot {_2P_2}$$

or

$$4! = (4 \cdot 3) \cdot (2 \cdot 1)$$

$$_9P_9 = {_9P_3} \cdot {_6P_6}$$

or

$$9! = (9 \cdot 8 \cdot 7) \cdot (6!)$$

Let's rewrite these examples:

$$_4P_2 = {_4P_4} \div {_2P_2}$$
$$= \frac{4!}{2!}$$

$$_9P_3 = {_9P_9} \div {_6P_6}$$
$$= \frac{9!}{6!}$$

In the same way, rewriting the equation $_nP_n = {_nP_r} \cdot {_{n-r}P_{n-r}}$ gives us

$$_nP_r = {_nP_n} \div {_{n-r}P_{n-r}}$$

or

$$_nP_r = \frac{n!}{(n - r)!}$$

If $r = n$, this reduces to $_nP_n = n! \div 0!$. Since $0! = 1$, we have $_nP_n = n!$, which checks.

PROBLEM 3   In how many ways can 13 successive cards be dealt from a 52-card deck?

SOLUTION   This is a problem in sampling without replacement. The number of ways of taking the sample is

$$_{52}P_{13} = \frac{52!}{39!}$$

PROBLEM 4   A conservative portfolio manager knows of 37 stocks that meet her investment criterion. (Each of these stocks pays a well-protected dividend in excess of 6%.) She will choose 9 of them for investment, and her choices will be made one by one. In how many ways can she make the 9 choices?

SOLUTION The 9-stock portfolio is a sample from a population of 37. Since the sample is ordered and without replacement, it can be chosen in

$$_{37}P_9 = \frac{37!}{9!} \qquad \frac{37!}{28!}$$

ways.

Problems 5, 6, and 7 use the ideas of sampling with and without replacement in calculating probabilities.

PROBLEM 5 There are 10 digits: 0, 1, 2, ..., 9. If we choose 4 of these digits randomly, one after the other, what is the probability that all 4 are different?

SOLUTION Since the choices are made randomly, each of the 10 outcomes is equally likely. Therefore the probability of the event

$$E = \{\text{all 4 digits are different}\}$$

will be given by

$$P(E) = \frac{n(E)}{n(S)}$$

The sample space S is made up of all possible outcomes of 4 successive choices from among the 10 digits. Repetitions are possible. In other words, S is a sample *with replacement*. Therefore

$$n(S) = 10^4$$

By contrast, $n(E)$ is the number of ways of taking a sample of size 4 from a population of size 10 *without replacement*. This means that

$$n(E) = {}_{10}P_4$$

Our result is

$$P(E) = \frac{n(E)}{n(S)} = \frac{{}_{10}P_4}{10^4} = \frac{10!}{10^4 \cdot 6!} = .504$$

PROBLEM 6 Four weary Christmas shoppers have spent hours at the Newington Mall. Each of the 4 will have something to eat before leaving the mall. There is a choice of 6 eating places. If each of the 6 is an equally likely choice, what is the probability that the 4 shoppers will eat at different eating places?

SOLUTION   The outcomes are equally likely. If we define

$$E = \{\text{each shopper eats at a different place}\}$$

then $n(E)$ is the number of ways of taking a sample of size 4 from a population of size 6 without replacement. And $n(S)$ is the number of ways of taking a sample of size 4 from a population of size 6 with replacement. Therefore

$$P(E) = \frac{n(E)}{n(S)} = \frac{{}_6P_4}{6^4} = \frac{6!}{6^4 \cdot 2!} = .2778$$

PROBLEM 7   Flight 47 is finally airborne after an aircraft repair delay of close to two hours. The 60 passengers are slightly upset, and the stewardesses try to calm them by running a game, offering a prize to the winner. Every passenger writes down his or her name and birthday on a slip of paper. All these slips are then collected and compared. If two or more passengers have the same birthday, each of them receives a prize. This game does not seem very generous, since there are 365 days in the year and only 60 people. In fact one passenger offers to bet \$100 that no one gets a prize. Another passenger (who once studied probability in a math course) snaps up the bet. He wins the \$100, and he is not one bit surprised. Can you explain?

SOLUTION   The first passenger is betting that no 2 passengers among 60 have the same birthday.

To keep things simple, we assume that each of 365 days is an equally likely birthday for a passenger. (February 29 is ignored.) We define

$$E = \{\text{no 2 passengers have the same birthday}\}$$

$$S = \{365 \text{ possible birthdays}\}$$

We will calculate $P(E)$. If the first passenger has a poor bet, then $P(E)$ will of course be very small.

For the calculation, we use the same reasoning as in Problems 5 and 6. We find that

$$P(E) = \frac{{}_{365}P_{60}}{365^{60}} = \frac{365!}{365^{60} \cdot 60!}$$

$P(E)$ is certainly small. The precise (computer-calculated) result is:

$$P(E) = .006$$

The first passenger certainly had a poor bet.

Notice that we can say this another way by defining the complement E^C of the event E. We have

$$E^C = \{\text{at least 2 passengers have the same birthday}\}$$

and

$$P(E^C) = 1 - P(E) = 1 - .006 = .994.$$

In other words: The passenger who snapped up the first passenger's $100 bet had something very close to a sure thing.

EXERCISES *for Section 7.2*

Evaluate each of the following:

1. $_9P_6$ **2.** $_7P_5$ **3.** $_6P_1$

4. $_8P_3$ **5.** $_{11}P_7$ **6.** $_{15}P_{13}$

Express in terms of factorials:

7. $_{22}P_{11}$ **8.** $_{16}P_4$ **9.** $_9P_9$

10. $_{100}P_{95}$ **11.** $_{1000}P_{1000}$ **12.** $_8P_5$

Find the number of permutations of:

13. the three numbers 3, 5, and 7

14. the four numbers 7, 11, 13, and 17

$(4)(3)(2)(1) = 24$ Sampling w̄ō Replacint

---

15. The *Handbook of Statistics* is a 5-volume reference work. Volumes 1, 2, 3, 4, and 5 are left on a library table and replaced on the shelf by a librarian who thinks, "There is only one correct way to arrange these 5 volumes on the shelf. I wonder how many incorrect ways there are." How many incorrect arrangements are there?

$(5)(4)(3)(2)(1)$ $-1 = 120-1$

$= 119$

Find the number of permutations of:

16. the three numbers 3, 5, and 7, taken two at a time

17. the four numbers 7, 11, 13, and 17, taken three at a time

---

18. A panel of wine tasters is asked to taste 16 May wines and to choose the ones that rank 1, 2, 3, and 4 in fruitiness. In how many different ways can the panel make such a choice?

19. Don Corleone has business concessions worth $100,000 per year, $75,000 per year, and $50,000 per year to award to loyal members of his family. Ten family members qualify. No one is to receive more than one concession. How many different ways are there to make the three awards?

Cultural historians tell us that the practice of referring to an organization or government agency by initials marks a certain stage in cultural evolution. Whatever that stage may be, we have long since reached it in the land of GE, UP, EPA, IBM, and HEW, and the home of NYSE, NCAA, AAUP, VISTA, ACTION, and NASDAQ. With all this in mind, we ask:

20. If letters can be repeated, then: (a) How many different two-initial names are possible? (b) How many three-initial names? (c) How many names with at most four initials?

21. If letters are not to be repeated: (a) How many different two-initial names are possible? (b) How many three-initial names? (c) How many names with at most four initials?

22. Using your answers to Exercises 20 and 21 (and assuming that all letter choices are equally likely), calculate the probability that the initials that may be used to identify an organization or government agency will all be different if the number of initials is: (a) 2; (b) 3; (c) at least 4.

---

23. The numbers 1, 2, 3, 4, 5, and 6 are arranged in random order. What is the probability that the 6-digit arrangement contains the numbers 1, 2 in that order?

HINT: Find the number of arrangements of the 6 digits in which 1, 2 in that order occupy the first and second of the 6 places. Then find the number of arrangements in which 1, 2 in that order occupy the second and third of the 6 places, and so on to the number of arrangements in which 1 is in the fifth place and 2 is in the sixth.

24. If the numbers 1, 2, 3, 4, 5, 6, 7, 8, 9, and 10 are arranged in random order, what is the probability that the arrangement contains the numbers 1, 2 in that order?

25. The numbers 1, 2, 3, 4, 5, and 6 are randomly arranged. What is the probability that the numbers 1, 2, 3 occur in the arrangement in that order?

26. The numbers 1, 2, 3, 4, 5, 6, 7, 8, 9, 10 are randomly arranged. What is the probability that the numbers 1, 2, 3 occur in the arrangement in that order?

27. Ten discs numbered 0, 1, 2, 3, 4, 5, 6, 7, 8, 9 are mixed in a revolving drum. A disc is drawn and its number is recorded. Then the disc is returned to the drum and the drum is revolved before the next drawing. This procedure is repeated 6 times. What is the probability that 6 differently numbered discs are drawn?

28. Five skiers have arrived at a crossing where 7 ski trails meet. Each skier then makes his or her own random choice of trail to follow. What is the probability that no 2 skiers follow the same trail away from the crossing?

See P. 338

The Opera Awards Board (OAB) is about to choose the opera of the year in 4 categories: best music, best libretto, best integration of music and libretto, and greatest overall originality. Twelve operas are being considered for these awards.

29. If no opera is to receive OAB's award in more than one category, how many possible choices are there for OAB to make?

30. If one opera can receive OAB's award in 2, 3, or all 4 categories, how many possible choices are there for OAB to make?

31. Suppose that one opera may win all 4 awards, as in Exercise 30. And suppose that OAB makes its awards at random. What is the probability that each of the 4 awards goes to a different opera?

In the next three exercises, we assume that each of the 12 months of the year is an equally likely birth month.

32. Two secretaries are having lunch together. What is the probability that both were born in the same month?

33. Three junior executives are discussing a recently televised hockey game. What is the probability that at least 2 of them were born in the same month?

34. Four middle-level executives and 5 union representatives are holding a bargaining session. What is the probability that: (a) At least 2 of the executives were born in the same month? (b) At least 2 of the union representatives were born in the same month? (c) At least 2 of the 9 people in the room were born in the same month?

7.3 UNORDERED SAMPLES AND COMBINATIONS

In Section 7.2 we always assumed that samples were ordered. Now we turn to the case of unordered samples.

SEC. 7.3 UNORDERED SAMPLES AND COMBINATIONS

PROBLEM 1   The sample space

$$S = \{G, F, M, J\}$$

contains 4 outcomes. How many 2-outcome events are there in S?

SOLUTION   At a glance, we might decide that the answer is

$$_4P_2 = 4 \cdot 3 = 12$$

But this would give us the number of *ordered* 2-outcome samples that can be taken from the 4-outcome sample space. And we recognize that $\{G, F\}$ and $\{F, G\}$ are *not* distinct events. In other words: We are interested in the number of *unordered* 2-outcome samples that can be taken from S.

The number of orderings (or permutations) of 2 objects is 2!.

To unorder, we merely *divide* by 2!. The number of 2-outcome events in S is therefore

$$\frac{_4P_2}{2!} = \frac{4 \cdot 3}{2 \cdot 1} = 6$$

Check: The sample space S appears in Example 1 of Section 6.2. All the events in S are listed on p. 291, and there are 6 two-outcome events.

An unordered sample without replacement of size r from a population of size n is called a *combination of n objects taken r at a time.*

The number of different combinations of n objects taken r at a time will be written $_nC_r$ (read "NCR"). As Problem 1 suggests, the number $_nC_r$ of combinations or unordered samples is related to the number $_nP_r$ of permutations or ordered samples:

HOW $_nC_r$ AND $_nP_r$ ARE RELATED

1. The number of *ordered* size-r samples from a size-n population is $_nP_r$.

2. There are $r!$ orderings (permutations) of each size-r sample.

3. To *un-order,* we divide by $r!$ The result is

$$_nC_r = \frac{_nP_r}{r!}$$

For an example we have (as was shown in Problem 1):

$$_4C_2 = \frac{_4P_2}{2!}$$

Since we know that

$$_nP_r = \frac{n!}{(n-r)!}$$

we can express $_nC_r$ by means of factorials.

> The number of combinations of n things taken r at a
> time is
>
> $$_nC_r = \frac{n!}{r!(n-r)!}$$

To repeat: *Combination* is another word for *unordered sample*. Therefore $_nC_r$ is the number of ways of choosing an unordered sample without replacement of size r from a population of size n.

PROBLEM 2   A sample space S contains 52 outcomes. How many 5-outcome events are there in S? How many 13-outcome events?

SOLUTION   The 5-outcome and 13-outcome events are unordered samples. Their respective numbers are

$$_{52}C_5 = \frac{52!}{5!47!}$$

$$_{52}C_{13} = \frac{52!}{13!39!}$$

PROBLEM 3   The 9 directors of the Wyotex Energy Corporation are about to elect a 3-member Solar Energy Committee. How many ways are there of electing the committee?

SOLUTION   Three different people are to be on the committee. But the order in which they are chosen is unimportant. We therefore want to know the number of ways of choosing an unordered sample without replacement of size 3 from a population of size 9. The answer is

$$_9C_3 = \frac{9!}{3!6!} = \frac{9 \cdot 8 \cdot 7}{3 \cdot 2 \cdot 1} = 84$$

NOTE: This problem should be compared with part (b) of Problem 1 in Section 7.2. In that case the sample was *ordered* and the number of ways to take the sample was therefore

$$_9P_3 = 3! \cdot {}_9C_3$$

PROBLEM 4 A well-balanced coin is tossed 10 times. What is the probability of exactly 4 heads? of exactly 5 heads? of exactly 6 heads?

SOLUTION The outcomes of each toss are H (heads) and T (tails). We assume that

$$P(H) = P(T) = \tfrac{1}{2}$$

The sample space S for the experiment contains all possible outcomes of 10 tosses: H or T on the first toss, the second toss, and so on to the tenth toss. This is a case of sampling with replacement (both H and T are available on each toss), and we therefore have

$$n(S) = 2^{10}$$

Next we look at

$$E = \{4 \text{ of the outcomes are heads}\}$$

Since order is irrelevant (we do not care which 4 tosses give us heads), we want the number of combinations of 10 outcomes taken 4 at a time. (In terms of sampling: We want the number of ways of taking an unordered sample without replacement of size 4 from a population of size 10.) The number is

$$n(E) = {}_{10}C_4$$

Our result for the probability of 4 heads is

$$P(E) = \frac{{}_{10}C_4}{2^{10}}$$

In the same way, we find that the events F (5 heads) and G (6 heads) have probabilities

$$P(F) = \frac{{}_{10}C_5}{2^{10}}$$

and

$$P(G) = \frac{_{10}C_6}{2^{10}}$$

For numerical results we use factorials:

$$_{10}C_4 = \frac{10!}{4!6!} = 210$$

$$_{10}C_5 = \frac{10!}{5!5!} = 252$$

$$_{10}C_6 = \frac{10!}{6!4!} = 210$$

Since $2^{10} = 1024$, we have:

$$P(E) = \frac{210}{1024} = .205$$

$$P(F) = \frac{252}{1024} = .246$$

$$P(G) = \frac{210}{1024} = .205$$

Since $P(E)$ is the probability of 4 heads in 10 tosses and $P(G)$ is the probability of 4 tails in 10 tosses—and heads and tails are equally likely—it is not surprising that $P(E) = P(G)$.

The next problem deals with the game of bridge. To understand the problem you need to know three facts. A standard 52-card bridge deck contains 4 suits: spades, hearts, clubs, and diamonds. Each suit contains 13 cards: 2, 3, 4, 5, 6, 7, 8, 9, 10, J (Jack), Q (Queen), K (King), A (Ace). In the game of bridge, each of 4 players is dealt 13 cards.

PROBLEM 5   What is the probability that 10 of the 13 cards in a bridge hand are spades?

SOLUTION   We assume that the deck is well shuffled, so that all outcomes are equally likely. The sample space S contains all possible 13-card hands that can be dealt from a 52-card deck. Since the order of the cards is irrelevant, $n(S)$ is the number of combinations of 52 things taken 13 at a time:

$$n(S) = {}_{52}C_{13}$$

We are interested in the event

$$E = \{10 \text{ of the } 13 \text{ cards dealt to one player are spades}\}.$$

There are 13 spades in the deck. Any 1 of the 4 players may receive any 10 of these among the 13 cards he is dealt, and he may receive them in any order. The remaining 3 cards in that player's hand are non-spades. In other words, E is a 2-stage event. The first stage (receiving 10 of the 13 spades in the deck) can occur in ${}_{13}C_{10}$ ways. The second stage (receiving 3 of the 39 non-spades in the deck) can occur in ${}_{39}C_3$ ways. By the multiplication principle:

$$n(E) = {}_{13}C_{10} \cdot {}_{39}C_3$$

Finally:

$$P(E) = \frac{n(E)}{n(S)} = \frac{{}_{13}C_{10} \cdot {}_{39}C_3}{{}_{52}C_{13}}$$

In Problem 6, we will have 5 cards dealt from a bridge deck. The solution of the problem uses a fact explained in Section 6.3: If an event is the *union* of two other events, as in

$$E = E_1 \cup E_2$$

and if E_1 and E_2 are disjoint events ($E_1 \cap E_2 = \emptyset$), then

$$P(E) = P(E_1) + P(E_2)$$

In Problem 6, we define an event that is the union of 4 events:

$$E = E_1 \cup E_2 \cup E_3 \cup E_4$$

The events will be disjoint (none of the 4 has outcomes in common with any of the others) and we will therefore have

$$P(E) = P(E_1) + P(E_2) + P(E_3) + P(E_4)$$

PROBLEM 6   Five cards are dealt from a well-shuffled 52-card bridge deck. What is the probability that all 5 cards are of the same suit?

SOLUTION   We assume that all outcomes are equally likely. The sample space S consists of all possible 5-card deals from a 52-card deck. Since order is irrelevant,

$$n(S) = {}_{52}C_5$$

We are interested in the event E that consists of any 1 of the 4 events

$$E_1 = \{\text{all 5 cards are spades}\}$$
$$E_2 = \{\text{all 5 cards are hearts}\}$$
$$E_3 = \{\text{all 5 cards are diamonds}\}$$
$$E_4 = \{\text{all 5 cards are clubs}\}$$

Since there are 13 spades and order is again irrelevant, we see that

$$n(E_1) = {}_{13}C_5$$

In the same way:

$$n(E_2) = n(E_3) = n(E_4) = {}_{13}C_5$$

But E can be any 1 of the 4 events, so that the total number of ways for E to occur is:

$$n(E) = 4 \cdot {}_{13}C_5$$

Finally:

$$P(E) = \frac{n(E)}{n(S)} = \frac{4 \cdot {}_{13}C_5}{{}_{52}C_5}$$

If we use factorials, we have

How DOES This HAPPEN?

$$P(E) = \frac{4(13!)(5!)(47!)}{(52!)(5!)(8!)} = .0019807$$

$$\frac{(4)(13!)}{5!\,(8!)}$$
$$\frac{52!}{5!\,(47!)}$$

This means that there are about 2 chances in 1000 that 5 cards dealt from a well-shuffled deck will all be of the same suit.

PROBLEM 7 What is the probability that a 13-card bridge hand contains 7 spades, 3 hearts, 2 diamonds, and 1 club?

SOLUTION We assume that the 52-card bridge deck has been well shuffled, so that all outcomes are equally likely. Our sample space S contains all possible outcomes in the dealing of 13 cards from a 52-card deck. Therefore

$$n(S) = {}_{52}C_{13}$$

We are interested in the event

$$E = \{\text{7 spades, 3 hearts, 2 diamonds, 1 club}\}$$

The 7 spades can be dealt in $_{13}C_7$ ways, the 3 hearts in $_{13}C_3$ ways, the 2 diamonds in $_{13}C_2$ ways, and the club in $_{13}C_1$ ways. The multiplication principle says that

$$n(E) = {}_{13}C_7 \cdot {}_{13}C_3 \cdot {}_{13}C_2 \cdot {}_{13}C_1$$

We therefore have

$$P(E) = \frac{n(E)}{n(S)} = .0001$$

(The result was obtained by expressing $n(E)$ and $n(S)$ in terms of factorials and carrying out the needed multiplication and division on a hand-held calculator). In other words: There is 1 chance in 10,000 that a bridge hand dealt from a well-shuffled deck will contain 7 spades, 3 hearts, 2 diamonds, and 1 club.

The ideas we use in solving card-dealing problems like Problems 5, 6, and 7 are also applied in solving real-world random sampling problems. (Remember: A sample is *random* if each outcome in the sample space is equally likely to be included in the sample.) Problems 8, 9, and 10 are examples.

PROBLEM 8   Big Oil Bank (BOB), like most other major banks, took a long bath in the 1972–1974 real estate binge. BOB made 20 substantial loans to real estate developers, 5 of which had to be charged off as total losses. (Since the 20 loans—including the 5 bad ones—averaged $89 million each, that was a lot to charge off.) Before these disastrous facts were generally known, a regulatory agency examined a random sample consisting of 5 of BOB's 20 real estate loans. What is the probability that the agency's sample contained:

a.   2 bad loans?
b.   at least 1 bad loan?
c.   more than 3 bad loans?

SOLUTION   Since the 5-loan sample is a random sample, each of the 20 loans on BOB's books was equally likely to be selected for examination.

The sample space S contained all possible ways of selecting an unordered sample without replacement of size 5 from a population of size 20. Therefore

$$n(S) = {}_{20}C_5 = 15,504$$

To answer question a, we define the event

$$E = \{2 \text{ bad loans, 3 good loans in the sample}\}$$

BOB's 20 loans include 5 bad ones and 15 good ones. The number of ways of choosing 2 bad loans is $_5C_2 = 10$, and the number of ways of choosing 3 good loans is $_{15}C_3 = 455$. The multiplication principle gives us

$$n(E) = 10 \cdot 455 = 4550$$

so that

$$P(E) = \frac{n(E)}{n(S)} = \frac{4550}{15,504} = .2934726$$

The event described in question b is

$$F = \{\text{at least 1 of the sampled loans is bad}\}$$

The easy way to calculate $P(F)$ is to work with the complementary event

$$F^C = \{0 \text{ bad loans, 5 good loans in the sample}\}$$

We have

$$n(F^C) = {}_5C_0 \cdot {}_{15}C_5 = 1 \cdot 3003 = 3003 \quad \text{Same as}$$
$$\text{cards}$$
$$\text{Sample must} = \mathcal{N} \text{ choices}$$

so that

$$P(F^C) = \frac{n(F^C)}{n(S)} = \frac{3003}{15,504} = .1936919$$

and

$$P(F) = 1 - P(F^C) = .8063081$$

Question c asks for the probability of the event

$$G = G_1 \cup G_2$$

where $G_1 = \{4 \text{ bad loans, 1 good loan in the sample}\}$
$G_2 = \{5 \text{ bad loans, 0 good loans in the sample}\}$

We find that

$$n(G_1) = {}_5C_4 \cdot {}_{15}C_1 = 5 \cdot 14 = 70$$
$$n(G_2) = {}_5C_5 \cdot {}_{15}C_0 = 1 \cdot 1 = 1$$

Therefore

$$P(G_1) = \frac{70}{15,504} \qquad P(G_2) = \frac{1}{15,504}$$

and

$$P(G) = P(G_1) + P(G_2) = \frac{71}{15,504} = .0045794$$

REAL-WORLD INTERPRETATION   The solution of Problem 8 shows us that the regulatory agency's random sample was not very likely to contain exactly 2 bad loans, and almost certainly did not contain more than 3 bad loans. But there was a high probability that the sample contained at least 1 bad loan, and this should have been enough to tell the regulatory agency that BOB was taking a real beating in real estate.

PROBLEM 9   Aztec Motors is determined to make its Tigre model the Rolls-Royce of North American automobiles. As a first step, quality control people will inspect a full 50% of total Tigre production. Each car that is inspected will be classified as G (good), F (fair), M (marginal), or J (junk). This is the same classification used in Rolls-Royce inspections.

M. Figueroa, a quality control expert at Aztec's San Diego plant, inspected a random sample of 10 cars out of 20 produced by a certain assembly group. If he had inspected all 20 cars, he would have classified them as follows:

G	M	F	J
8	6	4	2

What is the probability that M. Figueroa's 10-car random sample contains 4 cars he classifies as G, 3 cars he classifies as M, 2 cars he classifies as F, and 1 car he classifies as J?

SOLUTION   We will use the same approach that we used in solving Problem 7. The sample space S contains all possible outcomes in M. Figueroa's random selection of 10 cars out of 20. Therefore

$$n(S) = {}_{20}C_{10} = 184,756$$

The event we are interested in is

$$E = \{4G, 3M, 2F, 1J\}$$

Since there are 8 G-classified cars to choose from, the number of ways of choosing 4 G-cars is

$$_8C_4 = 70$$

Similarly, the number of ways of choosing 3 M-cars is

$$_6C_3 = 20$$

The number of ways of choosing 2 F-cars is

$$_4C_2 = 6$$

and the number of ways of choosing 1 J-car is

$$_2C_1 = 2$$

The multiplication principle tells us that

$$n(E) = 70 \cdot 20 \cdot 6 \cdot 2 = 16{,}800$$

Therefore

$$P(E) = \frac{n(E)}{n(S)} = \frac{16{,}800}{184{,}756} = .0909307$$

PROBLEM 10 (This problem is a continuation of Problem 9.) M. Figueroa's assembly group has an off day. Out of 20 cars produced, 9 are bad enough to be classified J. When M. Figueroa inspects a randomly chosen 10 cars of the 20, what is the probability that he gives the J classification to:

a. fewer than 4?
b. exactly 4?
c. more than 5?

SOLUTION As in Problem 9, we have

$$n(S) = {}_{20}C_{10} = 184{,}756$$

To answer question a, we need to define an event

$$E = E_1 \cup E_2 \cup E_3 \cup E_4$$

where
$$E_1 = \{0 \text{ J, } 10 \text{ non-J}\}$$
$$E_2 = \{1 \text{ J, } 9 \text{ non-J}\}$$
$$E_3 = \{2 \text{ J, } 8 \text{ non-J}\}$$
$$E_4 = \{3 \text{ J, } 7 \text{ non-J}\}$$

Since the 20-car population contains 9 J-cars and 11 non-J cars, we have

$$n(E_1) = {}_9C_0 \cdot {}_{11}C_{10} = 1 \cdot 11 = 11$$

$$n(E_2) = {}_9C_1 \cdot {}_{11}C_9 = 9 \cdot 55 = 495$$

$$n(E_3) = {}_9C_2 \cdot {}_{11}C_8 = 36 \cdot 165 = 5940$$

$$n(E_4) = {}_9C_3 \cdot {}_{11}C_7 = 84 \cdot 330 = 27{,}720$$

Since

$$n(E) = n(E_1) + n(E_2) + n(E_3) + n(E_4) = 34{,}166$$

we have

$$P(E) = \frac{n(E)}{n(S)} = \frac{34{,}166}{184{,}756} = .1849249$$

For question b, we define the event

$$F = \{4 \text{ J}, 6 \text{ non-J}\}$$

and we have

$$n(F) = {}_9C_4 \cdot {}_{11}C_6 = 126 \cdot 462 = 58{,}212$$

so that

$$P(F) = \frac{n(F)}{n(S)} = \frac{58{,}212}{184{,}756} = .315075$$

To calculate the probability of the event

$$G = \{\text{more than 5 J-cars}\}$$

we consider the complementary event

$$G^C = \{0, 1, 2, 3, 4, \text{ or } 5 \text{ J-cars}\}$$

which is the union of 3 events:

$$G_1{}^C = E_1$$

as defined in the answer to question a;

$$G_2{}^C = F$$

as defined in the answer to question b; and

$$G_3{}^C = \{5 \text{ J}, 5 \text{ non-J}\}$$

Since

$$n(G_3{}^C) = {}_9C_5 \cdot {}_{11}C_5 = 126 \cdot 462 = 58{,}212$$

we have $P(G_3{}^C) = P(F)$ and

$$P(G^C) = P(E) + P(F) + P(F) = .8150749$$

Therefore

$$P(G) = 1 - P(G^C) = .1849251$$

<hr>

EXERCISES *for Section 7.3*

Evaluate:

1. $_8C_6$ **2.** $_9C_7$ **3.** $_{11}C_{10}$

4. $_{13}C_0$ **5.** $_{17}C_2$ **6.** $_{666}C_{665}$

<hr>

7. You are told that $_{11}P_5 = 55440$. What is $_{11}C_5$?

8. You are told that $_{19}P_4 = 92880$. What is $_{19}C_4$?

<hr>

9. The sample space $S = \{G, M, F, J\}$ contains 4 outcomes. How many 2-outcome events are there in S? How many 3-outcome events? Check your answers by listing the events.

10. The sample space $S = \{A_1, A_2, \ldots, A_{27}\}$ contains 27 outcomes. How many 4-outcome events are there in S? How many 12-outcome events? How many 23-outcome events?

11. The Association of New England Pizza Houses (ANEPH), an organization of franchise owners, formed an 11-member committee to negotiate certain matters with national Pizza House management. The committee sent 4 of its members to national headquarters for preliminary talks. In how many ways could that 4-person group have been chosen?

12. ANEPH (as defined in Exercise 11) wanted to exchange ideas with ANYPH (Association of New York Pizza Houses). A 3-person group was sent to New York for that purpose. The 3-person group was chosen from the 11-member committee mentioned in Exercise 11. In how many ways could that 3-person group *and* the 4-person group sent to national headquarters be chosen from the 11-member committee, if no one could belong to both the 3-person group and the 4-person group?

<hr>

A Chrysler-Plymouth dealer has 58 new cars in stock. Of these, 13 are Plymouths, 23 are Volarés, and 22 are Chryslers. The dealer plans to display 4 cars in the showroom.

13. If the cars displayed may be Chryslers, Plymouths, or Volarés, how many ways does the dealer have to choose the 4 cars?

14. Suppose that 2 of the cars displayed are to be Chryslers and the other 2 Plymouths or Volarés. Now how many ways are there to make the choice?

15. Finally, suppose that the dealer decides to display 2 Volarés, 1 Chrysler, and 1 Plymouth. How many ways are there to make this choice?

---

16. Winnipesaukee National Bank (WNB) was founded to meet the needs of vacationers in the Lake Winnipesaukee area. Business has been good, and WNB is about to become a year-round full-service bank. The first step is to elect a board of directors. There will be 8 of them: 3 local lawyers and 5 local businessmen. If 6 lawyers and 11 businessmen are being considered for the board, how many different 8-member boards can be appointed?

17. U. K. Featherstone, the most successful account executive at Fenton Carlsbad Kelley, has just retired. Nine of Featherstone's accounts are to be handed on to 3 younger account executives. Each of them will be given 3 of the 9 accounts. In how many ways can this be done?

18. Writerite manufactures ball point pens and packages them in boxes of 12. If the company has 12,000 pens ready for packaging and 30 of these are defective, then:

    a. How many different packages containing *no* defective pens can the company put together?

    b. How many different packages of 12 pens containing *at least 1* defective pen can be put together?

19. A well-balanced coin is tossed 7 times. What is the probability that:

    a. exactly 2 heads are observed?

    b. exactly 3 heads are observed?

    c. at least 4 heads are observed?

20. Every few months (except in the winter) an intrepid balloonist attempts to make it over the Atlantic. As of this writing, there have been no successes. Assuming that the next 13 balloonists to make the attempt all come down in mid-Atlantic and assuming that the probability of rescue within 12 hours is $\frac{1}{2}$, what is the probability that exactly 5 of the 13 will be rescued within 12 hours? exactly 6? at least 7?

21. Cleopatra sometimes marries for love and sometimes marries for money. In the language of probability: the probability experiment of marriage by Cleopatra has the two outcomes L (marries for love) and M (marries for money). The sample space S for the experiment is

$$S = \{L, M\}$$

Observers of Cleopatra's career have assigned equal probabilities to L and M:

$$P(\text{L}) = P(\text{M}) = \tfrac{1}{2}$$

If these probabilities are correct (and if they remain correct) *and* if Cleopatra marries 6 more times, what is the probability that:

a. she will marry for love exactly 2 of the 6 times?
b. she will marry for love exactly 3 of the 6 times?
c. she will marry for love at least 4 of the 6 times?

22. Mickey McLinehan is studying TV culture. Before writing his book, McLinehan plans to conduct in-depth interviews with 12 U.S. families to see what they think about various TV shows. The 12 families will be selected from a panel of 48 families (12 big-city families, 12 small-city families, 12 suburban families, and 12 rural families). If the 12 families are selected at random, find the probability that:

a. all 12 of them will belong to one group (big-city, small-city, suburban, or rural)
b. 6 will belong to one of the 4 groups, and 6 to another of the 4 groups
c. 4 will belong to each of 3 groups (leaving one group unrepresented)
d. 4 will belong to one of the 4 groups, 3 to a second, 3 to a third, and 2 to the fourth group
e. 3 will belong to each of the 4 groups

A bridge hand is a random selection of 13 cards from a 52-card deck. The deck consists of 13 spades, 13 hearts, 13 diamonds, and 13 clubs.

23. Find the probability that a bridge hand contains exactly 7 hearts.

24. Find the probability that a bridge hand contains exactly 9 black cards (spades or clubs).

25. Find the probability that a bridge hand contains exactly 5 spades and exactly 4 hearts.

26. Find the probability that a bridge hand contains 4 clubs, 3 hearts, 3 diamonds, and 3 spades.

27. Find the probability that a bridge hand contains 5 clubs, 3 hearts, 3 diamonds, and 2 spades.

A poker hand is a random selection of 5 cards from a 52-card bridge deck. The 52 cards are divided into 4 suits (spades, hearts, diamonds, and clubs) and each suit contains 13 cards: 2, 3, 4, 5, 6, 7, 8, 9, 10, J (Jack), Q (Queen), K (King), A (Ace).

28. What is the probability that a poker hand consists of 5 spades?

HINT: A related but not identical question was asked and answered in worked-out Problem 6 of Section 7.3.

29. What is the probability that a poker hand consists of 5 spades *or* 5 hearts?

30. What is the probability that a poker hand contains 4 cards of a kind (4 Aces, 4 tens, etc.)?

31. A *full house* in poker is a hand containing 3 cards of one kind and 2 cards of a second kind. (Examples: 3 Aces, 2 Kings; 3 sevens, two sixes; etc.) Find the probability that a poker hand is a full house.

---

32. WMNB (White Mountain National Bank) made 17 big loans, and it lost money on 4 of them. If a state regulatory agency looks over the bank's books and randomly selects 4 of its 17 loans for examination, what is the probability that the 4-loan sample will contain:

    a. no bad loans?
    b. 1 bad loan?
    c. 2 bad loans?
    d. at least 3 bad loans?
    e. 4 bad loans?

33. Stella Ukridge, one of the account executives at Fenton Carlsbad Kelley, has a list of 16 municipal bonds to recommend to clients. Ukridge and her firm believe that all 16 of these are conservative investments, but in fact this is true of only 10 of the 16. Of the other 6 bonds, 4 are slightly risky and 2 are extremely risky. If a client selects 3 of the recommended 16 at random, what is the probability that:

    a. all 3 are conservative (that is, low-risk) investments?
    b. all 3 are slightly risky?
    c. 2 of them are extremely risky?
    d. at least 1 is slightly or extremely risky?
    e. more than 1 is slightly or extremely risky?

34. Oil wildcatter Ranald MacKenzie plans to sink exploratory wells in 11 promising locations. If 8 of these will turn out to be dry holes and 3 will be big strikes, what is the probability that MacKenzie's first 4 (randomly selected) exploratory wells give him:

    a. 4 dry holes?
    b. 3 dry holes, 1 big strike?
    c. at least 2 dry holes?
    d. 1 dry hole, 3 big strikes?

35. Eye in the Sky is a new-idea TV set. It is a 4-by-6-foot screen installed in the ceiling. The manufacturer's management expected to sell a few thousand sets, but actual sales are in the hundreds of thousands, which makes for a quality control problem. There just are not enough trained personnel to inspect more than 10% of the sets being produced. In a recent week an Eye in the Sky plant produced 110 sets. If every one of these had been inspected and classified by the company's system (Z: zero defects; A: annoying but minor defects; B: major defects; X: set cannot be operated), the results would have been:

Z	A	B	X
20	50	30	10

Zeno Smith, the plant's inspector, actually inspected and classified 11 of the 110 sets. If the 11 sets he inspected were a random sample, find the probability that Zeno Smith classified them as follows:

Z	A	B	X
2	5	3	1

36. (Continuation of Exercise 35). Eye in the Sky gave all its production workers a vacation in the first 2 weeks of July. But demand for the company's TV sets was so great that management hired temporary workers to keep the production line going during those weeks. Out of 84 sets produced by the temporary workers, 50 fall into the B classification (major defects). If Zeno Smith inspects a randomly chosen 8 sets out of the 84, what is the probability that he gives the B classification to:

a. fewer than 5 of the 8?
b. exactly 5 of the 8?
c. more than 5 of the 8?

37. There is some suspicion that a harmful chemical has found its way into the feeding troughs of dairy cows in Guernsey County. The County Health Department acts quickly to check milk samples for traces of the chemical. If there are 20,000 regularly milked cows in Guernsey County, and if 300 of them show traces of the harmful chemical in their milk, what is the probability that the Health Department's random selection of 400 samples will contain:

a. fewer than 6 with traces of the chemical?
b. exactly 6 with traces of the chemical?
c. more than 6 with traces of the chemical?

38. Joan Powers is the daughter of a movie star of the thirties. Joan has inherited a large collection of rare old films—some starring her mother, some featuring other famous old-time stars. The collection contains 220 films in various states of preservation:

40 E films (excellent condition)
60 G films (good condition)

70 R films (restorable condition)

50 B films (beyond restoration)

A museum is prepared to make an offer for the Powers collection, but first it would like to have some idea of the condition of the films. (The museum does not have the information we do.) Joan is willing to have the museum examine 11 of her films. If the sample of 11 is taken randomly, what is the probability that it contains:

a.   2 films in E condition, 3 in G, 3 in R, and 3 in B?
b.   more than 2 in E condition?
c.   more than 8 in E, G, or R condition?
d.   at least 2 in B condition?

THE BINOMIAL FORMULA

Our counting methods—including the combination concept—lead to easy solutions of certain algebra problems. For examples, we give some calculations that will be applied in Chapter 8. (As you will see in a moment, counting methods are *not* the easy way in Problems 1 and 2. But those problems lead into Problem 3, where counting methods are both easy and useful.)

PROBLEM 1   A 2-term algebraic expression like $x + y$ is known as a *binomial*. Use counting methods to calculate the *square* $(x + y)^2$.

SOLUTION   By definition,

$$(x + y)^2 = (x + y)(x + y)$$

We want to multiply out the 2 factors on the right side. Notice that:

1.   By the multiplication principle, the product contains $2 \cdot 2 = 2^2$ terms. (There are 2 factors and 2 choices, x or y, to be made from each factor.)

2.   Each of the 2^2 terms is made up of 2 factors. The first factor is either x or y, and the second factor is either x or y. Each term can therefore be written in the form

$$x^k y^{2-k} \qquad (k = 2, 1, 0)$$

where $k = 2$ means 2 x-factors and 0 y-factors; $k = 1$ means 1 x-factor and 1 y-factor; and $k = 0$ means 0 x-factors and 1 y-factor.

NOTE: When we write $x^k y^{2-k}$, we are using *exponents*, or *powers*. By definition: $x^2 = x \cdot x$, $y^2 = y \cdot y$; $x^1 = x$, $y^1 = y$; $x^0 = y^0 = 1$. For example: If we set $k = 2$ in $x^k y^{2-k}$, the result is $x^2 y^0 = x^2$.

3. The number of times that a term $x^k y^{2-k}$ occurs in the product is equal to the number of ways of taking an unordered sample of size k (k x-factors) from a population of size 2 (2 factors ($x + y$)). This means that the term $x^k y^{2-k}$ occurs $_2C_k$ times.

Putting together the results of our 3 steps, we have

$$(x + y)^2 = {_2C_2}x^2 + {_2C_1}xy + {_2C_0}y^2$$
$$= x^2 + 2xy + y^2$$

Check:

$$
\begin{array}{r}
x + y \\
x + y \\
\hline
x^2 + xy \\
+ xy + y^2 \\
\hline
x^2 + 2xy + y^2
\end{array}
$$

PROBLEM 2   Use counting methods to calculate the *cube* $(x + y)^3$.

SOLUTION   By definition,

$$(x + y)^3 = (x + y)(x + y)(x + y)$$

The multiplication principle tells us that the product contains $2 \cdot 2 \cdot 2 = 2^3$ terms. These terms have the form

$$x^k y^{3-k} \qquad (k = 3, 2, 1, 0)$$

The number of times that each term occurs in the product is equal to the number of ways of choosing an unordered sample of size k (k x-factors) from a population of size 3 (3 ($x + y$)-factors). Therefore the term $x^k y^{3-k}$ occurs in $_3C_k$ ways. Our result is:

$$(x + y)^3 = {_3C_3}x^3 + {_3C_2}x^2y + {_3C_1}xy^2 + {_3C_0}y^3$$
$$= x^3 + 3x^2y + 3xy^2 + y^3$$

Check: $(x + y)^3 = (x + y)^2(x + y) = (x^2 + 2xy + y^2)(x + y)$

Multiply:

$$x^2 + 2xy + y^2$$
$$\underline{ x + y}$$
$$x^3 + 2x^2y + xy^2$$
$$\underline{ + x^2y + 2xy^2 + y^3}$$
$$x^3 + 3x^2y + 3xy^2 + y^3$$

The methods we used in Problems 1 and 2 can also be applied to calculate higher powers of $(x + y)$, such as $(x + y)^{40}$ or $(x + y)^{197}$. It will be convenient to have a formula to cover all cases.

PROBLEM 3   Use counting methods to find a formula for $(x + y)^n$, where n can be any positive integer.

SOLUTION   We define

$$(x + y)^n = \underbrace{(x + y)(x + y) \cdots (x + y)}_{n \text{ factors}}$$

The multiplication principle tells us that the product of the n factors contains 2^n terms. (In each of the n factors, we choose either x or y. This gives

$$\underbrace{2 \cdot 2 \cdot 2 \cdot \ldots \cdot 2}_{n \text{ factors}} = 2^n$$

choices.) Each of these terms has the form

$$x^k y^{n-k} \qquad (k = n, n - 1, n - 2, \ldots, 1, 0)$$

The number of times each term $x^k y^{n-k}$ occurs in the product is equal to the number of ways of choosing an unordered sample of size k (k x-factors) from a population of size n (n $(x + y)$-factors). This number is $_nC_k$. Our result is:

$$
\begin{aligned}
(x + y)^n = {}&_nC_n x^n + {}_nC_{n-1} x^{n-1} y + {}_nC_{n-2} x^{n-2} y^2 \\
&+ \cdots + {}_nC_0 y^n
\end{aligned}
$$

This formula (known as the *binomial formula*) holds for any positive integer n. The formula gives us $(x + y)^1 = x + y$, and it also agrees with the results of Problems 1 and 2.

PROBLEM 4   Use the binomial formula to expand $(2x + 3y)^5$. Simplify the result.

SOLUTION   In the binomial formula, replace x by $2x$, y by $3y$, and n by 5. The result is:

$$(2x + 3y)^5 = {}_5C_5(2x)^5 + {}_5C_4(2x)^4(3y) + {}_5C_3(2x)^3(3y)^2$$
$$+ {}_5C_2(2x)^2(3y)^3 + {}_5C_1(2x)(3y)^4 + {}_5C_0(3y)^5$$
$$= 32x^5 + 240x^4y + 720x^3y^2 + 1080x^2y^3 + 810xy^4 + 243y^5$$

PROBLEM 5   Write the term involving a^5 in the expansion of $(\frac{1}{2}a + 4b)^9$.

SOLUTION   In the binomial formula, replace x by $\frac{1}{2}a$, y by $4b$, and n by 9. The term involving a^5 is therefore

$${}_9C_4(\tfrac{1}{2}a)^{9-4}(4b)^4$$
$$= 126 \left(\frac{a}{2}\right)^5 (4b)^4$$
$$= 1008a^5b^4$$

EXERCISES *for Section 7.4*

In each of the following cases, use the binomial formula to expand the given expression. Then simplify the result.

1. $(x + y)^8$ 2. $(x + 4)^5$ 3. $(x - y)^4$

4. $(a^2 + b^3)^6$ 5. $(1 + x)^7$ 6. $(p + 2q)^5$

7. $(x + 1)^9$ 8. $(2x + 1)^{10}$ 9. $(x + 2)^5$

10. $(x^2 + 1)^6$ 11. $(\frac{1}{3}m + \frac{1}{4}n)^5$ 12. $(x + 0.01)^{10}$

13. $(1 + 0.01)^{10}$ 14. $(1 + 0.04)^{10}$

15.   Write the third term in the expansion of $(2x + 3y)^7$.

16.   Write the fourth term in the expansion of $(8p + \frac{1}{16}q)^{11}$.

17.   Write the ninth term in the expansion of $(3c^2 + 4d^3)^{15}$.

18. Write the nineteenth term in the expansion of $(\frac{1}{4}x + 2y)^{25}$.

---

19. Write the term involving x^3 in the expansion of $(2x + 3y)^7$.

20. Write the term involving q^4 in the expansion of $(8p + \frac{1}{16}q)^{11}$.

21. Write the term involving d^9 in the expansion of $(3c^2 + 4d^3)^{15}$.

22. Write the term involving x^{17} in the expansion of $(\frac{1}{4}x + 2y)^{25}$.

23. Write the term involving x^{29} in the expansion of $(x + y)^{44}$.

24. Write the term involving x^{101} in the expansion of $(x + y)^{103}$.

---

25. Show that
$$(x + 1)^n = {}_nC_0 x^n + {}_nC_1 x^{n-1} + {}_nC_2 x^{n-2} + \cdots + {}_nC_{n-1} x + {}_nC_n$$
for $n = 1, 2, 3, \ldots$.

26. Use the result of Exercise 25 to show that
$$2^n = {}_nC_0 + {}_nC_1 + {}_nC_2 + \cdots + {}_nC_{n-1} + {}_nC_n$$
for $n = 1, 2, 3, \ldots$. Check the formula for the cases $n = 4$ and $n = 7$.

27. Show that
$$(\tfrac{3}{2})^n = {}_nC_0 + {}_nC_1(\tfrac{1}{2})$$
$$+ {}_nC_2(\tfrac{1}{2})^2 + {}_nC_3(\tfrac{1}{2})^3$$
$$+ \cdots + {}_nC_{n-1}(\tfrac{1}{2})^{n-1}$$
$$+ {}_nC_n(\tfrac{1}{2})^n$$
for $n = 1, 2, 3, \ldots$. Check the formula for the cases $n = 3$, $n = 6$.

28. A sample space S contains n outcomes. How many events (including the empty event) are there in S? Check your answer for the cases $n = 2$, $n = 3$, and $n = 4$.

chapter eight

PROBABILITY
CONTINUED

I F we assign a probability to a real-world event, we do so on the basis of conditions affecting the occurrence or nonoccurrence of that event. If the conditions change, the assigned probability changes. In this sense, all real-world probabilities are *conditional probabilities*. Section 8.1 explains how conditional probabilities are calculated, and how changes in conditions lead to changes in probabilities. *Bayes' rule,* at the end of Section 8.1, is a technique for assigning probable causes to events that have occurred. (If this month's figures show a surging demand for steel, Bayes' rule might be used to decide how probable it is that the appliance business has been booming.)

Probability experiments are sometimes repeated under identical conditions. (Two real-world examples are the random selection of subjects for opinion research, and the random selection of manufactured objects for quality control inspection.) In such cases the successive outcomes are unrelated, or independent. Section 8.2 defines and studies *independent events* in a sample space. There are many examples of *independent trials,* or repeated probability experiments under identical conditions. Section 8.3 considers independent trials with two possible outcomes. Probabilities associated with this case are called *binomial probabilities*. They are especially useful in applications of probability to opinion research, quality control, and acceptance sampling.

8.1 CONDITIONAL PROBABILITY; BAYES' RULE

Year-round, the Northeastern Air Lines shuttle flight from Boston to New York has a very good record of taking off on time. But there are seasonal variations. (For example, the runways at Logan Airport are sometimes blocked by snow, ice or, fog in winter. Table 8.1 summarizes the data for 1977.

TABLE 8.1

	Takeoff on Time	Late Takeoff	Total
Winter	494	156	650
Spring	608	42	650
Summer	516	34	550
Fall	607	43	650
Total	2225	275	2500

The shuttle flight's takeoff from Boston can be described as a probability *experiment,* whose *sample space* consists of two *outcomes:*

$$E = \text{on-time takeoff}$$

$$F = \text{late takeoff}$$

By looking at the Total row of Table 8.1, we see that the year-round empirical probability of an on-time takeoff is

$$P(E) = \tfrac{2225}{2500} = .89 \qquad \text{(year-round)}$$

From the Winter row in Table 8.1, we see that the winter-season empirical probability of an on-time takeoff is

$$P(E) = \tfrac{494}{650} = .76 \qquad \text{(winter)}$$

The probability that E occurs under the condition that it is winter is called a *conditional probability.* If W denotes the event "it is winter," we may write the conditional probability as

$$P(E, \text{given } W)$$

or more briefly as

$$P(E|W)$$

(read "P of E, given W.")

Notice that the difference between $P(E)$ and $P(E|W)$ is not in the outcome E but in the number of experiments used in calculating the empirical probability. In the case of $P(E)$, we look at all 2500 shuttle flights. To impose the condition W ("it is winter"), we remove 1850 spring, summer, and fall flights from consideration. Then $P(E|W)$ is the relative frequency of the outcome E among the remaining 650 (winter) flights. That is:

$$P(E|W) = \frac{494}{650} = .76$$

Example 1 is similar to the shuttle flight example. It also introduces a formula for calculating conditional probabilities.

EXAMPLE 1: SANDRO COSMETICS DOES A CUSTOMER SURVEY

Sandro, the cosmetics manufacturer, has two main product lines: Simonetta, which is a "tomorrow" look in eye and face make-up; and Primavera, which is a "today" look. It has been found that the Simonetta line does better among women under 29 and that the Primavera line sells mostly to women of 29 and over. A survey of 100 Sandro customers gave the results shown in Table 8.2.

TABLE 8.2

Age	Simonetta	Primavera
Under 29	53	9
29 and Over	11	27

To calculate some probabilities, we define the events

$$E = \text{customer uses Simonetta line}$$

$$F = \text{customer is under 29}$$

By adding the entries in the first column of Table 8.2, we see that $n(E) = 64$. From the first row of Table 8.2, $n(F) = 62$. And the number of customers in the survey is $n(S) = 100$. The empirical probabilities of E and F are therefore given by:

$$P(E) = \frac{n(E)}{n(S)} = \frac{64}{100} = .64$$

$$P(F) = \frac{n(F)}{n(S)} = \frac{62}{100} = .62$$

Now let's ask the question: What is the probability that an under-29 customer uses the Simonetta line?

For an answer, we first count the number of under-29 customers. The number is $n(F)$, or 62. Then we notice that 53 of these women use Simonetta. The probability that an under-29 customer uses Simonetta is therefore

$$\tfrac{53}{62} = .85,$$

approximately. This is much larger than $P(E)$. Since the Simonetta-using percentage is higher in the 62 under-29s than in the 100 all-age customers, we are not surprised.

Just what is this probability we have calculated? Since

$$E \cap F = \{\text{customer uses Simonetta line } and \text{ is under 29}\}$$

can we say that we have calculated $P(E \cap F)$? Let's check that one out. From Table 8.2, $n(E \cap F) = 53$. And $n(S) = 100$. Therefore

$$P(E \cap F) = \tfrac{53}{100}$$

which is not the same thing as $\tfrac{53}{62}$.

So we ask again: If the probability we have calculated is *not* $P(E \cap F)$, just what is it?

It is a *conditional probability*. That is: It is the probability of E (Simonetta-using) on *condition* that the customer is F (under 29). The way to write this is

$$P(E|F)$$

which we read as: *the probability of E, given F.* What we are saying is that our knowledge that F has occurred is extra information, or an extra condition, which we take into account when we calculate $P(E|F)$.

In the Sandro example,

$$P(E|F) = \frac{n(E \cap F)}{n(F)}$$

Check: $n(E \cap F) = 53$, $n(F) = 62$.

Since

$$P(E \cap F) = \frac{n(E \cap F)}{n(S)}, \qquad P(F) = \frac{n(F)}{n(S)}$$

we can also write

$$P(E|F) = \frac{P(E \cap F)}{P(F)}$$

Check: $P(E \cap F) = .53$, $P(F) = .62$, and $.53 \div .62 = \frac{53}{62} = P(E|F)$. This illustrates the definition of conditional probability:

DEFINITION   Conditional Probability

If E and F are any two events, then the conditional probability of E—given the fact that F has occurred—is

$$P(E|F) = \frac{P(E \cap F)}{P(F)} \qquad [P(F) \neq 0]$$

The definition was suggested by the Sandro example, in which all the probabilities are *empirical* probabilities. But we can use the same definition when the probabilities are *subjective*. In such cases it is very helpful to know that we can calculate $P(E|F)$ if we are given $P(E \cap F)$ and $P(F)$. Example 2 will show how it is done.

EXAMPLE 2:   WINNING AT VANCOUVER

Evita Smith is among the top women figure skaters who are competing in the annual Vancouver figure skating event. Her coach believes that Evita is one of only four women who might realistically be expected to win the compulsory (or "school figures") part of the event. He also thinks that Evita's probability of winning the compulsory competition *and* being the overall winner is $\frac{1}{5}$.

The coach then watches the competition. When it turns out that Evita Smith has won the compulsory competition, he nervously calculates the probability that she will be the overall winner. He defines the events

$$E = \{\text{Evita wins the compulsory competition}\}$$

$$F = \{\text{Evita is the overall Vancouver winner}\}$$

and

$$E \cap F = \{\text{Evita is the compulsory competition winner} \\ \textit{and} \text{ the overall Vancouver winner}\}$$

According to his reading of the situation,

$$P(E) = \frac{1}{4} \qquad P(E \cap F) = \frac{1}{5}$$

Since E has in fact occurred, the thing to calculate is the conditional probability $P(F|E)$. By the definition:

$$P(F|E) = \frac{P(F \cap E)}{P(E)} = \frac{1/5}{1/4} = \frac{4}{5}$$

FIRST NOTE: Since $F \cap E$ and $E \cap F$ are the same event, $P(F \cap E) = P(E \cap F)$.

SECOND NOTE: The conditional probabilities $P(F|E)$ and $P(E|F)$ are usually (but not always) different. In the two definitions

$$P(F|E) = \frac{P(F \cap E)}{P(E)} \qquad [P(E) \neq 0]$$

$$P(E|F) = \frac{P(E \cap F)}{P(F)} \qquad [P(F) \neq 0]$$

the numerators are the same, but the denominators are usually different. [To be precise: If $E \neq F$, we usually have $P(E) \neq P(F)$. But not always. If a symmetrical coin is tossed, H (heads) and T (tails) are different events, but $P(H) = P(T) = \frac{1}{2}$.] In the special case $F = E$, we have (since $E \cap E = E$):

$$P(E|E) = \frac{P(E \cap E)}{P(E)} = 1 \qquad [P(E) \neq 0]$$

This result checks with common sense: If we are given the fact that E has occurred, then $P(E) = 1$.

In a real-world problem, $P(E \cap F)$ may be harder to find than $P(E|F)$ or $P(F|E)$. If we have such a problem, our definitions of conditional probabilities are worse than useless. Or are they?

What we have in mind is this: If it is easier to find $P(E|F)$ [or $P(F|E)$] than it is to find $P(E \cap F)$, then why not use the conditional probability to find the unconditional one? To do this, we rewrite the definitions of $P(E|F)$ and $P(F|E)$ as the *multiplication rules*.

MULTIPLICATION RULES

$$P(E \cap F) = P(E|F) \cdot P(F)$$

$$P(E \cap F) = P(F|E) \cdot P(E)$$

Notice that we do not need to assume $P(F) \neq 0$ for the first multiplication rule or $P(E) \neq 0$ for the second. Why not? Suppose, for example, that $P(F) = 0$. Then the first rule gives $P(E \cap F) = 0$, which is absolutely correct. After all, $E \cap F$ cannot occur if F cannot occur.

The next example shows how we can calculate an unconditional probability by using a multiplication rule.

EXAMPLE 3:   SMITH ON SEMICONDUCTORS

Semiconductors are the key to new and improved electronic devices: hand-held calculators, digital watches, TV games, microcomputers. Understandably, the semiconductor industry is one of the most dynamic in the U.S. It is also one of the most volatile. This is because semiconductor prices seem to go down 25% to 30% every year. (Texas Instruments, the giant of the industry, improves its technology and cuts its prices all the time. Other companies have to do the same to stay competitive.) Each price cut leads to a dip in profits. But each price cut also opens new markets—and this in turn leads to new profitability.

This has been the pattern of the last several years. Things may or may not continue in the same way. Smith, a semiconductor industry analyst, defines the events

$E = \{$semiconductor prices go down 25% or more this year$\}$

$F = \{$average earnings of leading semiconductor companies go up
13% or more next year$\}$

Past experience leads Smith to assign the probabilities

$$P(E) = .62$$

$$P(F|E) = .58$$

By applying the second multiplication rule, he then has:

$$P(E \cap F) = (.58)(.62) = .3596$$

Smith on Semiconductors (the eagerly awaited quarterly report on the industry) therefore advises clients as follows: "There is a probability of .3596, or slightly more than $\frac{1}{3}$, that semiconductor prices will go down 25% or more this year *and* that leading companies like Texas Instruments and National Semiconductor will increase their earnings by 13% or more next year."

This gives us:

The two multiplication rules can be written in the form

$$P(E|F) \cdot P(F) = P(E \cap F) = P(F|E) \cdot P(E)$$
$$P(E|F) \cdot P(F) = P(F|E) \cdot P(E)$$

If we divide both sides of the equation by $P(F)$ [it is understood that $P(F) \neq 0$], we have *Bayes' rule.*

BAYES' RULE

$$P(E|F) = P(F|E) \cdot \frac{P(E)}{P(F)}$$

Bayes' rule is often applied in the drawing of inferences from data. An example will explain how it is done.

EXAMPLE 4: CHECKING OUT A DIAGNOSTIC DEVICE

A leading social psychologist estimates that 1 in every 1000 Americans is maladjusted—that is, unable to fit in with friends, neighbors, and society.

There is a new microelectronic device for diagnosing maladjustment. This device—which can be connected to any TV set—scans TV viewers and delivers the signal U (meaning "unhappy") for each one who is maladjusted.

More precisely: The electronic device gives the signal U with probability .98 for actual sufferers from maladjustment, and with probability .07 for non-sufferers.

Question: What is the probability that a person who is electronically labeled U is actually M (maladjusted) and not A (adjusted)?

The social psychologist defines the events M, A, and U as just described. The probability that a person is maladjusted is, as we have noted, estimated at 1 in 1000:

$$P(M) = .001$$

The probability that a maladjusted person is labeled U is

$$P(U|M) = .98$$

and the probability that an adjusted person is labeled U is

$$P(U|A) = .07$$

Bayes' rule then gives the probability that a person labeled U is actually maladjusted:

$$P(M|U) = \frac{P(U|M) \cdot P(M)}{P(U)}$$

Just one point is not clear: How is $P(U)$ to be calculated? Since any U-labeled person is *either* (U ∩ M), which means U-labeled and maladjusted, *or* (U ∩ A), which means U-labeled and adjusted, we have

$$U = (U \cap M) \cup (U \cap A)$$

Since (U ∩ M) and (U ∩ A) are mutually exclusive, we therefore have:

$$P(U) = P(U \cap M) + P(U \cap A)$$

From the multiplication rules:

$$P(U \cap M) = P(U|M) \cdot P(M)$$
$$= (.98)(.001) = .00098$$

$$P(U \cap A) = P(U|A) \cdot P(A)$$
$$= (.07)(.999) = .06993$$

(*NOTE:* A = M^c. Therefore $P(A) = 1 - P(M) = 1 - .001 = .999$.) Our result is:

$$P(U) = .00098 + .06993 = .07091$$

and this gives us

$$P(M|U) = \frac{P(U|M) \cdot P(M)}{P(U)}$$
$$= \frac{(.98)(.001)}{(.07091)} = \frac{.00098}{.07091}$$
$$= .0138203$$

In words: Approximately 14 out of 1000 U-labeled persons are actually maladjusted. At first sight, this looks like a mistake. After all, the two probabilities $P(U|M) = .98$ and $P(U|A) = .07$ tell us that maladjusted persons are (correctly) labeled U 98 times out of 100, and that adjusted persons are (incorrectly) labeled U only 7 times out of 100. A device that gives such results sounds fairly good. But $P(M|U) = .0138203$ sounds fairly bad.

The explanation of all this is fairly simple. If we had an error-free device, it would attach the U label to exactly 1 person out of 1000, which is the proportion of maladjusted persons.

The actual device would attach the U label 7 times out of 100, or 70 times out of 1000, to a population that contained *no* maladjusted persons.

Conclusion: Errors committed by the device are far more frequent than maladjusted persons. It is not at all surprising that only about 14 out of 1000 U-labeled persons are actually maladjusted.

Dave Munrow, president of the Winnepesaukee National Bank (WNB), thinks that his bank will grow if the Lake Winnepesaukee region grows. When he is making business loans, he therefore favors high-growth businesses like manufacturing over low-growth businesses like small retail stores. The table summarizes Dave Munrow's responses to 187 loan requests:

Loan	High-growth Business	Low-growth Business
Granted	102	29
Refused	34	22

Define A, A^C, B, and B^C as follows:

$$A = \{\text{loan request from high-growth business}\}$$
$$A^C = \{\text{loan request from low-growth business}\}$$
$$B = \{\text{loan granted}\}$$
$$B^C = \{\text{loan refused}\}$$

Then explain the meaning of each of the following probabilities, and find the numerical value of each one:

1. $P(B|A)$ **2.** $P(B|A^C)$ **3.** $P(B^C|A)$

4. $P(B^C|A^C)$ **5.** $P(A|B)$ **6.** $P(A|B^C)$

7. $P(A^C|B)$ **8.** $P(A^C|B^C)$ **9.** $P(A \cap B)$

10. $P(A^C \cap B^C)$

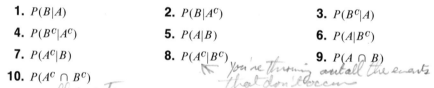 *you're throwing out all the events that don't occur* *all events*

11. Among the late-afternoon shoppers at North Shore Mall, 47% shop at the department store, while 18% shop at the department store *and* have a snack at the ice cream store. A randomly selected late-afternoon shopper who is on the way out of the mall is asked: "Did you shop at the department store?" The answer is yes. What is the probability that this shopper has also had a snack at the ice cream store?

12. The United Nuclear Workers (UNW) unionizes workers at nuclear power plants, nuclear submarine yards, and so on. This is work that no one wants to disrupt. UNW contract negotiations are usually fairly brisk: the probability of a timely settlement (within 30 days and without a strike) is .57. Nevertheless, the UNW tries to have an adequate strike fund in case it is needed. The UNW's probability of having such a fund is .74. The probability that there will be a timely settlement *and* an adequate strike fund is .26. If it is known that the UNW has an adequate strike fund one year, what is the probability that there will be a timely settlement of that year's contract negotiations?

13. An HEW study of unemployment in one of the largest metropolitan areas in the U.S. showed that 40% of the unemployed were young people aged 18 to 24. The study also showed that 11% of the unemployed were not only young (18 to 24) but also had had no job training of any kind. What is the probability that a randomly selected unemployed person in that area is without job training of any kind *if* the person selected is 18 to 24 years of age?

14. *Women in the Job Market,* a recent statistical survey, defines "level 2 women" as married women who do not have a child below school age. The statistics show (a) that there is a probability of .47 that a level 2 woman will both have a job *and* contribute more than 36% of the family income; and (b) that there is a probability of .71 that a level 2 woman will have a job. What is the probability that a level 2 woman who has a job will contribute more than 36% of the family income?

15. Twenty-three percent of the voting-age citizens in a certain congressional district are registered to vote *and* opposed to gun control. Of all the voting-age citizens in the district, 55% are registered to vote. What is the probability that a randomly selected registered voter in the district is opposed to gun control?

16. High Technologies—a manufacturer of aircraft engines, microcomputers, and solar energy hardware—has a large technical staff: mechanical and electrical engineers, physicists, mathematicians, and chemists. Among technical people who have been with the company for more than 11 years, exactly 7.9% earn more than $43,000 per year. Among all technical people working for High Technologies, exactly 11.3% earn more than $43,000 per year. If someone on the technical staff is paid more than $43,000 per year, what is the probability that this person has worked for the company for more than 11 years?

17. Among executives from Ohio who relocated in Florida this year—selling a family home in Ohio, and buying a family home in Florida—it was found (a) that in 79% of the cases, the Florida home was bought for more than twice the selling price of the Ohio home; and (b) that in 53% of the cases, the Florida home was inferior to the Ohio home in living space and quality of construction. What is the probability that an executive's Florida home, bought for more than twice the price of the Ohio home it replaced, is inferior in living space and quality of construction?

"Trash" is a new TV series that is widely considered to be in poor taste. Calder Motor Company (CMC) is one of the principal sponsors of Trash, but Calder management is now having second thoughts. It decides to do some opinion research among 350,000 owners of CMC cars. The question asked is: "Should CMC continue to sponsor Trash?" and answers are recorded as : Yes, No, or Don't care. Answers are also recorded separately for owners of compact, intermediate-sized and full-sized CMC cars. The results are shown in the following table. Calculate the probability that a randomly selected CMC car owner:

Car Type	Yes	No	Don't care
Compact	75,000	25,000	5000
Intermediate	50,000	40,000	4000
Full	65,000	85,000	1000

18. Favors continued CMC sponsorship of "Trash" if the size of car owned is: (a) compact; (b) intermediate; (c) full.

19. Opposes continued CMC sponsorship of "Trash" if the size of car owned is: (a) compact; (b) intermediate; (c) full.

20. Does not care whether or not CMC sponsors "Trash" if the size of car owned is: (a) compact; (b) intermediate; (c) full.

An insurance company used the table on pp. 298–99 in calculating premiums for a 20-year-old person. The company found that the events

$$E_1 = \{\text{the person dies by age 40}\}$$
$$E_2 = \{\text{the person dies by age 50}\}$$
$$E_3 = \{\text{the person dies by age 70}\}$$

had the following probabilities:

$$P(E_1) = .15685$$
$$P(E_2) = .24647$$
$$P(E_3) = .58462$$

(See p. 300.) Of course, the probabilities change if the 20-year-old person lives to be 30, 40, 50, or 60. The new probabilities are conditional probabilities. We define the following events:

$$F_1 = \{\text{the person lives to age 30}\}$$
$$F_2 = \{\text{the person lives to age 40}\}$$
$$F_3 = \{\text{the person lives to age 50}\}$$
$$F_4 = \{\text{the person lives to age 60}\}$$

Notice that the probabilities of these events are calculable from the probabilities of the outcomes A_1, A_2, A_3, and A_4 listed on p. 299. That is: $P(F_1) = 1 - P(A_1)$, $P(F_2) = 1 - P(A_1) - P(A_2)$, etc.

The insurance company continues to use the table on pp. 298–99. Calculate the numbers it will assign to the following probabilities:

21. $P(F_1)$ $P(E_1 \cap F_1)$ $P(E_1|F_1)$
              $P(E_2 \cap F_1)$ $P(E_2|F_1)$
              $P(E_3 \cap F_1)$ $P(E_3|F_1)$

22. $P(F_2)$ $P(E_2 \cap F_2)$ $P(E_2|F_2)$
              $P(E_3 \cap F_2)$ $P(E_3|F_2)$

23. $P(F_3)$ $\qquad$ $P(E_3 \cap F_3)$ $\qquad$ $P(E_3|F_3)$

24. $P(F_4)$ $\qquad$ $P(E_3 \cap F_4)$ $\qquad$ $P(E_3|F_4)$

---

25. E and F are any two events in the same sample space. You know that $P(E) = .37$, $P(F) = .74$, and $P(F|E) = .42$. Calculate:

a. $P(E \cap F)$ $\qquad$ b. $P(E|F)$ $\qquad$ c. $P(E \cup F)$

26. Analysis shows that there is a probability of .73 that the stock market will be down next year. And long experience shows that Granite State Fund, a mutual fund run by cautious New Englanders, has a probability of .65 of increasing its assets 10% or more in a down-market year. What is the probability that the stock market will be down *and* that Granite State Fund will increase its assets by 10% or more next year?

27. The Small Business Administration (SBA) says that 83% of all small businesses in the U.S. are undercapitalized. The required capital must be provided at some point—either through the owner's resources *or* through profits that can be plowed back into the business. SBA figures show that 46% of undercapitalized small businesses do not get the capital injection they need. In that case the small business fails. What is the probability that a small business will fail in this way?

28. Suppose that political experts say that there is a probability of .43 that the next major war will occur in the Far East. If there is a major war in the Far East, there is a probability of .39 that it will be in Korea. What is the probability that the next major war will be in the Far East *and* that it will be in Korea?

29. Winter City Home Improvement Company is launching a big campaign to sell its Styrofoam-Fiberglas home insulation to local homeowners. The campaign consists of TV commercials on the regional TV station. Market research shows that the probability that a local homeowner has seen one of these commercials is .32. The probability that a homeowner who sees the commercial will *buy* Winter City's Styrofoam-Fiberglas insulation is .007. What is the probability that a randomly selected local homeowner will see the commercial *and* buy the Styrofoam-Fiberglas insulation?

30. A and B are any two events in the same sample space. You know that $P(A) = .169$ and $P(B) = .26$. Calculate $P(A|B)$ if:

a. $P(B|A) = .09$ $\qquad$ b. $P(B|A) = .21$ $\qquad$ c. $P(B|A) = .34$

31. Public health physicians suspect that there has been an outbreak of X-strain pneumonic virus in Sonora County. (X-strain is a pneumonic virus that is resistant to all known antibiotics.) Tests for the detection of X-strain are 92.3% effective. (The tests fail to detect the virus in 7.7% of infected cases.) If a person is not infected, the tests will incorrectly show infection in 0.9% of the cases. (The tests will correctly show absence of the virus in 99.1% of the uninfected cases.) Suppose that 0.3% of the population in Sonora County is actually infected with X-strain. A randomly selected county resident is tested, and the tests show that X-strain is there. What is the probability that the tested person is actually infected with X-strain pneumonic virus?

Insurance companies like to collect and analyze data. Illinois General Mutual Assurance (IGMA) supplied the data in the following three exercises.

32. The policy writers who put IGMA group policies into words are intelligent and well-educated people. They are liberal arts graduates, who have been selected for their ability to write clearly and correctly. But they are not trained in mathematics or in law, and they sometimes make mathematical or legal mistakes. Of the policies written in one department, George writes 39%, Eddie writes 33%, and Liz writes 28%. There are mathematical or legal mistakes in 8% of George's policies, in 9% of Eddie's policies, and in 3% of Liz's policies. If a policy is chosen at random from the ones written by the George–Eddie–Liz group, and if the policy has a mathematical or legal mistake in it, what is the probability that it was written by George?

NOTE: IGMA points out that policies do not go directly from policy writers to policy holders. Before any IGMA policy is issued, it is carefully reviewed for mathematical accuracy by staff actuaries, and for legal accuracy by staff lawyers.

33. There are many departments at IGMA, and therefore many heads of departments. IGMA people have noticed that a surprising number of department heads are former college football players if they are men, or former team sport players (field hockey, ice hockey, basketball, crew) if they are women. Of all IGMA's college-trained male employees, 4.6% are former college football players while 95.4% did not play college football. IGMA's data-keeping people also report that 78% of all former college football players at IGMA are department heads or promising candidates for department headships; but only 3.8% of men who did not play college football are either department heads or promising candidates. Suppose that a male college-trained IGMA employee is chosen at random, and is found to be a department head or a promising candidate. What is the probability that the man played football in college?

34. Among IGMA's college-trained female employees, 6.2% were on athletic teams at college and 93.8% were not. But 87.7% of the former team sport players are department heads or promising candidates, while only 1.4% of the college-trained women who were not on athletic teams are department heads or promising candidates. If a randomly selected college-trained woman is an IGMA department head or a promising candidate, what is the probability that she played a team sport at college?

35. Appliance City sells a large number of microwave ovens. Purchasers learn how to use the new oven in one of three ways: (a) 15% of them by reading the microwave cookbook that every company packs with its oven; (b) 55% of them by attending the hour-long demonstration that Appliance City provides for every new owner who wants it; (c) 20% of them by attending the day-long microwave school that is offered to new owners by the major manufacturers. Ten percent of the purchasers simply *use* their new ovens but no one seems to become an expert at microwave cooking in that way. Probabilities of becoming an expert for those who follow method a, b, or c are .63 for method a; .54 for method b and .96 for method c. If an owner is an expert microwave cook, what is the probability that this is a person who has attended the day-long microwave school?

8.2 INDEPENDENT EVENTS AND INDEPENDENT TRIALS

Two events E, F in the same sample space are *independent* if they do not influence one another. This means that the information that F *has* occurred does not affect the probability that E *will* occur, and conversely. In the language of probability: the conditional probabilities $P(E|F)$ and $P(F|E)$ are really unconditional probabilities when E and F are independent:

$$P(E|F) = P(E)$$

shows that E is independent of F, and

$$P(F|E) = P(F)$$

shows that F is independent of E.

If we substitute $P(E|F) = P(E)$ in the multiplication rule $P(E \cap F) = P(E|F) \cdot P(F)$, we have the formula for *independent events*.

DEFINITION Independent Events

Two events E, F in a sample space S are independent if and only if

$$P(E \cap F) = P(E) \cdot P(F)$$

The examples that follow will explain why this definition seems to be a reasonable one.

EXAMPLES: INDEPENDENT EVENTS

1. The Queen of Hearts is well travelled: among other places, she appears in Mother Goose (where she baked some tarts) and also in every 52-card bridge deck. If a card is chosen at random from a well-shuffled bridge deck, we can define the events

$$E = \{\text{the card is a heart}\}$$

$$F = \{\text{the card is a Queen}\}$$

$$E \cap F = \{\text{the card is the Queen of Hearts}\}$$

We have

$$P(E) = \tfrac{1}{13} \qquad P(F) = \tfrac{1}{4} \qquad P(E \cap F) = \tfrac{1}{52}$$

so that

$$P(E \cap F) = P(E) \cdot P(F)$$

The events E and F are independent.

2. A pair of dice is given a fair roll. The dice are symmetrical. One die is green, one red. We define the events

$$E = \{\text{green die shows an even number}\}$$

$$F = \{\text{red die shows an odd number}\}$$

$$E \cap F = \{\text{the (green, red) outcome is one of the pairs} \\ (2, 1), (2, 3), (2, 5), (4, 1), (4, 3), (4, 5), \\ (6, 1), (6, 3), (6, 5)\}$$

Since there are 6 possible outcomes for the green die and 6 possible outcomes for the red die, the multiplication principle shows that there are $6 \cdot 6 = 36$ outcomes for the pair of dice. Since there are 3 even-number outcomes, 3 odd-number outcomes, and 9 even-odd outcomes, we see that

$$P(E) = \tfrac{3}{6} = \tfrac{1}{2} \qquad P(F) = \tfrac{3}{6} = \tfrac{1}{2} \qquad P(E \cap F) = \tfrac{9}{36} = \tfrac{1}{4}$$

and

$$P(E \cap F) = P(E) \cdot P(F)$$

The events E and F are independent.

3. We arrived at our definition of independent events by substituting $P(E|F) = P(E)$ in the multiplication rule $P(E \cap F) = P(E|F) \cdot P(F)$. Common sense suggests that

$$P(F|E) = P(F)$$

should be an equally good starting point. Is it? To find the answer, we apply the multiplication rule in the form

$$P(E \cap F) = P(F|E) \cdot P(E)$$

Since $P(F|E) = P(F)$, we have

$$P(E \cap F) = P(F) \cdot P(E)$$

which is our definition of independent events. (The order of the factors on the right is different, but this changes nothing.) In other words: $P(F|E) = P(F)$ and $P(E|F) = P(E)$ are alternative ways of saying the self-same thing—that E and F are independent.

4. What if one of the events E, F has zero probability? We would certainly want to say that E and F are independent. (If an event has probability zero—that is, if the event is impossible—common sense tells us it cannot possibly influence another event.) Let's see if our definition works. Suppose that $P(F) = 0$. Then $P(F|E) = 0$, no matter what E is. Therefore

$$P(E \cap F) = P(F|E) \cdot P(E)$$
$$= 0$$
$$= P(E) \cdot P(F)$$

Our definition works.

The concept of independent events can be extended to more than two events. We say that three events E_1, E_2, E_3 are independent if any two of them are independent and if, in addition,

$$P(E_1 \cap E_2 \cap E_3) = P(E_1) \cdot P(E_2) \cdot P(E_3)$$

Similarly, four events E_1, E_2, E_3, E_4 are independent if any three of them are independent and if

$$P(E_1 \cap E_2 \cap E_3 \cap E_4) = P(E_1) \cdot P(E_2) \cdot P(E_3) \cdot P(E_4)$$

Proceeding in this way, we can define independence for any finite number of events.

PROBLEM 1   The quality control people at the Tigre division of Aztec Motors are constantly trying to improve their product. Each Tigre automobile passes through four assembly lines: chassis, transmission, engine and cooling system, body and trim. The probability that a Tigre comes off one of these lines without a defect is

.99 for the chassis line

.97 for the transmission line

.98 for the engine and cooling system line

.96 for the body and trim line

What is the probability that a Tigre emerges with no defect?

SOLUTION   We define the events

$$E_1 = \{\text{no chassis defect}\}$$
$$E_2 = \{\text{no transmission defect}\}$$
$$E_3 = \{\text{no engine and cooling system defect}\}$$
$$E_4 = \{\text{no body and trim defect}\}$$

in the manufacture of a Tigre. Since the four assembly lines are separate, we assume that the four events are independent. The probability of a no-defect Tigre is therefore given by

$$P(E_1 \cap E_2 \cap E_3 \cap E_4) = P(E_1) \cdot P(E_2) \cdot P(E_3) \cdot P(E_4)$$
$$= (.99)(.97)(.98)(.96)$$
$$= .90345024$$

PROBLEM 2   A pair of dice—one green die, one red—is rolled. We define the events

$$E_1 = \{\text{green die shows an odd number}\}$$
$$E_2 = \{\text{red die shows an odd number}\}$$
$$E_3 = \{\text{sum of numbers shown on the 2 dice is odd}\}$$

Are E_1, E_2, and E_3 independent events?

SOLUTION   Each of the three events can occur in 18 ways. (To see this for E_1, notice that the green die has 3 odd numbers on it and that the red die has 6 numbers on it. By the multiplication principle, $n(E_1) = 3 \cdot 6 = 18$. Similarly, $n(E_2) = n(E_3) = 18$.) Therefore

$$P(E_1) = P(E_2) = P(E_3) = \tfrac{1}{2}$$

(The number of outcomes in the sample space S is $n(S) = 6 \cdot 6 = 36$. This gives $P(E_1) = \dfrac{n(E_1)}{n(S)} = \tfrac{18}{36} = \tfrac{1}{2}$, etc.) Next, each of the three events $(E_1 \cap E_2)$, $(E_1 \cap E_3)$, $(E_2 \cap E_3)$ can occur in 9 ways. This gives

$$P(E_1 \cap E_2) = P(E_1 \cap E_3) = P(E_2 \cap E_3) = \tfrac{1}{4}$$

The equations

$$P(E_1 \cap E_2) = \tfrac{1}{4} = P(E_1) \cdot P(E_2)$$
$$P(E_1 \cap E_3) = \tfrac{1}{4} = P(E_1) \cdot P(E_3)$$
$$P(E_2 \cap E_3) = \tfrac{1}{4} = P(E_2) \cdot P(E_3)$$

then show that the pairs of events (E_1, E_2), (E_1, E_3), and (E_2, E_3) are independent. But the three events E_1, E_2, E_3 cannot possibly occur simultaneously. To signify this, we write

$$E_1 \cap E_2 \cap E_3 = \phi$$

This gives

$$P(E_1 \cap E_2 \cap E_3) = 0$$

By contrast,

$$P(E_1) \cdot P(E_2) \cdot P(E_3) = \tfrac{1}{8}$$

The events E_1, E_2, E_3 are not independent.

In Section 7.1, we defined two-stage and three-stage probability experiments. Then we applied the multiplication principle to count outcomes.

Using the same ideas, we now say: If a probability experiment has k stages, and if the successive stages have $m_1, m_2, \ldots, m_k$ outcomes, then the total number of outcomes of the experiment is the product $m_1 m_2 \cdots m_k$.

In other words: If we know the number of outcomes of each stage of a multistage experiment, then the multiplication principle tells us the number of outcomes of the experiment.

Now we go a little further: If each stage of a multistage probability experiment is independent of all the other stages, then the probability of each outcome of the experiment can be calculated by multiplying the probabilities of the outcomes of the individual stages.

The same idea of multiplying individual probabilities applies if we have a number of independent repetitions of the same experiment.

In either case—k independent stages or k independent repetitions— we apply the multiplication rule in the form

$$P(E_1 \cap E_2 \cap \cdots \cap E_k) = P(E_1) \cdot P(E_2) \cdots P(E_k)$$

and we say that we have k *independent trials*.

EXAMPLES: INDEPENDENT TRIALS

1. The simultaneous roll of 12 dice can be regarded as a 12-stage experiment, or as 12 repetitions of a single experiment. In either case we have 12 independent trials. Since each trial has 6 possible outcomes, the 12-trial experiment has 6^{12} outcomes.

2. For an example of 100 independent trials, we imagine the simultaneous roll of 100 dice. This experiment has 6^{100} possible outcomes.

3. If nearly everything produced by a factory is of high quality, then the ocassional defective item may be thought of as occurring by chance. And the occurrence or nonoccurrence of defects in one item would be independent of the occurrence of defects in any other item. If such a factory produces 1394 items (each of which is graded A, B, C, D, or E) in a day, then we have an example of 1394 independent trials. Since 5 outcomes are possible for each trial, we have a total of 5^{1394} outcomes for the day's production.

4. My Old Kentucky Home (MOKH) is a trailer park in northern Kentucky. Tornadoes in this area are a yearly threat to MOKH. There are 4 possibilities: Trailers may come through a tornado unharmed, they may suffer minor damage, they may suffer major damage, or they may be blown away. Since tornadoes are notoriously capricious, the fate of one MOKH trailer during a tornado is entirely independent of the fate of every other MOKH trailer. If there are 376 trailers in MOKH, then each tornado passing through the area gives an example of 376 independent trials. There are 4 possible outcomes for each trailer and 4^{376} possible outcomes for the whole trailer park.

Here is an illustration of the independent trials concept.

PROBLEM 3   A poll-taker is conducting a survey in a city of over 1 million households. The question that will be asked in each household visited is: "How does this household get its news of the world around it?" Actual percentages are TV, 39%; radio, 22%; newspapers, 15%; no source of news, 24%. The poll-taker visits a large number of households. Find the probability that the following responses will be given, in order, at some point: 3 TV, 1 radio, 1 newspaper, 1 no source.

SOLUTION   The probabilities of the answers TV, radio, newspapers, and no source are .39, .22, .15, and .24, respectively. Since the city has over 1 million households, it can be assumed that each trial is independent and that the given probabilities hold for each trial. Because of the independence, probabilities multiply. The probability of the event that is asked for is:

$$(.39)^3(.22)(.15)(.24) = .00046981$$

EXERCISES *for Section 8.2*

1. A card is chosen from a well-shuffled bridge deck. Define the events

$$A = \{\text{the card is an Ace}\}$$
$$B = \{\text{the card is a spade}\}$$

Are A and B independent events?

2. A symmetrical pair of dice is given a fair roll. One die is green, the other red. Define the events

$E = \{\text{the green die shows the number 6}\}$
$F = \{\text{the sum of the numbers in the (green, red) outcome is odd}\}$

Are E and F independent?

3. A green die and a red die are rolled at the same time. Define the events

$M = \{\text{the green die shows the number 3}\}$
$N = \{\text{the sum of the numbers in the (green, red) outcome is 5}\}$

Are M and N independent?

4. Being a millionaire is not as good as it used to be (inflation, you know) but brothers Don and Julian Smith are old-fashioned enough to want to be millionaires anyway. Don owns a small but growing airline in Kentucky. Julian does very well in Indiana real estate. If bankers and other knowledgeable people had to guess, they would say that Don's probability of becoming a millionaire is .3 and that Julian's probability of becoming a millionaire is .25. If the two probabilities are correct—and independent—then find the probability that:

a. Don and Julian will both become millionaires
b. at least one of the two will become a millionaire
c. Don will, Julian will not
d. Don will not, Julian will

5. Belmont House is a major publisher of both fiction and nonfiction. In any one publishing season, probabilities of a Belmont House bestseller in these two categories are .27 in fiction and .31 in nonfiction. Let's assume that bestsellers in fiction and nonfiction are independent. For any one publishing season, what is the probability that Belmont House authors and editors will turn out bestsellers in:

a. both fiction and nonfiction?
b. at least one of the two categories?
c. one category but not both?
d. neither category?

Potentials in Marketing is a trade magazine for executives in advertising, marketing, and promotion. Media Probabilities, the opinion research giant, runs ads in three successive issues of the magazine. Probabilities for the audience appeal of these ads are as follows:

		Appeals to:	
Ad Number	Ad Executives	Marketing Executives	Promotion Executives
1	.52	.38	.13
2	.31	.49	.14
3	.46	.17	.11

Assume that the impact of these three ads is independent. Then calculate the probabilities that:

6. Ads 1, 2, and 3 will appeal to advertising executives.

7. Ad 1 will appeal to advertising executives, ad 2 to marketing executives, and ad 3 to advertising executives.

8. Ad 1 will appeal to promotion executives, ad 2 to advertising executives, and ad 3 to marketing executives.

---

9. According to the rules of "Monopoly," a player who rolls doubles three times in succession must go to jail. What is the probability of rolling doubles three times in succession with a pair of dice?

10. Freddie "Feets" Follansbee, the soccer player turned place-kicker, is known to kick points after touchdown successfully 90% of the time. What is the probability that Freddie will miss 4 successive points after touchdown? (*NOTE:* In the real world, Freddie would get nervous after missing 2 or 3 kicks. Here, we assume that every kick is independent of the others.)

11. Roger Jannine, chief executive officer of a major corporation, allows that his big decisions are blunders "about 10 percent of the time." Of course he makes a number of big decisions in a year. If the 10% figure holds, and if the decisions are independent, what is the probability that 4 successive big decisions are *not* blunders?

12. For Smith Steel to stay in business, it must do one of two things: (a) persuade customers that Smith's specialty steels cannot be matched by foreign suppliers; or (b) persuade the U.S. government to restrict steel imports. Suppose that these two exercises in persuasion are independent, that the customer-persuading has a probability of .3 of succeeding and that the government-persuading has a probability of .25 of succeeding. What is the probability that Smith Steel will not be able to stay in business? What is the probability that it will be able to stay in business because it persuades both customers and government? What is the probability that it will persuade at least one of the two?

13. Buyers of new cars in Fayetta County make the following choices: 32% buy Chrysler products, 30% buy Ford products, 11% buy General Motors cars, 3% buy American Motors cars, and 24% buy imported cars. Suppose that these percentages continue to hold, and that all purchases are independent. Then:

    a. What is the probability that the next 5 new cars bought in Fayetta County will be (in this order) 1 Chrysler product, 1 Ford product, 1 GM product, 1 AMC product, 1 import?

    b. What is the probability that the next 5 new cars bought in Fayetta County will be (in this order) 2 Chrysler products, 1 AMC product, 2 imports?

14. A symmetrical die is rolled 6 times. What is the probability that each of the numbers 1, 2, 3, 4, 5, 6 will show on the upper face exactly once? [*HINT:* Find the number $n(E)$ of favorable outcomes and also the number $n(S)$ of outcomes in the sample space.]

15. Surgical nurses keep track of the sponges used in an operation, but somehow these sponges get lost anyway. (Usually they are discarded with bandages and dressings. The reason the sponges are counted is to make sure they have not been left inside the patient.) At West Side Hospital, the probabilities for sponge loss in an operation are: 0 sponges lost, .29; 1 sponge lost, .33; 2 sponges lost, .17; 3 sponges lost, .21. If 5 randomly selected operations at West Side Hospital are independent, what is the probability that the number of sponges lost in those 5 operations will be:

    a. 0, 1, 1, 2, 2, 2?

    b. 1 or more every time?

    c. 1, 2, 3, 3, 3?

8.3   BINOMIAL PROBABILITIES

In many real-world applications of the independent trials model, there are only 2 possible outcomes for each individual trial. (If there are n repetitions, this gives a total of 2^n outcomes.) It is convenient to use a uniform terminology in the 2-outcome independent-trials case:

1. The 2 outcomes are dubbed *success* and *failure*.

2. The probability of success for an individual trial is denoted by p. The probability of failure for an individual trial is denoted by q.

   NOTE: Since there are just 2 outcomes in the sample space for an individual trial, we have $p + q = 1$, or $q = 1 - p$.

For an example of independent trials with 2 outcomes, imagine a coin being tossed. The sample space for an individual trial is $S = \{H, T\}$. If the outcome H is referred to as *success* and the outcome T as *failure,* then we denote

$$P(H) = p \qquad P(T) = q$$

For a well-balanced coin, $p = q = \frac{1}{2}$. For a coin that is not well balanced, $p \neq q$ (but $p + q = 1$). If there are n trials (n coins tossed once, or a single coin tossed n times in succession), then the sample space contains 2^n outcomes. Since the trials are independent, *probabilities multiply.*

PROBLEM 1 A coin is tossed 15 times. If $P(H) = p$ and $P(T) = q$, find the probability that the successive outcomes are HHTHHHHTTHHHHTTT.

SOLUTION The trials are independent and the probabilities multiply. Therefore $P(\text{HHTHHHHTTHHHHTTT}) = ppqppppqqppppqqq = p^9 q^6$.

Problem 1 asks for the probability that 15 independent trials lead to 9 successes and 6 failures in a specified order. We are often interested in the *number of successes,* but *not their order.*

PROBLEM 2 In 15 independent trials, each with 2 outcomes, what is the probability of 9 successes and 6 failures?

SOLUTION We make use of our uniform terminology: The probability of success in each trial is p, and the probability of failure is q. The event of interest is

$$E = \{15 \text{ trials result in 9 successes and 6 failures}\}$$

Since the trials are independent, probabilities multiply. We have probability p^9 for 9 successes, q^6 for 6 failures, and p^9q^6 for 9 successes *and* 6 failures.

The number p^9q^6 checks with the probability we found in solving Problem 1. But the order of successes and failures specified in Problem 1 is only one of many possible arrangements of 9 successes and 6 failures. As we know from Section 7.3, the totality of possible arrangements is the number of unordered samples without replacement of size 9 that can be taken from a population of size 15. This number is $_{15}C_9$. The probability we want is $_{15}C_9$ times the probability p^9q^6 of each arrangement. Therefore

$$P(E) = {}_{15}C_9 p^9 q^6$$

is the probability that 15 independent trials result in 9 successes and 6 failures.

Probabilities like the one we have just calculated are known as *binomial probabilities*. There is a convenient notation:

DEFINITION   The Binomial Probability $B(r; n, p)$

The binomial probability $B(r; n, p)$ is the probability that n 2-outcome independent trials, each with probability p of success and $q = 1 - p$ of failure, lead to r successes and $n - r$ failures ($0 \le r \le n$).

In solving Problem 2, we calculated $B(9; 15, p)$. The ideas we used in that calculation can be applied to give a general formula for $B(r; n, p)$.

CALCULATING THE BINOMIAL PROBABILITY $B(r; n, p)$

STEP 1   Since the trials are independent, probabilities multiply. Each way of achieving r successes and $n - r$ failures has probability $p^r q^{n-r}$.

STEP 2   The number of ways of labeling r of n trials "success" is $_nC_r$.

CONCLUSION $B(r; n, p) = {}_nC_r p^r q^{n-r}$

The formula for $B(r; n, p)$ shows that binomial probabilities are related to the binomial formula. To see this we expand $(q + p)^n$ by the binomial formula (Section 7.4, p. 366):

$$(q + p)^n = {}_nC_0q^n + {}_nC_1q^{n-1}p + \cdots + {}_nC_rq^{n-r}p^r + \cdots + {}_nC_np^n$$

The term containing p^r is precisely $B(r; n, p)$. If we rewrite the formula in terms of binomial probabilities, and remember that $(q + p)^n = 1^n = 1$, we find:

$$B(0; n, p) + B(1; n, p) + \cdots + B(n; n, p) = 1$$

The equation says that the sum of all $n + 1$ of the probabilities $B(r; n, p)$ is 1. This checks with the basic ideas of probability. (The sum of the probabilities of all outcomes in a sample space must be equal to 1.) It also checks with common sense: there must be r successes in n trials, where r is one of the $n + 1$ numbers $0, 1, 2, \ldots, n$.

Binomial probabilities are useful in giving answers to two questions:

1. What is the probability of *exactly r successes* in n 2-outcome independent trials?

2. What is the probability of *at least r successes* in n 2-outcome independent trials?

PROBLEM 3   A speculator has bought futures contracts in 5 commodities: corn, wheat, cocoa, soybeans, and pork bellies. According to his estimates, each of the 5 contracts has a probability of .1 of returning a profit. He thinks he is making a reasonable speculation, since a profit on just 1 of the 5 commodities contracts will more than make up for losses on the other 4 contracts. Assuming that the price movements of the 5 commodities are independent, what are his chances? That is: (a) What is the probability that *none* of the 5 contracts will return a profit? (b) What is the probability that *at least 1* of the 5 contracts will return a profit?

SOLUTION   To answer the first question, we need the probability of 0 successes in 5 independent 2-outcome trials. Each trial has probability $p = .1$ of success and probability $q = .9$ of failure. The probability of 0 successes is

$$B(0; 5, 0.1) = {}_5C_0(0.9)^5 = .59049$$

The complementary event (at least 1 success in 5 trials) has probability

$$1 - B(0; 5, 0.1) = 1 - .59049 = .40951$$

In words: The probability that the speculator will lose his entire investment is approximately $\frac{3}{5}$. The probability that his investment will be profitable is approximately $\frac{2}{5}$.

NOTE: CALCULATING $B(r; n, p)$ Appendix Table 1 gives values of $B(r; n, p)$ for n from 1 to 20 (and $0 \le r \le n$ in each case) and for $p = .05, .10, .20, .25, .30, .40,$ and $.50$. The table shows, for example, that $B(0; 5, 0.1) = .5905$. This agrees (to four figures) with the value just given. $B(0; 5, 0.1) = .59049$, was found with the aid of a hand-held calculator, as were the binomial probabilities needed for Problems 4, 5, 6, and 7. Most, but not all, of these calculations can be checked against Table 1. Every one of the binomial probabilities that you will need to do the exercises at the end of the section can be found in Table 1.

The following four examples illustrate the variety of applications of binomial probabilities.

PROBLEM 4   Over the years, top auto industry executive R. G. Brewster has made 10 important yes-or-no decisions. (These related to such matters as whether to produce a subcompact car in the U.S.A. or have it produced in Japan; whether to go along with Federal emission regulations or to fight them; and so on.) With the wisdom of hindsight, his fellow executives now see that Brewster made the correct decision 8 out of 10 times. They warmly congratulate him on his excellent judgment. Brewster replies: "I just flipped a coin." Is this believable?

SOLUTION   Brewster made 10 decisions. We assume that the decisions were independent, and that each had 2 outcomes: success (a correct decision) and failure (an incorrect decision). If he flipped a coin in each case, he had probability $p = .5$ of success and $q = .5$ of failure. The probability that exactly 8 out of the 10 decisions were correct is

$$B(8; 10, 0.5) = {}_{10}C_8(0.5)^8(0.5)^{10-8} = 45(0.5)^{10} = .04394531$$

The probability that at least 8 of the 10 decisions were correct is

$$B(8; 10, 0.5) + B(9; 10, 0.5) + B(10; 10, 0.5)$$
$$= {}_{10}C_8(0.5)^{10} + {}_{10}C_9(0.5)^{10} + {}_{10}C_{10}(0.5)^{10}$$
$$= .0546875$$

Conclusion: Brewster's reply is not believable—unless he had an amazing run of luck.

PROBLEM 5 (continuation of Problem 4) R. G. Brewster's actual decision-making method was to refer all problems to the men and women on his quantitative analysis staff, and to follow their advice, whether or not it seemed to agree with common sense. Assuming that this method had the same probability p of success in each of the 10 independent decisions, just how large a value of p would explain Brewster's 8-out-of-10 success record?

SOLUTION Brewster's record makes sense if the probability that he has at least 8 successes out of 10 is greater than the probability that he has fewer than 8 successes.

In other words: We want p to be large enough so that the sum of the three probabilities

$$B(8; 10, p) + B(9; 10, p) + B(10; 10, p)$$

is greater than .5.

The solution of Problem 4 shows that $p = .5$ is far too small. We try $p = .9$. (As before, we do the arithmetic on a hand-held calculator.) The results are:

$$B(8; 10, 0.9) = {}_{10}C_8(0.9)^8(0.1)^2 = .1937$$

$$B(9; 10, 0.9) = {}_{10}C_9(0.9)^9(0.1) = .3874$$

$$B(10; 10, 0.9) = {}_{10}C_{10}(0.9)^{10} = .3487$$

Since the sum of the three probabilities is .9298, we do not have to assume that $p = .9$ to make an 8-out-of-10 success record believable.

If $p = .7$, we find that the sum of the three probabilities is .3828. This does not seem to be large enough.

Finally we try $p = .75$. This gives

$$B(8; 10, 0.75) + B(9; 10, 0.75) + B(10; 10, 0.75)$$
$$= .2815 + .1878 + .0563 = .5256$$

which is large enough to explain Brewster's excellent record.

Our last two examples apply binomial probabilities to product testing.

PROBLEM 6 The new artificial sweetener Toot Sweet has been proposed as a safer substitute for saccharin. Actually, Toot Sweet is more dangerous than saccharin: it causes tumors in 6% of the laboratory rats who eat it. What is the probability that this fact will not be discovered if a laboratory tests Toot Sweet on a group of 10 rats? 20 rats? 50 rats?

SOLUTION   In this experiment "success" means "tumor," and "fail-ure" means "no tumor." The success probability $p = .06$ and the failure probability $q = .94$. Our first question is: What is the proba-bility of 0 successes in 10 trials? The answer is

$$B(0;\ 10, 0.6) = {}_{10}C_0(0.06)^0(0.94)^{10} = (0.94)^{10} = .5386$$

The probabilities of 0 successes in 20 trials, and in 50 trials, are

$$B(0;\ 20, 0.6) = (0.94)^{20} = .2901$$

$$B(0;\ 50, 0.6) = (0.94)^{50} = .0453$$

These results show that potentially dangerous products need to be tested on relatively large groups of laboratory animals.

PROBLEM 7   Secretaries (and executives) who cannot spell make an unfortunate impression on corporate clients who *can* spell. Comp-utype manufactures an intelligent typewriter that checks the spelling of every typed word against an on-line dictionary. (If a word is not spelled correctly, the typewriter talks back to the typist.) In the first production run, 1 out of 10 of these typewriters is defective. A company has ordered 1200 intelligent typewriters and will actually test a random sample of 20. If 2 or more of these 20 typewriters are defective, the company will reject the entire shipment. What is the probability that the company will in fact reject the 1200 typewriters?

SOLUTION   The shipment will be *accepted* if the number of defective typewriters in the 20-typewriter random sample is 0 or 1.

In this example "success" means "defective typewriter," and "failure" means "typewriter with no defects." The success probability $p = .1$ and the failure probability $q = .9$.

The probabilities for 0 and 1 successes in 20 trials are:

$$B(0;\ 20, 0.1) = {}_{20}C_0(0.1)^0(0.9)^{20} = (0.9)^{20} = .1215767$$

$$B(1;\ 20, 0.1) = {}_{20}C_1(0.1)(0.9)^{19} = 20(0.1)(0.9)^{19} = .2701704$$

Therefore the probability that the shipment will be accepted is

$$B(0;\ 20, 0.1) + B(1;\ 20, 0.1) = .3917471$$

and the probability that the shipment will be rejected is

$$1 - .3917471 = .6082529$$

In words: Acceptance is chancy, rejection is likely. Computype has a good idea, but it will have to tighten up its quality control if it wants to stay in business.

NOTE: Product testing of the type described in Problem 7 is called *acceptance sampling.* The idea behind acceptance sampling is that an entire shipment is accepted (or rejected) on the basis of test results for a random sample.

EXERCISES *for Section 8.3*

1. Ten well-balanced coins are tossed simultaneously. What is the probability that the result is:

a. exactly 7 heads?
b. at least 7 heads?
c. at most 4 heads?

2. Eleven symmetrical dice are rolled simultaneously. Find the probability that the result is:

a. four 6's, seven other numbers
b. seven 6's, four other numbers
c. at least four 6's
d. at most seven 6's

3. Half of the cards in a 52-card bridge deck are *black* (spades or clubs) and half are *red* (hearts or diamonds). Suppose that we randomly select a 20-card sample from such a deck, and suppose that the sample is *with replacement.* That is, we choose a card from the well-shuffled deck; record the color of the card; replace the card; shuffle the deck; choose a card and note its color before replacing it and reshuffling the deck; and so on. Under these conditions, find expressions for each of the following probabilities in terms of binomial probabilities. Do not calculate the probabilities numerically.

a. the probability that 10 of the cards selected are black
b. the probability that no more than 15 of the cards selected are black
c. the probability that no fewer than 8 of the cards selected are black

4. A history professor gave a multiple-choice exam. There were 8 questions, each counting 12.5 points, and there were 5 possible answers (only 1 of which was correct) for each question. For a grade of C, a student had to have the right answer for 6 of the 8 questions. If a student chose multiple-choice answers at random (not even reading the questions), what was his or her probability of getting a grade of C or better on the exam?

5. CPC Chemical has a 20% success ratio in its R&D (research and development). If the company has 17 R&D projects going on right now, what is the probability that at least 3 of them will be successful? What is the probability that more than 4 of them will be successful?

6. Bob Wiswell is a back-country Florida man who earns a living taking tourists alligator-hunting, which is not exactly an armchair sport. Five percent of the hunters are injured by alligators. If Bob Wiswell has 20 customers in a season, what is the probability that one of them will be injured? What is the probability that two or more will be injured?

7. Quality means everything at the Tigre division of Aztec Motors. In a report to management, the quality control department head says that 90% of Tigre cars come out of the factory with no defects of any kind. Assuming that this is true, use Table 1 to find the probabilities that the number of no-defect Tigre cars out of 19 randomly chosen ones that come out of the factory is 0, 1, 2, ..., 19.

A fair number of Americans have summer places in the Ozark Mountains in Arkansas. Not everyone who buys such a place remains satisfied with it. The satisfaction percentages for people from Omaha, Chicago, and Louisville are: 80% for families from Omaha, 90% for families from Chicago, 75% for families from Louisville. Translate these percentages into probabilities, and use Table 1 to answer the following questions.

8. For 15 families from Omaha, find the probabilities that the number satisfied with the family summer place in Arkansas is 0, 1, 2, ..., 15.

9. For 19 families from Chicago, find the probability that 0, 1, 2, ..., 19 are satisfied with their Arkansas summer place.

10. Of 18 families from Louisville, find the probabilities that 0, 1, 2, ..., 18 find their Arkansas summer place satisfying.

---

11. A pharmaceutical company has developed a new and very powerful tranquilizer. It was found that this tranquilizer had undesirable side effects 10% of the time. An improved version of the tranquilizer had undesirable side effects only 5% of the time.

   a. The tranquilizer was prescribed for 10 patients. What is the probability that at least 1 of these patients experienced the undesirable side effects?
   b. The *improved* tranquilizer was prescribed for 10 patients. What is the probability that at least 1 of those patients experienced the undesirable side effects?

12. Somnium is a tranquilizer that has been found useful in the treatment of 4 medical emergencies: heart attacks, severe asthmatic attacks, hypertensive flareups, and acute colitis. Clinical experience showed that Somnium would provide important relief in any one of these emergencies exactly 40% of the time.

   In a recent week, the resident physician at West Side Hospital used Somnium in the treatment of 3 heart attacks, 1 severe asthmatic attack, 2 hypertensive flareups, and 1 case of acute colitis. What is the probability that Somnium provided important relief in:

a. all 7 of the medical emergencies?
b. 6 of them?
c. 5 of them?
d. more than 3 of the 7?

A team of sociologists is studying homeowning patterns in a medium-sized U.S. city. Preliminary data seems to show that 40% of homeowners under the age of 35 are the children of homeowners. And 25% of homeowners under the age of 30 are the grandchildren of homeowners. Finally, 70% of non-homeowning heads of families over the age of 25 are actively looking for a first home to buy. In answering the questions in the next three exercises, assume that these preliminary figures are correct.

13. One of the sociologists studies a randomly chosen group of 19 under-35 homeowners. What is the probability that 7 or more of these people are the children of homeowners? What is the probability that fewer than 9 of them are? Only 5?

14. A second sociologist studies a randomly selected group of 17 under-30 homeowners. What is the probability that 4 or more of these are grandchildren of homeowners? What is the probability that fewer than 7 of them are? Only 3?

15. A third member of the team of sociologists studies a randomly chosen group of 16 non-homeowners. All of these are heads of families, and they are all over 25. What is the probability that 5 or more of them are *not* actively looking for a first home to buy? What is the probability that 5 or more of them *are* actively looking for a first home to buy? What is the probability that 11 or more *are* actively looking for a first home to buy?

chapter nine

MARKOV CHAINS

$\mathbf{C}$HAPTER 8 introduced the idea of repeated trials of a probability experiment. It was assumed that the outcome of any trial was unaffected by the outcomes of prior trials. This chapter makes the slightly different assumption that the outcome of a trial may be affected by the outcome of the immediately preceding trial (but not by any other). Under that assumption, a sequence of trials is said to form a *Markov chain*. This chapter will show you how to calculate the probabilities of the various outcomes in Markov chains. In the special case of a *regular Markov chain,* you will see how to predict the long-term behavior (or *steady state*) of the chain.

Among the real-world Markov chains discussed in the examples and exercises of this chapter, we want to call attention to the market competition examples given in Example 2 of Section 9.1 and Example 1 of Section 9.2. The second of these is based on actual data.

9.1 PROBABILITY VECTORS AND TRANSITION MATRICES

In Chapter 8 we defined repeated *independent* trials. Here we work with repeated trials under a different assumption: we assume that the outcome of each trial (after the first) is independent of all the other trials *except possibly the immediately preceding trial.* If outcomes are linked in this manner, we say that the repeated trials form a *Markov chain.*

You remember that coin-tossing provides an example of independent trials with two outcomes. The trials are independent because a coin has no memory. By contrast, coin-tossing with a coin that remembers the immediately preceding toss would provide an example of a Markov chain. Such a coin can be constructed with the aid of microelectronic technology.

EXAMPLE 1: THE COIN WITH A MEMORY

Midwest Microelectronics has produced a coin with a memory.* An initial toss (with $P(H) = P(T) = .5$) activates the coin's microcircuits. The outcomes of later tosses are as follows:

1. If the outcome of a coin toss is H, then the probability of H on the next toss is .6.

2. If the outcome of a coin toss is T, then the probability of T on the next toss is .8.

Notice that the coin with a memory is very different from an unbalanced coin: if a coin is unbalanced, then $P(H)$ and $P(T)$ are unequal, but they have the same numerical value on each trial. In the present case, $P(H)$ can be either .6 or .2, and $P(T)$ can be either .4 or .8, depending on the outcome of the immediately preceding trial.

Our second example describes a Markov chain in which each experiment has three possible outcomes.

---

*Midwest Microelectronics technicians construct the coin with a memory by cutting a normal coin in half, removing some of the metal, and implanting a microminiaturized power pack and a silicon chip containing transistors, diodes, and memory circuits. When the coin is put together again, it is perfectly balanced. (This is why $P(H) = P(T) = .5$ on the initial toss.) After the circuits are activated by the initial toss, the coin behaves like a miniaturized space ship: the memory circuit gives commands for later tosses (one toss at a time), and the power pack supplies the energy required to overbalance the coin in either the H or the T direction.

EXAMPLE 2: THE HAIRSPRAY MARKET

Holdfast, Wonder Web, and Lively Look are the three leading hairspray brands. All three are good products, and all three are relentlessly advertised and aggressively marketed. Interested ad agencies have noticed that hairspray market leadership *one* month influences market leadership the *next* month. The observed facts are as follows:

1. If Holdfast is the leader one month, then the probabilities that Holdfast, Wonder Web, and Lively Look will be next month's leader are .40, .25, and .35 in that order.

2. If Wonder Web leads one month, then the probabilities for Holdfast, Wonder Web, and Lively Look to be next month's leader are .35, .35, and .30 in that order.

3. If Lively Look leads the market one month, then the probabilities for Holdfast, Wonder Web, and Lively Look to lead in the next month are .30, .25, and .45 in that order.

It is convenient to list these probabilities in a matrix:

$$
\begin{array}{c}
 \\ H \\ W \\ L
\end{array}
\begin{array}{ccc}
H & W & L \\
\begin{pmatrix} .40 & .25 & .35 \\ .35 & .35 & .30 \\ .30 & .25 & .45 \end{pmatrix}
\end{array}
$$

Each of the nine probabilities listed is the probability of a change, or *transition*, in market leadership. (Maintenance of market leadership is a transition from leadership by one of the brands *one* month to leadership by the same brand the *next* month.) Each of the probabilities is therefore called a *transition probability*. The matrix of transition probabilities is called the *transition matrix* of the problem. Notice that the entries in each row of the transition matrix add up to 1. This is as it should be. For example: Row 1 of the matrix contains the probabilities of all possible outcomes for next month, given that Holdfast is this month's leader. If we think of row 1 of the matrix as a row vector, then we call it a *probability vector.*

DEFINITION Probability Vector

A row vector all of whose entries are non-negative is called a *probability vector,* if the sum of those entries is 1.

All the rows of our transition matrix are probability vectors. This property is shared by every transition matrix.

DEFINITION   **Transition Matrix**

A square matrix is a *transition matrix* if every one of its rows is a probability vector.

For an application of the concepts of probability vector and transition matrix, let's return to Example 1. We will formulate and solve some probability problems for the Markov chain described in that example.

EXAMPLE 1 CONTINUED: TOSSING THE COIN WITH A MEMORY

When we first toss the coin with a memory, the coin is perfectly balanced and we have $P(H) = P(T) = .5$. These probabilities are listed as the two entries of the *initial probability vector*

$$\mathbf{p}^{(0)} = (.5 \quad .5)$$

The transition matrix **P** listing the transition probabilities for the outcomes of later tosses is:

$$\begin{array}{cc} & \begin{array}{cc} H & T \end{array} \\ \begin{array}{c} H \\ T \end{array} & \begin{pmatrix} .6 & .4 \\ .2 & .8 \end{pmatrix} \end{array} = \mathbf{P}$$

What are the probabilities of the outcomes H and T on the first, second, and later tosses after the initial toss? For an answer, we draw a tree diagram (Figure 9.1), whose branches are labeled with the appropriate transition probabilities. The sample space for the initial toss is $\{H, T\}$ and the corresponding probabilities are $P(H) = .5$, $P(T) = .5$ as shown. In other words: The first two branches of the tree diagram contain precisely the same information that we have recorded in the initial probability vector

$$\mathbf{p}^{(0)} = (.5 \quad .5)$$

On the first toss after the initial toss, we can arrive at the outcome H along either of two paths: HH or TH. By multiplying transition probabilities along the corresponding branches of the tree, we find that

$$P(HH) = (.5)(.6) = .3$$
$$P(TH) = (.5)(.2) = .1$$

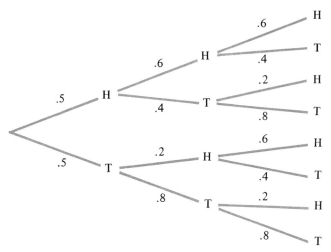

FIGURE 9.1 Tree Diagram: Initial Toss and Two Later Tosses of the Coin with a Memory

Therefore the probability of the outcome H is

$$P(\text{HH}) + P(\text{TH}) = .3 + .1 = .4$$

Similarly, the probability of the outcome T on the first toss after the initial toss is given by

$$P(\text{HT}) + P(\text{TT}) = (.5)(.4) + (.5)(.8) = .2 + .4 = .6$$

The *first-step probability vector*

$$\mathbf{p}^{(1)} = (.4 \quad .6)$$

records our results for the probabilities of H and T on the first toss.

To find probabilities for the second toss after the initial toss, we again look at the tree diagram. We see that there are four branches corresponding to the outcome H. The probabilities we want are obtained by multiplying transition probabilities along the branches of the tree:

$$P(\text{HHH}) = (.5)(.6)(.6) = .18$$

$$P(\text{HTH}) = (.5)(.4)(.2) = .04$$

$$P(\text{THH}) = (.5)(.2)(.6) = .06$$

$$P(\text{TTH}) = (.5)(.8)(.2) = .08$$

By adding the four numbers, we find that the probability of H on the second toss is .36. The probability of T on the second toss is therefore .64. (*Check:* Multiply transition probabilities along the four paths (HHT, HTT, THT, TTT) leading to the outcome T on the second toss. The sum of the probabilities is $.12 + .16 + .04 + .32 = .64$.) We record these results by writing the *second-step probability vector*

$$\mathbf{p}^{(2)} = (.36 \quad .64)$$

We can go on to calculate $\mathbf{p}^{(3)}$, $\mathbf{p}^{(4)}$, etc., but the tree diagram for such calculations will soon be much too large. For a more convenient approach, we look back over what we have done. To find $\mathbf{p}^{(1)}$ and $\mathbf{p}^{(2)}$, we had to:

1. multiply transition probabilities along the appropriate branches of the tree in Figure 9.1; and

2. add the results corresponding to H and T outcomes on the first and second tosses.

We were really doing matrix multiplication. To find $\mathbf{p}^{(1)}$, we multiplied $\mathbf{p}^{(0)}$ by the transition matrix $\mathbf{P}$:

$$\mathbf{p}^{(0)}\mathbf{P} = (.5 \quad .5) \begin{pmatrix} .6 & .4 \\ .2 & .8 \end{pmatrix}$$

$$= (.4 \quad .6) = \mathbf{p}^{(1)}$$

To find $\mathbf{p}^{(2)}$, we multiplied $\mathbf{p}^{(1)}$ by $\mathbf{P}$:

$$\mathbf{p}^{(1)}\mathbf{P} = (.4 \quad .6) \begin{pmatrix} .6 & .4 \\ .2 & .8 \end{pmatrix}$$

$$= (.36 \quad .64) = \mathbf{p}^{(2)}$$

We summarize by writing

$$\mathbf{p}^{(1)} = \mathbf{p}^{(0)}\mathbf{P}$$

$$\mathbf{p}^{(2)} = \mathbf{p}^{(1)}\mathbf{P}$$

Since $\mathbf{p}^{(1)} = \mathbf{p}^{(0)}\mathbf{P}$, the equation for $\mathbf{p}^{(2)}$ can be rewritten as

$$\mathbf{p}^{(2)} = \mathbf{p}^{(0)}\mathbf{P}^2$$

Notice that the raised 2 in $\mathbf{P}^2$ is a *power,* with the meaning that the matrix $\mathbf{P}$ is to be *squared.* The superscripts (2) and (0) have a different meaning: they are simply identifying labels.

Check:

$$\mathbf{P}^2 = \begin{pmatrix} .6 & .4 \\ .2 & .8 \end{pmatrix} \begin{pmatrix} .6 & .4 \\ .2 & .8 \end{pmatrix}$$

$$= \begin{pmatrix} .44 & .56 \\ .28 & .72 \end{pmatrix}$$

$$\mathbf{p}^{(0)}\mathbf{P}^2 = (.5 \quad .5)\begin{pmatrix} .44 & .56 \\ .28 & .72 \end{pmatrix}$$

$$= (.36 \quad .64)$$

We can find the step-3 probability vector, and all the higher probability vectors, in the same way:

$$\mathbf{p}^{(3)} = \mathbf{p}^{(0)}\mathbf{P}^3$$

$$\mathbf{p}^{(4)} = \mathbf{p}^{(0)}\mathbf{P}^4$$

and so on.

The general formula is

$$\mathbf{p}^{(k)} = \mathbf{p}^{(0)}\mathbf{P}^k \qquad (k = 1, 2, \ldots)$$

where the raised k in $\mathbf{P}^k$ indicates that the matrix $\mathbf{P}$ is to be multiplied by itself k times. The superscripts (k) and (0) are identifying labels.

EXAMPLE 1 CONCLUDED: STARTING FROM A KNOWN STATE

In real-world applications of the Markov chain model, we usually know the initial outcome of a probability experiment and want to calculate the probability of that outcome (or some other outcome) two or three steps down the chain.

Before showing how to carry out such calculations, note that it is customary to refer to the various possible outcomes of Markov chain trials as *states*. In the case of the coin with a memory, the two states are H and T. If the outcome of the initial toss is H, we say that *the system is in state H at step 0*. The initial probability vector would then be a *state vector*

$$\mathbf{S}_H^{(0)} = (1 \quad 0)$$

giving the information that the initial toss leads to the outcome (or state) H with probability 1, and to the state T with probability 0. As a second example, suppose that we know that the outcome of the third toss is T. The state vector conveying this information would be

$$\mathbf{S}_T^{(3)} = (0 \quad 1)$$

Problems 1 and 2 show how to calculate Markov chain probabilities when the chain starts from a known state.

PROBLEM 1   The outcome of the initial toss of the coin with a memory is H. What is the probability that the outcome of the second toss is H?

SOLUTION   We use the general formula $\mathbf{p}^{(k)} = \mathbf{p}^{(0)}\mathbf{P}^k$. Here we have $k = 2$, and

$$\mathbf{p}^{(0)} = \mathbf{S}_H^{(0)} = (1 \quad 0)$$

The second-step probability vector corresponding to $\mathbf{S}_H^{(0)}$ as initial probability vector is

$$\mathbf{S}_H^{(0)}\mathbf{P}^2 = (1 \quad 0)\begin{pmatrix} .44 & .56 \\ .28 & .72 \end{pmatrix}$$

$$= (.44 \quad .56)$$

In other words, if $\mathbf{S}_H^{(0)} = (1 \quad 0)$ is the initial state vector, then the probability of the outcome H at the second step is .44.

NOTE: If the initial state vector is $\mathbf{S}_T^{(0)} = (0 \quad 1)$, then we have

$$\mathbf{S}_T^{(0)}\mathbf{P}^2 = (.28 \quad .72)$$

which says that the probability of the outcome H at the second step (after an initial T) is .28. The difference between .28 and .44 is considerable. Finally: If we do not know the initial outcome, but know only that $\mathbf{p}^{(0)} = (.5 \quad .5)$, then the probability of the outcome H at the second step is .36. This result (found on p. 405) lies midway between .28 and .44, as we would expect.

PROBLEM 2   The outcome of the fourth toss of the coin with a memory is T. What are the probabilities for the sixth toss?

SOLUTION   The state vector for the fourth toss is

$$\mathbf{S}_T^{(4)} = (0 \quad 1)$$

From $\mathbf{p}^{(k)} = \mathbf{p}^{(0)}\mathbf{P}^k$, we find that

$$\mathbf{p}^{(6)} = \mathbf{p}^{(0)}\mathbf{P}^6 = \mathbf{p}^{(4)}\mathbf{P}^2$$

In the present case, our sixth-step probability vector is:

$$\mathbf{S}_T^{(4)}\mathbf{P}^2 = (0 \quad 1)\begin{pmatrix} .44 & .56 \\ .28 & .72 \end{pmatrix}$$

$$= (.28 \quad .72)$$

In other words: If the outcome of toss 4 is T, then the probabilities for toss 6 are .28 for H and .72 for T.

We conclude this section with some illustrative problems based on Example 2.

EXAMPLE 2 CONTINUED: COMPETING IN THE HAIRSPRAY MARKET

The three possible outcomes (or *states*) of the monthly hairspray competition are: H (Holdfast leads), W (Wonder Web leads), and L (Lively Look leads). An initial probability vector for this example woud be a three-dimensional vector

$$\mathbf{p}^{(0)} = (\mathbf{p_H}^{(0)} \mathbf{p_W}^{(0)} \mathbf{p_L}^{(0)})$$

where $\mathbf{p_H}^{(0)}$, $\mathbf{p_W}^{(0)}$, and $\mathbf{p_L}^{(0)}$ are the probabilities of the outcomes H, W, and L on the initial experiment. (Also, $\mathbf{p_H}^{(0)} + \mathbf{p_W}^{(0)} + \mathbf{p_L}^{(0)} = 1$ by the definition of a probability vector.) If we are given such an initial probability vector, then we can calculate higher probability vectors by the equation

$$\mathbf{p}^{(k)} = \mathbf{p}^{(0)}\mathbf{P}^k \qquad (k = 1, 2, \ldots)$$

where $\mathbf{p}^{(k)}$ is the kth-step probability vector, $\mathbf{p}^{(0)}$ is the given initial probability vector, and $\mathbf{P}^k$ is the kth power of the transition matrix (see p. 403):

$$\mathbf{P} = \begin{array}{c} \\ \text{H} \\ \text{W} \\ \text{L} \end{array} \begin{array}{ccc} \text{H} & \text{W} & \text{L} \\ \begin{pmatrix} .40 & .25 & .35 \\ .35 & .35 & .30 \\ .30 & .25 & .45 \end{pmatrix} \end{array}$$

In solving Problems 3 and 4, we assume that month-to-month transition probabilities are given by the matrix **P**.

PROBLEM 3   According to the best available market research, Holdfast and Wonder Web each have probability .30 of being the market leader in February 1979. The probability that Lively Look will be the leader is .40. What are the leadership probabilities for April 1979?

SOLUTION   The initial (February 1979) probability vector is:

$$\mathbf{p}^{(0)} = (.30 \quad .30 \quad .40)$$

and the second-step (April 1979) probability vector is:

$$\mathbf{p}^{(2)} = \mathbf{p}^{(0)}\mathbf{P}^2$$

where

$$\mathbf{P}^2 = \begin{pmatrix} .40 & .25 & .35 \\ .35 & .35 & .30 \\ .30 & .25 & .45 \end{pmatrix}^2 = \begin{pmatrix} .3525 & .275 & .3725 \\ .3555 & .282 & .3625 \\ .3425 & .275 & .3825 \end{pmatrix}$$

Our result is:

$$\mathbf{p}^{(2)} = (.3494 \quad .2771 \quad .3735)$$

(*Check:* The product of two transition matrices is always a transition matrix—that is, a matrix whose rows are probability vectors. As a check on our calculation, we notice that $\mathbf{P}^2$ is a transition matrix. And $\mathbf{p}^{(2)}$ is a probability vector.)

The meaning of the result for $\mathbf{P}^2$ is that the probabilities for Holdfast, Wonder Web, and Lively Look to lead the market in April 1979 are .3494, .2771, and .3735 in that order.

PROBLEM 4   A hilarious TV commercial starring a bald actor propelled Wonder Web into market leadership in May 1979. What is the probability that Wonder Web will be the market leader in August 1979?

SOLUTION   The initial state vector

$$\mathbf{S}_W^{(0)} = (0 \quad 1 \quad 0)$$

describes the market situation (leadership by Wonder Web) in May 1979. Since August 1979 is three months (or three steps) further along, we have to calculate the third-step probability vector $\mathbf{p}^{(3)}$. The general formula is $\mathbf{p}^{(3)} = \mathbf{p}^{(0)}\mathbf{P}^3$. In the present case, $\mathbf{p}^{(0)} = \mathbf{S}_W^{(0)}$, and

$$\mathbf{p}^{(3)} = \mathbf{S}_W^{(0)}\mathbf{P}^3$$

We calculated $\mathbf{P}^2$ in solving Problem 3. Making use of that result, we have

$$\mathbf{P}^3 = \mathbf{P}^2\mathbf{P} = \begin{pmatrix} .34975 & .27675 & .3735 \\ .35055 & .27745 & .372 \\ .34875 & .27675 & .3745 \end{pmatrix}$$

If we premultiply by $\mathbf{S}_W^{(0)} = (0 \quad 1 \quad 0)$, we find:

$$\mathbf{p}^{(3)} = \mathbf{S}_W^{(0)} \mathbf{P}^3 = (.35055 \quad .27745 \quad .372)$$

(*Check:* $\mathbf{P}^3$ is a transition matrix and $\mathbf{p}^{(3)}$, which is simply the second row of $\mathbf{P}^3$, is a probability vector.)

Conclusion: The probability that Wonder Web will lead the market in August 1979, given that it is the leader in May, is .27745.

REAL-WORLD INTERPRETATION If we start with

$$\mathbf{p}^{(0)} = (.30 \quad .30 \quad .40)$$

instead of $\mathbf{S}_W^{(0)}$, we find that

$$\mathbf{p}^{(3)} = \mathbf{p}^{(0)} \mathbf{P}^3 = (.34959 \quad .27696 \quad .37345)$$

Subtraction gives us:

$$\mathbf{S}_W^{(0)} \mathbf{P}^3 - \mathbf{p}^{(0)} \mathbf{P}^3 = (.00096 \quad .00049 \quad -.00145)$$

From the point of view of probability of market leadership, the difference between the two vectors is insignificant. The assumed fact that the transition matrix $\mathbf{P}$ is unchanged for three steps (June, July and August) will be more important than Wonder Web's temporary market leadership in May. In real-world terms, the assumption that the transition matrix remains unchanged must mean one of two things: *Either* Wonder Web's ad agency will exhaust its hairspray creativity with the bald actor commercial *or* the Holdfast and Lively Look agencies will mount successful countercampaigns in a very short time. If Wonder Web's management wants to change the transition matrix in favor of its own product, then it must be ready to spend months (and megabucks) blanketing the air with one outstanding commercial after another.

EXERCISES *for Section 9.1*

1. State which of the following vectors are probability vectors:

$\mathbf{a} = (0 \quad 1)$

$\mathbf{b} = (.3 \quad .3 \quad .4)$

$\mathbf{c} = (.3 \quad .3 \quad .5 \quad -.1)$

$\mathbf{d} = (.79 \quad .05 \quad .06 \quad .10)$

$\mathbf{e} = (.33 \quad .33 \quad .33)$

$\mathbf{f} = (.25 \quad .25 \quad .45 \quad -.20)$

2. Which of the following matrices are transition matrices?

$$A = \begin{pmatrix} \frac{2}{3} & \frac{1}{3} \\ 0 & 1 \end{pmatrix}$$

$$B = \begin{pmatrix} .5 & .5 \\ .75 & .25 \end{pmatrix}$$

$$C = \begin{pmatrix} .5 & .75 \\ .5 & .25 \end{pmatrix}$$

$$D = \begin{pmatrix} .8 & .2 \\ .2 & .8 \end{pmatrix}$$

$$E = \begin{pmatrix} .125 & .875 \\ .425 & .675 \end{pmatrix}$$

$$F = \begin{pmatrix} .3 & .3 & .4 \\ 0 & .5 & .5 \\ 0 & 0 & 1 \end{pmatrix}$$

$$G = \begin{pmatrix} .5 & .4 & .1 \\ .6 & .4 & 0 \\ .7 & .4 & -.1 \end{pmatrix}$$

3. Find the values, if any, of the variables $(x, y,$ etc.$)$ that will make the matrix a transition matrix:

$$A = \begin{pmatrix} .4 & x \\ .7 & y \end{pmatrix}$$

$$B = \begin{pmatrix} 1 & x \\ .3745 & y \end{pmatrix}$$

$$C = \begin{pmatrix} .5 & x \\ .5 & .6 \end{pmatrix}$$

$$D = \begin{pmatrix} .47 & .23 & x \\ .61 & y & .19 \\ z & .08 & .09 \end{pmatrix}$$

$$E = \begin{pmatrix} x & .45 & .35 \\ .99 & y & .01 \\ .88 & .13 & z \end{pmatrix}$$

$$F = \begin{pmatrix} x & .45 & .35 \\ .99 & y & .01 \end{pmatrix}$$

4. The initial probability vector of a Markov chain is:

$$\mathbf{p}^{(0)} = (.5 \quad .5)$$

Transition probabilities for the chain are given by the transition matrix

$$\mathbf{P} = \begin{pmatrix} .35 & .65 \\ .55 & .45 \end{pmatrix}$$

Draw a tree diagram illustrating the initial step and two more steps in the chain. For convenience, use the labels H and T for the two possible outcomes at each step.

5. From the tree diagram of Exercise 4 (with outcomes labeled H and T):

a. What is P(H) at step 1? at step 2?
b. What is P(T) at step 1? at step 2?

6. The initial probability vector of a Markov chain is

$$\mathbf{p}^{(0)} = (.3 \quad .7)$$

and the transition matrix of the chain is

$$\mathbf{P} = \begin{pmatrix} .15 & .85 \\ .37 & .63 \end{pmatrix}$$

Label the two possible outcomes H and T. Then draw a tree diagram showing outcomes for the initial step and the next two steps in the chain.

7. Use the tree diagram you drew in Exercise 6 to find:

a. the probability of the outcome H at step 1 and at step 2
b. the probability of the outcome T at step 1 and at step 2

8. The initial probability vector of a Markov chain is

$$\mathbf{p}^{(0)} = (.25 \quad .75)$$

and the transition matrix of the chain is

$$\mathbf{P} = \begin{pmatrix} .5 & .5 \\ .6 & .4 \end{pmatrix}$$

Calculate the step-1, step-2, and step-3 probability vectors of the chain.

9.   A Markov chain has the transition matrix

$$\mathbf{P} = \begin{pmatrix} .66 & .34 \\ .33 & .67 \end{pmatrix}$$

and the initial probability vector

$$\mathbf{p}^{(0)} = (.4 \quad .6)$$

Find the probability vectors $\mathbf{p}^{(1)}$, $\mathbf{p}^{(2)}$, $\mathbf{p}^{(3)}$, and $\mathbf{p}^{(4)}$ of the chain.

10.   A Markov chain has two possible outcomes, or states: A and B. The transition matrix of the chain is

$$\begin{array}{cc} & A \quad B \\ \begin{matrix} A \\ B \end{matrix} & \begin{pmatrix} .1 & .9 \\ .8 & .2 \end{pmatrix} = \mathbf{P} \end{array}$$

Find the step-4 probability vector $\mathbf{p}^{(4)}$ in each of the following cases:

a.   The initial state vector is

$$\mathbf{S}_A^{(0)} = (1 \quad 0)$$

b.   The initial state vector is

$$\mathbf{S}_B^{(0)} = (0 \quad 1)$$

c.   The first-step state vector is

$$\mathbf{S}_A^{(1)} = (1 \quad 0)$$

d.   The second-step state vector is

$$\mathbf{S}_B^{(2)} = (0 \quad 1)$$

A Markov chain has three states: F, G, and H. The transition matrix of the chain is

$$\begin{array}{cccc} & F & G & H \\ \begin{matrix} F \\ G \\ H \end{matrix} & \begin{pmatrix} .32 & .28 & .40 \\ .19 & .54 & .27 \\ .05 & .34 & .61 \end{pmatrix} = \mathbf{P} \end{array}$$

11.   If the initial probability vector is

$$\mathbf{p}^{(0)} = (.3 \quad .4 \quad .3)$$

what is the probability that the outcome of the second trial after the initial trial is: F? G? H?

12. If the initial state vector is

$$\mathbf{S}_G{}^{(0)} = (0 \quad 1 \quad 0)$$

what is the probability that the outcome of the second trial after the initial trial is: F? G? H?

13. If the state vector for the fourth trial after the initial one is

$$\mathbf{S}_H{}^{(4)} = (0 \quad 0 \quad 1)$$

what is the probability that the outcome of the seventh trial will be: F? G? H?

---

14. A very long time ago, the only inhabited continents on this planet were Africa and Asia. The total population of both continents was 1 million persons. Of these, 40% lived in Africa and 60% lived in Asia. Suppose that the total population remained constant for 5 years (no births or deaths on either continent) but that there was a certain amount of migration: Each year, 8% of the African population moved to Asia and 7% of the Asian population moved to Africa. Use a Markov chain analysis to calculate the number of persons in Africa and in Asia after 1, 2, 3, 4, and 5 years.

Computer salesman Howell Smith has noted the following facts:

a. If a customer uses Howell Smith's brand of computer, there is a probability of .63 that the customer's next computer will be bought from Howell Smith.

b. If a potential customer decides against Howell Smith's brand of computer, there is a probability of .58 that the customer will again decide against Howell Smith's company when buying the next computer.

Suppose Smith's territory includes 100 computer-buying customers, that 50 of them initially own the brand he sells, and that the pattern just described continues through 5 rounds of computer-buying by these 100 possible customers.

15. Set up a Markov chain analysis for Howell Smith's computer-selling experience. Define the transition matrix and the initial probability vector.

16. (Use your answer to Exercise 15.) What is the probability that a customer who buys from Howell Smith on the first round will buy from him again on the third round? on the fifth round?

17. (Use your answer to Exercise 15.) What is the probability that a customer who does not buy from Howell Smith on the first round *will* buy from him on the third round? on the fifth round?

18. (Use your answer to Exercise 15.) What is the probability that a customer who buys from Howell Smith on the first round will not buy from him on the second round? on the fourth round?

All the houses in a certain earthquake-prone area are made of adobe, brick, or concrete. (Adobe is used for ranch houses, brick for traditional houses, and concrete for contemporary houses.) Families move from one type of house to another for various reasons—and everyone moves once every 3 years. Transition probabilities for these moves are listed in the transition matrix

$$
\begin{array}{c}
 \\
A \\
B \\
C
\end{array}
\begin{array}{ccc}
A & B & C \\
\begin{pmatrix}
0 & .53 & .47 \\
.71 & 0 & .29 \\
.33 & .67 & 0
\end{pmatrix}
\end{array} = \mathbf{P}
$$

The matrix $\mathbf{P}$ shows, for example, that a family living in an adobe house *now* has probability 0 of moving to an adobe house 3 years from now, probability .53 of moving to a brick house, and probability .47 of moving to a concrete house.

The following exercises are based on the adobe-brick-concrete situation, the regular moves every 3 years, and the transition matrix $\mathbf{P}$.

19. A family in the area owns a pickup truck. Amateur sociologists might therefore use the initial probability vector

$$\mathbf{p}^{(0)} = (.5 \quad .2 \quad .3)$$

to describe where the family is likely to live. (That is: There is a probability of .5 that it lives in an adobe ranch house, a probability of .2 that it lives in a brick traditional house, and a probability of .3 that it lives in a concrete contemporary house.) If a family's probable living place is described by $\mathbf{p}^{(0)}$, what is the probability that the family will be living in an adobe house 9 years (and 3 moves) from now?

20. A family lives in a concrete house. Community custom forces it to move at the regular 3-year intervals. What is the probability that the family will live in a concrete house again after 6 years? after 9 years?

21. If a family will live in a brick house 6 years from now, what is the probability that it will live in an adobe house 15 years from now?

The area map for one of the older cities in Mid-America shows that the city consists of a large number of neighborhoods. Each of these neighborhoods can be classified as L (low-density residential), H (high-density residential), or C (commercial). Many of these neighborhoods change character from year to year. The matrix showing transition probabilities for such year-to-year changes in that city is:

$$
\begin{array}{c}
 \\
L \\
H \\
C
\end{array}
\begin{array}{ccc}
L & H & C \\
\begin{pmatrix}
.45 & .40 & .15 \\
.02 & .78 & .20 \\
.01 & .12 & .87
\end{pmatrix}
\end{array} = \mathbf{P}
$$

Make use of the transition matrix $\mathbf{P}$ in answering the following three questions.

22. You live in a low-density neighborhood in the city just described. What is the probability that your neighborhood will still be a low-density neighborhood 2 years from now? 3 years from now? What is the probability that it will be a high-density residential neighborhood 4 years from now?

23. Your business is located in the so-called Stockyard area of the city—a commercial neighborhood. Do you have much reason to fear that the Stockyard area will become a residential area (in which case you would have to move your business) in the next 2 years? the next 3, 4, 5, or 6 years? the next 8 years?

24. Right now, the city's neighborhoods are 21% low-density residential, 46% high-density residential, and 33% commercial. Will the percentages have changed much next year? What will they be 2 years from now? 3 years from now? 4 years from now?

9.2 THE STEADY STATE VECTOR OF A REGULAR CHAIN

If market competition follows a Markov chain pattern, then it is possible to predict the probabilities of month-to-month shifts in market leadership. Problem 4 of Section 9.1, with its real-world interpretation (p. 411), showed how this predictability can lead to useful data for management decision-making.

Since corporations (and managements) rise or fall on their long-term results, it is especially useful to be able to predict the long-term consequences of a Markov chain pattern. Competitors may, for example, want to know if market positions (as expressed by successive probability vectors) will keep changing or if the market will eventually reach equilibrium.

If a Markov chain leads to equilibrium, then we say that the Markov chain has moved into a *steady state*. Once the steady state has been reached, probability vectors are unchanged from step to step of the chain. Each of these unchanging probability vectors is equal to the same *steady state vector*.

Some real-world Markov chains have steady state vectors and others do not. In this section we will study *regular Markov chains*. These chains occur frequently in real-world problems. And they always move toward a steady state. A regular Markov chain can be recognized by its transition matrix.

In other words: A chain is regular if every entry in its transition matrix **P** (or
in $\mathbf{P}^2$ or $\mathbf{P}^3$ or some higher power) is a *positive* probability.

EXAMPLE 1:   SEARS VERSUS K-MART

In the years 1972–76, Sears and K-Mart followed very different
merchandising policies.

Sears has three product lines (low-, middle-, and top-priced) in almost
everything it sells. Computer analysis showed that Sears customers tended to
prefer the middle-price line. Profit margins in this line are higher than in the
low-price line. But margins are highest for top-of-the-line products. Management's strategy, reinforced by the biggest ad budget in retail merchandising history, was to make household words (and automatic buying choices)
out of its top-line products: Die Hard batteries, Toughskin jeans, Cling-alon
pantyhose, etc.

K-Mart, in the same years, built an image as a store that sold mer-
chandise for less. Its advertising budget was modest. But shoppers noticed
that they could buy perfectly good K-Mart products at a fraction of Sears'
top-line prices. Sears' Cling-alon at $2.98 per pair was a TV star but K-Mart's
99¢ brand (discounted from $1.39) got a much bigger audience share.

And so it went. Sears looked for bigger profit margins by stressing its
top-quality, top-price line. K-Mart looked for high volume (and got it) by
merchandising good-quality products at low prices.

The month-by-month competition between Sears and K-Mart can be
studied as a *two-state Markov chain*. The states are:

S = the retail customer's shopping dollar is spent at Sears

K = the retail customer's shopping dollar is spent at K-Mart

At the beginning of 1972, the state probabilities were:

$$\mathbf{p}_S^{(0)} = .74 \qquad \mathbf{p}_K^{(0)} = .26$$

These probabilities can be interpreted as relative frequencies: Of every dollar
spent by shoppers at Sears or K-Mart in January 1972, $.74 was spent at
Sears and $.26 at K-Mart. The *initial probability vector* of the Markov chain
is therefore

$$\mathbf{p}^{(0)} = (\mathbf{p}_S^{(0)}\ \mathbf{p}_K^{(0)}) = (.74 \quad .26)$$

There were changes in shopping habits from 1972 to 1976. The four transition probabilities for month-by-month changes are given in the *transition matrix*

$$\mathbf{P} = \begin{array}{c} \\ S \\ K \end{array} \begin{array}{c} \quad S \quad\quad K \\ \begin{pmatrix} .70 & .30 \\ .53 & .47 \end{pmatrix} \end{array}$$

The transition probabilities are arranged in the usual way. For example: The probability that a person who is a Sears customer *one* month is a K-Mart customer the *next* month is .30. Notice also that every transition probability in **P** is positive. This defines the chain as a *regular Markov chain*.

To calculate the *first-step probability vector* $\mathbf{p}^{(1)}$, we multiply $\mathbf{p}^{(0)}$ by **P**:

$$\mathbf{p}^{(1)} = \mathbf{p}^{(0)}\mathbf{P} = (.74 \quad .26) \begin{pmatrix} .70 & .30 \\ .53 & .47 \end{pmatrix}$$

$$= (.6558 \quad .3442)$$

These are the February 1972 probabilities. If we subtract the initial (or January 1972) probability vector $\mathbf{p}^{(0)}$ from $\mathbf{p}^{(1)}$, we have

$$\mathbf{p}^{(1)} - \mathbf{p}^{(0)} = (.6558 \quad .3442) - (.74 \quad .26) = (-.0842 \quad .0842)$$

This says that Sears' share of the shopper's dollar decreases by \$.0842, while K-Mart's share increases by the same amount.

The Markov chain continues for another 45 steps (or 45 months, through December 1976). To see whether or not the chain moves toward a *steady state*, we calculate the probability vectors $\mathbf{p}^{(2)}$ through $\mathbf{p}^{(7)}$. These apply to the months March through September 1972. The results are:

$$\mathbf{p}^{(2)} = \mathbf{p}^{(1)}\mathbf{P} = (.6558 \quad .3442) \begin{pmatrix} .70 & .30 \\ .53 & .47 \end{pmatrix} = (.641486 \quad .358514)$$

$$\mathbf{p}^{(3)} = \mathbf{p}^{(2)}\mathbf{P} = (.641486 \quad .358514) \begin{pmatrix} .70 & .30 \\ .53 & .47 \end{pmatrix}$$

$$= (.63905262 \quad .36094738)$$

$$\mathbf{p}^{(4)} = \mathbf{p}^{(3)}\mathbf{P} = (.63905262 \quad .36094738) \begin{pmatrix} .70 & .30 \\ .53 & .47 \end{pmatrix}$$

$$= (.63863895 \quad .36136105)$$

$$\mathbf{p}^{(5)} = \mathbf{p}^{(4)}\mathbf{P} = (.63863895 \quad .36136105)\begin{pmatrix} .70 & .30 \\ .53 & .47 \end{pmatrix}$$

$$= (.63856862 \quad .36143138)$$

$$\mathbf{p}^{(6)} = \mathbf{p}^{(5)}\mathbf{P} = (.63856862 \quad .36143138)\begin{pmatrix} .70 & .30 \\ .53 & .47 \end{pmatrix}$$

$$= (.63855667 \quad .36144333)$$

$$\mathbf{p}^{(7)} = \mathbf{p}^{(6)}\mathbf{P} = (.63855667 \quad .36144333)\begin{pmatrix} .70 & .30 \\ .53 & .47 \end{pmatrix}$$

$$= (.63855463 \quad .36144537)$$

If we round off the decimals to four figures, we have

$$\mathbf{p}^{(4)} = \mathbf{p}^{(5)} = \mathbf{p}^{(6)} = \mathbf{p}^{(7)} = (.6386 \quad .3614)$$

The probability vector

$$(.6386 \quad .3614) = \mathbf{v}$$

is called the *steady state vector* of the Markov chain. The equation

$$\mathbf{vP} = (.6386 \quad .3614)\begin{pmatrix} .70 & .30 \\ .53 & .47 \end{pmatrix} = (.6386 \quad .3614) = \mathbf{v}$$

justifies the name steady state vector. It shows that $\mathbf{v}$ is repeated to the end of the chain:

$$\mathbf{p}^{(9)} = \mathbf{p}^{(8)}\mathbf{P} = \mathbf{vP} = \mathbf{v}$$
$$\mathbf{p}^{(10)} = \mathbf{p}^{(9)}\mathbf{P} = \mathbf{vP} = \mathbf{v}$$

and so on, up to

$$\mathbf{p}^{(47)} = \mathbf{p}^{(46)}\mathbf{P} = \mathbf{vP} = \mathbf{v}$$

The equation $\mathbf{vP} = \mathbf{v}$ also serves as a definition of the steady state vector of a regular Markov chain.

There are two points about steady state vectors that you should not miss. The first is that the definition tells you:

As an example, let's redo Sears versus K-Mart using this approach. The transition matrix is

$$\mathbf{P} = \begin{pmatrix} .70 & .30 \\ .53 & .47 \end{pmatrix}$$

The steady state vector (which we are assuming we do not know) has the form

$$\mathbf{v} = (v_1 \quad v_2)$$

The equation **vP** = **v** is:

$$(v_1 \quad v_2)\begin{pmatrix} .70 & .30 \\ .53 & .47 \end{pmatrix} = (v_1 \quad v_2)$$

which translates into:

$$-.30v_1 + .53v_2 = 0$$
$$.30v_1 - .53v_2 = 0$$

The system is dependent, but we are not finished. We get *one* independent equation out of **vP** = **v**. For a *second* independent equation, we remember that **v** is a probability vector. This means that $v_1 + v_2 = 1$. The result is the system

$$-.30v_1 + .53v_2 = 0$$
$$v_1 + \quad v_2 = 1$$

and the solution is

$$\mathbf{v} = (.6385543 \quad .3614457)$$

Notice that the probability vectors, $\mathbf{p}^{(1)}, \mathbf{p}^{(2)}, \mathbf{p}^{(3)}, \ldots, \mathbf{p}^{(7)}$, as calculated earlier, get closer and closer to the exact value of $\mathbf{v}$.

Rounding to four figures, we have

$$\mathbf{v} = (.6386 \quad .3614)$$

as before. Our first method of finding the steady state vector was lengthy: we had to calculate vector after vector after vector. Solving $\mathbf{vP} = \mathbf{v}$ is much easier.

There is another difference between the two methods. In our first calculation, we started with an initial probability vector $\mathbf{p}^{(0)}$ and went on from that to calculate $\mathbf{p}^{(1)} = \mathbf{p}^{(0)}\mathbf{P}$, $\mathbf{p}^{(2)} = \mathbf{p}^{(1)}\mathbf{P} = \mathbf{p}^{(0)}\mathbf{P}^2$, etc. In the second method, all we do is solve $\mathbf{vP} = \mathbf{v}$. We do not say a thing about the initial probability vector. Can it be that the steady state vector has nothing to do with the initial probability vector? It can. As the chain advances to the steady state, the initial probability vector has less and less effect. In the long run the initial probability vector *washes out*. This is the second point about steady state vectors that you do not want to miss:

THE WASHING-OUT PRINCIPLE

The steady state vector $\mathbf{v}$ of a regular Markov chain is fully determined by the transition matrix $\mathbf{P}$. Changing the initial probability vector $\mathbf{p}^{(0)}$ does *not* change the steady state vector $\mathbf{v}$.

To repeat: The effect of a change in $\mathbf{p}^{(0)}$ *washes out*. To illustrate the washing-out principle, let's suppose that the Sears versus K-Mart initial probability vector is not $\mathbf{p}^{(0)} = (.74 \quad .26)$ but instead an arbitrary probability vector

$$\mathbf{A}^{(0)} = (1 - a \quad a)$$

where $0 \le a \le 1$. (The choice $a = .26$ makes $\mathbf{A}^{(0)} = \mathbf{p}^{(0)}$; the choice $a = .5$ makes $\mathbf{A}^{(0)} = (.5 \quad .5)$; and so on.) We calculate higher order probability vectors by successive multiplications by the transition matrix $\mathbf{P}$. The first seven results are:

$$\mathbf{A}^{(1)} = \mathbf{A}^{(0)}\mathbf{P} = (1 - a \quad a) \begin{pmatrix} .70 & .30 \\ .53 & .47 \end{pmatrix} = (.70 + .17a \quad .30 - .17a)$$

$$\mathbf{A}^{(2)} = \mathbf{A}^{(1)}\mathbf{P} = (.70 + .17a \quad .30 - .17a)\begin{pmatrix} .70 & .30 \\ .53 & .47 \end{pmatrix}$$

$$= (.649 + .0289a \quad .351 - .0289a)$$

$$\mathbf{A}^{(3)} = \mathbf{A}^{(2)}\mathbf{P} = (.64033 + .004913a \quad .35967 - .004913a)$$

$$\mathbf{A}^{(4)} = \mathbf{A}^{(3)}\mathbf{P} = (.6388561 + .0008352a \quad .3611439 - .0008352a)$$

$$\mathbf{A}^{(5)} = \mathbf{A}^{(4)}\mathbf{P} = (.6386054 + .0001419a \quad .3613944 - .0001419a)$$

$$\mathbf{A}^{(6)} = \mathbf{A}^{(5)}\mathbf{P} = (.6385627 + .0000241a \quad .3614369 - .0000241a)$$

$$\mathbf{A}^{(7)} = \mathbf{A}^{(6)}\mathbf{P} = (.6385553 + .000004a \quad .3614441 - .000004a)$$

The successive probability vectors are closer and closer to the steady state vector $\mathbf{v}$. Even with the least favorable value of a ($a = 1$), there is five-figure agreement between $\mathbf{A}^{(7)}$ and $\mathbf{v}$. The effect of the choice of initial probability vector has washed out.

If we look at the successive probability vectors $\mathbf{A}^{(1)}$, $\mathbf{A}^{(2)}$, $\mathbf{A}^{(3)}$, etc., we can see the washing-out principle in action. The first-step effect of the choice of the number a is $\pm.17a$. The second-step effect is $\pm.17^2a = \pm.0289a$. The third-step effect is $\pm.17^3a = \pm.004913a$. And so on. Each step washes out one more significant figure.

EXAMPLE 1: REAL-WORLD INTERPRETATION

The purpose of the Markov chain analysis is to make a long-term prediction about the Sears versus K-Mart competition. Since the steady state vector is

$$\mathbf{v} = (.6386 \quad .3614)$$

the prediction is that Sears would get $\$.6386$ of the shopper's dollar in December 1976, and that K-Mart would get $\$.3614$. If sales of the two companies in December 1976 totalled $2.32 billion, then the prediction says that Sears's sales totalled $1.48 billion and K-Mart's sales totalled $0.84 billion in that month. Notice that the January 1972 market shares, as given by the initial probability vector $\mathbf{p}^{(0)} = (.74 \quad .26)$, were much more favorable to Sears. The Markov chain analysis, if carried out in 1972, would have shown Sears's management that it was following a dangerous policy in stressing quality instead of price. By contrast, K-Mart's merchandising policy looked just right.

In the real world, K-Mart's policy really was right. Sears lost a lot of ground to K-Mart in the years 1972–76.* (The dollar figures resemble the figures given here.) Sears also shifted its policy in an attempt to recapture the

* *Forbes*, 1 October 1974 and 15 June 1977.

low-price business it had lost. We do not know whether or not long-term predictions based on a Markov chain analysis persuaded management to make this shift.

Let's pause to see where we are and where we are going.

So far in this section, we have defined a *regular Markov chain* and a *steady state vector*. We have seen how the equation

$$\mathbf{vP} = \mathbf{v}$$

can be used to calculate the steady state vector **v** of a regular chain with transition matrix **P**. And we have seen how the *washing-out principle* applies to a regular chain.

The four worked-out problems that follow will provide another look at each of these concepts.

PROBLEM 1   Which of the following matrices is the transition matrix of a regular Markov chain?

$$\mathbf{A} = \begin{pmatrix} .1234567 & .8765433 \\ .3345985 & .6654015 \end{pmatrix}$$

$$\mathbf{B} = \begin{pmatrix} .875 & .125 & 0 \\ 0 & .9375 & .0625 \\ .875 & 0 & .125 \end{pmatrix}$$

$$\mathbf{C} = \begin{pmatrix} .234 & .345 & .421 \\ .178 & .596 & .236 \\ .458 & .397 & .145 \end{pmatrix}$$

SOLUTION   Since both rows of **A** are probability vectors, **A** is a transition matrix. Since all four entries are positive, **A** is the transition matrix of a regular Markov chain.

B is a transition matrix. It has 3 zero entries, but calculation shows that

$$\mathbf{B}^2 = \begin{pmatrix} .765625 & .2265625 & .0078125 \\ .0546875 & .8789063 & .0664062 \\ .875 & .109375 & .015625 \end{pmatrix}$$

Since all the entries in **B**^{2} are positive, **B** is the transition matrix of a regular Markov chain.

Rows 1 and 3 of **C** are probability vectors, but row 2 is not. **C** cannot be the transition matrix of any Markov chain.

PROBLEM 2   The coin with a memory was described in Example 1 of Section 9.1. Suppose that coin is tossed 100 times in succession. What are $P(H)$ and $P(T)$ on toss number 100?

SOLUTION 1   The transition matrix for tossing the coin with a memory is

$$\mathbf{P} = \begin{pmatrix} .6 & .4 \\ .2 & .8 \end{pmatrix}$$

Since all the entries are positive, the successive tosses form a regular Markov chain. Toss number 100 is far enough out in the chain so that the steady state will have been reached. We therefore want to find the steady state vector $\mathbf{v} = (v_1 \quad v_2)$. The entry v_1 will give $P(H)$, and the entry v_2 will give $P(T)$, for toss number 100.

The equation $\mathbf{vP} = \mathbf{v}$ leads to:

$$-.4v_1 + .2v_2 = 0$$

$$.4v_1 - .2v_2 = 0$$

We also have the condition

$$v_1 + v_2 = 1$$

The augmented matrix for the three equations is

$$\begin{pmatrix} -.4 & .2 & 0 \\ .4 & -.2 & 0 \\ 1 & 1 & 1 \end{pmatrix}$$

and the echelon form of the matrix is (after a change from decimals to fractions):

$$\begin{pmatrix} 1 & 0 & \frac{1}{3} \\ 0 & 1 & \frac{2}{3} \\ 0 & 0 & 0 \end{pmatrix}$$

The steady state vector of the chain is

$$\mathbf{v} = (\tfrac{1}{3} \quad \tfrac{2}{3})$$

Therefore $P(H) = \frac{1}{3}$ and $P(T) = \frac{2}{3}$ on toss number 100.

SOLUTION 2   Let $\mathbf{p}^{(n)}$ be the nth-step probability vector for tossing the coin with a memory. As n increases, $\mathbf{p}^{(n)}$ gets closer and closer to the steady state vector $\mathbf{v}$. We sometimes say that $\mathbf{p}^{(n)}$ *approaches* $\mathbf{v}$, and we write

$$\mathbf{p}^{(n)} \to \mathbf{v}$$

According to the washing-out principle, the approach of $\mathbf{p}^{(n)}$ to $\mathbf{v}$ has nothing to do with the choice of $\mathbf{p}^{(0)}$. Since

$$\mathbf{p}^{(n)} = \mathbf{p}^{(0)}\mathbf{P}^n$$

this means that $\mathbf{p}^{(n)}$ is determined by $\mathbf{P}^n$. By using a hand calculator, we find that

$$\mathbf{P}^{16} = \begin{pmatrix} \frac{1}{3} & \frac{2}{3} \\ \frac{1}{3} & \frac{2}{3} \end{pmatrix}$$

to six-figure accuracy. All higher powers of $\mathbf{P}$ have the same value. (This is easy to check.) We can calculate $\mathbf{p}^{(100)}$ by using $\mathbf{p}^{(0)} = \mathbf{S}_{\mathrm{H}}^{(0)} = (1 \quad 0)$. The result is

$$\mathbf{p}^{(100)} = \mathbf{S}_{\mathrm{H}}^{(0)}\mathbf{P}^{100} = (1 \quad 0) \begin{pmatrix} \frac{1}{3} & \frac{2}{3} \\ \frac{1}{3} & \frac{2}{3} \end{pmatrix} = (\tfrac{1}{3} \quad \tfrac{2}{3})$$

just as before.

NOTE: STEADY STATE MATRIX   Solution 2 to Problem 2 illustrates the following fact about the transition matrix $\mathbf{P}$ of any regular Markov chain:

As n increases, $\mathbf{P}^n$ approaches a *steady state matrix*. We will use the notation $\mathbf{M}$ for the steady state matrix, and we will write:

$$\mathbf{P}^n \to \mathbf{M}$$

Each row of $\mathbf{M}$ is equal to the same probability vector $\mathbf{v}$, and $\mathbf{v}$ is the steady state vector of the Markov chain.

In the case of the coin with a memory, we have just seen that the steady state matrix is

$$\mathbf{M} = \begin{pmatrix} \frac{1}{3} & \frac{2}{3} \\ \frac{1}{3} & \frac{2}{3} \end{pmatrix}$$

For another illustration, let's refer to Example 1. We had

$$\mathbf{P} = \begin{pmatrix} .70 & .30 \\ .53 & .47 \end{pmatrix}$$

and we find (using a hand calculator with a simple memory) that:

$$\mathbf{P}^2 = \begin{pmatrix} .649 & .351 \\ .6201 & .3799 \end{pmatrix}$$

$$\mathbf{P}^4 = \begin{pmatrix} .6388561 & .3611439 \\ .6380208 & .3619792 \end{pmatrix}$$

$$\mathbf{P}^8 = \begin{pmatrix} .6385544 & .3614456 \\ .6385536 & .3614464 \end{pmatrix}$$

Since the first and second rows of $\mathbf{P}^8$ agree to six figures, we can conclude that the steady state matrix of the chain is

$$\mathbf{M} = \begin{pmatrix} .638554 & .361446 \\ .638554 & .361446 \end{pmatrix}$$

to six figures. Each row is in six-figure agreement with the steady state vector **v,** as calculated on pp. 421–422.

PROBLEM 3   Calculate, if possible, the steady state matrix of the Markov chain whose transition matrix is

$$\mathbf{I} = \begin{pmatrix} 1 & 0 & 0 \\ 0 & 1 & 0 \\ 0 & 0 & 1 \end{pmatrix}$$

and the Markov chain whose transition matrix is

$$\mathbf{A} = \begin{pmatrix} 0 & 1 \\ 1 & 0 \end{pmatrix}$$

SOLUTION   **I** is the third-order identity matrix. Therefore

$$\mathbf{I}^n = \mathbf{I}$$

for every positive integer n. In other words, $\mathbf{I}^n$ does not approach a matrix whose rows are all equal. From the definition, this says that $\mathbf{I}^n$ does not approach a steady state matrix.

As for the matrix **A,** every odd power of **A** is equal:

$$\begin{pmatrix} 0 & 1 \\ 1 & 0 \end{pmatrix} = \mathbf{A} = \mathbf{A}^3 = \mathbf{A}^5 = \cdots$$

and every even power of **A** is equal:

$$\begin{pmatrix} 1 & 0 \\ 0 & 1 \end{pmatrix} = \mathbf{A}^2 = \mathbf{A}^4 = \mathbf{A}^6 = \cdots$$

Therefore $\mathbf{A}^n$ does not approach a steady state matrix.

PROBLEM 4   Example 2 of Section 9.1 discussed the hairspray market. Suppose that H (Holdfast), W (Wonder Web), and L (Lively Look) continue as the market leaders and that the transition matrix

$$\mathbf{P} = \begin{matrix} & \begin{matrix} H & \quad W & \quad L \end{matrix} \\ \begin{matrix} H \\ W \\ L \end{matrix} & \begin{pmatrix} .40 & .25 & .35 \\ .35 & .35 & .30 \\ .30 & .25 & .45 \end{pmatrix} \end{matrix}$$

continues to describe month-to-month changes in leadership for 12 months. A mutual fund manager gets the following stock-buying advice from one of the fund's securities analysts: "Lively Look is a winner because it creates more brand loyalty than Holdfast or Wonder Web. Everyone believes that Lively Look will have 40% of the market in 6 months, and that's why the stock is priced so high right now. But my analysis projects Lively Look for a 50% share in 12 months, and more than that later if the hairspray market stays the same. That stock's going up and up. The more we buy the more money we'll make." Is this view sensible?

QUESTIONS TO BE ANSWERED   Let's suppose that you, a beginner in the securities business, are given the job of checking all this out. The mutual fund manager asks you to look at three questions about Lively Look's market share:

a.   Will it have a 40% share in 6 months?
b.   Will it have a 50% share in 12 months?
c.   If the transition matrix does not change, will Lively Look have more than a 50% share at some time after 12 months?

It is understood that you are going to do a Markov chain analysis. It is also understood that *market share* means the same thing as *probability of being the market leader.*

Do you have any questions? Well, yes. In answering question a, what are you supposed to assume about Lively Look's market share as of right now? The fund manager suggests $\mathbf{p}^{(0)} = (.35 \quad .30 \quad .35)$ as a realistic initial probability vector.

SOLUTION   Using a hand-held calculator, you calculate:

$$\mathbf{p}^{(1)} = \mathbf{p}^{(0)}\mathbf{P} = (.35 \quad .30 \quad .35) \begin{pmatrix} .40 & .25 & .35 \\ .35 & .35 & .30 \\ .30 & .25 & .45 \end{pmatrix} = (.35 \quad .28 \quad .37)$$

Then you calculate five more steps:

$$\mathbf{p}^{(2)} = \mathbf{p}^{(1)}\mathbf{P} = (.349 \quad .278 \quad .373)$$

$$\mathbf{p}^{(3)} = \mathbf{p}^{(2)}\mathbf{P} = (.3488 \quad .2778 \quad .3734)$$

$$\mathbf{p}^{(4)} = \mathbf{p}^{(3)}\mathbf{P} = (.34877 \quad .27778 \quad .37345)$$

$$\mathbf{p}^{(5)} = \mathbf{p}^{(4)}\mathbf{P} = (.348766 \quad .277778 \quad .373456)$$

$$\mathbf{p}^{(6)} = \mathbf{p}^{(5)}\mathbf{P} = (.3487655 \quad .2777778 \quad .3734567)$$

The conclusion is that Lively Look will have less than a 40% share in 6 months. To be precise, it will have a 37.34567% share. So much for question a.

You suspect that you have really answered questions b and c as well. The probability vectors $\mathbf{p}^{(4)}$, $\mathbf{p}^{(5)}$, and $\mathbf{p}^{(6)}$ are in four-figure agreement. You therefore believe that the chain has a steady state vector $\mathbf{v}$ and that it is given by

$$\mathbf{v} = (.3488 \quad .2778 \quad .3735)$$

to four figures. Assuming that the four-figure probabilities are correct, you have got to say that Lively Look's market share will stay right at 37.35% just so long as the transition matrix does not change. And so much for questions b and c. The answers are *no* and *never*.

Naturally, you check your work. First you note that the Markov chain is regular. (There are no zero entries in the transition matrix **P**.) The equation $\mathbf{vP} = \mathbf{v}$ for calculating the steady state vector $\mathbf{v} = (v_1 \quad v_2 \quad v_3)$ leads to three equations:

$$-.6v_1 + .35v_2 + .30v_3 = 0$$

$$.25v_1 - .65v_2 + .25v_3 = 0$$

$$.35v_1 + .30v_2 - .55v_3 = 0$$

Since $\mathbf{v}$ is a probability vector, you also have the condition

$$v_1 + v_2 + v_3 = 1$$

The augmented matrix for your system of four equations in the three variables v_1, v_2, and v_3 is:

$$\begin{pmatrix} -.6 & .35 & .30 & 0 \\ .25 & -.65 & .25 & 0 \\ .35 & .30 & -.55 & 0 \\ 1 & 1 & 1 & 1 \end{pmatrix}$$

Legal row operations lead to the reduced echelon form

$$\begin{pmatrix} 1 & 0 & 0 & .348765 \\ 0 & 1 & 0 & .277778 \\ 0 & 0 & 1 & .373457 \\ 0 & 0 & 0 & 0 \end{pmatrix}$$

This means that

$$\mathbf{v} = (.348765 \quad .277778 \quad .373457)$$

It checks.

If you want to show the fund manager that you are super-careful, you finish things off by calculating the steady state matrix **M.** Using your hand-held calculator again, you square **P** to find **P²**, then square **P²** to find **P⁴**, and square **P⁴** to find

$$\mathbf{P}^8 = \begin{pmatrix} .3487652 & .2777777 & .3734571 \\ .3487652 & .2777777 & .3734571 \\ .3487652 & .2777776 & .3734572 \end{pmatrix}$$

If you round these numbers off to six figures, you have a matrix with three equal rows. The matrix is the steady state matrix **M** of the chain:

$$\mathbf{M} = \begin{pmatrix} .348765 & .277778 & .373457 \\ .348765 & .277778 & .373457 \\ .348765 & .277778 & .373457 \end{pmatrix}$$

Each of the three rows is equal to the steady state vector **v.** The steady state has been reached in eight steps—or eight months.

You have really nailed it down. As long as the transition matrix **P** gives the month-to-month facts, Lively Look cannot have more than a 37.35% market share.

NOTE: If you wanted to check your answer to question a in a slightly different way, you might have started with (1 0 0) or (0 0 1) as initial probability vector. The washing-out principle shows that this would have made no difference at all in your results.

EXERCISES *for Section 9.2*

Which of the following matrices is the transition matrix of a regular Markov chain?

1. $\begin{pmatrix} .4 & .6 \\ .5 & .5 \end{pmatrix}$ 2. $\begin{pmatrix} .4 & .5 \\ .6 & .5 \end{pmatrix}$ 3. $\begin{pmatrix} 0 & 1 \\ .4 & .6 \end{pmatrix}$

4. $\begin{pmatrix} .5 & .5 \\ 0 & 1 \end{pmatrix}$ 5. $\begin{pmatrix} 1 & 0 \\ .5 & .5 \end{pmatrix}$ 6. $\begin{pmatrix} .5 & .5 \\ 1 & 0 \end{pmatrix}$

7. $\begin{pmatrix} 0 & 1 \\ .3 & .7 \end{pmatrix}$ **8.** $\begin{pmatrix} .3 & .7 \\ 0 & 1 \end{pmatrix}$ **9.** $\begin{pmatrix} 1 & 0 \\ .3 & .7 \end{pmatrix}$

10. $\begin{pmatrix} .4 & .4 & .3 \\ .3 & .3 & .4 \\ .4 & .4 & .2 \end{pmatrix}$ **11.** $\begin{pmatrix} .4 & .6 & 0 \\ .3 & .3 & .4 \\ .4 & .4 & .2 \end{pmatrix}$ **12.** $\begin{pmatrix} 0 & 1 & 0 \\ 0 & 0 & 1 \\ .4 & .6 & 0 \end{pmatrix}$

13. $\begin{pmatrix} .4 & .6 & 0 \\ .3 & 0 & .7 \\ 0 & 1 & 0 \end{pmatrix}$

In Exercises 14–19 the given 2×2 matrix is the transition matrix of a regular Markov chain. For each of them:

a. Calculate the successive probability vectors $\mathbf{p}^{(1)}$, $\mathbf{p}^{(2)}$, $\mathbf{p}^{(3)}$, $\mathbf{p}^{(4)}$, $\mathbf{p}^{(5)}$, $\mathbf{p}^{(6)}$ corresponding to the initial probability vector $\mathbf{p}^{(0)} = (1 \quad 0)$.
b. Estimate the steady state vector of the chain.

14. $\begin{pmatrix} .4 & .6 \\ .6 & .4 \end{pmatrix}$ **15.** $\begin{pmatrix} .3 & .7 \\ .7 & .3 \end{pmatrix}$ **16.** $\begin{pmatrix} .9 & .1 \\ .2 & .8 \end{pmatrix}$

17. $\begin{pmatrix} .4 & .6 \\ 1 & 0 \end{pmatrix}$ **18.** $\begin{pmatrix} .9 & .1 \\ 1 & 0 \end{pmatrix}$ **19.** $\begin{pmatrix} 0 & 1 \\ .9 & .1 \end{pmatrix}$

In Exercises 20–25 the given 3×3 matrix is the transition matrix of a regular Markov chain. Starting with

$$\mathbf{p}^{(0)} = (0 \quad 1 \quad 0)$$

in each case:

a. Calculate $\mathbf{p}^{(1)}$, $\mathbf{p}^{(2)}$, $\mathbf{p}^{(3)}$, $\mathbf{p}^{(4)}$.
b. Estimate the steady state vector of the chain.

20. $\begin{pmatrix} .3 & .2 & .5 \\ .2 & .7 & .1 \\ .2 & .2 & .6 \end{pmatrix}$ **21.** $\begin{pmatrix} \frac{1}{2} & \frac{1}{4} & \frac{1}{4} \\ \frac{1}{3} & \frac{1}{3} & \frac{1}{3} \\ \frac{1}{5} & \frac{2}{5} & \frac{2}{5} \end{pmatrix}$

22. $\begin{pmatrix} 0 & 0 & 1 \\ .3 & .7 & 0 \\ 0 & .5 & .5 \end{pmatrix}$ **23.** $\begin{pmatrix} 0 & .5 & .5 \\ .3 & .4 & .3 \\ .2 & .3 & .5 \end{pmatrix}$

24. $\begin{pmatrix} 0 & 1 & 0 \\ 0 & 0 & 1 \\ .9 & .1 & 0 \end{pmatrix}$ **25.** $\begin{pmatrix} .2 & .8 & 0 \\ .8 & 0 & .2 \\ 0 & .1 & 0 \end{pmatrix}$

Use the defining equation $\mathbf{vP} = \mathbf{v}$, together with the fact that $\mathbf{v}$ is a probability vector, to find the steady state vector $\mathbf{v}$ corresponding to the transition matrix $\mathbf{P}$ given in:

26.	Exercise 14	**27.**	Exercise 15
28.	Exercise 16	**29.**	Exercise 17
30.	Exercise 18	**31.**	Exercise 19
32.	Exercise 20	**33.**	Exercise 21
34.	Exercise 22	**35.**	Exercise 23
36.	Exercise 24	**37.**	Exercise 25

Find the steady state matrix corresponding to the transition matrix in:

38. Exercise 14 (and compare with your result in Exercise 26)

39. Exercise 15 (and compare with your result in Exercise 27)

40. Exercise 16 (and compare with your result in Exercise 28)

41. Exercise 17 (and compare with your result in Exercise 29)

42. Exercise 18 (and compare with your result in Exercise 30)

43. Exercise 19 (and compare with your result in Exercise 31)

44. Exercise 20 (and compare with your result in Exercise 32)

45. Exercise 21 (and compare with your result in Exercise 33)

46. Exercise 22 (and compare with your result in Exercise 34)

47. Exercise 23 (and compare with your result in Exercise 35)

48. Exercise 24 (and compare with your result in Exercise 36)

49. Exercise 25 (and compare with your result in Exercise 37)

Searchlight is a weekly paper that is sold in supermarkets throughout the U.S. Sixty percent of the people who buy the paper one week will also buy it the next week. Among those who see *Searchlight* in their local supermarket and who do not buy it one week, 5% will buy it the next week.

Week-to-week probabilities of buying and not buying *Searchlight* can be studied as a two-state Markov chain.

50. What are the states? What is the transition matrix of the chain?

51. For every 100,000 people who see *Searchlight* one year from this week, how many people will buy a copy?

In one of her courses, a math professor collects and grades homework every week. Students in that course always get grades of A or B in their homework. The professor notices the following pattern:

The student who has an A one week has a probability of .65 of having a B the next week.

The student who has a B one week has a probability of .55 of having an A the next week.

52. Marina von Neumann had an A in her homework this week. What is the probability that she will have an A 3 weeks from now? 5 weeks from now? 8 weeks from now?

53. Tom Mann had a B in his homework this week. What is the probability that he will have an A 3 weeks from now? 5 weeks from now? 8 weeks from now?

54. The semester is 14 weeks long. What is the probability that a student will have an A on the last homework of the semester?

The latest news from the hairspray market is that two new products are now the top sellers: Condition Spray (heavy in amino acids and vitamin E) and Natureswept (for the windswept natural look, but with every hair in place all day long). Month-to-month competition follows a pattern:

If Condition Spray is the sales leader one month, then the probability that Natureswept will replace it as the leader next month is .45.

If Natureswept is the sales leader one month, then the probability that Condition Spray will take over sales leadership the next month is .30.

In answering the next three questions, assume that these sales patterns continue for the next two years.

55. If Condition Spray is the leader this month, what is the probability that it will be the leader 2 months from now? 4 months from now? 6 months from now?

56. If Natureswept is the leader this month, what is the probability that it will be the leader 2, 4, and 6 months from now?

57. What are the probabilities for hairspray sales leadership (Condition Spray or Natureswept) 24 months from now?

A new slogan ("You vote with your *head* for Condition Spray"), together with a suggestion that Natureswept is harmful to the health, has changed buying habits in the hairspray market. Month-to-month probabilities are now as follows:

If Condition Spray is the sales leader one month, the probability that Natureswept will take over the leadership next month is .15.

If Natureswept is the sales leader one month, the probability that it will be the leader again next month is .35.

If these conditions prevail for 18 months, then:

58. If Condition Spray leads this month, what are the probabilities that it will be the leader 2, 4, and 6 months from now?

59. If Natureswept is this month's leader, what are the probabilities that it will again be the leader 2, 4, and 6 months from now?

60. What are the probabilities for hairspray sales leadership 18 months from now?

According to some estimates, 10% of all the adults in the U.S. are interested in losing weight. There are three popular methods:

B: Behavioral modification (calorie-counting, exercise, conditioning against overeating by hypnotism and other means)

S: Single-product diets (for example, the liquid protein diet, in which a patient drinks a protein distilled from cowhide and eats nothing at all)

M: Medical approaches (hormone treatment, surgery of various types)

Most people find it very difficult to lose weight. If they succeed, they then find it even more difficult to maintain the weight loss. The typical weight-loser spends a lifetime going from one weight-loss method to another. A 20-year study in San Diego County led to the following data:

If a weight-loser follows method B (behavioral modification) one year, then the probabilities that this person will follow methods B, S, M the next year are .5, .4, .1 in that order.

If a weight-loser follows method S (single-product diet) one year, then that person's probabilities of following methods B, S, M the next year are .4, .2, .4 in that order.

If a weight-loser follows method M (medical approaches) one year, then the probabilities that this person will follow methods B, S, M the next year are .6, .1, .3 in that order.

61. List these transition probabilities in a matrix. Suppose that 20% of San Diego County's weight-losers follow method B this year, 50% follow method S, and 30% follow method M. Use your transition matrix to calculate the probabilities that weight-losers in San Diego County will follow methods B, S, M next year, 2 years from now, and 3 years from now.

62. If the transition probabilities remain the same for the next 20 years, what are the probabilities that weight-losers in San Diego County will be following methods B, S, M 20 years from now?

Great Lakes Tennis Camp offers excellent coaching and pleasant condominium housing for people who sincerely want to improve their tennis. The only problem is the camp's Great Lakes location. It seems to be rainy or foggy all the time—and no one likes to play tennis outdoors in the rain or fog. To be precise:

There are never 2 clear days in a row.

If a day is clear, the probability of rain the next day is .40 and the probability of fog is .60.

If a day is rainy, the probability that the next day will be clear is .4, the probability that it will be rainy is .4, and the probability that it will be foggy is .2.

If a day is foggy, the probability that the next day will be clear is .3, the probability that it will be rainy is .3, and the probability that it will be foggy is .4.

63. Write the transition matrix of a three-state Markov chain that describes weather change probabilities at Great Lakes Tennis Camp.

64. One rainy Sunday, Jim and Ginger Heffernan arrived at Great Lakes Tennis Camp for a tennis vacation. What is the probability that the Heffernans will have a clear day for tennis on Monday? on Tuesday? on Wednesday?

65. Suppose that the weather patterns continue for the next year. What is the probability that the weather at Great Lakes Tennis Camp, one year from today, will be clear? rainy? foggy? (*NOTE:* If you have a calculator, you will find it convenient to answer these questions by finding the steady state matrix of the Markov chain. Without a calculator, it is easier to solve for the steady state vector of the chain.)

chapter ten

FUNCTIONS AND FUNCTIONAL MODELS

THE relationship between two variable quantities may be recorded in a data table, a graph, or an algebraic equation. If certain conditions are satisfied, the relationship is called a *functional relationship* or, more briefly, a *function*. Sections 10.1 and 10.2 give definitions, notations, and examples for the function concept. Later sections study various useful functions and construct mathematical models based on these functions. Example 2 of Section 10.4 is a typical application: it shows how a company used a functional model to determine the pricing policy that would maximize company profits.

10.1 GRAPHS, RELATIONS, AND FUNCTIONS

Graphs like Figures 10.1 and 10.2 illustrate a relationship between the variables x and y. Such graphs are often used to describe or analyze real-

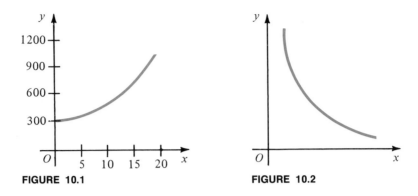

FIGURE 10.1 FIGURE 10.2

world situations. In fact, Figure 10.1 describes year-to-year changes in the GNP (Gross National Product) of the U.S. from 1951 to 1971. The variable x represents the year (0 represents 1951, 1 represents 1952, etc.) and the variable y represents GNP in billions of dollars.

Figure 10.2 shows the theoretical relationship between the unemployment rate (the variable x) and the inflation rate (the variable y). The meaning of Figure 10.2 is that the inflation rate goes up as the unemployment rate goes down. Remember, this is theoretical. The facts do not seem to be so simple. Figure 10.3 shows some observed data for a recent 10-year period.

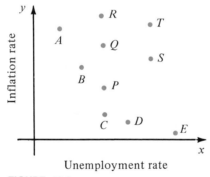

FIGURE 10.3

The points marked A, B, C, D, and E represent years in which the relationship between unemployment and inflation followed the theory illustrated by Figure 10.2. But the points P, Q, and R refer to years in which the unemployment rate was the same as in year A, while the inflation rate was different each time. Similarly, the years represented by the points S and T contradict the theory.

We now want to give a mathematical framework for studying graphs and the relationships they describe.

The graph in Figure 10.3 consists of 10 points. Each of these points can be represented by an *ordered pair*. (An ordered pair gives the *coordinates* of the corresponding point. In an *xy*-plane, the *first element* of an ordered pair of coordinates represents the *x*-coordinate of the point and the *second element* represents the *y*-coordinate. See p. 49.) Table 10.1 lists the 10 ordered pairs graphed in Figure 10.3.

TABLE 10.1

	A	B	C	D	E	P	Q	R	S	T
x	3.5	4.0	5.5	7.0	8.0	5.5	5.5	5.5	7.5	7.5
y	8.0	6.5	5.0	4.0	3.0	6.0	7.5	9.0	7.0	8.0

The relationship between *x* (unemployment rate) and *y* (inflation rate) is fully described by the ordered pairs in the table. This is an example of a *relation*.

DEFINITION Relation

A *relation* is a collection of ordered pairs.

There may be finitely or infinitely many ordered pairs in a relation. This means that any graph in the *xy*-plane defines a relation between the variables *x* and *y*.

To avoid the clumsiness of talking about the *x* values (or first-element values) and the *y*-values (or second-element values) in a relation, we introduce the terms *domain* and *range* for these collections of values.

DEFINITION Domain and Range of a Relation

Let the collection of ordered pairs making up a relation be given. Then the collection of first elements of these ordered pairs is called the *domain* of the relation and the collection of second elements is called the *range* of the relation.

As an example: The domain of the relation described by Table 10.1 is made up of the collection of first elements 3.5, 4.0, 5.5, 7.0, 7.5, 8.0. The range of the relation is the collection of second elements 8.0, 6.5, 5.0, 6.0, 7.5, 9.0, 4.0, 7.0, 8.0, 3.0. Figure 10.4 illustrates:

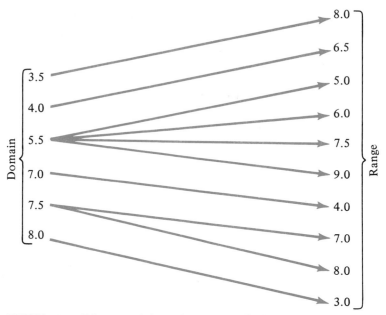

FIGURE 10.4 Diagram of the Relation Described in Figure 10.3 and Table 10.1

Figure 10.4 shows that one element in the domain of a relation can correspond to two or more elements in the range. It can also happen that each domain element corresponds to exactly one range element. For example, the relation

$$\{(1, 0.5), (2, 1.5), (3, 2.5), (4, 1.5), (5, 0.5)\}$$

has domain $\{1, 2, 3, 4, 5\}$ and range $\{0.5, 1.5, 2.5\}$. There are more domain elements than range elements, which means that different domain elements can correspond to the same range element. (See Figure 10.5.) But the key fact

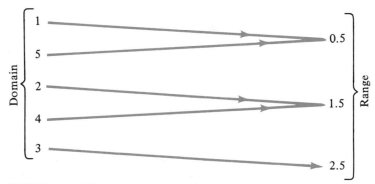

FIGURE 10.5 Diagram of the Relation
$$\{(1, 0.5), (2, 1.5), (3, 2.5), (4, 1.5), (5, 0.5)\}$$

is that each domain element corresponds to exactly one range element. A relation satisfying this condition is called a *function*.

DEFINITION Function

A relation is called a *function* if each element in the domain of the function corresponds to one and only one element in the range.

In other words: A function is a collection of ordered pairs, no two of which have the same first element.

EXAMPLE 1: Barnes & Noble (Fifth Avenue at Eighteenth, in New York City) has 2,545,000 books in stock. Each of these books has a retail price. The store's computerized inventory lists 2,545,000 (book, retail price) ordered pairs. This collection of ordered pairs defines a function. Domain: books. Range: retail prices. Each book has one and only one retail price.

EXAMPLE 2: Table 10.2 lists prices for domestic and imported crude oil from January 1974 to July 1975. (This was after OPEC's quadrupling of oil prices.) "Old" domestic oil is produced from existing wells. "New" domestic oil is produced from existing wells at an enhanced rate, or from newly drilled wells in an old or new field.

TABLE 10.2

Date	Price (*Dollars per Barrel*)		
	Old Domestic	*New Domestic*	*Imported*
Jan. 1974	5.25	9.82	9.59
Apr. 1974	5.25	9.88	12.72
July 1974	5.25	9.95	12.75
Oct. 1974	5.25	10.74	12.44
Jan. 1975	5.25	11.28	12.77
Apr. 1975	5.25	11.64	13.26
July 1975	5.25	12.30	14.03

Source: Federal Energy Administration.

Table 10.2 defines three functions: the (date, "old" domestic price) function; the (date, "new" domestic price) function; and the (date, imported price) function. Each of the three is specified by a list of seven ordered pairs. Since the price of "old" domestic crude was controlled, it remained at $5.25 a barrel during 1974 and 1975. The (date, "old" domestic price) function is an example of a *constant* function.

EXAMPLE 3: The graph in Figure 10.6 defines a function. Reason: No two points on the graph have the same *x*-coordinate.

The graph in Figure 10.7 does not define a function, but rather a relation. Reason: There are points on the graph with the same *x*-coordinate but different *y*-coordinates.

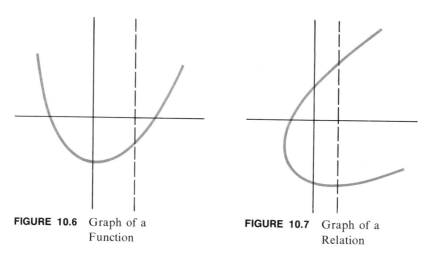

FIGURE 10.6   Graph of a
                 Function

FIGURE 10.7   Graph of a
                 Relation

The dashed vertical lines in Figures 10.6 and 10.7 plainly illustrate the difference between the two graphs. We formalize the difference by stating the *vertical line rule*.

VERTICAL LINE RULE

If no vertical line intersects a graph in more than one point, then the graph defines a *function*. Otherwise the graph defines a relation that is *not a function*.

Notice that the vertical line rule is merely a geometric way of saying that no two of the ordered pairs defining a function can have the same first element.

By applying the vertical line rule, we see that the graphs in Figures 10.1 and 10.2 represent functions. In each of these two cases the graph shows that one and only one *y*-value corresponds to each *x*-value.

Which of the following relations are functions?

1. $(-1, -5), (-6, 0), (-1, -1), (4, 3)$

2. $(-1, 4), (4, 3), (-1, 0), (6, 5)$

3. $(2, 2), (3, 4), (4, 6), (5, 4), (4, 2)$

4. $(-2, 2), (0, 0), (2, -2), (4, 0), (6, 2)$

5. $(6, -6), (4, -4), (2, -2), (4, 0), (6, 2)$

6. $(-2, 2), (-1, 1), (0, 0), (2, 0), (3, 1), (4, 2)$

7. $(4, -4), (3, -3), (2, -2), (2, 0), (3, 1), (4, 2)$

List the domain and range elements for each of the following relations. Which of them are functions?

8. $(-1, 0), (0, 1), (3, 2), (0, -1), (3, -2)$

9. $(-\frac{3}{2}, 0), (-1, 1), (\frac{1}{2}, 2), (3, 3) (-1, -1), (\frac{1}{2}, -2)$

10. $(0, 1), (1, 2), (-1, 2), (2, 5), (-2, 5)$

11. $(2, -0.2), (1, -0.9), (3, 1.7), (0, -1), (-1, -1.1)$

12. $(-0.9, 1), (-1, 0) (0.6, 2), (-0.9, -1), (0.6, -2)$

13. $(0.5, 0.75), (-0.5, 0.75), (0, 1), (1, 0), (0.5, -0.75), (-0.5, -0.75)$

---

14. Average wind speeds (measured in miles per hour) in 8 U.S. cities are:

Louisville	8.3
Denver	9.1
Oklahoma City	13.1
Minneapolis	10.7
Seattle	9.5
Chicago	10.3
Boston	13.1
Houston	10.8

Does the collection of (city, wind speed) pairs define a function? Does the collection of (wind speed, city) pairs define a function? Illustrate your answer with diagrams like those in Figures 10.4 and 10.5.

15. In a recent year, the U.S. Bureau of Labor Statistics gave the following figures for the percentage of women in the work force in 8 key industrial sectors:

Industry	Percent of Women Employees
Durable Goods Manufacturing	3
Nondurable Goods Manufacturing	5
Transportation and Public Vehicles	1
Wholesale Trade	1
Retail Trade	7
Finance, Insurance, and Real Estate	3
Services	9
Government	8

Is the relation defined by the 8 (industry, percent of women employees) pairs a function? Do the 8 (percent of women employees, industry) pairs define a function? As part of your answers to these questions, draw diagrams of the type shown in Figures 10.4 and 10.5.

A jeweler has a stock of 746 watches. Of these, 57 have conventional movements and the remaining 689 watches are battery-powered.

16. There is a ticket on each watch giving its retail price. Does the collection of (watch, price) pairs define a function? Does the collection of (price, watch) pairs define a function?

17. Conventional watches are hard to sell, and the jeweler decides that he is willing to discount them. He therefore marks a second and lower price on the ticket for each conventional watch. (If a customer appears price-conscious, a clerk may offer one of these watches at the lower price.) Does the collection of (watch, price) pairs for conventional watches now define a function? Does the collection of (price, watch) pairs for these watches define a function?

Farm Real Estate Developments, a publication of the United States Department of Agriculture, gives yearly figures for the average value of farm real estate in each of the states except Alaska and Hawaii. The values given are not in dollars but in index numbers. In a recent year, the index number for land and buildings per acre in the entire U.S. was 100.

18. Index numbers for the 8 states in the East South Central and West South Central regions were:

Ky.	Tenn.	Ala.	Miss.	Ark.	La.	Okla.	Tex.
103	111	112	112	111	111	105	104

Does the collection of (state, index number) pairs define a function? Does the collection of (index number, state) pairs define a function?

19. Index numbers for the 8 states in the South Atlantic region were:

Del.	Md.	Va.	W.Va.	N.C.	S.C.	Ga.	Fla.
105	112	110	109	102	118	133	105

Is the relation defined by the 8 (index number, state) pairs a function? Is the relation defined by the 8 (state, index number) pairs a function?

Which of the following graphs represent functions and which do not? In each case, explain your answer by reference to the domain and range of the function (or relation) represented by the graph.

20.

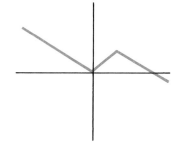

21.

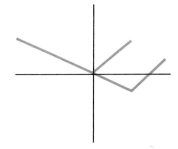

22.

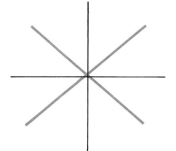

23.

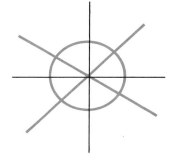

24.

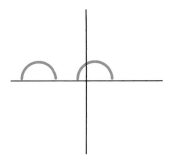

25.

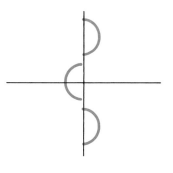

26.

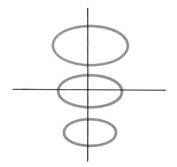

27.

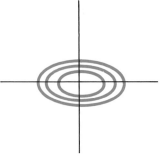

28.

29.

10.2 FUNCTIONAL NOTATION

If the domain and range elements of a function are real numbers, then the function can always be represented by a graph and can sometimes be represented by an equation.

EXAMPLE 1: THE SQUARING FUNCTION

If x is any real number, then the *squaring function is the collection of ordered pairs* (x, x^2). We take the *domain* of the squaring function to be *all real numbers*. Corresponding to this choice, the *range* will consist of *all nonnegative real numbers*.

NOTE: If we choose a different domain, we have a different function. For example: We might have the collection of ordered pairs (x, x^2) with domain of definition $-1 \leq x \leq 3$ and range of values $0 \leq x^2 \leq 9$.

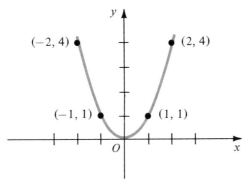

FIGURE 10.8 Graph of the Squaring Function. (Domain: all real numbers; range: all nonnegative real numbers.)

The graph in Figure 10.8 represents domain elements of the squaring function by the variable x, and range elements by the variable y. Since the range element corresponding to x is x^2, we have

$$y = x^2$$

as the equation representing the squaring function. The domain is made up of all real numbers. If we want to define the squaring function for the domain $-1 \leq x \leq 3$, we write:

$$y = x^2 \qquad (-1 \leq x \leq 3)$$

The graph of this function is shown in Figure 10.9.

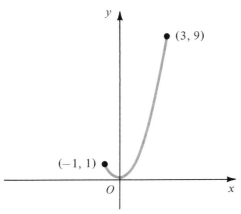

FIGURE 10.9 The Squaring Function with Domain $-1 \leq x \leq 3$ and Range $0 \leq x \leq 9$

EXAMPLE 2: THE LINEAR FUNCTION

If A and B are not both zero, then the linear equation in two variables

$$Ax + By + C = 0$$

is a *linear relation*. Suppose that we take the domain (the values of the variable x) to be all real numbers. Then the *range* (values of y) also consists of all real numbers. The graph of $Ax + By + C = 0$ is a *line*. We know from Chapter 2 that there are three cases (see pp. 63–64). If $A = 0$, the line is horizontal. If $B = 0$, the line is vertical. If $A \neq 0$ and $B \neq 0$, the line is neither horizontal nor vertical. Figures 10.10, 10.11, and 10.12 sketch the

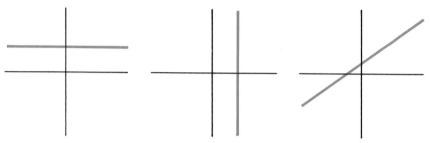

FIGURE 10.10 Graph of $Ax + By + C = 0$ ($A = 0$)

FIGURE 10.11 Graph of $Ax + By + C = 0$ ($B = 0$)

FIGURE 10.12 Graph of $Ax + By + C = 0$ ($A \neq 0, B \neq 0$)

three cases. The vertical line in Figure 10.11 is the graph of a relation that is not a function. (Reason: Every ordered pair in the graph has the same first element.) The other two graphs define functions. As we know from Chapter 2, any line that is not vertical has an equation

$$y = mx + b$$

where m is the *slope* of the line. The slope can be zero (for a horizontal line), positive (as in Figure 10.12), or negative. We do not define the slope of a vertical line. Since all lines except vertical lines represent functions, we will say that $y = mx + b$ is the equation of the *linear function*.

Before going on to further examples of functions, we want to introduce some useful notation.

Equations like $y = x^2$ and $y = mx + b$ tell us how to calculate the value of y corresponding to a given x. Sometimes we call the domain variable x the *independent variable* and the range variable y the *dependent variable*. This is simply another way of saying that y *depends on x,* or that y is a *function of x.*

The functional notation

$$y = f(x)$$

(read "y equals f of x") is a brief way of saying that y is a function of x. As examples of the $f(x)$ notation, we have the squaring function

$$f(x) = x^2 \qquad \text{(domain: all real } x)$$

the linear function

$$f(x) = mx + b \qquad \text{(domain: all real } x)$$

and the square root function

$$f(x) = +\sqrt{x} \qquad \text{(domain: all nonnegative real } x)$$

In these and other cases, the letter f (all by itself) is used to refer to the function. The function f being referred to is defined by the collection of ordered pairs $(x, f(x))$, where the domain of x has been specified. In other words:

---

f denotes the function: the correspondence between domain elements and range elements

$f(x)$ denotes the range element corresponding to the domain element x

---

NOTE: In our examples we have used the same letter f to describe three different functions. Similarly, the variable x is used to describe variables with different domains of definition. Not all variables are labeled x, and not all functions are labeled f. For example, linear functions are often symbolized by L. In using L we might be talking about the general linear function defined by $L(x) = mx + b$ or a particular linear function defined, for example, by $L(x) = 7x - 4$.

Functional notation is used because its meaning is very clear. If we define a function f by saying that the range element corresponding to any real x is

$$f(x) = x^2 + 2x + 3$$

then the range element corresponding to the choice $x = 3$ is written $f(3)$, where

$$f(3) = (3)^2 + 2(3) + 3 = 18$$

A function may be defined by different expressions in different parts of its domain. When such a function is graphed, the graph consists of several unconnected pieces.

EXAMPLE 3: THE ABSOLUTE VALUE FUNCTION

We define a function f by

$$f(x) = \begin{cases} x, & x \geq 0 \\ -x, & x < 0 \end{cases}$$

The domain of the function $[x, f(x)]$ consists of all real numbers x, but the range is restricted to the nonnegative real numbers. If we graph the equation $y = f(x)$ for $x \geq 0$, we have a semi-infinite line (or *ray*) bisecting the angle between the positive x-axis and the positive y-axis. Similarly, the graph for $x < 0$ is a ray bisecting the angle between the negative x-axis and the positive y-axis. The graphs are shown on one set of axes in Figure 10.13.

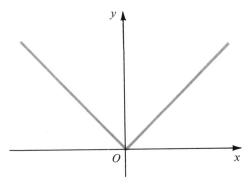

FIGURE 10.13   The Absolute Value Function. (Domain: all real numbers; range: all nonnegative real numbers.)

Since we define the *absolute value* of x by

$$|x| = \begin{cases} x, & x \geq 0 \\ -x, & x < 0 \end{cases}$$

the function f that we have graphed is the *absolute value function* defined by $f(x) = |x|$.

EXAMPLE 4: A STEP FUNCTION

The function f defined by

$$y = f(x) = \begin{cases} -1, & x < 0 \\ 1, & x > 0 \end{cases}$$

includes all real x except for $x = 0$ in its domain, but the range of f is restricted to two numbers: -1 (corresponding to $x < 0$) and 1 (corresponding to $x > 0$). To graph the function, we combine two graphs on one set of axes: for $x < 0$, we have the horizontal line graph of the constant function defined by $f(x) = -1$, and for $x > 0$ we have the horizontal line graph of the constant function defined by $f(x) = 1$. The result is shown in Figure 10.14. (As in Chapter 1, open dots indicate points that are not included in the

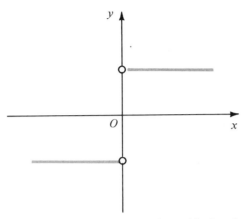

FIGURE 10.14 A Step Function with One Step

graph.) The appearance of the graph suggests the name *step function* for the function f of this example. Notice that f may be defined by

$$f(x) = \frac{|x|}{x} \qquad (x \text{ real and } x \neq 0)$$

The condition $x \neq 0$ excludes division by zero. Similarly, we might define a step function g by

$$g(x) = \frac{|x - 2|}{x - 2} \qquad (x \text{ real and } x \neq 2)$$

The graph of g looks like Figure 10.14, except for a shift of two units to the right. (See Figure 10.15.) In this case division by zero is excluded by the condition $x \neq 2$.

As an application of the step function concept we have:

EXAMPLE 5: PARK 'N SHOP

Park 'n Shop, Inc., is the owner-operator of parking lots in the high-priced shopping areas of several big cities. Shoppers at exclusive stores do not mind paying Park 'n Shop rates: $5.00 for the first hour or part

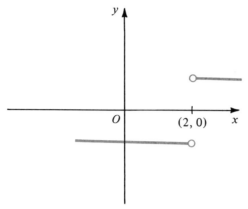

FIGURE 10.15 Graph of the Step Function *g*

thereof; $4.00 more for the second hour or part thereof; $3.00 more for the third hour or part thereof; a total of $15.00 for anything over 3 hours, in any one 12-hour period.

If *C* is the cost function for parking at a Park 'n Shop facility and *n* is the number of hours parked, then we define *C* by

$$C(n) = \begin{cases} 5, & 0 \le n \le 1 \\ 9, & 1 < n \le 2 \\ 12, & 2 < n \le 3 \\ 15, & n > 3 \end{cases}$$

Figure 10.16 graphs the Park 'n Shop cost function.

The *domain* of the function consists of all nonnegative real numbers

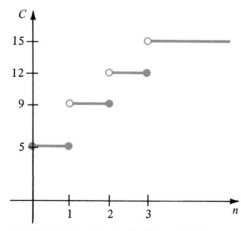

FIGURE 10.16 Graph for Example 5

from 0 to 12. The *range* of the function contains four elements: 5, 9, 12, and 15. [*NOTE:* A Park 'n Shop customer who drives in and drives out again without stopping has a parking time of zero hours—and pays $5.00. The functional notation is: $C(0) = 5$. Notice that the charge for one hour is the same as the charge for zero hours. In functional notation: $C(1) = 5$. Some other examples of functional notation are: $C(1.5) = 9$, $C(2) = 9$, $C(2.25) = 12$, $C(3.25) = 12$, and $C(15) = 12$.]

EXERCISES for Section 10.2

The collection of ordered pairs

$$(-1, 2), (0, -1), (1, 2), (2, -4), (-2, \tfrac{1}{2})$$

defines a function f.

1. Find $f(-1)$, $f(2)$, $f(0)$, and $f(1)$.

2. Find t if $f(t) = \tfrac{1}{2}$; if $f(t) = 2$.

3. Can you find $f(5)$? Can you find t if $f(t) = -2$?

Find $f(3)$, $f(0)$, and $f(-2)$ if:

4. $f(x) = 4x - 7$

5. $f(x) = 5x^2 - 11x + 12$

6. $f(x) = |x + 1| + |x - 1|$

---

7. Find the range of the function f defined by $f(x) = 8x + 5$ if the domain consists of the numbers -2, -1, 0, 1, 2.

8. Find the range of the function f defined by $f(x) = 3 + 5x - 2x^2$ if the domain elements are -2, -1, 0, 1, 2.

9. Find the range of the function f defined by $f(x) = \sqrt{1 - x}$ if the domain elements are 0, -3, -8, -15.

In each of the following cases: State whether or not the given equation defines a function $y = f(x)$; explain your answer.

10. $y = \dfrac{1}{x}$ **11.** $y = \dfrac{1}{x^2}$

12. $y^2 - x^2 = 1$ **13.** $y^2 - x = 1$

14. $y^2 + x^2 = 1$ **15.** $y^2 + x = 1$

To *find the domain* of a function f means to find all real values of x that lead to one and only one real value of $f(x)$. Find the domain of the function f defined by:

16. $f(x) = \dfrac{1}{x + 1}$ **17.** $f(x) = \dfrac{1}{x - 1}$

18. $f(x) = x^2 - 1$ **19.** $f(x) = \dfrac{1}{x^2 - 1}$

20. $f(x) = \sqrt{x + 7}$ **21.** $f(x) = \sqrt{x^2 - 1}$

22. $f(x) = \sqrt{1 - x^2}$ **23.** $f(x) = 3x - \dfrac{3}{x}$

24. $f(x) = \dfrac{1}{|x + 2|}$ **25.** $f(x) = \sqrt{|x - 2|}$

Graph the function f defined by:

26. $f(x) = |x - 1|$ **27.** $f(x) = |x + 1|$

28. $f(x) = +\sqrt{x}$ **29.** $f(x) = \begin{cases} 0, & x \le 0 \\ x^2, & x > 0 \end{cases}$

30. $f(x) = \begin{cases} x, & x \le 0 \\ -x, & x > 0 \end{cases}$ **31.** $f(x) = \begin{cases} -3, & 0 \le x < 3 \\ 3, & 3 \le x < 6 \\ 6, & 6 \le x < 9 \end{cases}$

32. $f(x) = \begin{cases} 9, & x \ge 3 \\ x^2, & -1 \le x < 3 \\ 1, & x < -1 \end{cases}$

33. The year is 1995. First-class mail is delivered every other Thursday. Letters and packages of x ounces are delivered for $C(x)$ dollars. The rules for determining $C(x)$ are: the first ounce (or part thereof) goes for \$3; the second ounce (or part thereof) goes for \$2; further ounces (or parts thereof) go for \$1. No letter or package can exceed 12 ounces. Graph the function $C(x)$.

34. County Ambulance is a private ambulance service that transports patients to the county hospital. If a patient is x miles from the hospital, then the ambulance fee $F(x)$ is:

a. $20 if the patient is less than 1 mile from the hospital
b. an extra $5 per mile (or part thereof) for patients who are 1 to 10 miles from the hospital
c. a flat $75 for patients who are 10 or more miles from the hospital

Graph the function $F(x)$.

10.3 QUADRATIC FUNCTIONS

The function f defined by

$$f(x) = ax^2 + bx + c \qquad \text{(domain: all real } x\text{)}$$

where a, b, and c are constants is called the *quadratic function*. The word "quadratic" means "square," and the squaring function $f(x) = x^2$ is a special case of the quadratic function. In studying the squaring function (see Example 1 of the last section), we have begun our study of quadratic functions. As you will soon see, the graph of the squaring function (Figure 10.8) has much in common with the graphs of other quadratic functions.

To begin with, the function defined for all real x by

$$y = f(x) = ax^2 \qquad (a > 0)$$

is the collection of ordered pairs (x, ax^2). If $a = 1$, this is the squaring function. If $a < 1$, we have a flattened squaring function, as in Figure 10.17. And if $a > 1$, we have a sharpened squaring function, as in Figure 10.18.

Changes of shape like flattening and sharpening are often called *stretching*. Multiplying the squaring function by a nonzero constant a therefore produces a *stretched squaring function*.

If $a < 0$, then the range of the function (x, ax^2) consists of all non-positive numbers. The graph in Figure 10.19 illustrates this case. We see that the graph of $y = (-a)x^2$ is the reflection in the x-axis of the graph of $y = ax^2$.

Before going on, you should know that the graph of $y = ax^2$ $(a \neq 0)$ is called a *parabola*. The parabola opens *upward* if $a > 0$ (as in Figures 10.8, 10.17, and 10.18) and *downward* if $a < 0$ (as in the graph of $y = -1.5x^2$; see Figure 10.19).

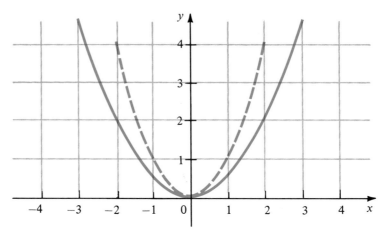

FIGURE 10.17   Graphs of the Squaring Function $y = x^2$
(Dashed Line) and the Flattened Squaring
Function $y = 0.5x^2$ (Solid Line)

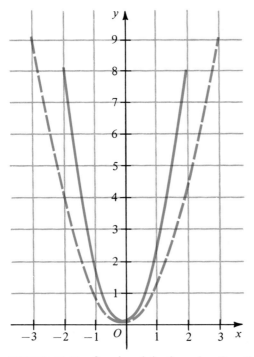

FIGURE 10.18   Graphs of the Squaring Function $y = x^2$
(Dashed Line) and the Sharpened Squaring
Function $y = 2x^2$ (Solid Line)

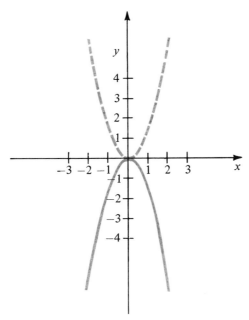

FIGURE 10.19 Graphs of the Stretched Squaring Function
$y = 1.5x^2$ (Dashed Line) and Its Reflection
$y = -1.5x^2$ (Solid Line)

The graph of $y = ax^2 + c$ is obtained by moving the graph of $y = ax^2$ up $|c|$ units (if $c > 0$) or down $|c|$ units (if $c < 0$). By graphing $y = ax^2 + c$ for various values of $|c|$, we obtain a *family* of parabolas. Figures 10.20 and 10.21 show families of upward-opening and downward-opening parabolas.

An upward-opening parabola has a lowest point (or *minimum*), and a downward-opening parabola has a highest point (or *maximum*). Such a minimum or maximum point of a parabola is called a *vertex*. For a parabola with the equation $y = ax^2$, the vertex is always at the origin $(0, 0)$. For a parabola with the equation $y = ax^2 + c$, the vertex is at $(0, c)$. As you will see in a moment, the graph of $y = ax^2 + bx + c$ is a parabola, and there is a simple method of determining its vertex as well. Finding the vertex of a parabola is useful in some of the real-world applications discussed in the next section.

We have one more special case. The graph of

$$y = a(x - h)^2$$

differs from that of $y = ax^2$ in only one way: the parabola is moved $|h|$ units to the right (if $h > 0$) or to the left (if $h < 0$). This case is illustrated in Figure 10.22. We take $a = 2$, and notice that the graph is moved to the right if $h = 3$ and to the left if $h = -2.5$.

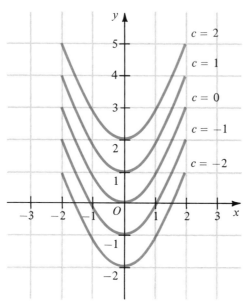

FIGURE 10.20 The Family of Parabolas $y = 0.75x^2 + c$. Curves Shown: $c = 0, \pm1, \pm2$

Now we can show that the graph of $y = ax^2 + bx + c$ (where $a \neq 0$) is always a parabola. By simple algebra (the technique is called *completing the square*),

$$ax^2 + bx = a\left(x + \frac{b}{2a}\right)^2 - \frac{b^2}{4a}$$

Therefore

$$ax^2 + bx + c = a\left(x + \frac{b}{2a}\right)^2 - \frac{b^2}{4a} + c = a\left(x + \frac{b}{2a}\right)^2 + \left(\frac{4ac - b^2}{4a}\right)$$

NOTE: Completing the square is easier to *do* than to talk about. Here are some examples:

$$x^2 + 12x + 17 = (x + 6)^2 - 36 + 17 = (x + 6)^2 - 19$$
$$2x^2 + 11x + 8 = 2(x + \tfrac{11}{4})^2 - \tfrac{121}{18} + 8 = 2(x + \tfrac{11}{4})^2 - \tfrac{57}{8}$$
$$3x^2 - 5x - 7 = 3(x - \tfrac{5}{6})^2 - \tfrac{25}{12} - 7 = 3(x - \tfrac{5}{6})^2 - \tfrac{109}{12}$$

Each of these can be checked against the general formula. In the third case, for example, $a = 3$, $b = -5$, and $c = -7$. The general formula gives

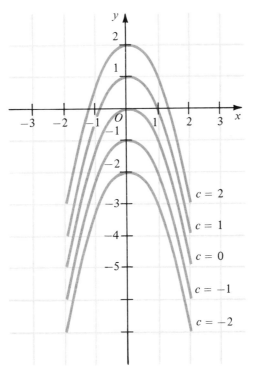

FIGURE 10.21 The Family of Parabolas $y = -1.25x^2 + c$.
Curves shown correspond to $c = 0, \pm1, \pm2$

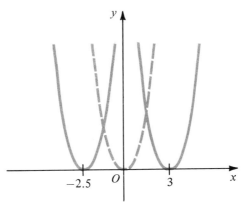

FIGURE 10.22 Graphs of $y = 2x^2$ (Dashed), $y = 2(x - 3)^2$ to
the Right, and $y = 2(x + 2.5)^2$ to the Left.

$$3x^2 - 5x - 7 = 3\left(x - \frac{5}{6}\right)^2 - \frac{25}{12} - 7 = 3\left(x - \frac{5}{6}\right)^2 + \left(\frac{-84 - 25}{12}\right)$$

which checks.

We sum up the algebra as follows:

> The equation $y = ax^2 + bx + c$ can be written in the form
> $$y = a(x - h)^2 + d$$
> where $h = -\dfrac{b}{2a}$, $d = \dfrac{4ac - b^2}{4a}$

To say it in terms of parabolas, we notice that
$$y = a(x - h)^2 + d$$
is the equation of a stretched squaring function that has been moved $|h|$ units to the right or left and $|d|$ units up or down. Therefore:

> The graph of $y = ax^2 + bx + c$ is a *parabola* with *vertex* at the point
> $$\left(-\frac{b}{2a}, \frac{4ac - b^2}{4a}\right)$$
> The parabola opens upward if $a > 0$ and downward if $a < 0$. (If $a = 0$, the parabola reduces to a line.)

PROBLEM 1   Discuss the graphs of the equations

(a) $\qquad\qquad\qquad y = (x - 2)^2$

(b) $\qquad\qquad\qquad y = -3(x - 2)^2$

(c) $\qquad\qquad\qquad y = -3(x - 2)^2 + 4$

SOLUTION   Each of the three graphs is a parabola, and each is related to the squaring function.

Equation (a) is of the form $y = a(x - h)^2$, with $a = 1$ and $h = 2$. Since $a = 1$, the graph has the squaring function shape. Since $h = 2$, the graph is *moved* 2 units to the right. That is: The parabola has vertex $(2, 0)$, and it opens upward.

Equation (b) is again of the form $y = a(x - h)^2$. In this case $a = -3$ and $h = 2$. Since $|a| > 1$, the graph shows a *stretched* (sharpened) squaring function. Since $a < 0$, the graph is *reflected* in the x-axis. Since $h = 2$, the graph is *moved* 2 units to the right. The parabola has vertex $(2, 0)$, and it opens downward.

Equation (c) is of the form $y = a(x - h)^2 + d$. Since $a = -3$ and $h = 2$ as in equation (b), we have to begin with the equation (b) graph. Since $d = 4$, the graph is *moved up* 4 units. The parabola has vertex $(2, 4)$, and it opens downward.

The graphs of equations (a), (b), and (c) are sketched on the same set of axes in Figure 10.23.

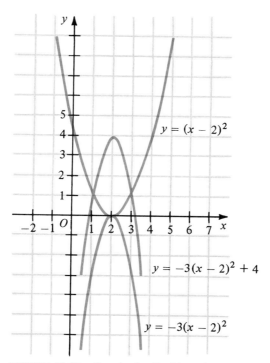

FIGURE 10.23 Graphs for Problem 1

PROBLEM 2 Find an equation for the upward-opening parabola with vertex $(4, -8)$ that passes through the origin.

SOLUTION   The equation

$$y = a(x - 4)^2 - 8 \qquad (a > 0)$$

represents an upward-opening parabola (it is upward-opening because $a > 0$) with vertex $(4, -8)$. If we substitute $(0, 0)$ in the equation, we have

$$0 = a(-4)^2 - 8 = 16a - 8$$

which gives $a = \frac{1}{2}$. The required equation is

$$y = (\tfrac{1}{2})(x - 4)^2 - 8$$

PROBLEM 3   Find an equation for the downward-opening parabola with vertex $(1, 9)$ that passes through the point $(3, 5)$.

SOLUTION   If $a < 0$, the equation

$$y = a(x - 1)^2 + 9$$

represents a downward-opening parabola with vertex $(1, 9)$. By substituting $(3, 5)$ in the equation, we find:

$$5 = a(3 - 1)^2 + 9 = 4a + 9$$

or $a = -1$. The equation we want is

$$y = -(x - 1)^2 + 9$$

PROBLEM 4   Discuss the graphs of:

(a) $$y = x^2 - 2x - 3$$

(b) $$y = -x^2 + x + 2$$

(c) $$y = x^2 + x + 1$$

SOLUTION   Each of the graphs is a parabola. We rewrite the three equations as follows:

(a) $$y = x^2 - 2x - 3 = (x - 1)^2 - 4$$

(b) $$y = -x^2 + x + 2 = -(x - \tfrac{1}{2})^2 + \tfrac{9}{4}$$

(c) $$y = x^2 + x + 1 = (x + \tfrac{1}{2})^2 + \tfrac{3}{4}$$

We see that each parabola has the same shape as the graph of the squaring function. The parabolas for cases (a) and (c) open upward, and the parabola in case (b) opens downward. The vertices are $(1, -4)$ for case (a); $(\frac{1}{2}, \frac{9}{4})$ for case (b); and $(-\frac{1}{2}, \frac{3}{4})$ for case (c).

Check: These results can be checked by using the boxed information on p. 460. In the case of equation (b), for example, we have $a = -1$, $b = 1$, $c = 2$. The vertex of the parabola is at

$$\left(-\frac{b}{2a}, \frac{4ac - b^2}{4a}\right) = \left(-\frac{1}{2}, \frac{9}{4}\right)$$

Since $a < 0$, the parabola opens downward.

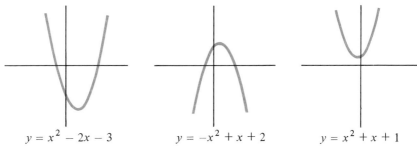

$y = x^2 - 2x - 3$ $y = -x^2 + x + 2$ $y = x^2 + x + 1$

FIGURE 10.24 Graphs for Problem 4

PROBLEM 5 Find the minimum value of the function f defined by

$$f(x) = 3x^2 - 7x + 11$$

and the maximum value of the function g defined by

$$g(x) = -8x^2 - 3x + 24$$

SOLUTION Since the graph of f is an upward-opening parabola, the minimum value of $f(x)$ is at the vertex of the parabola. Using the boxed information on p. 460, with $a = 3$, $b = -7$, and $c = 11$, we find that the vertex is at $(\frac{7}{6}, \frac{83}{12})$. Geometrically, the vertex is the lowest point on the upward-opening parabola. The minimum value of the function is defined as the lowest value assumed by any range element. This is

$$f(\tfrac{7}{6}) = \tfrac{83}{12}$$

The graph of g is a downward-opening parabola. We again make use of the boxed information on p. 460. In this case $a = -8$, $b = -3$, and $c = 24$. The vertex is at $(-\frac{3}{16}, \frac{777}{32})$. Geometrically, the vertex is the highest point of the downward-opening parabola. The maximum value of the function is the highest value assumed by a range element. This is

$$g(-\tfrac{3}{16}) = \tfrac{777}{32}$$

Graph each of the following equations:

1. $y = (x + 1)^2$ **2.** $y = (x + 2)^2 - 3$

      $y = -2(x + 1)^2$

      $y = -2(x + 1)^2 + 3$

3. $y - 2 = -3(x - 1)^2$ **4.** $y = x^2 - 2x + 1$

5. $y = 4 - 3x - x^2$ **6.** $y = x(x + 1)$

7. $y = 11 + 7x - 2x^2$ **8.** $y = 3x^2 - 6x + 13$

---

9. Find the equation of the quadratic function f [defined by $f(x) = ax^2 + bx + c$] if $f(0) = 2$, $f(1) = 6$, $f(-1) = 12$.

10. Find the equation of the quadratic function f [defined by $f(x) = ax^2 + bx + c$] if $f(-1) = -3$, $f(1) = 3$, $f(2) = 0$.

The vertex of an upward-opening parabola is at $(3, -2)$. Find the equation of the parabola if it passes through:

11. $(0, 0)$ **12.** $(4, 1)$

13. $(-6, 5)$ **14.** $(-3, 2)$

The vertex of a downward-opening parabola is at $(-3, 2)$. Find the equation of the parabola if it passes through:

15. $(0, 0)$ **16.** $(4, 1)$

17. $(6, -5)$ **18.** $(3, -2)$

Find the minimum (or maximum) value of the function f defined by:

19. $f(x) = x^2 - 3x + 2$ **20.** $f(x) = x^2 - 4x + 4$

21. $f(x) = 3x^2 + 3x$ **22.** $f(x) = -4x^2 + 7x - 7$

23. $f(x) = 3x^2 + 17x - 7$ **24.** $f(x) = -4x^2 + 11x - 10$

25. $f(x) = -2x^2 + x$ **26.** $f(x) = -3x^2 + 4x - 2$

27. $f(x) = 2x^2 - 5x + 6$ **28.** $f(x) = -\frac{1}{2}x^2 - 3x - 3$

29. $f(x) = -3x^2 + 17x - 8$ **30.** $f(x) = \frac{1}{2}x^2 + \frac{2}{3}x - 2$

31. $f(x) = -2x^2 - 6x + 5$ **32.** $f(x) = -x^2 - 3x - 4$

10.4 QUADRATIC MODELS

This section gives real-world applications of quadratic functions. In Example 1, a car dealer has a quadratic profit function. The maximum of the function (the highest point on its graph) is the maximum profit of the dealership.

EXAMPLE 1: MAXIMIZING PROFIT AT DUPONT CHRYSLER-PLYMOUTH

Bob and Mary Dupont own one of Ohio's smallest Chrysler-Plymouth dealerships. Bob takes care of sales and service and Mary runs the business. Bob would sell 10 cars a week if he could, but Mary's calculations show that selling too many cars is just as bad as selling too few. If Dupont Chrysler-Plymouth sells x cars per year, Mary figures that their profit will be

$$P(x) = -97{,}500 + 1860x - 6.2x^2$$

dollars. For example: If they sell no cars at all one year, they will lose $97,500. (This is the overhead. It consists of salaries, bank interest, heating, and so on.) If they sell 50 cars, the (negative) profit will be

$$P(50) = -97{,}500 + 1860(50) - 6.2(50)^2 = -20{,}000$$

dollars. They will still not be making enough to cover the overhead of the business. Things would look better if they sold 100 cars. Then the profit would be

$$P(100) = -97{,}500 + 1860(100) - 6.2(100)^2 = 26{,}500$$

dollars. "So okay," says Bob. "Let's see what happens if I sell 500 cars." Easy enough: the profit is

$$P(500) = -97{,}500 + 1860(500) - 6.2(500)^2 = -717{,}500$$

dollars. Note the minus sign. Selling 500 cars would be much much worse than selling no cars at all.

Why? Because that kind of volume would be too much for their service and business set-up. They would have to hire more mechanics and build more bays to take care of the service. For the business end, Mary would have to hire at least two secretaries and get them office space. That would mean still more building. Interest expense would zoom.

All of those negative factors are taken into account in the quadratic term $-6.2x^2$ *in* $P(x)$. As we have already mentioned, the constant term $-97{,}500$

in $P(x)$ is the business overhead. The only positive term in $P(x)$ is the linear term $1860x$. With the right choice of x, that term will keep the business running at a nice profit.

Question: What is the right choice of x? For an answer, we use what we know about graphs of quadratic expressions. Since $P(x)$ is of the form $ax^2 + bx + c$, its graph is a parabola. Since $a = -6.2 < 0$, the parabola opens downward. Its vertex (which gives the highest value of $P(x)$, or the maximum profit) can be located by the use of the boxed information on p. 460. With $b = 1860$, $a = -6.2$, and $c = -97,500$, we find that the vertex is at the point

$$\left(-\frac{b}{2a}, \frac{4ac - b^2}{4a}\right) = (150, 42,000)$$

In other words: If Dupont Chrysler-Plymouth delivers 150 cars per year, then its profit will be $42,000—and this is the maximum profit that the dealership can earn.

Example 1 shows that it does not make sense to increase the *revenue* (total sales) of a business if the *costs* of running the business climb even faster. Ideally, management wants to increase revenues and decrease costs. Example 2 studies the quadratic revenue function of a famous product. Management learns that the correct *price* for the product will maximize revenues. (Remarks at the end of Example 2 explain what management actually did and why, and how it worked out. See p. 467–68.)

EXAMPLE 2: AMERICAN CRACKER COMPANY'S QUADRATIC REVENUE FUNCTION

Back in 1974, American Cracker Company was about to raise its prices. (It had good reason to. The Nixon administration froze cracker prices for 18 months but allowed wheat to go from $1.65 to $6 a bushel, sugar from 10¢ to 70¢ a pound, etc.)

The American Cracker Company sales force was worried about the price increase. They were afraid of competition from no-name brands. They told management to raise prices if necessary, but to remember that every 1% price increase would cost 0.75% in sales.

Translated into boxes of Chococreme cookies, this meant: If 1 million cases of Chococremes could be sold at $7.00 (wholesale), then a wholesale price of $7.28 (up 4%) would cut sales to 970,000 (down 3%).

Assuming that these sales predictions were accurate, they did not sound that bad to American Cracker management. A staff economist prepared a table (Table 10.3), which suggested that a price somewhere between $8.12 and $8.40 a case would lead to the largest *revenue* (or gross sales). To

TABLE 10.3

Number of Cases Sold	Dollar Price per Case	Revenue (Dollars)
1,000,000	$7.00	$7,000,000
970,000	7.28	7,061,000
910,000	7.84	7,134,400
880,000	8.12	7,145,600
850,000	8.40	7,140,000
820,000	8.68	7,117,600
730,000	9.52	6,949,600

check this out, the economist constructed a *revenue function R*. By definition,

revenue = (number of cases sold) · (dollar price per case)

If the variable x represents the fractional increase in price (over $7.00), then $0.75x$ represents the functional decrease in sales (below 1 million cases). In other words:

dollar price per case = $(7.00)(1 + x)$

number of cases sold = $(1,000,000)(1 - 0.75x)$

The revenue function R is defined by

$R(x) = (1,000,000)(1 - 0.75x)(7.00)(1 + x)$
$$= (7,000,000)(1 + 0.25x - 0.75x^2)$$

The domain of $R(x)$ is the interval $0 \leq x \leq 1.33$. (A larger value of x would give a negative number of cases sold.)

Finding the largest revenue is the same as finding the maximum of $R(x)$. First we find the maximum of

$$f(x) = 1 + 0.25x - 0.75x^2$$

As we know from Section 10.3, the graph of $f(x)$ is a downward-opening parabola. The vertex is at (0.1666667, 1.0208333). The vertex is the highest point on the graph, which means that the maximum of $f(x)$ is reached at $x = 0.1666667$. Therefore the maximum revenue, realized at a price increase of $16\frac{2}{3}\%$, is

$$(7,000,000)(1.0208333) = \$7,145,833.10$$

A REAL-WORLD VIEW The study of American Cracker Company's quadratic revenue function shows that revenue is maximized if Chococreme cookie prices are increased $16\frac{2}{3}$%. Of course, management wanted to do more than maximize revenues: it wanted to maximize *profits*. By studying costs as well as revenues, management decided that it could meet its objective with a price increase of 30%. Assuming that the revenue function R still made sense, the calculation was that the revenue corresponding to this increase would be

$$R(0.3) = (7,000,000)\,[1 + (0.25)(0.3) - (0.75)(0.3)^2] = \$7,052,500$$

This would be on anticipated sales of 775,000 cases. Revenue would not be up very much, but raw materials costs would be down substantially. Management thought this would be the way to maximize profits.

NOTE: As it happened, American Cracker Company management was absolutely right, but for reasons not yet mentioned here. The sales force fought hard to overcome the handicap of the higher price, and advertising budgets were increased. Sales did not decrease as anticipated but actually went up slightly. Profits increased substantially.

Example 3 presents a model for the price behavior of a company's stock when there is large-scale demand for that stock. Supply and demand functions are quadratic. The graphs are parabolas. As the price per share of stock increases, the supply parabola curves upward and the demand parabola curves downward. The intersection point of the two parabolas is a point of *equilibrium:* equilibrium price, equilibrium supply, and equilibrium demand.

EXAMPLE 3: A QUADRATIC MODEL OF EQUILIBRIUM

Atlantis Realty owns shopping centers, condominiums, and assorted real estate all up and down the eastern seaboard. It has similar properties in Mexico, Venezuela, and Puerto Rico. Most of these holdings were glittering properties 10 years ago—before the real estate collapse. Nowadays Atlantis makes a living on its shopping centers and keeps trying to sell everything else.

Some investors think this is the time to pick up Atlantis's stock. The arithmetic is simple. Right now the stock is selling at $2.25 per share, and there are 28.6 million shares. That makes $64.35 million.

Sharp real estate professionals figure the Atlantis shopping centers for a liquidation value of $350 million to $400 million. Cut the $350 million in half, value the Atlantis condominiums, resort properties, etc., at zero, and you still have a rock-bottom $175 million. Each of the 28.6 million shares in Atlantis looks to be backed by $6.12 in assets.

All of this neglects possible future perils in the real estate market. But it looks good enough to tempt a few substantial investors. The *demand function D* (giving the number of millions of Atlantis shares these people will buy at x dollars a share) was calculated by an investment analyst. It is:

$$D(x) = 14.5 - 0.3x^2 \qquad (1 \leq x \leq 6.95)$$

Notice the restricted domain of the demand function. The meaning of the condition $x \geq 1$ is that no one will want to buy the stock if it falls below \$1 per share. The condition $x \leq 6.95$ is imposed because $D(x)$ becomes negative (which makes no sense) for $x > 6.95$.

   If the investors are offered all the Atlantis stock they want at the current market price of \$2.25 per share, they will buy

$$D(2.25) = 14.5 - 0.3(2.25)^2 = 12.98$$

million shares. Notice that 12.98 million is about 45% of 28.6 million. This is enough stock for effective control of Atlantis Realty. The investors are therefore willing to take over Atlantis at current prices.

   Of course, the fact that there are buyers for 12.98 million shares of stock will send prices up *above* current levels. The *supply function S* (showing how many million Atlantis shares will be supplied, or offered for sale, at x dollars per share), as calculated by an investment analyst, is

$$S(x) = 0.36x^2 - 0.44 \qquad (x \geq 0)$$

The fact that $S(0) = 0$ means that no shares will be given away. At the market price of \$2.25, there will be

$$S(2.25) = 0.36(2.25)^2 - 0.4(2.25) = 0.9225$$

million (or 922,500) shares for sale.

   There is a sizable difference between the 922,500 shares in *supply* (or for sale) and the 12.98 million shares that investors *demand* (or are willing to buy) at \$2.25 per share. To see what is happening, we graph the supply $S(x)$ and the demand $D(x)$ on the same set of axes. (See Figure 10.25.) The

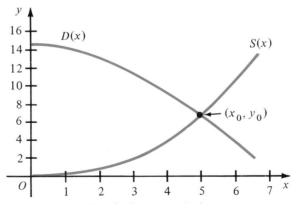

FIGURE 10.25   Graphs for Example 3

variables are x (price) and y (number of items). $D(x)$ is represented by a downward-opening parabola and $S(x)$ by an upward-opening parabola. We are interested only in positive values of x and y, and therefore show only the first-quadrant graphs of $S(x)$ and $D(x)$. As Figure 10.25 shows, the graphs intersect at a single point (x_0, y_0) in the first quadrant. Supply and demand are in balance, or in equilibrium, at that point:

$$S(x_0) = D(x_0) = y_0$$

We call x_0 the *equilibrium price* of the stock, $S(x_0)$ the *equilibrium supply*, and $D(x_0)$ the *equilibrium demand*.

REMARK: The idea of market equilibrium was introduced in Section 2.6. Supply and demand functions were linear in Chapter 2, and we therefore said we had a *linear model* of equilibrium. In the Atlantis example, supply and demand are quadratic functions, so we have a *quadratic model* of equilibrium.

The point of intersection (x_0, y_0) is found by equating $S(x) = 0.36x^2 - 0.4x$ and $D(x) = 14.5 - 0.3x^2$. This gives

$$0.36x^2 - 0.4x = 14.5 - 0.3x^2$$

or

$$0.66x^2 - 0.4x - 14.5 = 0$$

The positive solution is $x = 5$. (This is x_0.) The corresponding value of y is given by

$$D(5) = S(5) = 7$$

In real-world terms, this means that investors are willing to buy—and current stockholders are willing to sell—7 million Atlantis shares at $5 a share.

NOTE: It is easy to check that $x = 5$ is the equilibrium price. The number was found by the use of the *quadratic formula*. This states that the quadratic equation

$$ax^2 + bx + c = 0$$

has two solutions x_1, x_2 and that they are:

$$x_1 = \frac{-b + \sqrt{b^2 - 4ac}}{2a}, \quad x_2 = \frac{-b - \sqrt{b^2 - 4ac}}{2a}$$

We had $a = 0.66$, $b = -0.4$, and $c = -14.5$, and our result for the positive solution x_1 was

$$\frac{0.4 + \sqrt{(0.4)^2 + 4(0.66)(14.5)}}{1.32} = 5$$

The quadratic formula, by the way, is derived from the fact that $ax^2 + bx + c = 0$ can be rewritten (through completing the square; see p. 458) as

$$\left(x + \frac{b}{2a}\right)^2 = \frac{b^2 - 4ac}{4a^2}$$

Take square roots of both sides:

$$x + \frac{b}{2a} = \pm \frac{\sqrt{b^2 - 4ac}}{2a}$$

[The $\pm$ is used because every positive number has two square roots: one positive, one negative. For example: The number 9 has the positive square root 3, since $3^2 = 9$, and it has the negative square root -3, since $(-3)^2 = 9$. The symbol $\sqrt{9}$ means 3, the positive square root. And the negative square root -3 is written $-\sqrt{9}$.] Finally, rewrite:

$$x = \frac{-b \pm \sqrt{b^2 - 4ac}}{2a}$$

The plus sign gives x_1, and the minus sign gives x_2.

EXERCISES *for Section 10.4*

Betty's Barbeque Burger is not McDonald's, but it earns Betty a fair living. Monthly profits in dollars are:

$$P(x) = -7700 + 595x - 7x^2$$

where $x = $ the number of thousands of barbecued burgers sold during the month.

1. What is $P(0)$—and what does it mean?

2. What are the profits if monthly sales are 10,000? 20,000? 30,000? 40,000? 50,000?

3. Interpret your answers to Exercise 2 in real-world terms. Interpret them mathematically.

4. How many thousands of barbecued burgers must be sold per month to maximize Betty's profits? Does this make sense in terms of your answer to Exercise 2?

5. How large will the maximum monthly profit be?

6. Sketch the graph of $P(x)$, then interpret the graph.

Aggressor is a remote control toy fighter plane. The production and marketing cost for each plane (with its remote-control gear) is $150. If the selling price is x dollars per plane, then the manufacturer's market research says that

$$30,000 - 30x$$

planes will be sold. On hearing this, the manufacturer asked his accountant how many thousands of dollars he could expect to make from Aggressor. The accountant said: "If market research is right, your total profit will be

$$P(x) = -4500 + 34.5x - 0.03x^2$$

thousand dollars."

7. If the market research is correct, how many planes will be sold at $200? at $300? at $400? at $500? at $600?

8. Where did the accountant get that quadratic total profit function?

9. What is the manufacturer's total profit if Aggressor sells at $200? at $300? at $400? at $500? at $600? at $700?

10. What selling price x will give the largest total profit? How large will that total profit be?

11. How many planes are sold at the profit-maximizing price you found in answering Exercise 10? What are the manufacturer's total revenues when the plane is sold at that price? What are the total costs?

Energy Alert is a weekly newsletter for people in the energy business. It advises them about the latest developments in energy research, development, production, and marketing. *Energy Alert* has 1125 subscribers at the current yearly subscription rate of $275. The revenue function R showing the total revenues from subscriptions is

$$R(x) = 2106.3x - 3.57x^2$$

where x = yearly subscription rate.

NOTE: If you work it out, you will find that this gives 1124.55 subscribers at $275 per year. The number 1124.55 should of course be rounded off to 1125. Numbers you obtain as you answer the following questions should also be rounded off to whole numbers whenever that is appropriate.

12. Find the total revenue for subscription prices of $235, $255, $275, $295, $315, $335, and $355.

13. What subscription price gives the maximum revenue? How many subscribers will there be at this price?

The publishers of *Energy Alert* have certain fixed costs and certain variable costs. Their total costs are given by

$$C(x) = 176{,}900 - 77.5x + 0.01x^2$$

where x = yearly subscription rate.

The profit function P for the publishers of *Energy Alert* is then defined by

$$P(x) = R(x) - C(x) = -176{,}900 + 2183.8x - 3.58x^2$$

14. What subscription price gives the publishers the largest possible profit?

15. How much do the publishers lose if they act to maximize revenues instead of profits?

16. Sketch graphs of $C(x)$ and $R(x)$ on the same axes. Shade the part of the graph that represents profit. [The shaded area is not the same thing as the graph of $P(x)$.]

All over the U.S., farmland is being sold to developers who turn it into building lots. As the supply decreases, the price goes up. In the farm country around Ithaca, Indiana, the number of acres in supply at a price of x thousand dollars an acre is given by

$$S(x) = 10x^2 - 17x + 7$$

On the buyers' side, there is a demand for

$$D(x) = 420 - 45x - 11x^2$$

acres of the land at x thousand dollars an acre.

17. How much Ithaca farmland is available at $1000 an acre? at $2000 an acre? at $3000? at $4000?

18. Graph the equation $S(x) = 10x^2 - 17x + 7$.

19. How much land would local developers like to buy at $1000 an acre? at $2000 an acre? at $3000? at $4000?

20. Graph the equation $D(x) = 420 - 45x - 11x^2$ on the same axes you used for graphing $S(x)$.

21. From the graph in Exercise 20: What is the equilibrium price of the developable farmland in Ithaca, Indiana?

22. Use algebra to find the equilibrium price and the equilibrium supply/demand of the developable farmland.

Many families in Center Durham, New Hampshire, now use wood stoves to heat the kitchen–family room area in the early evening. Many families also cut their own wood. Those who do not find that the price of wood is coming to be a significant item. For 500 Center Durham families that do not cut their own wood, the demand function D for winter wood is defined by

$$D(x) = 5000 - 0.8x^2$$

where $D(x)$ is the number of cords of wood demanded by these 500 families, and

$$x = \text{dollar price of a cord of wood}$$

The supply that is available to these families at x dollars per cord is:

$$S(x) = 15x + 0.5x^2$$

23. How many cords of wood are the 500 families willing to buy at $30 per cord? at $40 per cord? at $50? at $60?

24. Among the families we are talking about, the average family needs 5 to 6 cords of wood to keep its stove going through the winter. From your answer to Exercise 23: What is the average family prepared to pay for its cordwood?

25. How many cords of wood are on the local market (and therefore available to these families) at $30 a cord? at $40 a cord? at $50? at $60?

26. Graph $S(x)$ and $D(x)$ on the same axes and interpret the graph.

27. Use algebra to find the equilibrium price and the equilibrium supply/demand of cordwood in Center Durham, New Hampshire. How do you interpret your answer, in light of your answer to Exercise 24?

10.5 POLYNOMIALS AND RATIONAL FUNCTIONS

Suppose that we define a function f for all real x by

$$f(x) = a_n x^n + a_{n-1} x^{n-1} + \cdots + a_2 x^2 + a_1 x + a_0$$

where the coefficients a_n, a_{n-1}, ..., a_2, a_1, a_0 are constants and n is a nonnegative integer. If $a_n \neq 0$, we call $f(x)$ a *polynomial of degree n*. (Examples: $2x^2 + 3x + 7$ is a polynomial of degree 2; $6x^7 - 5x + 1$ is a polynomial of degree 7.) So far, we have studied polynomials of degree 0, 1, and 2:

1. If $a_0 \neq 0$ and all higher coefficients vanish, then $f(x) = a_0$ defines a polynomial function of *degree 0*, or a *constant* function.

2. If $a_1 \neq 0$ and all higher coefficients vanish, then $f(x) = a_0 + a_1 x$ defines a polynomial function of *degree 1*, or a *linear* function.

3. If $a_2 \neq 0$ and all higher coefficients vanish, then $f(x) = a_0 + a_1 x + a_2 x^2$ defines a polynomial function of *degree 2*, or a *quadratic* function.

Among polynomials of higher degree, the most interesting for our applications are *power functions*. The *power function with integral exponent n* is defined by $f(x) = x^n$.

EXAMPLE 1: In the case of an *odd* exponent ($n = 1, 3, 5, \ldots$), the power function $f(x) = x^n$ is an *odd function*: $f(-x) = -f(x)$. Graphs of $f(x) = x$, $f(x) = x^3$, and $f(x) = x^5$ are shown in Figure 10.26. The pattern indicated in the three graphs of the figure continues through $n = 7, 9, 11$, etc. That is: As n increases, the graphs are successively flatter near the origin (that is, for $|x| < 1$) and successively steeper away from the origin (that is, for $|x| > 1$).

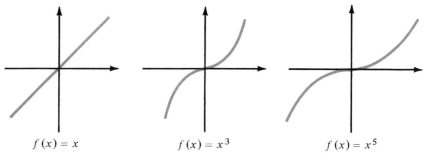

$f(x) = x$ $f(x) = x^3$ $f(x) = x^5$

FIGURE 10.26   Graphs of Odd Functions

EXAMPLE 2: In the case of an *even* exponent ($n = 2, 4, 6, \ldots$), the power function $f(x) = x^2$ is an *even* function: $f(-x) = f(x)$. Graphs of $f(x) = x^2$, $f(x) = x^4$, and $f(x) = x^6$ are shown in Figure 10.27. As the exponent n increases, the graph flattens in the interval $|x| < 1$ and grows steeper in $|x| > 1$. The pattern continues for $n = 8, 10$, etc.

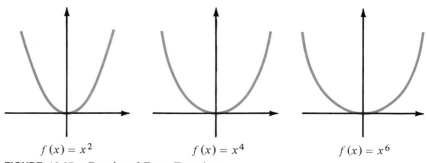

$f(x) = x^2$ $f(x) = x^4$ $f(x) = x^6$

FIGURE 10.27   Graphs of Even Functions

In Section 10.3, we moved from a study of $y = f(x) = x^2$ to $y = ax^2$, then to $y = ax^2 + c$, and finally to the general quadratic equation $y = ax^2 + bx + c$. We can generalize $y = x^3$ in a similar way, but this will *not* show us how to graph the general cubic $y = a_3x^3 + a_2x^2 + a_1x + a_0$. (Calculus is needed for that.)

PROBLEM 1   Discuss the graphs of:

(a) $y = ax^3$

(b) $y = ax^3 + c$

(c) $y = a(x - h)^3 + c$

SOLUTION   Each graph has the same general shape as the graph of $y = x^3$. In case (a), the graph is sharpened if $|a| > 1$, flattened if $|a| < 1$, and reflected in the x-axis if $a < 0$. In case (b), the graph is moved up or down $|c|$ units. In case (c), the graph is moved $|h|$ units to the right or left. Figure 10.28 illustrates these changes.

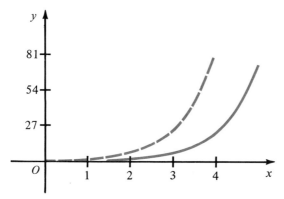

FIGURE 10.28   First-quadrant Graphs of $y = x^3$ (Dashed Line)
and $y = 2(x - 3)^3 + 12$ (Solid Line)

We next turn to functions that are obtained by dividing one polynomial by another.

If $p(x)$ and $q(x)$ are polynomials, then the function r defined by

$$r(x) = \frac{p(x)}{q(x)}$$

is called a *rational function*. Polynomials are defined for all real x. The domain of a rational function $r(x) = (p(x)/q(x))$ includes all real values of x for which $q(x)$ is nonzero.

EXAMPLE 3:   Any polynomial can be written as a quotient of itself and 1, as in

$$\frac{3x^5 + x^2 + 8}{1}$$

Therefore any polynomial is a rational function defined for all real x.

EXAMPLE 4: The domain of the rational function r defined by

$$r(x) = \frac{5x^2 + 29x - 12}{2x^2 - 24x + 70}$$

includes all real x *except* $x = 5$ and $x = 7$. (The quadratic in the denominator vanishes for these values.)

EXAMPLE 5: The rational function r defined by

$$r(x) = \frac{-17x^2 + 79x + 112}{x^2 + 1}$$

has all real x as its domain. There is no real x for which $x^2 + 1 = 0$.

EXAMPLE 6: The rational function r defined by

$$r(x) = \frac{x^2 - 1}{2x^2 - 2}$$

can be rewritten as

$$r(x) = \frac{x^2 - 1}{2(x^2 - 1)} = \frac{1}{2}$$

provided that $x \neq 1$, $x \neq -1$. In other words: The domain of the function includes all real x *except* $x = 1$ and $x = -1$. The function $r(x)$ can be written

$$r(x) = \tfrac{1}{2} \qquad (x \neq 1, x \neq -1)$$

and is *undefined* for $x = 1$ and $x = -1$.

In the first two examples of this section, we considered various cases of the power function with integral exponent n. The reciprocal of that power function is the rational function r defined by

$$r(x) = \frac{1}{x^n} \qquad (x \neq 0)$$

for $n = 1, 2, \ldots .$

As the condition $x \neq 0$ indicates, the domain of the reciprocal power function includes all real x except $x = 0$. This means that we are as usual excluding division by zero. But note that the study of the reciprocal power function is largely concerned with what happens when x is *close to zero*. In the case $n = 1$, for example, the equation of the function is

$$y = \frac{1}{x} \quad (x \neq 0)$$

and we have the following table of values:

x	2	$\frac{3}{2}$	1	$\frac{2}{3}$	$\frac{1}{2}$	$\frac{1}{3}$	$\frac{1}{4}$	$\frac{1}{5}$
y	$\frac{1}{2}$	$\frac{2}{3}$	1	$\frac{3}{2}$	2	3	4	5

We see that y gets larger as x gets smaller. A few more values will make the point more dramatically:

x	0.01	0.001	0.0001	0.00001	0.0000001
y	100	1000	10000	100000	10000000

The point (in words) is: As x takes on smaller and smaller positive values (without ever taking on the value 0), the corresponding positive y-values grow larger and larger and larger.

There is a convenient mathematical way of symbolizing what we have just said. The statement "as x takes on smaller positive values (without ever taking on the value 0)" translates into

$$x \rightarrow 0+$$

(That is: x approaches zero from the right—or through positive values. The value 0 is excluded.)

The translation of "positive y-values grow larger and larger" is:

$$y \rightarrow +\infty$$

which is read "y approaches positive infinity." (The symbol ∞ is read "infinity".)

CAUTION: The symbol ∞ does not represent an actual number. To say that a variable approaches positive infinity does not mean any more than that the numerical values of the variable grow larger than any number that can be assigned. In the case of $y = 1/x$, we can:

1. make y larger than 10 by setting $x = \frac{1}{11}$
2. make y larger than 100 by setting $x = \frac{1}{101}$
3. make y larger than 1,000,000 by setting $x = \frac{1}{1,000,001}$

and so on. In ordinary language: As x takes on smaller and smaller (positive) values, y takes on larger and larger (positive) values. In mathematical language: as $x \to 0+$, $y \to +\infty$.

In the next two examples, we graph $y = 1/x$ and $y = 1/x^2$. We make free use of the just-explained notations $x \to 0+$ and $y \to +\infty$, and of the related notations

$x \to 0-$ (x approaches 0 through negative values)

$y \to -\infty$ (y approaches negative infinity)

If the variable x gets larger and larger (through positive or negative values), we write

$$x \to +\infty \quad \text{or} \quad x \to -\infty$$

And if y approaches 0 (through positive or negative values), we write

$$y \to 0+ \quad \text{or} \quad y \to 0-$$

EXAMPLE 7: To graph

$$y = f(x) = \frac{1}{x} \quad (x \neq 0)$$

we begin with positive values of x (and of y). As we have seen,

$$y \to +\infty \quad \text{as} \quad x \to 0+$$

The table of values

x	1	2	3	4
y	1	$\frac{1}{2}$	$\frac{1}{3}$	$\frac{1}{4}$

illustrates what happens as x grows larger and larger. We have:

$$y \to 0+ \quad \text{as} \quad x \to +\infty$$

Figure 10.29 shows the first-quadrant graph of the function.

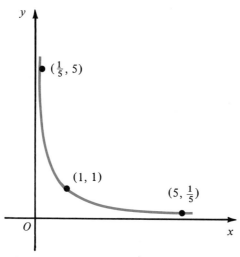

FIGURE 10.29 Graph of $y = 1/x$ for $x > 0$ and $y > 0$

Notice that the graph gets closer and closer to the y-axis (as $x \to 0+$) and to the x-axis (as $x \to +\infty$). Each of the two axes is called an *asymptote* of the graph. The y-axis is a *vertical asymptote* of the graph and the x-axis is a *horizontal asymptote*.

DEFINITION   Vertical Asymptote

A vertical line $x = a$ is called a *vertical asymptote* of $y = f(x)$ if $f(x) \to +\infty$ or $f(x) \to -\infty$ as $x \to a$.

In the case of $y = 1/x$, we have $(1/x) \to +\infty$ as $x \to 0+$.

DEFINITION   Horizontal Asymptote

A horizontal line $y = b$ is called a *horizontal asymptote* of $y = f(x)$ if $f(x) \to b$ as $x \to +\infty$ or as $x \to -\infty$.

In the case of $y = 1/x$, we have $(1/x) \to 0$ as $x \to +\infty$.

NOTE: The graphs of rational functions often have asymptotes. So do some other functions—as you will see in Chapter 11.

To graph $y = f(x) = 1/x$ for negative values of x (and of y), we note that $f(x)$ is an *odd* function: $f(-x) = -f(x)$. The graph for negative x and y is simply a third-quadrant reflection of the first-quadrant graph shown in Figure 10.29. As a check, notice that

$$y \to -\infty \quad \text{as} \quad x \to 0-$$

and that

$$y \to 0- \quad \text{as} \quad x \to -\infty$$

The complete graph of the function, showing both positive and negative values of x and y, is shown in Figure 10.30. Just as the *positive* x- and y-axes are asymptotes of the first-quadrant graph, the *negative* x- and y-axes are asymptotes of the third-quadrant graph.

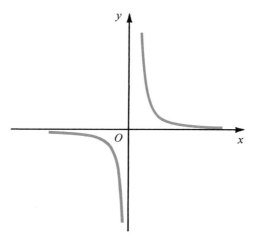

FIGURE 10.30   Graph of $y = 1/x$ $(x \neq 0)$

EXAMPLE 8:   To graph

$$y = f(x) = \frac{1}{x^2} \qquad (x \neq 0)$$

we notice first that the function is *even:* $f(-x) = f(x)$. We have

$$y \to +\infty \quad \text{as} \quad x \to 0+$$

and also

$$y \to +\infty \quad \text{as} \quad x \to 0-$$

As x becomes larger, y becomes smaller:

$$y \to 0+ \quad \text{as} \quad x \to +\infty$$

and

$$y \to 0+ \quad \text{as} \quad x \to -\infty$$

A few of the ordered pairs making up the function are shown in the following table:

x	100	10	1	0.1	0.01
y	.0001	0.01	1	100	10000

Figure 10.31 shows further points on the graph. The first-quadrant portion of the graph has the positive x- and y-axes as asymptotes. The second-quadrant portion of the graph has the negative x-axis and the positive y-axis as

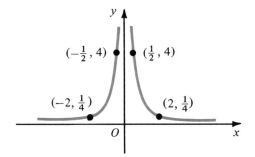

FIGURE 10.31   Graph of $y = \dfrac{1}{x^2} \; (x \neq 0)$

asymptotes. Since the function is even, its graph is restricted to the two upper quadrants: that is, to the half-plane $y > 0$.

To graph

$$y = f(x) = \frac{1}{x^n} \qquad (x \neq 0)$$

for $n > 2$, we follow the reasoning of Examples 7 and 8. If n is odd, then $f(x) = 1/x^n$ is odd and the graph resembles Figure 10.30. If n is even, then

$f(x) = 1/x^n$ is even and the graph resembles Figure 10.31. Of course, the graphs sharpen as n increases: that is, the asymptotes are approached more quickly for larger n.

In graphing a function f of the type

$$f(x) = \frac{1}{(x-h)^n} \qquad (x \neq h)$$

we follow a principle we have noted before: The *shape* of the graph is exactly the same as that of $f(x) = 1/x^n$. But the graph is moved $|h|$ units to the right or left. And adding a constant, as in

$$y = a + \frac{b}{x} \qquad (x \neq 0)$$

will move the graph $|a|$ units up or down. (*NOTE:* The graph being moved is that of $y = b/x$; the range elements are those of $y = 1/x$, multiplied by the constant b. If $b < 0$, the graph is reflected in the x-axis.)

PROBLEM 2   Discuss the graphs of:

(a) $$y = \frac{1}{(x-2)^2} \qquad (x \neq 2)$$

(b) $$y = 3 + \frac{7}{x} \qquad (x \neq 0)$$

(c) $$y = \frac{4x}{2x - 9} \qquad (x \neq \tfrac{9}{2})$$

SOLUTION   In case (a), the graph has the same shape as that of $y = 1/x^2$. See Figure 10.31. The graph is *moved* 2 units to the right. This means that the line $x = 2$ $(y > 0)$ is an asymptote for both the right and left branches of the graph:

$$y \to +\infty \quad \text{as} \quad x \to 2+$$

and

$$y \to +\infty \quad \text{as} \quad x \to 2-$$

The result is sketched in Figure 10.32. As in the case of $y = 1/x^2$, the x-axis is also an asymptote: $y \to 0+$ as $x \to +\infty$ and also as $x \to -\infty$.

For case (b), we begin by noting that the graph of $y = 7/x$ has the same general shape as that of $y = 1/x$. (There is a slight change of

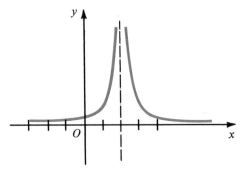

FIGURE 10.32 Graph of $y = \dfrac{1}{(x-2)^2}$

scale, as you can easily see, but the asymptotes and the boomerang shapes in the first and third quadrants are the same.) If the graph of $y = 7/x$ is then moved up 3 units, the result is the graph for case (b).

In case (c), we rewrite (we subtract and add 18 in the numerator, because of the 2 and -9 in the denominator):

$$y = \frac{4x}{2x-9} = \frac{4x-18+18}{2x-9} = \frac{4x-18}{2x-9} + \frac{18}{2x-9} = 2 + \frac{9}{x-\left(\frac{9}{2}\right)}$$

The basic shape is that of $y = 1/x$. Since we have $x - \left(\frac{9}{2}\right)$, the graph is moved $\left(\frac{9}{2}\right)$ units to the right. The multiplication by 9 changes the scale slightly. Finally, the graph is moved up 2 units. The curve is sketched in Figure 10.33. The point marked P in the figure has coordinates $\left(\frac{9}{2}, 2\right)$.

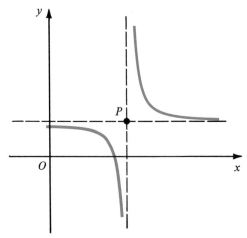

FIGURE 10.33 Graph of $y = \dfrac{(4x)}{(2x-9)}$

NOTE: Figure 10.33 says that the graph of

$$y = f(x) = \frac{4x}{2x - 9}$$

has a vertical asymptote at $x = \frac{9}{2}$, and a horizontal asymptote at $y = 2$. We can check these statements by using the definitions on p. 480. The fact that $f(x) \to +\infty$ as $x \to (\frac{9}{2})$ from the right, while $f(x) \to -\infty$ as $x \to (\frac{9}{2})$ from the left, defines $x = \frac{9}{2}$ as a vertical asymptote. The fact that $f(x) \to 2$, as $x \to +\infty$ or as $x \to -\infty$, defines $y = 2$ as a horizontal asymptote.

EXERCISES *for Section 10.5*

Discuss the graphs of:

1. $y = \frac{1}{5}x^3$, $y = \frac{1}{5}x^3 + 7$, $y = \frac{1}{5}(x + 1)^3 + 7$

2. $y = \frac{1}{3}x^4$, $y = \frac{1}{3}x^4 - 5$, $y = \frac{1}{3}(x - 2)^4 - 5$

3. $y = \frac{1}{5}x^5$, $y = \frac{1}{5}x^5 + 7$, $y = \frac{1}{5}(x + 1)^5 + 7$

4. $y = \frac{1}{3}x^6$, $y = \frac{1}{3}x^6 - 5$, $y = \frac{1}{3}(x - 2)^6 - 5$

Find the domain of each of the following rational functions:

5. $r(x) = \dfrac{x}{x^2 + 1}$ 6. $r(x) = \dfrac{x + 1}{x^2 + 1}$

7. $r(x) = \dfrac{x}{x^2 - 1}$ 8. $r(x) = \dfrac{x + 1}{x^2 - 1}$

9. $r(x) = \dfrac{x^2}{x^2 + 1}$ 10. $r(x) = \dfrac{x^2}{x^2 - 1}$

11. $r(x) = \dfrac{x^2 - 1}{x^2 + 1}$ 12. $r(x) = \dfrac{x^2 - 2x + 1}{x - 1}$

13. $r(x) = \dfrac{x^2 + 2x + 1}{x + 1}$ 14. $r(x) = \dfrac{x^3}{3x^2 - 4x^4}$

15. $r(x) = \dfrac{x^2 + 1}{x}$

16.   Which of the functions in Exercises 1 through 15 are even functions?

17.   Which of the functions in Exercises 1 through 15 are odd functions?

18. Which of the functions in Exercises 1 through 15 are neither even nor odd?

Discuss the graphs of the following functions. The finding of asymptotes (if any) should be part of your discussion.

19. $y = \dfrac{1}{(x-3)^2}$ $\quad (x \neq 3)$ $\qquad$ **20.** $y = 2 + \dfrac{3}{x}$ $\quad (x \neq 0)$

21. $y = -\dfrac{4}{x} + 5$ $\quad (x \neq 0)$ $\qquad$ **22.** $y = \dfrac{x}{2x-3}$ $\quad (x \neq \frac{3}{2})$

23. $y = \dfrac{x}{2x+3}$ $\quad (x \neq -\frac{3}{2})$ $\qquad$ **24.** $y = \dfrac{x}{x^2+1}$

25. $y = \dfrac{x^2+1}{x}$ $\quad (x \neq 0)$ $\qquad$ **26.** $y = \dfrac{x^2-1}{x}$ $\quad (x \neq 0)$

27. $y = \dfrac{x^2}{x+1}$ $\quad (x \neq -1)$ $\qquad$ **28.** $y = \dfrac{x^2}{x-1}$ $\quad (x \neq 1)$

29. $y = \dfrac{x^2}{x+2}$ $\quad (x \neq -2)$ $\qquad$ **30.** $y = \dfrac{x^2-1}{x^2+1}$

31. $y = \dfrac{x^2+1}{x^2-1}$ $\quad (x \neq 1, -1)$ $\qquad$ **32.** $y = \dfrac{x^2-1}{(x-3)^2}$ $\quad (x \neq 3)$

10.6 FITTING A RATIONAL CURVE TO REAL-WORLD DATA

In graphing a rational function f defined by

$$y = f(x) = a + \frac{b}{x-c} \qquad (x \neq c)$$

we always find that $x = c$ and $y = a$ are asymptotes. (The general shape of the graph is the familiar boomerang shape of the graph of $y = 1/x$.) In this section we will be interested only in *positive y-values*. With this in mind, we note that the graph of our function approaches $x = c$ from the right if $b > 0$ and from the left if $b < 0$. Figures 10.34 and 10.35 illustrate the two cases. The graph in Figure 10.34 is basically the first-quadrant graph of $y = 1/x$, moved 1 unit to the right and 1 unit upward. The graph in Figure 10.35 is basically the third-quadrant graph of $y = 1/x$, *reflected* in the x-axis and *then* moved 1 unit to the right and 1 unit upward.

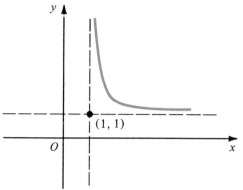

FIGURE 10.34 Graph of $y = 1 + \dfrac{1}{x-1}$ $(x \neq 1, y > 0)$

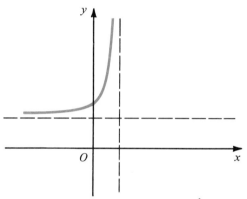

FIGURE 10.35 Graph of $y = 1 - \dfrac{1}{x-1}$ $(x \neq 1, y > 0)$

Rational functions like the ones graphed in Figures 10.34 and 10.35 are sometimes useful for describing real-world data. In particular, *cost data* may follow this functional model. Suppose, for example, that

$$x = \text{number of units produced}$$

$$y = \text{cost per unit}$$

As the number x of units produced grows larger, it sometimes happens that the unit cost y goes down sharply and eventually steadies at some constant level. In other cases, the unit cost y may go up and up and up as x increases.

EXAMPLES: COST DATA

1. As worldwide car production has gone up over the years, the unit cost (measured in "real," or uninflated, dollars) has gone down. The cost data curve would look like Figure 10.34.

2. Rolls-Royce production has been on the increase since 1974, mainly to meet demand from the Middle East. In that time the cost of the basic owner-driven Rolls-Royce has gone from $30,000 to $70,000 to $100,000. The cost data curve would have the same shape as Figure 10.35.

Problem 1 shows how a rational function can be fit to cost data. The solution of the problem uses the ideas of the *method of averages* (see Chapter 2, pp. 94–99). The curve that approximates the data is called a *rational curve of best fit*.

PROBLEM 1   Big Sur Airlines runs a Convair 880 on its flights from San Francisco to San Diego. The aircraft holds 50 passengers, and each flight costs Big Sur $1100. With a full payload, that means a cost per passenger of $1100 \div 50 = \$22$. Unfortunately for Big Sur, there is not always a full payload. For any given flight, let

$$x = \text{number of passengers carried}$$

$$y = \text{dollar cost per passenger}$$

Now find a functional model $y = f(x)$ relating the cost per passenger to the number of passengers carried.

SOLUTION   The table

x	50	40	30	22	15	11
y	22	27.50	36.57	50	73.33	100

and the graph in Figure 10.36 suggest that a rational function

$$y = a + \frac{b}{x}$$

may be fitted to the data. If we set

$$x' = \frac{1}{x}$$

then the equation of the rational function takes the form

$$y = a + bx'$$

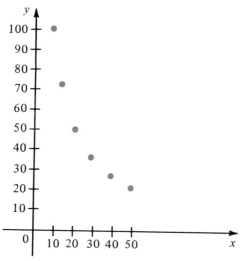

FIGURE 10.36   Graph for Problem 1

which is, of course, a linear equation. Now we can use the method of averages. First we construct a table:

x	50	40	30	22	15	11
$x' = 1/x$	.02	0.025	0.033	0.045	0.067	0.091
y	22	27.50	36.67	50	73.33	100

Then we substitute the coordinates of the six data points into the equation $y = a + bx'$. This gives

$$\begin{cases} 22 = a + 0.02b \\ 27.50 = a + 0.025b \\ 36.67 = a + 0.033b \end{cases}$$

$$\begin{cases} 50 = a + 0.045b \\ 73.33 = a + 0.067b \\ 100 = a + 0.091b \end{cases}$$

(If you are comparing this with Section 2.5, notice that the constants a and b play different roles here and there.) Now we add the three equations in the second group. This leads to a system of two equations:

$$86.17 = 3a + 0.078b$$

$$223.33 = 3a + 0.203b$$

Subtracting the first equation from the second, we have

$$137.16 = 0.125b$$

or:

$$b = 1097.28$$

The corresponding value for a is:

$$a = 0.1940533$$

Check: $3(0.1940533) + (0.078)(1097.28) = 86.169999$

$3(0.1940533) + (0.203)(1097.28) = 223.32999$

The results round off to 86.17 and 223.33.

We now have coefficients for the linear equation $y = a + bx'$. Since $x' = 1/x$, our rational function is:

$$y = 0.1940533 + \frac{1097.28}{x}$$

The following table compares values of y calculated from this equation with the values originally given:

x	50	40	30	22	15	11
calculated y	22.14	27.63	36.77	49.88	73.35	100.05
given y	22	27.50	36.67	50	73.33	100

There is good agreement between the calculated and the given points. If we graph the calculated curve on the same scale as Figure 10.36, the graph would appear to pass through the points shown in the figure. Notice, finally, that the calculated curve (like the real-world problem) makes sense only for a restricted domain: $1 \leq x \leq 50$.

Find a rational curve of best fit, of the form

$$y = a + \frac{b}{x}$$

(where *a* and *b* may be positive or negative) for the data in each of the following tables:

1.

x	44.5	23.4	14.3	12.0	9.7
y	132.08	142.57	156.31	163.58	173.59

2.

x	33.3	16.7	10.0	8.33	6.67
y	39.2	40.5	42.1	42.9	44.1

3.

x	143	118	100	87	77
y	57	46	36	26	15

4.

x	50	26.3	16.1	13.5	10.9
y	208.56	209.24	210.13	210.60	211.25

5.

x	4.05	2.70	2.03	1.62	1.50	1.39
y	79.1	80.8	82.0	83.4	84.5	84.9

6.

x	40	25	20	16.67	13.33	12.5	11.11
y	58	72	82	89	101	104	110

7.

x	52.9	43.7	37.0	32.2	28.5
y	80.6	65.1	50.9	36.8	21.2

8.

x	20.0	10.0	6.67	5.00	4.00	3.33	2.86	2.50
y	88.3	81.2	74.4	70.0	59.3	52.2	45.0	38.9

9.

x	52.63	40.00	33.33	27.78	25.00	22.22	20.00
y	178.22	182.44	186.08	190.18	193.11	196.28	200.26

Pike River Bleachery dumps toxic wastes into the Pike River. A court order requires a clean-up. The bleachery finds that it can eliminate

57% of the toxicity at a yearly cost of $22,500
66% of the toxicity at a yearly cost of $33,750
75% of the toxicity at a yearly cost of $56,250
85% of the toxicity at a yearly cost of $135,000
95% of the toxicity at a yearly cost of $270,000

10. Find a rational function of the form

$$y = \frac{ax}{b - x}$$

that approximates the given data.

11. Sketch the graph of the function you find.

12. According to the function and graph you found, what would it cost Pike River Bleachery to remove 50% of the toxicity? 70%? 90%? Can it remove *all* of the toxicity?

Frieda Franklin, the well-known dress designer and manufacturer, finds that her sales tend to go up every year as the prices she charges go up. The following table tells her story over the past 6 years: x represents the price of her basic black dress, and y represents her annual sales, in tens of thousands of dollars:

x	50	100	150	200	250	300
y	42	81	96	101	106	108

13. Find a rational curve of best fit for Frieda Franklin's data.

14. Suppose that Ms. Franklin continues to raise the price of her basic black dress $50 every year, and suppose that the sales pattern of the past 6 years continues. What will annual sales be when her basic black sells for $400? $500? $600?

15. When Frieda Franklin raised her basic price from $50 to $100, her annual sales jumped from $420,000 to $810,000. Later increases in sales seem to be much more modest. From your answers to Exercises 13 and 14: If present trends continue, do you anticipate any future large increases in Frieda Franklin's annual sales? If not, why not? If so, why?

chapter eleven

EXPONENTIAL AND LOGARITHMIC FUNCTIONS

THE exponential functions described in this chapter provide convenient models for growth and for decay. Exponential growth—of production, of profits, of costs, of population—is very rapid growth, as you will see. Conversely, exponential decay is very rapid decay. A typical example of exponential decay is the decline in the value of money in a period of high inflation.

Section 11.1 runs through the rules for exponents. These are things you learned in high school. If you have forgotten them, you can relearn them quickly.

Section 11.2 introduces the exponential function $y = f(x) = a^x$ where $a > 0$ and x can be any real number. Section 11.3 specializes this function to a particularly useful (and extensively tabulated) case, and gives real-world examples of exponential growth and decay.

Section 11.4 defines the logarithmic function, which is closely related to the exponential function. By using the logarithmic function, it is possible to find the exponential curve of best fit for appropriate data.

11.1 RULES FOR EXPONENTS

If a is a positive number and n is an integer, we have

$$a^n = \underbrace{a \cdot a \cdot \,\cdots\, \cdot a}_{n \text{ factors}}$$

The integer n is called the *exponent* of a^n, and the number a is called the *base*. In Section 11.2 we will study the function f defined by

$$f(x) = a^x$$

where the *base* a will be a constant and the *exponent* x an arbitrary real number. As a preliminary, let's go over the facts about a^x in three cases: when the exponent is a *positive integer*, a *negative integer* or *zero*, and a positive or negative *rational number* (that is, a *fraction*).

The positive integer case is familiar. We will just go over the rules.

RULES FOR POSITIVE INTEGRAL EXPONENTS

If a, b are nonzero real numbers and m, n are positive integers, then:

1. $a^m a^n = a^{m+n}$

2. $(ab)^n = a^n b^n$

3. $(a^m)^n = a^{mn}$

4. $\dfrac{a^m}{a^n} = \begin{cases} 1, & \text{if } m = n \\[2mm] a^{m-n}, & \text{if } m > n \\[2mm] \dfrac{1}{a^{n-m}}, & \text{if } n > m \end{cases}$

Let's take a closer look at rule 4. Suppose that we want to have

$$\frac{a^m}{a^n} = a^{m-n}$$

in all cases: that is, for $m \le n$ as well as $m > n$. This means, for example, that

$$\frac{a^5}{a^7} = a^{5-7} = a^{-2}$$

ought to make sense. It does, if a^{-2} means $\frac{1}{a^2}$. We will adopt that definition in general:

$$a^{-n} = \frac{1}{a^n} \qquad (a \neq 0)$$

for every positive integer n and every nonzero real constant a.

If we want rule 4 to work for the case $m = n$, we need

$$\frac{a^m}{a^m} = a^{m-m} = a^0 = 1$$

This gives a definition of a *zero exponent:*

$$a^0 = 1 \qquad (a \neq 0)$$

Now that negative and zero exponents have been defined, the four rules for positive integral exponents can be relabeled. They are really *rules for integral exponents*. That is, the exponents m, n in the rules can be any integers: positive, negative, or zero.

EXAMPLES: INTEGRAL EXPONENTS

1. $(7ab^2) \cdot (5a^3b^8) = (7 \cdot 5)(a \cdot a^3)(b^2 \cdot b^8) = 35a^4b^{10}$

2. $(-7xy)^3 = (-1)^3(7)^3x^3y^3 = -343x^3y^3$

3. $\dfrac{a^9b^{58}}{a^7b^{63}} = a^{9-7}b^{58-63} = a^2b^{-5}$

4. $(x^{-8}y^3)^{-2} = (x^{-8})^{-2}(y^3)^{-2} = x^{16}y^{-6}$

5. $11^0 = 1 \qquad\qquad (415)^0 = 1$

   $(-\pi)^0 = 1 \qquad\qquad (\sqrt{2})^0 = 1$

   0^0 is not defined

Rational (or fractional) exponents are defined in terms of nth roots. A precise definition of nth roots (ruling out various ambiguities) will be useful. If a and b are real numbers and n is a positive integer ($n > 1$), we will say that the equation

$$a^n = b$$

defines a as an nth root of b, written

$$a = \sqrt[n]{b}$$

REMARK: If b is a *positive* number, then $\sqrt[n]{b}$ means the positive nth root of b. For example, we define $\sqrt[4]{16}$ as the positive fourth root: $\sqrt[4]{16} = 2$. If n is an odd positive integer (3, 5, 7, etc.) and b is a *negative* number, then $\sqrt[n]{b}$ means the negative nth root of b. For example, we define $\sqrt[3]{-8}$ by $\sqrt[3]{-8} = -2$. Notice that the nth root of a negative number is not defined if n is even (2, 4, 6, etc.)

Now we can start defining rational exponents. The first, and simplest, definition is as follows: If n is a positive integer and a is a real number such that $\sqrt[n]{a}$ is a real number, then $a^{1/n}$ is defined by:

$$a^{1/n} = \sqrt[n]{a}$$

This means that $a^{1/n}$ is the real number whose nth power equals a:

$$(a^{1/n})^n = a$$

If we take the mth power (for some positive or negative integer m) of $a^{1/n}$, we have

$$(a^{1/n})^m = (\sqrt[n]{a})^m$$

And if we want the rules of exponents to hold for rational (or fractional) exponents, we will then define $a^{m/n}$ by:

$$a^{m/n} = (a^{1/n})^m = (\sqrt[n]{a})^m$$

To sum up, we have the following definition:

> **DEFINITION   Rational Exponents**
>
> If m and n are integers (with $n > 1$) and if a is a real number such that $\sqrt[n]{a}$ is a real number, then we define $a^{m/n} = (\sqrt[n]{a})^m$.

All the rules of exponents hold for rational as well as integral exponents. For example: Rule 3 on p. 494 generalizes to

$$(a^{m/n})^p = a^{mp/n}$$

with

$$(a^{m/n})^n = a^m$$

as a special case.

EXAMPLES: RATIONAL EXPONENTS

$$9^{1/2} = \sqrt{9} = 3$$

$$32^{1/5} = \sqrt[5]{32} = 2$$

$$27^{2/3} = (27^{1/3})^2 = (\sqrt[3]{27})^2 = 3^2 = 9$$

or

$$27^{2/3} = (27^2)^{1/3} = (729)^{1/3} = 9$$

The rules for exponents are often used in simplifying algebraic expressions.

PROBLEM   Simplify:

a. $(27x^{12})^{-4/3}$

b. $\left(\dfrac{x^5}{32y^{-125}}\right)^{1/5}$

SOLUTION   The rules for exponents lead to

a. $(27x^{12})^{-4/3} = ((27x^{12})^{1/3})^{-4}$

$$= (3x^4)^{-4}$$

$$= \dfrac{1}{81x^{16}}$$

b. $\left(\dfrac{x^5}{32y^{-125}}\right)^{1/5} = \dfrac{(x^5)^{1/5}}{(32y^{-125})^{1/5}}$

$$= \dfrac{x}{32^{1/5}y^{-125/5}}$$

$$= \dfrac{x}{2y^{-25}}$$

$$= \dfrac{xy^{25}}{2}$$

EXERCISES *for Section 11.1*

1.   Evaluate:

a. 4^2 b. 4^{-2} c. -4^2

d. $(-4)^2$ e. -4^{-2} f. $(-4)^{-2}$

2. Simplify:

a. $\dfrac{x^{11}}{x^7}$
b. $\dfrac{x^2y^3z^4}{x^7y^4z^2}$
c. $(xy^4)(x^5y)$

d. $\dfrac{(xy^3)^2(xy)^4}{(x^3y)^2(xy^2)^3}$

3. Simplify by removing the zero and negative exponents:

a. $3x^{-4}$
b. $(3x)^{-4}$
c. $3x^0$

d. $(3x)^0$
e. $\dfrac{x^{-1}}{y^{-1}}$
f. $\dfrac{y^{-1}}{x^{-1}}$

g. $(s^{-3})^{-4} + s^{-3}(s^4 + 2s^5 + 3s^6)$

4. Find the value of:

a. $16^{1/2}$
b. $16^{1/4}$
c. $16^{-1/2}$

d. $16^{3/4}$
e. $16^{-3/2}$
f. $16^{7/4}$

5. Use the rules for exponents in simplifying the following expressions. Assume that all variables are positive.

a. $x^{-2/3}x^{3/2}$
b. $\dfrac{a^{1/8}}{a^{3/4}}$

c. $7r^{-1}s^{-2}t^3$
d. $a^{6/7}a^{-7/6}a^{9/42}$

e. $(-x^{-8/3})^{-1/8}$
f. $\dfrac{(x^{2/3})^2(y^{1/2})^3}{(x^{2/3})^3(y^{3/8})^4}$

g. $(x^{-9}y^{5/4}z^{7/3})^{-1/7}$
h. $\left(\dfrac{x^{-9}y^{5/4}z^{7/3}}{x^{-2}y^0z^{-1}}\right)^{-1/7}$

i. $\left(\dfrac{r^{-4}s^{-2/3}t^{-4/3}}{r^{2/3}s^{-7/3}t^{-1/3}}\right)^{-3}$

11.2

THE EXPONENTIAL FUNCTION

Irrational numbers cannot be expressed as fractions, but they can be *approximated* as fractions (as decimals). Irrational exponents are handled in the same way. Just as $\sqrt{3}$ is approximated (to 3 figures) by 1.73, $2^{\sqrt{3}}$ is approximated by $2^{1.73}$. If a better approximation is wanted, more figures are used. With this in mind, we can define a^x for all positive a and all *real* x—rational or irrational. The result is known as the *exponential function*.

DEFINITION   Exponential Function

If a is a positive constant and x is any real number, then the function f defined by

$$f(x) = a^x$$

is the *exponential function* with *base a* and *exponent x*.

The best way to understand the exponential function is to draw some graphs. We start with:

PROBLEM 1   Graph $y = 2^x$.

SOLUTION   The y values corresponding to $x = 0, 1, 2, \ldots, 10$ are given by:

x	0	1	2	3	4	5	6	7	8	9	10
y	1	2	4	8	16	32	64	128	256	512	1024

By graphing these points on the axes shown in Figure 11.1 and then joining them with a smooth curve, we have (we think) graphed $y = 2^x$ for $0 \le x \le 10$. To check this out, let's look at a few intermediate points, as given by the following table:

x	2.5	4.5	6.5	8.5	9.5
y	5.66	22.6	90.5	362	724

(The calculations use $\sqrt{2} = 1.41$, as in $2^{4.5} = 2^4 \cdot 2^{.5} = (16)(1.41) = 22.6$, approximately.) The intermediate points lie on the smooth curve of Figure 11.1. As a final check, we give x some irrational values, and we find that the corresponding values of $y = 2^x$ are given by

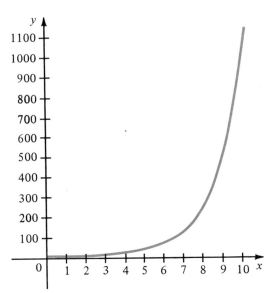

FIGURE 11.1 Graph of $y = 2^x$, $0 \leq x \leq 10$

x	$\sqrt{3}$	$\sqrt{47}$	$\sqrt{48}$	$\sqrt{50}$
y	3.32	116	122	134

In the calculations we used three-figure approximations for the irrational x-values. The corresponding y-values are also three-figure approximations. All of the calculated points agree with the smooth curve given in Figure 11.1. (*REMARK:* For a close-up view of the agreement, compare the values of 2^x for $x = \sqrt{47}$, $\sqrt{48}$, and $\sqrt{50}$ with the value 128 for $x = 7$.)

Looking at the evidence, we have to believe that the values of $y = 2^x$ corresponding to any and all x-values in $0 \leq x \leq 10$ will lie on the graph in Figure 11.1. *The smooth curve through points corresponding to integral values of x accurately represents the function* $f(x) = 2^x$. We will assume that the pattern continues for $x > 10$ and for $x < 0$.

If $x > 10$, the graph of range values 2^x corresponding to integer domain values shows a sharp rise: $2^{11} = 2048$, $2^{12} = 4096$, $2^{13} = 8192$, and so on. The smooth curve joining the points $(x, 2^x)$ keeps getting steeper as x increases.

To graph $y = 2^x$ for $x < 0$, we calculate the y-values corresponding to the negative integers $x = -1, -2, \ldots, -10$. The two-figure results are as follows:

x	-1	-2	-3	-4	-5	-6	-7	-8	-9	-10
y	0.50	0.25	0.13	0.06	0.03	0.02	0.01	0.00	0.00	0.00

Figure 11.2 shows a smooth curve through these points.

The difference in scale between Figures 11.1 and 11.2 is noticeable. Figure 11.2 (and the table on which it is based) show $y = 0$ from $x = -8$ leftward. This is nothing but a two-figure approximation to the truth. More accurate calculations show that $2^{-8} = 0.0039062$, $2^{-9} = 0.0019531$, $2^{-10} = 0.0009765$, and so on. As x moves further and further to the left, 2^x gets smaller and smaller. For example: $2^{-20} = 0.0000009$. But 2^x is never equal to zero. In the language of Section 10.5, $y = 0$ is an *asymptote* of the graph of $y = 2^x$.

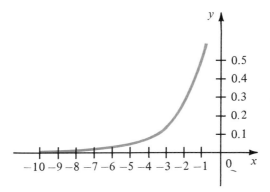

FIGURE 11.2   Graph of $y = 2^x$, $-10 \le x \le -1$

Now we can graph $y = 2^x$. It is done by combining the information in Figures 11.1 and 11.2. The result is shown in Figure 11.3. Notice that the x- and y-axes are drawn to the same scale in Figure 11.3. (By contrast, Figure 11.1 has a stretched-out x-axis and Figure 11.2 has a stretched-out y-axis.)

To summarize: Figure 11.3 shows that the graph of $y = 2^x$ increases rapidly as x increases through positive values, and decreases rapidly as x decreases through negative values. We have:

$$y \to +\infty \quad \text{as} \quad x \to +\infty$$

$$y \to 0+ \quad \text{as} \quad x \to -\infty$$

The line $y = 0$ is an asymptote.

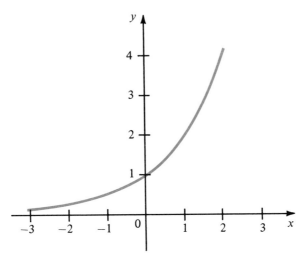

FIGURE 11.3 Graph of $y = 2^x$

The exponential curve in Figure 11.3 is a typical graph of $y = a^x$ when the base $a > 1$. Any such graph passes through the point $(0, 1)$, rises rapidly as x moves to the right, and falls rapidly toward its asymptote $y = 0$ as x moves to the left. The rise and fall are sharper as the base a increases, and more gradual as a decreases toward 1. Figure 11.4 illustrates this behavior.

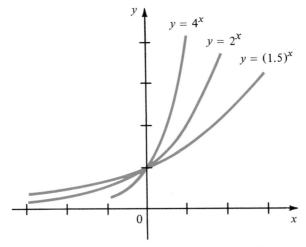

FIGURE 11.4 Graphs of $y = 1.5^x$, $y = 2^x$, $y = 4^x$

If $a = 1$, the exponential function $f(x) = a^x$ reduces to the constant function $f(x) = 1$. The case $a = 1$ is of no interest in itself, but it marks a dividing line. Exponential curves for $a < 1$ are quite different from the curves in Figure 11.4. The next problem gives an example.

PROBLEM 2   Graph $y = (\frac{1}{2})^x$.

SOLUTION   By the rules of exponents,

$$(\tfrac{1}{2})^x = 2^{-x}$$

The values of $(\frac{1}{2})^x$ at $x = 0, \pm 1, \pm 2, \pm 3, \ldots$, are therefore the same as the values of 2^x at $x = 0, \mp 1, \mp 2, \mp 3, \ldots$. We form a table:

x	-3	-2	-1	0	1	2	3
y	8	4	2	1	0.50	0.25	0.125

Graphing these points and joining them by a smooth curve, we have the exponential curve expressed by the solid line in Figure 11.5. The dashed line shows the graph of $y = 2^x$. Notice that the two graphs are reflections of one another in the positive y-axis.

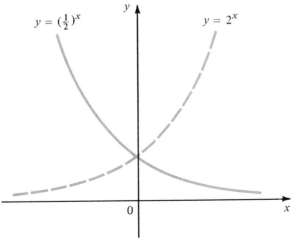

FIGURE 11.5   Graphs of $y = \frac{1}{2}^x$ (Solid Line) and $y = 2^x$ (Dashed Line)

The graph of $y = (\frac{1}{2})^x$ is typical of graphs of exponential functions $f(x) = a^x$ with base $a < 1$. Any such graph shows a rapid decrease as x increases. The curve always passes through the point $(0, 1)$ and always has $y = 0$ as an asymptote. Symbolically:

$$y \to +\infty \quad \text{as} \quad x \to -\infty$$

$$y \to 0+ \quad \text{as} \quad x \to +\infty$$

EXERCISES *for Section 11.2*

Each of the following points lies on the graph of an exponential function. Find the base a of the exponential function in each case.

1. $(2, 64)$ **2.** $(5, 243)$

3. $(3, 3.375)$ **4.** $(0, 1)$

5. $(-2, \frac{1}{16})$ **6.** $(-3, 0.008)$

Graph each of the following functions. In each case, state the domain and range of the function *and* the domain and range shown in your graph.

7. $y = 3^x$ **8.** $y = (\frac{1}{3})^x$

9. $y = 3^{-2x}$ **10.** $y = (1.5)^x$

11. $y = 2 \cdot 3^x$ **12.** $y = 2^x + 2^{-x}$

13. $y = 2^x - 2^{-x}$ **14.** $y = 2^{x-1}$

15. $y = \frac{1}{2}(2^x - 2^{-x})$ **16.** $y = 3^x - 2^x$

17. Exercise 11 asked you to graph $y = 2 \cdot 3^x$. What is the general shape of the graph of $y = ba^x$ when $b > 0$ and $a > 1$? when $b > 0$ and $0 < a < 1$?

18. What is the general shape of the graph of $y = ba^x$ when $b < 0$ and $a > 1$? when $b < 0$ and $0 < a < 1$? Give numerical examples for each of the two cases.

11.3

THE IRRATIONAL NUMBER *e*; EXPONENTIAL MODELS OF GROWTH AND DECAY

In many real-world applications of exponential functions, the number that is used as a base is an irrational number called *e*. There are practical reasons for choosing *e* as a base, one of which will be explained after we have drawn a graph of e^x. Meanwhile, note that the number *e* is approximately equal to 2.718. Since $e > 2$, the values of e^x rise and fall more sharply than those of 2^x. Here is a short comparative table:

x	-3	-2	-1	0	1	2	3
e^x	0.050	0.135	0.368	1	2.718	7.389	20.09
2^x	0.125	0.250	0.500	1	2	4	8

In Figure 11.6, $y = e^x$ and $y = 2^x$ are graphed on the same set of axes.

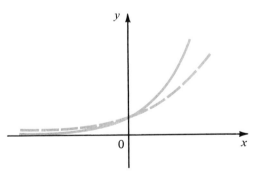

FIGURE 11.6 Graphs of $y = e^x$ (Solid Line) and $y = 2^x$ (Dashed Line)

To understand why the base *e* is so useful, you need to know that exponential curves are used as models for *growth*. As an example, look at Figure 11.7, which is a redrawn version of Figure 10.1 (the graph describing year-to-year changes in the U.S. GNP) with the addition of a superimposed *exponential growth curve* that has been fitted to the data. (Section 11.4 explains how exponential curves are fitted to data.)

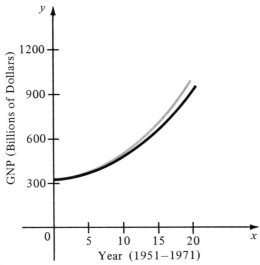

FIGURE 11.7   GNP (Gross National Product) of the United States, 1951–1971. The black line shows the exponential growth curve that has been fitted to the data.

If we are studying growth, we want to know the *rate of growth*. Notice, for example, that U.S. Commerce Department economists issue monthly figures on the rate of growth of GNP, the rate of increase in wholesale prices, etc. Sometimes the rate of growth is negative—GNP, prices, or any other quantity may fall rather than rise. Negative growth is usually referred to as *decay*.

There is a geometric method for calculating rates of growth or decay. Look at Figure 11.8. The dashed line PQ_1 is called a *secant* to the curve. (By definition, a secant intersects a curve at two points.) The dashed line PQ_2 is a second secant. Now imagine points Q_3, Q_4, etc., on the curve, closer and closer to P. Also imagine that secants PQ_3, PQ_4, etc., have been drawn. Then those imagined secants would come closer and closer to the solid color line in the figure. That color line, whose position represents a limiting position of secants through PQ_1, PQ_2, PQ_3, PQ_4, etc., is called the *tangent to the curve at P*.

The significance of the tangent is this: *The slope of the tangent to a curve at a point P gives the rate of increase (or decrease) of the curve at that point.*

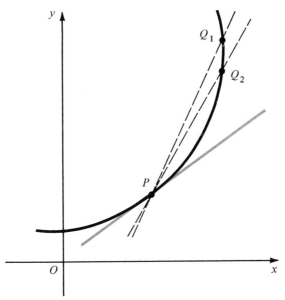

FIGURE 11.8 Tangent (Color) to a Curve at a Point P. The dashed lines PQ_1 and PQ_2 are secants.

The usefulness of the base e comes in right here. The slope of the tangent to $y = e^x$ at the point $x = c$ is precisely e^c. Therefore, the rate of increase (if $c > 0$) or decrease (if $c < 0$) of the exponential function with base e is known at once.

We will use the term *slope of* $y = e^x$ to refer to the slope of the tangent to $y = e^x$. Remember: Each time we refer to the slope of $y = e^x$, we are talking about the rate of increase or decrease of the exponential function with base e.

EXAMPLES: SLOPE OF $y = e^x$

1. The slope of $y = e^x$ at $x = 3$ is e^3.

2. The slope of $y = e^x$ at $x = -1$ is e^{-1}.

3. Every exponential curve $y = a^x$ $(a > 0)$ passes through the point $(0, 1)$. Of all these curves, the only one that passes through $(0, 1)$ with slope 1 is the curve $y = e^x$. (The slope of $y = e^x$ at $x = 0$ is $e^0 = 1$.)

In applications, the exponential curve that fits the data may have the form $y = e^{bx}$, where b is a positive or negative real number. Since $e^{bx} = (e^x)^b$, the curve $y = e^{bx}$ rises or falls $|b|$ times as fast as $y = e^x$. [*NOTE:* A positive

b multiplies the rate of increase by $|b|$, and a negative b multiplies the rate of decrease by $|b|$. The rate of increase (or decrease) is faster if $|b| > 1$ and slower if $|b| < 1$.] *The slope of* $y = e^{bx}$ *at the point* $x = c$ *is* be^{bc}. Notice that b occurs twice in be^{bc}.

EXAMPLES: SLOPE OF $y = e^{bx}$

1. The slope of $y = e^{2x}$ at $x = \sqrt{2}$ is $2e^{2\sqrt{2}}$

2. The slope of $y = e^{-3x}$ at $x = 4$ is $-3e^{(-3)(4)} = -3e^{-12}$

3. The exponential curve $y = e^{bx}$ is the only exponential curve that passes through $(0, 1)$ with slope b.

To sum up: If you know where you are on an exponential curve $y = e^x$ (or $y = e^{bx}$), then you also know the slope of the curve and therefore (by definition) the rate of increase or decrease. If the curve represents real-world growth or decay, then you know the rate of growth or rate of decay at any point on the curve.

EXAMPLE 1: AN EXPONENTIAL PRICE GROWTH CURVE

Prices of new single-family houses have gone up substantially in the past decade. In some areas of the U.S., the rise has been a steady 10% per year. In Center Durham, New Hampshire, the price rise has followed the formula

$$y = 27 + 0.0025e^x$$

where y = average price of a new single-family house, in thousands of dollars

x = year

In year 0 (1968), the average price was

$$y = 27 + 0.0025e^0 = 27.0025$$

or $27,002.50. In year 1 (1969), the average price was

$$y = 27 + 0.0025e$$
$$= 27 + (0.0025)(2.71828)$$
$$= 27.0068$$

or $27,006.80. Values of e^x, $0.0025e^x$, and $y = 27 + 0.0025e^x$ for years 0, 1, 2, ..., 10 are listed in Table 11.1.

TABLE 11.1

x (Year)	e^x	$0.0025e^x$	y (Price)
0	1	0.0025	27.0025
1	2.71828	0.0068	27.0068
2	7.38906	0.0185	27.0185
3	20.0855	0.0502	27.0502
4	54.5982	0.1365	27.1365
5	148.412	0.3710	27.3710
6	403.429	1.0086	28.0086
7	1096.63	2.7416	29.7416
8	2980.96	7.4524	34.4524
9	8103.08	20.2577	47.2577
10	22026.5	55.0663	82.0663

The tabulated values are graphed in Figure 11.9. As both the table and the graph show, prices were relatively steady for five years. Then the increases began: $636.60 in 1974, $1733.30 in 1975, $4710.80 in 1976, and far larger amounts in 1977 and 1978.

Price stability over a five-year period had masked an exponential growth process. The results were not startling until year 8 (1976), but from then on prices went up explosively. This is what exponential growth is like.

Mathematically, we can talk about what happened in terms of *rates of growth.* Since the price formula is

$$y = 27 + 0.0025e^x$$

the basic rate of growth is that of e^x. We know that the rate of increase of e^x is $e^1 = e = 2.71828$ in year 1, $e^2 = 7.38906$ in year 2, etc. But e^x is multiplied by 0.0025, and that small number masks the exponential increase. The observed rates of growth for the first five years are:

$$0.0025e = 0.0068 \text{ in year } 1$$
$$0.0025e^2 = 0.0185 \text{ in year } 2$$
$$0.0025e^3 = 0.0502 \text{ in year } 3$$
$$0.0025e^4 = 0.1365 \text{ in year } 4$$
$$0.0025e^5 = 0.3710 \text{ in year } 5$$

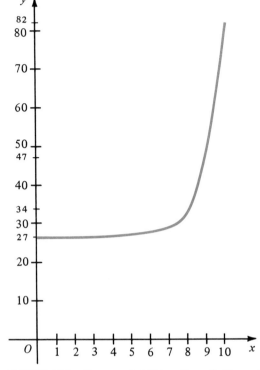

FIGURE 11.9 Exponential Price Growth Curve for Example 1

These figures show what the curve in Figure 11.9 shows: the rate of increase was slow for five years. The upturn began in year 6, and continued at an accelerated pace for the rest of the decade. For years 8, 9, and 10, the results were

$$0.0025e^8 = 7.4524 \text{ in year 8}$$

$$0.0025e^9 = 20.2577 \text{ in year 9}$$

$$0.0025e^{10} = 55.0663 \text{ in year 10}$$

In real-world terms, these increased rates of growth meant dramatic year-to-year price increases. If the pattern had continued, the average price of a new single-family house in Center Durham in 1979 would have been

$$y = 27 + 0.0025e^{11} = 176.68535$$

or $176,685.35.

REMARK: Prices did not climb that high. People in Center Durham simply did not have the money. This is typical. Unless there is runaway inflation, an exponential price growth curve like the one in Figure 11.9 cannot go on indefinitely.

Example 1 suggests that the Center Durham house that was bought for $27,002.50 in 1968 would sell for much more in 1978—not as much as $82,066.30 perhaps, but a lot more than the original cost. This is true. Local real estate agents say that the 1968 house is pulled up in value by the rising prices of comparable new houses. The $27,000 house of 1968 sold for about $74,000 in 1978. That $47,000 jump looks like a good profit. Of course it is not. Thanks to inflation, the 1978 selling price of $74,000 had about the same purchasing power as $27,000 in 1968. The purchasing power of the dollar dropped, or decayed, that much in 10 years. Example 2 gives the details.

EXAMPLE 2: EXPONENTIAL DECAY (PURCHASING POWER OF THE DOLLAR)

Everyone knows that the 1968 dollar bought more food, housing, transportation, and medical care than the 1978 dollar. These changes in the purchasing power of the dollar have been recorded month by month in publications of the U.S. Commerce Department.* Of course, these statistics are nationwide averages. For Center Durham, New Hampshire, the value of the dollar from 1968 to 1978 was given by

$$y = -0.938 + 1.938e^{-0.04x}$$

where y = value of the dollar, measured in 1968 dollars
$\quad x$ = year (0 = 1968, 1 = 1969, . . . , 10 = 1978)

The formula shows that the year 0 (1968) value of the dollar is

$$y = -0.938 + 1.938e^0 = -0.938 + 1.938 = 1$$

or $1.00, as it should be when we are measuring in 1968 dollars. In year 1 (1969), the value is

$$y = -0.938 + 1.938e^{-0.04} = -0.938 + 1.938(0.96079) = 0.924$$

or $.924. (The figure is carried to three places, to ensure accuracy in two-place calculations.) This says (accurately) that the goods and services bought for $1 in 1969 would have cost only 92.4 cents in 1968.

Table 11.2 gives the values of $e^{-0.04x}$, $1.938e^{-0.04x}$, and $y = -0.938 + 1.938e^{-0.04x}$ corresponding to $x = 0, 1, 2, \ldots, 10$. (*NOTE:* All the numbers in the table, including the various values of $e^{-0.04x}$, were calculated

---

*The yearly publication *Statistical Abstract of the United States* gives annual data, and historical summaries, for purchasing power and more than 1300 other quantities of interest to the U.S. business community, to economists, and to many social scientists.

TABLE 11.2

x (Year)	$e^{-0.04x}$	$1.938e^{-0.04x}$	y (Value of Dollar)
0	1	1.938	$1.000
1	0.96079	1.862	0.924
2	0.92312	1.789	0.851
3	0.88692	1.724	0.786
4	0.85214	1.651	0.713
5	0.81873	1.587	0.649
6	0.78663	1.522	0.584
7	0.75578	1.465	0.527
8	0.72615	1.407	0.469
9	0.69768	1.352	0.414
10	0.67032	1.299	0.361

on a hand-held calculator. The exercises at the end of this section will not require the use of such a calculator.)

The values of x and y shown in the table are graphed in Figure 11.10. (The solid-line curve passes through the tabulated values.) At a glance, the

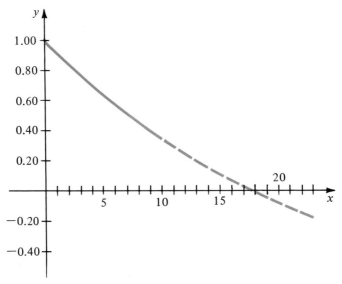

FIGURE 11.10 Graph for Example 2

curve may look like a straight line, but it is not. A straight line joining the endpoints (0, 1.000) and (10, 0.361) of our curve would be *above* the curve at $x = 1, 2, \ldots, 9$. To make the shape of the exponential decay curve more apparent, $y = -0.938 + 1.938e^{-0.04x}$ has been calculated for $x = 11, 12, \ldots, 23$ and the curve has been extended through these points. (See the dashed line in Figure 11.10.) Values of real-world dollars will *not* follow the dashed-line curve—not beyond $x = 18$, anyway.

The erosion in the value of the dollar shown by the solid-line curve was steady and also devastating. An average young family in Center Durham in 1968 lived moderately well on a $10,000 income. But the same $10,000 income did not go very far in 1978. It bought only as much as $3610 did in 1968. The average young family of 1978 needed an income of $27,700.83 to buy the goods and services that $10,000 bought in 1968. Two-income families often had that many dollars of income, but most other young families did not.

As another illustration, let's return to the Center Durham house bought for $27,000 in 1968 and sold for $74,000 in 1978. Let's suppose that the same realtor handled both sales. The commission was 6% both times. That gave the realtor $1620 in 1968 and $4440 in 1978. To find the purchasing power of the second commission in 1968 dollars, multiply by 0.361. This gives $(4440)(0.361) = \$1602.84$. The realtor keeps up with inflation (as many people do not) but certainly does not gain by it.

For a mathematical insight, look at the slope of the exponential decay curve. The slope (always negative, after $x = 0$) represents a *rate of decay*. Since

$$y = -0.938 + 1.938e^{-0.04x}$$

the basic rate of decay is that of $e^{-0.04x}$. As we saw on p. 508, the slope of e^{bx} at $x = c$ is be^{bc}. In the case of $e^{-0.04x}$, the slope (or rate of decay) at $x = c$ is $(-0.04)(e^{-0.04c})$. The rate is

$$-0.04e^{-0.04} = -0.0384 \text{ in year 1 (1969)}$$

$$-0.04e^{-0.08} = -0.0369 \text{ in year 2 (1970)}$$

and so on down to

$$-0.04e^{-0.4} = -0.0268 \text{ in year 10 (1978)}$$

In the formula, these numbers are multiplied by 1.938 to give

$$(1.938)(-0.0384) = -0.074$$

$$(1.938)(-0.0369) = -0.072$$

and so on to

$$(1.938)(-0.0290) = -0.056$$

$$(1.938)(-0.0279) = -0.054$$

$$(1.938)(-0.0268) = -0.052$$

The decreasing rate of decay shows that the value of the dollar went down less rapidly each year of the 1968–78 decade. These figures were observed in Center Durham. National trends were similar.

EXERCISES *for Section 11.3*

Graph the following functions. (Use Appendix Table 4.)

1. $y = e^{-0.2x}$ **2.** $y = e^{-0.3x}$

3. $y = 0.05e^{-0.2x}$ **4.** $y = e^{-x^2}$

5. $y = xe^x$ **6.** $y = xe^{-x}$

7. $y = x^2e^{-x^2}$

For each of the following functions: Sketch the graph; discuss the function's growth and decay; locate the asymptotes of the function.

8. $y = 10(1 - e^{-x})$ **9.** $y = 20(1 - e^{-0.2x})$

10. $y = 12 - 15e^{-0.2x}$ **11.** $y = 600(1 + e^{-0.7x})$

12. $y = 600 + 800e^{-0.7x}$ **13.** $y = 100 - 100(e^{5-3x})$

14. $y = 100 - 150(e^{5-3x})$ **15.** $y = 40 - 40(e^{7-0.07x})$

---

16. Wizz! Wizz! Janitorial Service took a little time to get on its feet, but it is now a well-established business with many regular customers. The history of Wizz! Wizz! over the past 10 years can be summarized by the equation

$$y = 67{,}542(1 - e^{-0.1x})$$

where y = annual profit
        x = year (1, 2, ..., 10)

Find the values of y corresponding to $x = 1$, $x = 2$, ..., $x = 10$. Is the rate of growth increasing or decreasing? Does the curve have an asymptote? If it does, what is it?

17. Calder Motor Corporation's new subcompact car is called the Coyote. A big TV campaign led to a healthy demand for the Coyote. If y = monthly demand for Coyote cars and x = number of months the TV campaign continued, then the function

$$y = 86{,}954 - 71{,}329e^{-0.2x}$$

describes what happened. To see what this demand curve looks like, calculate y after $0, 1, 2, \ldots, 11$ months, and sketch a graph. Does the curve have an asymptote? Would you expect the behavior shown by the curve to continue?

18. Sally Hansen has just received her license as a real estate broker. Since she is capable, good at talking to people, and good at managing people, she figures that she will earn

$$y = 240{,}000(e^{0.15x} - 1)$$

dollars in the next x years of her life. (This is total income, not annual income.) How much is this in money? That is: If she is right, how much will she have earned after 2 years, after 4 years, after 8 years, after 10 years, and after 20 years?

Midwest Microelectronics has a testing program to assign new employees to suitable jobs. Under this program, both assembly workers and service technicians need high test scores in manual dexterity and dependability, but they must have different psychological profiles. A recent error in recording test results is causing some difficulties. One of the company's assembly plants has been staffed with employees who are *not* psychologically suited for assembly work. After going through the company's training program, one of these employees will turn out 100 acceptable units of work a day. At first. After 6 weeks on the job, the employee will be turning out only about 50 acceptable units of work a day. (The employee cannot adjust to the sameness of the job. If the test scores had been properly recorded, such an employee would have been given a job with more variety—service or mainte-nance.) The loss in worker productivity is described by the function

$$y = -87.6 + 187.6e^{-0.05x}$$

where y = number of acceptable units per day turned out by the worker

x = number of weeks since worker's training was complete

19. Find the values of y corresponding to $x = 0$, $x = 4$, $x = 6$, $x = 8$, and $x = 10$.

20. Graph your results. Extend the graph by calculating further points. Interpret the results.

THE LOGARITHMIC FUNCTION

The exponential function f defined by

$$f(x) = y = a^x \qquad (a > 0, a \neq 1)$$

includes all real numbers in its *domain* and all positive real numbers in its *range*. If c is a positive real number, this means that

$$a^x = c$$

for *some* value of x. To find out *which* x makes $a^x = c$, we graph $y = a^x$ and $y = c$ on the same set of axes (Figure 11.11). This locates a point (b, c) such that $a^b = c$.

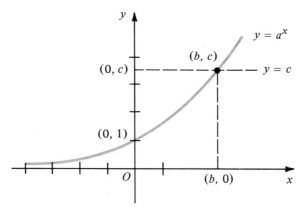

FIGURE 11.11 Locating the Point (b, c) such that $a^b = c$

An equation like $a^x = c$, in which the unknown variable x appears as an exponential, is called an *exponential equation*. The construction using Figure 11.11 shows that we can always solve such an equation—provided that $a > 0$, $a \neq 1$, and $c > 0$. The main fact to notice is that the line $y = c$ will intersect the curve $y = a^x$ in one and only one point: (b, c). In other words:

> If $c > 0$, there is one and only one real number b such that
>
> $$a^b = c$$
>
> The number b is called the *logarithm of c to the base a*. This is written
>
> $$\log_a c = b$$

Logarithms to the base a are defined for every $a > 0$ except $a = 1$. In each case the statement $\log_a c = b$ means exactly the same thing as $a^b = c$.

EXAMPLES: CALCULATING LOGARITHMS

1. $\log_2 8$. We know that $8 = 2^3$. Therefore, $\log_2 8 = 3$.

2. $\log_2 \sqrt[3]{4}$. If we write $\sqrt[3]{4} = 2^{2/3}$, we see that $\log_2 \sqrt[3]{4} = \frac{2}{3}$.

3. $\log_2 2.630757$. Using a calculator, we find that $2^{1.395478} = 2.630757$. Therefore, $\log_2 2.630757 = 1.395478$.

4. $\log_\pi 3836.661$. The base is the irrational number π, which we approximate by 3.1415927. Using a calculator, we find that $\pi^{7.209} = 3836.661$. This leads us to ask for $\log_\pi 3836.661$. The answer, of course, is 7.209.

5. $\log_{10} 6.57$. There are tables of logarithms to the base 10. (Since the base 10 is also the base of our commonly used decimal system, these logarithms are called *common logarithms.*) Using Appendix Table 2, we can find that $\log_{10} 6.57 = 0.8176$. In exponential notation, this means that $10^{0.8176} = 6.57$.

6. $\log_{10} 6570$. From the last example, we know that $10^{0.8176} = 6.57$. We also know that $6570 = (6.57)(1000)$, which can also be written as $6570 = (6.57)(10^3)$. By the rules for exponents,

$$6570 = (10^{0.8176})(10^3) = 10^{3.8176}$$

Therefore, $\log_{10} 6570 = 3.8176$.

7. $\log_e 1.43$. The base is the irrational number e. For certain theoretical reasons, the base e is the most natural and efficient base for logarithms. Such logarithms are therefore called *natural logarithms,* and they are extensively tabulated. Using Appendix Table 3, we can find that $\log_e 1.43 = 0.35767$. Notice that the table gives natural logarithms only for numbers from 1.00 to 9.99. The table can also be used to find the natural logarithm of any other positive number. The instructions at the beginning of the table tell you how it is done.

NOTE: Logarithms to the base 10, or common logarithms, are usually denoted "log" without mention of the base. If, for example, you see the equation $\log 3.64 = 0.5611$, you know that the logarithm is a logarithm to the base 10. Similarly, logarithms to the base e, or natural logarithms, are usually denoted "ln." For example: $\ln e = 1$, $\ln e^2 = 2$, $\ln 1.43 = 0.35767$.

We have now seen that the equation

$$y = a^x \qquad (a > 0, a \neq 1)$$

is equivalent to

$$x = \log_a y$$

The second equation defines x as a function of y. The function is called the *logarithmic function*. Its domain consists of all positive real numbers and its range consists of all real numbers. If we want a graph, we simply look at a graph of $y = a^x$ and remember that y is now the independent variable and x the dependent variable. To put things in the more usual way, we simply switch variables and axes. This is done in the following definition, and in Figure 11.12.

DEFINITION Logarithmic Function

The function f defined by

$$f(x) = y = \log_a x$$

is called the *logarithmic function with base a*. The variables x and y are related by

$$x = a^y \qquad (a > 0, a \neq 1)$$

The domain of the logarithmic function includes all positive real numbers x, and its range includes all real numbers y.

To graph the logarithmic function, we simply interchange the x- and y-axes in the graph of $y = a^x$. (In geometric terms, we *reflect* $y = a^x$ across the line $y = x$.) The result is shown in Figure 11.12.

The graph shows that

$$y \to +\infty \quad \text{as} \quad x \to +\infty$$

$$y \to -\infty \quad \text{as} \quad x \to 0+$$

In other words: The logarithmic function increases indefinitely as x increases indefinitely. (But the rate of increase is very slow.) And the logarithmic function decreases indefinitely as x approaches 0 through positive values. (The rate of decrease is rapid, as x comes close to 0.) The negative y-axis is an asymptote of the graph of the logarithmic function.

We give two applications of the logarithmic function. In the first, a real-world problem leads to an exponential equation that is then solved by the use of logarithms. In the second application, logarithms are used to fit an exponential curve to given data.

REMARK: Logarithms were invented as an aid to calculation. We omit this application, since anyone who does much calculating nowadays will use a

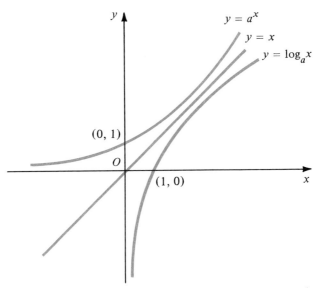

$y = a^x$

$y = x$

$y = \log_a x$

$(0, 1)$

O

$(1, 0)$

x

FIGURE 11.12 Graph of $y = \log_a x$, shown as the reflection of $y = a^x$ in the line $y = x$

hand-held calculator. But we do need to know the following rules for working with logarithms to the base a.

RULES FOR LOGARITHMS

1. $\log_a (x_1 x_2) = \log_a x_1 + \log_a x_2$

2. $\log_a (x_1/x_2) = \log_a x_1 - \log_a x_2$

3. $\log_a x^k = k \log_a x$

In these rules, x_1, x_2, and x are understood to be positive real numbers, k can be any real number, and the base a can be any positive real number except 1. To see where the rules come from, we use the basic fact that

$$\log_a x = y$$

means exactly the same thing as the exponential equation

$$x = a^y$$

With this in mind, look at rule 1. Write

$$\log_a x_1 = y_1 \qquad \log_a x_2 = y_2$$

The corresponding exponential equations are

$$x_1 = a^{y_1} \qquad x_2 = a^{y_2}$$

Therefore

$$x_1 x_2 = (a^{y_1})(a^{y_2}) = a^{y_1 + y_2}$$

and

$$\log_a (x_1 x_2) = \log_a (a^{y_1 + y_2}) = y_1 + y_2 = \log_a x_1 + \log_a x_2$$

So much for rule 1. Rules 2 and 3 also correspond to exponential equations.

In calculations, we will use $a = 10$ or $a = e$. That is, we will use logarithms to the base 10 ("common logarithms") or logarithms to the base e ("natural logarithms"). As noted on p. 517, common logarithms are denoted "log" without mention of the base, and natural logarithms are denoted "ln." In the examples that follow, values of common logarithms are taken from Table 2 (p. 563) and values of natural logarithms are taken from Table 3 (p. 565).

PROBLEM 1 Before it could locate its oil refinery in southeastern Maine, Wyotex had to file an environmental impact statement. The statement spelled out the amount of damage the refinery would do to air quality (not much, thanks to technology invented by Wyotex chemical engineers), and the building permit went through without trouble. Now Wyotex wants to expand its refinery. Studies by company engineers show that the planned expansion will lead to a 4% annual deterioration in southeastern Maine's air quality. (After the expansion stops, air quality will not deteriorate further.) On this basis, Wyotex has approval for its expansion so long as air quality deterioration does not exceed 50%.

Since a half-billion dollar investment is at risk, Wyotex management wants to look at this one very closely. Expanding according to plan will take eight more years. If this has to be cut short, the expansion will not pay off. Management therefore asks: How many years do we have?

SOLUTION If the pre-expansion air pollution index in southeastern Maine is 100, Wyotex has the go-ahead to keep expanding so long as the air pollution index does not go over 150.

The first year of expansion adds 4% to the index, giving a total of $100(1.04)$. The second year multiplies that number by 1.04 again, giving a total of $(100)(1.04)^2$, and so on. After x years of expansion, the air pollution index will be $(100)(1.04)^x$. To find out how many years of expansion will be permitted, we set

$$(100)(1.04)^x = 150$$

and solve for x. The one and only way to do this is to take logarithms of both sides of the equation. By using rules 1 and 3 for logarithms, we have

$$\log 100 + x \log (1.04) = \log 150$$

or

$$2 + 0.017x = 2.1761$$

(Notice that $100 = 10^2$, or $\log 100 = 2$. Also, $150 = (100)(1.5)$, which gives $\log 150 = \log 100 + \log 1.5 = 2 + 0.1761$.) Therefore

$$0.017x = 0.1761$$

or

$$x = 10.36$$

This shows that Wyotex has plenty of time for its planned eight-year expansion program.

NOTE: If we want to use natural logarithms to solve the exponential equation, we have

$$\ln 100 + x \ln(1.04) = \ln 150$$

or

$$4.60517 + x(.03922) = 5.01064$$

(Notice that we followed the instructions at the beginning of Appendix Table 3 in computing $\ln 100$ and $\ln 150$.) This leads to

$$0.03922x = 0.40547$$

or

$$x = 10.338348$$

This is more accurate than $x = 10.36$. (The reason is that Table 3 shows five places while Table 2 shows only four places.) The added accuracy is irrelevant in Problem 1 but might be helpful in another problem. If we really need accuracy, we can use a hand-held calculator, which gives us the equivalent of an eight-place table for $\log x$ (or $\ln x$). In the case of Problem 1, using the calculator leads to the solution $x = 10.338036$, which checks out to eight figures. That is: $(1.04)^{10.338036} = 1.5$, to eight figures. (The ninth figure is not 0.)

Problem 2 shows how to fit an exponential curve of the form

$$y = Ae^{Bx}$$

to given data. Notice that there are two questions to be answered, in any such use of an exponential curve to approximate data:

1. Is it *reasonable* to make such an approximation?

2. If it is, what values do we want for A and B?

Question 1 is answered in part 1 of the solution, and question 2 in part 2.

PROBLEM 2 Can the functional relationship expressed by the table

x	1	2	3	4	5	6	7	8
y	11.8	15.9	21.3	28.5	38.2	51.1	68.4	91.7

be approximated by an exponential function $y = Ae^{Bx}$? If so, what values would you assign to A and B?

SOLUTION

PART 1: If we assume that $y = Ae^{Bx}$ and take natural logarithms, we have

$$\ln y = \ln A + Bx$$

or (with $y' = \ln y$, $A' = \ln A$):

$$y' = A' + Bx$$

This shows that we must find values of $y' = \ln y$ corresponding to the values of y in the table. Then we must see if the points (x, y') appear to lie on a line. If they do, we can use the method of averages to find good values for A' and B.

The values of $y' = \ln y$ corresponding to $x = 1, 2, \ldots, 8$ are listed in the following table:

x	1	2	3	4	5	6	7	8
y'	2.47	2.77	3.06	3.35	3.64	3.93	4.23	4.52

Graphing the points will show if they appear to lie on a line. There is a quicker way. If $y' = A' + Bx$, then the values of y' corresponding to $x = 1, 2, 3, \ldots$ are

$$y'(1) = A' + B$$
$$y'(2) = A' + 2B$$
$$y'(3) = A' + 3B$$

and so on. This would give

$$\Delta y'_2 = y'(2) - y'(1) = B$$
$$\Delta y'_3 = y'(3) - y'(2) = B$$

etc. (The symbol Δ is the capital Greek letter *delta*. It stands for *difference*.) In other words: If we prepare a table of differences $(\Delta y_2, \Delta y_3, \Delta y_4, \ldots, \Delta y_8)$, then the differences will be equal if the points (x, y') lie on a straight line—and *almost* equal if the points (x, y') are close to lying on a straight line. The table of differences is:

x	1	2	3	4	5	6	7	8
y'	2 47	2.77	3.06	3.35	3.64	3.93	4.23	4.52
$\Delta y'$		0.30	0.29	0.29	0.29	0.29	0.30	0.29

The differences are very close to being equal. Therefore, the functional relationship between x and y' is very close to being linear. Finally, the functional relationship between x and y is very close to being exponential.

PART 2: Now we can apply the method of averages. We assume that $y' = A' + Bx$ and divide the eight equations into two equal groups:

$$\begin{cases} 2.47 = A' + B \\ 2.77 = A' + 2B \\ 3.06 = A' + 3B \\ 3.35 = A' + 4B \end{cases}$$

$$\begin{cases} 3.64 = A' + 5B \\ 3.93 = A' + 6B \\ 4.23 = A' + 7B \\ 4.52 = A' + 8B \end{cases}$$

Summing the equations in the first group, and then the equations in the second group, we have the system

$$11.65 = 4A' + 10B$$

$$16.32 = 4A' + 26B$$

The solution ($A' = 2.1828125$, $B = 0.291875$) tells us that

$$y' = 2.1828125 + 0.291875x$$

Since $A' = \ln A$, we have:

$$A = 8.8712215$$

The exponential curve that fits the data is therefore given by:

$$y = 8.8712215e^{0.291875x}$$

EXERCISES *for Section 11.4*

Find the logarithmic equation that corresponds to the exponential equation:

1.   a. $3^0 = 1$ b. $5^3 = 125$

2.   a. $2^{10} = 10.24$ b. $9^{5/2} = 243$

3.   a. $9^{-1} = \frac{1}{9}$ b. $(\frac{1}{9})^{-1} = 9$

4.   a. $(16807)^{0.2} = 7$ b. $32^{-0.6} = 0.125$

Find the exponential equation that corresponds to the logarithmic equation:

5.   a. $\log_2 4 = 2$ b. $\log_3 729 = 6$

6.   a. $\log_2 32 = 5$ b. $\log_{0.5} 32 = -5$

7.   a. $\log_{0.2} (0.008) = 3$ b. $\log_5 (0.008) = -3$

8.   a. $\log_\pi 15.601261 = 2.4$ b. $\log_\pi 1 = 0$

Solve for x:

9.   a. $\log_2 x = 4$ b. $\log_{10} x = 5$

10.   a. $\log_6 x = 3$ b. $\log_3 x = 6$

11.   a. $\log_{49} x = \frac{1}{2}$ b. $\log_{\frac{1}{2}} x = 49$

12.   a. $\log_{\frac{1}{5}} x = -3$ b. $\log_3 x = -\frac{1}{5}$

13.   a. $\log_2 16 = x$ b. $\log_3 27 = x$

14.   a. $\log_x 81 = 4$ b. $\log_x 32 = 2$

15.   a. $\log_x 1000 = -3$ b. $\log_x 27 = \frac{3}{5}$

Sketch the graph of:

16. $y = \log_2 x$

17. $y = \log_4 x$

18. $y = \log x$ ($\log x$ means $\log_{10} x$)

19. $y = \log_{1.5} x$

20. $y = \log_{\frac{1}{2}} x$

21. $y = \ln x$ ($\ln$ means $\log_e x$)

If A and B are positive numbers and $A > B$:

22.   Which is greater, $\log A$ or $\log B$?

23.   Which is greater, $\ln A$ or $\ln B$?

24.   Which is greater, $\log_{\frac{1}{2}} A$ or $\log_{\frac{1}{2}} B$?

25.   Which is greater, $\log_A 10$ or $\log_B 10$?

Make a table of:

26.   The common logarithms of 0.0001, 0.001, 0.01, 0.1, 1, 10, 100, 1000, 10,000.

27.   The natural logarithms of $e^{-4} = 0.01831564$, $e^{-3} = 0.04978707$, $e^{-2} = 0.13533528$, $e^{-1} = 0.36787944$, $e^0 = 1$, $e^1 = 2.7182818$, $e^2 = 7.3890561$, $e^3 = 20.085537$, $e^4 = 54.59815$.

28.   The logarithms base 2 of 0.0625, 0.125, 0.25, 0.5, 2, 4, 8, 16.

The next three exercises make use of Exercises 26, 27, and 28, respectively.

29.   Between which two consecutive integers does the common logarithm of a number lie, if the number is between 0.0001 and 0.001? between 0.1 and 1? between 1000 and 10,000?

30.   Between which two consecutive integers does the natural logarithm of a number lie, if the number is between 0.04978707 and 0.13533528? between 20.085537 and 54.59815? between 0.13533528 and 0.36787944?

31.   Between which two consecutive integers does the logarithm base 2 of a number lie, if the number is between 8 and 16? between 2 and 4? between 0.5 and 2? between 0.0625 and 0.125?

Use Appendix Table 2 and the rules for logarithms (when you need them) to find the common logarithms of the following numbers:

32. a. 286   b. $(286)^2$

33. a. $(777)^5$ b. $(777)^{0.85}$

34. a. $(955)(343)(679)$ b. $(955)^{0.15}(343)^{-0.87}(679)^{1.92}$

35. a. $\left(\dfrac{138}{297}\right)^{14}$ b. $\left(\dfrac{138}{297}\right)^{-14}$

Use Appendix Table 3 and the rules for logarithms (as needed) to find the natural logarithms of the following numbers. (If a number is outside the range of the table, make use of the instructions at the beginning of the table. Your answers to Exercises 29 and 30 may be a useful check for some of those logarithms.)

36. a. 7.87   b. 78.7   c. 787

37. a. 1.06   b. 10.6   c. 106

38. a. $(1.06)^2$ b. $(1.06)^3$ c. $(1.06)^{17}$

39. a. 0.856   b. 0.00856   c. 0.0000856

The exponential equation

$$y = 4,250,000x^{-0.8}$$

gives the number of families in a certain city whose annual incomes are x dollars or more. Use logarithms (Appendix Table 2 or Table 3, whichever you prefer) to answer the following questions.

40. How many families in the city have annual incomes of $5500 or more?

41. How many families in the city have annual incomes of $14,500 or more?

42. How many families in the city have annual incomes of $33,500 or more?

43. How many families in the city have annual incomes of $275,000 or more?

44. You are told that 1714 families in the city have annual incomes of x_1 dollars or more. What is x_1?

45. Figures show that 109 families in the city have annual incomes of x_2 dollars or more. What is x_2?

46. In the city we are talking about, *middle class* means a family income of $11,200 to $37,700. How many families in the city are middle class, according to that definition?

47. In the same city, physicians in private practice enjoy annual incomes in the range $85,000 to $979,000. How many families in the city have annual incomes in the physician-in-private-practice range?

The next two exercises are based on Problem 1, page 520.

48. Revised figures show that the planned oil refinery expansion will lead to a 4.5% annual deterioration in southeastern Maine's air quality. On this basis, how many years can the expansion continue before air quality deterioration exceeds 50%?

49. Expanding the oil refinery would affect water quality as well as air quality. Wyotex engineers find that the planned expansion will lead to a 3% annual deterioration in water quality. If the company is permitted to continue expanding so long as water quality deterioration does not exceed 40%, how many years does it have?

An Aztec Motors economist has discovered that annual U.S. sales of the subcompact Aztec Princess depend on three variables:

$x =$ the dollar difference in price between the Princess and the lowest-priced subcompact competitor

$y =$ the annual percentage rate of growth of the U.S. economy

$z =$ the advertising budget (in thousands of dollars, per year) for the Princess

The sales formula is:

$$S = x^{-0.29} y^{7.6} z^{0.32}$$

EXAMPLE: If the Princess costs $4100 and the lowest-priced subcompact competitor costs $3400, then $x = 700$. If the annual rate of GNP growth in the U.S. is 4.9%, then $y = 4.9$. If the annual ad budget is $650,000, then $z = 650$. With these figures, annual sales are:

$$S = (700)^{-0.29}(4.9)^{7.6}(650)^{0.32}$$
$$= (0.1496)(176,000)(7.946)$$
$$= 209,215$$

Use logarithms to calculate the answers to the following questions.

50. Calculate annual sales if: the Princess sells for $4200 and its lowest-priced competitor sells for $3300; the annual rate of GNP growth is 5.7%; the annual ad budget is $970,000.

51. Annual sales are 635,000. Suppose that the difference in price between the Princess and its lowest-priced competitor is $950, and that the annual GNP growth rate is 6.4%. What is the annual ad budget for the Aztec Princess?

52. Annual sales are 572,000. The difference in price between the Princess and its lowest-priced competitor is $1100. The annual ad budget for the Princess is $1,290,000. What is the annual rate of growth of the U.S. GNP?

For each of the following tables, answer two questions:

a. Can the functional relationship expressed by the table be approximated by an exponential function $y = Ae^{Bx}$?

b. If it can, what values would you assign to A and B?

53.

x	6	15	24	33	42	51	81	93
y	8.82	9.58	10.3	11.3	12.3	13.1	17.1	19.1

54.

x	0	4	12.5	21.6	31.5	48.2
y	0.682	0.659	0.614	0.568	0.523	0.455

55.

x	1	4	12.5	25	50	75	100
y	1.69	3.91	7.78	11.9	18.0	22.8	26.7

56.

x	0	1	2	3	4	5	6	7
y	4	6.6	10.9	18.0	29.6	48.8	80.4	132

57.

x	1	2	3	4	5	6
y	27.9	39.5	48.3	55.8	62.4	68.3

58.

x	0	1	2	3	4	5	6	7
y	23.7	21.9	20.1	18.5	17.2	16.1	15.2	14.5

chapter twelve

MATHEMATICS OF FINANCE

THE main topic in this chapter is *compound interest*. To understand compound interest, you have to know the material about exponential functions in Chapter 11. Once you do understand compound interest, all the other topics in this chapter—present value, annuities, sinking funds, car loans, home mortgages—will fall into place. You will not learn everything about these things here, but you will learn the basics. Most of the applications in this chapter are to personal finance. There are also applications to simple problems of corporate finance.

12.1 COMPOUND INTEREST AND PRESENT VALUE

Interest is a fee paid for the use of money. If you deposit $1000 in a bank at 5% annual interest, you expect that the $1000 will have grown to

$1050 by the end of the year. This easy example will introduce some terminology that will be useful in other problems. We call the amount originally deposited the *principal* and denote it by P. The amount you receive at the end of the time period is the *final amount*, and we will denote it by A. The interest paid will be I, which means that

$$A = P + I$$

In the example $A = \$1050$ and $P = \$1000$, which gives $I = \$50$. For another way of computing the interest, we can use

$$I = PRT$$

where P, as before, is the principal, R is the annual rate of interest, and T is the number of years. We have $R = 0.05$ and $T = 1$, so that $I = (1000)(0.05)(1) = \$50$.

The $\$1000$ that you leave on deposit for a year has become $\$1050$. You leave it on deposit for another year. The bank promises again to pay interest at the rate of 5% per year. But it can be done in two ways.

If the bank pays *simple interest*, which is interest on the principal amount only, then it will pay you $50 for the second year, as a fee paid for the use of your $\$1000$. The fact that you really have $\$1050$ on deposit will not be forgotten, but you will earn interest on only $\$1000$ of that amount. At the end of two years your $\$1000$ will have grown to $\$1100$. The formula used is $I = PRT$ as before, except that now $T = 2$.

If the bank pays *compound interest*, which is interest on both the principal and the accumulated interest, then your second year's interest will be 5% of $\$1050$, or $52.50. With compound interest, your $\$1000$ will have grown to $\$1102.50$ at the end of 2 years. If we want to develop a formula for compound interest, we note that you have

$$1000 + 1000(0.05) = 1000(1.05)$$

or $\$1050$ at the end of one year, and

$$1000(1.05) + 1000(1.05)(0.05) = 1000(1.05)(1 + 0.05) = 1000(1.05)^2$$

or $\$1102.50$ at the end of two years, and

$$1000(1.05)^2 + 1000(1.05)^2(0.05) = 1000(1.05)^2(1 + 0.05) = 1000(1.05)^3$$

or $\$1157.625$ at the end of three years, and so on. If the money is left on deposit for 10 years on the same terms, you will have $(1000)(1.05)^{10} = \$1628.89$ at the end of that period. The general formula is

$$A = P(1 + R)^n$$

where A is the final amount, P is the principal you started with, R is the annual rate of interest, and n is the number of years the money is left on deposit.

Most banks pay compound interest nowadays. In fact, most banks compound the interest more frequently than once a year. The compounding may be done quarterly, monthly, or daily. Suppose, for example, that your $1000 deposit earns 5% *compounded quarterly*. Then you will start earning interest on interest after the money has been on deposit for three months— and there will be interest on interest every three months thereafter. To calculate all this interest, we note that your 5% annual rate becomes a 5% ÷ 4, or 1.25%, quarterly rate and that n years become $4n$ quarter years. With these changes, your final amount after n years is

$$A = P\left(1 + \frac{R}{4}\right)^{4n}$$

If $P = \$1000$, $R = 0.05$, and $n = 10$, the dollar amount is

$$A = (1000)(1.0125)^{40} = \$1643.62$$

If compounding takes place m times a year, then the final amount after n years is

$$A = P\left(1 + \frac{R}{m}\right)^{mn}$$

which of course checks out for the case $m = 4$ of quarterly compounding. As further examples, we have $m = 12$ for monthly compounding, $m = 52$ for weekly compounding, and $m = 365$ for daily compounding. For a final example of how $1000 grows at a 5% annual interest rate, let's now assume that the interest is compounded daily for 10 years. The final amount is then

$$A = (1000)\left(1 + \frac{0.05}{365}\right)^{3650} = (1000)(1.000137)^{3650} = \$1648.66$$

To sum up, notice that 10 years of simple interest at a 5% rate would give you a total interest amount of $I = (1000)(0.05)(10) = \$500$, and therefore a final amount of $1500. Annual compounding would give $1628.89, or an extra $128.89. More frequent compounding would add smaller amounts: $14.73 for quarterly instead of annual compounding, and $5.04 for daily instead of quarterly compounding.

NOTE: The amounts just mentioned are approximations. That is, they are rounded off to the nearest cent. For example: $1000(1.05)^{10} = 1628.8945$, and $\$1628.89$ is the nearest-cent approximation. Similarly: $1000(1 + \frac{0.05}{4})^{40} = 1643.6195$, which is $\$1643.62$ to the nearest-cent approximation.

PROBLEM 1   A bank offers to pay an interest rate of 7.75% compounded monthly, on funds left on deposit for 7 years. You deposit $\$8743$ on these terms. How much will the bank pay you 7 years later?

SOLUTION   We use the formula

$$A = P\left(1 + \frac{R}{m}\right)^{mn}$$

for the final amount A. On the right side of the equation we have:

$$P = 8743$$
$$R = 7.75\% \,(= 0.0775)$$
$$m = 12$$
$$n = 7$$

The result is

$$A = (8743)\left(1 + \frac{0.0775}{12}\right)^{(12)(7)}$$
$$= (8743)(1.0064583)^{84}$$
$$= \$15,014.39$$

REMARK: The arithmetic for Problem 1 was done with a calculator. The exercises at the end of the section will not require a calculator. In some cases you will need Appendix Table 5. The next problem shows how Table 5 is used.

PROBLEM 2   A mutual fund pays dividends quarterly and automatically reinvests these dividends. (Since dividends can be regarded as interest, the mutual fund offers quarterly compounding of interest.) You invest $\$22,000$ in shares of that mutual fund, and the dividend continues at the rate of 12% (with quarterly compounding) for 11 years. How much has your $\$22,000$ investment grown?

To calculate the final amount, we again use

$$A = P\left(1 + \frac{R}{m}\right)^{mn}$$

where $P = 22,000$

$R = 12\% \ (= 0.12)$

$m = 4$

$n = 11$

The factor multiplying P on the right side of the equation is

$$(1 + 0.03)^{44} = (1.03)^{44} = 3.671452$$

according to Appendix Table 5. Therefore

$$A = (22,000)(3.671452) = \$80,771.95$$

Your initial $22,000 has grown by $58,771.95.

The mutual fund described in Problem 2 had an extraordinarily good 11-year record. (Of 604 mutual funds rated in the August 15, 1977, issue of *Forbes*, only 4 showed an 11-year average annual growth rate of 12% or more.) No mutual fund, and no investment of any kind at the present time, guarantees 12% a year compounded quarterly for the next 11 years. But suppose you must have $80,771.95 11 years from now. If you can get a guaranteed 8%, how much do you have to invest right now? Since 8% is much less than the 12% in Problem 2, you know you will need to invest more than $22,000. Problem 3 shows how to calculate the exact amount.

PROBLEM 3 To make the final payment on some real estate 11 years from now, you will need to have $80,771.95. Your bank offers 11-year certificates of deposit that pay 8%, compounded quarterly. How large a certificate must you buy if you want to have your $80,771.95 at the end of the 11 years?

SOLUTION Once more we use the compound interest formula

$$A = P\left(1 + \frac{R}{m}\right)^{mn}$$

We do not know the principal amount P that is to be invested, but we do know all the other quantities, and we can therefore determine P. We have:

$$A = 80{,}771.95$$

$$R = 8\% \ (= 0.08)$$

$$m = 4$$

$$n = 11$$

Therefore

$$80{,}771.95 = P(1.02)^{44}$$

Multiplying both sides of the equation by $(1.02)^{-44}$, we have

$$(80{,}771.95)(1.02)^{-44}$$

on the left side and

$$P(1.02)^{44}(1.02)^{-44} = P(1.02)^0 = P$$

on the right side. Therefore

$$P = (80{,}771.95)(1.02)^{-44}$$

Appendix Table 6 gives $(1.02)^{-44} = 0.418401$, so that

$$P = (80{,}771.95)(0.418401) = \$33{,}795.07$$

This initial investment is over 50% more than the $22,000 in Problem 2. The difference in return is explained by the difference in the interest rate. The difference between a guaranteed bank rate and a very chancy mutual fund rate explains why prudent money managers often buy certificates of deposit.

The solution $P = \$33{,}795.07$ in Problem 3 is called the *present value* of the *future amount* $A = \$80{,}771.95$. If you want the amount A right now, you must pay A dollars for it. But you can get your A dollars for the bargain price of P dollars if you are willing to wait 11 years. A dollars *then* are worth exactly as much as P dollars *now*.

As Problem 3 shows, the present value P corresponding to a future amount A is calculated by the formula

$$P = A\left(1 + \frac{R}{m}\right)^{-mn}$$

The formula is obtained (as in Problem 3) by multiplying both sides of the compound interest formula $A = P[1 + (R/m)]^{mn}$ by $[1 + (R/m)]^{-mn}$.

Here is a second illustration of the *present value* concept.

PROBLEM 4   Edward L. Francis has bought a luxurious house-boat. The agreed-upon price is $233,000, with $100,000 to be paid now and the remaining $133,000 to be paid three years from now. A moment after the contract has been signed—and the first $100,000 paid over—the seller makes a further offer. For a second $100,000 paid *now,* he will turn over the houseboat free and clear. Is this one a good offer?

SOLUTION   Mr. Francis is being offered a *future amount* of $133,000 and the question is whether or not the *present value* of the money is as much as $100,000.
    Since this is supposed to be a good offer, Mr. Francis will assume that his $100,000 *could* earn 15%, compounded 6 times a year. In 3 years, this would give him a final amount of

$$A = P\left(1 + \frac{R}{m}\right)^{mn}$$

dollars, where $P = 100,000$

$$R = 15\% \ (= 0.15)$$

$$m = 6$$

$$n = 3$$

The calculation leads to:

$$A = (100,000)\left(1 + \frac{0.15}{6}\right)^{18} = (100,000)(1.025)^{18} = \$155,965.87$$

It was not a very good offer.
    With a counteroffer in mind, Mr. Francis then calculates what *would* be a good offer. He needs to find the *present value P* of $133,000. This is given by

$$P = A\left(1 + \frac{R}{m}\right)^{-mn}$$

(notice the negative exponent on the right side), with

$$A = 133,000$$

$$R = 15\% \ (= 0.15)$$

$$m = 6$$

$$n = 3$$

The assumption, again, is that the Francis money can earn 15%, compounded 6 times a year. The calculation of P leads to:

$$P = (133,000)(1.025)^{-18} = (133,000)(0.6411659) = \$85,275.07$$

This is the present value of $133,000—provided that $R = 0.15$, $m = 6$, and $n = 3$.

EXERCISES *for Section 12.1*

Use Table 5 (p. 568) to calculate the *final amount* and the *interest earned* in each of the following cases:

1.   A principal of $11,000 earns 5%, compounded annually for 3 years.

2.   A principal of $14,000 earns 6%, compounded semiannually for 4 years.

3.   A principal of $11,000 earns 5%, compounded quarterly for 3 years.

4.   A principal of $14,000 earns 6%, compounded monthly for 4 years.

5.   A principal of $26,500 earns 8%, compounded annually for 12 years.

6.   A principal of $26,500 earns 10%, compounded every 2 months for 8 years.

7.   A principal of $26,500 earns 8%, compounded quarterly for 12 years.

8.   A principal of $26,500 earns 10.5%, compounded 7 times a year for 7 years.

9.   A principal of $39,750 earns 16%, compounded semiannually for 12 years.

10.   A principal of $39,750 earns 28%, compounded quarterly for 12 years.

Use Table 6 (p. 572) to calculate the present value corresponding to a future amount of $15,000 if:

11.   Interest is earned at a 6% rate, compounded annually for 4 years.

12.   Interest is earned at a 7% rate, compounded quarterly for 4 years.

13.   Interest is earned at an 8% rate, compounded quarterly for 4 years.

Environmental Structures has bought 2300 acres in Henry County, Kentucky. (The plan is to build a thousand or so houses within commuting distance of Louisville.) This land cost $3,400,000. Environmental Structures paid $500,000 down and has contracted to pay the remaining $2,900,000 three years from now. For tax reasons, the company prefers to put aside money to pay this debt right now. The amount put aside will depend on the interest that can be earned. Use the appropriate Table to calculate how much money Environmental Structures must put aside if its money can earn:

14. 5%, compounded annually.

15. 5%, compounded quarterly.

16. 6%, compounded annually.

17. 6%, compounded semiannually.

18. 6%, compounded quarterly.

19. 6%, compounded monthly.

20. 8%, compounded semiannually.

21. 8%, compounded quarterly.

22. 9%, compounded every 2 months.

---

23. Cattle ranchers in Nevada say that the wild horse population in that state grows at an annual rate of 14%, compounded every half year. If this is correct, and if there were 11,000 wild horses in Nevada 6 years ago, how many wild horses are there in Nevada at the present time?

In most parts of the U.S., rats are about as numerous as people. But they have recently become far more numerous than people on the west side of a certain large city. (See *Time,* October 10, 1977, p. 36. The rats have become immune to poisons used by the city's health department.) One year ago, there were 500,000 people and 500,000 rats living together on the west side. Since that time, the human population has increased at a high rate, for humans—an annual rate of 9%, compounded monthly. Meanwhile, the rat population has gone up the way rat populations can: at a 312% annual rate, compounded weekly.

24. How many humans live on the west side today?

25. How many rats live on the west side today? *HINT:* To use the Table, remember that $a^{n+2} = a^n a^2$.

There are 1,200 gray wolves in northern Minnesota. (This is the only significant gray wolf population in the contiguous United States today. There is a larger wolf population in Alaska.) These animals are legally protected, but their reproduction rate is slow and they are also illegally hunted.

26. Suppose that the gray wolf population of northern Minnesota shows a net increase of 1.25% a year for 10 years. How many gray wolves will be living in northern Minnesota at the end of that time?

27. Suppose that the gray wolf population of northern Minnesota shows a net decrease of 7% a year for 10 years. How many gray wolves will be left in northern Minnesota by the end of the 10 years?

---

28. A playwright received royalties amounting to $87,000 five years ago. He deposited the money in a Swiss bank account. The Swiss bank *charged* him 3% annual interest (compounded every 2 months) for keeping the money. (Swiss banks really do that with large foreign accounts.) How much was left of the $87,000 after the 5 years were up?

12.2 ANNUITIES AND SINKING FUNDS

An *annuity* is an amount of money that is received or paid annually. And since there is no better word for the purpose, *annuity* is also used to refer to a fixed amount of money that is received or paid at other fixed intervals—semiannually, quarterly, monthly.

This section explains the use of annuities to accumulate money. As examples: A family may make regular deposits in a savings account to accumulate the money to make a down payment on a house. A corporation may make regular deposits to accumulate the cash needed to replace depreciating equipment or to meet future obligations. Funds that are accumulated in this way include the amounts deposited and also the compound interest earned by the deposits. The total amount accumulated is called a *sinking fund*.

Before setting up the mathematical framework for annuities, let's try a simple problem.

> **PROBLEM 1** You want to accumulate $4100 for a skiing vacation in the Alps next winter. For that purpose, you deposit $500 in a savings account at the beginning of each month, starting May 1. You will make these deposits for 8 consecutive months (through December 1), for a total of $4000. Your bank pays interest at a 5% annual rate, compounded monthly. Will you have the $4100 in your account immediately after you make payment 8 on December 1?
>
> **SOLUTION** For a preliminary fix on the problem, let's consider how it would go if you had $4000 to deposit on May 1 and left that money

in the bank from May 1 to December 1. The final amount A could then be calculated from the compound interest formula

$$A = P\left(1 + \frac{R}{m}\right)^{mn}$$

with $P = 4000$, $R = 0.05$, $m = 12$, and $n = 7/12$. The result is:

$$A = (4000)(1.0041667)^7 = \$4118.14$$

Accumulated interest would give you the extra money you need for the trip.

If your $4000 is deposited in 8 monthly installments of $500, starting May 1, you should not expect interest to add the extra $100 you need. This is common sense: only the first $500 will earn interest for the full 7 months. The next $500 (deposited June 1) earns interest for only 6 months, the next after that earns interest for only 5 months, and so on. (The $500 deposit on December 1 will earn no interest at all.)

But let's see if we can determine exactly how much you will have. Repeated use of the compound interest formula will do it; see Table 12.1. The total accumulation of the annuity (the sum of the

TABLE 12.1

Deposit Number	Number of Months on Deposit	Grows to
1	7	$500(1.0041667)^7 = 514.77$
2	6	$500(1.0041667)^6 = 512.63$
3	5	$500(1.0041667)^5 = 510.51$
4	4	$500(1.0041667)^4 = 508.39$
5	3	$500(1.0041667)^3 = 506.28$
6	2	$500(1.0041667)^2 = 504.18$
7	1	$500(1.0041667)\ = 502.08$
8	0	$500(1)\qquad\quad = 500.$

deposits, together with the interest, if any, on each deposit) is the sum of the eight items in the third column of the table. The result is

$$514.77 + 512.63 + 510.51 + 508.39 + 506.28 + 504.18$$
$$+ 502.08 + 500 = \$4058.84$$

As expected, the sinking fund is not large enough. For a ski trip, you would undoubtedly make up the missing $41.16 and think no more about it. For another application, a sinking fund that is too small (or too large) might be a real embarrassment. We therefore need a convenient method for calculating the total accumulation of an annuity.

To develop a framework, let's suppose that each payment in an annuity is a dollars, that you deposit these dollars in a bank at the beginning of each of k periods, and that there is a rate of interest r for each period. Let's also assume that interest is compounded at the end of each of these periods.

Now we calculate the amount of money in the fund immediately after payment 1, immediately after payment 2, etc. We will denote these amounts by A_1, A_2, etc. The first two are easy:

$$A_1 = a$$

because the fund contains only the first deposit immediately after that has been made. Then

$$A_2 = a + a(1 + r)$$

where a is the second deposit and $a(1 + r)$ is the first deposit together with a month's interest on the first deposit. Next

$$A_3 = a + a(1 + r) + a(1 + r)^2$$
$$A_4 = a + a(1 + r) + a(1 + r)^2 + a(1 + r)^3$$

and so on to

$$A_k = a + a(1 + r) + \cdots + a(1 + r)^{k-1}$$

To get a useful formula for A_k, we now write two equations. The first equation simply repeats the expression for A_k. In the second equation, we multiply A_k by $(1 + r)$. The results are:

$$A_k = a + a(1 + r) + \cdots + a(1 + r)^{k-1}$$
$$(1 + r)A_k = \quad a(1 + r) + \cdots + a(1 + r)^{k-1} + a(1 + r)^k$$

Subtracting the second equation from the first, we have

$$[1 - (1 + r)]A_k = a - a(1 + r)^k$$

Since $[1 - (1 + r)] = -r$, the left side of the equation can be written $-rA_k$. Since $a - a(1 + r)^k = a[1 - (1 + r)^k]$, the right side of the equation can be written $-a[(1 + r)^k - 1]$. Making use of these results for the left and right sides, we write the equation as

$$-rA_k = -a[(1 + r)^k - 1]$$

If we then divide both sides by $-r$, we have a formula for A_k:

$$A_k = a \frac{(1 + r)^k - 1}{r}$$

As a check, let's use this formula for Problem 1. There we have $k = 8$, $a = 500$, and $r = 0.0041667$. The result is:

$$A_8 = 500 \frac{(1.0041667)^8 - 1}{0.0041667} = \$4058.82$$

(Rounding-off errors explain the slight difference between this amount and the solution of Problem 1.)

The formula for A_k tells us how much money you will accumulate if you make k periodic payments of a dollars, with a rate of interest r for each period.

Sometimes you know how much money you want to accumulate and also know k and r. Then you have to determine how large a must be. For such problems it is convenient to rewrite the annuity formula as:

$$a = A_k \frac{r}{(1 + r)^k - 1}$$

For an illustration, let's return to Problem 1. That problem showed that 8 monthly deposits of $500 each, plus interest, would *not* give you the $4100 you wanted. Slightly larger payments are needed. To find just how large they must be, we use the formula for the payment size a. Since $A_k = A_8 = 4100$ and $r = 0.0041667$, we have

$$a = 4100 \frac{0.0041667}{(1.0041667)^8 - 1} = \$505.07$$

NOTE: A hand-held calculator was used to find the monthly payment. When you do the exercises you will be able to refer to Appendix Tables 7 and 8, which give values of

$$\frac{(1 + r)^k - 1}{r}$$

and

$$\frac{r}{(1 + r)^k - 1}$$

for various values of r and k. The next problem makes use of Appendix Table 7.

PROBLEM 2   Dick and Dolly van Schacht have good jobs, and they are therefore able to deposit $2500 a month in their savings and loan association account. The account earns interest at a rate of 5.5%, compounded monthly. After 4 years of this, they think they may have enough to go house-hunting. How much have they accumulated immediately after their last (that is, their 48th) deposit?

SOLUTION   We use the annuity formula

$$A_k = a \frac{(1 + r)^k - 1}{r}$$

with $k = 48$, $a = 2500$, and $r = (5.5/12)\%$. From Appendix Table 7,

$$\frac{(1 + r)^k - 1}{r} = 53.5528$$

when $r = (5.5/12)\%$ and $k = 48$. Therefore

$$A_k = (2500)(53.5528) = \$133,882$$

The van Schachts have enough money for a down payment on the kind of house (with swimming pool) that they want.

Appendix Table 8 gives values of

$$\frac{r}{(1 + r)^k - 1}$$

for various choices of r and k. This table is useful in connection with the formula

$$a = A_k \frac{r}{(1 + r)^k - 1}$$

which tells you how large a periodic payment a will be needed to meet a given financial goal A_k in k periodic payments. Appendix Table 8 is used in the next problem.

PROBLEM 3   Llewellyn and Angharad Davis are Welsh emigrants to Australia who have made it big in uranium mining. They are thinking of returning to Wales to buy a castle that they have always admired. When they inquire through British real estate agents, they learn that the castle will be for sale 3 years from now at a price of 1.5 million pounds. (That is about 2.6 megabucks. The figures will be left in pounds in this problem.) That is all right with the Davises. They agree to buy the castle, and they start depositing regular monthly amounts in a British bank. The interest there is 9.5%, compounded monthly. How many pounds must they deposit each month if they want to have their 1.5 million pounds immediately after deposit number 36?

SOLUTION   The payment size a that is needed will be found from

$$a = A_k \frac{r}{(1 + r)^k - 1}$$

where $A_k = A_{36} = 1,500,000$, $r = (9.5/12)\%$, and $k = 36$. Appendix Table 8 shows that

$$a = (1,500,000)(0.024116) = 36,174$$

pounds (about $63,000) a month. The amount deposited would be

$$(36,174)(36) = 1,302,264$$

pounds. The high rate of interest would add 197,736 pounds, to make up the needed 1,500,000 pounds.

NOTE: British banks pay a high rate of interest because there is a high rate of inflation in Great Britain. No U.S. bank is permitted to pay such rates, but many Americans are locked into home mortgages at 9.5% or more. The interest expense for a 20-year mortgage at 9.5% is considerable. Home mortgages are studied in the next section.

The last example in this section is concerned with corporate finance. Most corporations set up sinking funds to cover the replacement cost of depreciating assets. In Problem 4 the depreciating asset is an expensive computer.

PROBLEM 4   Media Probabilities, the opinion research and forecasting giant, does much of its analytical work with a $26 million H-3000 computer. Management believes that this computer will be obsolete in 5 years. It will then be replaced by a new computer costing (at an educated guess) $33 million. At that time the old H-3000 should still be worth $9 million on the used-computer market. Media Probabilities has to be prepared to spend $33 - 9 = $24 million 5 years from now. The solution is to set up a *sinking fund*. Money will be invested every month in 30-day notes issued by the bluest blue-chip corporations (AT&T, General Motors, etc.). The proceeds of these notes will be reinvested (one month later) in similar 30-day notes. In effect, this means that interest will be compounded monthly. The average annual rate of interest earned in this way should be 8.5%. Suppose that Media Probabilities will invest the same amount each month for 5 years, and suppose that the 8.5% rate (compounded monthly) holds up. How large must the monthly investment be if the company is to have the $24 million it needs immediately after the last (60th) monthly investment?

SOLUTION   The monthly payment size will be given by

$$a = A_k \frac{r}{(1 + r)^k - 1}$$

where $A_k = A_{60} = 24{,}000{,}000$, $r = (8.5/12)\%$, and $k = 60$. From Table 8,

$$a = (24{,}000{,}000)(0.013433) = \$322{,}392$$

Notice that

$$(332{,}392)(60) = \$19{,}943{,}520$$

Media Probabilities would have earned $4,056,480 in interest over the 5-year period.

EXERCISES *for Section 12.2*

Use Appendix Table 7 to calculate the amount accumulated by an annuity consisting of k monthly payments of a dollars, with yearly interest rate r, if:

1. $k = 60$, $a = 87$, $r = 4.5\%$

2. $k = 96$, $a = 59$, $r = 5\%$

3. $k = 228$, $a = 136$, $r = 5.5\%$

4. $k = 108$, $a = 237$, $r = 8.5\%$

5. $k = 240$, $a = 381$, $r = 9.5\%$

6. $k = 336$, $a = 3465$, $r = 7.5\%$

Use Table 8 to calculate the monthly payment needed to accumulate:

7. $2000 in 3 years at a yearly rate of 4%.

8. $3000 in 4 years at a yearly rate of 5%.

9. $7320 in 11 years at a yearly rate of 6%.

10. $16,540 in 15 years at a yearly rate of 7%.

11. $34,033 in 19 years at a yearly rate of 8%.

12. $91,384 in 36 years at a yearly rate of 9%.

---

13. Jack Brown, a government employee, puts $250 in the bank every month. He does this for 40 years (and does not withdraw any of it). His bank pays interest at the rate of 5.5% per year, compounded monthly. How much does Brown have in his bank account at the end of the 40 years?

If the news media are to be believed, organized crime makes a very good thing out of smuggling cigarettes from low-tax states like North Carolina and Kentucky to high-tax northern cities. An organized crime figure who profits from all this puts $850,000 per month in each of two confidential bank accounts.

14. One account is in the Bahamas. It earns 4% per year, compounded monthly. How much is in the account after 5 years?

15. The other account is in a Swiss bank, which charges the account (or credits it with *negative* interest) at the rate of 3.5% per year, compounded monthly. How much is in this account after 5 years?

Sally Hansen has been earning a lot of money selling California real estate. When the head of the agency she works for offers her a partnership for $250,000, Sally asks if the offer is still good at the same price a year from now. "Why not?" is the answer. Sally assumes this means "yes."

16. If Sally Hansen can save $20,000 per month, and if her money earns 5% per year, compounded monthly, at her local savings and loan association, will she have the $250,000 at year's end?

17. How much should she deposit per month if she wants to have neither more nor less than $250,000 but *exactly* that sum?

18. At the end of the year, Sally Hansen decides she doesn't want to buy a partnership in the agency she works for. Instead, she buys herself a nice little house. But then she gets ambitious again and decides she wants to buy into a big Australian land-holding company. She signs a contract that gets her into the company, on her undertaking to invest 1 megabuck (U.S.) in 2 years. If she deposits her money in a certain Australian bank, it will earn interest at the rate of 7.5% per year, compounded monthly. How much must she deposit each month to have her $1 million in 2 years?

---

19. Kathy Pierce, a basketball coach at a medium-sized college, thinks it would help her image if she drove a Porsche. She is willing to spend 18 months saving up for the down payment. If the down payment (18 months from now) will be $3000, how much a month will she have to save in her credit union account if the interest earned is:

    a. 4% per year, compounded monthly?
    b. 4.5% per year, compounded monthly?
    c. 5% per year, compounded monthly?
    d. 5.5% per year, compounded monthly?

20. Dave Smith, the demon balloonist from Albuquerque, has just failed in his latest attempt to cross the Atlantic by balloon. As he is hauled out of the waters off Nova Scotia by the Canadian Coast Guard, he vows: "I'll be up there in another balloon 2 years from now." Since those ocean-crossing (or ocean-not-crossing) balloons cost $500,000 a throw, it looks as if Dave will have to do some serious money-saving if he wants to keep his promise. Assuming he does, how many dollars a month must he put aside, for the next 2 years, if his local thrift institution pays him 5% per year, compounded monthly? 6% per year, compounded monthly? 7% per year, compounded monthly?

Mineral Resources is a corporation that owns three important mines:

a short-life gold mine, valued at $57 million, but with only 6 years of useful life left

a uranium mine, valued at $123 million, which has 17 more years of useful life

a long-life gold mine, valued at $179 million, which has 25 more years of useful life

In other words: The three properties together are valued at $359 million. But the value will be down to $302 million in 6 years, down to $179 million in 17 years, and down to zero in 25 years.

    Mineral Resources will set up three sinking funds to replace these three important capital assets. Each sinking fund will be made up of investments in corporate 30-day notes, but interest rates will be different for the three sinking funds since interest rates vary from year to year and from decade to decade.

21. To replace the short-life gold mine, money is invested every month for 6 years. How large a monthly investment is needed if the investments earn 7% per year, compounded monthly? 7.5%? 8%? 8.5%?

22. The sinking fund to replace the uranium mine will be set up over a 17-year period. How much a month must be invested if the rate earned is 7% per year, compounded monthly? 7.5%? 8%? 8.5%?

23. The sinking fund to replace the long-life gold mine is made up of monthly investments over 25 years. How much a month must be invested if the annual rate earned is 6%, compounded monthly? 7%, compounded monthly? 8%, compounded monthly? 9%, compounded monthly?

The Mineral Resources sinking funds described in Exercises 21, 22, and 23 will replace the three mines at *today's* values. But dollar values will probably be higher when the mines are exhausted. As an example, the replacement cost for the short-life gold mine might be up as much as 100%. In that case the sinking fund has to have $114 million in it at the end of 6 years.

24. Answer Exercise 21, on the assumption that the replacement cost of the mine will be up by 50%, 75%, 100%, or 150% at the end of the 6 years.

25. Answer Exercise 21, on the assumption that the replacement cost of the mine goes up by 5%, 6%, 7%, or 8% a year.

26. Answer Exercise 22, on the assumption that the replacement cost of the uranium mine will be up by 300%, 350%, 400%, or 450% at the end of the 17 years.

27. Answer Exercise 22, on the assumption that the replacement cost of the uranium mine goes up by 2%, 3%, 4%, or 5% every six months.

28. Answer Exercise 23, on the assumption that the replacement cost of the long-life gold mine will be up by 500%, 550%, 600%, or 650% at the end of the 25 years.

29. What is the answer to Exercise 23, if the replacement cost of the long-life gold mine goes up 4% every 6 months for 10 years, and then 2% every 3 months for 15 years?

12.3 CAR LOANS AND MORTGAGES

If you borrow money to buy a car or a house, you expect to repay the money borrowed (plus interest) in monthly installments. Car loans are usually repaid in 3 or 4 years. Real estate loans, called *mortgages,* may run 10, 20, or 30 years.

The monthly payment for a car loan or a mortgage depends on the size of the loan, the number of payments, and the interest rate. You will know three quantities:

P = the principal (that is, the amount borrowed)

k = the number of monthly payments

r = the interest rate per month

and you will want to know:

a = the size of the monthly payment

A car loan example will show how it works.

PROBLEM 1   Your new compact car costs $5010.40. You make a down payment of $1010.40, which leaves $4000 to finance. If your bank gives you 36 months to repay the $4000, and if the interest rate is 9.31% (compounded monthly), what is your monthly payment?

SOLUTION   If the bank can get 9.31% compounded monthly for the money over the next 3 years, then the $4000 it lends you will grow according to the compound interest formula (with monthly compounding, for 36 months):

$$A = P(1 + r)^k$$

where $P = 4000$

$$r = \frac{9.31}{12}\% = \frac{0.0931}{12} = 0.0077583$$

$$k = 36$$

This would give the bank the final amount

$$A = (4000)(1.0077583)^{36} = (4000)(1.3207796) = \$5283.12$$

Now suppose that you pay the bank the $5283.12 in 36 monthly payments. To find the monthly payment a, we use the formula (p. 541)

$$a = A_k \frac{r}{(1 + r)^k - 1}$$

where $A_k = A_{30} = 5283.12$

$$r = 0.0077583$$

$$k = 36$$

The result is:

$$a = (5283.12)\frac{0.0077583}{(1.0077583)^{36} - 1} = (5283.12)(0.02418589)$$

$$= \$127.78$$

a month.

As a check, we multiply the monthly payment by 36. We have

$$(127.78)(36) = \$4600.08$$

This is not the same as the $5283.12 that the bank could have earned on the $4000 at 9.31% compounded monthly for 3 years. On the other hand, you did not get $4000 for 3 years. You reduced the debt every month and paid interest only on the amount still owed.

There is just one thing wrong with the solution to Problem 1. It seems too complicated.

As a matter of fact, we can do it a lot more easily. We simply combine our two formulas. The monthly payment is

$$a = A_k \frac{r}{(1 + r)^k - 1}$$

and the final amount A_k is exactly the same as the final amount A in the compound interest formula. That is:

$$A_k = A = P(1 + r)^k$$

Therefore

$$a = P \frac{(1 + r)^k r}{(1 + r)^k - 1}$$

If we multiply the numerator and denominator of the fraction by $(1 + r)^{-k}$, we have [since $(1 + r)^{-k}(1 + r)^k = (1 + r)^0 = 1$] the *monthly repayment formula*

$$a = P \frac{r}{1 - (1 + r)^{-k}}$$

which gives the monthly payment of a dollars required to repay a loan of P dollars, if the monthly rate is r and the repayment takes k months.

As a check on the monthly repayment formula, let's redo Problem 1. You have

$$P = 4000$$

$$r = 0.0931 \div 12 = 0.0077583$$

$$k = 36$$

The result is

$$a = 4000\left[\frac{0.0077583}{1 - (0.0077583)^{-36}}\right] = (4000)(0.03194419) = \$127.78$$

It checks.

NOTE: Table 9 gives values of the monthly repayment factor for monthly

$$\frac{r}{1 - (1 + r)^{-k}}$$

interest rates r from $(4/12)\%$ to $(9.5/12)\%$ and for values of k from 12 to 480. The value of r needed for Problem 1 is not in the table. (A calculator was used to find $a = \$127.78$.) Table 9 *does* give the monthly payment factors for $r = (9/12)\%$ and $r = (9.5/12)\%$. The factors are:

0.0318 for $r = \dfrac{9}{12}\%$, $k = 36$

0.032023 for $r = \dfrac{9.5}{12}\%$, $k = 36$

When multiplied by \$4000, these two factors give monthly payments of \$127.20 and \$128.09, respectively. The payment for $r = (9.31/12)\%$ lies in between, as we would expect.

The monthly repayment formula also works for other installment loans, including mortgage loans. We will look at some examples in a moment.

First, however, let's study the effect of a big change in interest rate. You paid your bank 9.31%. But you could have financed the car through the car dealer—at a rate of 13.22%. How much difference would this have made in the monthly payments? For an answer, we again use

$$a = P\frac{r}{1 - (1 + r)^{-k}}$$

with $P = 4000$ and $k = 36$. But now $r = 0.1322 \div 12 = 0.01101667$. Therefore

$$a = (4000)\frac{0.01101667}{1 - (1.01101667)^{-36}} = (4000)(0.03380019) = \$135.20$$

according to a calculator. Over the 36 months, that would have amounted to \$4867.20, or \$267.12 more than the \$4600.08 to be paid the bank.

Now let's see how the monthly repayment formula is applied if you want to own a driveway to go with the car you bought in Problem 1.

PROBLEM 2   The new house you want to buy has two bedrooms and a garage, and a few trees around it, and it is only half a mile from salt water. The realtor says, "This property is a steal at $98,000." Local lending institutions want a 20% down payment, and this $19,600 (if you can scrape it up) will leave $78,400 to be financed by a mortgage loan. You have the following mortgage choices:

a.   a 20-year mortgage at 8.75%
b.   a 20-year mortgage at 9%
c.   a 30-year mortgage at 9.25%

(All these interest rates are annual rates. Interest will be compounded monthly.) How will the monthly payments for mortgages a, b, and c compare? What will the total payments over the life of the mortgage be in each case?

NOTE ON TABLES: Table 9 contains only one of the monthly payment factors needed to solve this problem. A supplementary table (Table 10) gives monthly payment factors for values of $r\%$ from 7% to 11% (in steps of 0.25%), and for values of k from 120 to 420 months. The solution to this problem will show how Table 10 is used.

SOLUTION   We will apply the monthly repayment formula

$$a = P\frac{r}{1 - (1 + r)^{-k}}$$

with $P = 78{,}400$ in all three cases. Values of the monthly payment factor

$$\frac{r}{1 - (1 + r)^{-k}}$$

will be taken from Table 10.

In case a, we have $r = 8.75\%$ and $k = 240$. Therefore

$$a = (78{,}400)\frac{\dfrac{8.75}{1200}}{1 - \left(1 + \dfrac{8.75}{1200}\right)^{-240}} = (78{,}400)(0.0088371071)$$

with the monthly payment factor taken from Table 10. The result is

$$a = \$692.83$$

The total amount paid would be

$$(240)(692.83) = \$166,279.20$$

In case b, we have $r = 9\%$ and $k = 240$. This leads to

$$a = (78,400)(0.0089972596)$$

where the monthly payment factor has again been taken from Table 10. The monthly payment would be

$$a = \$705.38$$

and the total amount paid would be that number times 240, or $\$169,291.20$.

If you knew all along that mortgage a would be a better deal than mortgage b, these results spell it out. Getting an 8.75% rate instead of a 9% rate would save you $\$12.55$ per month in payments, and $\$3012$ over the life of the mortgage.

For case c, we have $r = 9\%$ and $k = 360$. We consult Appendix Table 10 for the monthly payment factor, and we have

$$a = (78,400)(0.0080462262) = \$630.82$$

for the monthly payment. Over the 30-year life of the mortgage, you would pay out

$$(360)(\$630.82) = \$227,095.20$$

This is a whopping $\$60,816.$ over the total payout under mortgage a. But the monthly payments would be $\$62.01$ lower. This might make a crucial difference in your budget. If it did, you would choose the 30-year mortgage and push that $\$60,816$ to the back of your mind.

REMARK: You may think it is curious to use the same repayment formula for car loans and for mortgage loans. The fact is that car loans (with the car as security) and mortgage loans (with the real estate as security) are legally very similar. In terms of mathematics of finance, the only difference is that real estate loans run over a longer period of time.

Notice, finally, that we have been using a *monthly* repayment formula. If a loan is paid off on some other terms—quarterly payments, annual payments, etc.—the formula can easily be adjusted. In the case of quarterly payments, you would have the very same formula:

$$a = P\frac{r}{1 - (1 + r)^{-k}}$$

with P as the principal amount. The number r would be the *quarterly* interest rate. (For example, a 9% annual rate would give $r = (9.00/400) = 0.0225$.) The number k would be the number of quarters required to repay the loan—that is, 4 times the number of years.

EXERCISES *for Section 12.3*

Interest rates in the following exercises are annual rates, and interest is always compounded monthly. Use Table 9 for car loan problems, and for mortgage problems whenever possible. Use Table 10 for mortgage problems when it is needed.

Bob buys a Jeep wagon for $8002. He gets $2300 for the old Bronco he trades in. Calculate the monthly payments and the total amount paid if he takes out his car loan with:

1. bank A, which will give him a 2-year loan at 8.5%

2. bank B, which will give him a 3-year loan at 9.0%

3. bank C, which will give him a 4-year loan at 9.5%

Carol's latest car is a Mark V in yellow-gold diamond fire paint. The price is $20,517. She has no trade, since she totaled her Eldorado. Calculate the monthly payments and the total amount paid if the loan for the Mark V is taken out with:

4. bank E, which will give a 1-year loan at 8%

5. bank F, which will give a 2-year loan at 9%

6. bank G, which will give a 3-year loan at 9.5%

Ted buys a Monte Carlo for $8875. He will make a 20% down payment on the car. Calculate his monthly payments and the total amount he pays if he finances the remaining sum with:

7. bank J, which offers a 1-year loan at 9.5%

8. bank K, which offers a 2-year loan at 8%

9. bank L, which offers a 3-year loan at 8.5%

Alice traces in her Volaré for a Cordoba. The price of the Cordoba is $8513, and the trade-in brings her $1950. Calculate her monthly payments and the total amount she pays if she does business with:

10. a credit union, which will give her a 2-year loan at 8.5%

11. the same credit union, which will give her a 3-year loan at 9%

12. A bank, which makes her the following offer: It will let her have a 3-year loan at 8%. After she has made those payments for 1 year, the bank will refinance the amount she has left to pay by giving her a 3-year loan at 8.5%. After she has made the payments for that loan for 1 year, the bank will refinance the amount she has left to pay by giving her a 3-year loan at 9.5%. (This may or may not be legal, but it is the offer Alice gets. She will have different monthly payments for the first year, the second year, and the last three years of the loan.)

Cage Realty has advertised some real estate for sale. Calculate the monthly payments for mortgage loans on each of the following advertised properties. Assume a 20% down payment in each case.

13. a 3-bedroom ranch for $48,500, available on an 18-year mortgage at 8.5%

14. a 7-room chalet for $53,000, available on a 15-year mortgage at 7.75%

15. a 4-bedroom contemporary for $103,000, available on a 20-year mortgage at 8.25%

16. a 143-acre farm with a small house and a large barn for $256,000, available on a 25-year mortgage at 8.75%

17. a 24-unit apartment house for $297,000, available on a 12-year mortgage at 10.5%

Bob and Carol are looking for a new house. Bob's choice has old-timey features like a movie projection room, an air-conditioned squash court, and a bomb shelter. The Bomb (as Carol calls it) can be had for $795,000, with 20% down.

18. If they make the 20% down payment, Bob and Carol can get a 20-year mortgage loan for the rest at an 8.5% rate. Or if they prefer, they can have a 25-year mortgage loan at a 9% rate. What are the monthly payments and the total payments, for each of these two loans?

19 If they will make a 25% down payment, Bob and Carol can get slightly better terms: a 20-year mortgage loan at 8.25%, or a 25-year mortgage loan at 8.75%. Find the monthly payments and total payments in these cases.

Carol's choice for a new house is heated (and cooled) by solar collectors, a heat pump, and (occasionally) utility company electricity. The mix is controlled by a built-in computer. And the house also has tennis courts, beach rights, indoor and outdoor swimming pools, a mud bath, a few saunas, and a $3,500,000 price tag. Bob is not sure that their budget will stretch that far, but he is willing to look at the options.

20. With a 10% down payment, Bob and Carol can have a 10-year mortgage loan at 9.75%, a 15-year loan at 10.25%, or a 20-year loan at 10.75%. Find the monthly payments and total payments in each of these cases.

21. With a 15% down payment, Bob and Carol are offered a 10-year mortgage loan at 9.25%, a 15-year loan at 9.5%, or a 20-year loan at 10%. Find their monthly payments and total payments for each of these loans.

Tables

TABLE 1 $B(r; n, p)$

n	r	.05	.10	.15	.20	.25	.30	.35	.40	.45	.50
1	0	.9500	.9000	.8500	.8000	.7500	.7000	.6500	.6000	.5500	.5000
	1	.0500	.1000	.1500	.2000	.2500	.3000	.3500	.4000	.4500	.5000
2	0	.9025	.8100	.7225	.6400	.5625	.4900	.4225	.3600	.3025	.2500
	1	.0950	.1800	.2550	.3200	.3750	.4200	.4550	.4800	.4950	.5000
	2	.0025	.0100	.0225	.0400	.0625	.0900	.1225	.1600	.2025	.2500
3	0	.8574	.7290	.6141	.5120	.4219	.3430	.2746	.2160	.1664	.1250
	1	.1354	.2430	.3251	.3840	.4219	.4410	.4436	.4320	.4084	.3750
	2	.0071	.0270	.0574	.0960	.1406	.1890	.2389	.2880	.3341	.3750
	3	.0001	.0010	.0034	.0080	.0156	.0270	.0429	.0640	.0911	.1250
4	0	.8145	.6561	.5220	.4096	.3164	.2401	.1785	.1296	.0915	.0625
	1	.1715	.2916	.3685	.4096	.4219	.4116	.3845	.3456	.2995	.2500
	2	.0135	.0486	.0975	.1536	.2109	.2646	.3105	.3456	.3675	.3750
	3	.0005	.0036	.0115	.0256	.0469	.0756	.1115	.1536	.2005	.2500
	4	.0000	.0001	.0005	.0016	.0039	.0081	.0150	.0256	.0410	.0625
5	0	.7738	.5905	.4437	.3277	.2373	.1681	.1160	.0778	.0503	.0312
	1	.2036	.3280	.3915	.4096	.3955	.3602	.3124	.2592	.2059	.1562
	2	.0214	.0729	.1382	.2048	.2637	.3087	.3364	.3456	.3369	.3125
	3	.0011	.0081	.0244	.0512	.0879	.1323	.1811	.2304	.2757	.3125
	4	.0000	.0004	.0022	.0064	.0146	.0284	.0488	.0768	.1128	.1562
	5	.0000	.0000	.0001	.0003	.0010	.0024	.0053	.0102	.0185	.0312
6	0	.7351	.5314	.3771	.2621	.1780	.1176	.0754	.0467	.0277	.0156
	1	.2321	.3543	.3993	.3932	.3560	.3025	.2437	.1866	.1359	.0938
	2	.0305	.0984	.1762	.2458	.2966	.3241	.3280	.3110	.2780	.2344
	3	.0021	.0146	.0415	.0819	.1318	.1852	.2355	.2765	.3032	.3125
	4	.0001	.0012	.0055	.0154	.0330	.0595	.0951	.1382	.1861	.2344
	5	.0000	.0001	.0004	.0015	.0044	.0102	.0205	.0369	.0609	.0938
	6	.0000	.0000	.0000	.0001	.0002	.0007	.0018	.0041	.0083	.0156
7	0	.6983	.4783	.3206	.2097	.1335	.0824	.0490	.0280	.0152	.0078
	1	.2573	.3720	.3960	.3670	.3115	.2471	.1848	.1306	.0872	.0547
	2	.0406	.1240	.2097	.2753	.3115	.3177	.2985	.2613	.2140	.1641
	3	.0036	.0230	.0617	.1147	.1730	.2269	.2679	.2903	.2918	.2734
	4	.0002	.0026	.0109	.0287	.0577	.0972	.1442	.1935	.2388	.2734
	5	.0000	.0002	.0012	.0043	.0115	.0250	.0466	.0774	.1172	.1641
	6	.0000	.0000	.0001	.0004	.0013	.0036	.0084	.0172	.0320	.0547
	7	.0000	.0000	.0000	.0000	.0001	.0002	.0006	.0016	.0037	.0078

TABLE 1 $B(r; n, p)$ 557

TABLE 1 *continued* **B(r; n, p)**

n	r	.05	.10	.15	.20	.25	.30	.35	.40	.45	.50
8	0	.6634	.4305	.2725	.1678	.1001	.0576	.0319	.0168	.0084	.0039
	1	.2793	.3826	.3847	.3355	.2670	.1977	.1373	.0896	.0548	.0312
	2	.0515	.1488	.2376	.2936	.3115	.2965	.2587	.2090	.1569	.1094
	3	.0054	.0331	.0839	.1468	.2076	.2541	.2786	.2787	.2568	.2188
	4	.0004	.0046	.0185	.0459	.0865	.1361	.1875	.2322	.2627	.2734
	5	.0000	.0004	.0026	.0092	.0231	.0467	.0808	.1239	.1719	.2188
	6	.0000	.0000	.0002	.0011	.0038	.0100	.0217	.0413	.0703	.1094
	7	.0000	.0000	.0000	.0001	.0004	.0012	.0033	.0079	.0164	.0312
	8	.0000	.0000	.0000	.0000	.0000	.0001	.0002	.0007	.0017	.0039
9	0	.6302	.3874	.2316	.1342	.0751	.0404	.0207	.0101	.0046	.0020
	1	.2985	.3874	.3679	.3020	.2253	.1556	.1004	.0605	.0339	.0176
	2	.0629	.1722	.2597	.3020	.3003	.2668	.2162	.1612	.1110	.0703
	3	.0077	.0446	.1069	.1762	.2336	.2668	.2716	.2508	.2119	.1641
	4	.0006	.0074	.0283	.0661	.1168	.1715	.2194	.2508	.2600	.2461
	5	.0000	.0008	.0050	.0165	.0389	.0735	.1181	.1672	.2128	.2461
	6	.0000	.0001	.0006	.0028	.0087	.0210	.0424	.0743	.1160	.1641
	7	.0000	.0000	.0000	.0003	.0012	.0039	.0098	.0212	.0407	.0703
	8	.0000	.0000	.0000	.0000	.0001	.0004	.0013	.0035	.0083	.0176
	9	.0000	.0000	.0000	.0000	.0000	.0000	.0001	.0003	.0008	.0020
10	0	.5987	.3487	.1969	.1074	.0563	.0282	.0135	.0060	.0025	.0010
	1	.3151	.3874	.3474	.2684	.1877	.1211	.0725	.0403	.0207	.0098
	2	.0746	.1937	.2759	.3020	.2816	.2335	.1757	.1209	.0763	.0439
	3	.0105	.0574	.1298	.2013	.2503	.2668	.2522	.2150	.1665	.1172
	4	.0010	.0112	.0401	.0881	.1460	.2001	.2377	.2508	.2384	.2051
	5	.0001	.0015	.0085	.0264	.0584	.1029	.1536	.2007	.2340	.2461
	6	.0000	.0001	.0012	.0055	.0162	.0368	.0689	.1115	.1596	.2051
	7	.0000	.0000	.0001	.0008	.0031	.0090	.0212	.0425	.0746	.1172
	8	.0000	.0000	.0000	.0001	.0004	.0014	.0043	.0106	.0229	.0439
	9	.0000	.0000	.0000	.0000	.0000	.0001	.0005	.0016	.0042	.0098
	10	.0000	.0000	.0000	.0000	.0000	.0000	.0000	.0001	.0003	.0010
11	0	.5688	.3138	.1673	.0859	.0422	.0198	.0088	.0036	.0014	.0005
	1	.3293	.3835	.3248	.2362	.1549	.0932	.0518	.0266	.0125	.0054
	2	.0867	.2131	.2866	.2953	.2581	.1998	.1395	.0887	.0513	.0269
	3	.0137	.0710	.1517	.2215	.2581	.2568	.2254	.1774	.1259	.0806
	4	.0014	.0158	.0536	.1107	.1721	.2201	.2428	.2365	.2060	.1611
	5	.0001	.0025	.0132	.0388	.0803	.1321	.1830	.2207	.2360	.2256
	6	.0000	.0003	.0023	.0097	.0268	.0566	.0985	.1471	.1931	.2256
	7	.0000	.0000	.0003	.0017	.0064	.0173	.0379	.0701	.1128	.1611

TABLE 1 *continued*   *B(r; n, p)*

n	r	.05	.10	.15	.20	.25	.30	.35	.40	.45	.50
11	8	.0000	.0000	.0000	.0002	.0011	.0037	.0102	.0234	.0462	.0806
	9	.0000	.0000	.0000	.0000	.0001	.0005	.0018	.0052	.0126	.0269
	10	.0000	.0000	.0000	.0000	.0000	.0000	.0002	.0007	.0021	.0054
	11	.0000	.0000	.0000	.0000	.0000	.0000	.0000	.0000	.0002	.0005
12	0	.5404	.2824	.1422	.0687	.0317	.0138	.0057	.0022	.0008	.0002
	1	.3413	.3766	.3012	.2062	.1267	.0712	.0368	.0174	.0075	.0029
	2	.0988	.2301	.2924	.2835	.2323	.1678	.1088	.0639	.0339	.0161
	3	.0173	.0852	.1720	.2362	.2581	.2397	.1954	.1419	.0923	.0537
	4	.0021	.0213	.0683	.1329	.1936	.2311	.2367	.2128	.1700	.1208
	5	.0002	.0038	.0193	.0532	.1032	.1585	.2039	.2270	.2225	.1934
	6	.0000	.0005	.0040	.0155	.0401	.0792	.1281	.1766	.2124	.2256
	7	.0000	.0000	.0006	.0033	.0115	.0291	.0591	.1009	.1489	.1934
	8	.0000	.0000	.0001	.0005	.0024	.0078	.0199	.0420	.0762	.1208
	9	.0000	.0000	.0000	.0001	.0004	.0015	.0048	.0125	.0277	.0537
	10	.0000	.0000	.0000	.0000	.0000	.0002	.0008	.0025	.0068	.0161
	11	.0000	.0000	.0000	.0000	.0000	.0000	.0001	.0003	.0010	.0029
	12	.0000	.0000	.0000	.0000	.0000	.0000	.0000	.0000	.0001	.0002
13	0	.5133	.2542	.1209	.0550	.0238	.0097	.0037	.0013	.0004	.0001
	1	.3512	.3672	.2774	.1787	.1029	.0540	.0259	.0113	.0045	.0016
	2	.1109	.2448	.2937	.2680	.2059	.1388	.0836	.0453	.0220	.0095
	3	.0214	.0997	.1900	.2457	.2517	.2181	.1651	.1107	.0660	.0349
	4	.0028	.0277	.0838	.1535	.2097	.2337	.2222	.1845	.1350	.0873
	5	.0003	.0055	.0266	.0691	.1258	.1803	.2154	.2214	.1989	.1571
	6	.0000	.0008	.0063	.0230	.0559	.1030	.1546	.1968	.2169	.2095
	7	.0000	.0001	.0011	.0058	.0186	.0442	.0833	.1312	.1775	.2095
	8	.0000	.0000	.0001	.0011	.0047	.0142	.0336	.0656	.1089	.1571
	9	.0000	.0000	.0000	.0001	.0009	.0034	.0101	.0243	.0495	.0873
	10	.0000	.0000	.0000	.0000	.0001	.0006	.0022	.0065	.0162	.0349
	11	.0000	.0000	.0000	.0000	.0000	.0001	.0003	.0012	.0036	.0095
	12	.0000	.0000	.0000	.0000	.0000	.0000	.0000	.0001	.0005	.0016
	13	.0000	.0000	.0000	.0000	.0000	.0000	.0000	.0000	.0000	.0001
14	0	.4877	.2288	.1028	.0440	.0178	.0068	.0024	.0008	.0002	.0001
	1	.3593	.3559	.2539	.1539	.0832	.0407	.0181	.0073	.0027	.0009
	2	.1229	.2570	.2912	.2501	.1802	.1134	.0634	.0317	.0141	.0056
	3	.0259	.1142	.2056	.2501	.2402	.1943	.1366	.0845	.0462	.0222
	4	.0037	.0349	.0998	.1720	.2202	.2290	.2022	.1549	.1040	.0611
	5	.0004	.0078	.0352	.0860	.1468	.1963	.2178	.2066	.1701	.1222
	6	.0000	.0013	.0093	.0322	.0734	.1262	.1759	.2066	.2088	.1833

TABLE 1 *B(r; n, p)*   559

TABLE 1 *continued* $B(r; n, p)$

n	r	.05	.10	.15	.20	.25	.30	.35	.40	.45	.50
14	7	.0000	.0002	.0019	.0092	.0280	.0618	.1082	.1574	.1952	.2095
	8	.0000	.0000	.0003	.0020	.0082	.0232	.0510	.0918	.1398	.1833
	9	.0000	.0000	.0000	.0003	.0018	.0066	.0183	.0408	.0762	.1222
	10	.0000	.0000	.0000	.0000	.0003	.0014	.0049	.0136	.0312	.0611
	11	.0000	.0000	.0000	.0000	.0000	.0002	.0010	.0033	.0093	.0222
	12	.0000	.0000	.0000	.0000	.0000	.0000	.0001	.0005	.0019	.0056
	13	.0000	.0000	.0000	.0000	.0000	.0000	.0000	.0001	.0002	.0009
	14	.0000	.0000	.0000	.0000	.0000	.0000	.0000	.0000	.0000	.0001
15	0	.4633	.2059	.0874	.0352	.0134	.0047	.0016	.0005	.0001	.0000
	1	.3658	.3432	.2312	.1329	.0668	.0305	.0126	.0047	.0016	.0005
	2	.1348	.2669	.2856	.2309	.1559	.0916	.0476	.0219	.0090	.0032
	3	.0307	.1285	.2184	.2501	.2252	.1700	.1110	.0634	.0318	.0139
	4	.0049	.0428	.1156	.1876	.2252	.2186	.1792	.1268	.0780	.0417
	5	.0006	.0105	.0449	.1032	.1651	.2061	.2123	.1859	.1404	.0916
	6	.0000	.0019	.0132	.0430	.0917	.1472	.1906	.2066	.1914	.1527
	7	.0000	.0003	.0030	.0138	.0393	.0811	.1319	.1771	.2013	.1964
	8	.0000	.0000	.0005	.0035	.0131	.0348	.0710	.1181	.1647	.1964
	9	.0000	.0000	.0001	.0007	.0034	.0116	.0298	.0612	.1048	.1527
	10	.0000	.0000	.0000	.0001	.0007	.0030	.0096	.0245	.0515	.0916
	11	.0000	.0000	.0000	.0000	.0001	.0006	.0024	.0074	.0191	.0417
	12	.0000	.0000	.0000	.0000	.0000	.0001	.0004	.0016	.0052	.0139
	13	.0000	.0000	.0000	.0000	.0000	.0000	.0001	.0003	.0010	.0032
	14	.0000	.0000	.0000	.0000	.0000	.0000	.0000	.0000	.0001	.0005
	15	.0000	.0000	.0000	.0000	.0000	.0000	.0000	.0000	.0000	.0000
16	0	.4401	.1853	.0743	.0281	.0100	.0033	.0010	.0003	.0001	.0000
	1	.3706	.3294	.2097	.1126	.0535	.0228	.0087	.0030	.0009	.0002
	2	.1463	.2745	.2775	.2111	.1336	.0732	.0353	.0150	.0056	.0018
	3	.0359	.1423	.2285	.2463	.2079	.1465	.0888	.0468	.0215	.0085
	4	.0061	.0514	.1311	.2001	.2252	.2040	.1553	.1014	.0572	.0278
	5	.0008	.0137	.0555	.1201	.1802	.2099	.2008	.1623	.1123	.0667
	6	.0001	.0028	.0180	.0550	.1101	.1649	.1982	.1983	.1684	.1222
	7	.0000	.0004	.0045	.0197	.0524	.1010	.1524	.1889	.1969	.1746
	8	.0000	.0001	.0009	.0055	.0197	.0487	.0923	.1417	.1812	.1964
	9	.0000	.0000	.0001	.0012	.0058	.0185	.0442	.0840	.1318	.1746
	10	.0000	.0000	.0000	.0002	.0014	.0056	.0167	.0392	.0755	.1222
	11	.0000	.0000	.0000	.0000	.0002	.0013	.0049	.0142	.0337	.0667
	12	.0000	.0000	.0000	.0000	.0000	.0002	.0011	.0040	.0115	.0278
	13	.0000	.0000	.0000	.0000	.0000	.0000	.0002	.0008	.0029	.0085
	14	.0000	.0000	.0000	.0000	.0000	.0000	.0000	.0001	.0005	.0018

TABLE 1 *continued* $B(r; n, p)$

n	r	.05	.10	.15	.20	.25	.30	.35	.40	.45	.50
16	15	.0000	.0000	.0000	.0000	.0000	.0000	.0000	.0000	.0001	.0002
	16	.0000	.0000	.0000	.0000	.0000	.0000	.0000	.0000	.0000	.0000
17	0	.4181	.1668	.0631	.0225	.0075	.0023	.0007	.0002	.0000	.0000
	1	.3741	.3150	.1893	.0957	.0426	.0169	.0060	.0019	.0005	.0001
	2	.1575	.2800	.2673	.1914	.1136	.0581	.0260	.0102	.0035	.0010
	3	.0415	.1556	.2359	.2393	.1893	.1245	.0701	.0341	.0144	.0052
	4	.0076	.0605	.1457	.2093	.2209	.1868	.1320	.0796	.0411	.0182
	5	.0010	.0175	.0668	.1361	.1914	.2081	.1849	.1379	.0875	.0472
	6	.0001	.0039	.0236	.0680	.1276	.1784	.1991	.1839	.1432	.0944
	7	.0000	.0007	.0065	.0267	.0668	.1201	.1685	.1927	.1841	.1484
	8	.0000	.0001	.0014	.0084	.0279	.0644	.1134	.1606	.1883	.1855
	9	.0000	.0000	.0003	.0021	.0093	.0276	.0611	.1070	.1540	.1855
	10	.0000	.0000	.0000	.0004	.0025	.0095	.0263	.0571	.1008	.1484
	11	.0000	.0000	.0000	.0001	.0005	.0026	.0090	.0242	.0525	.0944
	12	.0000	.0000	.0000	.0000	.0001	.0006	.0024	.0081	.0215	.0472
	13	.0000	.0000	.0000	.0000	.0000	.0001	.0005	.0021	.0068	.0182
	14	.0000	.0000	.0000	.0000	.0000	.0000	.0001	.0004	.0016	.0052
	15	.0000	.0000	.0000	.0000	.0000	.0000	.0000	.0001	.0003	.0010
	16	.0000	.0000	.0000	.0000	.0000	.0000	.0000	.0000	.0000	.0001
	17	.0000	.0000	.0000	.0000	.0000	.0000	.0000	.0000	.0000	.0000
18	0	.3972	.1501	.0536	.0180	.0056	.0016	.0004	.0001	.0000	.0000
	1	.3763	.3002	.1704	.0811	.0338	.0126	.0042	.0012	.0003	.0001
	2	.1683	.2835	.2556	.1723	.0958	.0458	.0190	.0069	.0022	.0006
	3	.0473	.1680	.2406	.2297	.1704	.1046	.0547	.0246	.0095	.0031
	4	.0093	.0700	.1592	.2153	.2130	.1681	.1104	.0614	.0291	.0117
	5	.0014	.0218	.0787	.1507	.1988	.2017	.1664	.1146	.0666	.0327
	6	.0002	.0052	.0301	.0816	.1436	.1873	.1941	.1655	.1181	.0708
	7	.0000	.0010	.0091	.0350	.0820	.1376	.1792	.1892	.1657	.1214
	8	.0000	.0002	.0022	.0120	.0376	.0811	.1327	.1734	.1864	.1669
	9	.0000	.0000	.0004	.0033	.0139	.0386	.0794	.1284	.1694	.1855
	10	.0000	.0000	.0001	.0008	.0042	.0149	.0385	.0771	.1248	.1669
	11	.0000	.0000	.0000	.0001	.0010	.0046	.0151	.0374	.0742	.1214
	12	.0000	.0000	.0000	.0000	.0002	.0012	.0047	.0145	.0354	.0708
	13	.0000	.0000	.0000	.0000	.0000	.0002	.0012	.0045	.0134	.0327
	14	.0000	.0000	.0000	.0000	.0000	.0000	.0002	.0011	.0039	.0117
	15	.0000	.0000	.0000	.0000	.0000	.0000	.0000	.0002	.0009	.0031
	16	.0000	.0000	.0000	.0000	.0000	.0000	.0000	.0000	.0001	.0006
	17	.0000	.0000	.0000	.0000	.0000	.0000	.0000	.0000	.0000	.0001
	18	.0000	.0000	.0000	.0000	.0000	.0000	.0000	.0000	.0000	.0000

TABLE 1 $B(r; n, p)$ 561

TABLE 1 continued   B(r; n, p)

n	r	.05	.10	.15	.20	.25	.30	.35	.40	.45	.50
19	0	.3774	.1351	.0456	.0144	.0042	.0011	.0003	.0001	.0000	.0000
	1	.3774	.2852	.1529	.0685	.0268	.0093	.0029	.0008	.0002	.0000
	2	.1787	.2852	.2428	.1540	.0803	.0358	.0138	.0046	.0013	.0003
	3	.0533	.1796	.2428	.2182	.1517	.0869	.0422	.0175	.0062	.0018
	4	.0112	.0798	.1714	.2182	.2023	.1491	.0909	.0467	.0203	.0074
	5	.0018	.0266	.0907	.1636	.2023	.1916	.1468	.0933	.0497	.0222
	6	.0002	.0069	.0374	.0955	.1574	.1916	.1844	.1451	.0949	.1518
	7	.0000	.0014	.0122	.0443	.0974	.1525	.1844	.1797	.1443	.0961
	8	.0000	.0002	.0032	.0166	.0487	.0981	.1489	.1797	.1771	.1442
	9	.0000	.0000	.0007	.0051	.0198	.0514	.0980	.1464	.1771	.1762
	10	.0000	.0000	.0001	.0013	.0066	.0220	.0528	.0976	.1449	.1762
	11	.0000	.0000	.0000	.0003	.0018	.0077	.0233	.0532	.0970	.1442
	12	.0000	.0000	.0000	.0000	.0004	.0022	.0083	.0237	.0529	.0961
	13	.0000	.0000	.0000	.0000	.0001	.0005	.0024	.0085	.0233	.0518
	14	.0000	.0000	.0000	.0000	.0000	.0001	.0006	.0024	.0082	.0222
	15	.0000	.0000	.0000	.0000	.0000	.0000	.0001	.0005	.0022	.0074
	16	.0000	.0000	.0000	.0000	.0000	.0000	.0000	.0001	.0005	.0018
	17	.0000	.0000	.0000	.0000	.0000	.0000	.0000	.0000	.0001	.0003
	18	.0000	.0000	.0000	.0000	.0000	.0000	.0000	.0000	.0000	.0000
	19	.0000	.0000	.0000	.0000	.0000	.0000	.0000	.0000	.0000	.0000
20	0	.3585	.1216	.0388	.0115	.0032	.0008	.0002	.0000	.0000	.0000
	1	.3774	.2702	.1368	.0576	.0211	.0068	.0020	.0005	.0001	.0000
	2	.1887	.2852	.2293	.1369	.0669	.0278	.0100	.0031	.0008	.0002
	3	.0596	.1901	.2428	.2054	.1339	.0716	.0323	.0123	.0040	.0011
	4	.0133	.0898	.1821	.2182	.1897	.1304	.0738	.0350	.0139	.0046
	5	.0022	.0319	.1028	.1746	.2023	.1789	.1272	.0746	.0365	.0148
	6	.0003	.0089	.0454	.1091	.1686	.1916	.1712	.1244	.0746	.0370
	7	.0000	.0020	.0160	.0545	.1124	.1643	.1844	.1659	.1221	.0739
	8	.0000	.0004	.0046	.0222	.0609	.1144	.1614	.1797	.1623	.1201
	9	.0000	.0001	.0011	.0074	.0271	.0654	.1158	.1597	.1771	.1602
	10	.0000	.0000	.0002	.0020	.0099	.0308	.0686	.1171	.1593	.1762
	11	.0000	.0000	.0000	.0005	.0030	.0120	.0336	.0710	.1185	.1602
	12	.0000	.0000	.0000	.0001	.0008	.0039	.1036	.0355	.0727	.1201
	13	.0000	.0000	.0000	.0000	.0002	.0010	.0045	.0146	.0366	.0739
	14	.0000	.0000	.0000	.0000	.0000	.0002	.0012	.0049	.0150	.0370
	15	.0000	.0000	.0000	.0000	.0000	.0000	.0003	.0013	.0049	.0148
	16	.0000	.0000	.0000	.0000	.0000	.0000	.0000	.0003	.0013	.0046
	17	.0000	.0000	.0000	.0000	.0000	.0000	.0000	.0000	.0002	.0011
	18	.0000	.0000	.0000	.0000	.0000	.0000	.0000	.0000	.0000	.0002
	19	.0000	.0000	.0000	.0000	.0000	.0000	.0000	.0000	.0000	.0000
	20	.0000	.0000	.0000	.0000	.0000	.0000	.0000	.0000	.0000	.0000

TABLE 2 Common Logarithms

x	0	1	2	3	4	5	6	7	8	9
1.0	0.0000	.0043	.0086	.0128	.0170	.0212	.0253	.0294	.0334	.0374
.1	.0414	.0453	.0492	.0531	.0569	.0607	.0645	.0682	.0719	.0755
.2	.0792	.0828	.0864	.0899	.0934	.0969	.1004	.1038	.1072	.1106
.3	.1139	.1173	.1206	.1239	.1271	.1303	.1335	.1367	.1399	.1430
.4	.1461	.1492	.1523	.1553	.1584	.1614	.1644	.1673	.1703	.1732
.5	.1761	.1790	.1818	.1847	.1875	.1903	.1931	.1959	.1987	.2014
.6	.2041	.2068	.2095	.2122	.2148	.2175	.2201	.2227	.2253	.2279
.7	.2304	.2330	.2355	.2380	.2405	.2430	.2455	.2480	.2504	.2529
.8	.2553	.2577	.2601	.2625	.2648	.2672	.2695	.2718	.2742	.2765
.9	.2788	.2810	.2833	2856	.2878	.2900	.2923	.2945	.2967	.2989
2.0	0.3010	.3032	.3054	.3075	.3096	.3118	.3139	.3160	.3181	.3201
.1	.3222	.3243	.3263	.3284	.3304	.3324	.3345	.3365	.3385	.3404
.2	.3424	.3444	.3464	.3483	.3502	.3522	.3541	.3560	.3579	.3598
.3	.3617	.3636	.3655	.3674	.3692	.3711	.3729	.3747	.3766	.3784
.4	.3802	.3820	.3838	.3856	.3874	.3892	.3909	.3927	.3945	.3962
.5	.3979	.3997	.4014	.4031	.4048	.4065	.4082	.4099	.4116	.4133
.6	.4150	.4166	.4183	.4200	.4216	.4232	.4249	.4265	.4281	.4298
.7	.4314	.4330	.4346	.4362	.4378	.4393	.4409	.4425	.4440	.4456
.8	.4472	.4487	.4502	.4518	.4533	.4548	.4564	.4579	.4594	.4609
.9	.4624	.4639	.4654	.4669	.4683	.4698	.4713	.4728	.4742	.4757
3.0	0.4771	.4786	.4800	.4814	.4829	.4843	.4857	.4871	.4886	.4900
.1	.4914	.4928	.4942	.4955	.4969	.4983	.4997	.5011	.5024	.5038
.2	.5051	.5065	.5079	.5092	.5105	.5119	.5132	.5145	.5159	.5172
.3	.5185	.5198	.5211	.5224	.5237	.5250	.5263	.5276	.5289	.5302
.4	.5315	.5328	.5340	.5353	.5366	.5378	.5391	.5403	.5416	.5428
.5	.5441	.5453	.5465	.5478	.5490	.5502	.5514	.5527	.5539	.5551
.6	.5563	.5575	.5587	.5599	.5611	.5623	.5635	.5647	.5658	.5670
.7	.5682	.5694	.5705	.5717	.5729	.5740	.5752	.5763	.5775	.5786
.8	.5798	.5809	.5821	.5832	.5843	.5855	.5866	.5877	.5888	.5899
.9	.5911	.5922	.5933	.5944	.5955	.5966	.5977	.5988	.5999	.6010
4.0	0.6021	.6031	.6042	.6053	.6064	.6075	.6085	.6096	.6107	.6117
.1	.6128	.6138	.6149	.6160	.6170	.6180	.6191	.6201	.6212	.6222
.2	.6232	.6243	.6253	.6263	.6274	.6284	.6294	.6304	.6314	.6325
.3	.6335	.6345	.6355	.6365	.6375	.6385	.6395	.6405	.6415	.6425
.4	.6435	.6444	.6454	.6464	.6474	.6484	.6493	.6503	.6513	.6522
.5	.6532	.6542	.6551	.6561	.6571	.6580	.6590	.6599	.6609	.6618
.6	.6628	.6637	.6646	.6656	.6665	.6675	.6684	.6693	.6702	.6712
.7	.6721	.6730	.6739	.6749	.6758	.6767	.6776	.6785	.6794	.6803
.8	.6812	.6821	.6830	.6839	.6848	.6857	.6866	.6875	.6884	.6893
.9	.6902	.6911	.6920	.6928	.6937	.6946	.6955	.6964	.6972	.6981
5.0	0.6990	.6998	.7007	.7016	.7024	.7033	.7042	.7050	.7059	.7067
.1	.7076	.7084	.7093	.7101	.7110	.7118	.7126	.7135	.7143	.7152
.2	.7160	.7168	.7177	.7185	.7193	.7202	.7210	.7218	.7226	.7235
.3	.7243	.7251	.7259	.7267	.7275	.7284	.7292	.7300	.7308	.7316
.4	.7324	.7332	.7340	.7348	.7356	.7364	.7372	.7380	.7388	.7396

TABLE 2 COMMON LOGARITHMS   563

TABLE 2 *continued*   Common Logarithms

x	0	1	2	3	4	5	6	7	8	9
5.5	.7404	.7412	.7419	.7427	.7435	.7443	.7451	.7459	.7466	.7474
.6	.7482	.7490	.7497	.7505	.7513	.7520	.7528	.7536	.7543	.7551
.7	.7559	.7566	.7574	.7582	.7589	.7597	.7604	.7612	.7619	.7627
.8	.7634	.7642	.7649	.7657	.7664	.7672	.7679	.7686	.7694	.7701
.9	.7709	.7716	.7723	.7731	.7738	.7745	.7752	.7760	.7767	.7774
6.0	0.7782	.7789	.7796	.7803	7810	.7818	.7825	.7832	.7839	.7846
.1	.7853	.7860	.7868	.7875	.7882	.7889	.7896	.7903	.7910	.7917
.2	.7924	.7931	.7938	.7945	.7952	.7959	.7966	.7973	.7980	.7987
.3	.7993	.8000	.8007	.8014	.8021	.8028	.8035	.8041	.8048	.8055
.4	.8062	.8069	.8075	.8082	.8089	.8096	.8102	.8109	.8116	.8122
.5	.8129	.8136	.8142	.8149	.8156	.8162	.8169	.8176	.8182	.8189
.6	.8195	.8202	.8209	.8215	.8222	.8228	.8235	.8241	.8248	.8254
.7	.8261	.8267	.8274	.8280	.8287	.8293	.8299	.8306	.8312	.8319
.8	.8325	.8331	.8338	.8344	.8351	.8357	.8363	.8370	.8376	.8382
.9	.8388	.8395	.8401	.8407	.8414	.8420	.8426	.8432	.8439	.8445
7.0	0.8451	.8457	.8463	.8470	.8476	.8482	.8488	.8494	.8500	.8506
.1	.8513	.8519	.8525	.8531	.8537	.8543	.8549	.8555	.8561	.8567
.2	.8573	.8579	.8585	.8591	.8597	.8603	.8609	.8615	.8621	.8627
.3	.8633	.8639	.8645	.8651	.8657	.8663	.8669	.8675	.8681	.8686
.4	.8692	.8698	.8704	.8710	.8716	.8722	.8727	.8733	.8739	.8745
.5	.8751	.8756	.8762	.8768	.8774	.8779	.8785	.8791	.8797	.8802
.6	.8808	.8814	.8820	.8825	.8831	.8837	.8842	.8848	.8854	.8859
.7	.8865	.8871	.8876	.8882	.8887	.8893	.8899	.8904	.8910	.8915
.8	.8921	.8927	.8932	.8938	.8943	.8949	.8954	.8960	.8965	.8971
.9	.8976	.8982	.8987	.8993	.8998	.9004	.9009	.9015	.9020	.9025
8.0	0.9031	.9036	.9042	.9047	.9053	.9058	.9063	.9069	.9074	.9079
.1	.9085	.9090	.9096	.9101	.9106	.9112	.9117	.9122	.9128	.9133
.2	.9138	.9143	.9149	.9154	.9159	.9165	.9170	.9175	.9180	.9186
.3	.9191	.9196	.9201	.9206	.9212	.9217	.9222	.9227	.9232	.9238
.4	.9243	.9248	.9253	.9258	.9263	.9269	.9274	.9279	.9284	.9289
.5	.9294	.9299	.9304	.9309	.9315	.9320	.9325	.9330	.9335	.9340
.6	.9345	.9350	.9355	.9360	.9365	.9370	.9375	.9380	.9385	.9390
.7	.9395	.9400	.9405	.9410	.9415	.9420	.9425	.9430	.9435	.9440
.8	.9445	.9450	.9455	.9460	.9465	.9469	.9474	.9479	.9484	.9489
.9	.9494	.9499	.9504	.9509	.9513	.9518	.9523	.9528	.9533	.9538
9.0	0.9542	.9547	.9552	.9557	.9562	.9566	.9571	.9576	.9581	.9586
.1	.9590	.9595	.9600	.9605	.9609	.9614	.9619	.9624	.9628	.9633
.2	.9638	.9643	.9647	.9652	.9657	.9661	.9666	.9671	.9675	.9680
.3	.9685	.9689	.9694	.9699	.9703	.9708	.9713	.9717	.9722	.9727
.4	.9731	.9736	.9741	.9745	.9750	.9754	.9759	.9763	.9768	.9773
.5	.9777	.9782	.9786	.9791	.9795	.9800	.9805	.9809	.9814	.9818
.6	.9823	.9827	.9832	.9836	.9841	.9845	.9850	.9854	.9859	.9863
.7	.9868	.9872	.9877	.9881	.9886	.9890	.9894	.9899	.9903	.9908
.8	.9912	.9917	.9921	.9926	.9930	.9934	.9939	.9943	.9948	.9952
.9	.9956	.9961	.9965	.9969	.9974	.9978	.9983	.9987	.9991	.9996

Source: This table is reproduced from S. Selby, *Standard Mathematical Tables*, 20th edition (Cleveland, Ohio: The Chemical Rubber Company, 1972). Used by permission.

TABLE 3 Natural Logarithms

To find the natural logarithm of a number which is 1/10, 1/100, 1/1000, etc. of a number whose logarithm is given, subtract from the given logarithm $\log_e 10$, $2\log_e 10$, $3\log_e 10$, etc.

To find the natural logarithm of a number which is 10, 100, 1000, etc. times a number whose logarithm is given, add to the given logarithm $\log_e 10$, $2\log_e 10$, $3\log_e 10$, etc.

$1\log_e 10 =\ \ 2.30259$	$6\log_e 10 = 13.81551$
$2\log_e 10 =\ \ 4.60517$	$7\log_e 10 = 16.11810$
$3\log_e 10 =\ \ 6.90776$	$8\log_e 10 = 18.42068$
$4\log_e 10 =\ \ 9.21034$	$9\log_e 10 = 20.72327$
$5\log_e 10 = 11.51293$	$10\log_e 10 = 23.02585$

N	0	1	2	3	4	5	6	7	8	9
1.0	0.00000	.00995	.01980	.02956	.03922	.04879	.05827	.06766	.07696	.08618
.1	.09531	.10436	.11333	.12222	.13103	.13976	.14842	.15700	.16551	.17395
.2	.18232	.19062	.19885	.20701	.21511	.22314	.23111	.23902	.24686	.25464
.3	.26236	.27003	.27763	.28518	.29267	.30010	.30748	.31481	.32208	.32930
.4	.33647	.34359	.35066	.35767	.36464	.37156	.37844	.38526	.39204	.39878
.5	.40547	.41211	.41871	.42527	.43178	.43825	.44469	.45108	.45742	.46373
.6	.47000	.47623	.48243	.48858	.49470	.50078	.50682	.51282	.51879	.52473
.7	.53063	.53649	.54232	.54812	.55389	.55962	.56531	.57098	.57661	.58222
.8	.58779	.59333	.59884	.60432	.60977	.61519	.62058	.62594	.63127	.63658
.9	.64185	.64710	.65233	.65752	.66269	.66783	.67294	.67803	.68310	.68813
2.0	0.69315	.69812	.70310	.70804	.71295	.71784	.72271	.72755	.73237	.73716
.1	.74194	.74669	.75142	.75612	.76081	.76547	.77011	.77473	.77932	.78390
.2	.78846	.79299	.79751	.80200	.80648	.81093	.81536	.81978	.82418	.82855
.3	.83291	.83725	.84157	.84587	.85015	.85442	.85866	.86289	.86710	.87129
.4	.87547	.87963	.88377	.88789	.89200	.89609	.90016	.90422	.90826	.91228
.5	.91629	.92028	.92426	.92822	.93216	.93609	.94001	.94391	.94779	.95166
.6	.95551	.95935	.96317	.96698	.97078	.97456	.97833	.98208	.98582	.98954
.7	.99325	.99695	.00063	.00430	.00796	.01160	.01523	.01885	.02245	.02604
.8	1.02962	.03318	.03674	.04028	.04380	.04732	.05082	.05431	.05779	.06126
.9	.06471	.06815	.07158	.07500	.07841	.08181	.08519	.08856	.09192	.09527
3.0	1.09861	.10194	.10526	.10856	.11186	.11514	.11841	.12168	.12493	.12817
.1	.13140	.13462	.13783	.14103	.14422	.14740	.15057	.15373	.15688	.16002
.2	.16315	.16627	.16938	.17248	.17557	.17865	.18173	.18479	.18784	.19089
.3	.19392	.19695	.19996	.20297	.20597	.20896	.21194	.21491	.21788	.22083
.4	.22378	.22671	.22964	.23256	.23547	.23837	.24127	.24415	.24703	.24990
.5	.25276	.25562	.25846	.26130	.26413	.26695	.26976	.27257	.27536	.27815
.6	.28093	.28371	.28647	.28923	.29198	.29473	.29746	.30019	.30291	.30563
.7	.30833	.31103	.31372	.31641	.31909	.32176	.32442	.32708	.32972	.33237
.8	.33500	.33763	.34025	.34286	.34547	.34807	.35067	.35325	.35584	.35841
.9	.36098	.36354	.36609	.36864	.37118	.37372	.37624	.37877	.38128	.38379
4.0	1.38629	.38879	.39128	.39377	.39624	.39872	.40118	.40364	.40610	.40854
.1	.41099	.41342	.41585	.41828	.42070	.42311	.42552	.42792	.43031	.43270
.2	.43508	.43746	.43984	.44220	.44456	.44692	.44927	.45161	.45395	.45629
.3	.45862	.46094	.46326	.46557	.46787	.47018	.47247	.47476	.47705	.47933
.4	.48160	.48387	.48614	.48840	.49065	.49290	.49515	.49739	.49962	.50185
.5	.50408	.50630	.50851	.51072	.51293	.51513	.51732	.51951	.52170	.52388
.6	.52606	.52823	.53039	.53256	.53471	.53687	.53902	.54116	.54330	.54543
.7	.54756	.54969	.55181	.55393	.55604	.55814	.56025	.56235	.56444	.56653
.8	.56862	.57070	.57277	.57485	.57691	.57898	.58104	.58309	.58515	.58719
.9	.58924	.59127	.59331	.59534	.59737	.59939	.60141	.60342	.60543	.60744

TABLE 3 NATURAL LOGARITHMS   565

TABLE 3 *continued*   Natural Logarithms

N	0	1	2	3	4	5	6	7	8	9
5.0	1.60944	.61144	.61343	.61542	.61741	.61939	.62137	.62334	.62531	.62728
.1	.62924	.63120	.63315	.63511	.63705	.63900	.64094	.64287	.64481	.64673
.2	.64866	.65058	.65250	.65441	.65632	.65823	.66013	.66203	.66393	.66582
.3	.66771	.66959	.67147	.67335	.67523	.67710	.67896	.68083	.68269	.68455
.4	.68640	.68825	.69010	.69194	.69378	.69562	.69745	.69928	.70111	.70293
.5	.70475	.70656	.70838	.71019	.71199	.71380	.71560	.71740	.71919	.72098
.6	.72277	.72455	.72633	.72811	.72988	.73166	.73342	.73519	.73695	.73871
.7	.74047	.74222	.74397	.74572	.74746	.74920	.75094	.75267	.75440	.75613
.8	.75786	.75958	.76130	.76302	.76473	.76644	.76815	.76985	.77156	.77326
.9	.77495	.77665	.77834	.78002	.78171	.78339	.78507	.78675	.78842	.79009
6.0	1.79176	.79342	.79509	.79675	.79840	.80006	.80171	.80336	.80500	.80665
.1	.80829	.80993	.81156	.81319	.81482	.81645	.81808	.81970	.82132	.82294
.2	.82455	.82616	.82777	.82938	.83098	.83258	.83418	.83578	.83737	.83896
.3	.84055	.84214	.84372	.84530	.84688	.84845	.85003	.85160	.85317	.85473
.4	.85630	.85786	.85942	.86097	.86253	.86408	.86563	.86718	.86872	.87026
.5	.87180	.87334	.87487	.87641	.87794	.87947	.88099	.88251	.88403	.88555
.6	.88707	.88858	.89010	.89160	.89311	.89462	.89612	.89762	.89912	.90061
.7	.90211	.90360	.90509	.90658	.90806	.90954	.91102	.91250	.91398	.91545
.8	.91692	.91839	.91986	.92132	.92279	.92425	.92571	.92716	.92862	.93007
.9	.93152	.93297	.93442	.93586	.93730	.93874	.94018	.94162	.94305	.94448
7.0	1.94591	.94734	.94876	.95019	.95161	.95303	.95445	.95586	.95727	.95869
.1	.96009	.96150	.96291	.96431	.96571	.96711	.96851	.96991	.97130	.97269
.2	.97408	.97547	.97685	.97824	.97962	.98100	.98238	.98376	.98513	.98650
.3	.98787	.98924	.99061	.99198	.99334	.99470	.99606	.99742	.99877	.00013
.4	2.00148	.00283	.00418	.00553	.00687	.00821	.00956	.01089	.01223	.01357
.5	.01490	.01624	.01757	.01890	.02022	.02155	.02287	.02419	.02551	.02683
.6	.02815	.02946	.03078	.03209	.03340	.03471	.03601	.03732	.03862	.03992
.7	.04122	.04252	.04381	.04511	.04640	.04769	.04898	.05027	.05156	.05284
.8	.05412	.05540	.05668	.05796	.05924	.06051	.06179	.06306	.06433	.06560
.9	.06686	.06813	.06939	.07065	.07191	.07317	.07443	.07568	.07694	.07819
8.0	2.07944	.08069	.08194	.08318	.08443	.08567	.08691	.08815	.08939	.09063
.1	.09186	.09310	.09433	.09556	.09679	.09802	.09924	.10047	.10169	.10291
.2	.10413	.10535	.10657	.10779	.10900	.11021	.11142	.11263	.11384	.11505
.3	.11626	.11746	.11866	.11986	.12106	.12226	.12346	.12465	.12585	.12704
.4	.12823	.12942	.13061	.13180	.13298	.13417	.13535	.13653	.13771	.13889
.5	.14007	.14124	.14242	.14359	.14476	.14593	.14710	.14827	.14943	.15060
.6	.15176	.15292	.15409	.15524	.15640	.15756	.15871	.15987	.16102	.16217
.7	.16332	.16447	.16562	.16677	.16791	.16905	.17020	.17134	.17248	.17361
.8	.17475	.17589	.17702	.17816	.17929	.18042	.18155	.18267	.18380	.18493
.9	.18605	.18717	.18830	.18942	.19054	.19165	.19277	.19389	.19500	.19611
9.0	2.19722	.19834	.19944	.20055	.20166	.20276	.20387	.20497	.20607	2.0717
.1	.20827	.20937	.21047	.21157	.21266	.21375	.21485	.21594	.21703	.21812
.2	.21920	.22029	.22138	.22246	.22354	.22462	.22570	.22678	.22786	.22894
.3	.23001	.23109	.23218	.23324	.23431	.23538	.23645	.23751	.23858	.23965
.4	.24071	.24177	.24284	.24390	.24496	.24601	.24707	.24813	.24918	.25024
.5	.25129	.25234	.25339	.25444	.25549	.25654	.25759	.25863	.25968	.26072
.6	.26176	.26280	.26384	.26488	.26592	.26696	.26799	.26903	.27006	.27109
.7	.27213	.27316	.27419	.27521	.27624	.27727	.27829	.27932	.28034	.28136
.8	.28238	.28340	.28442	.28544	.28646	.28747	.28849	.28950	.29051	.29152
.9	.29253	.29354	.29455	.29556	.29657	.29757	.29858	.29958	.30058	.30158

Source: This table is reproduced from S. Selby, *Standard Mathematical Tables,* 20th edition (Cleveland, Ohio: The Chemical Rubber Company, 1972). Used by permission.

TABLE 4   Exponential Functions

x	e^x	e^{-x}	x	e^x	e^{-x}
.1	1.10517	.904837	5.1	164.022	.006097
.2	1.2214	.818731	5.2	181.272	.005517
.3	1.34986	.740818	5.3	200.337	.004992
.4	1.49183	.67032	5.4	221.406	.004517
.5	1.64872	.606531	5.5	244.692	.004087
.6	1.82212	.548811	5.6	270.427	.003698
.7	2.01375	.496585	5.7	298.867	.003346
.8	2.22554	.449329	5.8	330.3	.003028
.9	2.4596	.40657	5.9	365.037	.002739
1.0	2.71828	.367879	6.0	403.429	.002479
1.1	3.00417	.332871	6.1	445.859	.002243
1.2	3.32012	.301194	6.2	492.749	.002029
1.3	3.6693	.272532	6.3	544.572	.001836
1.4	4.0552	.246597	6.4	601.845	.001662
1.5	4.48169	.22313	6.5	665.142	.001503
1.6	4.95303	.201897	6.6	735.095	.00136
1.7	5.47395	.182684	6.7	812.406	.001231
1.8	6.04965	.165299	6.8	897.848	.001114
1.9	6.6859	.149569	6.9	992.275	.001008
2.0	7.38906	.135335	7.0	1096.63	.000912
2.1	8.16617	.122456	7.1	1211.97	.000825
2.2	9.02501	.110803	7.2	1339.43	.000747
2.3	9.97419	.100259	7.3	1480.3	.000676
2.4	11.0232	.090718	7.4	1635.98	.000611
2.5	12.1825	.082085	7.5	1808.04	.000553
2.6	13.4637	.074274	7.6	1998.2	.0005
2.7	14.8797	.067205	7.7	2208.35	.000453
2.8	16.4447	.06081	7.8	2440.61	.00041
2.9	18.1741	.055023	7.9	2697.28	.000371
3.0	20.0855	.049787	8.0	2980.96	.000335
3.1	22.198	.045049	8.1	3294.47	.000304
3.2	24.5325	.040762	8.2	3640.95	.000275
3.3	27.1126	.036883	8.3	4023.87	.000249
3.4	29.9641	.033373	8.4	4447.07	.000225
3.5	33.1155	.030197	8.5	4914.77	.000203
3.6	36.5983	.027324	8.6	5431.66	.000184
3.7	40.4473	.024724	8.7	6002.92	.000167
3.8	44.7012	.022371	8.8	6634.25	.000151
3.9	49.4025	.020242	8.9	7331.98	.000136
4.0	54.5982	.018316	9.0	8103.09	.000123
4.1	60.3403	.016573	9.1	8955.3	.000112
4.2	66.6863	.014996	9.2	9897.14	.000101
4.3	73.6998	.013569	9.3	10938	.000091
4.4	81.4509	.012277	9.4	12088.4	.000083
4.5	90.0172	.011109	9.5	13359.7	.000075
4.6	99.4844	.010052	9.6	14764.8	.000068
4.7	109.947	.009095	9.7	16317.6	.000061
4.8	121.51	.00823	9.8	18033.7	.000055
4.9	134.29	.007447	9.9	19930.4	.00005
5.0	148.413	.006738	10.0	22026.5	.000045

TABLE 4   EXPONENTIAL FUNCTIONS

567

TABLE 5 $(1 + R)^k$

$k =$	$R = 0.005$	$R = 0.0075$	$R = 0.01$	$R = 0.0125$	$R = 0.015$	$R = 0.02$
1	1.005000	1.007500	1.010000	1.012500	1.015000	1.020000
2	1.010025	1.015056	1.020100	1.025156	1.030225	1.040400
3	1.015075	1.022669	1.030301	1.037971	1.045678	1.061208
4	1.020150	1.030339	1.040604	1.050945	1.061364	1.082432
5	1.025251	1.038067	1.050110	1.064082	1.077284	1.104081
6	1.030378	1.045852	1.061520	1.077383	1.093443	1.126162
7	1.035529	1.053696	1.072135	1.090850	1.109845	1.148686
8	1.040707	1.061599	1.082857	1.104486	1.126493	1.171659
9	1.045911	1.069561	1.093685	1.118292	1.143390	1.195093
10	1.051140	1.077583	1.104622	1.132271	1.160541	1.218994
11	1.056396	1.085664	1.115668	1.146424	1.177949	1.243374
12	1.061678	1.093807	1.126825	1.160755	1.195618	1.268242
13	1.066986	1.102010	1.138093	1.175264	1.213552	1.293607
14	1.072321	1.110276	1.149474	1.189955	1.231756	1.319479
15	1.077683	1.118603	1.160969	1.204829	1.250232	1.345868
16	1.083071	1.126992	1.172579	1.219890	1.268986	1.372786
17	1.088487	1.135445	1.184304	1.235138	1.288020	1.400241
18	1.093929	1.143960	1.196147	1.250577	1.307341	1.428246
19	1.099399	1.152540	1.208109	1.266210	1.326951	1.456811
20	1.104896	1.161184	1.220190	1.282037	1.346855	1.485947
21	1.110420	1.169893	1.232392	1.298063	1.367058	1.515666
22	1.115972	1.178667	1.244716	1.314288	1.387564	1.545980
23	1.121552	1.187507	1.257163	1.330717	1.408377	1.576899
24	1.127160	1.196414	1.269735	1.347351	1.429503	1.608437
25	1.132796	1.205387	1.282432	1.364193	1.450945	1.640606
26	1.138460	1.214427	1.295256	1.381245	1.472710	1.673418
27	1.144152	1.223535	1.308209	1.398511	1.494800	1.706886
28	1.149873	1.232712	1.321291	1.415992	1.517222	1.741024
29	1.155622	1.241957	1.334504	1.433692	1.539981	1.775845
30	1.161400	1.251272	1.347849	1.451613	1.563080	1.811362

TABLE 5 *continued* $(1 + R)^k$

$k =$	$R = 0.005$	$R = 0.0075$	$R = 0.01$	$R = 0.0125$	$R = 0.015$	$R = 0.02$
31	1.167207	1.260656	1.361327	1.469759	1.586526	1.847589
32	1.173043	1.270111	1.374941	1.488131	1.610324	1.884541
33	1.178908	1.279637	1.388690	1.506732	1.634479	1.922231
34	1.184803	1.289234	1.402577	1.525566	1.658996	1.960676
35	1.190727	1.298904	1.416603	1.544636	1.683881	1.999890
36	1.196681	1.308645	1.430769	1.563944	1.709140	2.039887
37	1.202664	1.318460	1.445076	1.583493	1.734777	2.080685
38	1.208677	1.328349	1.459527	1.603287	1.760798	2.122299
39	1.214721	1.338311	1.474123	1.623328	1.787210	2.164745
40	1.220794	1.348349	1.488864	1.643619	1.814018	2.208040
41	1.226898	1.358461	1.503752	1.664165	1.841229	2.252200
42	1.233033	1.368650	1.518790	1.684967	1.868847	2.297244
43	1.239198	1.378915	1.533978	1.706029	1.896880	2.343189
44	1.245394	1.389256	1.549318	1.727354	1.925333	2.390053
45	1.251621	1.399676	1.564811	1.748946	1.954213	2.437854
46	1.257879	1.410173	1.580459	1.770808	1.983526	2.486611
47	1.264168	1.420750	1.596263	1.792943	2.013279	2.536344
48	1.270489	1.431405	1.612226	1.815355	2.043478	2.587070
49	1.276842	1.442141	1.628348	1.838047	2.074130	2.638812
50	1.283226	1.452957	1.644632	1.861022	2.105242	2.691588
51	1.289642	1.463854	1.661078	1.884285	2.136821	2.745420
52	1.296090	1.474833	1.677689	1.907839	2.168873	2.800328
53	1.302571	1.485894	1.694466	1.931687	2.201406	2.856335
54	1.309083	1.497038	1.711410	1.955833	2.234428	2.913461
55	1.315629	1.508266	1.728525	1.980281	2.267944	2.971731
56	1.322207	1.519578	1.745810	2.005034	2.301963	3.031165
57	1.328818	1.530975	1.763268	2.030097	2.336493	3.091786
58	1.335462	1.542457	1.780901	2.055473	2.371540	3.153624
59	1.342139	1.554026	1.798710	2.081167	2.407113	3.216697
60	1.348850	1.565681	1.816697	2.107181	2.443220	3.281031

TABLE 5 $(1 + R)^k$ 569

TABLE 5 *continued* $(1 + R)^k$

$k =$	$R = 0.03$	$R = 0.04$	$R = 0.05$	$R = 0.06$	$R = 0.07$	$R = 0.08$
1	1.030000	1.040000	1.050000	1.060000	1.070000	1.080000
2	1.060900	1.081600	1.102500	1.123600	1.144900	1.166400
3	1.092727	1.124864	1.157625	1.191016	1.225043	1.259712
4	1.125509	1.169859	1.215506	1.262477	1.310796	1.360489
5	1.159274	1.216653	1.276282	1.338226	1.402552	1.469328
6	1.194052	1.265319	1.340096	1.418519	1.500730	1.586874
7	1.229874	1.315932	1.407100	1.503630	1.605781	1.713824
8	1.266770	1.368569	1.477455	1.593848	1.718186	1.850930
9	1.304773	1.423312	1.551328	1.689479	1.838459	1.999005
10	1.343916	1.480244	1.628895	1.790848	1.967151	2.158925
11	1.384234	1.539454	1.710339	1.898299	2.104852	2.331639
12	1.425761	1.601032	1.795856	2.012196	2.252192	2.518170
13	1.468534	1.665074	1.885649	2.132928	2.409845	2.719624
14	1.512590	1.731676	1.979932	2.260904	2.578534	2.937194
15	1.557967	1.800944	2.078928	2.396558	2.759032	3.172169
16	1.604706	1.872981	2.182875	2.540352	2.952164	3.425943
17	1.652848	1.947900	2.292018	2.692773	3.158815	3.700018
18	1.702433	2.025817	2.406619	2.854339	3.379932	3.996020
19	1.753506	2.106849	2.526950	3.025600	3.616528	4.315701
20	1.806111	2.191123	2.653298	3.207135	3.869684	4.660957
21	1.860295	2.278768	2.785963	3.399564	4.140562	5.033834
22	1.916103	2.369919	2.925261	3.603537	4.430402	5.436540
23	1.973587	2.464716	3.071524	3.819750	4.740530	5.871464
24	2.032794	2.563304	3.225100	4.048935	5.972367	6.341181
25	2.093778	2.665836	3.386355	4.291871	5.427433	6.848475

TABLE 5 *continued* $(1 + R)^k$

$k =$	$R = 0.03$	$R = 0.04$	$R = 0.05$	$R = 0.06$	$R = 0.07$	$R = 0.08$
26	2.156591	2.772470	3.555673	4.549383	5.807353	7.396353
27	2.221289	2.883369	3.733456	4.822346	6.213868	7.988061
28	2.287928	2.998703	3.920129	5.111687	6.648838	8.627106
29	2.356566	3.118651	4.116136	5.418388	7.114257	9.317275
30	2.427263	3.243398	4.321942	5.743491	7.612255	10.062657
31	2.500080	3.373133	4.538039	6.088101	8.145113	10.867669
32	2.575083	3.508059	4.764941	6.453387	8.715271	11.737083
33	2.652335	3.648381	5.003186	6.840590	9.325340	12.676050
34	2.731905	3.794316	5.253348	7.251025	9.978114	13.690134
35	2.813862	3.946089	5.516015	7.686087	10.676581	14.785344
36	2.898278	4.103933	5.791816	8.147252	11.423942	15.968172
37	2.985227	4.268090	6.081407	8.636087	12.223618	17.245626
38	3.074783	4.438813	6.385477	9.154252	13.079271	18.625276
39	3.167027	4.616366	6.704751	9.703507	13.994820	20.115298
40	3.262038	4.801021	7.039989	10.285718	14.974458	21.724522
41	3.359899	4.993061	7.391988	10.902861	16.022670	23.462483
42	3.460696	5.192784	7.761588	11.557033	17.144258	25.339482
43	3.564517	5.400495	8.149667	12.250455	18.344355	27.366640
44	3.671452	5.616515	8.557150	12.985482	19.628460	29.555972
45	3.781596	5.841176	8.985008	13.764611	21.002452	31.920449
46	3.895044	6.074823	9.434258	14.590487	22.472623	34.474085
47	4.011895	6.317816	9.905971	15.465917	24.045707	37.232012
48	4.132252	6.570528	10.401270	16.393872	25.728907	40.210573
49	4.256219	6.833349	10.921333	17.377504	27.529930	43.427419
50	4.383906	7.106683	11.467400	18.420154	29.457025	46.901613

TABLE 5 $(1 + R)^k$ 571

TABLE 6 $(1 + R)^{-k}$

$k =$	$R = 0.005$	$R = 0.0075$	$R = 0.01$	$R = 0.0125$	$R = 0.015$	$R = 0.02$
1	0.995025	0.992556	0.990099	0.987654	0.985222	0.980392
2	0.990074	0.985167	0.980296	0.975461	0.970662	0.961169
3	0.985149	0.977833	0.970590	0.963418	0.956317	0.942322
4	0.980248	0.970554	0.960980	0.951524	0.942184	0.923845
5	0.975371	0.963329	0.951466	0.939777	0.928260	0.905731
6	0.970518	0.956158	0.942045	0.928175	0.914542	0.887971
7	0.965690	0.949040	0.932718	0.916716	0.901027	0.870560
8	0.960885	0.941975	0.923483	0.905398	0.887711	0.853490
9	0.956105	0.934963	0.914340	0.894221	0.874592	0.836755
10	0.951348	0.928003	0.905287	0.883181	0.861667	0.820348
11	0.946615	0.921095	0.896324	0.872277	0.848933	0.804263
12	0.941905	0.914238	0.887449	0.861509	0.836387	0.788493
13	0.937219	0.907432	0.878663	0.850873	0.824027	0.773033
14	0.932556	0.900677	0.869963	0.840368	0.811849	0.757875
15	0.927917	0.893973	0.861349	0.829993	0.799852	0.743015
16	0.923300	0.887318	0.852821	0.819746	0.788031	0.728446
17	0.918707	0.880712	0.844377	0.809626	0.776385	0.714163
18	0.914136	0.874156	0.836017	0.799631	0.764912	0.700159
19	0.909588	0.867649	0.827740	0.789759	0.753607	0.686431
20	0.905063	0.861190	0.819544	0.780009	0.742470	0.672971
21	0.900560	0.854779	0.811430	0.770379	0.731498	0.659776
22	0.896080	0.848416	0.803396	0.760868	0.720688	0.646839
23	0.891622	0.842100	0.795442	0.751475	0.710037	0.634156
24	0.887186	0.835831	0.787566	0.742197	0.699544	0.621721
25	0.882772	0.829609	0.779768	0.733034	0.689206	0.609531
26	0.878380	0.823434	0.772048	0.723984	0.679021	0.597579
27	0.874010	0.817304	0.764404	0.715046	0.668986	0.585862
28	0.869662	0.811220	0.756836	0.706219	0.659099	0.574375
29	0.865335	0.805181	0.749342	0.697500	0.649359	0.563112
30	0.861030	0.799187	0.741923	0.688889	0.639762	0.552071

TABLE 6 *continued* $(1 + R)^{-k}$

$k =$	$R = 0.005$	$R = 0.0075$	$R = 0.01$	$R = 0.0125$	$R = 0.015$	$R = 0.02$
31	0.856746	0.793238	0.734577	0.680384	0.630308	0.541246
32	0.852484	0.787333	0.727304	0.671984	0.620993	0.530633
33	0.848242	0.781472	0.720103	0.663688	0.611816	0.520229
34	0.844022	0.775654	0.712973	0.655494	0.602774	0.510028
35	0.839823	0.769880	0.705914	0.647402	0.593866	0.500028
36	0.835645	0.764149	0.698925	0.639409	0.585090	0.490223
37	0.831487	0.758461	0.692005	0.631515	0.576443	0.480611
38	0.827351	0.752814	0.685153	0.623719	0.567924	0.471187
39	0.823235	0.747210	0.678370	0.616018	0.559531	0.461948
40	0.819139	0.741648	0.671653	0.608413	0.551262	0.452890
41	0.815064	0.736127	0.665003	0.600902	0.543116	0.444010
42	0.811008	0.730647	0.658419	0.593484	0.535089	0.435304
43	0.806974	0.725208	0.651900	0.586157	0.527182	0.426769
44	0.802959	0.719810	0.645445	0.578920	0.519391	0.418401
45	0.798964	0.714451	0.639055	0.571773	0.511715	0.410197
46	0.794989	0.709133	0.632728	0.564714	0.504153	0.402154
47	0.791034	0.703854	0.626463	0.557742	0.496702	0.394268
48	0.787098	0.698614	0.620260	0.550856	0.489362	0.386538
49	0.783182	0.693414	0.614119	0.544056	0.482130	0.378958
50	0.779286	0.688252	0.608039	0.537339	0.475005	0.371528
51	0.775409	0.683128	0.602019	0.530705	0.467985	0.364243
52	0.771551	0.678043	0.596058	0.524153	0.461069	0.357101
53	0.767713	0.672995	0.590156	0.517682	0.454255	0.350099
54	0.763893	0.667986	0.584313	0.511291	0.447542	0.343234
55	0.760093	0.663013	0.578528	0.504979	0.440928	0.336504
56	0.756311	0.658077	0.572800	0.498745	0.434412	0.329906
57	0.752548	0.653178	0.567129	0.492587	0.427992	0.323438
58	0.748804	0.648316	0.561514	0.486506	0.421667	0.317095
59	0.745079	0.643490	0.555954	0.480500	0.415435	0.310878
60	0.741372	0.638700	0.550450	0.474568	0.409296	0.304782

TABLE 6 $(1 + R)^{-k}$ 573

TABLE 6 *continued* $(1 + R)^{-k}$

$k =$	$R = 0.03$	$R = 0.04$	$R = 0.05$	$R = 0.06$	$R = 0.07$	$R = 0.08$
1	0.970874	0.961538	0.952381	0.943396	0.934579	0.925926
2	0.942596	0.924556	0.907029	0.889996	0.873439	0.857339
3	0.915142	0.888996	0.863838	0.839619	0.816298	0.793832
4	0.888487	0.854804	0.822702	0.792094	0.762895	0.735030
5	0.862609	0.821927	0.783526	0.747258	0.712986	0.680583
6	0.837484	0.790315	0.746215	0.704961	0.666342	0.630170
7	0.813092	0.759918	0.710681	0.665057	0.622750	0.583490
8	0.789409	0.730690	0.676839	0.627412	0.582009	0.540269
9	0.766417	0.702587	0.644609	0.591898	0.543934	0.500249
10	0.744094	0.675564	0.613913	0.558395	0.508349	0.463193
11	0.722421	0.649581	0.584679	0.526788	0.475093	0.428829
12	0.701380	0.624597	0.556837	0.496969	0.444012	0.397114
13	0.680951	0.600574	0.530321	0.468839	0.414964	0.367698
14	0.661118	0.577475	0.505068	0.442301	0.387817	0.340461
15	0.641862	0.555264	0.481017	0.417265	0.362446	0.315242
16	0.623167	0.533908	0.458112	0.393646	0.338735	0.291890
17	0.605016	0.513373	0.436297	0.371364	0.316574	0.270269
18	0.587395	0.493628	0.415521	0.350344	0.295864	0.250249
19	0.570286	0.474642	0.395734	0.330513	0.276508	0.231712
20	0.553676	0.456387	0.376889	0.311805	0.258419	0.214548
21	0.537549	0.438834	0.358942	0.294155	0.241513	0.198656
22	0.521892	0.421955	0.341850	0.277505	0.225713	0.183941
23	0.506692	0.405726	0.325571	0.261797	0.210947	0.170315
24	0.491934	0.390121	0.310068	0.246979	0.197147	0.157699
25	0.477606	0.375117	0.295303	0.232999	0.184249	0.146018

TABLE 6 *continued* $(1 + R)^{-k}$

$k =$	$R = 0.03$	$R = 0.04$	$R = 0.05$	$R = 0.06$	$R = 0.07$	$R = 0.08$
26	0.463695	0.360689	0.281241	0.219810	0.172195	0.135212
27	0.450189	0.346817	0.267848	0.207368	0.160930	0.125187
28	0.437077	0.333477	0.255094	0.195630	0.150402	0.115914
29	0.424346	0.320651	0.242946	0.184557	0.140563	0.107328
30	0.411987	0.308319	0.231377	0.174110	0.131367	0.099377
31	0.399987	0.296460	0.220359	0.164255	0.122773	0.092016
32	0.388337	0.285058	0.209866	0.154957	0.114741	0.085200
33	0.377026	0.274094	0.199873	0.146186	0.107235	0.078889
34	0.366045	0.263552	0.190355	0.137912	0.100219	0.073045
35	0.355383	0.253415	0.181290	0.130105	0.093663	0.067635
36	0.345032	0.243669	0.172657	0.122741	0.087535	0.062625
37	0.334983	0.234297	0.164436	0.115793	0.081809	0.057986
38	0.325226	0.225285	0.156605	0.109239	0.076457	0.053690
39	0.315754	0.216621	0.149148	0.103056	0.071455	0.049713
40	0.306557	0.208289	0.142046	0.097222	0.066780	0.046031
41	0.297628	0.200278	0.135282	0.091719	0.062412	0.042621
42	0.288959	0.192575	0.128840	0.086527	0.058329	0.039464
43	0.280543	0.185168	0.122704	0.081630	0.054513	0.036541
44	0.272372	0.178046	0.116861	0.077009	0.050946	0.033834
45	0.264439	0.171198	0.111297	0.072650	0.047613	0.031328
46	0.256737	0.164614	0.105997	0.068538	0.044499	0.029007
47	0.249259	0.158283	0.100949	0.064658	0.041587	0.026859
48	0.241999	0.152195	0.096142	0.060998	0.038867	0.024869
49	0.234950	0.146341	0.091564	0.057546	0.036324	0.023027
50	0.228107	0.140713	0.087204	0.054288	0.033948	0.021321

TABLE 6 $(1 + R)^{-k}$ 575

TABLE 7

$$\frac{(1 + r)^k - 1}{r}$$

k =	r = (4/12)%	r = (4.5/12)%	r = (5/12)%	r = (5.5/12)%
12	12.2226	12.2509	12.2787	12.3072
24	24.9432	25.0647	25.1855	25.3086
36	38.182	38.4671	38.7527	39.0433
48	51.9602	52.4852	53.014	53.5528
60	66.2996	67.1474	68.0049	68.8808
72	81.2234	82.483	83.7628	85.0734
84	96.7553	98.5234	100.327	102.179
96	112.92	115.301	117.738	120.25
108	129.743	132.848	136.041	139.34
120	147.252	151.203	155.279	159.508
132	165.473	170.4	175.502	180.812
144	184.438	190.479	196.76	203.319
156	204.175	211.481	219.105	227.095
168	224.716	233.447	242.593	252.212
180	246.094	256.423	267.283	278.745
192	268.343	280.454	293.236	306.776
204	291.498	305.589	320.517	336.388
216	315.597	331.88	349.194	367.67
228	340.678	359.377	379.338	400.717
240	366.78	388.138	411.024	435.627
252	393.946	418.221	444.331	472.507
264	422.218	449.685	479.342	511.468
276	451.643	482.595	516.144	552.626
288	482.266	517.017	554.83	596.105
300	514.138	553.02	595.494	642.037
312	547.307	590.677	638.239	690.56
324	581.828	630.064	683.17	741.821
336	617.755	671.261	730.401	795.973
348	655.146	714.35	780.047	853.179
360	694.061	759.419	832.234	913.612
372	734.561	806.558	887.091	977.454
384	776.711	855.863	944.754	1044.9
396	820.578	907.433	1005.37	1116.14
408	866.233	961.373	1069.08	1191.41
420	913.748	1017.79	1136.06	1270.92
432	963.198	1076.8	1206.46	1354.92
444	1014.66	1138.52	1280.46	1443.66
456	1068.23	1203.07	1358.25	1537.4
468	1123.97	1270.6	1440.02	1636.43
480	1181.98	1341.22	1525.97	1741.04

TABLE 7 *continued* $\dfrac{(1+r)^k - 1}{r}$

k =	r = (6/12)%	r = (6.5/12)%	r = (7/12)%	r = (7.5/12)%
12	12.336	12.3639	12.3928	12.421
24	25.4328	25.5559	25.6814	25.6063
36	39.3374	39.6314	39.9307	40.2306
48	54.0998	54.6495	55.2101	55.7748
60	69.7726	70.6734	71.5941	72.5257
72	86.412	87.7705	89.1624	90.5769
84	104.078	106.013	108.001	110.03
96	122.833	125.476	128.201	130.992
108	142.746	146.243	149.862	153.582
120	163.886	168.402	173.088	177.926
132	186.331	192.044	197.994	204.16
144	210.159	217.269	224.699	232.43
156	235.458	244.184	253.336	262.895
168	262.317	272.901	284.043	295.725
180	290.832	303.542	316.969	331.103
192	321.107	336.234	352.276	369.228
204	353.249	371.116	390.135	410.313
216	387.373	408.334	430.731	454.587
228	423.502	448.045	474.262	502.298
240	462.066	490.415	520.94	553.713
252	502.902	535.623	570.992	609.12
264	546.256	583.858	624.662	668.827
276	592.285	635.324	682.213	733.17
288	641.153	690.236	743.923	802.508
300	693.036	748.826	810.095	877.229
312	748.118	811.34	881.051	957.75
324	806.597	878.041	957.135	1044.52
336	868.684	949.208	1038.72	1138.03
348	934.601	1025.14	1126.2	1238.8
360	1004.58	1106.16	1220.01	1347.39
372	1078.88	1192.61	1320.6	1464.41
384	1157.76	1284.84	1428.46	1590.52
396	1241.51	1383.25	1544.12	1726.41
408	1330.42	1488.26	1668.14	1872.85
420	1424.82	1600.29	1801.12	2030.67
432	1525.03	1719.83	1943.72	2200.73
444	1631.43	1847.37	2096.62	2384.
456	1744.4	1983.46	2260.58	2581.49
468	1864.33	2128.65	2436.4	2794.32
480	1991.65	2283.58	2624.92	3023.67

TABLE 7 $\dfrac{(1+r)^k - 1}{r}$ 577

TABLE 7 continued $\dfrac{(1 + r)^k - 1}{r}$

k =	r = (8/12)%	r = (8.5/12)%	r = (9/12)%	r = (9.5/12)%
12	12.4499	12.4788	12.5075	12.5366
24	25 9331	26.0606	26.1883	26.3175
36	40.5353	40.8429	41.1525	41.4661
48	56.3496	56.9317	57.5204	58.1181
60	73.4765	74.4428	75.4237	76.4228
72	92.0248	93.5016	95.0065	96.5443
84	112.113	114.245	116.426	118.663
96	133.868	136.822	139.855	142.976
108	157.428	161.395	165.482	169.703
120	182.945	188.139	193.513	199.083
132	210.579	217.248	224.173	231.378
144	240.507	248.93	257.71	266.878
156	272.918	283.412	294.392	305.902
168	308.02	320.942	334.516	348.799
180	346.035	361.789	378.403	395.953
192	387.206	406.246	426.407	447.787
204	431.794	454.634	478.914	504.766
216	480.082	507.298	536.347	567.4
228	532.378	564.618	599.167	636.25
240	589.015	627.004	667.881	711.933
252	650.352	694.904	743.04	795.128
264	716.781	768.806	825.249	886.58
276	788.723	849.241	915.171	987.108
288	866.636	936.785	1013.53	1097.61
300	951.016	1032.07	1121.11	1219.09
312	1042.4	1135.77	1238.78	1352.61
324	1141.37	1248.64	1367.5	1499.4
336	1248.55	1371.49	1508.29	1660.74
348	1364.63	1505.2	1662.28	1838.11
360	1490.34	1650.72	1830.72	2033.07
372	1626.49	1809.11	2014.96	2247.39
384	1773.93	1981.5	2216.49	2482.97
396	1933.62	2169.12	2436.91	2741.94
408	2106.56	2373.34	2678.02	3026.61
420	2293.85	2595.6	2941.74	3339.53
432	2496.69	2837.5	3230.21	3683.51
444	2716.36	3100.79	3545.73	4061.63
456	2954.26	3387.35	3890.85	4477.28
468	3211.92	3699.25	4268.34	4934.18
480	3490.95	4038.71	4681.25	5436.42

From T. Marll McDonald, *Mathematical Methods for Social and Management Scientists.*
Copyright © 1974 by Houghton Mifflin Company. Reprinted by permission.

TABLES

TABLE 8 $\dfrac{r}{(1 + r)^k - 1}$

k =	r = (4/12)%	r = (4.5/12)%	r = (5/12)%	r = (5.5/12)%
12	0.08182	0.081631	0.081447	0.081258
24	0.040096	0.039901	0.03971	0.039517
36	0.026195	0.026001	0.025809	0.025617
48	0.01925	0.019057	0.018867	0.018678
60	0.015088	0.014897	0.014709	0.014522
72	0.012316	0.012128	0.011943	0.011759
84	0.01034	0.010154	0.009972	0.009791
96	0.00886	0.008677	0.008498	0.00832
108	0.007712	0.007532	0.007355	0.007181
120	0.006796	0.006618	0.006445	0.006274
132	0.006048	0.005873	0.005702	0.005535
144	0.005426	0.005254	0.005087	0.004923
156	0.004902	0.004733	0.004569	0.004408
168	0.004455	0.004288	0.004127	0.003969
180	0.004068	0.003904	0.003746	0.003592
192	0.003731	0.00357	0.003415	0.003264
204	0.003435	0.003277	0.003124	0.002977
216	0.003173	0.003018	0.002868	0.002724
228	0.00294	0.002787	0.002641	0.0025
240	0.002731	0.002581	0.002437	0.0023
252	0.002543	0.002396	0.002255	0.002121
264	0.002373	0.002228	0.002091	0.00196
276	0.002219	0.002077	0.001942	0.001814
288	0.002078	0.001939	0.001807	0.001682
300	0.00195	0.001813	0.001684	0.001562
312	0.001832	0.001697	0.001571	0.001453
324	0.001723	0.001592	0.001468	0.001353
336	0.001623	0.001494	0.001374	0.001261
348	0.001531	0.001404	0.001286	0.001177
360	0.001445	0.001321	0.001206	0.001099
372	0.001366	0.001244	0.001132	0.001028
384	0.001292	0.001173	0.001063	0.000962
396	0.001223	0.001107	0.000999	0.0009
408	0.001159	0.001045	0.00094	0.000844
420	0.001099	0.000987	0.000885	0.000791
432	0.001043	0.000933	0.000833	0.000743
444	0.00099	0.000883	0.000785	0.000697
456	0.000941	0.000836	0.000741	0.000655
468	0.000894	0.000792	0.000699	0.000616
480	0.000851	0.00075	0.00066	0.000579

TABLE 8 $\dfrac{r}{(1 + r)^k - 1}$ 579

TABLE 8 continued $\dfrac{r}{(1+r)^k - 1}$

k =	r = (6/12)%	r = (6.5/12)%	r = (7/12)%	r = (7.5/12)%
12	0.081068	0.080885	0.080697	0.080513
24	0.039324	0.039134	0.038943	0.038755
36	0.025426	0.025237	0.025048	0.024861
48	0.018489	0.018303	0.018117	0.017934
60	0.014337	0.014154	0.013972	0.013793
72	0.011577	0.011398	0.01122	0.011045
84	0.009613	0.009437	0.009264	0.009093
96	0.008146	0.007974	0.007805	0.007639
108	0.00701	0.006842	0.006677	0.006516
120	0.006106	0.005943	0.005782	0.005625
132	0.005371	0.005212	0.005055	0.004903
144	0.004763	0.004607	0.004455	0.004307
156	0.004252	0.0041	0.003952	0.003808
168	0.003817	0.003669	0.003525	0.003386
180	0.003443	0.003299	0.003159	0.003025
192	0.003119	0.002979	0.002843	0.002713
204	0.002835	0.002699	0.002568	0.002442
216	0.002586	0.002453	0.002326	0.002204
228	0.002365	0.002236	0.002113	0.001995
240	0.002169	0.002044	0.001924	0.00181
252	0.001993	0.001871	0.001756	0.001646
264	0.001835	0.001717	0.001605	0.0015
276	0.001693	0.001579	0.00147	0.001368
288	0.001564	0.001453	0.001349	0.001251
300	0.001447	0.00134	0.001239	0.001144
312	0.001341	0.001237	0.00114	0.001049
324	0.001244	0.001143	0.001049	0.000962
336	0.001156	0.001058	0.000967	0.000883
348	0.001074	0.00098	0.000892	0.000812
360	0.001	0.000909	0.000824	0.000747
372	0.000931	0.000843	0.000762	0.000687
384	0.000868	0.000783	0.000705	0.000633
396	0.00081	0.000727	0.000652	0.000584
408	0.000756	0.000676	0.000604	0.000538
420	0.000706	0.000629	0.00056	0.000497
432	0.00066	0.000586	0.000519	0.000459
444	0.000617	0.000546	0.000481	0.000424
456	0.000578	0.000509	0.000447	0.000392
468	0.000541	0.000474	0.000415	0.000362
480	0.000507	0.000442	0.000385	0.000335

TABLE 8 *continued*

$$\frac{r}{(1 + r)^k - 1}$$

k =	r = (8/12)%	r = (8.5/12)%	r = (9/12)%	r = (9.5/12)%
12	0.080322	0.080136	0.079952	0.079766
24	0.038561	0.038372	0.038185	0.037998
36	0.02467	0.024484	0.0243	0.024116
48	0.017746	0.017565	0.017385	0.017206
60	0.01361	0.013433	0.013258	0.013085
72	0.010867	0.010695	0.010526	0.010358
84	0.00892	0.008753	0.008589	0.008427
96	0.00747	0.007309	0.00715	0.006994
108	0.006352	0.006196	0.006043	0.005893
120	0.005466	0.005315	0.005168	0.005023
132	0.004749	0.004603	0.004461	0.004322
144	0.004158	0.004017	0.00388	0.003747
156	0.003664	0.003528	0.003397	0.003269
168	0.003247	0.003116	0.002989	0.002867
180	0.00289	0.002764	0.002643	0.002526
192	0.002583	0.002462	0.002345	0.002233
204	0.002316	0.0022	0.002088	0.001981
216	0.002083	0.001971	0.001864	0.001762
228	0.001878	0.001771	0.001669	0.001572
240	0.001698	0.001595	0.001497	0.001405
252	0.001538	0.001439	0.001346	0.001258
264	0.001395	0.001301	0.001212	0.001128
276	0.001268	0.001178	0.001093	0.001013
288	0.001154	0.001067	0.000987	0.000911
300	0.001052	0.000969	0.000892	0.00082
312	0.000959	0.00088	0.000807	0.000739
324	0.000876	0.000801	0.000731	0.000667
336	0.000801	0.000729	0.000663	0.000602
348	0.000733	0.000664	0.000602	0.000544
360	0.000671	0.000606	0.000546	0.000492
372	0.000615	0.000553	0.000496	0.000445
384	0.000564	0.000505	0.000451	0.000403
396	0.000517	0.000461	0.00041	0.000365
408	0.000475	0.000421	0.000373	0.00033
420	0.000436	0.000385	0.00034	0.000299
432	0.000401	0.000352	0.00031	0.000271
444	0.000368	0.000322	0.000282	0.000246
456	0.000338	0.000295	0.000257	0.000223
468	0.000311	0.00027	0.000234	0.000203
480	0.000286	0.000248	0.000214	0.000184

TABLE 8

TABLE 9
$$\frac{r}{1 - (1 + r)^{-k}}$$

k =	r = (4/12)%	r = (4.5/12)%	r = (5/12)%	r = (5.5/12)%
12	0.085154	0.085381	0.085613	0.085841
24	0.043429	0.043651	0.043877	0.0441
36	0.029528	0.029751	0.029976	0.0302
48	0.022583	0.022807	0.023034	0.023261
60	0.018421	0.018647	0.018876	0.019106
72	0.01565	0.015878	0.01611	0.016342
84	0.013673	0.013904	0.014139	0.014375
96	0.012194	0.012427	0.012665	0.012904
108	0.011045	0.011282	0.011522	0.011765
120	0.010129	0.010368	0.010611	0.010857
132	0.009381	0.009623	0.009869	0.010118
144	0.00876	0.009004	0.009254	0.009506
156	0.008236	0.008483	0.008735	0.008991
168	0.007788	0.008038	0.008293	0.008553
180	0.007401	0.007654	0.007913	0.008175
192	0.007064	0.00732	0.007581	0.007848
204	0.006768	0.007027	0.007291	0.007561
216	0.006506	0.006768	0.007035	0.007308
228	0.006273	0.006537	0.006807	0.007083
240	0.006064	0.006331	0.006604	0.006883
252	0.005876	0.006146	0.006422	0.006704
264	0.005706	0.005978	0.006257	0.006543
276	0.005552	0.005827	0.006109	0.006397
288	0.005411	0.005689	0.005974	0.006265
300	0.005283	0.005563	0.00585	0.006145
312	0.005165	0.005447	0.005738	0.006036
324	0.005057	0.005342	0.005635	0.005936
336	0.004957	0.005244	0.00554	0.005844
348	0.004864	0.005154	0.005453	0.00576
360	0.004779	0.005071	0.005373	0.005682
372	0.004699	0.004994	0.005298	0.005611
384	0.004625	0.004923	0.00523	0.005545
396	0.004556	0.004857	0.005166	0.005484
408	0.004492	0.004795	0.005107	0.005427
420	0.004432	0.004737	0.005051	0.005375
432	0.004376	0.004683	0.005	0.005326
444	0.004323	0.004633	0.004952	0.005281
456	0.004274	0.004586	0.004907	0.005238
468	0.004228	0.004542	0.004866	0.005199
480	0.004184	0.0045	0.004826	0.005162

TABLE 9 continued $\dfrac{r}{1 - (1 + r)^{-k}}$

k =	r = (6/12)%	r = (6.5/12)%	r = (7/12)%	r = (7.5/12)%
12	0.086068	0.086302	0.08653	0.086763
24	0.044324	0.044551	0.044777	0.045005
36	0.030426	0.030654	0.030881	0.031111
48	0.023489	0.02372	0.02395	0.024184
60	0.019337	0.019571	0.019805	0.020043
72	0.016577	0.016815	0.017053	0.017295
84	0.014613	0.014854	0.015097	0.015343
96	0.013146	0.013391	0.013638	0.013889
108	0.01201	0.012259	0.012511	0.012766
120	0.011106	0.011359	0.011615	0.011875
132	0.010371	0.010628	0.010889	0.011153
144	0.009763	0.010024	0.010288	0.010557
156	0.009252	0.009516	0.009785	0.010058
168	0.008817	0.009085	0.009358	0.009636
180	0.008443	0.008716	0.008993	0.009275
192	0.008119	0.008395	0.008677	0.008963
204	0.007835	0.008116	0.008401	0.008692
216	0.007586	0.00787	0.008159	0.008454
228	0.007365	0.007653	0.007946	0.008245
240	0.007169	0.00746	0.007757	0.00806
252	0.006993	0.007288	0.007589	0.007896
264	0.006835	0.007134	0.007439	0.00775
276	0.006693	0.006995	0.007304	0.007618
288	0.006564	0.00687	0.007182	0.007501
300	0.006447	0.006757	0.007072	0.007394
312	0.006341	0.006654	0.006973	0.007299
324	0.006244	0.00656	0.006883	0.007212
336	0.006156	0.006475	0.006801	0.007133
348	0.006074	0.006397	0.006726	0.007062
360	0.006	0.006325	0.006657	0.006997
372	0.005931	0.00626	0.006595	0.006937
384	0.005868	0.006199	0.006538	0.006883
396	0.00581	0.006144	0.006485	0.006834
408	0.005756	0.006093	0.006437	0.006788
420	0.005706	0.006046	0.006393	0.006747
432	0.00566	0.006003	0.006352	0.006709
444	0.005617	0.005962	0.006315	0.006674
456	0.005578	0.005925	0.00628	0.006642
468	0.005541	0.005891	0.006248	0.006612
480	0.005507	0.005859	0.006219	0.006585

TABLE 9 $\dfrac{r}{1 - (1 + r)^{-k}}$

583

TABLE 9 continued

$$\frac{r}{1 - (1 + r)^{-k}}$$

k =	r = (8/12)%	r = (8.5/12)%	r = (9/12)%	r = (9.5/12)%
12	0.086989	0.087219	0.087452	0.087683
24	0.045227	0.045456	0.045685	0.045914
36	0.031337	0.031567	0.0318	0.032033
48	0.024413	0.024648	0.024885	0.025123
60	0.020276	0.020516	0.020758	0.021002
72	0.017533	0.017778	0.018026	0.018275
84	0.015586	0.015836	0.016089	0.016344
96	0.014137	0.014392	0.01465	0.014911
108	0.013019	0.013279	0.013543	0.013809
120	0.012133	0.012399	0.012668	0.01294
132	0.011415	0.011686	0.011961	0.012239
144	0.010825	0.011101	0.01138	0.011664
156	0.010331	0.010612	0.010897	0.011186
168	0.009913	0.010199	0.010489	0.010784
180	0.009557	0.009847	0.010143	0.010442
192	0.009249	0.009545	0.009845	0.01015
204	0.008983	0.009283	0.009588	0.009898
216	0.00875	0.009055	0.009364	0.009679
228	0.008545	0.008854	0.009169	0.009488
240	0.008364	0.008678	0.008997	0.009321
252	0.008204	0.008522	0.008846	0.009174
264	0.008062	0.008384	0.008712	0.009045
276	0.007935	0.008261	0.008593	0.00893
288	0.007821	0.008151	0.008487	0.008828
300	0.007718	0.008052	0.008392	0.008737
312	0.007626	0.007964	0.008307	0.008656
324	0.007543	0.007884	0.008231	0.008584
336	0.007468	0.007812	0.008163	0.008519
348	0.007399	0.007748	0.008102	0.008461
360	0.007338	0.007689	0.008046	0.008409
372	0.007281	0.007636	0.007996	0.008362
384	0.00723	0.007588	0.007951	0.008319
396	0.007184	0.007544	0.00791	0.008281
408	0.007141	0.007505	0.007873	0.008247
420	0.007103	0.007469	0.00784	0.008216
432	0.007067	0.007436	0.00781	0.008188
444	0.007035	0.007406	0.007782	0.008163
456	0.007005	0.007379	0.007757	0.00814
468	0.006978	0.007354	0.007734	0.008119
480	0.006953	0.007331	0.007714	0.008101

From T. Marll McDonald, *Mathematical Methods for Social and Management Scientists.* Copyright © 1974 by Houghton Mifflin Company. Reprinted by permission.

TABLES

TABLE 10 $\dfrac{r}{1 - (1 + r)^{-k}}$: Supplementary Table

Annual Rate $r\%$	Number of Months, k					
	120	180	240	300	360	420
7.00	.0116108479	.0089882827	.0077529894	.0070677920	.0066530250	.0063885636
7.25	.0117401041	.0091286288	.0079037598	.0072280686	.0068217628	.0065646724
7.50	.0118701769	.0092701236	.0080559319	.0073899118	.0069921451	.0067424260
7.75	.0120010631	.0094127575	.0082094856	.0075532876	.0071641225	.0069217594
8.00	.0121327594	.0095565208	.0083644007	.0077181622	.0073376457	.0071026088
8.25	.0122652625	.0097014036	.0085206565	.0078845013	.0075126660	.0072849114
8.50	.0123985689	.0098473956	.0086782324	.0080522708	.0076891348	.0074686057
8.75	.0125326750	.0099944865	.0088371071	.0082214364	.0078670041	.0076536314
9.00	.0126675774	.0101426658	.0089972596	.0083919636	.0080462262	.0078399297
9.25	.0128032722	.0102919229	.0091586683	.0085638184	.0082267543	.0080274432
9.50	.0129397558	.0104422468	.0093213119	.0087369666	.0084085421	.0082161160
9.75	.0130770242	.0105936266	.0094851685	.0089113742	.0085915441	.0084058939
10.00	.0132150737	.0107460512	.0096502165	.0090870075	.0087757157	.0085967243
10.25	.0133539002	.0108995092	.0098164339	.0092638328	.0089610130	.0087885561
10.50	.0134934997	.0110539892	.0099837989	.0094418171	.0091473929	.0089813402
10.75	.0136338680	.0112094798	.0101522895	.0096209272	.0093348136	.0091750290
11.00	.0137750011	.0113659693	.0103218839	.0098011308	.0095232340	.0093695765

Source: This table was calculated on the UNH DEC System 1099 computer. The computer program was written by Dr. D. Bergeron, whose help is gratefully acknowledged.

TABLE 10   585

answers to selected exercises

Section 1.1

15. one solution, 0
17. one solution, $\dfrac{17}{2} = 8\dfrac{1}{2}$
19. infinitely many solutions
21. one solution, 0
23. no solution
25. infinitely many solutions (note: $x \neq 1$)

Section 1.2

1. $\dfrac{24}{5}$ or $4\dfrac{4}{5}$
3. 4
5. $-\dfrac{3}{2}$ or $-1\dfrac{1}{2}$
7. $\dfrac{5}{2}$ or $2\dfrac{1}{2}$
9. $\dfrac{11}{24}$
11. -5

13. $-\dfrac{184}{15}$ or $-12\dfrac{4}{15}$
15. 22
17. 6
19. 1
21. $\dfrac{16}{7}$ or $2\dfrac{2}{7}$
23. 9
25. $\dfrac{1}{3}$
27. $-\dfrac{2}{9}$

Section 1.3

1. 8
3. -7
5. 7
7. -1
9. $2 - \sqrt{2}$
11. 12
13. 2
15. 1

17. 19

19. $-(x+1)$ or $-x-1$

21. -6 is to the right of -13
[might just write $-13 < -6$]

23. $\frac{4}{8}$ is to the right of $-\frac{5}{8}$
$$\left[-\frac{5}{8} < \frac{4}{8}\right]$$

25. $-\frac{2}{5} > -\frac{5}{7}$

27. $-.333 > -\frac{1}{3}$

29. $-\pi < -3.14$

31. $|-7+3| > 6-3$

Section 1.4

1. $x < \frac{7}{2}$ or $x < 3\frac{1}{2}$

3. $x > \frac{6}{5}$ or $x > 1\frac{1}{5}$

5. $x < 10$

7. $-\frac{9}{7} > x$, or $x < -\frac{9}{7}$, or
$-1\frac{2}{7} > x$, or $x < -1\frac{2}{7}$

9. all positive real numbers, $x > 0$

11. $x > \frac{25}{2}$ or $x > 12\frac{1}{2}$

13. no solution

15. $x < \frac{18}{5}$ or $x < 3\frac{3}{5}$

17. $-\frac{1}{12} < x$

19. $x > 0$

Section 1.5

1. $x \geq -\frac{3}{2}$ or $x \geq -1\frac{1}{2}$

3. $x \geq \frac{3}{2}$ or $x \geq 1\frac{1}{2}$

5. $21 \geq x$

7. $x \geq -4$

9. $2 \leq x$

11. $-\frac{3}{2} \leq x \leq \frac{3}{2}$

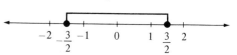

13. $2 \leq x \leq 4\frac{2}{3}$

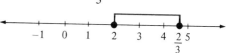

15. $7 < x < 13$

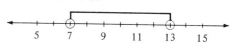

17. $\frac{4}{3} > x > 0$

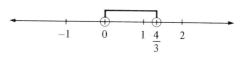

19. $x < -1$ or $\frac{1}{2} < x$

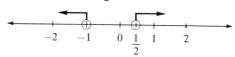

21. $5 < x \leq 35$

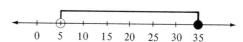

23. $x < -\frac{27}{11}$ or $-\frac{4}{3} < x$
$x < -2\frac{5}{11}$ or $-1\frac{1}{3} < x$

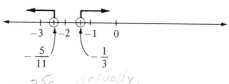

$-2\frac{5}{11}$ Actually,
$-1\frac{1}{3}$

Section 1.6

1. middle income : 1900
   high income : 900
3. 10
5. $705,000
7. 182,000 copies of the novel; 3,000
   of the poems
9. 23
11. No more than 24,000
13. $50 < x < 70$

Section 1.7

1. 15 hours after the baboons start
3. 6.2 years
5. 4 years, 6 months, 1 week

Section 1.8

11. $7\frac{7}{8}$ or better $7\frac{881}{1008}$

Section 2.1

1.

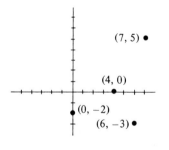

3.

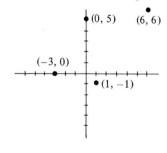

5.

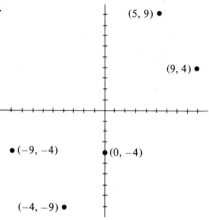

7. $y - 2 = 0$

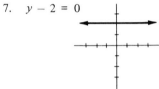

9. $3y + 15 = 0$

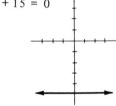

11. $y > 2$

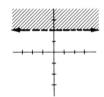

13. $2x + 6 > 0$

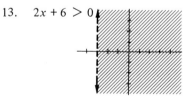

15. $\frac{1}{y} < 3$

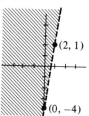

17. $-\infty < x \le 0, -\infty < y \le 0$

19. $-\infty < x < +\infty, -\infty < y \le -3$
    or $y \le -3$

21. $-7 \le x < +\infty, -\infty < y < +\infty$
    or $-7 \le x$

23. $5x - 2y = 8$

(2, 1)

(0, −4)

25. $3y - 8x = 16$

(1, 8)

(−2, 0)

27. $2x + 10y = 5$

(−5, 1½)

(0, ½)

29. $5x - 2y < 8$

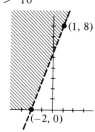

(2, 1)

(0, −4)

31. $3y - 8x > 16$

(1, 8)

(−2, 0)

33. $2x + 10y > 5$

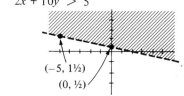

(−5, 1½)

(0, ½)

35. $3x - 5y + 6 < 0$

37. $3x - 6y + 4 < 0$

39. $-1 \le x \le 1$

41. $1 < x < 4$

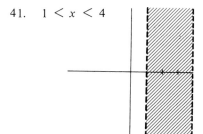

43. $-2 \leq y \leq 2$

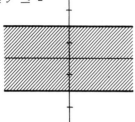

3.

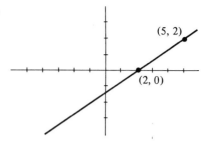

(5, 2)

(2, 0)

45. $x > 0, -2 \leq y < 2$

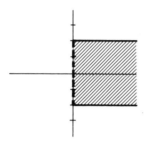

5. The three graphs are parallel lines. The term $-3x$ is the same in all three equations.

47. $x < -1, y < 1$

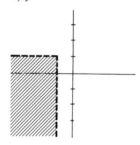

Section 2.2B

1. Any equation of the form $y = b$, e.g. $y = 2$
3. Any equation of the form $y = mx + b$, where $m > 0$
5. Any equation of the form $y = mx$
7. Any equation of the form $x = a$, $a > 0$
9. Any equation of the form $y = .75x + b$
11. $3x + 4y = 9$

Section 2.2A

1.

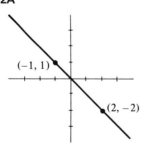

(-1, 1)

(2, -2)

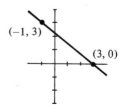

(-1, 3)

(3, 0)

15. $y = 2x$
17. $x = 2$
19. $m = -1$
21. $m = 1$
23. $m = -\dfrac{1}{3}$
25. They are not collinear
27. No
29. $y = -1$
31. $y = -\dfrac{1}{2}x + 1$
33. $y = -\dfrac{3}{5}x - 3\dfrac{2}{5}$

Section 2.2C

1. $y \le 3x + 2$

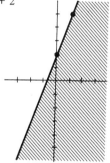

3. $x + 2y < 2$

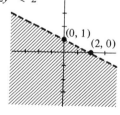

5. $y > -4x + 5$

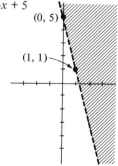

7. $8x + 4y \ge 5$

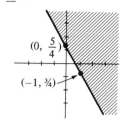

9. $3y - 9x + 4 > 0$

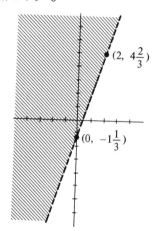

11. $2y - 8x + 5 > 0$
13. $2x - 5y + 7 \le 0$
15. $7x + 8y - 10 \ge 0$ or
    $7x + 8y - 10 \le 0$

Section 2.3

1. $y = 1\dfrac{3}{4}x + 90$
3. $y = 11x + 480$
5. Yes; 111,000 boxes
7. Yes. Linear predictions based on Table 3 give a sales estimate of 3,441,000 boxes over the 6 months. The equation $y = 97x + 535$ gives 5,247,000 boxes for the 6 months, a 52% increase.
8. $y = 11x - 2$
10. $y = 115x - 22$
12. Yes; Yes, 50,000 boxes.

14. $c = 10N + 1,000,000$

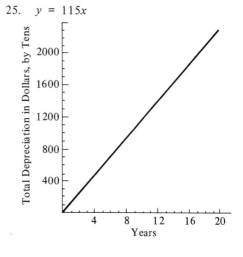

In Millions

In Millions

16. After one month, $1,082,212
After three months, $3,216,937
After six months, $6,293,063

18. After one month, $99,138
After three months, $261,600.50
After six months, $353,399.50

20.

22. $15 per month; After 9 months, $415;
After 11 months, $385; After 13
months, $355

23. $y = 2300 - 115x$
Each year: $115

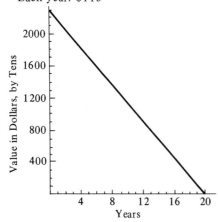

Value in Dollars, by Tens

Years

25. $y = 115x$

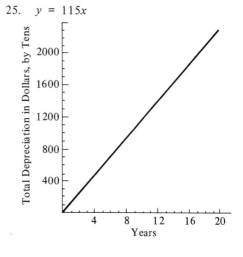

Total Depreciation in Dollars, by Tens

Years

Section 2.4

1. Inconsistent

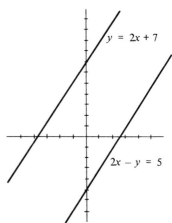

$y = 2x + 7$

$2x - y = 5$

3. Consistent

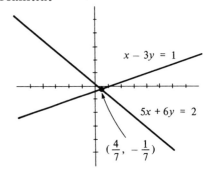

$x - 3y = 1$

$5x + 6y = 2$

$\left(\frac{4}{7}, -\frac{1}{7}\right)$

5. Consistent

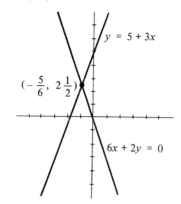

$y = 5 + 3x$

$(-\frac{5}{6}, 2\frac{1}{2})$

$6x + 2y = 0$

7. Consistent; (1, 0)

9. Consistent; $(40, 51\frac{1}{2})$

11. Consistent; $(6\frac{12}{23}, 11\frac{16}{23})$

13. Consistent; $(-1, 5)$

15. Consistent; $(-\frac{2}{3}, -3)$

17. Dependent

19. Inconsistent

21. Consistent; $(\frac{35}{47}, \frac{19}{47})$

23. Consistent; $(-\frac{3}{2}, -\frac{11}{6})$ or $(-1\frac{1}{2}, -1\frac{5}{6})$

25. Consistent; $(0, 3\frac{1}{2})$

27. Consistent; (4, 0)

29. Dependent

31. Inconsistent

Section 2.5

1. (a) graphical method: $y = -2.118x + 36$
   (b) method of averages: $y = -2.272x + 37.203$

3. (a) graphical method: $y = \frac{9}{10}x + 13$
   (b) method of averages: $y = .911x + 11.089$

5. (a) graphical method: $y = 2x - 40$
   (b) method of averages: $y = 1.909x - 35.9$

7. $y = -1.064x + 102.3$

9. $y = .062x + 120.227$

11. $y = .163x + 1.887$

13. $y = .150x + 75.117$

15. $y = 3.578x + 12.822$

17. $y = 12.556x + 470.777$

Answers to question 4.
Yes, Good Morning is growing faster.
Yes, Good Morning will outsell Sugar Yummies after 176 months or 14 years, 8 months. (rounded to the nearest month)

Section 2.6

3. and 5.

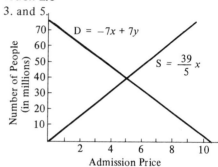

$D = -7x + 7y$

$S = \frac{39}{5}x$

Number of People (in millions)

Admission Price

7. (5, 39)
   $5 and 39 million people

8. $D(1000) = 22,000,000$
   $D(5000) = 6,000,000$

10. $S(3000) = 700,000$
    $S(10,000) = 2,100,000$

12. $(6166\frac{2}{3}, 1,333,333\frac{1}{3})$ or thereabouts

14. 1470 scientists

16.

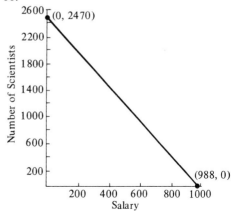

(0, 2470)

(988, 0)

Number of Scientists

Salary

18. 1419 scientists

20. (748,600)

22. No

24.

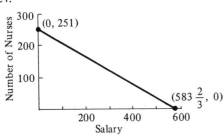

26. 30 nurses

28. (567, 8)

11. $9x + y = 1$
    $4x + 6y = 8$

13. $6x + 7y + 2z = 1$
    $\phantom{6x + {}}6y + 9z = 5$

15. $\begin{pmatrix} 3 & 4 & 5 \\ 1 & 1 & 8 \\ 1 & -5 & -6 \end{pmatrix}$

17. $\begin{pmatrix} 2 & 3 & -2 & 4 \\ 1 & 4 & -3 & 6 \end{pmatrix}$

19. $\begin{pmatrix} 2 & 6 \\ 1 & 9 \end{pmatrix}$

21. $\begin{pmatrix} 2 & 12 \\ 2 & 6 \end{pmatrix}$

Section 3.1

1.

City	Total Budget	Food	Shelter	Transportation	Clothing
Boston	27,000	4363	5943	1607	1435
Chicago	22,592	3967	4198	1575	1335
Houston	20,090	3967	3794	1393	1376

$\begin{pmatrix} 27{,}000 & 4363 & 5943 & 1607 & 1435 \\ 22{,}592 & 3967 & 4198 & 1575 & 1335 \\ 20{,}090 & 3967 & 3794 & 1393 & 1376 \end{pmatrix}$

3. Matrix **A** has 2 rows and 5 columns
   A(2, 3) = 0
   Matrix **B** has 4 rows and 4 columns
   B(2, 3) = −6
   Matrix **C** has 3 rows and 3 columns
   C(2, 3) = 3141

5. **B**(2, 3) = −6
   B(3, 1) = **B**(3, 4) = 3
   B(4, 3) = 5
   B(2, 2) = **B**(2, 4) = 1

7. $\begin{pmatrix} 2 & 4 \\ 1 & -1 \\ 3 & 5 \end{pmatrix}$

9. $\begin{pmatrix} 5 & 7 \\ 2 & 4 \\ 6 & 5 \end{pmatrix}$

23. $\begin{pmatrix} \frac{10}{17} & 0 & \frac{20}{17} \\ 5 & 7 & 3 \\ 8 & 3 & 4 \\ 13\frac{1}{2} & 9 & -3 \end{pmatrix}$

25. $\begin{pmatrix} 5 & 0 & 8 & 1 & 8 \\ 9 & 6 & 8 & 2 & 1 \\ 2 & 4 & 1 & 5 & 7 \end{pmatrix}$

27. $\begin{pmatrix} 2 & 4 & 1 & 5 & 7 \\ 9 & 6 & 8 & 2 & 1 \\ 9 & 8 & 10 & 11 & 22 \end{pmatrix}$

29. (5, −6)

31. (−2, 3)

33. $(32, -35)$

35. $(6, -4)$

37. No solution, the system is inconsistent.

39. No unique solution, the system is dependent.

41. $(\frac{11}{4}, -\frac{1}{2})$

43. $(-\frac{35}{16}, \frac{7}{16})$

45. No solution, the system is inconsistent.

Section 3.2

1. (a) Yes　　(b) Yes

3. (a) Yes　　(b) No, the numbers on the diagonal are not one.
   　　　　　　Also, the second column has a nonzero entry above 4.

5. (a) No, all rows except two should have zero entries.

7. (a) No, the rows after row 1 do not have more zeroes than row 1 preceding its first nonzero entry.

9. $\begin{pmatrix} 1 & 2 \\ 0 & -2 \end{pmatrix}, \begin{pmatrix} 1 & 0 \\ 0 & 1 \end{pmatrix}$

11. $\begin{pmatrix} 1 & 2 & 3 \\ 0 & -3 & -6 \end{pmatrix}, \begin{pmatrix} 1 & 0 & -1 \\ 0 & 1 & 2 \end{pmatrix}$

13. $\begin{pmatrix} 1 & 2 & 3 & -1 \\ 0 & -3 & -6 & 2 \end{pmatrix}, \begin{pmatrix} 1 & 0 & -1 & \frac{1}{3} \\ 0 & 1 & 2 & -\frac{2}{3} \end{pmatrix}$

15. $\begin{pmatrix} 1 & 2 & 1 & 7 \\ 0 & -1 & 1 & 2 \\ 0 & 0 & 1 & 3 \end{pmatrix}, \begin{pmatrix} 1 & 0 & 0 & 2 \\ 0 & 1 & 0 & 1 \\ 0 & 0 & 1 & 3 \end{pmatrix}$

17. $\begin{pmatrix} 2 & 1 & 3 & 9 \\ 0 & 1 & 1 & 5 \\ 0 & 0 & 2 & -62 \end{pmatrix}, \begin{pmatrix} 1 & 0 & 0 & 33 \\ 0 & 1 & 0 & 36 \\ 0 & 0 & 1 & -31 \end{pmatrix}$

19. $\begin{pmatrix} 1 & -2 & 1 & 4 \\ 0 & 1 & -1 & -3 \\ 0 & 0 & 4 & 10 \end{pmatrix}, \begin{pmatrix} 1 & 0 & 0 & \frac{1}{2} \\ 0 & 1 & 0 & -\frac{1}{2} \\ 0 & 0 & 1 & \frac{5}{2} \end{pmatrix}$

21. $\begin{pmatrix} 2 & -3 & 5 & 8 \\ 0 & 12 & -8 & -15 \\ 0 & 0 & 0 & -19 \end{pmatrix}, \begin{pmatrix} 1 & 0 & \frac{3}{2} & 0 \\ 0 & 1 & -\frac{2}{3} & 0 \\ 0 & 0 & 0 & 1 \end{pmatrix}$

23. $\begin{pmatrix} 4 & 4 & 3 & 3 & 3 \\ 0 & 1 & \frac{11}{4} & -\frac{1}{4} & \frac{23}{4} \\ 0 & 0 & -\frac{1}{4} & -\frac{1}{4} & -\frac{13}{4} \end{pmatrix}, \begin{pmatrix} 1 & 0 & 0 & 3 & 2 \\ 0 & 1 & 0 & -3 & 30 \\ 0 & 0 & 1 & 1 & 13 \end{pmatrix}$

25.
$$\left(\begin{array}{cccc} 1 & 0 & 2 & -6 \\ 0 & -1 & -9 & 28 \\ 0 & 0 & -36 & 107 \end{array}\right) \quad \left(\begin{array}{cccc} 1 & 0 & 0 & -\dfrac{1}{18} \\ 0 & 1 & 0 & -\dfrac{5}{4} \\ 0 & 0 & 1 & -\dfrac{107}{36} \end{array}\right)$$

27.
$$\left(\begin{array}{cccc} 1 & 0 & -4 & 2 \\ 0 & 2 & 11 & 1 \\ 0 & 0 & -29 & 8 \end{array}\right) \quad \left(\begin{array}{cccc} 1 & 0 & 0 & \dfrac{26}{29} \\ 0 & 1 & 0 & \dfrac{117}{29} \\ 0 & 0 & 1 & -\dfrac{8}{9} \end{array}\right)$$

29.
$$\left(\begin{array}{cccccc} 3 & 2 & 4 & -6 & 8 & 15 \\ 0 & -9 & -20 & 25 & -33 & -16 \\ 0 & 0 & -674 & 838 & 771 & 791 \end{array}\right)$$

$$\left(\begin{array}{cccccc} 1 & 0 & 0 & -\dfrac{336}{1011} & \dfrac{160}{3033} & \dfrac{3681}{1011} \\ 0 & 1 & 0 & -\dfrac{15}{1011} & \dfrac{6277}{1011} & \dfrac{4434}{1011} \\ 0 & 0 & 1 & -\dfrac{419}{337} & -\dfrac{771}{337} & -\dfrac{791}{337} \end{array}\right)$$

31. (2, 1)
33. Infinitely many solutions
35. (7, 5)
37. (2, −1, 2)
39. (−5, 0, 4)
41. (−1, 2, 4)
43. (−2, 1, 3)
45. no unique solution

Section 3.3
1. (36, 41)

3. a. 36 megabucks should be invested in white paper production expansion
24 megabucks in bleached board expansion
37 megabucks in pulp mill expansion
   b. 14 megabucks in Sunbelt
31 megabucks in Mid-America
52 megabucks in East
5. 60 assistant chefs
410 kitchen workers
7. steak : poultry : mutton the ratio is 1:1:4

9. a. He was absolutely right. If x_3 is greater than 69, then x_3 is negative (which is impossible).

   b. He was not. For example, x_4 can certainly be 100.

   c. It could happen, if the fourth master chef is not working, or hardly working. For example, if $x_3 = 60$ and $x_4 = 3$, then $x_1 = 503$.

11. $x_1 = 98, S_1 = D_1 = 1178$
    $x_2 = 126, S_2 = D_2 = 3314$

13. $x_1 = 93, S_1 = D_1 = 2388$
    $x_2 = 128, S_2 = D_2 = 2464$

Section 4.1

1. $x = 10$
3. There is no x that will work
5. $x = 1, y = 7$
7. $x = 2, y = 7$
9. $\begin{pmatrix} 1 & 1 \\ 5 & -1 \end{pmatrix}$

11. $\begin{pmatrix} 6 & 9 \\ 27 & 12 \end{pmatrix}$

13. $\begin{pmatrix} 7 & 14 \\ 28 & 35 \end{pmatrix}$

15. $\begin{pmatrix} 2 & 3 \\ 9 & 4 \end{pmatrix}$

17. $\begin{pmatrix} 10.5 & -2.1 & 4.2 \\ 1.4 & 2.8 & 2.1 \end{pmatrix}$

19. $\begin{pmatrix} 1 & -\dfrac{1}{2} \\ -\dfrac{3}{4} & -\dfrac{1}{4} \end{pmatrix}$

21. $\dfrac{1}{10} \begin{pmatrix} \dfrac{3}{2} & -\dfrac{3}{10} & \dfrac{3}{5} \\ \dfrac{1}{5} & \dfrac{2}{5} & \dfrac{3}{10} \end{pmatrix}$

23. $x = \dfrac{1}{10}$

25. No

27.

Amount	30 days	60 days	90 days
0 to 20,000	2141	1275	925
20,001 to 50,000	1232	837	744
50,001 to 100,000	1083	792	479

29.

Amount	30 days	60 days	90 days
0 to 20,000	915	334	258
20,001 to 50,000	526	288	266
50,001 to 100,000	491	349	110

31. $\begin{pmatrix} 142.50 & 11.99 & 5.99 \\ 69.90 & 7.57 & 3.00 \\ 102.60 & 4.80 & 2.46 \\ 25.50 & 2.77 & 1.09 \\ 57.90 & 4.30 & 1.56 \\ 12.90 & 1.52 & .48 \end{pmatrix} \begin{pmatrix} 23.75 & 2.00 & 1.00 \\ 11.65 & 1.26 & .50 \\ 17.10 & .80 & .41 \\ 4.25 & .46 & .18 \\ 7.34 & .72 & .26 \\ 2.15 & .25 & .08 \end{pmatrix}$

33. 1.2**A** and 0.2**A** are the matrices obtained in exercise 31.
They are not the matrices obtained in exercise 32.

$$1.2\mathbf{A} - \mathbf{B} = \begin{bmatrix} 0 & 0 & 1.00 \\ 0 & 0 & .50 \\ 0 & 0 & .41 \\ 0 & 0 & .18 \\ 0 & 0 & .26 \\ 0 & 0 & .08 \end{bmatrix} \qquad 0.2\mathbf{A} - \mathbf{C} = \begin{bmatrix} 0 & 0 & 1.00 \\ 0 & 0 & .50 \\ 0 & 0 & .41 \\ 0 & 0 & .18 \\ 0 & 0 & .26 \\ 0 & 0 & .08 \end{bmatrix}$$

35.

Pet Food	Boston	Indianapolis	Phoenix
TLC	36.84	21.05	21.93
Simba	39.47	28.95	27.19
Call of the Wild	25.44	42.98	26.32
White Fang	18.42	46.49	29.82

Date: November 18, 1974

Section 4.2

1. $\begin{bmatrix} 2 & 6 & 6 & 7 \\ 1 & 0 & 7 & 1 \end{bmatrix}$

3. $\begin{bmatrix} 7 & 8 & 8 \\ 4 & 1 & 7 \\ 2 & 2 & 6 \end{bmatrix}$

5. (2)

7. $(4 - 7 - 35 \ 9)$

9. (-14)

11. (156)

13. Impossible

15. Impossible

17. (89)

19. $\mathbf{A} = (4 \ 5 \ 7); \mathbf{X} = \begin{pmatrix} x_1 \\ x_2 \\ x_3 \end{pmatrix}; b = 7$

21. $\mathbf{A} = (5 \ 5 \ 8); \mathbf{X} = \begin{pmatrix} x_1 \\ x_2 \\ x_3 \end{pmatrix}; b = 0$

23. $\mathbf{A} = (-3 \ -1 \ 2); \mathbf{X} = \begin{pmatrix} x_1 \\ x_2 \\ x_3 \end{pmatrix}; b = -8$

25. $(4 \ -12)$

27. $\begin{pmatrix} 50 \\ -30 \end{pmatrix}$

29. $\begin{pmatrix} 4 \\ -18 \end{pmatrix}$

31. $(-56 \ 4)$

33. $(-53 \ -30)$

35. (-57)

37. Impossible

39. **AB** is defined
BA is not defined

41. **AB** is not defined
BA is defined

43. Neither **AB** nor **BA** is defined

45. **C** is a 3×4 matrix
D is a 4×3 matrix

47. **C** is a 4×1 matrix
D is a 1×4 matrix

49. **C** is a $3 \times w$ matrix
D is a $w \times 5$ matrix

51. $\mathbf{A} = \begin{pmatrix} 1 & 1 \\ 4 & 3 \end{pmatrix}; \mathbf{X} = \begin{pmatrix} x \\ y \end{pmatrix}; \mathbf{B} = \begin{pmatrix} 4 \\ 5 \end{pmatrix}$

53. $\mathbf{A} = \begin{bmatrix} 1 & 8 & 8 & 6 \\ 2 & 1 & 9 & 9 \\ 1 & 0 & 0 & 7 \\ 3 & 4 & 8 & -8 \end{bmatrix}$;

$\mathbf{X} = \begin{bmatrix} x_1 \\ x_2 \\ x_3 \\ x_4 \end{bmatrix}; \quad \mathbf{B} = \begin{bmatrix} 2 \\ 8 \\ 3 \\ 0 \end{bmatrix}$

55. $\begin{bmatrix} 3 & 24 \\ 11 & -28 \end{bmatrix}$

57. $\begin{bmatrix} 12 & 27 \\ 49 & 29 \end{bmatrix}$

59. $\begin{bmatrix} 22 & 17 \\ -46 & -6 \end{bmatrix}$

61. $\begin{bmatrix} 26 & 14 \\ 25 & -20 \end{bmatrix}$

63. $\begin{bmatrix} -36 & -60 \\ 39 & -51 \end{bmatrix}$

65. $\begin{bmatrix} -21 & -39 \\ -39 & -21 \end{bmatrix}$

67. $\begin{bmatrix} -14 & 6 & 26 \\ 70 & -74 & -22 \end{bmatrix}$

69. $\begin{bmatrix} 2 & -32 & 6 \\ 1 & -72 & 16 \end{bmatrix}$

71. $\begin{bmatrix} 35 & 0 & 7 \\ 1 & 0 & 0 \\ 28 & -24 & 11 \end{bmatrix}$

Section 4.3 (cont.)

9. $\begin{bmatrix} 4 & 6 & 8 \\ 3 & 7 & 5 \end{bmatrix}$

11. $\begin{bmatrix} 1 & 1 & 9 \\ 3 & 4 & 6 \\ 8 & 7 & 5 \end{bmatrix}$

13. $\begin{bmatrix} 2 & -1 \\ -5 & 3 \end{bmatrix}$

15. $\begin{bmatrix} 7 & -11 \\ -5 & 8 \end{bmatrix}$

17. $\begin{bmatrix} -\dfrac{1}{12} & \dfrac{1}{4} \\ \dfrac{1}{18} & \dfrac{1}{6} \end{bmatrix}$

19. $\begin{bmatrix} -1 & 2 \\ -\dfrac{3}{2} & \dfrac{5}{2} \end{bmatrix}$

21. $x = 1; y = -1$ and $x = -3, y = 3$
23. Neither matrix is the inverse.
25. $x = \dfrac{1}{8}$

73.

	30 days	60 days	90 days
Waiting	1277	1063	839
Refusing	1481	1232	975
Discipline	1375	1131	922

75.

	Price	Earnings per share	Dividends per year
I	409.14	32.87	14.54
II	434.07	35.31	15.67
III	422.59	34.20	14.81
IV	428.82	34.95	15.49

Section 4.3

1. (1 2)
3. not defined
5. $\begin{bmatrix} 5 & 6 \\ 7 & 8 \end{bmatrix}$
7. not defined

27. $\begin{bmatrix} 1 & 3 & -17 \\ 0 & 1 & -5 \\ 0 & 0 & 1 \end{bmatrix}$

29. $\begin{bmatrix} -8 & 24 & 1 \\ 1 & -4 & 0 \\ 0 & 1 & 0 \end{bmatrix}$

31. $\begin{bmatrix} 1 & 0 & 1 \\ -2 & -\frac{1}{2} & -4 \\ 1 & \frac{1}{2} & 2 \end{bmatrix}$

33. $x_1 = -9, x_2 = 9, x_3 = 2;$
and $x_1 = 15, x_2 = 0, x_3 = -12$

35. $\begin{bmatrix} \frac{2}{3} & -\frac{5}{9} \\ -\frac{1}{3} & \frac{4}{9} \end{bmatrix}$;

$x_1 = 95, x_2 = 135; x_1 = 68,$
$x_2 = 170; x_1 = 96, x_2 = 161$

37. $\begin{bmatrix} -1 & -1 & 0 \\ -27 & -16 & -5 \\ 4 & 2 & 1 \end{bmatrix}$;

$x_1 = -1, x_2 = -20, x_3 = 3;$
$x_1 = 1, x_2 = 2, x_3 = 0$

Section 4.4

1. $A = \begin{bmatrix} .10 & .20 \\ .30 & .40 \end{bmatrix}$; $D = \begin{bmatrix} 86 \\ 30 \end{bmatrix}$; $X = \begin{bmatrix} 120 \\ 110 \end{bmatrix}$

3. $A = \begin{bmatrix} .40 & .60 \\ .20 & .10 \end{bmatrix}$; $D = \begin{bmatrix} 4428 \\ 120 \end{bmatrix}$;

$X = \begin{bmatrix} 9660 \\ 2280 \end{bmatrix}$

5. $A = \begin{bmatrix} .70 & .60 \\ .04 & .20 \end{bmatrix}$; $D = \begin{bmatrix} 2421 \\ 642 \end{bmatrix}$;

$X = \begin{bmatrix} 10750 \\ 1340 \end{bmatrix}$

7. $\begin{bmatrix} 6000 \\ 3600 \end{bmatrix}$

9. $\begin{bmatrix} 3150 \\ 2166\frac{2}{3} \end{bmatrix}$

11.

Inputs			D	Output
12	22	16	70	120
36	44	24	6	110
12	22	16	30	80

13.

Inputs			D	Output
3864	1368	950	3478	9660
1932	228	19	101	2280
966	228	190	516	1900

15.

Inputs			D	Output
7525	804	1300	1121	10,750
430	268	260	382	1340
215	67	104	2214	2600

Section 5.1

1. $(-3, 3); (-4, 0)$
3. $(7, -4); (-12, -8)$
5. $(-6, 2); (-3, 3)$
7. The region is the one between the lines which includes the origin.

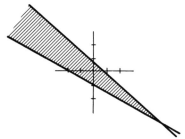

9. The region to the left of both lines.

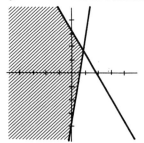

11. The region is to the left and below $x - y = 0$ and above and to the left of $x - 3y = 6$.
13. There is no region which satisfies all the inequalities.
15. The region is the closed first quadrant region above $x + y = 4$.
17. There is no region which satisfies both inequalities.

19. The region is below $x + y = 3$ and $x - y = 0$.
21. The region is the triangle bounded by $5x + 2y = 8$, $x - y = 3$, and $3x - 6y = 4$.
23. The region is the box bounded by $x + y = 4$, $x - y = 3$, $-x + y = 2$, and $-x - y = 1$.
25. $6x - 10y < 12$
$3x - 5y > 8$

27. $2x - 5y \leq 11$
$x - y \geq 0$
$x + y \leq 7$
29. $x \geq -1$
$y \leq 3$
$8y \geq 7x - 3$
$14x - 16y \leq 24$
31. $2x + y \leq 10$
$3x + 4y \leq 20$
$x \geq 0$
$y \geq 0$

Section 5.2

1.

	Per share Etreit	Per share Lamfund	Total
Cost	80,000	100,000	minimum
Dividend	8,000	9,000	at least 72,000

x: no. of shares of Etreit
y: no. of shares of Lamfund
$C = 80,000x + 100,000y$
$x \geq 0, y \geq 0$
$8000x + 9000y \geq 72,000$

3.

	Per 100 grams of chicken	Per 100 grams of dessert	Total
Fat (grams)	3	3	at least 12
Sugar (grams)	6	15	at least 42
Cost (dollars)	.80	1.20	minimum

x: no. of 100 grams of chicken
y: no. of 100 grams of dessert
$3x + 3y \geq 12$
$6x + 15y \geq 42$
$C = .80x + 1.20y$

5.

	Per A Group	Per B Group	Total
Doctors	1	1	2700 (less than or equal to)
Nurses	5	3	10,800 (less than or equal to)
Flu Shots	950	650	maximize

x: no. of A groups
y: no. of B groups
F: no. of flu shots
$x + y \leq 2700$
$5x + 3y \leq 10,800$
$F = 950x + 650y$

7.

	Per Effective Presentation Job	Per Whole New Image Job	Total
Greene	.4	1.2	less than or equal to 24
Blacklock	1.2	.6	less than or equal to 24
Grant	1.0	1.0	less than or equal to 24
Cost	11,000	25,000	maximum

x: no. of Effective Presentation jobs
y: no. of Whole New Image jobs
$.4x + 1.2y \leq 24$
$1.2x + .6y \leq 24$
$x + y \leq 24$
Maximize
$C = 11,000x + 25,000y$

9.

	Per "Improved" S	Per "Improved" E	Total
Front-brain pleasure	2	1	at most 12
Mid-brain pleasure	5	8	at least 24
Rear-brain pleasure	1	6	at most 28
Number of pills	1	1	minimize

x: no. of "Improved" S pills
y: no. of "Improved" E pills
N: total number of pills
$2x + y \leq 12$
$5x + 8y \geq 24$
$x + 6y \leq 28$
Minimize
$N = x + y$

11.

	Bavaria	Regensburg	Total
Nitrogen	1	3	at least 900
Potassium	1	1	at least 500
Phosphate	2	1	at least 600
Cost	30	50	minimize

x: no. of kilograms of Bavaria
y: no. of kilograms of Regensburg
$x + 3y \geq 900$
$x + y \geq 500$
$2x + y \geq 600$
$C = 30x + 50y$

Section 5.3

1. (0, 5)
3. (0, 5)
5. (3, 4)
7. $(0, 13\frac{1}{3})$

9. (6, 0)
11. (9, 0)
13. (2, 2)
15. (1350, 1350)

Section 5.4

1. (3, 0)
3. $(\frac{3}{2}, \frac{1}{2})$ or $(\frac{3}{4}, \frac{3}{4})$
5. (1, 5)
7. (3, 6)
9. (3, 6) or (6, 4) for maximum;
   (6, 2) or (3, 0) for minimum
11. (6, 18)
13. (0, 3)
15. (300, 200)

Section 5.5

1. Yes
3. No, the origin is not a feasible corner
5. No, not a maximum problem
6. $6x + y + u = 66$
   $x + 6y + v = 48$
   $-5x - 4y + P = 0$

	x	y	u	v	P	
u	6	1	1	0	0	66
v	1	6	0	1	0	48
P	-5	-4	0	0	1	0

9. $2x + 5y + u = 95$
   $6x + 7y + v = 56$
   $-45x - 110y + P = 0$

	x	y	u	v	P	
u	2	5	1	0	0	95
v	6	7	0	1	0	56
P	-45	-110	0	0	1	0

11.

	x	y	u	P	
u	9	29	1	0	58
P	-76	-85	0	1	0

Basic variables: u, P
Nonbasic variables: x, y

13.

	x	y	u	v	P	
u	4	2	1	0	0	8
v	1	1	0	1	0	6
P	-0.4	-0.6	0	0	1	0

Basic variables: u, v, P
Nonbasic variables: x, y

15.

	x_1	x_2	x_3	u	v	P	
u	2	3	4	1	0	0	27
v	3	2	2	0	1	0	39
P	-2	-3	-4	0	0	1	0

Basic variables: u, v, P
Nonbasic variables: x_1, x_2, x_3

17. $P = 9x + 29y$
    $8x + 2y \leq 7$
    $x \geq 0, y \geq 0$
19. $P = 8x + 61y$
    $4x + 2y \leq 45$
    $7x + 3y \leq 73$
21. $P = 157x + 822y$
    $12x + 3y \leq 32$
    $7x + 98y \leq 88$
    $55x + 86y \leq 211$
23. $P = 8x_1 + 9x_2 + 10x_3$
    $2x_1 + 7x_2 + 6x_3 \leq 33$
    $6x_1 + 7x_3 \leq 35$
    $6x_1 + 5x_2 + 7x_3 \leq 48$
25. incoming variable: x
    pivot: (row 1) 1
    outgoing variable: u
27. incoming variable: x
    pivot: (row 2) 3
    outgoing variable: v
29. incoming variable: y
    pivot: (row 3) 40
    outgoing variable: w
31. incoming variable: x_1
    pivot: (row 1) 6
    outgoing variable: u
33.

	x	y	u	P	
	1	1	$\frac{1}{6}$	0	6
	0	7	$\frac{3}{2}$	1	54

old corner variables: x, y

basic variables: u, P
new corner variables: y, u
basic variables: x, P

35.

$$\begin{array}{ccccc} x & y & u & v & P \\ \begin{bmatrix} 0 & 4 & 1 & -1 & 0 & 2 \\ 1 & 2 & 0 & \frac{1}{2} & 0 & 8 \\ 0 & 19 & 0 & 8 & 1 & 128 \end{bmatrix} \end{array}$$

old corner variables: x, y
basic variables: u, v, P
new corner variables: y, u
basic variables: x, u, P

37. $x = 9, P = 261$
39. $x = 4; y = 3; P = 47$
41. $x_2 = 4; P = 236$
43. $x_1 = \frac{24}{7}, x_2 = \frac{6}{7}, x_3 = 0; P = \frac{174}{7}$
45. 25 megabucks on commercial TV
5 megabucks on public TV
15 megabucks on print media

Section 6.1

1. $S = \{M, D\}$ M: they match
   D: they don't match
3. $S = \{0, 1, \ldots, 100\}$
   100 or some other appropriate limit
   (assuming there are no more than 100
   violent crimes in a night)
5. $S = \{0, 1, \ldots, 12\}$
7. $S = \{45, 46, \ldots, 58\}$
9. $S = \{-5000, -4000, -3000, \ldots, 8000\}$
   assuming the same restrictions as no. 7
   and that the price went up or down by
   whole dollar amounts.
11. $\frac{1}{7}$
13. $\frac{1}{3}$
15. (a) $\frac{3}{5}$ (b) $\frac{39}{50}$ (c) $\frac{11}{50}$

17. (a) $\frac{1}{6}$ (b) $\frac{1}{6}$ (c) $\frac{1}{6}$
    (d) $\frac{1}{6}$ (e) $\frac{1}{6}$ (f) 0
    (g) $\frac{1}{2}$ (h) $\frac{1}{2}$; no
19. (a) relative frequency
    (b) relative frequency
    (c) subjective approach
    (d) subjective approach
    (e) equal likelihood approach
21. (a)

Outcome	Number
Healthy at 50	250
Death before 50 not linked to smoking	100
Lung cancer not linked to smoking	160
Heart disease not linked to smoking	270
Death or disease linked to smoking	210

(b) The number of people who are healthy is significantly different. This also throws off the other totals.
(c) No, the probabilities do not add to 1.

Section 6.2

1. 0 outcomes; A; B; C; A, B; A, C;
   B, C; A, B, C
3. (a) .50 (b) .50 (c) .20
5. (a) .24 (b) .55 (c) .54
7.

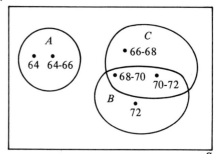

9. $\{(P,P,P), (P,P,F), (P,F,P), (F,P,P),$
$(P,F,F), (F,F,P), (F,F,F), (F,P,F)\}$

(P, P, P)   (P, F, P)
• •
(P, P, F)   (F, P, P)
•   •
(P, F, F)   (F, P, F)
•   •
(F, F, P)
•

(F, F, F)
•

S

11. (a) You may have many answers
(b) $P(E_1) = P(P,P,F) + P(P,F,P)$
$+ P(F,P,P)$
$P(E_2) = P(P,P,F) + P(P,F,P)$
$+ P(F,P,P) + P(P,P,P)$
$P(E_3) = P(P,P,F) + P(P,F,P)$
$+ P(F,P,P) + P(P,F,F)$
$+ P(F,P,F) + P(F,F,P)$
$+ P(F,F,F)$

13. $P(E_1) = \dfrac{1697}{10,000} = .1697$

$P(E_2) = \dfrac{2901}{10,000} = .2901$

$P(E_3) = \dfrac{4124}{10,000} = .4124$

$P(E_4) = \dfrac{8428}{10,000} = .8428$

Section 6.3

1. $\{A_2, A_4, A_6, A_8, A_{10}\}$
3. $\{A_1, A_2, A_3, A_4\}$
5. $\{A_5, A_7, A_9\}$
7. $\{A_1, A_3, A_5\}$
9. $\{A_5, A_6\}$
11. $\{A_1, A_3, A_5, A_6, A_7, A_8, A_9, A_{10}\}$
13. $\{A_7, A_9\}$
15. $\{A_8, A_{10}\}$
17. $\{A_6, A_8, A_{10}\}$
19. $\{A_1, A_2, A_3, A_4\}$

21. $\emptyset$
23. $\{A_1, A_3, A_5, A_7, A_8, A_9, A_{10}\}$
25. $\{A_2, A_4, A_5, A_6, A_7, A_8, A_9, A_{10}\}$
27. $\{A_1, A_2, A_3, A_4, A_6, A_8, A_{10}\}$
29. $\{A_1, A_2, A_3, A_4\}$
31. S
33. G
35. $\emptyset$
37. F
39. $F^c = \{A_7, A_8, A_9, A_{10}\}$
41. $E \cup F$
43. $E^c \cap F^c$
45.

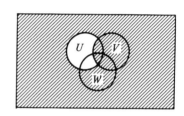

47.

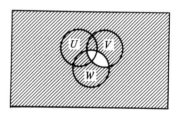

49. $P(E) = .75$
$P(F) = .55$
$P(G) = .49$
51. $P(E \cup F) = 1$
$P(E \cup G) = .88$
53. $P(E \cap F) = .3$
55. $P(F \cap G) = .27$
57. $P(E^c \cap G^c) = .12$
59. $P(F_1) = .8303$
$P(F_2) = .7099$
$P(F_3) = .5876$
$P(F_4) = .1576$
61. $P(M \cup D) = .93$
63. $P(I^c \cap D^c) = .06$
65. $P(M^c \cap D^c) = .08$
67. $P(F^c \cap E^c) = .16$

Section 6.4

1. $P(\text{at least one head}) = \dfrac{3}{4}$

   $P(\text{two heads}) = \dfrac{1}{4}$

3. (a) $P(A) = \dfrac{1}{3}$

   (b) $P(B) = \dfrac{1}{2}$

   (c) $P(C) = \dfrac{1}{3}$

5. $P(\text{chose a prime}) = \dfrac{1}{2}$

7.

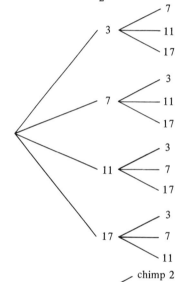

9.

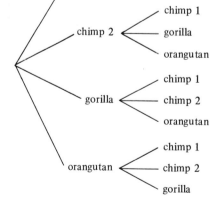

11. C: Cordoba keys
    G: Granada keys
    Z: Z-car keys
    V: Volaré keys

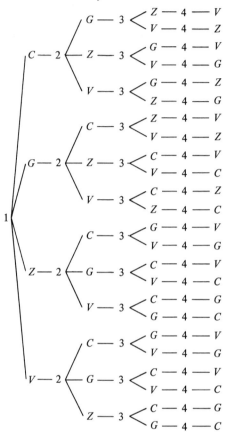

13. $\dfrac{3}{7}$

Section 7.1

1. (a) 16
   (b) 12
3. 63
5. 105
7. 4; 8; 16
9. 432
11. 136; 156

13. (a) $\dfrac{20}{432} = .04630$

(b) $\dfrac{80}{432} = .18519$

15. (a) $\dfrac{196}{432} = .45370$

(b) $\dfrac{276}{432} = .63889$

Section 7.2

1. 60,480
3. 6
5. 1,663,200
7. $\dfrac{22!}{11!}$
9. $\dfrac{9!}{0!} = 9!$
11. $\dfrac{1000!}{0!} = 1000!$
13. 6
15. 119
17. 24
19. 720
21. (a) 650
    (b) 15,600
    (c) 375,050
23. $\dfrac{120}{720} = .1667$
25. $\dfrac{24}{720} = .0333$
27. .1512
29. 11,880
31. .57292
33. .2361

Section 7.3

1. 28
3. 11
5. 136
7. 462
9. 6; 4; $\{$(G,M), (G,F), (G,J), (M,F), (M,J), (F,J)$\}$, $\{$(G,M,F), (G,M,J), (M,F,J), (G,F,J)$\}$
11. 330

13. 424,270
15. 72,358
17. 1680
19. .1641; .2734; .5000
21. (a) .2344
    (b) .3125
    (c) .3438
23. .0088
25. .0217
27. .01293
29. .00099
31. .0014
33. (a) .2143
    (b) .0071
    (c) .0250
    (d) .7857
    (e) .3036
35. .0383
36. (a) .4145
    (b) .2908
    (c) .2947
37. (a) .4445
    (b) .1618
    (c) .3937
38. (a) .0252
    (b) .6274
    (c) .5254
    (d) .7589

Section 7.4

1. $x^8 + 8x^7y + 28x^6y^2 + 56x^5y^3$
   $+ 70x^4y^4 + 56x^3y^5 + 28x^2y^6$
   $+ 8xy^7 + y^8$
3. $x^4 - 4x^3y + 6x^2y^2 - 4xy^3 + y^4$
5. $1 + 7x + 21x^2 + 35x^3 + 35x^4 + 21x^5$
   $+ 7x^6 + x^7$
7. $x^9 + 9x^8 + 36x^7 + 84x^6 + 126x^5$
   $+ 126x^4 + 84x^3 + 36x^2 + 9x + 1$
9. $x^5 + 10x^4 + 40x^3 + 80x^2 + 80x + 32$
11. $\dfrac{1}{243} m^5 + \dfrac{5}{324} m^4 n + \dfrac{5}{216} m^3 n^2$
    $+ \dfrac{5}{288} m^2 n^3 + \dfrac{5}{768} mn^4 + \dfrac{1}{1024} n^5$

13. $1 + 10(1)^9(.01) + 45(1)^8(.01)^2$
     $+ 120(1)^7(.01)^3 + 210(1)^6(.01)^4$
     $+ 252(1)^5(.01)^5 + 210(1)^4(.01)^6$
     $+ 120(1)^3(.01)^7 + 45(1)^2(.01)^8$
     $+ 10(1)(.01)^9 + (.01)^{10}$

     Simplified 1.10462212541120451001

15. $21(2x)^5(3y)^2 = 6048x^5y^2$

17. $6435(3c^2)^8(4d^3)^7$
     $= (6435)(6561)(16,384)c^{16}d^{21}$

19. $22,680x^3y^4$

21. $1,547,556,192c^{24}d^9$

23. $229,911,617,054x^{29}y^{15}$

Section 8.1

1. The probability of a loan being granted given that it was requested by a high-growth business. .75
3. The probability of a loan being refused given that it was requested by a high-growth business. .25
5. The probability of a loan being requested by a high-growth business given that the loan was granted. .78
7. The probability of a loan being requested by a low-growth business given that the loan was granted. .22
9. The probability of a loan requested from a high-growth business and the loan was granted. .55
11. .38
13. .275
15. .42
17. .53
19. (a) .24
     (b) .43
     (c) .56
21. $P(F_1) = .92233$
     $P(E_1 \cap F_1) = .08585$
     $P(E_2 \cap F_1) = .18301$
     $P(E_3 \cap F_1) = .54964$
     $P(E_1 \mid F_1) = .09308$
     $P(E_2 \mid F_1) = .19842$
     $P(E_3 \mid F_1) = .59593$

23. $P(F_3) = .75353$
     $P(E_3 \cap F_3) = .44875$
     $P(E_3 \mid F_3) = .59554$
25. (a) $P(E \cap F) = .1554$
     (b) $P(E \mid F) = .21$
     (c) $P(E \cup F) = .9546$
27. .3818
29. .00224
31. .00297
33. .04386
35. .32905

Section 8.2

1. Yes
3. No; $P(M) = \frac{1}{6}$; $P(N) = \frac{1}{9}$;
    $P(M \cap N) = \frac{1}{36}$
5. (a) .0837
    (b) .4963
    (c) .4126
    (d) .5037
7. .117208, round to .12
9. .0046
11. .6561
13. (a) .000076032
     (b) .00017695
15. (a) .000155
     (b) .18042
     (c) .0005195

Section 8.3

1. (a) .1172
    (b) .1719
    (c) .3770
3. (a) $B(10; 20, .5)$
    (b) $B(0; 20, .5) + B(1; 20, .5)$
         $+ B(2; 20, .5) + \cdots + B(15; 20, .5)$
    (c) $B(8; 20, .5) + B(9; 20, .5) + \cdots$
         $+ B(20; 20, .5)$
5. .6904

7. For the number of no-defects cars from 0 to 10 the probability is .0000; 11 no-defects cars .0002; 12, .0014; 13, .0069; 14, .0266; 15, .0798; 16, .1796; 17, .2852; 18, .2852; 19, .1351

9. 0 satisfied through 10 satisfied the probability is .0000; 11, .0002; 12, .0014; 13, .0069; 14, .0266; 15, .0798; 16, .1796; 17, .2852; 18, .2852; 19, .1351

11. (a) .6513
    (b) .4013

13. .6918; .6676; .0933

15. .5502; .9998; .6597

15.
$$\begin{array}{c} \quad\quad \text{H.S.}\quad \text{not H.S.} \\ \begin{array}{c}\text{H.S.}\\ \text{not H.S.}\end{array} \begin{pmatrix} .63 & .37 \\ .42 & .58 \end{pmatrix} \begin{array}{l}\text{transition}\\ \text{matrix}\end{array} \end{array}$$

initial probability vector $P^{(0)}$ (H.S., not H.S.) = (.5, .5)

17. third round: .473278
    fifth round: .4685715598

19. .3120437

21. .515247

23. No, after two years .2176 is the probability that the area will be residential
    3 years .276572
    4 years .31624744
    5 years .31624744
    6 years .3429300768
    8 years .3729306627

Section 9.1

1. a, b, d

3. A $x = .6$, $y = .3$
   B $x = 0$, $y = .6255$
   C $x = .5$
   D $x = .3$, $y = .2$, $z = .83$
   E $x = .2$, $y = 0$, z impossible
   F $x = .2$, $y = 0$

5. (a) Step 1, P(H) = .5;
       Step 2, P(H) = .45
   (b) Step 1, P(T) = .5;
       Step 2, P(T) = .55

7. (a) Step 1, P(H) = .3;
       Step 2, P(H) = .304
   (b) Step 1, P(T) = .7;
       Step 2, P(T) = .696

9. $P^{(1)} = (.462 \quad .538)$
   $P^{(2)} = (.48246 \quad .51754)$
   $P^{(3)} = (.4892118 \quad .5107882)$
   $P^{(4)} = (.491439894 \quad .508560106)$

11. P(F) = .187
    P(G) = .402
    P(H) = .411

13. P(F) = .136697
    P(G) = .414334
    P(H) = .448969

Section 9.2

1. Yes

3. Yes, $P^{(2)}$ is without zero entries

5. No

7. Yes, $P^{(2)}$ is without zero entries

9. No

11. Yes, $P^{(2)}$ is without zero entries

13. Yes, $P^{(4)}$ is without zero entries

15. (a) $P^{(1)} = (.3 \quad .7)$
       $P^{(2)} = (.58 \quad .42)$
       $P^{(3)} = (.468 \quad .532)$
       $P^{(4)} = (.5128 \quad .4872)$
       $P^{(5)} = (.49488 \quad .50512)$
       $P^{(6)} = (.502048 \quad .497952)$
    (b) steady state vector (.5 .5)

17. (a) $P^{(1)} = (.4 \quad .6)$
       $P^{(2)} = (.76 \quad .24)$
       $P^{(3)} = (.544 \quad .456)$
       $P^{(4)} = (.6736 \quad .3264)$
       $P^{(5)} = (.59584 \quad .40416)$
       $P^{(6)} = (.642496 \quad .357504)$
    (b) steady state vector (.6 .4)

19. (a) $P^{(1)} = (0 \quad 1)$
$P^{(2)} = (.9 \quad .1)$
$P^{(3)} = (.09 \quad .91)$
$P^{(4)} = (.819 \quad .181)$
$P^{(5)} = (.1629 \quad .8371)$
$P^{(6)} = (.75339 \quad .24661)$
(b) steady state vector $(.5 \quad .5)$

21. (a) $P^{(1)} = (\frac{1}{3} \quad \frac{1}{3} \quad \frac{1}{3})$
$P^{(2)} = (.344444 \quad .327778$
$.327778)$
$P^{(3)} = (.347037 \quad .326481$
$.326481)$
$P^{(4)} = (.347641 \quad .326179$
$.326179)$
(b) steady state vector $(.347 \quad .326$
$.326)$

23. (a) $P^{(1)} = (.3 \quad .4 \quad .3)$
$P^{(2)} = (.18 \quad .4 \quad .42)$
$P^{(3)} = (.204 \quad .376 \quad .42)$
$P^{(4)} = (.1968 \quad .3784 \quad .4248)$
(b) steady state vector $(.2 \quad .38 \quad .42)$

25. (a) $P^{(1)} = (.8 \quad 0 \quad .2)$
$P^{(2)} = (.16 \quad .84 \quad 0)$
$P^{(3)} = (.704 \quad .128 \quad .168)$
$P^{(4)} = (.2432 \quad .7312 \quad .0256)$
(b) steady state vector $(.47 \quad .43 \quad .10)$

27. $(.5 \quad .5)$

29. $(.625 \quad .375)$

31. $\left(\dfrac{10}{19} \quad \dfrac{9}{19} \right)$

33. $\left(\dfrac{8}{23} \quad \dfrac{15}{46} \quad \dfrac{15}{46} \right)$

35. $(.198113 \quad .377358 \quad .424528)$

37. $(.454545 \quad .454545 \quad .090909)$

39. $\begin{pmatrix} .500000 & .500000 \\ .500000 & .500000 \end{pmatrix}$

41. $\begin{pmatrix} .625000 & .375000 \\ .625000 & .375000 \end{pmatrix}$

43. $\begin{pmatrix} .473684 & .526316 \\ .473684 & .526316 \end{pmatrix}$

45. $\begin{pmatrix} .347826 & .326087 & .326087 \\ .347826 & .326087 & .326087 \\ .347826 & .326087 & .326087 \end{pmatrix}$

47. $\begin{pmatrix} .198113 & .377359 & .424528 \\ .198113 & .377359 & .424528 \\ .198113 & .377359 & .424528 \end{pmatrix}$

49. $\begin{pmatrix} .454545 & .454545 & .090909 \\ .454545 & .454545 & .090909 \\ .454545 & .454545 & .090909 \end{pmatrix}$

51. $(.111111 \quad .888889)$ is the steady state vector; 11, 111 will buy a copy

53. $.462; .45816; .458326$

55. $.4375; .402344; .400146$

57. $.4$ for Condition spray; $.6$ for Natureswept

59. $.625; .6015625; .600098$

61. $(.48 \quad .21 \quad .31); (.51 \quad .265 \quad .225);$
$(.496 \quad .2795 \quad .2245)$

63.
	C	R	F
C	0	.4	.6
R	.4	.4	.2
F	.3	.3	.4

65. Clear: $.258621$
Rainy: $.362069$
Foggy: $.379310$

Section 10.1

1. Not a function
3. Not a function
5. Not a function
7. Not a function

9. Domain: $\left\{ -\dfrac{3}{2}, -1, \dfrac{1}{2}, 3 \right\}$
Range: $\{0, 1, 2, 3, -1, -2\}$
Not a function

11. Domain: $\{2, 1, 3, 0, -1\}$
Range: $\{-.2, -.9, 1.7, -1, -1.1\}$
A function

13. Domain: $\{.5, -.5, 0, 1, .5, -.5\}$
Range: $\{.75, .75, 1, 0, -.75, -.75\}$

15. Yes; No

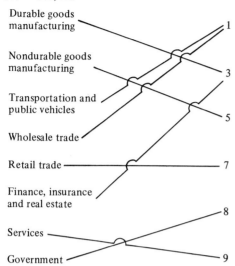

17. No; probably not
19. No; Yes
21. Not a function; when $x > 0$ there are two y's.
23. Not a function; near $x = 0$, there are four y's.
25. Not a function; when $x > 0$, there are two y's.
27. Not a function; when x is near 0, there are six y's.
29. Not a function; the left curve doubles back on itself, all the curves overlap.

21. $x \leq -1$ or $1 \leq x$
23. All real numbers, except $x = 0$
25. All real numbers
27.

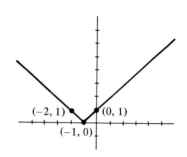

29.

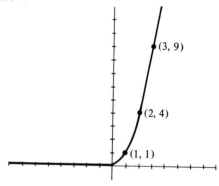

Section 10.2

1. $f(-1) = 2$; $f(2) = -4$; $f(0) = -1$; $f(1) = 2$
3. No; No
5. $f(3) = 24$; $f(0) = 12$; $f(-2) = 54$
7. Range $\{-11, -3, 5, 13, 21\}$
9. Range $\{1, 2, 3, 4\}$
11. Yes
13. No; when $x = 0$, $y = 1$ or -1
15. No; when $x = 0$, $y = 1$ or -1
17. All real numbers, except $x = 1$
19. All real numbers, except $x = 1$ or -1

31.

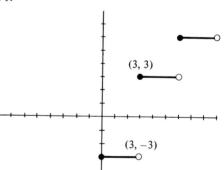

33.

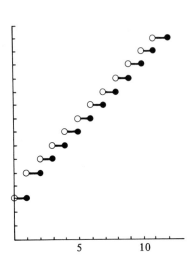

3.

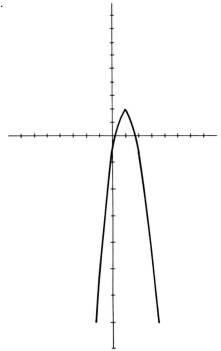

Section 10.3

1.

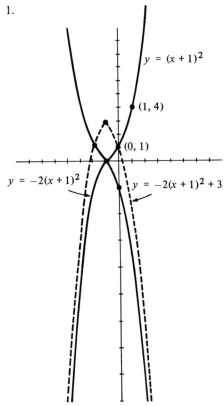

$y = (x + 1)^2$

$(1, 4)$

$(0, 1)$

$y = -2(x + 1)^2$

$y = -2(x + 1)^2 + 3$

5.

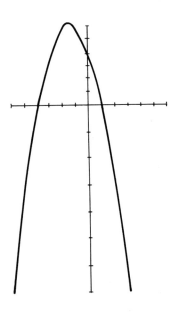

7.

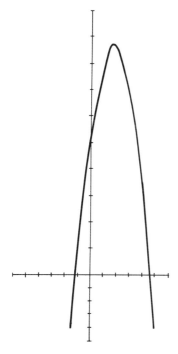

9. $f(x) = 7x^2 - 3x + 2$

11. $y = \frac{2}{9}(x - 3)^2 - 2$

13. $y = \frac{7}{81}(x - 3)^2 - 2$

15. $y = -\frac{2}{9}(x + 3)^2 + 2$

17. $y = -\frac{7}{81}(x + 3)^2 + 2$

19. $f(\frac{3}{2}) = -\frac{1}{4}$

21. $f(-\frac{1}{2}) = -\frac{3}{4}$

23. $f(-\frac{17}{6}) = -\frac{373}{12}$ or $-31\frac{1}{12}$

25. $f(\frac{1}{4}) = \frac{1}{8}$

27. $f(\frac{5}{4}) = \frac{23}{8}$ or $2\frac{7}{8}$

29. $f(\frac{17}{6}) = \frac{193}{12}$ or $16\frac{1}{12}$

31. $f(-\frac{3}{2}) = \frac{19}{2}$ or $9\frac{1}{2}$

Section 10.4

1. $P(0) = -7700$. It costs $7700 just to set the restaurant up, even if you sell nothing.

3. Betty should sell something more than 10,000 burgers. To maximize profit she should sell somewhere between 30,000 and 50,000 burgers. Mathematically, $y = P(x)$ is a downward opening parabola whose vertex occurs somewhere between $x = 30$ and $x = 50$.

5. $4943.75

7. (200, 24,000); (300, 21,000); (400, 18,000); (500, 15,000); (600, 12,000)

9. $P(200) = 1200$ $P(500) = 5250$
   $P(300) = 3150$ $P(600) = 5400$
   $P(400) = 4500$ $P(700) = 4950$

11. 12,750 planes; total revenue $7,331,250; total cost $86,250

12. $R(235) = \$297,827.25$
    $R(255) = \$304,967.25$
    $R(275) = \$309,251.25$
    $R(295) = \$310,679.25$
    $R(315) = \$309,251.25$
    $R(335) = \$304,967.25$
    $R(355) = \$297,827.25$

14. $305

16.

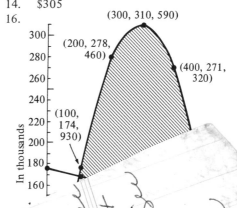

17. $S(1) = 0$; $S(2) = 13$; $S(3) = 46$;
    $S(4) = 99$
19. $D(1) = 364$; $D(2) = 286$;
    $D(3) = 186$; $D(4) = 64$
21. 3.8
23. $D(30) = 4280$ $D(50) = 3000$
    $D(40) = 3720$ $D(60) = 2120$
25. $S(30) = 900$ $S(50) = 2000$
    $S(40) = 1400$ $S(60) = 2700$
27. $56.52, 2444.39 cords
    This averages about 4.9 cords per
    family. Therefore either the families
    won't be able to buy enough wood, or
    they will have to change their minds
    and be willing to pay more.

21. asymptotes
    vertical $x = 0$
    horizontal $y = 5$

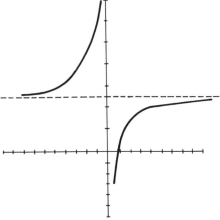

Section 10.5

1. Each has the same shape. The second
   is the same as the first only moved up
   7 units. The third is the same as the
   first only moved up 7 and 1 to the
   left.
2. Each has the same shape. The second
   is the same as the first only moved
   down 5 units. The third is the same as
   the first only moved five units down
   and 2 to the right.
5. All real numbers
7. $x \neq 1, -1$
9. All real numbers
11. All real numbers
13. $x \neq -1$
15. $x \neq 0$
17. 1(a); 3(a); 5, 7, 14, 15
19. asymptotes
    vertical $x = 3$
    horizontal $y = 0$

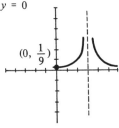

23. asymptotes
    vertical $x = -\dfrac{3}{2}$
    horizontal $y = \dfrac{1}{2}$

25.   vertical asymptote: $x = 0$
    no horizontal

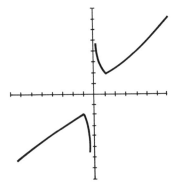

27. vertical asymptote: $x = -1$
no horizontal

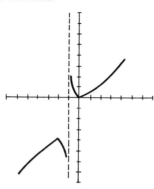

29. vertical asymptote: $x = -2$
no horizontal

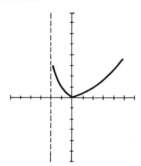

31. asymptotes
vertical $x = -1, 1$
horizontal $y = 1$

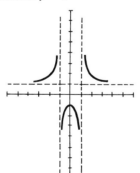

Section 10.6

1. $y = 1357.25 - \dfrac{1831.84}{x}$

3. $y = 104.889 - \dfrac{6888.89}{x}$

5. $y = 76.1200 + \dfrac{12.1992}{x}$

7. $y = 147.943 - \dfrac{3593.44}{x}$

9. $y = 164.872 + \dfrac{703.947}{x}$

11. $y = \dfrac{18,230x}{b - x}$

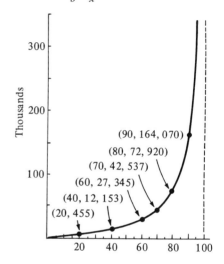

13. $y = 121.131 - \dfrac{3934.43}{x}$

15. No, the curve is slowly approaching a horizontal asymptote so there will not be any more big changes.

Section 11.1

1. (a) 16 (b) $\dfrac{1}{16}$ (c) -16 (d) 16

(e) $-\dfrac{1}{16}$ (f) $\dfrac{1}{16}$

3. (a) $\dfrac{3}{x^4}$ (b) $\dfrac{1}{(3x)^4}$ (c) 3 (d) 1

(e) $\dfrac{y}{x}$ (f) $\dfrac{x}{y}$

(g) $s^{12} + s + 2s^2 + 3s^3$

5. (a) $x^{5/6}$ (b) $\dfrac{1}{a^{1/4}}$ (c) $\dfrac{7t^3}{rs}$

(d) $\dfrac{1}{a^{2/21}}$ (e) $-x^{1/3}$

(f) $\dfrac{x^{4/3}\,y^{3/2}}{x^{6/3}\,y^{12/8}} = \dfrac{1}{x^{2/3}}$

(g) $x^{9/7}\,y^{-5/28}\,z^{-1/3}$

(h) $(x^{-7}\,y^{5/4}\,z^{10/3})^{-1/7} =$

$xy^{-5/28}\,z^{-10/21}$

(i) $\dfrac{r^{12}\,s^2\,t^4}{r^{-2}\,s^7\,t^1} = \dfrac{r^{14}\,t^3}{s^5}$

Section 11.2
1. 8
3. 1.5
5. 4
7. domain: all real numbers
    range: $0 < y$

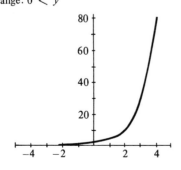

9. domain: all real numbers
    range: $0 < y$

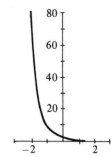

11. domain: all real numbers
     range: $0 < y$

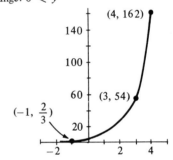

13. domain: all real numbers
     range: all real numbers

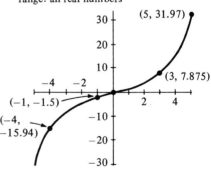

15.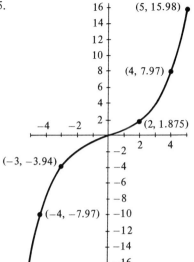

(5, 15.98)

(4, 7.97)

(2, 1.875)

(−3, −3.94)

(−4, −7.97)

3.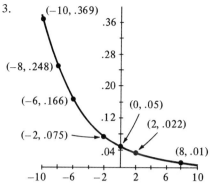

(−10, .369)

(−8, .248)

(−6, .166)

(0, .05)

(2, .022)

(−2, .075)

(8, .01)

17.

1 < a

0 < a < 1

(0, b)

(0, b)

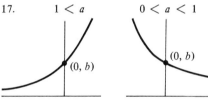

5.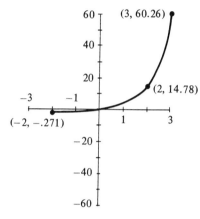

(3, 60.26)

(2, 14.78)

(−2, −.271)

7.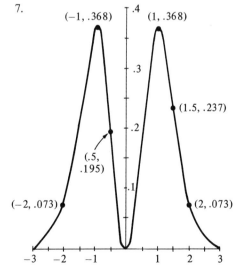

(−1, .368)

(1, .368)

(1.5, .237)

(.5, .195)

(−2, .073)

(2, .073)

Section 11.3

1.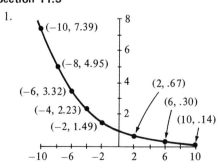

(−10, 7.39)

(−8, 4.95)

(−6, 3.32)

(2, .67)

(−4, 2.23)

(6, .30)

(−2, 1.49)

(10, .14)

9. horizontal asymptote: $y = 20$

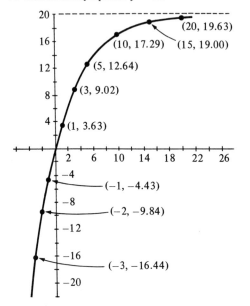

13. horizontal asymptote: $y = 100$

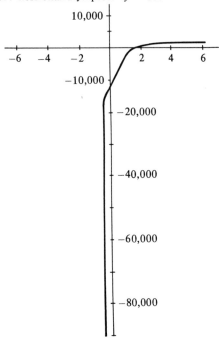

11. horizontal asymptote: $y = 600$

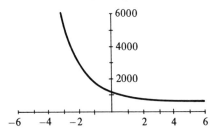

15. horizontal asymptote: $y = 40$

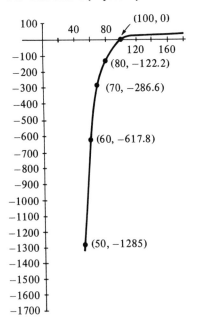

17.

x	0	1	2
y	15,625	29,711	41,016

3	4	5
50,088	57,368	63,211

6	7	8
67,900	71,662	74,682

9	10	11
77,106	79,051	80,611

The asymptote is $y = 86,954$.
Probably yes, or it might decrease.

19.

x	0	4	6	8	10
y	100	66	51	38	26

19.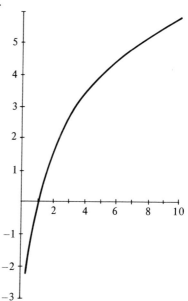

Section 11.4

1. (a) $\log_3 1 = 0$ (b) $\log_5 125 = 3$

3. (a) $\log_9 (\frac{1}{9}) = -1$ (b) $\log_{\frac{1}{9}} 9 = -1$

5. (a) $2^2 = 4$ (b) $3^6 = 729$

7. (a) $.2^3 = .008$ (b) $5^{-3} = .008$
9. (a) $x = 16$ (b) $x = 100,000$

11. (a) $x = 7$ (b) $x = \dfrac{1}{2^{49}}$

13. (a) $x = 125$ (b) $x = 3$
15. (a) $x = .1$ (b) $x = 243$

17.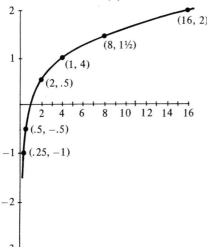

21.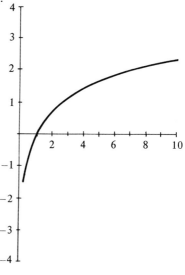

23. In A

25. $\log_B 10$

27.

x	-4	-3
e^x	.01831564	.04978707

-2	-1
.13533528	.36787944

0	1	2
1	2.7182818	7.3890561

3	4
20.085537	54.59815

29. $-4, -3; -1, 0; 3, 4$

31. $3,4; 1,2; -1,1$ (not consecutive integers); $-4, -3$

33. (a) 14.4521   (b) 2.45686

35. (a) -4.66028 (b) 4.66028

37. (a) .058269   (b) 2.360854
    (c) 4.663439

39. (a) $-.155485$ (b) -4.76065
    (c) -9.36582

41. 1992

43. 189

45. 547,902

47. 415

49. 11.38 years

51. $48,468

53. $y = 8.3e^{.009x}$

55. (a) No

57. (a) No

Section 12.1

1. $12,733.88
3. $12,768.30
5. $66,731.51
7. $68,557.37
9. $252,061.93
11. $11,881.40
13. $10,926.69
15. $2,498,374.94
17. $2,428,704.34
19. $2,423,370.27
21. $2,286,630.21

23. 24,774
25. 10,348,443
27. 581

Section 12.2

1. $5841.66
3. $54,497.46
5. $271,242.87
7. $52.38
9. $39.29
11. $63.93
13. $435,260
15. $46,849,360
17. $20,360
19. (a) $162
    (b) $161.42
    (c) $160.84
    (d) $160.27
21. $639,293; $629,286; $619,395; $609,618
23. $258,300; $220,968; $188,218; $159,661
25. 5% increase in cost: $856,714; $843,304; $830,048; $816,946
    6% increase in cost: $906,850; $892,655; $878,623; $864,755
    7% increase in cost: $959,407; $944,389; $929,544; $914,872
    8% increase in cost: $1,014,478; $998,598; $982,902; $967,387
27. 2% increase every 6 months: $618,167; $587,737; $588,510; $530,460
    3% increase every 6 months: $861,322; $818,923; $778,199; $739,115
    4% increase every 6 months: $1,196,282; $1,137,394; $1,080,833; $1,026,550
    5% increase every 6 months: $1,656,289; $1,574,757; $1,496,447; $1,421,290
29. $3,298,565; $3,136,190; $2,980,233; $2,830,554

Section 12.3

1. $259.19; $6220.52
3. $143.25; $6876.10
5. $937.31; $22,495.53
7. $622.55; $7470.64
9. $322.74; $7745.65
11. $208.70; $7513.26
13. $351.32; $75,884.58
15. $702.10; $168,504.50
17. $2908.56; $418,832.39
19. 20 year mortgage $5080.44;
    $1,219,306
    25 year mortgage $4902.03;
    $1,470,609
21. 10 year $38,089.73; $4,570,768
    15 year $31,065.68; $5,591,823
    20 year $28,709.39; $6,890,255

index

Legal operations: 5, 7; example, 5

Legal row operations: 118, examples, 118–121. *See also* Linear systems, higher order

Leontief, Wassily: 193

Line, equation of: 58, 63–66; of best fit, 94–99; horizontal, 63–64; horizontal asymptote, 480; vertical, 63–64; vertical asymptote, 480. *See also* Slope

Line of best fit: 94–99; examples, 95–99; method of averages, 95

Linear equation: 115; graphing and examples, 58–62; real-world problems, 75–81; use of matrices, 115–117. *See also* Linear equations, systems of two

Linear equation in one variable: 2; definition, 7; examples, 2–3, 7–11; graphing, 53–56; solving, 4. *See also* Word problems, translating and solving

Linear equation in two variables: 63; graph, 64

Linear equations, systems of two: addition method and examples, 88, 91–93, 116; consistent, 89, 91–93; dependent, 90–93; flow chart used in, 91; inconsistent, 89, 91–93; solution, 88. *See also* Linear equations; Linear systems

Linear function: 448–449

Linear inequalities, graphing: 71–75

Linear inequalities in two variables, systems of: graphical solution and examples, 207–210; more than two inequalities, 210–212. *See also* Linear programming

Linear model of equilibrium, in the marketplace. *See* Equilibrium, linear models

Linear programming: constraints and examples, 215; definition, 215; feasible solutions and examples, 215; optimal solutions and examples, 215. *See also* Corner point principle; Linear inequalities in two variables, systems of; Linear programming problems

Linear programming problems: feasible region, 231; geometrical solutions and examples, 230–235; geometrical step-by-step solution rule and examples, 241–247; maximum problem, 230, 232–235; minimum problem and examples, 230–232; no solution possibilities, 241; real-world problems, 230–235; translating real-world problems, 216–225. *See also* Linear programming problems, simplex method

Linear programming problems, algebraic approach. *See* Linear programming, simplex method

Linear programming problems, geometrical solutions. *See* Linear programming problems

Linear programming problems, simplex method: a clever method, 253–254; corner variable, 252; examples, 258–265; examples in three variables, 263–265; first-round conditions, 257; flow chart, 259; matrix method, 254–256; pivot, 258; rules, 257–258; rules locating corner, 251; slack variable, 257; start-up, 252

Linear systems: dependent, 121; higher order, 127–128; inconsistent, 121, 183; matrix multiplication, 169–170; real-world problems, 127, 137–146; solving, 118–121; two-by-two, 120–121; use of inverses, 179–180, 186–188. *See also* Echelon method; Matrix, inverse of

Lines of constant cost: 232

Logarithmic functions: applications, 520–524; definition, 518; graphing, 518; real-world problems, 519–522. *See also* Exponential functions; Logarithms

Logarithms: 516; calculating, 517; common, 517, 520; natural, 517, 520; rules, 519–520. *See also* Logarithmic functions

Venn diagram: 294; in complement of
an event, 305; in equiprobable
models, 322; examples, 309–314;
in union of two events, 309, 310
Vertex: 457–460
Vertical asymptote: 480
Vertical line: 63–64; rule, 442

Washing-out principle: definition, 422;
examples, 422–431; real-world
problems, 423–424
Word problems, translating and solving:
24; examples, 25–30

Zero exponent: 495
Zero matrix: 154